T0156210

Microsoft®
VISUAL BASIC® 2017
for Windows®, Web, and Database Applications

COMPREHENSIVE

CORINNE HOISINGTON

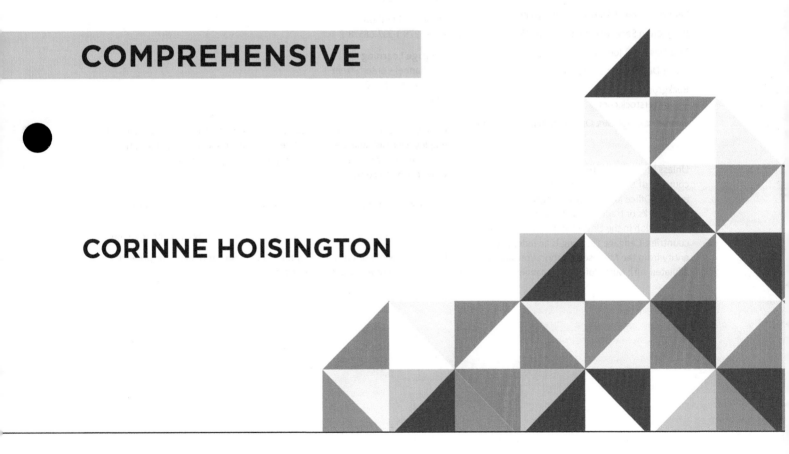

CENGAGE
Learning·

SHELLY CASHMAN SERIES®

Australia • Brazil • Mexico • Singapore • United Kingdom • United States

CENGAGE
Learning·

Windows®, Web, and Database Applications Comprehensive
Corinne Hoisington

SVP, GM Science, Technology & Math:
  Balraj S. Kalsi

Product Director: Kathleen McMahon

Product Team Manager: Kristin McNary

Associate Content Developer: Brianna Vorce

Marketing Manager: Stephanie Albracht

Senior Content Project Manager:
  Jennifer K. Feltri-George

Art Director: Diana Graham

Project Manager: Hemalatha Velayutham,
  Lumina Datamatics Inc.

Manufacturing Planner: Julio Esperas

Development Editor: Lisa Ruffolo

QA Manuscript Reviewer: John Freitas

IP Analyst: Amber Hill

Senior IP Project Manager: Kathryn Kucharek

Production Service: Lumina Datamatics, Inc.

Text Designer: Joel Sadagursky

Cover Designer: Diana Graham

Background Cover Image: Piotr Zajc/
  Shutterstock.com

Geometric image: Mrs. Opossum/Shutterstock.com

Unless otherwise stated, all screenshots
courtesy of Microsoft Corporation. Microsoft
and the Office logo are either registered
trademarks or trademarks of Microsoft
Corporation in the United States and/or other
countries. Cengage Learning is an independent
entity from the Microsoft Corporation, and not
affiliated with Microsoft in any manner.

For product information and technology assistance, contact us at
Cengage Learning Customer & Sales Support, 1-800-354-9706

For permission to use material from this text or product,
submit all requests online at **www.cengage.com/permissions**.
Further permissions questions can be emailed to
permissionrequest@cengage.com.

Library of Congress Control Number: 2017938500

Student Edition:
ISBN: 978-1-337-10211-7

Loose-Leaf Edition:
ISBN: 978-1-337-68578-8

Cengage Learning
20 Channel Center Street
Boston, MA 02210
USA

Cengage Learning is a leading provider of customized learning solutions with
employees residing in nearly 40 different countries and sales in more than
125 countries around the world. Find your local representative at
www.cengage.com.

Cengage Learning products are represented in Canada by Nelson Education, Ltd.

To learn more about Cengage Learning Solutions, visit **www.cengage.com**.

Purchase any of our products at your local college store or at our preferred
online store **www.cengagebrain.com**.

Printed at CLDPC, USA, 04-18

CONTENTS

CHAPTER 7
Using Procedures and
Exception Handling

CHAPTER 8
Using Arrays and File
Handling

The Shelly Cashman Series® offers the finest textbooks in computer education. This *Microsoft Visual Basic 2017* book utilizes an innovative step-by-step pedagogy, which integrates demonstrations of professional-quality programs with in-depth discussions of programming concepts and techniques and opportunities for hands-on practice and reinforcement. The new volume retains popular features and pedagogy from past editions, while emphasizing the changing development process in an increasingly mobile-oriented world. The popular Guided Program Development section supports students as they work independently to create useful, realistic, and appealing applications, building their confidence and skills while guiding them to select appropriate Visual Basic 2017 programming methods. Marginal elements, such as In the Real World boxes, provide expert tips to add interest and depth to topics. A robust and varied collection of exercises, including a series of practical case-based programming projects, ensures students gain the knowledge and expertise they need to succeed when developing professional programs.

Visual Basic 2017 builds on the features of Visual Basic 2015, which emphasized coding once and deploying on multiple devices. Some of the major enhancements to Visual Basic 2017 include cross-platform coding, including the ability to develop apps for Android, iOS, Windows, Linux, web, and cloud platforms. Visual Studio 2017 also allows you to extend and customize its environment by building your own extensions. Using Visual Basic 2017, you can design, create, and deploy Windows, Mobile, Web, Database, and cloud applications. Visual Studio 2017 includes several productivity enhancements such as debugging tools, mobile templates for both smartphones and tablet design, more powerful searching tools, a built-in suite of Azure tools for creating cloud-first apps, and more.

Objectives of This Textbook

Microsoft Visual Basic 2017 for Windows, Web, and Database Applications Comprehensive is intended for a year-long course that introduces students to the correct ways to design and write programs using Visual Basic 2017. The goal of this text is to provide a rigorous and comprehensive course in computer programming for students with little or no previous programming experience. The objectives of this book are as follows:

- To teach the fundamentals of the Microsoft Visual Basic 2017 programming language
- To understand and apply graphical user interface design principles
- To emphasize the development cycle when creating applications, which mirrors the same approach that professional developers use
- To illustrate well-written and readable programs using a disciplined coding style, including documentation and indentation standards
- To create Visual Basic applications that are deployed on multiple platforms such as mobile computers (smartphones and tablets) and webpages

- To demonstrate how to implement logic involving sequence, selection, and repetition using Visual Basic 2017
- To encourage the use of critical thinking skills in the application development process
- To write useful, well-designed programs for personal computers and mobile computers that solve practical business problems
- To create appealing, interactive Web applications that can be delivered and executed on the Internet on any device from scratch or using built-in templates
- To organize complex programs by using procedures and to anticipate and prevent errors by managing exceptions
- To produce sophisticated, professional programs by using arrays and files that handle data and to make programs more robust by defining classes and using the power of inheritance
- To encourage independent study and help those who are working on their own in a distance education environment

The Shelly Cashman Approach

Features of this *Microsoft Visual Basic 2017* book include the following:

- **Realistic, Up-to-Date Applications** Each programming chapter focuses on building a sample project, a complete, useful application that showcases Visual Basic 2017 features and the latest technology.
- **Guided Steps to Encourage Independence** After observing how a professional developer would build the chapter project and exploring related programming concepts and Visual Basic 2017 techniques, students create the sample application on their own in the Guided Program Development section. This step-by-step section provides enough guidance for students to work independently, with Hint Screens that verify students are performing the tasks correctly.
- **More Than Step-by-Step** Each chapter offers clear, thorough discussions of the programming concepts students need to understand to build the sample application. Important Visual Basic 2017 design and programming features are also highlighted, including time-saving techniques such as using IntelliSense, code snippets, and the Toolbox. As appropriate, students design and prepare for applications the way professional developers do — by creating or analyzing requirements documents, use case definitions, and event-planning documents.
- **Heads Up Boxes** Heads Up boxes appear in the margin to give advice for following best programming practices and tips about alternative ways of completing the same task.
- **In the Real World Boxes** This marginal feature provides insight into how developers use Visual Basic tools or programming techniques to save time or enhance professional development projects.
- **Watch Out For Boxes** These boxes explain how to avoid common pitfalls when using a particular command, programming structure, or technique.
- **Consider This Boxes** This element encourages independent problem solving by posing thought-provoking questions and providing answers related to programming and Visual Basic.

- **Critical Thinking Boxes** Critical thinking is an essential part of the programming process; developers need to be able to reason strategically and justify their decisions to craft an effective program. The Critical Thinking boxes encourage students to further explore the ideas in the chapters.

Organization of This Textbook

Microsoft Visual Basic 2017 for Windows, Web, and Database Applications Comprehensive provides detailed instructions on how to use Visual Basic 2017 to build authentic, effective, and appealing applications for Microsoft Windows personal computers and mobile devices. The material is divided into 11 chapters and two appendices as follows:

Chapter 1 — Introduction to Visual Basic 2017 Programming
Chapter 1 provides an overview of programming with Visual Basic 2017. The chapter defines a computer program, describes the role of a developer in creating computer programs, and discusses event-driven programs that have a graphical user interface (GUI). The chapter also explains the roles of input, processing, output, and data when running a program on a computer; examines the basic arithmetic and logical operations a program can perform; and explores the use of databases and computer programming languages in general. Finally, the chapter introduces Visual Studio 2017 and the .NET 4.6.2 Framework, including the .NET class libraries and related features, and surveys the types of Visual Basic 2017 applications.

Chapter 2 — Program and Graphical User Interface Design
Chapter 2 introduces students to the major elements of the Visual Studio 2017 integrated development environment (IDE) while designing a graphical user interface mock-up. Topics include opening Visual Studio 2017, creating a Windows Forms App project, adding objects to a Windows form, assigning properties to objects, aligning objects on the Windows form, and saving Visual Basic projects. The chapter also discusses how to apply GUI design principles and examines the first two phases of the program development life cycle (PDLC).

Chapter 3 — Program Design and Coding
Chapter 3 provides students with the skills and knowledge necessary to complete phases 2, 3, and 4 of the PDLC by enhancing a GUI mock-up, designing program processing objects, and coding a program. Topics include using IntelliSense when writing code and enhancing a Visual Basic 2017 form by changing the BackColor property of an object and displaying images. This chapter also explains how to enter Visual Basic 2017 code, correct errors, and run a completed program. Finally, the chapter discusses the value of creating an event-planning document.

Chapter 4 — Variables and Arithmetic Operations
Chapter 4 introduces variables and arithmetic operations used in the coding of a Visual Basic application. The chapter provides in-depth coverage of declaring variables, gathering input for an application, differentiating data types, performing mathematical calculations, and understanding the proper scope of variables. The chapter also shows how to use various types of TextBox objects.

Chapter 5 — Decision Structures Chapter 5 explains how to create a Visual Basic 2017 Windows application that uses decision structures to take different actions depending on the user's input. Topics include using If...Then statements, If... Then...Else statements, nested If statements, logical operators, and Case statements. The chapter also explores how to use the GroupBox object, place RadioButton objects, display a message box, insert code snippets, and test input to ensure it is valid.

Chapter 6 — Loop Structures Chapter 6 presents another type of fundamental programming structure — the repetition structure, including Do While, Do Until, For... Next, For Each...Next, and While...End While loops. Topics include repeating a process using the For...Next and Do loops; priming a loop; creating a nested loop; selecting the best type of loop; avoiding infinite loops; validating data; and understanding compound operators, counters, and accumulators. The chapter also shows how to insert a MenuStrip object, use the InputBox function, display data using the ListBox object, debug programs using DataTips at breakpoints, and publish a finished application using ClickOnce technology.

Chapter 7 — Using Procedures and Exception Handling Chapter 7 focuses on using procedures to organize complex programs and handling exceptions to prevent errors. The chapter begins by demonstrating how to create a splash screen that is displayed as a program loads. It then explores how to organize long, complex programs into procedures, including Sub and Function procedures, and shows how to pass an argument to a procedure by value and by reference, how to code a Function procedure to return a value, and how to create a class-level variable. The chapter concludes by discussing exception handling and using Try-Catch blocks to detect errors and take corrective actions.

Chapter 8 — Using Arrays and File Handling Chapter 8 explains how to develop applications that maintain data for later processing, including sorting, calculating, and displaying the data. The chapter project demonstrates an application that reads data from a file, displays the data in a ComboBox object, and then uses the data in calculations. This chapter also shows how to create a Windows application that uses more than one form.

Chapter 9 — Creating Web Applications Chapter 9 explains how to create a Web application by building an interactive web form, a page displayed in a browser that requests data from users. The chapter examines ASP.NET technology and explores tools that help to create appealing, useful Web applications, including web form properties, CheckBox, DropDownList, and Calendar objects and custom tables. The chapter also explains how to validate data on web forms and format text using the HTML <br> tag and the string manipulation properties and procedures in the Visual Basic String class.

Chapter 10 — Incorporating Databases with ADO.NET Chapter 10 examines databases and explores the ADO.NET 5 technology. The chapter discusses how to take advantage of the data access technology of ADO.NET to connect to databases and update, add, and delete data and retrieve database information for viewing and decision making. The chapter project demonstrates how to create a professional application that connects to a Microsoft Access database, temporarily stores data from the database, and lets users add, select, and delete records.

Chapter 11 — Multiple Classes and Inheritance Chapter 11 explores the advanced topics of defining classes, using inheritance, and designing a three-tier structure for a program. The chapter begins by introducing the three-tier program structure and thoroughly defining classes and the object-oriented programming concepts related to classes. The chapter project shows how to create a class, instantiate an object, write a class constructor, call a procedure in a separate class, and use inheritance to code a base class and a subclass. Other topics include calling procedures in a base and subclass, writing overridable and overrides procedures, and creating and writing a comma-delimited text file.

Appendices This book concludes with two appendices. Appendix A explains the purpose of Unicode and provides a table two Unicode characters and their equivalents. Appendix B examines the My namespace element of Visual Basic 2017 in detail. Naming convention for the three-character prefix preceding variable names.

End-of-Chapter Activities

A notable strength of this Microsoft Visual Basic 2017 book is the extensive student activities at the end of each chapter. Well-structured student activities can make the difference between students merely participating in a class and retaining the information they learn. These end-of-chapter activities include the following:

- **Knowledge Check** The Knowledge Check section includes short exercises and review questions that reinforce concepts and provide opportunities to practice skills.

- **Debugging Exercises** In these exercises, students examine short code samples to identify errors and solve programming problems.

- **Program Analysis** The Program Analysis exercises let students apply their knowledge of Visual Basic 2017 and programming techniques. In some exercises, students write programming statements that meet a practical goal or solve a problem. In other exercises, students analyze code samples and identify the output.

- **Case Programming Assignments** Six programming assignments for each chapter challenge students to create applications using the skills learned in the chapter. Each assignment presents a realistic business scenario and requires students to create programs of varying difficulty.

  - Easiest: The first two assignments provide most of the program design information, such as a requirements document and use case definition, for a business application. Students design an application, create an event-planning document, and write the code for the application.

  - Intermediate: The next two assignments provide some of the program design information, such as a requirements document. Students create other design documents, such as a use case definition and event-planning document and then build the user interface and code the application.

  - Challenging: The final two assignments provide only a description of a business problem, and students create all the design documents, design the user interface, and code the application.

To the Instructor

Each chapter in this book focuses on a realistic, appealing Visual Basic 2017 application. A chapter begins with a completed application, which you can run to demonstrate how it works, the tasks it performs, and the problems it solves. The chapter introduction also identifies the application's users and their requirements, such as running the program on a mobile computer or validating input data.

The steps in the next section of a chapter show how to create the user interface for the application. You can perform these steps in class — each step clearly explains an action, describes the results, and includes a figure showing the results, with callouts directing your attention to key elements on the screen. Some marginal features, such as the Heads Up boxes, provide additional tips for completing the steps.

This section also explains the Visual Basic 2017 tools and properties needed to understand and create the user interface. For example, while placing a text box in an application, the chapter describes the purpose of a text box and why you should set its maximum and minimum size. You can discuss these ideas and strategies and then continue your demonstration to show students how to apply them to the chapter application.

After completing the user interface, the chapter explores the programming concepts students should understand to create the application, such as proper syntax, variables, data types, conditional statements, and loops. This section uses the same types of steps, figures, and marginal features to demonstrate how to enter code to complete and test the application.

To prepare students for building the application on their own, the chapter next considers the program design and logic by examining planning documents:

- *Requirements document* — The requirements document identifies the purpose, procedures, and calculations of the program and specifies details such as the application title, restrictions, and comments that help to explain the program.
- *Use case definition* — The use case definition describes what the user does and how the program responds to each action.
- *Event-planning document* — The event-planning document lists each object in the user interface that causes an event, the action the user takes to trigger the event, and the event processing that must occur.

You can discuss these documents in class and encourage students to review them as they create a program, reinforcing how professional developers create applications in the modern workplace.

In the innovative Guided Program Development section, students work on their own to create the chapter application. They complete the tasks within each numbered step, referring to Hint Screens when they need a reminder about how to perform a step or which method to use. Many tasks reference figures are shown earlier in the chapter. Students can refer to these figures for further help — they show exactly how to use a particular technique for completing a task. Steps end with a results figure, which illustrates how the application should look if students performed the tasks correctly. To reinforce how students learned the chapter material, the Guided Program Development section also focuses first on designing the user interface and then on coding the application. A complete program listing appears at the end of this section, which students can use to check their work.

At the end of each chapter, you'll find plenty of activities that provide review, practice, and challenge for your students, including exercises ranging from short, focused review questions to assignments requiring complete programs and related planning documents. You can assign the Knowledge Check, Debugging Exercises, and Program Analysis activities as necessary to reinforce and assess learning. Depending on the expertise of your class, you can assign the Case Programming assignments as independent projects, selecting one from each level of difficulty (easiest, intermediate, and challenging) or concentrating on the level that is most appropriate for your class.

INSTRUCTOR RESOURCES

The following resources are available through www.cengage.com to instructors who have adopted this book. Search for this title by ISBN, title, author, or keyword. From the Product Overview page, select the Instructor's Companion Site to access your complementary resources.

- **Instructor's Manual** The Instructor's Manual consists of Microsoft Word files, which include chapter objectives, lecture notes, teaching tips, classroom activities, lab activities, quick quizzes, figures and boxed elements summarized in the chapters, and a glossary page.

- **Syllabus** Sample syllabi, which can be customized easily to a course, cover policies, assignments, exams, and procedural information.

- **Figure Files** Illustrations for every figure in the textbook are available in electronic form. Figures are provided both with and without callouts.

- **PowerPoint Presentation** PowerPoint is a multimedia lecture presentation system that provides slides for each chapter. Presentations are based on chapter objectives. Use this presentation system to present well-organized lectures that are both interesting and knowledge based. PowerPoint presentations provide consistent coverage at schools that use multiple lecturers.

- **Solutions to Exercises** Solutions are included for all end-of-chapter and chapter reinforcement exercises.

- **Test Bank and Test Engine** Test Banks include a wide range of questions for every chapter, featuring objective-based and critical-thinking question types, and include page number references and figure references, when appropriate. The test engine, Cognero, is a flexible, online system that allows you to author, edit, and manage test bank content from multiple Cengage Learning solutions; create multiple test versions in an instant; and deliver tests from your LMS, your classroom, or wherever you want.

- **Printed Test Bank** A printable Rich Text File (.rtf) version of the test bank is also included.

- **Data Files for Students** Includes all the files that are required by students to complete the exercises.
- **Additional Activities for Students** These additional activities consist of Chapter Reinforcement Exercises, which are true/false, multiple-choice, and short answer questions that help students gain confidence in the material learned.

To the Student

Getting the Most Out of Your Book

Welcome to *Microsoft Visual Basic 2017 for Windows, Web, and Database Applications Comprehensive.* To save yourself time and gain a better understanding of the elements in this text, spend a few minutes reviewing the descriptions and figures in this section.

Introduction and Initial Chapter Figures Each chapter presents a programming project and shows the solution in the first figure of the chapter. The introduction and initial chapter figure let you see firsthand how your finished product will look and illustrate your programming goals.

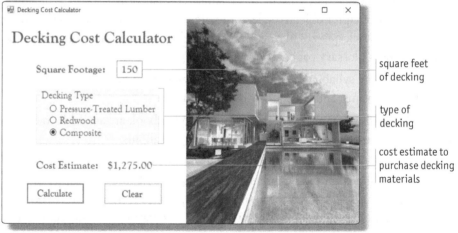

Franck Boston/Shutterstock.com

Guided Program Development After reading through the chapter and observing how to create the chapter application, the Guided Program Development section takes you through building the chapter project step by step. As you perform each task, you can refer to Hint Screens that remind you how to complete a step or use a particular technique. If you need further help, some steps include references to figures shown earlier in the chapter — you can revisit these figures to review exactly how to perform a task. Each step ends with a results figure, so you can make sure your application is on the right track. A complete program listing also appears at the end of the Guided Program Development section, which you can use to check your work.

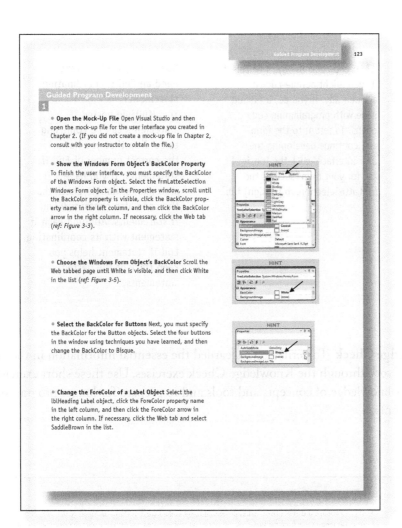

Marginal Boxes Marginal elements include Heads Up boxes, which offer tips and programming advice, In the Real World boxes, which indicate how professional developers use Visual Basic 2017 tools, Watch Out For boxes, which identify common errors and explain how to avoid them, and Critical Thinking boxes, which help you go beyond the reading to think critically about the development process.

HEADS UP

Unlike some programming languages, the capitalization of object names, properties, property values, and other values is not important in Visual Basic. Therefore, the object name picPumpkin is equivalent to the object name picpumpkin. Capitalization is used within the object name to make the name easier to read.

IN THE REAL WORLD

Some developers use the AutoSize property for a Button object to ensure that the button always is large enough for the text. By setting the AutoSize property for a Button object to True in the Properties window, the Button object will expand or contract when you change the text so it fits precisely in the button.

WATCH OUT FOR

When you click an object to select it, you might double-click it accidentally. If you do, a tabbed page with programming code opens. To return to the form and continue developing the user interface, click the [Design] tab for your form, such as the frmLatteSelection.vb [Design] tab.

CRITICAL THINKING

Does every If statement need an End If coordinating statement?
Yes. Multiple nested If statements can be confusing to confirm that you have the correct number of End If statements. If you have 9 If statements, double-check that the code also contains 9 End If statements. Aligning each If statement with its coordinating End If statement helps you keep track of the nested statements.

Knowledge Check To verify you've learned the essential information in the chapter, you can work through the Knowledge Check exercises. Use these short exercises to test your knowledge of concepts and tools and to prepare for longer programming assignments.

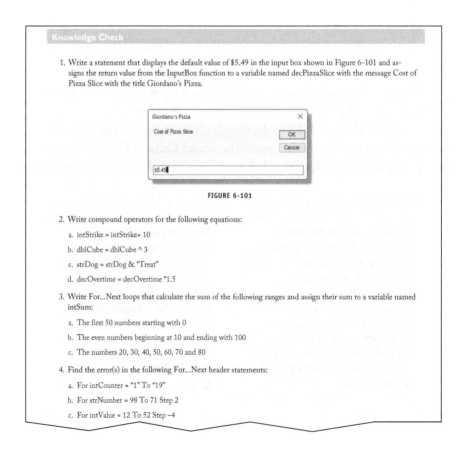

Knowledge Check

1. Write a statement that displays the default value of $5.49 in the input box shown in Figure 6-101 and assigns the return value from the InputBox function to a variable named decPizzaSlice with the message Cost of Pizza Slice with the title Giordano's Pizza.

FIGURE 6-101

2. Write compound operators for the following equations:

   a. intStrike = intStrike+ 10

   b. dblCube = dblCube ^ 3

   c. strDog = strDog & "Treat"

   d. decOvertime = decOvertime *1.5

3. Write For...Next loops that calculate the sum of the following ranges and assign their sum to a variable named intSum:

   a. The first 50 numbers starting with 0

   b. The even numbers beginning at 10 and ending with 100

   c. The numbers 20, 30, 40, 50, 60, 70 and 80

4. Find the error(s) in the following For...Next header statements:

   a. For intCounter = "1" To "19"

   b. For strNumber = 98 To 71 Step 2

   c. For intValue = 12 To 52 Step –4

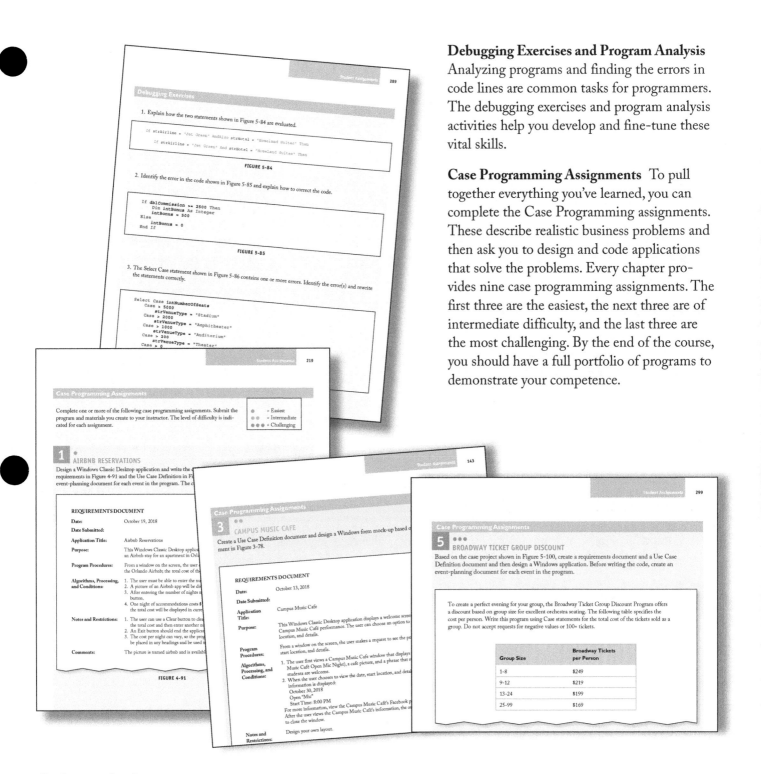

Debugging Exercises and Program Analysis
Analyzing programs and finding the errors in code lines are common tasks for programmers. The debugging exercises and program analysis activities help you develop and fine-tune these vital skills.

Case Programming Assignments To pull together everything you've learned, you can complete the Case Programming assignments. These describe realistic business problems and then ask you to design and code applications that solve the problems. Every chapter provides nine case programming assignments. The first three are the easiest, the next three are of intermediate difficulty, and the last three are the most challenging. By the end of the course, you should have a full portfolio of programs to demonstrate your competence.

Acknowledgments

To Tim, my husband, for sharing this wonderful world filled with moments under the Northern Lights of Tromso. To Liam, Lochlan, Colin, and Jackson, my grandsons, without whose loving attention this book would have been finished in half the time. To my six children Timothy, Brittany, Ryan, Daniel, Bre, and Eric, who are no longer children but my dear friends. To Lisa Ruffolo, my editor, for being the motivating master of her detailed craft. And lastly, my mother, who will be remembered for her tenacity, strength, and hard work.

—Corinne Hoisington

CHAPTER 1

Introduction to Visual Basic 2017 Programming

OBJECTIVES

You will have mastered the material in this chapter when you can:

- Understand software and computer programs

- State the role of a developer in creating computer programs

- Specify the use of a graphical user interface and describe an event-driven program

- Specify the roles of input, processing, output, and data when running a program on a computer

- Explain the logical operations a computer program can perform

- Define and describe the use of a database

- Identify the use of a computer programming language in general and Visual Basic 2017 in particular

- Explain the use of Visual Studio 2017 when developing Visual Basic 2017 programs

- Specify the programming languages available for use with Visual Studio 2017

- Explain .NET Framework 4.6.2

- Explain RAD

- Describe classes, objects, and the .NET Framework class libraries

- Explain ADO.NET, ASP.NET, MSIL, and CLR

- Specify the types of Visual Basic 2017 applications

Introduction

A computer is an electronic device that completes tasks under the direction of a sequence of instructions to produce useful results for people. Computers include desktop models, laptops, tablets, and smartphones. The set of instructions that directs a computer to perform tasks is called **computer software**, or a **computer program**. A computer program on a mobile device or on a Windows 10 computer is also called an **app**. In addition, programs are being developed for wearable devices, augmented reality headsets, smart TVs, automobiles, and smart devices (Internet of Things) such as home thermostats and refrigerators.

When controlled by programs, computers and mobile devices can accomplish a wide variety of activities. For example, computers can interpret and display a webpage, compute and write payroll checks for millions of employees, display video and play audio from the web, post to a social network on a smartphone, and engage in an augmented reality experience using a virtual reality headset such as the HoloLens (Figure 1-1).

Source: Microsoft

FIGURE 1-1

Two vital components of a computer must interact with each other for any activity to be performed. These components are computer hardware and computer software. **Computer hardware** is the physical equipment associated with a computer. It includes the keyboard (traditional or on-screen), mouse, touch screen or monitor, central processing unit (CPU), random access memory (RAM), and hard disk (Figure 1-2). A **mobile device** is portable computer hardware such as a smartphone, tablet computer, or wearable device such as a smart watch or headset.

A computer program, or app, is a set of electronic instructions that directs the hardware to perform tasks such as displaying a character on the screen when a key is pressed on the keyboard, adding an employee's regular pay and overtime pay to

FIGURE 1-2

calculate the employee's total pay, or displaying a picture from an attached digital camera. Computer hardware cannot perform any activity unless an instruction directs that hardware to act. In most cases, the instruction is part of a computer program a developer has created to carry out the desired activity. A third component required is data. **Data** includes words, numbers, videos, graphics, and sound that programs manipulate, display, and otherwise process. The basic function of many programs is to accept some form of data (sometimes called **input data**), manipulate the data in some manner (sometimes called **processing**), and create some form of data that is usable by people or other computers (sometimes called **output data**, or **information**). In short, many computer programs perform the following general steps: accept input data, process the data, and create output data. The data that acts as input to a program, the processing that occurs, and the output that is created vary with the requirements of the program.

In order for the computer to execute a program, both the program and the data must be placed in the computer's **random access memory (RAM)** (Figure 1-3). Once the program is stored in RAM, the computer's **central processing unit (CPU)** can access the program instructions and the data in RAM to perform activities as directed by the program.

FIGURE 1-3

iStockphoto.com/NorasitKaewsai

Another activity that hardware and software typically carry out is saving both the data and other software. **Saving**, or **storing**, data refers to placing the data or software electronically on a storage medium such as a hard disk or a Universal Serial Bus (USB) drive or saving to a cloud storage server. The software and data are stored so they can be accessed and retrieved at a later time. Stored local data is said to be **persistent** because it remains available even after the computer power is turned off.

Computer Programmers and Developers

A computer program is designed and developed by people known as **computer programmers**, or developers. **Developers** are people skilled in designing computer programs and creating them using programming languages. Some computer programs are small and relatively simple, but often a problem to be solved on a computer requires more than one program. Thus, developers speak of developing an **application**, which can mean several computer programs working together to solve a problem.

When designing a program, developers analyze the problem and determine how to solve it. Once a computer program or an application is designed, the developer must create it so it can be executed on a computer. In most cases, the developer creates the program by writing its code using a **programming language**, which is a set of words and symbols that can be interpreted by special computer software and eventually executed as instructions by a computer. In this book, you will learn the skills required both to design and to create computer programs and apps using the Visual Basic 2017 programming language (Figure 1-4).

FIGURE 1-4

CONSIDER THIS

Will I be able to find a job in computer programming?

According to Robert Half Technology, the following technology positions are in highest demand:

- Data scientists with a coding background
- Big data engineers
- Network security engineers
- Mobile application developers
- Software developers
- Software engineers

(www.roberthalf.com/technology/it-salary-center)

Event-Driven Computer Programs with a Graphical User Interface

Most Visual Basic 2017 programs are **event-driven programs** that communicate with the user through a **graphical user interface (GUI)**. The GUI usually consists of a window that contains a variety of objects and that can be displayed on various devices such as a computer monitor or a smartphone screen. Users employ GUI objects to select options, enter data, and cause events to occur. An **event** means the user has initiated an action that causes the program to perform a type of processing in response to that action. For example, a user might enter data into the program, and then click a button. The button action triggers an event, resulting in the program performing the appropriate processing in response.

To illustrate the process of entering data when using a GUI and then triggering an event, consider the window shown in Figure 1-5.

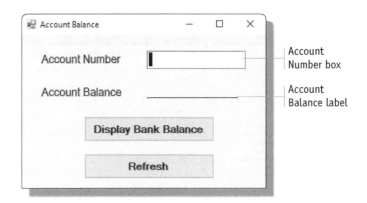

FIGURE 1-5

This window is part of a banking application. When it is displayed, the teller at the bank or a user on the web can enter an account number. Next, the user can click the Display Bank Balance button (which triggers an event) and the program displays the account balance. The following steps illustrate the dynamics of the interaction with the program:

STEP 1 The user enters the account number in the Account Number box.

The account number the user entered is displayed in the Account Number text box (Figure 1-6). The Account Balance label displays no information.

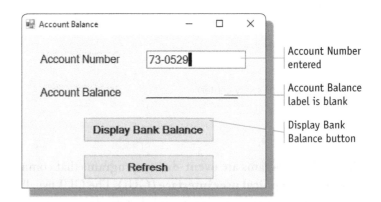

FIGURE 1-6

STEP 2 The user clicks the Display Bank Balance button.

The account balance is displayed in the Account Balance label (Figure 1-7). Clicking the Display Bank Balance button triggered the event that caused the program to determine and display the account balance based on data that the program accessed.

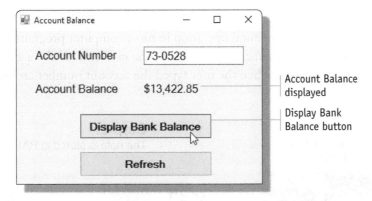

FIGURE 1-7

STEP 3 The user clicks the Refresh button to clear the text box and the label, and prepare the user interface for the next account number.

Clicking the Refresh button triggers another event. The text box and the label are cleared and the insertion point is placed in the Account Number text box (Figure 1-8). The user now can enter a new account number to determine the account balance.

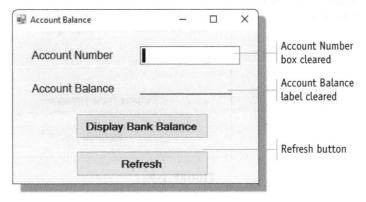

FIGURE 1-8

The events in the previous example consist of clicking the Display Bank Balance button and clicking the Refresh button. The program reacts to the events by performing specific actions (showing the account balance and resetting the text box and label). This is an example of an event-driven program. The Visual Basic developer designs the user interface and writes the program code that performs these event-triggered actions.

Basic Program Operations

All programs, regardless of their size and complexity, execute only a few fundamental operations: input, output, basic arithmetic operations, and logical operations. These operations can be combined in countless different ways to accomplish the tasks required of the program. The following pages describe these basic program operations.

Input Operation

As noted previously, a fundamental operation in most computer programs involves a user who enters data. For instance, in Figure 1-6, the user entered the account number. The steps that occurred when the user typed the account number are shown in Figure 1-9.

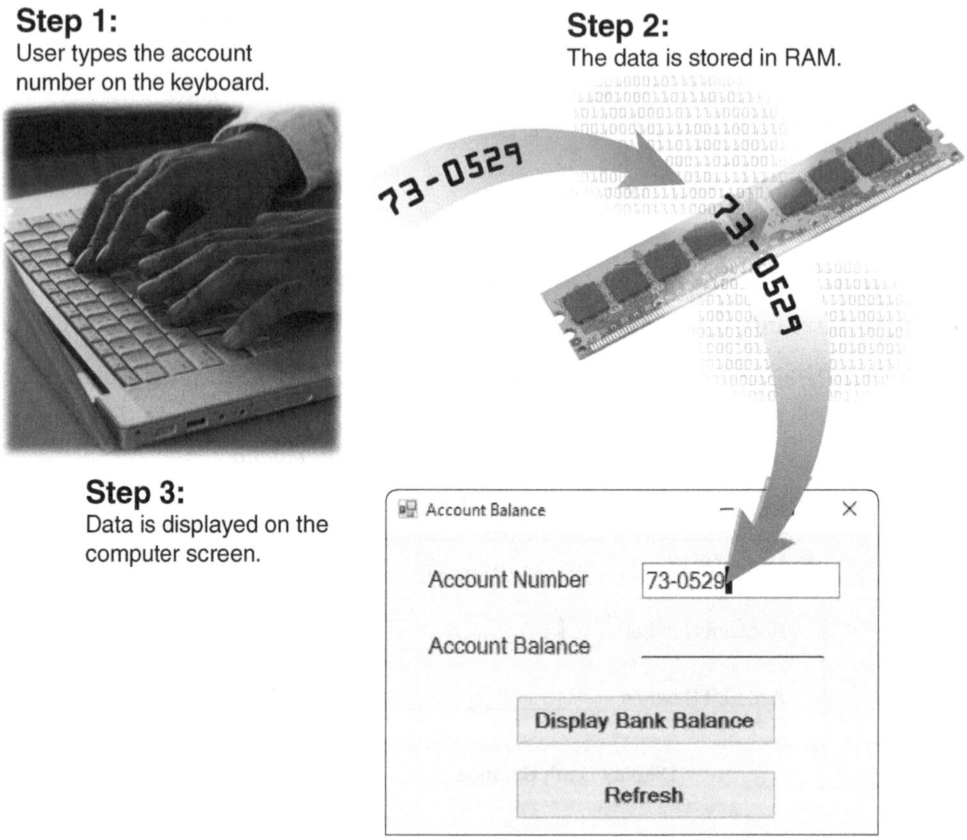

Step 1:
User types the account number on the keyboard.

Step 2:
The data is stored in RAM.

Step 3:
Data is displayed on the computer screen.

FIGURE 1-9

iStockphoto.com/Wesley Thornberry; iStockphoto.com/TPopova

In Figure 1-9, the banking computer program that processes the user's request is stored in RAM. The data entered by the user also is stored in RAM. Depending on the input device, the entered data might also be displayed on the computer screen. The input device used to enter data depends on the application. In Figure 1-9, the user typed the account number on a traditional keyboard or mobile device keyboard. Other applications might allow data to be entered with a scanner, touch screen, digital camera, video camera, mouse, or other device. In each instance, the data is stored in the computer's RAM. When the data is in RAM, instructions in the program can operate on the data.

Output Operation

The second basic program operation is creating output, or information. As you learned previously, a major goal of most computer programs is to create output data, or information, that is useful to people. In Figure 1-7 on page 7, the information requested of the program is the account balance. The process of creating output is shown in Figure 1-10.

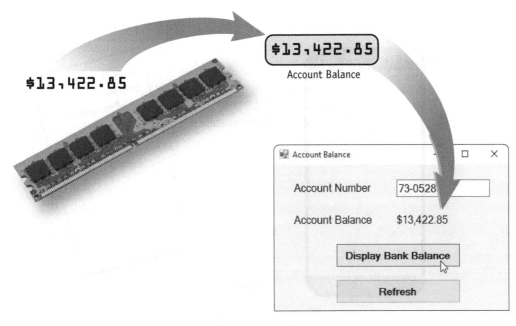

FIGURE 1-10

iStockphoto.com/TPopova

As always, the program must be stored in RAM to control the operations of the computer. In the example, the program sets the text of the Account Balance label equal to the account balance, and then displays it on the screen.

As with input operations, a variety of devices can present output. In addition to computer monitors, common output devices include printers, gaming console screens, and smartphone screens (Figure 1-11).

Basic Arithmetic Operations

After data is stored in main memory as a result of an input operation, the program can process it in some manner. In many programs, arithmetic operations (addition, subtraction, multiplication, and division) are performed on numeric data to produce useful output.

Prior to performing arithmetic operations, the numeric data used in calculations must be stored in RAM. Then, program instructions that also are stored in RAM can direct the computer to add, subtract, multiply, or divide the numbers. The answers from arithmetic operations can be used in additional calculations and processing, stored for future use, and used as output from the program.

Logical Operations

The ability of a computer to perform logical operations separates it from other types of calculating devices. Computers, through the use of programs, can compare numbers, letters of the alphabet, and special characters. Based on the result of these comparisons, the program can perform one processing task if the tested condition is true

Smartphones

Printer

FIGURE 1-11
iStockphoto.com/nixki; iStockphoto.com/guvendemir; iStockphoto.com/scorpion26

and another processing task if the condition is not true. Using a program to compare data and perform alternative operations allows the computer to complete sophisticated tasks such as predicting weather, formatting and altering digital photographs, editing digital video, and running high-speed games.

A program can perform the following types of logical operations:

* Comparing to determine if two values are equal
* Comparing to determine if one value is greater than another value
* Comparing to determine if one value is less than another value

Based on the results of these comparisons, the program can direct the computer to take alternative actions.

Saving Software and Data

When you develop and write a program, the code you write and other features, such as the GUI, must be saved on disk. Then, when you want the program to run, you can have the program loaded into RAM and executed. By saving the program on disk, you can execute the same program many times without rewriting it each time you want to run it.

The program you write, however, also can save data. This data, which can be generated from the processing in the program, can be saved on disk for future use. For example, in a banking application, a customer might open an account. The computer program that is used to open the account saves the customer's information, such as name, address, account number, and account balance, to a local file on the device or in the cloud on a remote server. Later, when the customer makes a deposit or withdrawal, the customer information will be retrieved and modified to reflect the deposit or withdrawal.

In most cases, data such as a customer's name and address is saved in a database. A **database** is a collection of data organized in a manner that allows access, retrieval, and use of that data. Once the data is saved in the database, any programs with permission can reference the data. You will learn more about databases and their use when programming using Visual Basic 2017 later in this textbook.

Visual Basic 2017 and Visual Studio 2017

To write a computer program, a developer uses a programming language. As you learned previously, a programming language is a set of written words, symbols, and codes, following a strict set of usage rules called the language **syntax**, that a developer uses to communicate instructions to a computer. An example of code statements in the Visual Basic 2017 programming language is shown in Figure 1-12.

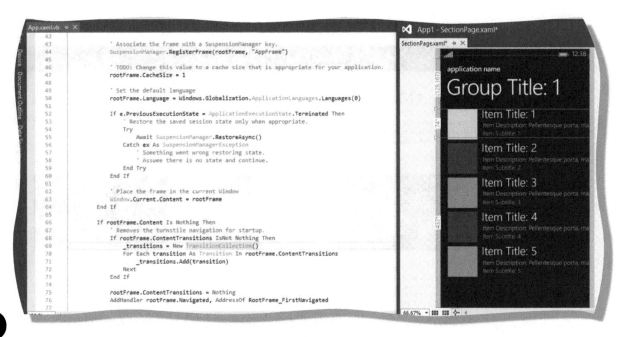

FIGURE 1-12

Each program statement causes the computer to perform one or more operations. When written, these instructions must conform to the rules of the Visual Basic 2017 language. Coding a program is a precise skill. The developer must follow the syntax, or **programming rules**, of the programming language precisely. Even a single coding error can cause a program to execute improperly. Therefore, the developer must pay strict attention to coding an error-free program.

When writing Visual Basic 2017 programs, most developers use a tool called Visual Studio 2017. **Visual Studio 2017** is a software application that allows you to develop Visual Basic 2017 programs using the code you write, code prewritten by others that can be incorporated into your program, and sophisticated tools that speed up the programming process significantly while building better executing and more reliable programs. In this book, you will use Visual Studio 2017 to write Visual Basic 2017 programs.

Visual Studio 2017 is a type of **integrated development environment (IDE)**, which provides services and tools that enable a developer to code, test, and implement a single program, or sometimes a series of programs that comprise an application. Visual Studio 2017, which was developed by Microsoft Corporation, works specifically with Visual Basic 2017 as well as other programming languages to develop program code.

Visual Basic, part of Visual Studio, can be installed on a computer running Windows 7 with Service Pack 1, Windows 8, Windows 10, or Windows Server 2016. Visual Studio 2017 can be installed on a 32-bit or 64-bit computer. Students, educators, and academic institutions can access a free copy of Visual Studio 2017 at *imagine. microsoft.com*. Microsoft Imagine (Figure 1-13) is a Microsoft program that supports technical education by providing access to Microsoft software for learning, teaching, and research purposes such as Visual Studio. This text uses the Microsoft Visual Studio 2017 Community version to present the programming topics. Microsoft Visual Studio Professional and Enterprise can also be used in teaching this textbook course.

FIGURE 1-13

After you start the Visual Studio 2017 application, the Visual Studio 2017 window is displayed. In this window, you can develop and write your Visual Basic program, as shown in Figure 1-14.

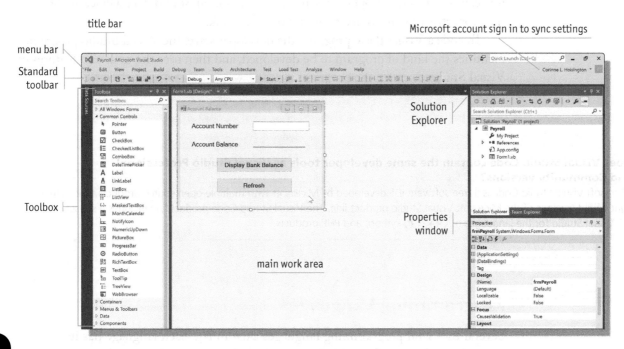

FIGURE 1-14

The following elements help you use the Visual Studio 2017 window. In subsequent chapters, you will learn to use each of the elements found in this window.

Title bar: The title bar identifies the window and the application open in the window. In Figure 1-14, the open application is named Payroll.

Menu bar: The menu bar displays the Visual Studio 2017 menu names. The menus contain lists of commands that allow you to create, edit, save, print, test, and run a Visual Basic program, and to perform other functions that are critical to developing Visual Basic programs.

Standard toolbar: The Standard toolbar contains buttons that execute frequently used commands such as Open Project, New Project, Save, Cut, Copy, Paste, and Undo.

Toolbox: The Toolbox contains **.NET components** that help you develop the GUI for your program. For example, you can use the Toolbox to place buttons, picture boxes, labels, radio buttons, and other Windows GUI objects in the windows of your program.

Main work area: The main work area contains the item you are currently developing. In Figure 1-14, this area contains the Account Balance window of the Payroll program.

Solution Explorer: The Solution Explorer window displays the elements of the Visual Basic **solution**, which is the name for the Visual Basic program and other items generated by Visual Studio to help the program execute properly. You will learn about these items and how to use the Solution Explorer window throughout this book.

Properties window: An item that is a visible part of a GUI, such as the Display Bank Balance button in Figure 1-14, is called an **object** or **control**. Each object in a Visual Basic program has a set of characteristics called the **properties** of the object. These properties, such as the size of the button and the text displayed within the button, can be set in the Properties window within Visual Studio. You will learn about the properties of many objects throughout this book.

To code a Visual Basic program, the developer starts the Visual Studio program, identifies the kind of program to be developed, and then uses the tools and features of Visual Studio to create the program.

Does Visual Studio Code contain the same developer tools as Visual Studio Professional and Community versions?
Microsoft Visual Studio Code is a free software IDE developed by Microsoft with multiple open source products that include lightweight versions of the Microsoft Visual Studio product line. The Visual Studio Code product line includes a subset of the full Visual Studio for the languages of C++, C#, Python, and PHP products.

Programming Languages

Several thousand programming languages exist today. Each language has its own rules and syntax for writing instructions. Languages often are designed for specific purposes, such as scientific applications, business solutions, or webpage development.

Visual Studio can be used to write programs in five languages: Visual Basic, Visual C++ (pronounced see plus plus and called C++ for short), Visual C# (pronounced see sharp and called C# for short), JavaScript, and Visual F# (pronounced eff sharp and called F# for short). You can develop a Windows Universal app for Windows 8/10 or a Windows smartphone coded with Visual Basic, C++, or C#. Each of these languages is described in the following sections.

Visual Basic

Visual Basic is a programming language that allows developers to easily build complex Windows and web programs, as well as other software tools. Visual Basic 2017 is based on the Visual Basic programming language that Microsoft developed in the early 1990s. Visual Basic was created from the BASIC (Beginner's All-purpose Symbolic Instructional Code) language, which was developed in the 1960s.

Visual Basic's popularity evolved from the wide range of productivity features that enabled developers to quickly generate high-quality software applications for Windows. Today, Visual Basic is one of the most widely used programming languages in the world because it is English-like and is considered one of the easier enterprise-level programming languages to learn. Visual Basic is the only language in Visual

Studio that is not case sensitive, which makes it easy for entry-level programmers. It is as powerful as the other programming languages in the Visual Studio suite, such as C++ or C#. An example of Visual Basic 2017 code is shown in Figure 1-12 on page 11.

In this book, you will learn to become a proficient Visual Basic developer.

Visual C++

C++ is a derivative of the programming language C, which originally was developed at Bell Labs in the 1970s. It gives developers exacting control of their applications through optimized code and access to system-provided services. It contains powerful language constructs, though at the price of added complexity. C++ provides unrivaled performance and precision for applications that require a high degree of control.

Visual C#

Introduced in 2001 by Microsoft, Visual C# offers a synthesis of the elegance and syntax of C++ with many of the productivity benefits enjoyed in Visual Basic. Visual C# can be used to create both Windows and Web applications, as well as other types of software tools. Microsoft designed Visual C# to overcome some of the limitations of C++ while still providing the depth of control that C++ developers demand. The language includes aspects of several other programming languages, such as C++, Java, and Delphi, with a strong emphasis on code simplification.

JavaScript

Fully included in the Visual Studio 2017 version, JavaScript (JS) is an open-source client-side scripting language that enhances web browser user interfaces and dynamic websites. Visual Studio 2017 provides complete IntelliSense and debugging support for all the JavaScript objects and its methods.

Visual F#

A Microsoft .NET object-oriented language that debuted with Visual Studio 2010 is called F#. A multipurpose language similar to Visual Basic and C#, the F# language is known for its math-intensive focus, making it perfect for heavy-duty scientific programming applications. The language is relatively new and is just beginning to gain popularity in the business and science environments.

.NET Framework 4.6.2

In the year 2000, Microsoft announced a set of software technologies and products under the umbrella name of .NET. The .NET technologies and products were designed to work together to allow businesses to connect information, people, systems, and devices through software. Much of this connection occurs over the Internet.

The software environment in which programs and applications can be developed for .NET is called the **.NET Framework**, which provides tools and processes developers can use to produce and run programs. The .NET Framework is a development platform for building apps for Windows, Windows Phone, Windows Server, and Windows Azure (the Microsoft professional cloud computing platform). The most recent version is called **.NET Framework 4.6.2**. Visual Studio 2017 provides the development environment for the developer to have access to the .NET Framework 4.6 tools and processes.

Major features of .NET Framework 4.6.2 include the .NET class library, ADO.NET (provides the ability to read and write data in databases), ASP.NET (provides the ability to develop web applications across desktop, tablet, and mobile browsers), Azure Cloud, Windows services, and the Common Language Runtime (CLR: allows programs to run on different computers under different operating systems). Each of these features is explained in the following sections.

.NET Class Library

As you have learned, most programs written using Visual Basic 2017 are event-driven programs in which a user performs an action, such as clicking a button, and the program executes the appropriate instructions. The instructions a program executes when a user clicks a button are normally written by the Visual Basic developer and are unique to the processing required by the program. For example, when a user clicks a button in one program, the overtime pay is calculated for an employee, whereas in another program parking fees are calculated. Each program responds to the events triggered by users with unique processing based on the requirements of the program.

In many programs, however, much of the programming code that must be developed is common for all the programs. For example, in all the programs you have seen in this chapter, a button was used to trigger an event in the program. The button appears in a window on a screen and senses when it has been clicked through the use of program instructions.

When code is common to multiple programs, the best approach is to write the code once and then reuse it when appropriate. For example, when a button is required in the GUI of a program, it is more efficient to use common programming code to insert the button than to require a developer to write all the code for a button each time one is required. When a common task must be performed or a new object such as a button is required, a developer can write the code once and save it as a class. That class can then be referenced by all other programs when the task or object is required.

In short, the coding required for a button can be placed in a class. A **class** is a named group of program code. Once the class is coded, it can be stored in a **class library**, which makes the class available to all developers who need to use it. For example, when you as a developer need to place a button in the user interface, you can use the Button class stored in a class library to create the button without writing all the programming code associated with the button (Figure 1-15).

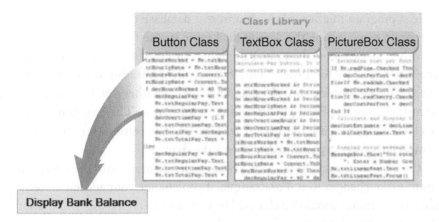

FIGURE 1-15

A button created from a class is called an **object**, or sometimes an **instance** of a class. In programming terminology, the process of creating a Button object from the Button class is called **instantiation**. In other words, a class acts as a general template, while an object is a specific item that is generated based on the class template. Thus, all buttons can be generated, or instantiated, from the Button class. The Display Bank Balance button in Figure 1-15 is a specific Button object instantiated from the Button class.

To create a Button object from the Button class in Visual Studio 2017, you only need to drag the Button .NET component from the Toolbox to a Windows Form object, as you will learn in Chapter 2.

A button in a GUI is only a single example of using classes and class libraries. The .NET Framework class library contains thousands of classes and many class libraries for Visual Basic developers who use Visual Studio to create programs.

With so many classes available in .NET Framework, developers use a method of program development called rapid application development. **Rapid application development (RAD)** refers to the process of using prebuilt classes to make application development faster, easier, and more reliable. Throughout this book, you will gain a further understanding of classes and their use in modern computer programming, and will see how the classes in the .NET Framework class libraries can be used for RAD.

ADO.NET

Often, programs you write must access data stored in a database. A set of prewritten classes called ADO.NET (ADO stands for ActiveX Data Objects) provides the functionality for a program to perform the four primary tasks required when working with a database: getting the data, examining the data, editing the data, and updating the data.

Getting the data refers to retrieving it from the database and making it available to the program. Once the data is retrieved from the database, ADO.NET provides the tools for the program to examine the data and determine how to use it. For example, a program might retrieve data from a database to create a printed report. The program can examine the data to determine its use for the report.

In other applications, the program might examine the data to determine if it is appropriate to display for a user. Thus, in a payroll application the program might require the user to enter a special value, such as her mother's maiden name, to verify her identity before displaying the requested information. The program, using ADO.NET classes, can compare the special value to the data retrieved from the database to determine if the user is permitted to access the data.

A third facility provided by ADO.NET is the ability to edit the data, which means to make changes to it. For example, if you change your address or telephone number, those values should be changed in your account database information. ADO.NET supports the ability to make those changes.

Finally, once changes have been made to data, ADO.NET enables a program to update the database with the new information by writing the data into the database.

ASP.NET

The Internet and the web are integral technological resources. Modern websites provide services from selling products to sharing the latest medical research on any known disease. The development and maintenance of these websites is a constant requirement and consumes many developer hours.

Recognizing the importance of the web, Microsoft developed .NET Framework 4.6.2 to include a programming framework called ASP.NET. Developers can use this framework through Visual Studio 2017 to build powerful and sophisticated web applications on a web server. Using ASP.NET classes, Visual Basic 2017 programmers can create websites that perform any function available on the web today. In addition to traditional websites, you can automatically adapt web applications to target mobile devices with enhanced ASP.NET support for mobile browsers. ASP.NET is designed for cloud technologies and server-side applications. **Cloud computing** is the connection of remote servers hosted on the Internet to store and process data, instead of storing the information locally on a personal computer or device.

ASP.NET offers several advantages for developers. First, almost all the objects available in the .NET framework, such as buttons, text boxes, and picture boxes, are available in ASP.NET. So, developers can use the same techniques to create a web application that they use to create Windows applications such as those shown in this chapter. In addition, ASP.NET is dedicated to mobile-first and cloud-first development. The code footprint for mobile webpages have been slimmed down to open quickly within mobile browsers. The ASP.NET within Visual Studio provides tools to develop interactive HTML5 web applications easily and efficiently with JavaScript and jQuery. Instead of coding separate webpages for each type of mobile device, a single programming model is available for designing webpages and services.

Important web requirements such as performance and security are enhanced and maximized through use of the tools offered with ASP.NET. In short, ASP.NET offers a complete solution for developing modern web applications and cloud services for computers, tablets, and smartphones.

Microsoft Intermediate Language and Common Language Runtime

After a developer writes a program in a programming language such as Visual Basic 2017 using Visual Studio 2017, the programming statements must be translated into a collection of instructions that eventually can be understood by the electronics of the computer. These electronic instructions are executed by the computer to carry out the tasks of the program. This process of translation is called **program compilation**.

Program compilation for a Visual Basic 2017 program creates a set of electronic code expressed in an intermediate language called the **Microsoft Intermediate Language (MSIL)**. When the program is executed, a portion of .NET called the **Common Language Runtime (CLR)** reads the MSIL and causes the instructions within the program to be executed (Figure 1-16).

In Figure 1-16, the Visual Basic program written by a developer is compiled, which translates the human-readable statements in Visual Basic into MSIL, the set of electronic code that forms the input to CLR. Then, when the program is ready for execution, the CLR reads the MSIL in RAM in a form that allows the computer's CPU to execute the instructions in the program.

The use of MSIL and CLR offers multiple benefits that provide speed and flexibility for both the development and execution environments of a program. Utmost among these benefits is that a program written using Visual Studio 2017 and compiled into MSIL can be executed on any computer using any operating system, as long as .NET Framework is available on the computer. So, with no changes to a program you write, the program could be executed on a Dell computer running Windows 10, a mobile smartphone, an older operating system, or an IBM computer using the Linux operating system. This ability to execute programs on different computers running different operating systems is a primary benefit of using .NET Framework.

Types of Visual Basic 2017 Applications

When you begin creating a new Visual Basic 2017 program in Visual Studio 2017, you must choose the type of application you will be developing. Based on your choice, Visual Studio 2017 provides the classes, tools, and features required for that type of application.

Five major types of applications are Windows Classic Desktop applications, Universal Windows apps, Web/Cloud applications, database applications, and HoloLens headset apps. A **Windows Classic Desktop application** means the program will run on a computer or other device that supports the Windows GUI. You can run Windows Classic Desktop applications on a variety of computers.

```
Public Class frmPayroll

    Private Sub frmPayroll_Load(ByVal sender As System.Object, ByVal e As System.EventArgs) Handles MyBase.Load
        ' The eventhandler is executed when the form is loaded.  It
        ' clears the Label objects for the hours worked and weekly pay.

        lblHoursWorked.Text = ""
        lblExtraMinutesWorked.Text = ""
        lblRegularPay.Text = ""
        txthoursWorked.Focus()
    End Sub

    Private Sub btnWeeklyPay_Click(ByVal sender As System.Object, ByVal e As System.EventArgs) Handles btnWeeklyPay.Click
        ' This event handler is executed when the user clicks the Weekly
        ' Pay button.  It calculates and displays the hours worked, minutes
        ' worked, and weekly pay.

        Dim strHoursWorked As String
        Dim strHourlyPay As String
        Dim decHourlyPay As Decimal
        Dim intHoursWorked As Integer
        Dim decRegularPay As Decimal
        Dim decOverTimeHours As Decimal
        Dim decOvertimePay As Decimal

        ' Convert the user input from string to a numeric value
        strHourlyPay = txtHourlyPayRate.Text
        decHourlyPay = Convert.ToDecimal(strHourlyPay)
        strHoursWorked = txtHoursWorked.Text
        intHoursWorked = Convert.ToInt32(strHoursWorked)
        If intHoursWorked > 40 Then
            decRegularPay = decHourlyPay * 40
            lblRegularPay.Text = decRegularPay.ToString("C")
            decOvertimePay = 1.5D * decOverTimeHours + decHourlyPay
        Else
            decRegularPay = decHourlyPay * decHourlyPay

        End If
```

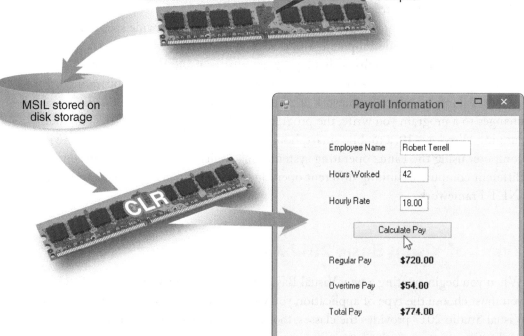

FIGURE 1-16

You can also create **Windows Universal apps** that are designed to run on Windows 8 or Windows 10 computers and mobile devices such as smartphones and tablets. Windows Universal apps have a new look and feel; run on a variety of devices such as a desktop, Windows tablet, or Windows phone; and can be sold in the Windows Store. To develop a Windows Universal app, you must have Visual Studio 2017 installed on a Windows 8 or Windows 10 computer. You cannot develop Windows Universal apps on Windows 7 or Windows Server products. You must obtain a free developer license to develop and test Windows Universal apps before the Windows Store can certify them. The free developer license is provided on a per-machine basis and for a fixed amount of time using a Microsoft account.

When you open Visual Studio 2017 to create any type of application, you can sign in to Visual Studio with a Microsoft account to enable features such as synchronized settings that roam with you to your other Visual Studio devices. If you do not have a Microsoft account, Visual Studio provides the opportunity to sign up for an account for free.

In addition to Visual Studio's Universal App development, Microsoft has a separate app development platform, **Xamarin**, which enables you to develop a mobile app and deploy it to Android, iOS, and Windows devices. Microsoft Xamarin builds native apps for any platform in C#.

You create a **Web application** using ASP.NET. The application runs on a web server. It produces HTML5 code that is downloaded to the client computer, where the browser interprets the HTML and displays the contents of a webpage in a traditional or mobile browser. In a web application, the developer can include items such as security and forms processing to provide all the cloud and local services required of a modern website on a computer or mobile device.

A **database application** is written using ADO.NET to reference, access, display, and update data stored in a database. The Visual Basic 2017 developer writes the code to process the data.

CRITICAL THINKING

Do you have a great idea for an app for the App Store? Creating a mobile app and selling it in the Windows Store provides an exciting way to make money online. You do not need a storefront to sell your idea or worry about distribution. To create an income stream, you need to come up with a unique idea and make that idea a reality by learning to build an app.

Microsoft HoloLens Development

Display technology is rapidly moving beyond two dimensions. **HoloLens** is the augmented reality headset shown in Figure 1-1 on page 2 that places 3-D holographic images in your scope of vision. HoloLens apps are being developed using Visual Studio to select car options at Volvo dealerships, create a custom kitchen at Lowe's Home Centers, explore other planets at NASA, and replace a flat screen TV with a much larger holographic display. Holographic apps in the Windows Store can be monetized in the same way that all other apps are sold.

Microsoft Visual Studio works with Unity software to build HoloLens apps and test them on a built-in HoloLens emulator (Figure 1-17) without the need for a physical HoloLens headset. The emulator uses a Hyper-V virtual machine to run the app. The human and environmental inputs that would usually be read by the sensors on the HoloLens are instead simulated using your keyboard, mouse, or Xbox controller.

FIGURE 1-17

Source: Microsoft

Summary

In this chapter, you have learned the fundamentals of computer programming and have been introduced to the Visual Studio 2017 and Visual Basic 2017 program development environments. In subsequent chapters, you will learn to use Visual Studio 2017 and Visual Basic 2017 to create Windows Classic Desktop applications, Windows Universal apps, database applications, Web/Cloud applications for computer and mobile devices, and HoloLens apps.

Knowledge Check

1. The basic functions of many programs are: a. _____; b. _____; c. _____.

2. Explain the differences between computer hardware and computer software.

3. Match the following terms and their definitions:

   a. Developer

   b. Persistent data

   c. Programming language

   d. Graphical user interface

   e. HoloLens

   f. Database

   g. Rapid application development (RAD)

   h. Cloud computing

   1. A headset designed to view augmented reality

   2. Someone skilled in designing computer programs and implementing them in programming languages

   3. A window with a variety of objects that can be displayed on a variety of devices

   4. Data that is stored on a storage medium

   5. The process of using prebuilt classes to make application development faster, easier, and more reliable

   6. A collection of data organized in a manner that allows access, retrieval, and use of that data

   7. The connection of remote servers hosted on the Internet to store and process data instead of storing the information locally on a personal computer or device

   8. A set of words and symbols that can be interpreted by special computer software and eventually can be executed as instructions by a computer

4. Explain what an event is in the context of event-driven programs. Give two examples.

5. Give examples of the differences between an input operation and an output operation.

6. Describe three different databases where you think information about yourself might be stored.

7. What is programming language syntax? Why is it important?

8. What is a Toolbox in Visual Studio 2017? Why is it valuable?

9. Name two properties that a Button object can possess.

10. What are the five programming languages you can use with Visual Studio 2017?

11. Where can you sell the Windows Universal apps that you develop?

12. State three reasons that Visual Basic is one of the most widely used programming languages in the world.

13. Name two purposes of creating a Microsoft account for use in Visual Studio 2017.

14. Why is a class developed? How are classes organized and stored?

(continues)

15. Differentiate between a class and an object. Give three examples each of classes and objects.

16. What is the primary use of ADO.NET?

17. What do you call the process of translating statements written by a developer? What is the result of this process?

18. What are five types of applications you can create in Visual Basic 2017?

19. Find three YouTube videos that give an excellent overview of different HoloLens examples. Copy and the paste the URL of each of these videos and write a sentence after each URL explaining the video.

20. Research the cost of a HoloLens device and list the specifications.

CHAPTER 2

Program and Graphical User Interface Design

OBJECTIVES

You will have mastered the material in this chapter when you can:

- Create a Visual Basic 2017 Windows Classic Desktop application project

- Name and set the title bar text in a Windows Form object and resize a Windows Form object

- Add a Label object to a Windows Form object, name the Label object, set the text in the Label object, and change the Font properties of the text in the Label object

- Add a PictureBox object to the Windows Form object, name the PictureBox object, and resize the PictureBox object

- Add a Button object to the Windows Form object, name the Button object, set the text in the Button object, and change the Button object's size

- Align objects on the Windows Form object

- Save, close, and open Visual Basic projects

- Understand and implement design principles of the graphical user interface

- Understand and implement the first two phases of the program development life cycle

Introduction

Before a program can be coded using Visual Basic 2017, it must be designed. Designing a program can be compared to constructing a building. Before cement slabs are poured, steel beams are put in place and walls are built. Architects and engineers must design a building to ensure it will perform as required and be safe and reliable. The same holds true for a computer program or app. Once the program is designed, it can be implemented through the Visual Basic 2017 programming language to perform its intended functions.

To illustrate the process of creating a computer program in Visual Basic 2017 using **Visual Studio 2017** as the integrated development environment, you will design and implement the application shown in Figure 2-1 throughout this chapter and Chapter 3.

The application in Figure 2-1 could be part of a larger menu application used to select a coffee latte order at your favorite coffee shop. The program that creates the window in Figure 2-1 will run on a personal computer using the Windows operating system. Similar design principles for desktop computers and mobile devices taught in

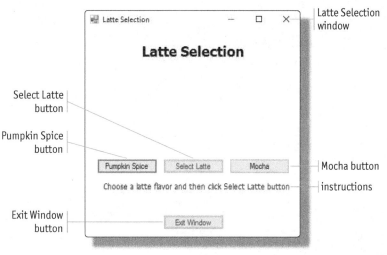

FIGURE 2-1a

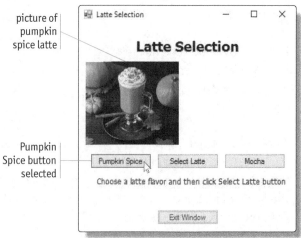

FIGURE 2-1b

this chapter assist with graphic and text layout on any user interface to deliver a consistent experience across touch screens or a desktop's keyboard and mouse interaction. The program will allow customers to select their favorite latte type between the two options of pumpkin spice latte and mocha latte.

In Figure 2-1a, the program begins by displaying the Latte Selection window. The program provides instructions for the user to choose the latte flavor by clicking the Pumpkin Spice or Mocha button, and then to complete the selection by clicking the Select Latte button. If the user clicks the Pumpkin Spice button, a picture of a pumpkin spice latte is displayed (Figure 2-1b). If the user clicks the Mocha button, a picture of a mocha latte is displayed (Figure 2-1c). After choosing a latte flavor, the user can click the Select Latte button and the program informs the user that a flavored latte has been selected (Figure 2-1d). To close the window and exit the program, the user can click the Exit Window button after making a latte selection.

By the end of Chapter 3, you will have completed the design and implementation of this program.

FIGURE 2-1c

Africa Studio/Shutterstock.com

FIGURE 2-1d

Africa Studio/Shutterstock.com

Using Visual Studio 2017

When designing an event-driven program that uses a graphical user interface (GUI), such as the program in this chapter, one of the first steps after defining the purpose for the program is to design the user interface itself. Recall that the user interface is the window that appears on the screen when the program is running. The user interface includes a variety of objects such as buttons that are displayed in the window. Before beginning to design the user interface, however, the developer should know how to use Visual Studio and Visual Basic **rapid application development** (**RAD**) tools in the design process. For example, you use the Visual Studio tools to place a button on the window. Before starting the design of the program shown in Figure 2-1, you should know how to accomplish the Visual Studio tasks described on the following pages. In this text, you can complete steps by tapping if you are using a touch screen or by clicking if you are using a mouse or touchpad.

CONSIDER THIS

Can I store code and other files in the Visual Studio Cloud?

Microsoft provides an online storage cloud for the Visual Studio 2017 community. This optional storage space allows you to store your code, collaborate with team server members, test your code in the cloud, and sync your personal settings such as themes or keyboard shortcuts across various computers. The first time Visual Studio 2017 is launched, your Microsoft account sign-in and password information is requested. If you do not have a Microsoft account, you can create one for free at outlook.com. Signing into your Microsoft account is optional for Windows Classic Desktop applications, but is necessary for creating a Windows Store app. After signing into your Microsoft account, Visual Studio 2017 requests the user interface settings and color theme. These options can be changed at a later time in the Options menu of Visual Studio. To confirm that you are connected to your Microsoft account, check the profile name in the upper-right corner of Visual Studio.

Create a New Visual Basic 2017 Windows Classic Desktop Project

A **project** is equivalent to a single program created using Visual Studio. A **Windows Classic Desktop project** is a program that includes a user interface whose windows are created using the Windows operating system. When the program is executed, the user interacts with the program by using its windows and components (the user interface).

To create a new project using Visual Studio, you must specify the programming language you want to use and the type of program or application you will create. To create a new Visual Basic Windows Classic Desktop project, you can complete the following steps:

STEP 1   In Windows 10, click the Start button on the Windows taskbar, type `Visual Studio`, and then click Visual Studio 2017 in the search results. When the Start Page opens, click the New Project button on the Standard toolbar.

Visual Studio opens the New Project window (Figure 2-2). The New Project window on your computer might be displayed differently, depending on selections made when Visual Studio was installed on your computer. The left pane contains the programming languages and other types of templates available in Visual Studio. The middle pane contains the types of applications you can create within each programming language. The right pane displays a description of the selected application. At this point, you want to create a Windows Classic Desktop project using Visual Basic.

New Project window   description of the selected application

types of
applications

templates
installed
by default

FIGURE 2-2

STEP 2 If necessary, expand Visual Basic and Windows in the left pane, and then click Windows Classic Desktop so it is selected. If necessary, click Windows Forms App in the middle pane.

Windows Classic Desktop is highlighted in the left pane and the types of Windows Classic Desktop projects you can create using Visual Basic are listed in the middle pane. Windows Forms App is selected in the middle pane (Figure 2-3). By making this selection, you specify you are creating a program that runs under the Windows operating system using the Windows Classic Desktop GUI.

Windows Forms App

Windows
Classic Desktop
selected

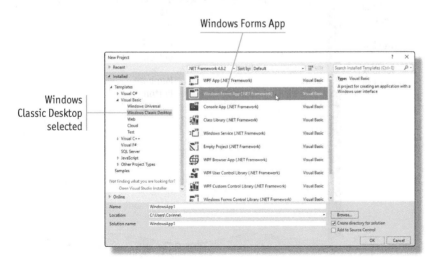

FIGURE 2-3

STEP 3   Type the project name. For this example, you could type `Latte Selection` as the name.

The project name appears in the Name text box (Figure 2-4).

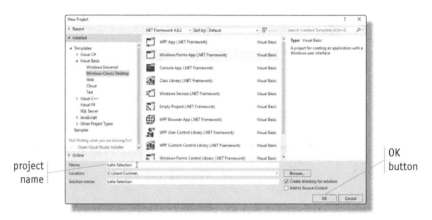

project
name

OK
button

FIGURE 2-4

STEP 4   Click the OK button in the New Project window.

Visual Studio creates a new project (Figure 2-5). The project name is displayed in the title bar of the window.

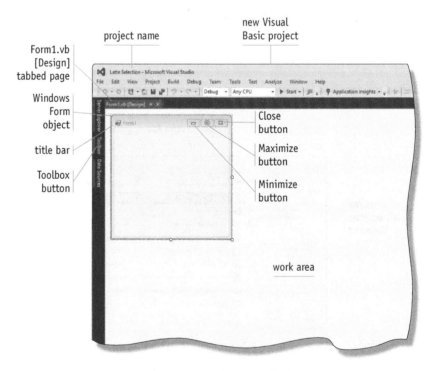

project name

new Visual
Basic project

Form1.vb
[Design]
tabbed page

Windows
Form
object

title bar

Toolbox
button

Close
button

Maximize
button

Minimize
button

work area

FIGURE 2-5

The Visual Studio window contains several important features you should know. First, in the portion of the window known as the **work area**, a tabbed page named Form1.vb [Design] contains a Windows Form object called Form1. A **Windows Form object** is the window you will use to build the program and then display it on your screen when you execute the program. The Windows Form object is the fundamental object in the GUI you will create using Visual Studio tools. Notice in Figure 2-5 that the Windows Form object contains a title bar, a window title (Form1), a Minimize button, a Maximize button, and a Close button.

A second important element is displayed on the left side of the window. Depending on the settings in Visual Studio, the left portion of the window will appear as shown in Figure 2-5 or Figure 2-6. In Figure 2-5, the left margin contains the Toolbox button. The Toolbox button also appears on the Standard toolbar.

Display the Toolbox

You can use the **Toolbox button** to display the Toolbox. The **Toolbox** is the primary tool you use to place objects such as buttons on the Windows Form object. Items in the Toolbox are grouped into sections called **tabs**. To display the Toolbox, you can complete the following steps:

STEP 1   If the window does not already display the Toolbox, click the Toolbox button in the left margin of the window. If necessary, click Common Controls to display the Common Controls tab.

When you point to the Toolbox button, the Toolbox is displayed on the window (Figure 2-6). Notice that the Toolbox hides the Form1 Windows Form object.

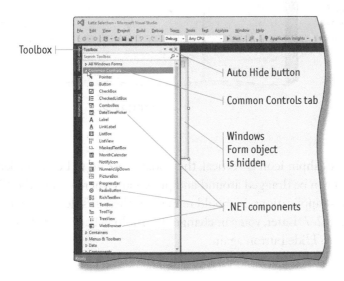

FIGURE 2-6

WATCH OUT FOR

In Figure 2-6, the Common Controls category of tools is open and all its tools are visible. If the Common Controls tab is not expanded, a right triangle appears to the left of the Common Controls tab. To open the tab, click the right triangle.

Among other things, the Toolbox contains many graphical elements called **controls** that you can place on the Windows Form object as GUI objects. For example, the Toolbox contains buttons that can be placed on the Windows Form object. You will learn how to perform this activity in the next section of this chapter.

Permanently Display the Toolbox

When you click outside the Toolbox, it no longer is displayed. When you are designing the GUI, normally it helps to display the Toolbox at all times. To always display the Toolbox, you can complete the following step:

STEP 1   If necessary, click the Toolbox button in the left margin of the window to display the Toolbox. Then, click the Auto Hide button (Pushpin icon) on the Toolbox title bar.

When you click the Auto Hide button, the Pushpin icon on the button changes from being horizontal, which indicates Auto Hide, to vertical, which indicates the Toolbox has been pinned to the window and will remain there (Figure 2-7). Form1 is moved to the right so you can see both the Toolbox and all of Form1.

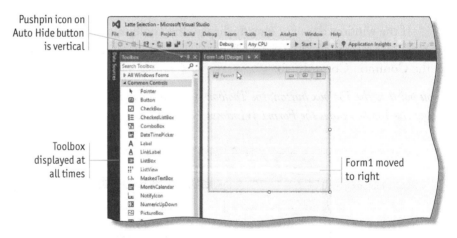

FIGURE 2-7

When the Pushpin icon is vertical, the Toolbox is said to be in Dockable mode, which means it can be dragged around and placed anywhere within the Visual Studio window. In most applications, it should remain on the left side of the window, as shown in Figure 2-7. Later, you can change the Toolbox back to Auto Hide mode by clicking the Auto Hide button again.

View Object Properties

Every object you create in the user interface, including the Windows Form object, has properties. **Properties** can describe a multitude of characteristics about the object, including its color, size, name, and position on the screen. You will learn about the properties of all the objects you create using the Toolbox.

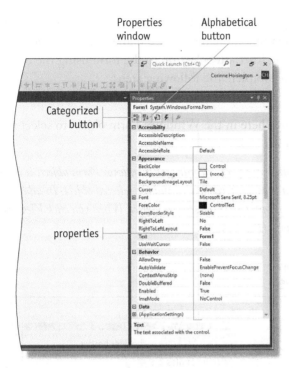

FIGURE 2-8

To view the properties for an object in Visual Studio, you use the Properties window. By default, the Properties window is displayed in the right section of the Visual Studio window (Figure 2-8). Your window might display the Solution Explorer window above the Properties window.

In the **Properties window** shown in Figure 2-8, the property names in the left list appear in Alphabetical view. Many developers find the Alphabetical view the easiest to use when searching for properties. Some developers, however, prefer the Categorized view, in which properties are organized according to type. You can change the order of the properties to Categorized if you click the Categorized button on the Properties window toolbar (see Figure 2-8). In this book, the properties are shown in Alphabetical view, which you select by clicking the Alphabetical button on the Properties window toolbar.

Name the Windows Form Object

Visual Studio assigns a default name to every object in a Visual Basic GUI. For example, the first Windows Form object in a project is named Form1. In virtually every instance, a developer should assign a meaningful name to an object so the program can reference it if required. The name of an object should reflect the object's use. For example, a good name for the Latte Selection window might be frmLatteSelection. Notice in the name that each word is capitalized and the remaining letters are lowercase. You should always follow this naming method when naming objects.

No spaces or other special characters are allowed in the object name. Also, by convention, each object name should begin with a prefix that identifies the type of object. For Windows Form objects, the prefix is frm. Therefore, the complete name

HEADS UP

If you want to reset your Visual Basic window to its original installed layout, you can complete the following steps:

1. Click Window on the menu bar.
2. Click Reset Window Layout on the Window menu.

for the Windows Form object would be frmLatteSelection. The form name should be changed from Form1 to a more descriptive name in the Solution Explorer.

To give the name frmLatteSelection to the form using the Solution Explorer in Figure 2-8, you can complete the following steps:

STEP 1   Click anywhere in the Windows Form object to select it and then click View on the menu bar.

When you click within any object, including a Windows Form object, it is selected (Figure 2-9). Sizing handles and a heavier border surround the selected object. In addition, the Properties window displays the properties of the selected object. When you click View on the menu bar, the View menu is displayed (Figure 2-9).

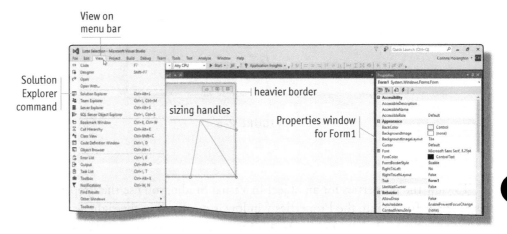

FIGURE 2-9

STEP 2   If necessary, click Solution Explorer on the View menu to display the Solution Explorer. In the Solution Explorer window, right-click the Form1.vb file name to display a shortcut menu with the Rename command.

The shortcut menu for the Form1.vb file appears in the Solution Explorer (Figure 2-10).

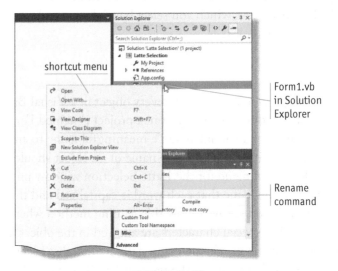

FIGURE 2-10

STEP 3 Click Rename. Type `frmLatteSelection.vb` and press the ENTER key.

The Form1.vb form file is given the new name frmLatteSelection.vb in the Solution Explorer window (Figure 2-11).

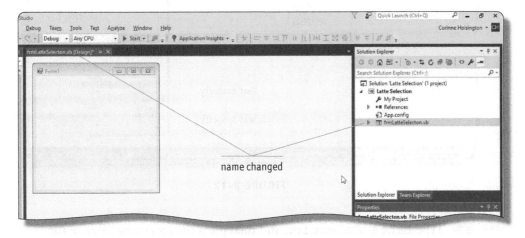

name changed

FIGURE 2-11

Why should you name the Form object?
Later in this text, you add multiple Form objects. It can become confusing if you do not have unique identifying names for each of the Form objects within the project.

CONSIDER THIS

Set the Title Bar Text in a Windows Form Object

After you name the Windows Form object, often the next step in GUI design is to change the title bar text to reflect the function of the program. In this example, the name used is Latte Selection. The **Text property** in the Properties window for the Windows Form object contains the value displayed in the title bar of the window. You can set the Text property using the following steps:

STEP 1 Click the Windows Form object and then scroll in the Properties window as necessary until you find the Text property. (Remember that the properties are in alphabetical order.) Then, double-click the Text property in the right column.

The text, Form1, is selected in the Properties window (Figure 2-12). Form1 is the default text value for the first Windows Form object created in a project. Whenever a property is selected, you can change it.

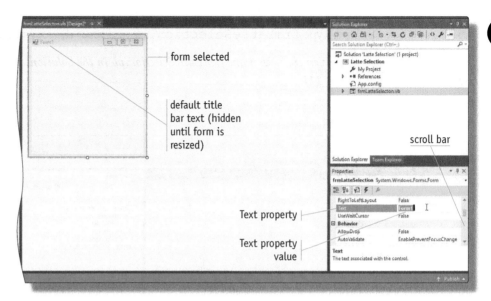

form selected

default title
bar text (hidden
until form is
resized)

scroll bar

Text property

Text property
value

FIGURE 2-12

STEP 2   Type Latte Selection and then press the ENTER key. Resize the
Form object to view the text at the top.

*The value Latte Selection is displayed for the Text property in the Properties window and is
partially displayed in the title bar of the Windows Form object (Figure 2-13). You can enter
any value you like for the Text property of the Windows Form object.*

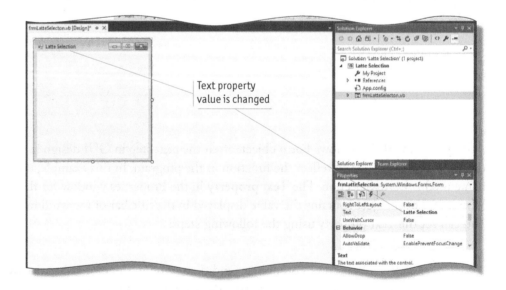

Text property
value is changed

FIGURE 2-13

You can change many of the properties for any object in the GUI using the techniques
just illustrated.

Resize a Form

To resize a Windows Form object, you can change the **Size property** in the Properties window to the exact number of horizontal and vertical pixels you desire. As an alternative, you can drag the vertical border to change the width of the window and the horizontal border to change the height. Another way to change the size is to drag a corner sizing handle, which allows you to change the width and height at the same time.

The following step illustrates how to change the Size property of the Windows Form object shown in Figure 2-14:

STEP 1 With the Windows Form object selected, double-click the Size property in the right column. Type 730, 700 and then press the ENTER key.

The Windows Form object has been resized (Figure 2-14). The exact size of the Windows Form object is shown on the status bar as (number of horizontal pixels, number of vertical pixels). In Figure 2-14, the size of the Windows Form object is 730 pixels horizontally by 700 pixels vertically.(Figure 2-14).

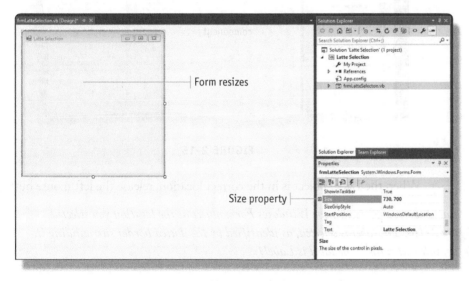

FIGURE 2-14

Adding GUI Objects

After setting up the Windows Form object as necessary for a project, you continue working on the user interface design by adding GUI objects to the form, such as labels, picture boxes, and buttons. Format and position the objects to make the form appealing and easy to use.

Add a Label Object

After sizing the Windows Form object, you can use the Toolbox to add other GUI objects as required. For example, a GUI often displays a message or labels an item in the window. To accomplish this, you can use the **Label .NET component** in the

Toolbox to place a **Label object** on the Windows Form object. To add a Label object to a Windows Form object, you can complete the following steps:

STEP 1   Drag the Label .NET component from the Common Controls tab in the Toolbox over the Windows Form object to the approximate location where you want to place the Label object.

The pointer changes to a crosshair and small rectangle when you place it over the Windows Form object (Figure 2-15). The Label object will be placed on the form at the location of the small rectangle in the pointer.

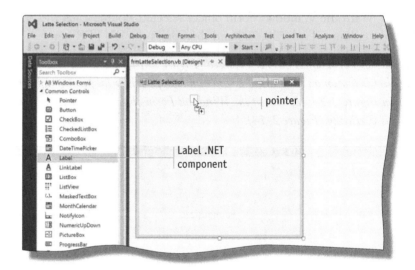

FIGURE 2-15

STEP 2   When the Label object is in the correct location, release the left mouse button.

The Label object is placed on the Windows Form object at the location you selected (Figure 2-16). The label is selected, as identified by the dotted border surrounding it. The default text within the label is Label1.

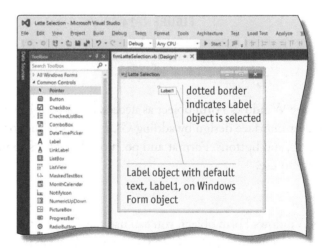

FIGURE 2-16

Name the Label Object

As with most objects you place on the Windows Form object, the first step after creating the object should be to name it. To give the Label object the name Heading with the Label prefix lbl, complete the following step:

STEP 1 With the Label object selected, scroll in the Properties window until you find the (Name) property. Then, double-click the (Name) property in the right column. Type the new name as `lblHeading` and then press the ENTER key.

The name you entered is displayed in the (Name) property in the Properties window (Figure 2-17). You now can reference the Label object by its name in other parts of the program.

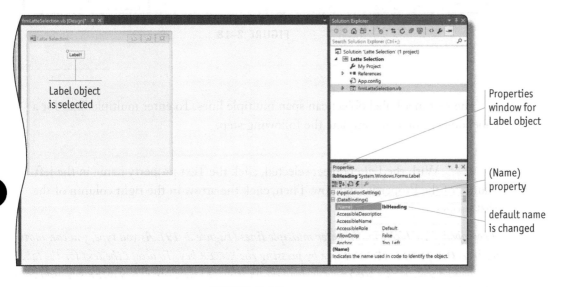

FIGURE 2-17

Change the Text in a Label Object

The default text in a Label object, Label1, normally is not the text you want to display in the label. Therefore, you should change the Text property for the Label object to the value you want. To change the text on the label in Figure 2-16 to Latte Selection, you can complete the following step:

STEP 1 With the Label object selected, scroll in the Properties window until you find the Text property. Then, double-click the value for the Text property in the right column. Type `Latte Selection` for the Text property and press the ENTER key.

The text you entered, Latte Selection, is displayed in the Text property and in the label itself (Figure 2-18). By default, the font size of the text is approximately 8 points. The Label object automatically expanded horizontally to accommodate the text you typed. By default, Label objects change to be the right size for the text in the Text property.

WATCH OUT FOR

If you make an error while typing a property value, such as the name, you can press the BACKSPACE key to erase your mistake and then type the correct data. You also can double-click the property you want to change and start over.

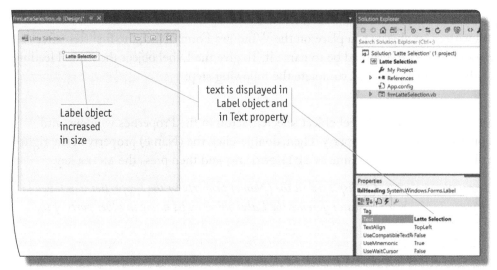

FIGURE 2-18

The text in a Label object can span multiple lines. To enter multiple lines for a Label object, you can complete the following step:

STEP 1   With the Label object selected, click the Text property name in the left column of the Properties window. Then, click the arrow in the right column of the Text property.

A box opens in which you can enter multiple lines (Figure 2-19). As you type, you can move the insertion point to the next line by pressing the ENTER key. To accept the text for the label, press CTRL+ENTER. (In other words, hold down the CTRL key, press the ENTER key, and then release both keys.)

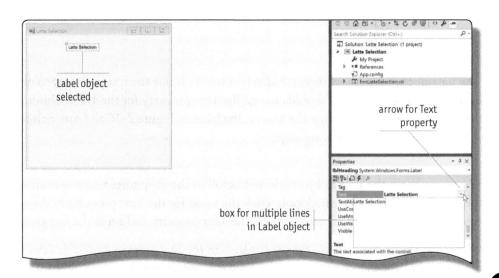

FIGURE 2-19

Change the Label Font, Font Style, and Font Size

The default font, font style, and font size of the text in a Label object often must be changed to reflect the purpose of the label. For example, in a label used as a heading for a window, the text should be larger than the default 8-point font size used for Label objects, and it should be bold to stand out as a heading. To change the font, font style, and font size of a label, you can select the label and then use the **Font property** to make the changes. To change the text in the lblHeading label to Tahoma font, make the font bold, and increase the font size to 16 points, you can complete the following steps:

WATCH OUT FOR

When you click an object to select it, you might double-click it accidentally. If you do, a tabbed page with programming code opens. To return to the form and continue developing the user interface, click the [Design] tab for your form, such as the frmLatteSelection.vb [Design] tab.

STEP 1   Click the Label object to select it. Scroll until you find the Font property in the Properties window. Click the Font property in the left column of the Properties window. Click the ellipsis button for the Font property.

When you click the Font property in the Properties window, a button with an ellipsis (three dots) is displayed in the right column. In the Properties window, an ellipsis button indicates that multiple choices for the property will be made available when you click the button. The Font dialog box is displayed (Figure 2-20). Using the Font dialog box, you can change the font, font style, and size of the text in the Label object.

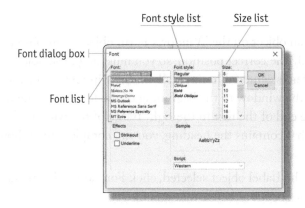

FIGURE 2-20

STEP 2   In the Font dialog box, scroll in the Font list until you find Tahoma and then click it. Click Bold in the Font style list. Click 16 in the Size list.

The selections are highlighted in the Font dialog box (Figure 2-21).

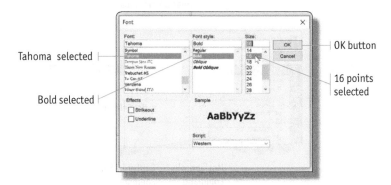

FIGURE 2-21

STEP 3 Click the OK button.

The font, font style, and font size in the Label object are changed as specified in the Font dialog box (Figure 2-22). The Label object automatically expands to accommodate the changed font. The changes also are made for the Font property in the Properties window.

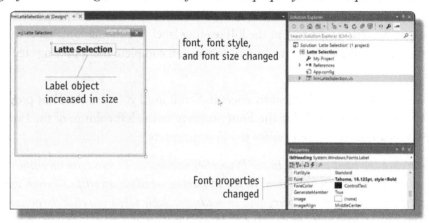

FIGURE 2-22

Center a Label Object in the Windows Form Object

When you place an object on the Windows Form object, your object may not be located in precisely the correct position, so you must align the object in the window. A single label often is centered horizontally in the window; that is, the distance from the left frame of the window to the beginning of the text should be the same as the distance from the end of the text to the right frame of the window. To horizontally center the label that contains the heading, you can complete the following steps:

STEP 1 With the Label object selected, click Format on the menu bar and then point to Center in Form on the Format menu.

The Format menu is displayed and the pointer is located on the Center in Form command (Figure 2-23). The Center in Form submenu also is displayed. The two choices on the Center in Form submenu are Horizontally and Vertically. Horizontally means the label will be centered between the left and the right edge of the window. Vertically means the label will be centered between the top edge and the bottom edge of the window.

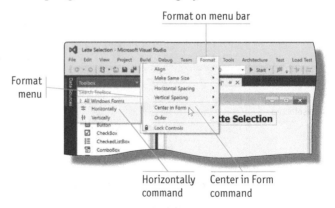

FIGURE 2-23

STEP 2 Click Horizontally on the Center in Form submenu.

The Label object is centered horizontally in the window (Figure 2-24).

FIGURE 2-24

Aligning objects is an important aspect of user interface design because it makes objects and the interface easy to use. Centering within the Windows Form object is the first of several alignments you will make in this chapter.

Delete GUI Objects

In some instances, you might add an object to the Windows Form object and later discover you do not need the object in the user interface. When this occurs, you should delete the object from the Windows Form object. Visual Studio provides two primary ways to delete an object from the Windows Form object: the keyboard and a shortcut menu. An object can be selected and then deleted by pressing the Delete key on the keyboard.

A second way to delete an object is to use a shortcut menu. To do so, right-click the object to be deleted and then select Delete on the shortcut menu.

Use the Undo Button on the Standard Toolbar

As you work in Visual Studio to create a GUI, you might delete an object or perform another activity that you realize was an error. You can undo an action you just performed by clicking the Undo button on the Standard toolbar.

Add a PictureBox Object

When you want to display a picture in a window, such as the latte pictures shown in Figure 2-1b and Figure 2-1c on pages 26 and 27, respectively, you must place a Picture-Box object on the Windows Form object. Then, you place the picture in the PictureBox object. In this section, you will learn to add a PictureBox object to the Windows Form object. In Chapter 3, you will learn how to place a picture in the PictureBox object.

A **PictureBox** is an object much like a label. To add a PictureBox object to the window, you can use the Toolbox, as shown in the following steps:

STEP 1   With the Toolbox visible, drag the PictureBox .NET component on the Toolbox over the Windows Form object to the approximate location where you want the PictureBox object to be displayed.

The pointer changes when you place it over the Windows Form object (Figure 2-25). The upper-left corner of the PictureBox object will be placed on the form at the location of the small square in the pointer.

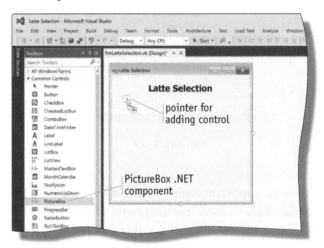

FIGURE 2-25

STEP 2   When the pointer is in the correct location, release the left mouse button.

A PictureBox object is placed on the Windows Form object in the default size (Figure 2-26). The PictureBox object is selected, as indicated by the sizing handles and the heavier border. Notice that when the pointer is inside the PictureBox object, it changes to a crosshair with four arrowheads. This indicates you can drag the PictureBox object anywhere on the Windows Form object.

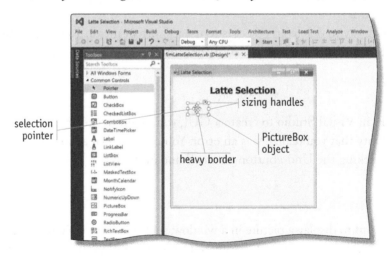

FIGURE 2-26

As you can see, placing a PictureBox object on the Windows Form object is similar to placing a Label object on the Windows Form object. You can use the same technique for most objects within the Toolbox.

Name a PictureBox Object

When you add an object to the Windows Form object, your next action should be to name the object. The technique for naming a PictureBox object is identical to that for a Label object, except that the prefix for a PictureBox object is pic. For example, to give the name picPumpkin to the PictureBox object just added to the form, you can complete the following steps:

Step 1: Select the PictureBox object.

Step 2: Locate the (Name) property in the Properties window for the PictureBox object.

Step 3: Double-click the value in the right column for the (Name) property, type picPumpkin as the name, and then press the ENTER key.

Resize a PictureBox Object

When you place a PictureBox object on the Windows Form object, it often is not the size required for the application. You can resize a PictureBox object using the same technique you used to resize the Windows Form object. Complete the following step to resize the PictureBox object:

STEP 1 Double-click to the right of the Size property of the PictureBox object, type 300, 250, and then press the ENTER key.

When you change the Size property, the width and height of the PictureBox object are changed. In Figure 2-27, the width and height of the PictureBox object are increased. The actual size of the PictureBox object in pixels (300 horizontal pixels, 250 vertical pixels) is shown on the status bar.

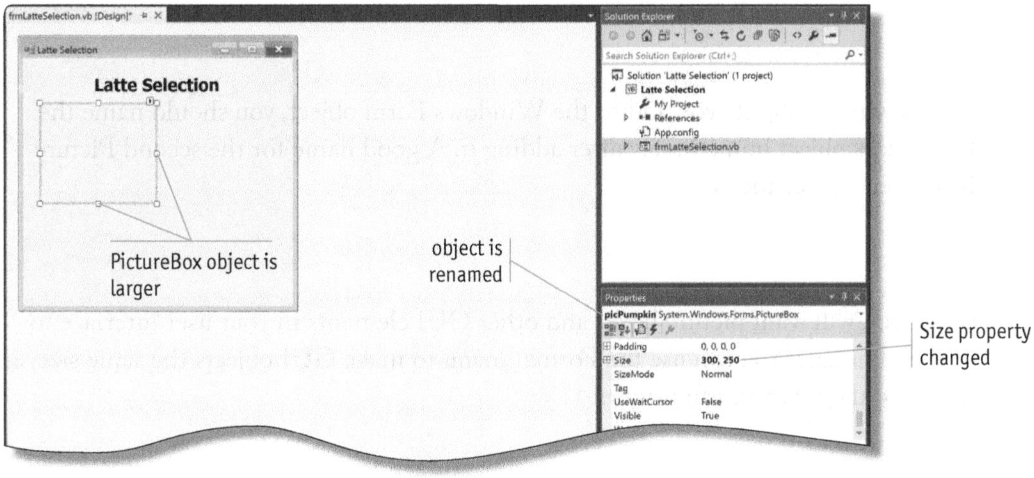

CRITICAL THINKING

If I want to place an image as the background of a Form object, should a PictureBox object be stretched to cover the entire form?
Instead of placing a form-sized image as the background, click the Form object and select the BackgroundImage property.

HEADS UP

The Size property will change to the new size in the Properties window. If you know the exact size you want, you can enter it directly in the Size property for that object.

FIGURE 2-27

Add a Second PictureBox Object

You can add a second PictureBox object to the Windows Form object by performing the same technique you used previously, as in the following step:

STEP 1 Drag the PictureBox .NET component in the Toolbox to any location in the Windows Form object, and then release the left mouse button.

The PictureBox object is placed on the Windows Form object (Figure 2-28). Notice that the PictureBox objects in Figure 2-28 are of different sizes. If you see a blue line as you drag the PictureBox object onto the Windows Form object, ignore it. You will learn about these lines later in this chapter.

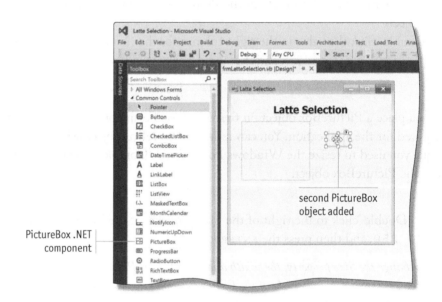

PictureBox .NET component

second PictureBox object added

FIGURE 2-28

As with all objects you add to the Windows Form object, you should name the PictureBox object immediately after adding it. A good name for the second Picture-Box object is picMocha.

Make Objects the Same Size

Often you will want picture boxes and other GUI elements in your user interface to be the same size. You can use the Format menu to make GUI objects the same size, as shown in the following steps:

STEP 1 Select the object whose size you want to duplicate (in this example, the left PictureBox object in the window), hold down the CTRL key, and then click the object you want to resize (the right PictureBox object in the window).

The left and right PictureBox objects are selected (Figure 2-29). The left PictureBox object is surrounded by white sizing handles and the right PictureBox object is surrounded by black sizing handles, which indicates the left PictureBox object is the controlling object when sizing or alignment commands are executed. The first object selected always is the controlling object.

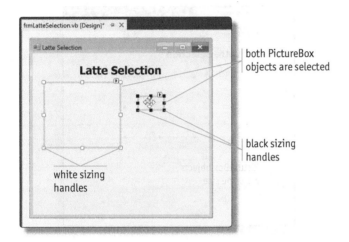

FIGURE 2-29

STEP 2   Click Format on the menu bar and then point to the Make Same Size command on the Format menu.

The Format menu and the Make Same Size submenu are displayed (Figure 2-30). The Make Same Size submenu provides commands to make the width, height, or both dimensions the same as the controlling object.

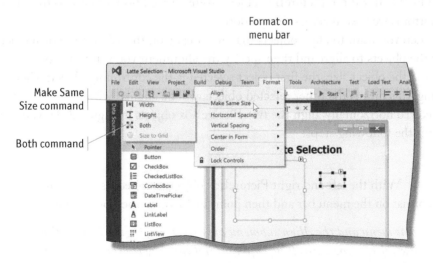

FIGURE 2-30

STEP 3   Click Both on the Make Same Size submenu.

Visual Studio changes the size of the right PictureBox object to match the size of the left PictureBox object (Figure 2-31). Both the width and the height of the right PictureBox object are changed.

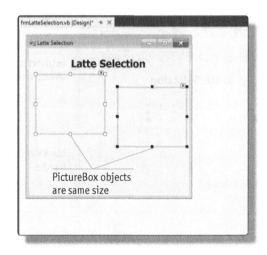

FIGURE 2-31

Align the PictureBox Objects

Notice in Figure 2-31 that the left PictureBox object is higher in the form than the right PictureBox object. When designing a GUI, you should consider aligning the elements to create a clean, uncluttered look for the user. **Alignment** means one element in the GUI is lined up horizontally (left and right) or vertically (up and down) with another element in the window. For example, in Figure 2-31 the GUI would look better if the PictureBox objects were aligned horizontally so their tops and bottoms were even across the window.

When you want to align objects that are already on the Windows Form object, select the objects to align and then specify the alignment you want. As you saw when changing the object size, the first object selected is the controlling object; when aligning, this means the other selected objects will be aligned with the first object selected. To horizontally align the two PictureBox objects in Figure 2-31, you can perform the following steps:

STEP 1   With the left and right PictureBox objects selected, as shown in Figure 2-31, click Format on the menu bar and then point to Align on the Format menu.

The Format menu and the Align submenu are displayed (Figure 2-32). The left PictureBox object is the controlling object, as indicated by the white sizing handles, so the right PictureBox object will be aligned horizontally with the left PictureBox object.

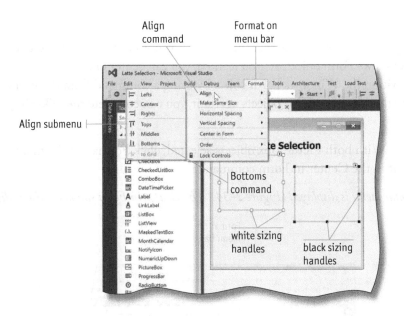

FIGURE 2-32

STEP 2 Click Bottoms on the Align submenu.

The bottom of the right PictureBox object is aligned horizontally with the bottom of the left PictureBox object (Figure 2-33). Because the PictureBox objects are the same size, the tops also are aligned.

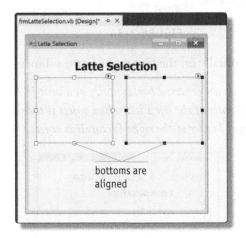

FIGURE 2-33

Notice on the Align submenu in Figure 2-32 that Visual Studio offers seven choices for alignment. When you are aligning objects horizontally, you should choose from the Tops, Middles, and Bottoms group. When you are aligning objects vertically, you should choose from the Lefts, Centers, and Rights group. You will learn how to align to a grid later in this book.

Center Multiple Objects Horizontally in the Window

From Figure 2-33, you can see that the PictureBox objects are not centered horizontally in the Windows Form object. As you learned, you can center one or more objects horizontally within the Windows Form object by using a command from the Format menu. To center the two PictureBox objects as a unit, you can complete the following steps:

STEP 1   With both PictureBox objects selected, click Format on the menu bar and then point to the Center in Form command.

The Format menu is displayed (Figure 2-34). The Center in Form submenu also is displayed.

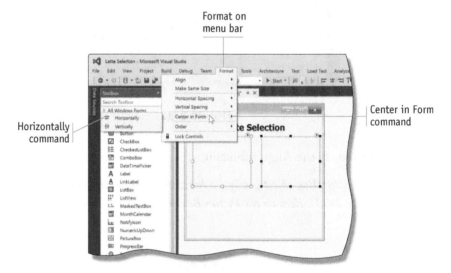

FIGURE 2-34

STEP 2   Click Horizontally on the Center in Form submenu.

The two PictureBox objects are centered horizontally as a unit in the Windows Form object (Figure 2-35). The left border of the left PictureBox object is the same distance from the window frame as the right border of the right PictureBox object.

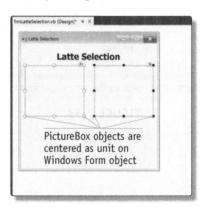

FIGURE 2-35

Adding an object, naming it, sizing it, and aligning it are basic to GUI design.

Add a Button Object

A **Button object** is commonly used in a GUI. For example, you probably are familiar with the OK button used in many applications. Generally, when the program is executing, buttons are used to cause an event to occur. To place a Button object on the Windows Form object, you use the Toolbox. To create a Button object, you can complete the following steps:

STEP 1 With the Toolbox displayed in the Visual Studio window, drag the Button control in the Toolbox over the Windows Form object to the position where you want to place the button below the first PictureBox object.

When you drag the button over the Windows Form object, the pointer changes (Figure 2-36). The upper-left corner of the Button object will be placed at the lower-left corner of the rectangle.

FIGURE 2-36

STEP 2 When the pointer is positioned properly, release the left mouse button.

A standard-sized Button object is added to the Windows Form object (Figure 2-37). The text on the button is the default, Button1. The button is selected, as indicated by the heavier border and sizing handles.

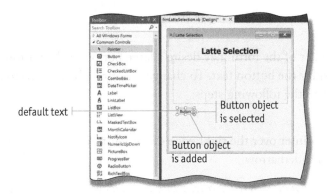

FIGURE 2-37

Name and Set Text for a Button Object

As with other objects you add to the Windows Form object, the first step after adding the Button object is to name it. A Button object name should begin with the prefix btn. For example, the name for the button you just added could be btnPumpkin.

In most cases, you also will change the text that appears on the Button object. To change the text on the btnPumpkin button, you can do the following:

STEP 1 With the Button object selected, scroll in the Properties window until you find the Text property. Double-click the Text value in the right column, type Pumpkin Spice, and then press the ENTER key.

The text for the Pumpkin Spice button is changed on the button and in the Properties window (Figure 2-38). Notice that the text in the button is not fully displayed.

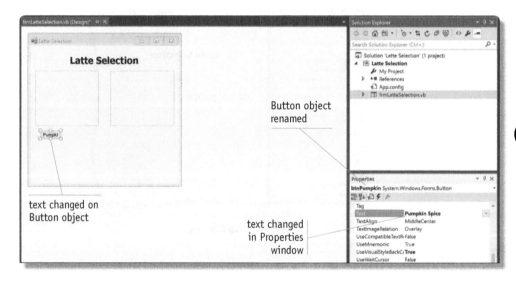

FIGURE 2-38

Change a Button Object's Size

Sometimes, the designer of the form may desire a large button or the button may not be big enough to display the button text. To change a Button object's size to a larger width, you can perform the following steps:

STEP 1 Place the pointer over the right edge of the Button object until the pointer changes to a double-headed arrow.

The pointer changes to a double-headed arrow, which indicates you can drag the border of the button to increase or decrease its size (Figure 2-39).

FIGURE 2-39

STEP 2   Drag the pointer to the right to increase the button's width, and then release the left mouse button.

As you drag the pointer to the right, the button becomes wider (Figure 2-40).

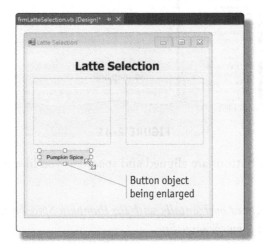

FIGURE 2-40

To move a Button object, first place the pointer on the button; when the pointer changes to a crosshair with four arrowheads, drag the button to any location on the Windows Form object. You can move other objects on the Windows Form object using the same technique.

Add and Align a Second Button

Often, a window requires more than one button. When a second button is added to the window, a normal requirement is to align the buttons. As with PictureBox objects, you can align Button objects horizontally or vertically.

With the PictureBox objects, you saw that you can align objects after placing them on the Windows Form object. You also can align objects when you place them on the Windows Form object. To add a second button to the Windows Form object in Figure 2-40 and align it horizontally at the same time, you can complete the following steps:

STEP 1   Drag the Button .NET component from the Toolbox to the right of the Pumpkin Spice button on the Windows Form object. Release the mouse button, and then align the top of the rectangle in the pointer to the top of the Pumpkin Spice button until a red line appears under the text of the buttons.

*The red line, called a **snap line**, indicates the text on the Pumpkin Spice button is aligned with the text on the Button object being added to the Windows Form object (Figure 2-41). You can drag the Button object left or right to obtain the desired spacing between the buttons. If the red line disappears while you are dragging, move the pointer up or down until the red line reappears, signaling the objects are aligned horizontally.*

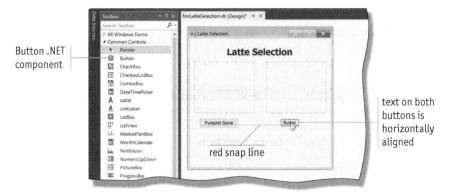

Button .NET component

text on both buttons is horizontally aligned

red snap line

FIGURE 2-41

STEP 2   When the buttons are aligned and spaced as you like, release the left mouse button.

The Button object is aligned horizontally with the Pumpkin Spice button (Figure 2-42). The text of each button is on the same line.

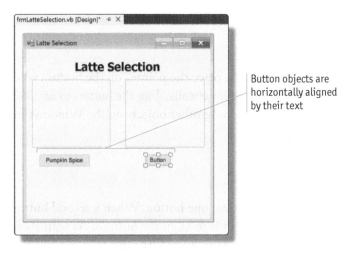

Button objects are horizontally aligned by their text

FIGURE 2-42

After adding the second Button object, you should name it, change the text as needed, and size the Button object if necessary. Assume you have named the second Button object btnMocha, changed the button text to Mocha, and made the two buttons the same size. Recall that you can make the Mocha button the same size as the Pumpkin Spice button by completing the following steps:

Step 1: Click the Pumpkin Spice button and then, while holding down the CTRL key, click the Mocha button.

Step 2: Click Format on the menu bar, point to Make Same Size on the Format menu, and then click Both on the Make Same Size submenu.

Step 3: To deselect the Button objects, click anywhere on the Windows Form object except on another object.

Align Objects Vertically

The buttons in Figure 2-42 are aligned horizontally, but they also can be aligned vertically. To illustrate this point and to use snap lines to align objects that are already on the Windows Form object, assume that the Pumpkin Spice and Mocha buttons are aligned vertically on the left side of the Windows Form object, with the Pumpkin Spice button above the Mocha button. To align the Button objects vertically, you can complete the following steps:

STEP 1 If necessary, click anywhere in the Windows Form object to deselect any other objects. Then, slowly drag the Mocha button below the Pumpkin Spice button until vertical blue snap lines are displayed.

*As you drag, **blue snap lines** indicate when the sides of the objects are aligned vertically. In Figure 2-43, the buttons are the same size, so when the left side of the Pumpkin Spice button is aligned with the left side of the Mocha button, the right sides are aligned as well. As a result, two blue vertical lines are displayed. If you drag the button a little more to the left or right, the buttons will not be aligned and the blue lines will disappear.*

FIGURE 2-43

STEP 2   When the blue lines appear, indicating the buttons are aligned vertically, drag the Mocha button up or down to create the proper spacing between the buttons, and then release the left mouse button.

The proper vertical distance between the buttons is a judgment call based on the needs of the application, the size of the Windows Form object, and the number of other elements in the window (Figure 2-44). As with many aspects of GUI design, the eye of the developer is critical when placing objects in the window.

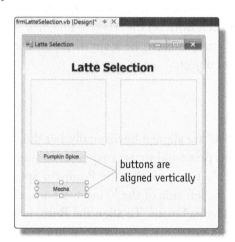

FIGURE 2-44

The use of red and blue snap lines allows you to align objects on the Windows Form object by dragging instead of selecting the objects and using the Format menu.

Visual Studio offers a variety of tools to create and align elements in the GUI, and to make the user interface as effective and useful as possible.

Saving, Closing, and Opening a Visual Basic Project

As you are working on a Visual Basic project, you must save your work on a regular basis. Some developers save every 10 to 20 minutes, while others might wait for a natural break to save their work. Regardless, it is important to develop the habit of regularly saving your work.

To save the work you have completed, you can click the Save All button on the Standard toolbar.

Select the location where you want to store your program. You might use a USB drive, the hard drive on your computer, or a network drive. If you have questions about where to store your program, check with your instructor or network administrator. After you save the program the first time, click the Save All button on the Standard toolbar to save your program in the same location with the same name.

Close Visual Studio 2017

To close Visual Studio, you can click the Close button to the right of the title bar in the Visual Studio window.

Open a Visual Basic Project

After you save a project and close Visual Studio, you often will want to open the project and work on it again. To open a saved project, you can use one of several methods:

Method 1: Double-click the solution file in the folder where it is stored. This method opens the solution and allows you to continue your work.

Method 2: With Visual Studio open, click the Open File button on the Standard toolbar, locate the solution file, and open it in the same manner you do for most Windows programs.

Method 3: With Visual Studio open, click File on the menu bar and then point to Recent Projects and Solutions on the File menu. A list of recent projects is displayed. Click the name of the project you want to open. This method might not work well if you are not using your own computer because other projects might be listed.

After using one of these methods, you can continue working on your project.

WATCH OUT FOR

Sometimes when you open a Visual Basic project, the Form1.vb[Design] tabbed page is not displayed. (This page is renamed frmLatteSelection.vb in your project.) To display the page, double-click Form1 or the new name of this project, frmLatteSelection.vb, which appears in the Solution Explorer window in the upper-right section of the Visual Studio window.

Program Development Life Cycle

Now that you have learned the necessary skills to design a user interface in Visual Studio and Visual Basic, you are ready to learn about the program development life cycle. The **program development life cycle** is a set of phases and steps that developers follow to design, create, and maintain a computer program. The phases of the program development life cycle are as follows:

1. **Gather and Analyze the Program Requirements** — The developer must obtain information that identifies the program requirements and then document these requirements.
2. **Design the User Interface** — After the developer understands the program requirements, the next step is to design the user interface. The user interface provides the framework for the processing that will occur within the program.
3. **Design the Program Processing Objects** — A computer program consists of one or more processing objects that perform the tasks required by the program. The developer must determine what processing objects are required and then determine the requirements of each object.
4. **Code the Program** — After a processing object has been designed, the object must be implemented in program code. **Program code** is the set of instructions, written using a programming language such as Visual Basic 2017, that a computer executes.
5. **Test the Program** — As the program is being coded, and after the coding is completed, the developer should test the program code to ensure it is executing properly. The testing process is ongoing and includes a variety of stages.
6. **Document the Program/System** — As a program is being designed and coded, and after the process is completed, the developer should document the program. **Documenting a program** means using a prescribed method to write down the instructions for using the program, the way the program performs its tasks, and other items that users, developers, and management might require.

7. **Maintain the Program/System** — After a program is put into use, it probably will have to be modified in the future. For example, if a third type of latte is added to the Latte Selection program, it must be changed to reflect the new latte type. The process of changing and updating programs is called **program and system maintenance**.

The program development life cycle rarely is accomplished in a linear fashion, with one phase completed before the next phase starts. Rather, programs are developed iteratively, which means phases and steps within phases might have to be repeated several times before the program is completed. For example, the requirements for a program might change after the developer has begun coding the program. If so, the developer must return to Phase 1 and gather and document the new requirements. Then, changes might be needed to the user interface or other parts of the program to accommodate the updated requirements. This process of moving back and forth within the program development cycle is normal when developing a computer program.

The next sections in this chapter explain Phase 1 and Phase 2 of the program development life cycle in more detail. The remaining phases are explained in Chapter 3.

Phase I: Gather and Analyze the Program Requirements

An old programming adage states, "If you don't understand the problem to be solved, you will never develop a solution." While this seems self-evident, too often a program does not perform as desired because the designer did not understand the problem to be solved. Before beginning the user interface design, it is mandatory that the developer understands the problem.

In many programming projects, the developer is responsible for gathering program requirements by interviewing users, reviewing current procedures, and completing other fact-gathering tasks. The emphasis in this book is on learning to program using the Visual Basic 2017 language, so the process of gathering program requirements is beyond the scope of the book. You will be given the program requirements for each program in this book.

When the requirements have been determined, they must be documented so the developers can proceed to design and implement the program. The exact form of the requirements documentation can vary significantly. The format and amount of documentation might be dictated by the application itself or by the documentation standards of the organization for which the program is being developed. For Windows Classic Desktop applications in this book, two types of requirements documentation will be provided for you. The first is the requirements document.

A **requirements document** identifies the purpose of the program being developed, the application title, the procedures to be followed when using the program, any equations and calculations required by the program, any conditions within the program that must be tested, notes and restrictions that the program must follow, and any other comments that would be helpful to understanding the problem.

Recall that the program being developed in this chapter and Chapter 3 is the Latte Selection program (see Figure 2-1 on pages 26 and 27). The requirements document for the Latte Selection program is shown in Figure 2-45.

REQUIREMENTS DOCUMENT

Date Submitted:	January 23, 2019
Application Title:	Latte Selection
Purpose:	The Latte Selection program will allow a user to select a type of latte.
Program Procedures:	From a window on the screen, the user should view two different latte types and then make a latte selection.
Algorithms, Processing, and Conditions:	1. The user must be able to view choices for a pumpkin spice and mocha latte until the user selects a latte type.
	2. When the user chooses a latte type, a picture of the selected type should appear in the window.
	3. Only one picture should be displayed at a time, so if a user chooses pumpkin spice latte, only its picture should be displayed. If a user then chooses mocha latte, its picture should be displayed instead of pumpkin spice latte.
	4. When the user makes a latte selection, a confirming message should be displayed. In addition, the user should be prevented from identifying a latte flavor after making the latte selection.
	5. After the user makes a latte selection, the only allowable action is to exit the window.
Notes and Restrictions:	The user should be able to make a latte selection only after choosing a latte type.
Comments:	The pictures shown in the window should be selected from pictures available on the web.

FIGURE 2-45

The requirements document contains all the information a developer needs to design the program. In an event-driven program such as the Latte Selection program, however, one additional document often is needed to clarify for the developer what should occur in the program. This document is the Use Case Definition.

A **use case** is a sequence of actions a user will perform when using the program. The **Use Case Definition** specifies each of these sequences by describing what the user will do and how the program will respond. The Use Case Definition for the Latte Selection program is shown in Figure 2-46.

IN THE REAL WORLD

The general term *users* in this text can refer to widely different groups of people. In some cases, actual users of the program, such as bank tellers and their management for a banking application, must approve the user interface design. Not every teller must approve the design, of course, but a representative group should be involved in the process.

In other cases, *users* might refer to people who represent the actual users. For example, in the Latte Selection program in this chapter, not all the people who might order at a coffee shop have to approve the user interface design. The coffee shop chain might select certain customers to participate in a focus group, review the user interface, and make their comments.

The important point is that actual users or their representatives should review the interface. Then, management can give the final approval.

USE CASE DEFINITION

1. User clicks Pumpkin Spice or Mocha button.
2. Program displays a picture of the latte chosen by the user and enables the latte selection button.
3. User clicks latte flavor buttons to view the flavors of latte as desired. Program displays the picture of the chosen latte flavor.
4. User clicks the Select Latte button.
5. Program displays a latte selection confirmation message, and disables both latte flavor buttons and the Select Latte button. The Exit Window button becomes active.
6. User exits the program by clicking the Exit Window button.

FIGURE 2-46

As you can see, the Use Case Definition specifies the actions that the user performs and the actions the program must take in response.

The Use Case Definition is an important part of the requirements documentation for two reasons: (1) It defines for the developer exactly what will occur as the user operates the program. (2) It allows users to review the requirements documentation and ensure that the specifications are correct before the developer begins designing the program.

When gathering and documenting the program requirements, it is critical that users be involved. After all, the program is being developed for their use. When the users concur that the requirements documentation is correct, the developer can move forward into the design phases of the program with confidence that it will fulfill users' needs.

For the programs you will design in this book, the program requirements, including the requirements document and the Use Case Definition, will be provided to you. However, be aware that in many cases in the industry, an experienced developer must gather the requirements as well as implement them in a program.

Phase 2: Design the User Interface

Virtually all programs developed for a GUI are driven by the user's actions within the interface. These actions dictate the processing that the program should execute. Therefore, by designing the user interface, the developer will obtain a foundation for designing the rest of the program. By designing the user interface early in the design process, the developer also can interact with users and ensure that the interface will fulfill their requirements.

Expert program developers recognize the importance of the GUI. These developers spend 25 to 40 percent of program design on the user interface, which sometimes is called the **presentation layer** of the program because it is so critical to the program's success. Mobile devices use small screens, so an easy-to-follow user interface assists in clear navigation that relies on fingers instead of keyboard input.

In the past, developers would draw the user interface on paper and present the drawings to users for their approval. When using Visual Studio 2017, however, the developer should use the program's rapid application development tools to create the user interface. The interface is created with no functionality; that is, none of the buttons or other GUI elements will cause processing to occur. Often, these interface designs are called **mock-ups** because they are provided only for approval of the design. When the users or others approve the interface design, the developer can design the program elements required to implement the functions of the program.

An additional benefit of using Visual Studio to design the user interface is that you can use the completed design in the actual program; you do not have to re-create the design using other software.

My boss at my programming job asked me to design a prototype for the layout of the user interface. What is a prototype?

A prototype is a model of a software product or information system built for customer approval. It is similar to a mock-up of a user interface.

CONSIDER THIS

Principles of User Interface Design

Because the presentation layer of the program is so important, a number of principles and guidelines have been developed over the years for user interface design. **User experience design (UX)** is the process of enhancing user satisfaction by improving the usability and accessibility provided in the interaction between the user and the program or website. While the intent of this book is not to create experts in user interface design, you should understand some of the principles so you can develop programs that are useful and usable. The following are some **design principles** you should incorporate into your user interface designs:

1. The most important principle to remember is that the user's ability to operate the program effectively depends on the design of the interface. If the GUI is easy to use and follow, the user will have a productive and enjoyable experience. On the other hand, if the user struggles to figure out how to enter data or which button to click, the user interface design is defeating the purpose of the program.
2. If the user interface is not easy to use, the user will not be satisfied with the application regardless of how well it works.
3. The user interface includes the windows, graphics, and text shown on the screen, as well as the methods that interact with your program and cause operations to occur. Four primary means of interacting with a user interface are the keyboard, a pointing device such as a mouse, a touch interface, and voice input. The correct use of these tools significantly increases the probability of success for a traditional or touch-based user interface.

4. Using the interface should feel natural and normal. The developer must be aware of who the user is and how the user is accustomed to working. For example, the interface for a banking program in which a teller enters account information will be different from that of a graphic arts program that allows manipulation of graphics and photographs. Each must reflect the needs of the user.

5. Visual Studio contains a wide variety of objects, many of which can be used for similar purposes in the GUI. A good user interface provides the most appropriate object for each requirement. You will learn about all these objects and their correct use throughout this text.

6. Once an object is used for a particular purpose in the user interface, such as a button that causes a particular action, the object should be used for the same purpose throughout the program interface.

7. Objects must be arranged in the sequence in which they are used so the user can move from item to item on the screen in a logical, straightforward manner. Following this principle helps create an interface that is clean and easy to use. Again, the developer must understand the needs of the user.

8. The interface should be kept as simple as possible while containing all required functionality. Generally, the simpler the interface is, the more effective it will be. Consider using colors that are easy on the eyes to prevent eye fatigue.

9. When implemented, the user interface should be intuitive, which means the user should be able to use it with little or no instruction. In fact, the user should feel that no other interface could have been designed because the one they are using is the most natural.

By following these principles, you will create user interfaces that assist the user. The success of your program can depend on the user interface you design.

Sample Program

As you learned earlier, the Latte Selection program is the sample program for this chapter and Chapter 3 (see Figure 2-1 on pages 26 and 27). The requirements document for this program is shown in Figure 2-45 on page 59, and the Use Case Definition is shown in Figure 2-46 on page 60. With these documents in hand, the first phase of the program development cycle is complete.

Sample Program — Phase 2: Design the User Interface

When beginning the design of the user interface, the primary sources of reference are the requirements document and the Use Case Definition for the program. Using these documents, the developer must analyze the program requirements and determine which elements are required in the user interface.

On a line-for-line basis, the analysis of the requirements document in Figure 2-45 on page 59 could proceed as follows:

1. The application will be presented in a window on the screen, so a Windows Forms App using a Windows Form object is the appropriate means for creating the program.

2. The user will review the choices — a pumpkin spice or a mocha latte — and then make a selection. When a latte flavor is selected, a picture of the latte should be displayed. To choose each latte, the program uses a Button object, a common tool that is familiar to users. When a user clicks a button, the user has made a choice and the program responds appropriately. In this application, a good design decision is to use buttons so the user can decide between latte types and then make a latte selection. When the user clicks the Pumpkin Spice button, a picture of pumpkin spice latte will be displayed. When the user clicks the Mocha button, a picture of mocha latte will be displayed. The user then clicks the Select Latte button to make the selection.

3. Two pictures must be displayed in the user interface — a pumpkin spice picture and a mocha picture. Although it is possible to display two different pictures in a single PictureBox object depending on the user's choice, you can develop a simpler and more easily understood user interface if a PictureBox object and a button work together. In other words, when the user clicks the Pumpkin Spice button, the pumpkin spice picture is displayed in the Pumpkin Spice PictureBox object; when the user clicks the Mocha button, the mocha picture is displayed in the Mocha PictureBox object. In this way, the user can associate a button with a picture box location and the user interface is intuitive and easy to use.

4. When the user makes a latte selection by clicking the Select Latte button, a message must be displayed to confirm the latte selection. Therefore, a Label object must be included for the confirmation message.

5. After the user makes a latte selection, the only action available to the user is to exit the window, so an Exit Window button is required.

6. In addition to the requirements in the program requirements document, standard procedure usually dictates that a heading should appear in the program window. Also, it is common practice to include simple instructions in the window so the user is not confused while using the interface. The heading and instructions can be included as Label objects.

7. As a result of this analysis, the user interface should include the following items: a Windows Form object that will contain all the other objects, two PictureBox objects to contain pictures of pumpkin spice and mocha lattes, four Button objects (Pumpkin Spice button, Mocha button, Select Latte button, and Exit Window button), and three Label objects (Heading, Instructions, and Latte Selection Confirmation).

After determining the elements required for the user interface, the developer can use Visual Studio 2017 to create a mock-up of the user interface. The exact placement of objects in the window is a creative process, and is guided by the principles of user interface design you have learned. Usually, no right answer exists because each developer will see a slightly different solution, but you must adhere to the principles of a good user interface design. Figure 2-47 shows the mock-up created for the Latte Selection program.

FIGURE 2-47

Guided Program Development

This section on guided program development takes you step by step through the process of creating the sample program in this chapter. To create the mock-up shown in Figure 2-48, complete the steps on the following pages.

● **Open Visual Studio 2017** Open Visual Studio and sign in to your Microsoft account if necessary. Change your Development settings to Visual Basic, and then maximize the Visual Studio window, if necessary.

● **Create a New Visual Basic Windows Forms App**
Create a new Visual Basic Windows Forms App project by clicking the New Project button, selecting Windows Classic Desktop in the left pane, selecting Windows Forms App in the middle pane, naming the project `Latte Selection`, and then clicking the OK button in the New Project window *(ref: Figure 2-2)*.

● **Keep the Toolbox Visible** If necessary, click the Auto Hide button to keep the Toolbox visible *(ref: Figure 2-7)*.

The Visual Studio application opens and a new project is displayed in the window (Figure 2-48). The Toolbox remains visible regardless of the location of the pointer.

RESULT OF STEP I

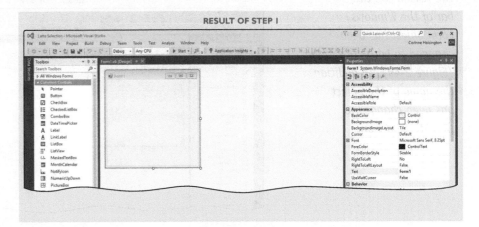

FIGURE 2-48

(continues)

● **Name the Windows Form Object** Click View on the
menu bar and select Solution Explorer to display the Solution
Explorer. In the Solution Explorer window, right-click
Form1.vb. On the shortcut menu, click Rename.
Name the form `frmLatteSelection` *(ref: Figure 2-11)*.

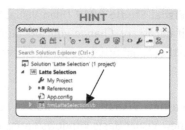

● **Change the Windows Form Object Text Property** With the
Windows Form object selected, double-click the text value for
the Windows Form object in the Text property of the Properties
window. Change the title bar text for the Windows Form object
to `Latte Selection` *(ref: Figure 2-13)*.

*The text in the title
bar of the Windows
Form object has been
changed to Latte Selection
(Figure 2-49). In addition,
the name of the object
has been changed to
frmLatteSelection.*

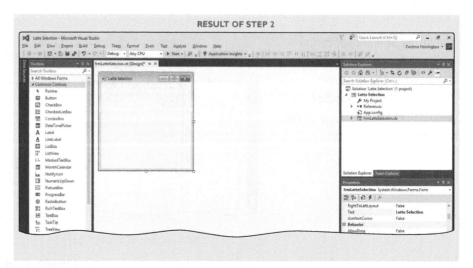

FIGURE 2-49

3

● **Resize the Windows Form Object** Resize the Windows Form
object to the approximate size shown in Figure 2-47 (730 × 700)
by changing the Size property in the Properties window
to 730, 700 *(ref: Figure 2-14)*.

4

● **Add a Label Object** Add a Label object by dragging the Label .NET component
from the Toolbox to the Windows Form object. Place the label near the center
and top of the Windows Form object.

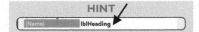

● **Name the Label Object** Change the name of the Label object to lblHeading
by using the (Name) property in the Properties window for the Label object
(ref: Figure 2-17).

● **Change the Label Object Text Property** Double-click the text value for the
Label object in the Text property of the Properties window, and then change the
Text property of the lblHeading Label object to Latte Selection
(ref: Figure 2-18).

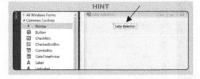

● **Open the Font Dialog Box** Click the Font property for the Label object in the
Properties window, and then click the ellipsis button (...) for the Font property
(ref: Figure 2-20).

● **Change the Font for the Label Object** In the Font list of the Font dialog box,
change the font in the lblHeading Label object to Tahoma *(ref: Figure 2-21)*.

● **Change the Font Style for the Label Object** Using the Font style
list in the Font dialog box, change the font style in the lblHeading Label
object to Bold *(ref: Figure 2-21)*.

● **Change the Size for the Label Object** Using the Size list in the Font
dialog box, change the font size in the lblHeading Label object to 16 points
(ref: Figure 2-21).

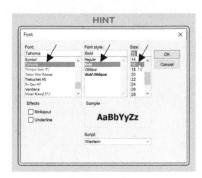

(continues)

● **Center the Heading Horizontally** If necessary, select the
lblHeading Label object. Using the Center in Form command on
the Format menu, click the Horizontally command on the Center
in Form submenu to center the lblHeading Label object horizontally
on the Windows Form object *(ref: Figure 2-23)*.

*The lblHeading Label object text has been changed and the label object is centered horizontally on the Windows Form
object (Figure 2-50). The vertical placement of the label (that is, the distance from the top of the window frame)
depends on the eye of the developer, the size of the Windows Form object, and the other objects in the GUI.*

RESULT OF STEPS 3 AND 4

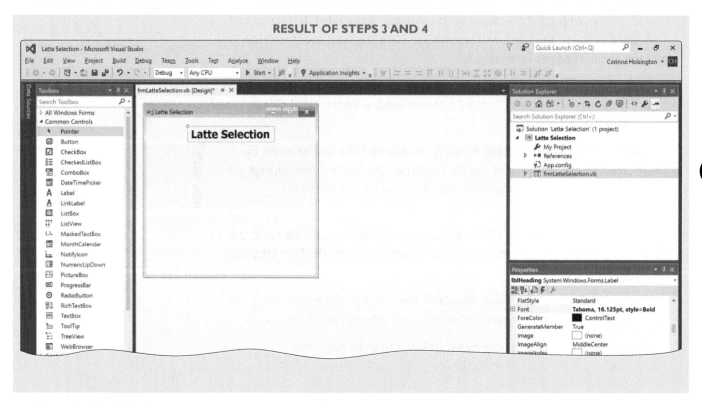

FIGURE 2-50

● **Add a PictureBox Object** Add a PictureBox object to the
Windows Form object by dragging a PictureBox .NET component
from the Toolbox to the Windows Form object. Place the
PictureBox object below and to the left of the heading
label, as shown in Figure 2-51 *(ref: Figure 2-26)*.

● **Name the PictureBox Object** Using the (Name) property in
the PictureBox Properties window, name the PictureBox object
`picPumpkin`.

● **Resize the PictureBox Object** Resize the PictureBox object
by changing its Size property to `300, 250` *(ref: Figure 2-27)*.

*A properly sized PictureBox object is displayed in the Windows Form object (Figure 2-51). This PictureBox object will
display a picture of a pumpkin spice latte when the program is completed in Chapter 3.*

RESULT OF STEP 5

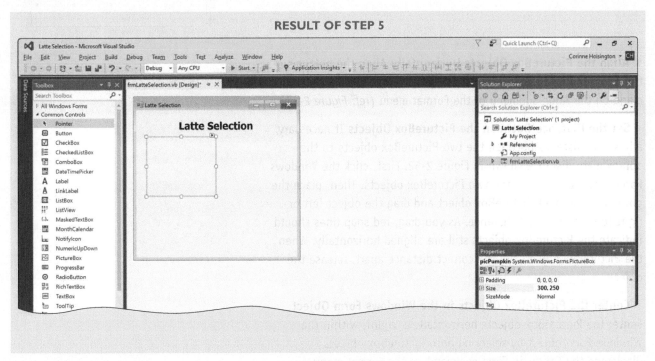

FIGURE 2-51

(continues)

● **Add a PictureBox Object** Add a second PictureBox object to the Windows Form object by dragging a PictureBox .NET component from the Toolbox to the Windows Form object. Place it to the right of the first PictureBox object in the Windows Form object *(ref: Figure 2-28)*.

● **Name the PictureBox Object** Using the (Name) property in the PictureBox Properties window, name the PictureBox object `picMocha`.

● **Size the PictureBox Object** Make the second PictureBox object on the Windows Form object the same size as the first by using the Both command on the Make Same Size submenu of the Format menu *(ref: Figure 2-31)*.

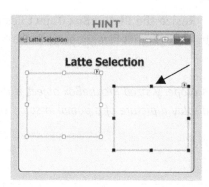

● **Align the PictureBox Objects Horizontally** Align the bottoms of the two PictureBox objects horizontally by using the Bottoms command on the Align submenu of the Format menu *(ref: Figure 2-33)*.

● **Set the Distance Between the PictureBox Objects** If necessary, adjust the distance between the two PictureBox objects to the approximate distance shown in Figure 2-52. First, click the Windows Form object to deselect the two PictureBox objects. Then, place the pointer in the right PictureBox object and drag the object left or right to set the correct distance. As you drag, red snap lines should indicate the PictureBox objects still are aligned horizontally. When the PictureBox objects are the correct distance apart, release the object.

● **Center the PictureBox Objects in the Windows Form Object** Center the PictureBox objects horizontally as a unit within the Windows Form object by selecting both PictureBox objects, displaying the Center in Form command on the Format menu, pointing to the Center in Form command, and then clicking Horizontally on the Center in Form submenu *(ref: Figure 2-35)*.

The PictureBox objects are sized and located properly within the Windows Form object (Figure 2-52).

RESULT OF STEP 6

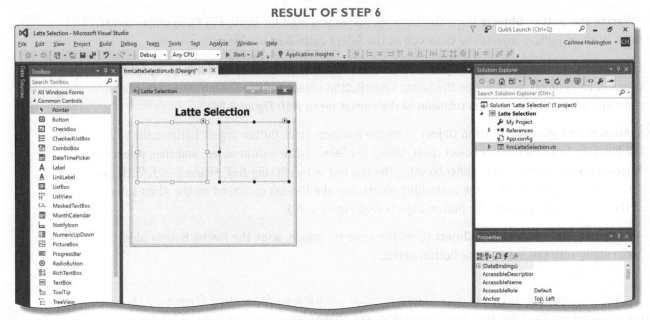

FIGURE 2-52

7

● **Add Three Button Objects to the Windows Form Object** Add three Button objects by dragging them onto the Windows Form object. Align them horizontally below the PictureBox objects at about the same locations shown in Figure 2-47 on page 64. Use red snap lines to align horizontally the buttons on the Windows Form object as you drag them onto the form *(ref: Figures 2-36 and 2-41).*

● **Name the Three Button Objects** Using the (Name) property in the Properties window, name the left Button object btnPumpkin, the center Button object btnSelect, and the right Button object btnMocha.

● **Change the Text Property for the Three Button Objects** Using the Text property in the Properties window, change the text for the left Button object to Pumpkin Spice, the text for the middle Button object to Select Latte, and the text for the right Button object to Mocha *(ref: Figure 2-47).*

(continues)

Guided Program Development *continued*

- **Change the Button Object Size** Change the size of the Select Latte button to accommodate the Select Latte text with extra room on each side of the text *(ref: Figure 2-39)*.

- **Resize the Button Objects** Using the same technique you used for sizing the PictureBox objects, make all three Button objects the same size as the Select Latte Button object.

- **Center the btnSelect Button Object** Center the Select Latte Button object horizontally within the Windows Form object by selecting the Select Latte Button object and then using the Horizontally command on the Center in Form submenu of the Format menu *(ref: Figure 2-24)*.

- **Align the btnPumpkin Button Object** Align the Pumpkin Spice Button object horizontally with the Pumpkin Spice PictureBox object. First, select the Select Latte Button object and then select the Pumpkin Spice Button object, either by using the CTRL key or by clicking *(ref: Figure 2-29)*. With the Select Latte Button object as the controlling object, use the Middles command on the Align submenu of the Format menu to align the Button objects *(ref: Figure 2-32)*.

- **Align the btnMocha Button Object** Using the same technique, align the Mocha Button object horizontally with the Select Latte Button object.

The Button objects are sized and placed properly within the Windows Form object (Figure 2-53). All three buttons are the same size. The three buttons are aligned horizontally, and the Select Latte button is centered in the Windows Form object.

RESULT OF STEP 7

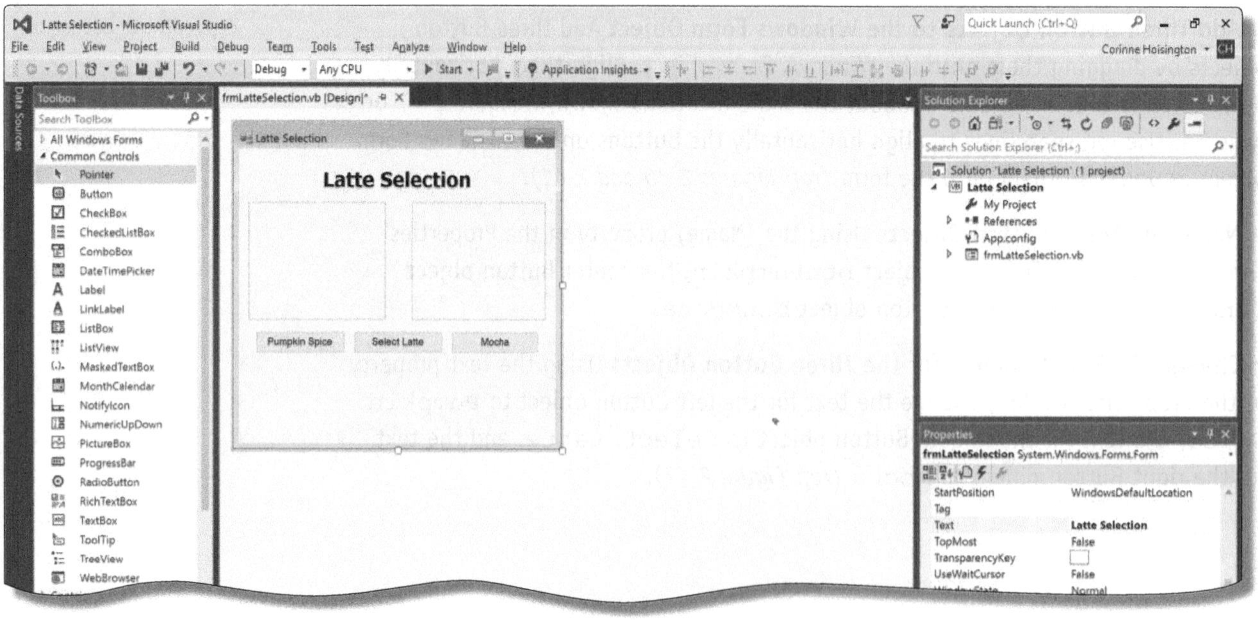

FIGURE 2-53

8

- **Add a Label Object** Add the instructions Label object to the Windows Form object by dragging a Label .NET object from the Toolbox to the Windows Form object. Place it below the Button objects at the approximate location shown.

- **Name a Label Object** Using the techniques you have learned, name the Label object `lblInstructions`.

- **Change the Label Object Text Property** Using the techniques you have learned, change the text in the lblInstructions Label object to `Choose a latte flavor and then click Select Latte button`.

- **Change the Label Object Font** Using the techniques you have learned, change the font for the lblInstructions Label object to Tahoma, change the font style to Regular, and change the size to 9 points.

- **Center the Label Object** Using the techniques you have learned, center the lblInstructions Label object horizontally within the Windows Form object.

- **Add a Label Object** Using the techniques you have learned, add the final message Label object to the Windows Form object. The text of the label should read `Enjoy your latte selection`. Place the Label object in the location shown in Figure 2-54. Name it `lblConfirmation`. Change the font to Tahoma, the font style to Regular, and the size to 9 points. Center the Label object within the Windows Form object.

The two Label objects contain the correct text and are centered horizontally in the Windows Form object (Figure 2-54).

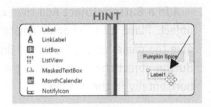

HINT

RESULT OF STEP 8

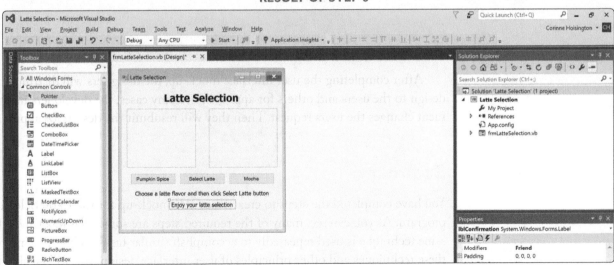

FIGURE 2-54

(continues)

● **Add a Button Object** Add the Exit Window Button object by dragging a Button control onto the Windows Form
object. Place it in the approximate location shown in Figure 2-55. Then, using the techniques you have learned,
give the name btnExit to the Button object, change its text to Exit Window, make the Exit Window
Button object the same size as the other Button objects in the window, and center the Exit Window Button object
horizontally in the window.

The user interface mock-up is complete (Figure 2-55).

RESULT OF STEP 9

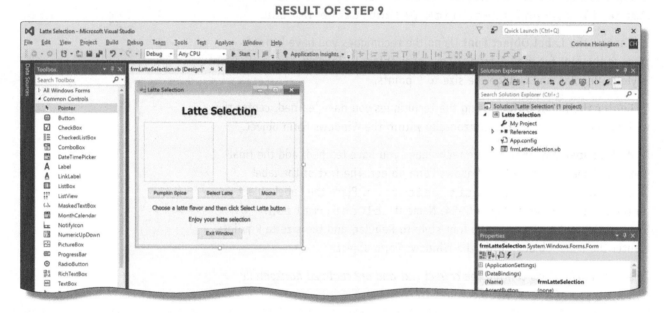

FIGURE 2-55

After completing the user interface mock-up, the designers will distribute the
design to the users and others for approval. In many cases, the developers must implement changes the users request. Then they will resubmit the design for approval.

Summary

You have completed the steps to create the GUI mock-up for the Latte Selection
program. As you can see, many of the required steps are somewhat repetitive; the
same technique is used repeatedly to accomplish similar tasks. When you master
these techniques and other principles of user interface design, you will be able to
design user interfaces for a variety of programs.

Knowledge Check

1–5. Label the following parts of the window shown in Figure 2-56:

1. _____ 2. _____ 3. _____

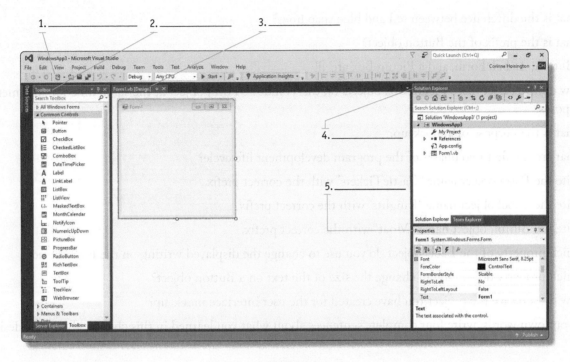

4. _____

5. _____

FIGURE 2-56

(continues)

6. Why would you sign in with a Microsoft account when opening Visual Studio?

7. What does RAD stand for?

8. What is the difference between red and blue snap lines?

9. What is the prefix of the Button object?

10. A Button, Label, Form, and a PictureBox are all _____.

11. How do you select three PictureBox objects on the Windows Form object at the same time for alignment purposes?

12. What is the purpose of a mock-up?

13. What are the first two phases of the program development life cycle?

14. Write the Form object name "CastleTickets" with the correct prefix.

15. Write the Label object name "Knights" with the correct prefix.

16. Write the Button object name "Moat" with the correct prefix.

17. Which property of the Label object do you use to change the displayed writing on the Form object?

18. Which property do you use to change the size of the text on a Button object?

19. How do you save the project you have created for the user interface mock-up?

20. In your own words, write four complete sentences about what you learned in this chapter about UX design.

Debugging Exercises

1. List the steps required to change the poorly aligned buttons on the left (Figure 2-57a) to the properly aligned buttons on the right (Figure 2-57b).

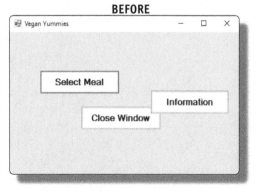

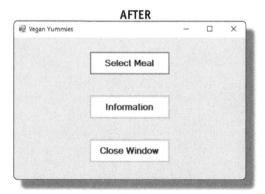

BEFORE   AFTER

FIGURE 2-57a   FIGURE 2-57b

Debugging Exercises *continued*

2. Change the order of the numbered Use Case Definition steps to correspond to the following problem definition: A college provides every incoming freshman with a gift card for a choice of two specialty restaurants within the cafeteria. Students should select one specialty restaurant they want. A program opens a window that displays each specialty restaurant one picture at a time when a student clicks the corresponding button. After making a decision, the student should click the Select Restaurant button. After selecting a restaurant, the student should exit the application.

USE CASE DEFINITION

1. User clicks the Select Restaurant button.
2. User clicks the Teppanyaki button or Sushi button.
3. User exits the program by clicking the Close button.
4. User clicks the button not selected in Step 2.
5. Program displays a confirmation message and disables both restaurant type buttons. The Close button becomes active.
6. Program displays a picture of the first selected specialty restaurant selected by the user and enables the Select Restaurant button.
7. Program displays a picture of the second selected specialty restaurant selected by the user.

Program Analysis

1. After you have placed objects on the Windows Form object (Figure 2-58), list the steps you would follow to change the font for the Order Cupcakes label to Tahoma font, Bold style, 20 points.

2. List the steps you would perform to center the Order Cupcakes label horizontally.

3. List the steps you would perform to center the PictureBox object horizontally on the Windows Form object in Figure 2-58.

4. List the steps you would perform to change the font for the Purchase Now button in Figure 2-58 to Tahoma, 14 points.

5. List the steps you would perform to align the two Button objects horizontally by the bottoms of the buttons.

6. List the steps you would perform to make the Purchase Now button the same size as the Close Window button.

7. In the real world, why is it important to have a user interface mock-up approved before proceeding with the rest of the project?

FIGURE 2-58

Ruth Black/Shutterstock.com

Complete one or more of the following case programming assignments. Submit the program and materials you create to your instructor. The level of difficulty is indicated for each assignment.

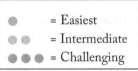

● = Easiest
●● = Intermediate
●●● = Challenging

1 ● VIRTUAL REALITY HEADSETS

Create a Windows form mock-up for the requirements document shown in Figure 2-59 and the Use Case Definition shown in Figure 2-60. The Windows Form object and the other objects in the user interface are shown in Figure 2-61.

REQUIREMENTS DOCUMENT

Date:	October 13, 2018
Date Submitted:	
Application Title:	Virtual Reality Headsets
Purpose:	This Windows Classic Desktop application displays an order screen for two types of virtual reality headsets. The user can choose either a crown VR headset or earbud VR headset.
Program Procedures:	From a window on the screen, the user makes a request to see one of the two VR headset types.
Algorithms, Processing, and Conditions:	1. The user first views a Virtual Reality Headset window that displays the VR Headset company (VR Forward). When the user chooses to click the first headset button for the Crown VR, the crown.jpg image is displayed. When the user chooses to view the second headset for the Earbud VR, the earbud.jpg image is displayed. 2. After the user views one of the two images, the user can select the other image or exit the window.
Notes and Restrictions:	The images should not be displayed at the same time.
Comments:	The picture shown in the window can be found on CengageBrain.com. The name of the pictures are crown and earbud. Images will be added in Chapter 3.

FIGURE 2-59

Virtual Reality Headsets

USE CASE DEFINITION

1. The window opens, displaying the name of the company. The two VR image buttons are enabled.
2. User clicks either the VR Crown or VR Earbud button.
3. The user can continue to click each VR button.
4. The Exit Window button is enabled after the user views an image. User clicks the Exit Window button to exit the application.

FIGURE 2-60

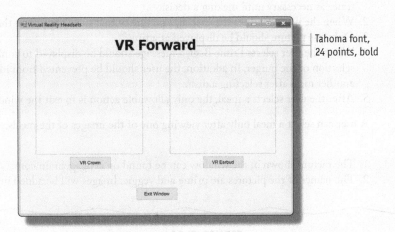

Tahoma font, 24 points, bold

FIGURE 2-61

2 BURGER SPECIALS

Create a Windows Form mock-up for the requirements document in Figure 2-62 and the Use Case Definition shown in Figure 2-63. The Windows Form object and the other objects in the user interface are shown in Figure 2-64.

REQUIREMENTS DOCUMENT

Date:	January 10, 2019
Date Submitted:	
Application Title:	Burger Specials
Purpose:	This Windows Classic Desktop application displays the burger specials for a restaurant named Farm Burger. The user can select one of two specials: Prime Beef or Veggie.
Program Procedures:	From a window on the screen, the user orders one of two special burgers and the program confirms the order with a message.
Algorithms, Processing, and Conditions:	1. The user must be able to identify the Prime Beef or Veggie burger special name as many times as necessary until making a decision.
	2. When the user identifies the special, a picture of that meal appears in the window.
	3. Only one picture should be displayed at a time.
	4. When the user selects Prime Beef, a message should be displayed to confirm the selection of the burger. In addition, the user should be prevented from identifying another meal after selecting a dish.
	5. After the user selects a meal, the only allowable action is to exit the window.
Notes and Restrictions:	A user can select a meal only after viewing one of the images of the meals.
Comments:	1. The picture shown in the window can be found on cengagebrain.com.
	2. The names of the pictures are prime and veggie. Images will be added in Chapter 3.

FIGURE 2-62

Case Programming Assignments *continued*

Burger Specials

USE CASE DEFINITION

1. User clicks the Prime Beef button or Veggie button.
2. Program displays a picture of the burger identified by the user and enables the burger selection button.
3. User clicks meal buttons to view meals as desired. Program displays the picture of the identified burger.
4. User clicks the Select Meal button.
5. Program displays a meal confirmation message and disables both burger buttons and the Select Meal button.
6. The Exit Window button becomes active. User exits the program by clicking the Exit Window button.

FIGURE 2-63

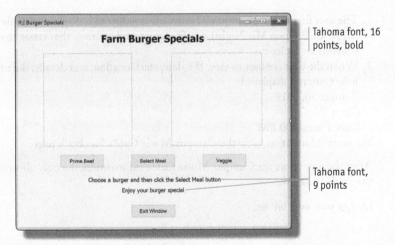

FIGURE 2-64

3 ●●
CAMPUS MUSIC CAFE

Create a Use Case Definition document and design a Windows form mock-up based on the requirements document in Figure 2-65.

REQUIREMENTS DOCUMENT

Date:	October 13, 2018
Date Submitted:	
Application Title:	Campus Music Cafe
Purpose:	This Windows Classic Desktop application displays a welcome screen to market the Campus Music Café performance. The user can choose an option to view the date, start location, and details.
Program Procedures:	From a window on the screen, the user makes a request to see the performance's date, start location, and details.
Algorithms, Processing, and Conditions:	1. The user first views a Campus Music Cafe window that displays the title (Campus Music Café Open Mic Night), a cafe picture, and a phrase that states that all college students are welcome. 2. When the user chooses to view the date, start location, and details, the following information is displayed: October 30, 2018 Open "Mic" Start Time: 8:00 PM For more information, view the Campus Music Café's Facebook page. After the user views the Campus Music Café's information, the only allowable action is to exit the window.
Notes and Restrictions:	Design your own layout.
Comments:	Locate your own image online for use in Chapter 3.

FIGURE 2-65

4 SPRING BREAK TRAVEL SPECIALS

Create a Use Case Definition document and design a Windows Form mock-up based on the requirements document in Figure 2-66.

REQUIREMENTS DOCUMENT

Date:	March 21, 2018
Date Submitted:	
Application Title:	Spring Break Travel Specials
Purpose:	The Student Center on campus has created special Spring Break travel specials on three trips. A student can choose one of three Spring Break trips. The program must display each of the Spring Break travel specials upon request. The student can then select a trip for purchase.
Program Procedures:	From a window on the screen, the user selects one of three trips. A picture of the selected trips is displayed in the window. The user then can choose a trip for purchase.
Algorithms, Processing, and Conditions:	1. The user selects a trip. Then, a picture of the trip location is displayed in the window.
	2. The user can select any of the three trips. Only the picture of the selected trip should be displayed.
	3. The user can select trips as many times as necessary and display the pictures of the destinations.
	4. The user finds a trip, chooses it for purchase, and clicks the Book Trip button.
	5. After the user chooses a trip, a message stating "Enjoy your trip" should be displayed.
	6. After the user chooses a trip, the only allowable action is to exit the window.
Notes and Restrictions:	The user should not be able to choose a trip until viewing at least one trip image.
Comments:	1. The available trips are to Myrtle Beach, Key West, or Venice Beach. Select your own pictures online. Images will be added in Chapter 3.

FIGURE 2-66

5 ●●●
INTERNATIONAL SNACKS

Create a requirements document and a Use Case Definition document and then design a Windows Form mock-up based on the case project shown in Figure 2-67.

> The international club on campus requests a computer application that will run on a kiosk during the International Festival where students can select a healthy international snack. The application should request which free snack you would like, display the choices as buttons, and then display an image of the snack you select. Another button allows you to make your final snack selection and display a confirmation message.
>
> | Snack |
> | --- |
> | Bean Burrito |
> | Falafel |
> | Greek Yogurt |
> | Spring Rolls |

FIGURE 2-67

6 ●●●
COSTUME SHOP

Create a requirements document and a Use Case Definition document and then design a Windows Form mock-up based on the case project shown in Figure 2-68.

> A costume shop requests a computer application that advertises costume rentals. This week's costume rental specials are as follows:
>
> | Destination | Price |
> | --- | --- |
> | Renaissance Fair | $40 week rental |
> | Stormtrooper | $49 week rental |
> | Batman/Batgirl | $36 week rental |
> | Pirate | $29 week rental |
>
> Write an application that allows the user to select any of the five costume rental specials. When the user selects a costume, the corresponding cost and a picture of the costume should be displayed. Clear each prior price and picture when the user selects a different costume. After selecting a costume, the user should be able to book the costume rental and then exit the window.

FIGURE 2-68

CHAPTER 3

Program Design and Coding

OBJECTIVES

You will have mastered the material in this chapter when you can:

- Change the color properties of an object

- Add images to a PictureBox object

- Locate and save an image from the web

- Import an image into the Program Resources folder

- Size an image

- Set the Visible property in the Properties window

- Set the Enabled property in the Properties window

- Run a Visual Basic 2017 program

- Enter Visual Basic 2017 code

- Understand Visual Basic 2017 code statement formats

- Use IntelliSense to enter Visual Basic 2017 code statements

- Use code to set the Visible property of an object

- Use code to set the Enabled property of an object

- Enter comments in Visual Basic 2017 code

- Correct errors in Visual Basic 2017 code

- Write code to use the Close() procedure

- Print code

- Prepare an event-planning document

Introduction

In Chapter 2 you completed the design of a graphical user interface (GUI) mock-up. While users and others can approve the mock-up as being functional, the developer normally must make a variety of changes to the GUI to prepare it for the actual production version of the program. Among these changes are the following:

- Adding color to the interface to make it more visually appealing
- Acquiring and including images that are required for the program
- Setting interface object properties in accordance with the needs of the program

Once these tasks have been completed, Phase 2 of the program development life cycle (PDLC) is complete.

The next two phases of the PDLC are as follows:

- Phase 3: Design the program processing objects
- Phase 4: Code the program

This chapter will provide the skills and knowledge necessary to complete Phase 2 of the PDLC and then complete Phases 3 and 4.

Sample Program

You will recall that the sample program for Chapter 2 and this chapter is the Latte Selection program. Windows for the program are shown in Figure 3-1.

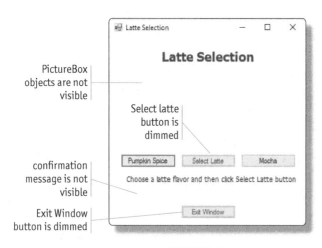

FIGURE 3-1a

FIGURE 3-1b

Africa Studio/Shutterstock.com

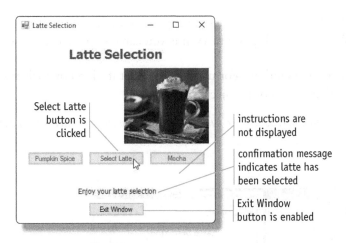

FIGURE 3-1c

Africa Studio/Shutterstock.com

In the opening window (Figure 3-1a), no images appear in the PictureBox objects, and the Select Latte button and Exit Window button are dimmed, which means they are disabled (visible, but not available for selection) when the program begins. In Figure 3-1b, the user clicked the Mocha button, so the picture is displayed. In addition, the Select Latte button is enabled. The Exit Window button still is dimmed. In Figure 3-1c, the user has selected a flavored latte, so the latte selection confirmation message is displayed. The Pumpkin Spice, Select Latte, and Mocha buttons are dimmed and the Exit Window button is enabled. When the program runs, each of these changes occurs through the use of Visual Basic code you enter into the program, as you will discover later in this chapter.

Fine-Tune the User Interface

You learned about some properties of Visual Basic objects in Chapter 2, including the Name property and the Text property. As you probably noted while viewing the Properties window in Chapter 2, more properties are available for each of the objects in a GUI. In many cases, you set these properties to fine-tune the user interface and make it more usable. In the sample program, the BackColor and ForeColor properties make the user interface more attractive and effective.

BackColor and ForeColor Properties

The **BackColor** of an object is the color displayed in its background. For example, in Figure 3-1 on pages 86 and 87 the BackColor of the Windows Form object is white instead of the default gray color, and the BackColor of the Button objects is a Bisque shade. You can select the BackColor of an object by using the **BackColor property** in the Properties window. The **ForeColor** of an object is the color displayed in the text of the object. The heading Label object that displays the Latte Selection text uses a text color called Firebrick. To change the BackColor of a Windows Form object from its default color of Control (gray) to White, you can complete the following steps:

STEP 1   Click the Windows Form object to select it. (Do not click any of the objects on the Windows Form object.)

The Windows Form object is selected, as indicated by the thick border and the sizing handles (Figure 3-2).

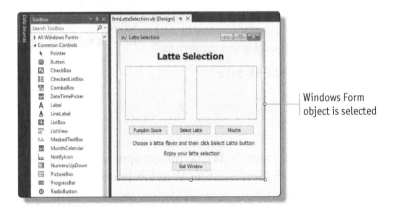

Windows Form object is selected

FIGURE 3-2

STEP 2   If necessary, scroll in the Properties window until the BackColor property is displayed, and then click the right column of the BackColor property.

The BackColor property is selected, and the BackColor arrow is displayed (Figure 3-3).

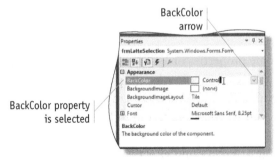

BackColor arrow

BackColor property is selected

FIGURE 3-3

STEP 3   Click the BackColor arrow. Then, click the Web tab to display the Web tabbed page.

The color window opens within the Properties window (Figure 3-4). The Web tabbed page contains more than 100 named colors you can display as the BackColor for the selected object, which in this case is the Windows Form object.

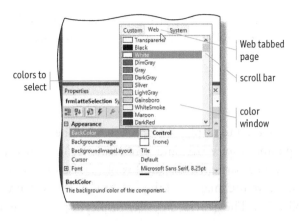

FIGURE 3-4

STEP 4 If necessary, scroll until White is displayed in the list of colors.

The name and a sample of the White color are displayed (Figure 3-5).

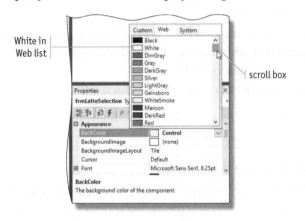

FIGURE 3-5

STEP 5 Click White on the color list.

The background color in the Windows Form object is changed to White (Figure 3-6).

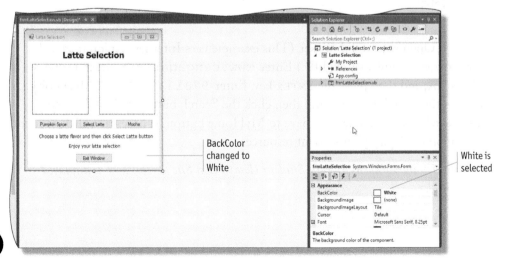

FIGURE 3-6

You can use the same technique to change the BackColor or ForeColor of any object that contains the BackColor or ForeColor properties, including Button and Label objects.

Add Images to a PictureBox Object

PictureBox objects are used to display a graphic image. The sample program can display pictures of a pumpkin spice latte and a mocha latte. You must specify the image that will be displayed in a particular PictureBox object. Before specifying the image, however, you must locate the image and then place it in the Resources folder that is linked to the application. The general steps for displaying an image in a PictureBox object are as follows:

1. Locate the image to be displayed in the PictureBox object. You might locate this image on the web, in which case you must store the image in a folder on your computer, or the image might already be stored on your computer or a local school network.
2. Import the image into the **Resources folder**. This step makes the image available for display within the PictureBox object. Multiple images can be placed in the Resources folder.
3. Specify the image to be displayed within the PictureBox object.

Each of these steps will be explained on the following pages.

Locate and Save an Image from the Web

Images are available from a multitude of sources, from your own digital camera to millions of publicly available images on the web. If you work for a company, it might have photos and graphic logo images that can be used in company applications.

In this book, you can use the Student Companion Site to retrieve an image. For example, to retrieve the pumpkin image from this site, you can complete the following steps:

STEP 1   Open your web browser. (This example uses Internet Explorer; steps for other browsers might vary slightly.) Enter www.cengagebrain.com in the Address box, and then press the ENTER key. Enter 9781337102117 (the book's ISBN) in the Search text box, and then click the Search button. Select the Free Materials tab, and then click the Save to MyHome button. If necessary, click Student Companion to display your student resources.

The browser window opens and the Student Companion Site for this book is displayed (Figure 3-7).

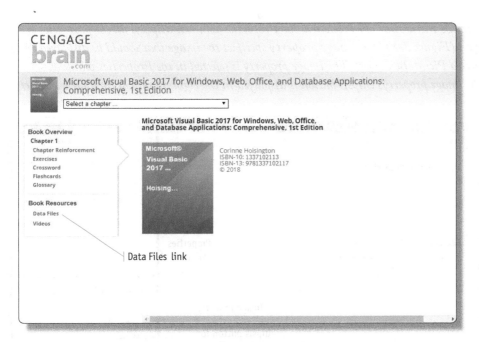

Data Files link

FIGURE 3-7

STEP 2 In the left pane, click Data Files. Click the Download Now link, click Save as, and then navigate to the location on your computer where you store downloaded files. Click the Save button to save the zipped file. Navigate to the location of the downloaded file, and then click the file. Click the Extract all button on the Extract tab to extract the files to the selected folder. Click the Browse button, navigate to the folder where you want to store files for this book, and then click the Extract button. Open the extracted folder for Chapter 3 to display its contents.

In the Save As dialog box you must identify the drive and folder in which you want to store the zipped files containing the Data Files. The location depends on your computer and drives. The image files for Chapter 3 are displayed in a folder window. Remember where you save the images because later you must locate and import them into the Resources folder for use in the program. In all sample programs in this book, images are stored on a USB drive that is designated as drive E. Image file names should not contain spaces.

HEADS UP

When selecting an image, you should choose one that is the same approximate size of the PictureBox object where you will place the image. You can determine the size (in pixels) of a selected PictureBox object by looking at the Size property in the Properties window. To determine the size of the image on the web, press and hold or right-click the image and then click Properties on the menu. The size in pixels is displayed in the Properties dialog box. By choosing an image of the same approximate size, you minimize image distortion when it is fitted into the PictureBox object. If you cannot find an image of the same size, less distortion will occur if you select a larger image with approximately the same relative dimensions as the PictureBox object. In general, avoid selecting an image that is considerably smaller than the PictureBox object.

Import the Image into the Program Resources Folder

After you have saved an image on a storage device that is available to your computer, you should import the image into the program's Resources folder so the image is available for use. To import the Pumpkin image into the Resources folder, you can complete the following steps:

STEP 1 If necessary, open Visual Studio 2017 and the Latte Selection Visual Basic program. Select the picPumpkin PictureBox object by clicking it. Scroll in the PictureBox Properties window until the Image property is visible. Click the Image property name in the left list of the Properties window.

With the PictureBox object selected, the Properties window displays all the properties of the object (Figure 3-8). The **Image property** specifies the image that should be displayed in the selected PictureBox object. The Image property is selected in the Properties window. The Image property's ellipsis button is displayed in the right column of the Image property.

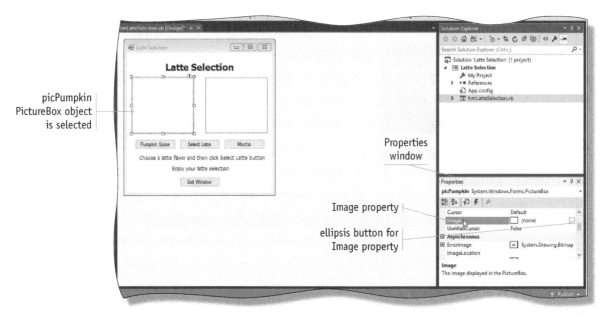

FIGURE 3-8

STEP 2   Click the ellipsis button in the right column of the Image property.

The **Select Resource dialog box** opens (Figure 3-9) and displays the resources that have been imported for the program. In Figure 3-9, no resources have been imported.

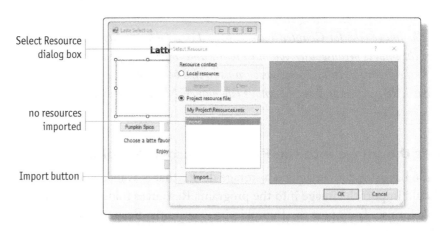

FIGURE 3-9

STEP 3   Click the Import button in the Select Resource dialog box. Use the features of the Open dialog box to locate the file you want to import into the program. In this case, you want to import the pumpkin.jpg file stored on drive E, which is a USB drive. Select pumpkin.jpg. Click the Open button in the Open dialog box.

The Select Resource dialog box is displayed again, but now the pumpkin image is identified in the Project resource file list (Figure 3-10). The image appears in the preview window. This means the image is now part of the resources for the program. You no longer need to locate the image on the USB drive to include the image in a Picture Box object.

Select Resource
dialog box

pumpkin image
is selected

pumpkin image in
preview window

FIGURE 3-10

Anna_Pustynnikova/Shutterstock.com

STEP 5 With the pumpkin file name selected in the Project resource file list, click the OK button in the Select Resource dialog box.

The pumpkin image is displayed in the picPumpkin PictureBox object (Figure 3-11). In addition, the Resources folder is added to the Solution Explorer window, indicating the Resources folder now is part of the program.

Resources
folder

pumpkin image in
picPumpkin
PictureBox object

FIGURE 3-11

Anna_Pustynnikova/Shutterstock.com

Size an Image

In most cases, when you import an image into a program, the image will not fit in the PictureBox object perfectly because the two items have different sizes or dimensions. The developer must adjust the size of the image to fit in the PictureBox object or adjust the size of the PictureBox object to accommodate the image.

By comparing the images in Figures 3-10 and 3-11, you can see that the image is larger than the PictureBox object. Because the PictureBox object must remain its current size, the image must be adjusted using the **SizeMode property**. To adjust an image's size to fit in a PictureBox object, you can complete the following steps:

STEP 1 Select the PictureBox object that contains the pumpkin image, and then scroll in the picPumpkin Properties window until you see the SizeMode property. Click the SizeMode property name in the left column, and then click the SizeMode arrow in the right column of the SizeMode property.

The SizeMode property list is displayed (Figure 3-12). The list contains five choices you can use to change either the size of the image or the size of the PictureBox object. Normal is selected because it is the default value.

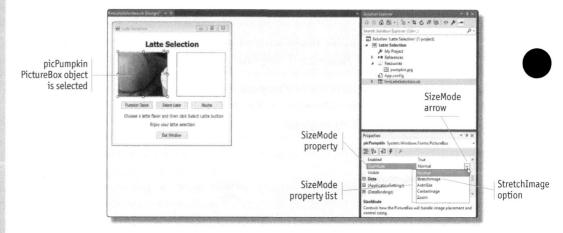

FIGURE 3-12

Anna_Pustynnikova/Shutterstock.com

STEP 2 Click StretchImage in the SizeMode list.

*The SizeMode list is closed and the image is resized to fit within the picPumpkin Picture-Box object (Figure 3-13). When you use the **StretchImage option**, some image distortion might occur to make it fit within the PictureBox object. Therefore, you should select an image that has the same approximate dimensions (or at least the same aspect ratio) as the selected PictureBox object.*

image is resized

StretchImage is selected

FIGURE 3-13

Anna_Pustynnikova/Shutterstock.com

Set the Visible Property

As you have learned, when the Latte Selection program begins, neither of the two latte types is pictured in the window. When the user clicks the Pumpkin Spice button, the program displays the appropriate picture in the Pumpkin Spice PictureBox object. When the user clicks the Mocha button, the program displays the appropriate picture in the other PictureBox object.

The **Visible property** controls whether an object is displayed on the Windows Form object. By default, the Visible property is set to True so that any object you place on the Windows Form object is displayed when the program runs. If you do not want an object to be displayed, you must set the Visible property to False. To set the Visible property to False for the picPumpkin PictureBox object, you can complete the following steps:

STEP 1   If necessary, select the picPumpkin PictureBox object. Scroll in the Properties window until the Visible property is displayed. Click the Visible property name in the left column, and then click the Visible arrow in the right column of the Visible property.

When you click the Visible arrow, the list displays the options True and False (Figure 3-14). To make the object visible when the program starts, select True. If you do not want the object to be visible when the program starts, select False.

FIGURE 3-14

Anna_Pustynnikova/Shutterstock.com

STEP 2   Click False in the Visible property list.

The Visible property is set to False (Figure 3-15). When the program begins, the pumpkin picture will not be displayed on the Windows Form object. Note that the image and object are displayed on the frmLatteSelection.vb [Design] tabbed page regardless of the Visible property setting.

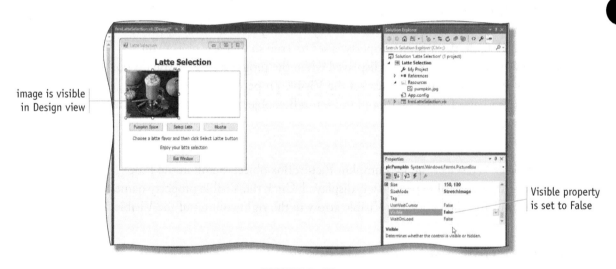

FIGURE 3-15

Anna_Pustynnikova/Shutterstock.com

Once you have set an object's Visible property to False, the only way to display the object on the Windows Form object while the program is running is to set the Visible property to True. You can do this by writing code, as you will see later in this chapter.

Set the Enabled Property

In an event-driven program, objects such as Button objects can be used to make events occur. For example, when you click the Pumpkin Spice button, a picture of a pumpkin spice latte is displayed in the PictureBox object. In addition, the Select Latte Button object becomes **enabled**, which means it can be clicked to make an event occur. When the program begins, however, the Select Latte button is **disabled**, which means nothing will happen when you click the button. A disabled button is displayed as dimmed (see Figure 3-1a on page 86).

The **Enabled property** controls when a Button object is enabled. The property also controls when a Button object is not enabled, which means clicking the button causes no action. The default selection for the Enabled property is True, which means the associated Button object is enabled. To set the Enabled property to False for the Select Latte button, you can complete the following steps:

STEP 1   Select the btnSelect object. Scroll in the Properties window until the Enabled property is displayed. Click the Enabled property name in the left column, and then click the Enabled arrow in the right column of the Enabled property.

When you click the Enabled arrow, the list contains the words True and False (Figure 3-16). To make the object enabled when the program starts, select True. If you do not want the object to be enabled when the program starts, select False.

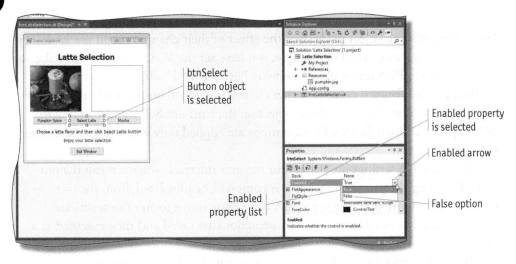

FIGURE 3-16

Anna_Pustynnikova/Shutterstock.com

STEP 2   Click False in the Enabled property list.

The Enabled property is set to False (Figure 3-17). When the program begins, the btnSelect Button object will not be enabled on the Windows Form object.

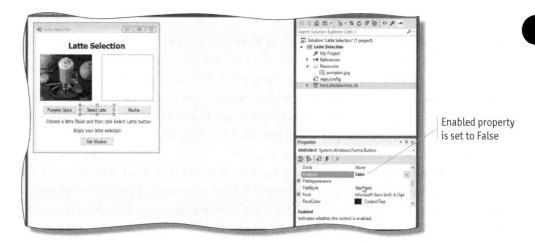

FIGURE 3-17

Anna_Pustynnikova/Shutterstock.com

Enabled property
is set to False

Once you have set the Enabled property to False, the only way to enable a Button object on the Windows Form object while the program is running is to set the Enabled property to True. You can do this by writing code, as you will see later in this chapter.

Run a Program

When you set some object properties, the effect of their changes might not be evident until you run the program. For example, you have set the Visible property to False for the picPumpkin PictureBox object, and you have set the Enabled property to False for the btnSelect Button object. Neither change is evident, however, when you view the Latte Selection Windows Form object on the frmLatteSelection.vb [Design] tabbed page in Visual Studio. These settings are applied only when you actually run the program.

To ensure the settings are correct for the user interface, you must run the program. **Running the program** means it is compiled, or translated, from the instructions you have written or generated in Visual Basic into a form of instructions that the computer can execute. These instructions are saved and then executed as a program.

To run the program you have created, you can click the Start button on the Standard toolbar, as shown in the following steps:

STEP 1 Point to the Start button on the Standard toolbar.

The pointer appears over the Start button (Figure 3-18).

Start
button

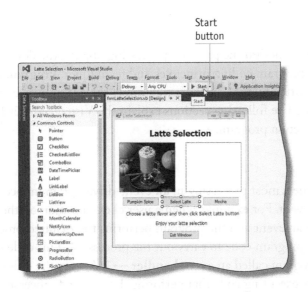

FIGURE 3-18

Anna_Pustynnikova/Shutterstock.com

STEP 2   Click the Start button on the Standard toolbar.

The program is compiled and saved, and then it runs on the computer. When the program runs, the Latte Selection window is displayed on the screen (Figure 3-19). Notice that the pumpkin image is not displayed in the window because the Visible property was set to False for the picPumpkin PictureBox object (see Figure 3-15). Notice also that the Select Latte button is dimmed, which indicates its Enabled property is set to False. The Diagnostic Tools button pane opens on the right.

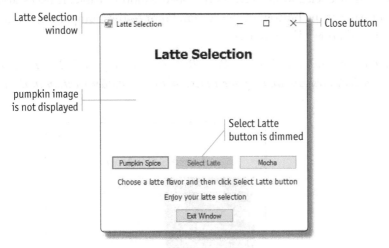

Latte Selection window | Close button
pumpkin image is not displayed | Select Latte button is dimmed

FIGURE 3-19

Once you start running the program, it continues to run until you exit it. To exit a program, click the Close button on the right side of the window title bar (see Figure 3-19).

After you set all the properties for the objects in the user interface, the design of the user interface is complete. You now are ready to move to the next phase of the PDLC — designing the program processing objects.

Visual Basic Program Coding

Before beginning to design the program processing objects, the developer must understand certain program coding principles and techniques. **Program code** is the set of instructions written by the developer that direct the program to carry out its required processing. The following sections explain the Visual Basic 2017 code required for the Latte Selection program.

Enter Visual Basic Code for Event Handling

As you have learned, most processing in an event-driven program occurs when the user triggers an event. For example, when a user clicks a button on the GUI, the activity can trigger an event and the program performs the required processing. The developer writes program code to carry out the processing. This code is placed in a section of the program called an **event handler** — it *handles* the event that the user action triggers by executing code that performs the required processing.

To write the code for an event handler, the developer first must identify the GUI object that will be used to trigger the event. For example, when the Pumpkin Spice button is clicked in the sample program, the Pumpkin picture should appear in the picPumpkin PictureBox object. To write the code that will display the pumpkin picture, the developer must inform Visual Studio that the Pumpkin Spice button is the object for which the code is being written and that an event handler must be created for the click event. You can create the event handler using the following steps:

STEP 1   If necessary, open Visual Studio 2017 and the Latte Selection program and make the frmLatteSelection.vb [Design] tabbed window visible. If necessary, close the Output pane at the bottom of the screen. Point to the Pumpkin Spice Button object in the Windows Form object.

The pointer appears over the Pumpkin Spice Button object (Figure 3-20). The four-headed arrow pointer indicates you can drag the Button object to another location in the window.

pointer is on Pumpkin Spice Button object

FIGURE 3-20

Anna_Pustynnikova/Shutterstock.com

STEP 2 Double-click the Pumpkin Spice Button object.

The code window is displayed on the frmLatteSelection.vb* tabbed page (Figure 3-21). The code in the window is generated by Visual Studio. This code identifies an event handler, which is the code that executes when an event is triggered. When the Pumpkin Spice button is clicked, the program will execute the code in this event handler. The list box at the top of the tabbed page identifies the object for which the event handler will execute — in this case, the btnPumpkin object. The list box in the upper-right corner of the tabbed page identifies the event that must occur to execute the code in the event handler. The event identified in Figure 3-21 is "Click." When the user clicks the Pumpkin Spice button, the program executes the code between the Private Sub statement and the End Sub statement. The insertion point is located where the developer should begin entering the code that executes when the user clicks the btnPumpkin Button object.

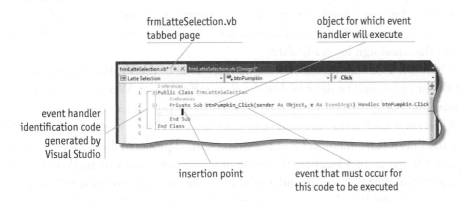

FIGURE 3-21

Visual Basic 2017 Coding Statements

A Visual Basic 2017 coding statement contains instructions that the computer eventually executes. Visual Basic has a set of rules, or **syntax,** that specifies how each statement must be written.

When the user clicks the Pumpkin Spice button while the Latte Selection program is running, the pumpkin image should be displayed in the picPumpkin Picture-Box object. Figure 3-22 shows a Visual Basic coding statement that sets the Visible property to True for the picPumpkin PictureBox object so the image is displayed in the picture box after the statement executes.

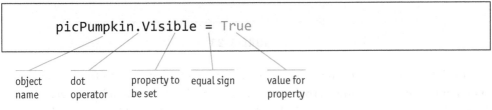

FIGURE 3-22

The first part of the statement, picPumpkin, identifies the object that contains the property to set. The name of the object is followed by the **dot operator** (period) with no intervening spaces. The dot operator separates the name of the object from the next entry in the statement and is required.

Following the dot operator is the name of the property to set. In Figure 3-22 on page 101, the name of the property is Visible. You will recall that the Visible property determines whether an image is displayed in the PictureBox object when the program is running. In Figure 3-15 on page 96, the Visible property was set to False for the picPumpkin PictureBox object so the image would not be displayed when the program started. This statement sets the Visible property to True so the image will be displayed.

The property name is followed by a space and then an equal sign. The space is not required, but good coding practice dictates that elements within a statement should be separated by a space so the statement is easier to read. One or more spaces can be used, but most developers use only one space. The equal sign is required because it indicates that the value to be used for setting the property follows. A space follows the equal sign for readability.

The word *True* follows the space. The value True in the Visible property indicates that the image should be displayed in the PictureBox object. When the program is running and the Visible property is set to True, the image appears in the picture box.

Each entry within the program statement must be correct or the program will not compile. This means the object name must be spelled properly, the dot operator must be placed in the correct location, the name of the property must be spelled properly, the equal sign must be present, and a valid entry for the property must follow the equal sign. For the Visible property, the only valid entries are True and False.

General Format of a Visual Basic Statement

The general format of the Visual Basic statement shown in Figure 3-22 appears in Figure 3-23.

General Format: Property Value Assignment Statement
`objectname.property = propertyvalue`

EXAMPLE	*RESULT*
picPumpkin.Visible = True	Picture is visible
btnSelectLatte.Enabled = False	Button is dimmed

FIGURE 3-23

In the general format, the object name always is the first item in the Visual Basic statement. The object name is the name you specified in the (Name) property of the Properties window. In Figure 3-22, the object name is picPumpkin because that name was given to the pumpkin PictureBox object.

The dot operator (period) is required. It follows the object name with no space between them. Immediately following the dot operator is the name of the property that will be set by the statement. The property name must be spelled correctly and must be a valid property for the object named in the statement. Valid properties that can be specified in the statement are identified in the Properties window associated with the object.

The equal sign must follow the property name in the statement. Visual Basic statements do not require spaces, nor is there a limit to how many spaces you can place between elements in the statement. The equal sign identifies the statement as an **assignment statement**, which means the value on the right side of the equal sign is assigned to the element on the left side of the equal sign. When setting properties, the element on the left side of the equal sign is the property.

The property value specified in the assignment statement must be a valid value for the property identified on the left side of the equal sign. You can see the valid values for a given property by looking in the Properties window for the object whose property you are setting.

After you have entered the property value, the Visual Basic statement is complete. Because correct programming protocol dictates that only one statement should appear on a line, the next step is to press the ENTER key to move the insertion point to the next line in the code window.

The general statement format shown in Figure 3-23 is used for all statements in which the code sets the value of an object property.

IntelliSense

In Figure 3-21 on page 101, the insertion point is located in the code window. To enter the statement shown in Figure 3-22 into the program using the code window, you can type the entire statement. Visual Studio, however, provides help so that you will be less prone to make a typing error when entering the statement. This help feature is called IntelliSense.

IntelliSense displays all allowable entries you can make in a Visual Basic statement each time a dot (period), an equal sign, or another special character is required for the statement. When you type the prefix pic as shown in Figure 3-24, an IntelliSense window opens with all the objects that begin with the prefix. Instead of possibly misspelling the object name, you can select it from the IntelliSense list. The complete Visual Basic statement is shown in Figure 3-24.

```
picPumpkin.Visible = True
```

FIGURE 3-24

When you type the first few letters of the object name, IntelliSense displays a list of all the objects and other entries that can be specified in the statement.

HEADS UP

Unlike some programming languages, the capitalization of object names, properties, property values, and other values is not important in Visual Basic. Therefore, the object name picPumpkin is equivalent to the object name picpumpkin. Capitalization is used within the object name to make the name easier to read.

IN THE REAL WORLD

Microsoft created IntelliSense in response to the demands of rapid application development so statements can be entered accurately and easily. Most developers use IntelliSense; it is the standard within the software industry.

Enter a Visual Basic Statement

To enter the Visual Basic statement in Figure 3-24 using IntelliSense, you can complete the following steps:

STEP 1   With the code window open and the insertion point positioned as shown in Figure 3-21 on page 101, type pic.

The characters "pic" are displayed in the code window (Figure 3-25). IntelliSense displays a list of all the entries that can follow the prefix in the statement. Sometimes the selected entry is correct for the statement you are entering, but often it is not. Therefore, you must identify the correct statement in the list before entering it.

characters *pic* typed

IntelliSense list

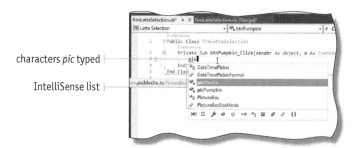

FIGURE 3-25

STEP 2   To identify the correct entry, type its next letter until the entry is selected. In this case, type p.

As you type, IntelliSense highlights an entry in the list that begins with the letters you enter (Figure 3-26). When you enter picp, IntelliSense highlights the only term in the list that begins with picp, which is picPumpkin. This is the object name you want to enter into the Visual Basic statement.

picp typed

picPumpkin
is highlighted

FIGURE 3-26

STEP 3   When IntelliSense highlights the correct object name, press the key corresponding to the entry that follows the object name. In this case, press the PERIOD key.

IntelliSense automatically enters the entire object name into the Visual Basic statement and the period you typed following the object name (Figure 3-27). In addition, IntelliSense realizes that the dot you entered means more information is required in the statement, so it displays a list of the allowable entries following the dot.

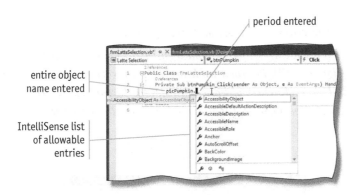

period entered

entire object
name entered

IntelliSense list
of allowable
entries

FIGURE 3-27

STEP 4 As with the object name in Step 2, the next step is to enter one or more characters until IntelliSense highlights the desired property in the list. Type the letter v for the Visible property.

IntelliSense highlights the properties in the list that begin with the letter v (Visible) (Figure 3-28). Because the Visible property is highlighted, no further action is required to select it. The red curly line below the code indicates that the line of code is not complete.

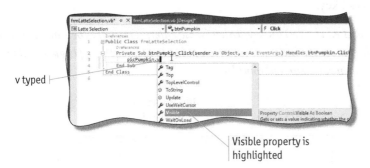

v typed

Visible property is
highlighted

FIGURE 3-28

STEP 5 Press the key for the character that follows the property name. In this case, press the SPACEBAR.

IntelliSense enters the highlighted property name (Visible) followed by the space you typed (Figure 3-29). The space indicates to Visual Basic that the object name and property name entry is complete. In Figure 3-29, the statement gets or sets a value indicating whether the control is displayed. This means the Visible property indicates whether the picPumpkin PictureBox object is displayed.

Visible property
name is entered

space entered

FIGURE 3-29

STEP 6   Press the EQUAL SIGN key and then press the SPACEBAR and the letter t.

The equal sign and a space are displayed and then IntelliSense displays a list of the entries you can make (Figure 3-30). For the Visible property, the correct entries following the equal sign are False and True. An entry of False indicates the PictureBox object should not be visible; True indicates the opposite. IntelliSense highlights the True entry.

equal sign and
space entered

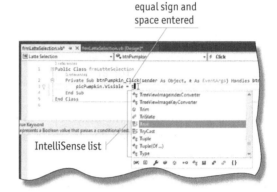

IntelliSense list

FIGURE 3-30

STEP 8   Press the key for the character that follows the True entry. In this case, press the ENTER key.

Because you pressed the ENTER key, IntelliSense enters True into the statement and then Visual Studio moves the indented insertion point to the next line (Figure 3-31). The Visual Basic statement now is entered completely.

True is entered
in statement

FIGURE 3-31

Can I turn on line numbers to receive assistance while creating my program?

Line numbers help identify each line of code in the code window. If line numbers do not appear in the code window on your computer, you can display them by completing the following steps:

1. Click Tools on the menu bar.
2. Click Options on the Tools menu.
3. If necessary, click the triangle next to Text Editor in the Options dialog box.
4. If necessary, click the triangle next to Basic in the list below Text Editor.
5. Click General in the list below Basic.
6. Place a check mark in the Line numbers check box.
7. Click the OK button in the Options dialog box.

Do professional programming teams immediately sit down at a laptop and start typing in code?

Professional programmers first design the program by thinking about the numerous ways the problem's solution may be found. One of the most common is called top-down design. Top-down design divides the program into sub-tasks. Each sub-task is a smaller problem that must be solved.

Visual Studio and IntelliSense automatically create the indentations in the program statements in Figure 3-31 because indentations make the statements easier to read and understand. As programs become more complex, proper indentation of program statements can be an important factor in developing error-free programs.

The following general steps summarize the procedure for using IntelliSense to enter a Visual Basic statement that sets a property:

1. In the IntelliSense list, type the first letter(s) of the name of the object whose property will be set.
2. When the object name is selected in the list, press the PERIOD key.
3. Type the first letter(s) of the name of the property to be set until the name is highlighted in the IntelliSense list.
4. Press the SPACEBAR to complete the first portion of the statement.
5. Press the EQUAL SIGN key.
6. Press the SPACEBAR.
7. Press the first letter(s) of the entry you want to select in the list until the entry is highlighted. If IntelliSense does not display a list, type the value for the property.
8. Press the ENTER key.

Using IntelliSense to enter a Visual Basic statement provides two significant advantages. First, it is faster to enter a statement using IntelliSense than it is to type the statement. Second, using IntelliSense drastically reduces the number of errors when entering statements. By using only the entries in the IntelliSense lists, the developer seldom will make an invalid entry. In addition, because the entry is chosen from a list, it cannot possibly be misspelled or mistyped.

Entering a programming statement is a fundamental skill for a Visual Basic programmer. You should thoroughly understand how to enter a programming statement using IntelliSense.

Set the Visible Property to False

In Figure 3-31, the programming statement set the Visible property to True for the picPumpkin PictureBox object, which will display the image in the picture box when the statement is executed. The statement will execute when the user clicks the Pumpkin Spice button because the statement is part of the btnPumpkin_Click event handler.

When the user clicks the Pumpkin Spice button, the Visible property also must be set to False for the picMocha PictureBox so the mocha picture is not displayed alongside the Pumpkin picture. To set the Visible property to False for the picMocha PictureBox object, you can complete the following steps:

STEP 1   Click the Close button to close the Toolbox. With the insertion point on the next line of the code window for the Pumpkin Spice button click event, type pic.

The letters you typed are displayed in the code window and the IntelliSense list shows the valid entries you can choose (Figure 3-32). The entry picPumpkin is highlighted because it is the last entry that was selected from this list.

FIGURE 3-32

STEP 2   Type m to highlight the picMocha entry in the IntelliSense list.

IntelliSense highlights picMocha in the list because it is the only entry that starts with the characters "picm" (Figure 3-33).

FIGURE 3-33

STEP 3   Press the key for the character that follows the object name. In this case, press the PERIOD key and type a v to highlight Visible.

The picMocha entry is placed in the statement followed by the dot operator (period) you typed. The Visible entry is highlighted in the list (Figure 3-34).

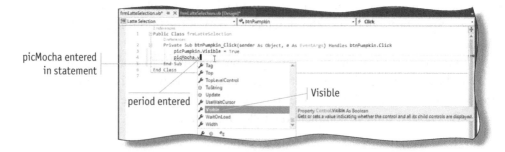

FIGURE 3-34

STEP 4 Press the SPACEBAR, press the EQUAL SIGN key, and then press the SPACEBAR.

IntelliSense places the Visible entry in the statement (Figure 3–35). Next, the space you typed appears, followed by the equal sign and the second space you typed. When you typed the equal sign, IntelliSense displayed the list of allowable entries following the equal sign.

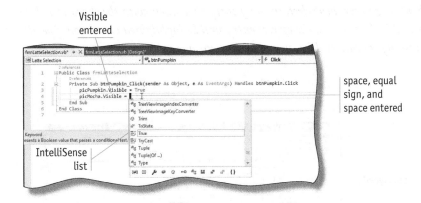

FIGURE 3-35

STEP 5 Type f and then press the ENTER key.

When you type the letter f, IntelliSense highlights False in the list. When you press the enter key, IntelliSense inserts False at the insertion point (Figure 3–36).

FIGURE 3-36

Again, using IntelliSense to enter a Visual Basic programming statement results in a correct statement entered in minimal time with a reduced chance of errors.

Set the Enabled Property

You learned earlier that if the Enabled property is True for a Button object, the click event code will be executed for the button when the user clicks it. If the Enabled property is False for a Button object, the event code for the button will not be executed. In Figure 3-17 on page 98, the Enabled property was set to False for the Select Latte button so that the button is not active when the program begins. When the user clicks a picture button such as the Pumpkin Spice button, however, the Enabled property must be set to True so the Select Latte button is active. To set the Enabled property to True, the developer must enter a coding statement for the btnSelect Button object. To enter the coding statement into the btnPumpkin_Click event handler, you can complete the following steps:

STEP 1   Type `btns` to display the IntelliSense list until IntelliSense highlights the btnSelect entry in the list.

IntelliSense highlights btnSelect, the only entry that starts with the characters "btns" (Figure 3-37). Sometimes, the correct entry will be highlighted before you type all the distinguishing characters. If so, you need not type more characters.

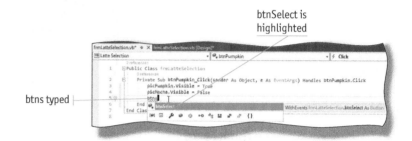

btnSelect is highlighted

btns typed

FIGURE 3-37

STEP 2   Type a period, type `e`, press the SPACEBAR, press the EQUAL SIGN key, press the SPACEBAR again, and then type `t` to select True in the IntelliSense list.

IntelliSense places the highlighted entry (btnSelect) in the statement and displays a list of the next allowable entries. When you typed e, Enabled was selected in the list. Pressing the SPACEBAR caused IntelliSense to place Enabled and then the space in the statement. When you typed the equal sign and second space, IntelliSense inserted both and displayed the list of entries that can follow the equal sign (Figure 3-38).

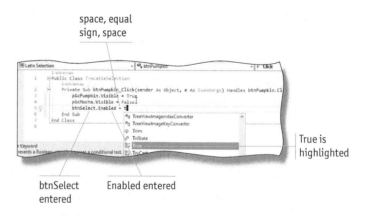

space, equal sign, space

True is highlighted

btnSelect entered

Enabled entered

FIGURE 3-38

STEP 3   Press the ENTER key to enter the completed statement and place the insertion point on the next line.

IntelliSense enters True in the statement (Figure 3-39). Pressing the ENTER key completes the statement and moves the indented insertion point to the next line.

indented
insertion point

True entered

FIGURE 3-39

Learning how to enter program statements using IntelliSense is fundamental to writing programs using the Visual Basic 2017 language.

Comments in Program Statements

A well-written Visual Basic program normally contains **comment statements** within the code itself to document what the code is doing. The general purpose of comments is to help code readers understand the code and how it accomplishes its tasks. An example of comment statements used in code is shown in Figure 3-40.

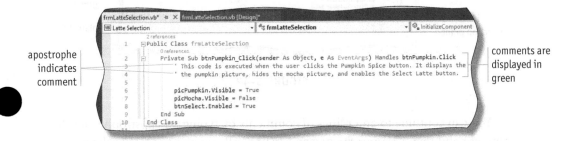

apostrophe
indicates
comment

comments are
displayed in
green

FIGURE 3-40

A comment is preceded by an apostrophe. Whenever the Visual Basic compiler encounters an apostrophe in the code, it ignores the remaining characters on the line. To the compiler, it's as if the comments do not exist.

The comments in the code are displayed in green text and describe the processing that will occur in the code that follows. Because comments are ignored by the Visual Basic compiler, developers must not include programming language syntax in the comments. Any letters or characters are allowed within comments.

To enter comments, first type an apostrophe in the code. All characters following the apostrophe on a line of code are considered a comment. To enter the comment code shown in Figure 3-40, you can complete the following steps:

STEP 1   To insert a blank line following the event code generated by Visual Studio that begins with the word Private, click anywhere in that line and then press the END key. Press the ENTER key.

Visual Studio inserts a blank line in the code and then moves the insertion point to the blank line (Figure 3-41). The comments can be inserted on the blank line.

FIGURE 3-41

STEP 2   Type the first line of the comments, beginning with an apostrophe as shown in Figure 3-40, and then press the ENTER key. Type the next line of comments, and then press the ENTER key.

The apostrophe identifies the rest of the line as a comment. The comment lines are displayed in green text (Figure 3-42).

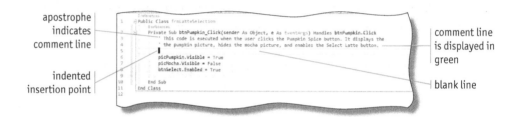

FIGURE 3-42

You can continue to enter lines of comments by typing an apostrophe and the comment and then pressing the ENTER key until all comments are completed.

Same-Line Comments

Because the Visual Basic compiler treats all characters following an apostrophe as comments, it is possible to place a comment on the same line as executable code. In Figure 3-43, a comment is shown on the same line as the statement that sets the btnSelect Enabled property to True.

FIGURE 3-43

In Figure 3-43, the apostrophe specifies that subsequent characters on the line are to be treated as comments. Therefore, the Enable button text is displayed in green and is treated as a comment. To enter a comment on any line, enter an apostrophe and then type the comment. Remember that all characters after an apostrophe are treated as comments on a line of code.

Introductory Comments

Every program should begin with comments that state the name of the program, the developer's name, the date, and the purpose of the program. These introductory comments should precede all code in the program — even the code generated by Visual Studio (Figure 3-44).

FIGURE 3-44

To enter introductory comments, you can complete the following steps:

STEP 1   Click to the left of the word Public on line 1 of the program to place the insertion point on that line. Press the ENTER key and then press the UP ARROW key.

When you press the ENTER key, Visual Studio inserts a blank line on line 1 of the code and moves the line that begins with the words Public Class down to line 2 (Figure 3-45). Visual Studio also moves the insertion point to line 2 when you press the ENTER key. When you press the UP ARROW key, the insertion point moves to the first line, which is blank.

FIGURE 3-45

STEP 2   Type an apostrophe, a space, the text `Program Name:`, and then press the TAB key.

The apostrophe identifies all characters and words that follow as comments, so those characters are displayed in green (Figure 3-46). The first line of introductory comments normally specifies the name of the program. Pressing the TAB key moves the insertion point to the right.

FIGURE 3-46

STEP 3 Type Latte Selection as the name of the program, and then press the ENTER key.

The program name appears in the first line of comments and the insertion point is moved to line 2 (Figure 3-47).

FIGURE 3-47

CONSIDER THIS

What do the yellow and green lines to the left of the code represent?

The yellow lines indicate lines of code that have not been saved. The green lines indicate the changes in code that have been saved. The yellow and green lines are a method of tracking your most recent changes in code.

You can enter the remaining comments using the same techniques. Press the TAB key one or more times to vertically align the paragraphs on the right so they appear as shown in Figure 3-44 on page 113.

Correct Errors in Code

Using IntelliSense to help you enter code reduces the likelihood of coding errors considerably. Nevertheless, because you could create errors when entering code, you should understand what to do when a coding error occurs.

One possible error would be to forget an apostrophe in a comment statement. In Figure 3-48, a comment was entered without a leading apostrophe.

In Figure 3-48, the comment words are displayed in black and red text, which indicates an error because comment characters normally are displayed in green text. Visual Studio gives no other indication that an error has occurred.

From the point where the error occurred, the developer might take any course of action. For example, she might immediately run the program. Or she might click anywhere in the window to move the insertion point, or press the ENTER key to insert a blank line. If the program in Figure 3-48 is executed immediately by clicking the Start button on the Standard toolbar, the window shown in Figure 3-49 will be displayed.

apostrophe omitted

comment appears in black text

FIGURE 3-48

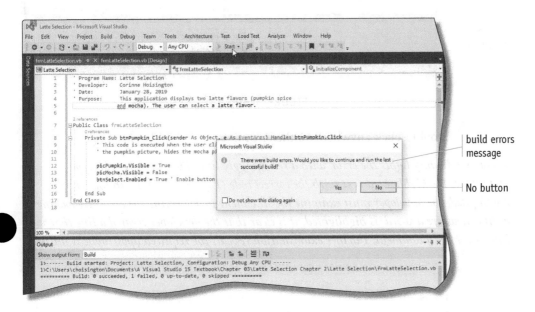

build errors message

No button

FIGURE 3-49

The **build errors message** means the Visual Basic compiler detected a coding error in the program. An absolute requirement when creating Visual Basic programs is that when you see the build errors message, you *always click the No button*. Under no circumstances should you click the Yes button in the dialog box. When you click the No button, you can perform the following steps to make corrections in your program:

STEP 1 Click the No button in the Microsoft Visual Studio dialog box that informs you of a build error (Figure 3-49).

*When you click the No button, Visual Studio displays the program code and the Error List window (Figure 3-50). The **Error List window** identifies the number of errors that occurred and displays descriptions of the errors. For example, the Syntax error means Visual Studio expected to find a different type of statement. The window also contains the file name in which the error occurred (frmLatteSelection.vb) and the line number of the statement in error (5). In the code window, the location of the error is noted by a red squiggly line.*

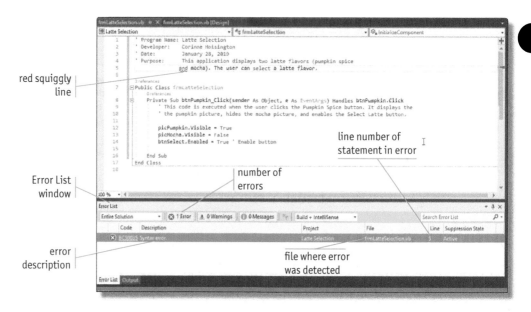

FIGURE 3-50

STEP 2   Double-click anywhere on the error line.

Visual Studio highlights the error with a red squiggly line. The developer can type and replace the highlighted text with the correct code (Figure 3-51). With the error highlighted, the developer must examine the statement to determine the error. By looking at line 5, where a word is highlighted, it is clear that the developer created a line that was intended to be a comment. Further examination reveals the required apostrophe is missing.

FIGURE 3-51

STEP 3   Click in the far left column on line 5 to place the insertion point there. Type an apostrophe.

The apostrophe is placed in the first column on line 5 of the program (Figure 3-52). If the statement has been corrected, the error line is removed from the Error List window, and the number of errors is reduced by one. The number of errors now is zero because the one error found in the program has been corrected. Multiple errors can be detected when the program is compiled.

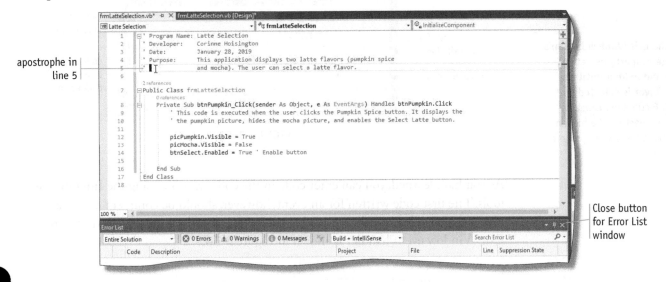

apostrophe in line 5

Close button for Error List window

FIGURE 3-52

You can close the Error List window by clicking its Close button (see Figure 3-52).

In Figure 3-49 on page 115, the example assumed that the developer made an error and then immediately ran the program. If the developer moved the insertion point to another part of the program or clicked any other element in the window before running the program, then Visual Studio would provide a visual cue that an error occurred by displaying a red squiggly line under the error (Figure 3-50). You do not have to run the program to find coding errors. If a red squiggly line appears, you must correct the error.

CRITICAL THINKING

When a program displays an error and a line number, is it possible that the error is on another line?
Yes. When an error is detected, review the line of code before the statement in error.

Additional Click Events

In the sample program in this chapter, multiple buttons can trigger events. For example, when the user clicks the Exit Window button, the program window should close and the program should terminate. To indicate that clicking the Exit Window button will trigger an event, and to prepare to write the code for the event, complete the same steps for the Exit Window button that you learned for the Pumpkin Spice button, as shown in the following example:

STEP 1   On the frmLatteSelection.vb [Design] tabbed page, double-click the Exit Window Button object.

Visual Studio opens the code window and displays the frmLatteSelection.vb tabbed page (Figure 3-53). Visual Studio also inserts the event handler code for the click event on the btnExit object. One horizontal line separates the event handler code for the btnExit object from code for other event handlers that might be in the program. The developer must write the code that will be executed when the click event occurs. The insertion point is located in the proper place to begin writing code.

event handler
code for
btnExit object

insertion point

event that
must occur

code for
btnExit
click event

FIGURE 3-53

Enter Comments

As you have learned, you can enter code in the code window using the IntelliSense tools. The first code written for an event, however, should be comment code that identifies the event and the processing that will occur. The comment code for the Exit Window event handler is shown in Figure 3-54.

comments for
btnExit event
handler

FIGURE 3-54

Close Procedure

The Visual Basic statement to close the window and terminate the program calls a procedure that performs the actual processing. A **procedure** is a set of prewritten code that can be called by a statement in the Visual Basic program. When the procedure is called, the program processes the code. The procedure used to close a window and terminate a program is the Close procedure.

You can use the statement in Figure 3-55 to call the Close procedure.

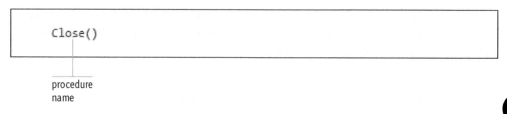

```
Close()
```

procedure
name

FIGURE 3-55

The word Close specifies the name of the procedure to be called. The left and right parentheses immediately following the procedure name identify the Visual Basic statement as a **procedure call statement**.

When the statement in Figure 3-55 is executed, the Close procedure will be called and control will be given to the prewritten programming statements in the Close procedure. These statements will close the window and end the application.

To enter the Close statement into the program, you can type "clo" and then select Close in the IntelliSense list, as shown in the following steps:

STEP 1 With the insertion point positioned as shown in Figure 3-54, type clo to highlight Close in the IntelliSense list.

When you type the letters "clo," IntelliSense highlights the word Close in the IntelliSense list (Figure 3-56).

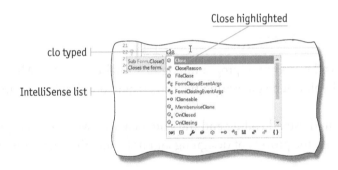

Close highlighted

clo typed

IntelliSense list

FIGURE 3-56

STEP 2 Press the ENTER key.

IntelliSense enters Close in the statement and, because it knows Close is a procedure call, automatically appends the open and closed parentheses to the statement (Figure 3-57). Then, Visual Studio returns the insertion point to the next line.

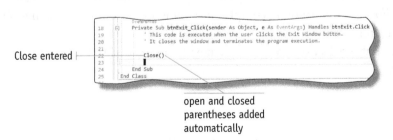

Close entered

open and closed
parentheses added
automatically

FIGURE 3-57

Prewritten procedures are an important element when using rapid application development in Visual Basic and Visual Studio because the developer is not required to write the procedure code. The developer merely writes a single statement to call the procedure. You will use many procedures in this book for a variety of reasons.

Print Code

In some instances, you will need to print the code in the program. While reviewing code, you might find it easier to read and understand the code on a printed page rather than on your computer screen. In other cases, you might want to share the code with another developer; the printed page often is a better tool for sharing than a monitor screen. To print the code in a program, you can complete the following steps:

1. Click File on the menu bar to display the File menu.
2. Click Print on the File menu to display the Print dialog box.
3. Make any other needed selections in the Print dialog box.
4. Click the OK button in the Print dialog box to print the code.

If you have a color printer, the code will be printed with correct color. Otherwise, shades of gray will represent the colors shown in the code window. If a line of code extends beyond one printed line, an arrow will appear at the end of the first line to indicate it continues to the next printed line.

Coding Summary

Writing code is the essence of programming in Visual Basic 2017. Much of the emphasis in this book will be on writing the code required to implement applications of all kinds.

Once you understand coding and the statements shown in this chapter, you are ready to continue the process of designing and implementing the Latte Selection program.

Phase 3 — Design the Program Processing Objects

The next phase in the PDLC requires determining the processing objects for the program and creating the event-planning document. In the Latte Selection program and programs of similar complexity, the designer need not be concerned about determining the processing objects. The only processing object required for the program is the Windows Form object. In more complex programs, determining processing objects will become important.

For the Latte Selection program, the next task is to design the event-planning document.

Event-Planning Document

As you have learned, programs written using a GUI normally are event-driven programs. An **event** means the user has initiated an action that causes the program to perform the appropriate type of processing in response. Once the mock-up has been created for the user interface, the developer must document the events that can occur based on the user interface.

HEADS UP

Visual Studio 2017 does not provide a tool to print the user interface designed on the frmLatteSelection.vb [Design] tabbed page. You can implement a workaround to print the user interface using the following steps: (1) open Microsoft Word; (2) make Visual Studio 2017 the active program window; (3) with the user interface displayed on the frmLatteSelection.vb [Design] tabbed page, hold down the ALT key and then press the PRINT SCREEN key; (4) make Microsoft Word the active window; (5) click the Paste button on the Word Home tab. The screen shot created in Step 3 will be pasted into the Word document; (6) print the Word document. The Snipping Tool is another option to take a screen shot.

The **event-planning document** is a table that specifies objects in the user interface that will cause events, the actions taken by the user to trigger the events, and the event processing that must occur. The event-planning document for the Latte Selection program is shown in Figure 3-58.

EVENT PLANNING DOCUMENT

Program Name:	Developer:	Object:	Date:
Latte Selection	Corinne Hoisington	frmLatteSelection	January 28, 2019

Object	Event Trigger	Event Processing
btnPumpkin	Click	Display the pumpkin picture Hide the mocha picture Enable the Select Latte button
btnSelect	Click	Disable the Pumpkin Spice button Disable the Select Latte button Disable the Mocha button Hide the Instructions label Display the Confirmation Message label Enable the Exit Window button
btnMocha	Click	Display the mocha picture Hide the pumpkin picture Enable the Select Latte button
btnExit	Click	Close the window and exit the program

FIGURE 3-58

The left column in the event-planning document identifies the object in the GUI that can trigger an event. In the Latte Selection program, each of the four Button objects can be used to trigger an event, so each must be included in the event-planning document. Notice each Button object is identified by its name. Using this technique ensures that the documentation is precise and provides little room for error when the developer creates the code to implement these events.

The middle column identifies the event trigger, which is the action a user takes to cause the event. In all four event cases in Figure 3-58, clicking a button triggers the event. As you will learn in this book, users can perform a variety of acts to trigger an event. For example, a user might point to an object, right-click the object, or double-click the object. Each event trigger could trigger a different event.

The right column in the event-planning document specifies the event processing that the program must perform when the event occurs. This list of tasks for each event is a critical element in the program design. It must be precise and accurate. No processing step that must occur should be left out of the event-processing column. The tasks should be listed in the same sequence as they will be performed in the program.

For example, the first task for the btnPumpkin_Click event is to display the pumpkin picture. This is the primary task for the Pumpkin Spice button. However, several other tasks must be completed. When the program begins, the mocha picture is not visible, but if the user clicks the Mocha button, then the picture is displayed. When the user clicks the Pumpkin Spice button, however, the mocha picture should not be visible. Therefore, each time the user clicks the Pumpkin Spice button, the processing must hide the mocha picture.

You also will recall that when the program begins, the Select Latte button is dimmed (disabled). After the user clicks a latte flavor button, the Select Latte button must be enabled. For example, each time the user clicks the Pumpkin Spice button, the Select Latte button must be enabled.

As you review the event-planning document in Figure 3-58, be sure you understand the processing that must occur for each event.

You should note that the event-processing tasks in the right column identify *what* processing must be done when the event occurs. *How* these tasks will be accomplished is not identified specifically, although the information in the event-planning document must be precise enough that the developer can easily write the code to implement the specified tasks.

Phase 4 — Code the Program

After the events and tasks within the events have been identified, the developer is ready to code the program. As you have learned in this chapter, coding the program means entering Visual Basic statements to accomplish the tasks specified in the event-planning document. As the developer enters the code, she also will implement the logic to carry out the required processing.

Guided Program Development

To fine-tune the user interface in the Latte Selection program and enter the code required to process each event in the program, complete the following steps to create the program shown in Figure 3-1 on pages 86 and 87.

NOTE TO THE LEARNER

In the following activity, you should complete the tasks within the specified steps. Each of the tasks is accompanied by a Hint Screen. The purpose of the Hint Screen is to indicate where you should perform the activity in the Visual Studio window and to remind you which method to use. If you need further help completing a step, refer to the figure identified by *ref:*.

1

● **Open the Mock-Up File** Open Visual Studio and then open the mock-up file for the user interface you created in Chapter 2. (If you did not create a mock-up file in Chapter 2, consult with your instructor to obtain the file.)

● **Show the Windows Form Object's BackColor Property** To finish the user interface, you must specify the BackColor of the Windows Form object. Select the frmLatteSelection Windows Form object. In the Properties window, scroll until the BackColor property is visible, click the BackColor property name in the left column, and then click the BackColor arrow in the right column. If necessary, click the Web tab (*ref: Figure 3-3*).

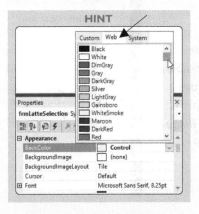

● **Choose the Windows Form Object's BackColor** Scroll the Web tabbed page until White is visible, and then click White in the list (*ref: Figure 3-5*).

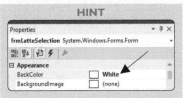

● **Select the BackColor for Buttons** Next, you must specify the BackColor for the Button objects. Select the four buttons in the window using techniques you have learned, and then change the BackColor to Bisque.

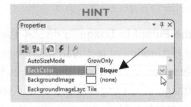

● **Change the ForeColor of a Label Object** Select the lblHeading Label object, click the ForeColor property name in the left column, and then click the ForeColor arrow in the right column. If necessary, click the Web tab and select SaddleBrown in the list.

(continues)

1

The BackColor for the Windows Form object is changed to White, the ForeColor of the heading is changed to SaddleBrown, and the BackColor for the buttons in the window is changed to Bisque (Figure 3-59).

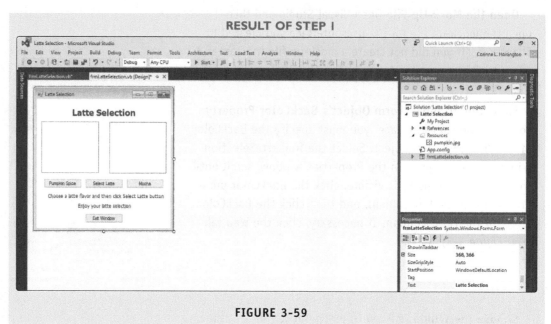

RESULT OF STEP 1

FIGURE 3-59

2

● **Download the Pumpkin Image** To display the pictures in the PictureBox object, you might need to use your web browser to download the pictures from the book's webpage at CengageBrain.com and store them on your computer. After downloading the files for Chapter 3, save the pumpkin image on a USB drive or other available storage media on your computer.

● **Download the Mocha Image** Save the mocha image on a USB drive or other storage media on your computer.

- **Display the Select Resource Dialog Box** After acquiring the pictures, you must import them into the Resources folder and specify the PictureBox object where they will be displayed. Select the picPumpkin PictureBox object. In the Properties window, click Image and then click the ellipsis button in the right column (*ref: Figure 3-8*).

- **Import the Pumpkin Image** In the Select Resource dialog box, click the Import button, import the pumpkin image from its saved location, and then click the OK button (*ref: Figure 3-9*).

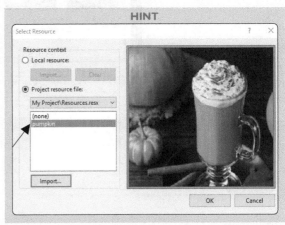

HINT

Anna_Pustynnikova/Shutterstock.com

- **Import the Mocha Image** Using the same technique, specify the mocha image as the image for the picMocha PictureBox object.

- **Set the SizeMode Property to StretchImage for the Pumpkin Image** When you import a picture, normally you must resize it or the PictureBox object so the picture is displayed properly. To resize the pumpkin image, select the picPumpkin PictureBox object. In the Properties window for the picPumpkin PictureBox object, click the SizeMode property name, click the SizeMode arrow, and then set the property to StretchImage (*ref: Figure 3-12*).

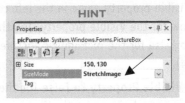

HINT

- **Set the SizeMode Property to StretchImage for the Mocha Image** Using the same technique, set the SizeMode property to StretchImage for the picMocha PictureBox object.

(continues)

The images are displayed in the correct PictureBox objects (Figure 3-60).

RESULT OF STEPS 2 & 3

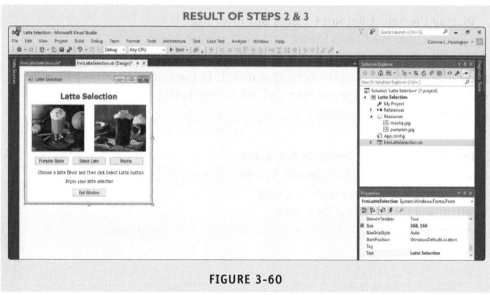

FIGURE 3-60

Anna_Pustynnikova/Shutterstock.com, Africa Studio/Shutterstock.com

4

● **Set the Visible Property to False for the Pumpkin Image**
When the program begins, the pictures are not displayed in
the window, so you must set their Visible property to False. In
the Properties window for the picPumpkin PictureBox object,
click the Visible property name in the left column, click the
Visible arrow for the Visible property, and then set the Visible
property to False for the picPumpkin PictureBox object (*ref:
Figure 3-14*).

● **Set the Visible Property to False for the Mocha Image**
Using the same technique, set the Visible property to False
for the picMocha PictureBox object (*ref: Figure 3-14*).

HINT

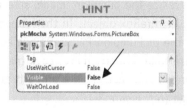

● **Set the Visible Property to False for the Confirmation
Message** The confirmation message is not displayed when the
program begins, so you must set its Visible property to False.
In the Properties window, set the Visible property to False for
the lblConfirmation Label object (*ref: Figure 3-14*).

● **Run the Program** After you make changes to a program,
you should run it to ensure your changes work properly and
are correct (*ref: Figure 3-18*).

In Figure 3-61, the latte pictures are not displayed. In addition, the confirmation message is not displayed.

RESULT OF STEP 4

FIGURE 3-61

5

● **Set the Select Latte Button's Enabled Property to False**
Initially, the Select Latte button and the Exit Window button must be dimmed. In the Properties window for the btnSelect object, click the Enabled property name, click the Enabled arrow, and then set the Enabled property to False for the btnSelect Button object (*ref: Figure 3-16*).

● **Set the Exit Window Button's Enabled Property to False**
Using the same technique, set the Enabled property to False for the btnExit Button object (*ref: Figure 3-16*).

● **Run the Program** Again, after you make changes, always ensure the changes are correct. Run the program.

● *Both the Select Latte button and the Exit Window button are dimmed, indicating the Enabled property for both buttons is False (Figure 3-62).*

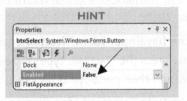

HINT

RESULT OF STEP 5

FIGURE 3-62

(continues)

6

● **Open the Code Window for the btnPumpkin Event Handler** The user interface now is complete, so you should begin writing the code for the program. To write code, you must open the code window. Double-click the Pumpkin Spice button to open the code window for the btnPumpkin_Click event (*ref: Figure 3-20*).

● **Position the Insertion Point** Close the Toolbox window. When you begin writing the code for a program, the first step is to write the introductory comments. Click in the far left position of the first line of code (Public Class)

● **Create a Blank Line and Position the Insertion Point** Press the ENTER key and then press the UP ARROW key (*ref: Figure 3-45*).

● **Enter the First Line of the Introductory Comments** The introductory comments provide the code reader with important information about the program. The first line normally specifies the name of the program. Type an apostrophe, press the SPACEBAR, type Program Name:, press TAB, type Latte Selection, and then press the ENTER key and the BACKSPACE key to return to the left position (*ref: Figure 3-47*).

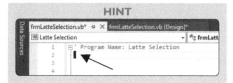

● **Enter the Developer Identification Comment Line** Type an apostrophe, press the SPACEBAR, type Developer:, press TAB, type your name, and then press the ENTER key.

● **Enter the Date Comment Line** Type an apostrophe, **press** the SPACEBAR, type Date:, press TAB three times, enter the current date, and then press the ENTER key.

● **Enter the First Program Purpose Comment Line** Type an apostrophe, press the SPACEBAR, type Purpose:, press TAB two times, enter the first line of your own comments about the program, and then press the ENTER key.

● **Enter the Remaining Program Purpose Comment Lines** Insert additional lines of comments about the purpose of the program as you see fit.

The comments appear at the top of the program code (Figure 3-63).

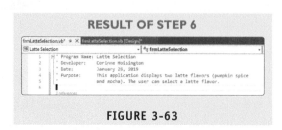

FIGURE 3-63

● **Position the Insertion Point Inside the Click Event Handler** With the insertion point located on the line above the line of code that begins with Public Class (see Figure 3-63), press the DOWN ARROW key three times and then press TAB two times to position the insertion point in the btnPumpkin_Click event handler

● **Enter the First Line of the Event Handler Comments** Each event handler should begin with comments describing what the event handler accomplishes. Type an apostrophe, press the SPACEBAR, and then enter the first line of comments for the btnPumpkin_Click event handler. Press the ENTER key (*ref: Figure 3-42*).

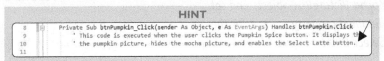

● **Enter the Remaining Event Handler Comments** Enter the remaining comments for the btnPumpkin_Click event handler.

● **Make the Pumpkin Spice PictureBox Object Visible** The first executable line of code in the Pumpkin Spice Button object click event handler must make the Pumpkin Spice PictureBox object visible. Using IntelliSense, enter the Visual Basic code statement to set the Visible property to True for the picPumpkin PictureBox object (*ref: Figure 3-28*).

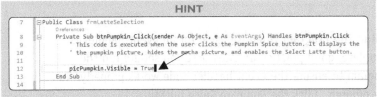

● **Make Sure the Mocha PictureBox Object is Not Visible** As documented in the event-planning document, the next task is to make sure the mocha picture is not visible in the window. Using IntelliSense, enter the Visual Basic code statement to set the Visible property to False for the picMocha PictureBox object (*ref: Figure 3-35*).

● **Enable the Select Latte Button Object** The last task for the btnPumpkin_Click event handler is to enable the Select Latte button. Using IntelliSense, enter the Visual Basic code statement to set the Enabled property to True for the btnSelect Button object (*ref: Figure 3-38*).

(continues)

The lines of code are entered in the Pumpkin Spice Button object's click event handler (Figure 3-64). The code will set the Visible property to True for the picPumpkin PictureBox object, set the Visible property to False for the picMocha PictureBox object, and set the Enabled property to True for the btnSelect Button object.

RESULT OF STEP 7

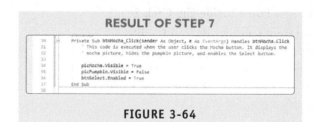

```
30    Private Sub btnMocha_Click(sender As Object, e As EventArgs) Handles btnMocha.Click
31        ' This code is executed when the user clicks the Mocha button. It displays the
32        ' mocha picture, hides the pumpkin picture, and enables the Select button.
33
34        picMocha.Visible = True
35        picPumpkin.Visible = False
36        btnSelect.Enabled = True
37    End Sub
38
```

FIGURE 3-64

HEADS UP

As you enter executable code, you should refer to the event-planning document to ensure the code implements the identified tasks. The event-planning document is the guide to the code you write in each event handler.

8

• **Run the Program** When the code for an event handler is complete, good practice dictates that you should run the program to ensure the event handler code works properly. Run the program. Click the Pumpkin Spice button.

When you click the Pumpkin Spice button, the pumpkin picture is displayed, the mocha picture is not displayed, and the Select Latte button is enabled (Figure 3-65). These are the correct results. Note that if you click any of the other buttons in the window, nothing happens because you have not yet written the event handler code for these objects.

RESULT OF STEP 8

FIGURE 3-65

● **Display the Design Window** When the code for an event handler is completed, the next task is often to write the code for another event handler. To do so, you must go to the De- sign tabbed page and indicate the object for which the code will be written. Click the frmLatteSelection.vb [Design] tab to return to the Design tabbed page.

● **Open the Code Window for the btnSelect Event Handler** You must open the code window for the btnSelect Button object to enter code for the event handler. Double-click the Select Latte button to open the code window for the btnSe- lect_Click event (*ref: Figure 3-20*).

● **Enter Event Handler Comments** When beginning the code for an event handler, the first step is to enter the event handler comments. Enter the comments that describe the processing in the btnSelect_Click event handler.

● **Disable the btnPumpkin Button Object** According to the event-planning document (Figure 3-58 on page 121), the next task is to disable the Pumpkin Spice button. Using IntelliSense, enter the Visual Basic code statement to set the Enabled property to False for the btnPumpkin Button object (*ref: Figure 3-37*).

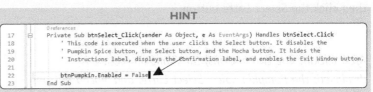

● **Disable the btnSelect Button Object** The next task is to disable the Select Latte button. Using IntelliSense, enter the Visual Basic code statement to set the Enabled property to False for the btnSelect Button object (*ref: Figure 3-37*).

● **Disable the btnMocha Button Object** Using IntelliSense, enter the Visual Basic code statement to set the Enabled property to False for the btnMocha Button object (*ref: Figure 3-37*).

● **Hide the Instructions Label Object** When the Select Latte button is clicked, the instructions should not be displayed. Using IntelliSense, enter the Visual Basic code statement to set the Visible property to False for the lblInstructions Label object (*ref: Figure 3-28*).

(continues)

● **Display the Confirmation Message** The confirmation message must be displayed when the user clicks the Select Latte button. Using IntelliSense, enter the Visual Basic code statement to set the Visible property to True for the lblConfirmation Label object (*ref: Figure 3-30*).

● **Enable the Exit Window Button** After the user clicks the Select Latte button, the only allowable action is to click the Exit Window button and exit the application. Therefore, the Exit Window button must be enabled. Using IntelliSense, enter the Visual Basic code statement to set the Enabled property to True for the btnExit Button object (*ref: Figure 3-37*).

● **Run the Program** Save and then run the program to ensure that it works correctly. Click the Pumpkin Spice button and then click the Select Latte button.

After clicking the two buttons, the Pumpkin picture is displayed; the Pumpkin Spice, Select Latte, and Mocha buttons are disabled; the Instructions label is not displayed; the Confirmation Message label is displayed; and the Exit Window button is enabled (Figure 3-66).

RESULT OF STEP 9

FIGURE 3-66

Anna_Pustynnikova/Shutterstock.com

● **Display the Design Window** The next task is to write the code for the btnMocha event handler. To return to the Design tabbed page so you can select the Mocha button, click the frmLatteSelection.vb [Design] tab.

● **Open the Code Window for the btnMocha Event Handler** Double-click the Mocha button to open the code window for the btnMocha_Click event (*ref: Figure 3-20*).

● **Enter the Event Handler Comments** Using the techniques you have learned, enter the comments that describe the processing in the btnMocha_Click event handler.

● **Make the Mocha PictureBox Object Visible** According to the event-planning document, the next task is to make the mocha picture visible. Using IntelliSense, enter the Visual Basic code statement to set the Visible property to True for the picMocha PictureBox object (*ref: Figure 3-30*).

● **Make Sure the Pumpkin Picture Is Not Visible** Using IntelliSense, enter the Visual Basic code statement to set the Visible property to False for the picPumpkin PictureBox object (*ref: Figure 3-36*).

● **Enable the Select Latte Button** Using IntelliSense, enter the Visual Basic code statement to set the Enabled property to True for the btnSelect Button object (*ref: Figure 3-39*).

● **Run the Program** Run the program and then click the Mocha button to ensure your code works correctly.

The completed code for the Select Latte button event handler and the Mocha button event handler is shown in Figure 3-67.

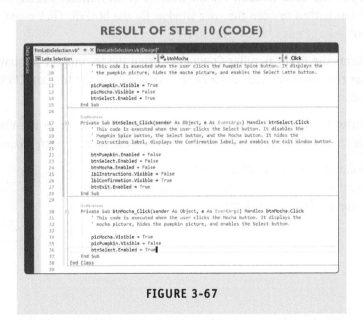

RESULT OF STEP 10 (CODE)

FIGURE 3-67

(continues)

When you click the Mocha button, the mocha picture is displayed, the Pumpkin picture is not displayed, and the Select Latte button is enabled (Figure 3-68). The program is working properly.

RESULT OF STEP 10 (PROGRAM EXECUTION)

FIGURE 3-68

Africa Studio/Shutterstock.com

11

- **Display the Design Window** Click the frmLatteSelection.vb [Design] tab to return to the Design tabbed page.

- **Open the Code Window for the btnExit Event Handler** Double-click the Exit Window button to open the code window for the btnExit_Click event (*ref: Figure 3-20*).

- **Enter the Event Handler Comments** Using the techniques you have learned, enter the comments that describe the processing in the btnExit_Click event handler.

- **Enter the Close() Procedure Call** Using IntelliSense, enter the Visual Basic code statement to close the window and exit the program (*ref: Figure 3-57*).

The Close() procedure call statement is entered (Figure 3-69). When the procedure call is executed, the application will be closed.

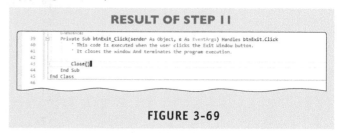

RESULT OF STEP 11

```
39        Private Sub btnExit_Click(sender As Object, e As EventArgs) Handles btnExit.Click
40            ' This code is executed when the user clicks the Exit Window button.
41            ' It closes the window And terminates the program execution.
42
43            Close()
44        End Sub
45    End Class
46
```

FIGURE 3-69

12

- **Run the Program** Run the program to ensure that it works correctly. Click the Pumpkin Spice button, the Mocha button, the Select Latte button, and the Exit Window button.

Code Listing

The complete code for the sample program is shown in Figure 3-70.

Summary

In this chapter you have learned to fine-tune a GUI to maximize its usefulness and to enter code for object event handlers.

```vbnet
VB Latte Selection                                              ▼    frmLatteSelection
 1    ' Program Name:  Latte Selection
 2    ' Developer:     Corinne Hoisington
 3    ' Date:          January 28, 2019
 4    ' Purpose:       This application displays two latte flavors (pumpkin spice
 5    '                and mocha). The user can select a latte flavor.
 6
      2 references
 7    Public Class frmLatteSelection
        0 references
 8        Private Sub btnPumpkin_Click(sender As Object, e As EventArgs) Handles btnPumpkin.Click
 9            ' This code is executed when the user clicks the Pumpkin Spice button. It displays the
10            ' the pumpkin picture, hides the mocha picture, and enables the Select Latte button.
11
12            picPumpkin.Visible = True
13            picMocha.Visible = False
14            btnSelect.Enabled = True
15        End Sub
16
        0 references
17        Private Sub btnSelect_Click(sender As Object, e As EventArgs) Handles btnSelect.Click
18            ' This code is executed when the user clicks the Select button. It disables the
19            ' Pumpkin Spice button, the Select button, and the Mocha button. It hides the
20            ' Instructions label, displays the Confirmation label, and enables the Exit Window button.
21
22            btnPumpkin.Enabled = False
23            btnSelect.Enabled = False
24            btnMocha.Enabled = False
25            lblInstructions.Visible = False
26            lblConfirmation.Visible = True
27            btnExit.Enabled = True
28        End Sub
29
        0 references
30        Private Sub btnMocha_Click(sender As Object, e As EventArgs) Handles btnMocha.Click
31            ' This code is executed when the user clicks the Mocha button. It displays the
32            ' mocha picture, hides the pumpkin picture, and enables the Select button.
33
34            picMocha.Visible = True
35            picPumpkin.Visible = False
36            btnSelect.Enabled = True
37        End Sub
38
        0 references
39        Private Sub btnExit_Click(sender As Object, e As EventArgs) Handles btnExit.Click
40            ' This code is executed when the user clicks the Exit Window button.
41            ' It closes the window and terminates the program execution.
42
43            Close()
44        End Sub
45    End Class
46
```

FIGURE 3-70

1. When the Latte Selection program was executed, was the Enabled property of the Mocha button set to True or False?

2. Which property controls the background color of the Button object?

3. Which property controls the text color of a Label object?

4. Which color palette is guaranteed to be displayed properly on every computer?

5. When a PictureBox object is placed on the form, what is the default SizeMode property setting?

6. When you place a PictureBox object on a Windows form, in which project folder is the image stored in the Solution Explorer?

7. Which option should be selected in the SizeMode property to align the center of the image with the center of the PictureBox object?

8. Which option should be selected in the SizeMode property to make the image fit within the PictureBox object?

9. Which property has been set to False if a PictureBox object is hidden in a window when the program begins?

10. Which property has been set to False if a Button object is dimmed when you run the application?

11. What two options can you select for the Visible property in the Properties window?

12. Write a line of code that would set the Visible property to False for a PictureBox object named picCaptainAmerica.

13. Write a line of code that would set the Enabled property to True for a Button object named btnSuperman.

14. Write a line of code that would set the Visible property to True for a PictureBox object named picWonderWoman.

15. Write a comment line of code that states, "This code displays the superhero images."

16. What color is used to display comments in the code window of Visual Basic 2017?

17. Write a line of code that will close an application window and exit the application.

18. What does a red squiggly line mean in the code window?

19. Which symbol is associated with the assignment statement?

20. Why is it best to use IntelliSense when you enter code in the code window? List two reasons.

1. Fix the following line of code to set the Enabled property to True for the btnCharacter Button object.

   ```
   btnCharacter.Enable.True
   ```

2. Fix the following line of code to change the visibility of the btnExitProgram Button object so that you can view it when the program runs.

   ```
   btnExitProgram.Visibilty = Yes
   ```

3. Fix the following line of code to set the Visible property to False for the lblGotham Label object.

   ```
   lblGotham.Visible = ' False
   ```

4. Fix the following comment line of code.

   ```
   The ' following line of code makes the Batman logo visible
   ```

5. Fix the following line of code.

   ```
   Close;
   ```

6. Examine the code below. Then, write a line of code to replace the erroneous line.

   ```
   btnMarvelProgram.Enabled = True
   picSpiderman.Visibilty = Enable
   picThor.Visible = False
   ```

1. For the Yellowstone National Park application shown in Figure 3-71, write the Visual Basic 2017 coding statement to view the picture when the user clicks the btnParkImage button, assuming the Visible property had been set to False for the picParkBison PictureBox object in the Properties window.

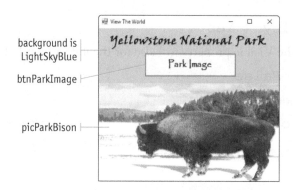

background is LightSkyBlue

btnParkImage

picParkBison

FIGURE 3-71

Photo courtesy of Corinne Hoisington

2. Which property in the Properties window controls whether the picParkBison image is displayed when the program begins? Which option for the property would you select to make the button dimmed when the program begins?

3. When you import the picture into the Resources folder and select the image to use in the picParkBison PictureBox object, which SizeMode property option would you select to view the complete picture?

4. Write the Visual Basic coding statement for the btnParkImage click event that would cause the image to be displayed.

5. To change the window background color to LightSkyBlue as shown in Figure 3-71, what property should you modify?

6. What property is used to display the text "View the World" in the window title bar?

Complete one or more of the following case programming assignments. Submit the program and materials you create to your instructor. The level of difficulty is indicated for each assignment.

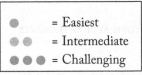

●   = Easiest
● ●   = Intermediate
● ● ● = Challenging

1 VIRTUAL REALITY HEADSETS

Create a Windows form mock-up for the requirements document shown in Figure 3-72 and the Use Case Definition shown in Figure 3-73. The Windows Form object and the other objects in the user interface are shown in Figure 3-74.

REQUIREMENTS DOCUMENT

Date:	October 13, 2018
Date Submitted:	
Application Title:	Virtual Reality Headsets
Purpose:	This Windows Classic Desktop application displays an order screen for two types of virtual reality headsets. The user can choose either a crown VR headset or earbud VR headset.
Program Procedures:	From a window on the screen, the user makes a request to see one of the two VR headset types.
Algorithms, Processing, and Conditions:	1. The user first views a Virtual Reality Headset window that displays the VR Headset company (VR Forward). When the user chooses to click the first headset button for the Crown VR, the crown.jpg image is displayed. When the user chooses to view the second headset for the Earbud VR, the earbud.jpg image is displayed. 2. After the user views one of the two images, the user can select the other image or close the window.
Notes and Restrictions:	The images should not be displayed at the same time.
Comments:	The pictures shown in the window can be found on CengageBrain.com. The name of the pictures are crown and earbud.

FIGURE 3-72

(continues)

Virtual Reality Headsets

USE CASE DEFINITION

1. The window opens, displaying the name of the company. The two VR image buttons are enabled.
2. User clicks either the VR Crown or VR Earbud button.
3. The user can continue to click each VR button.
4. The Exit Window button is enabled after the user views an image. User clicks the Exit Window button to exit the application.

FIGURE 3-73

In Figure 3-74a, no button has been clicked. In Figure 3-74b, the user has clicked the VR Crown button.

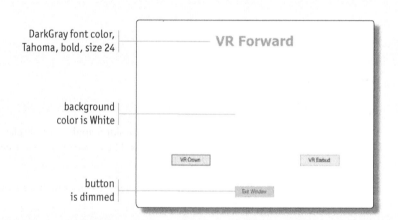

FIGURE 3-74a

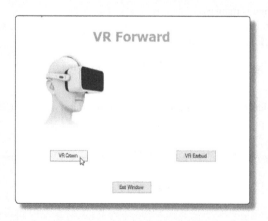

FIGURE 3-74b

2 BURGER SPECIALS

Create a Windows form mock-up for the requirements document shown in Figure 3-75 and the Use Case Definition shown in Figure 3-76. The Windows Form object and the other objects in the user interface are shown in Figure 3-77.

REQUIREMENTS DOCUMENT

Date:	January 10, 2019
Date Submitted:	
Application Title:	Burger Specials
Purpose:	This Windows Classic Desktop application displays the burger specials for a restaurant named Farm Burger. The user can select one of two specials: Prime Beef or Veggie.
Program Procedures:	From a window on the screen, the user orders one of two special burgers and the program confirms the order with a message.
Algorithms, Processing, and Conditions:	1. The user must be able to identify the Prime Beef or Veggie burger special name as many times as necessary until making a decision. 2. When the user identifies the special, a picture of that meal appears in the window. 3. Only one picture should be displayed at a time. 4. When the user selects Prime Beef, a message should be displayed to confirm the selection of the burger. In addition, the user should be prevented from identifying another meal after selecting a dish. 5. After the user selects a meal, the only allowable action is to close the window.
Notes and Restrictions:	A user can select a meal only after viewing one of the images of the meals.
Comments:	1. The pictures shown in the window can be found on cengagebrain.com. 2. The names of the pictures are prime and veggie.

FIGURE 3-75

(continues)

Burger Specials

USE CASE DEFINITION

1. User clicks the Prime Beef button or Veggie button.
2. Program displays a picture of the burger identified by the user and enables the burger selection button.
3. User clicks burger buttons to view burgers as desired. Program displays the picture of the identified burger.
4. User clicks the Select Meal button.
5. Program displays a meal confirmation message and disables both burger buttons and the Select Meal button.
6. The Exit Window button becomes active. User exits the program by clicking the Exit Window button.

FIGURE 3-76

In Figure 3-77a, no button has been clicked. In Figure 3-77b, the user has clicked the Veggie button. In Figure 3-77c, the user has clicked the Select Meal button.

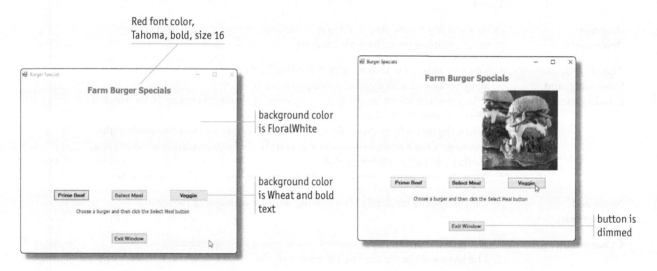

FIGURE 3-77a

FIGURE 3-77b

Olga Miltsova/Shutterstock.com

FIGURE 3-77c

Olga Miltsova/Shutterstock.com

Case Programming Assignments

3 ●● CAMPUS MUSIC CAFE

Create a Use Case Definition document and design a Windows form mock-up based on the requirements document in Figure 3-78.

REQUIREMENTS DOCUMENT

Date:	October 13, 2018
Date Submitted:	
Application Title:	Campus Music Cafe
Purpose:	This Windows Classic Desktop application displays a welcome screen to market the Campus Music Café performance. The user can choose an option to view the date, start location, and details.
Program Procedures:	From a window on the screen, the user makes a request to see the performance's date, start location, and details.
Algorithms, Processing, and Conditions:	1. The user first views a Campus Music Cafe window that displays the title (Campus Music Café Open Mic Night), a cafe picture, and a phrase that states that all college students are welcome. 2. When the user chooses to view the date, start location, and details, the following information is displayed: October 30, 2018 Open "Mic" Start Time: 8:00 PM For more information, view the Campus Music Café's Facebook page. After the user views the Campus Music Café's information, the only allowable action is to close the window.
Notes and Restrictions:	Design your own layout.
Comments:	Locate your own image online.

FIGURE 3-78

4 ●●

SPRING BREAK TRAVEL SPECIALS

Create a Use Case Definition document and design a Windows form mock-up based on the requirements document in Figure 3-79.

REQUIREMENTS DOCUMENT

Date:	March 21, 2019
Date Submitted:	
Application Title:	Spring Break Travel Specials
Purpose:	The Student Center on campus has created special Spring Break travel specials on three trips. A student can choose one of three Spring Break trips. The program must display each of the Spring Break travel specials upon request. The student can then select a trip for purchase.
Program Procedures:	From a window on the screen, the user selects one of three trips. A picture of the selected trip is displayed in the window. The user then can choose a trip for purchase.
Algorithms, Processing, and Conditions:	1. The user selects a trip. Then, a picture of the trip location is displayed in the window. 2. The user can select any of the three trips. Only the picture of the selected trip should be displayed. 3. The user can select trips as many times as necessary and display the pictures of the destinations. 4. The user finds a trip, chooses it for purchase, and clicks the Purchase button. 5. After the user chooses a trip, a message stating "Enjoy your trip!" should be displayed. 6. After the user chooses a trip, the only allowable action is to close the window.
Notes and Restrictions:	The user should not be able to choose a trip until viewing at least one trip image.
Comments:	The available trips are to Myrtle Beach, Key West, or Venice Beach. Select your own pictures online.

FIGURE 3-79

5

HEALTHY SNACK SELECTION

Create a requirements document and a Use Case Definition document and then design a Windows form mock-up based on the case project shown in Figure 3-80:

The international club on campus requests a computer application that will run on a kiosk during the International Festival where students can select a healthy international snack. The application should request which free snack you would like, display the choices as buttons, and then display an image of the snack you select. Another button allows you to make your final snack selection and display a confirmation message.

Snack
Bean Burrito
Falafel
Greek Yogurt
Spring Rolls

FIGURE 3-80

6 •••
COSTUME PARTY RENTALS

Create a requirements document and a Use Case Definition document and then design a Windows form mock-up based on the case project shown in Figure 3-81:

A costume shop requests a computer application that advertises costume rentals. This week's costume rental specials are as follows:

Costume	Price per Week
Renaissance Fair	$40
Stormtrooper	$49
Batman/Batgirl	$36
Pirate	$29

Write an application that allows the user to select any of the five costume rental specials. When the user selects a costume, the corresponding cost and a picture of the costume should be displayed. Clear each prior price and picture when the user selects a different costume. After selecting a costume, the user should be able to book the costume rental and then close the window.

FIGURE 3-81

CHAPTER 4

Variables and Arithmetic Operations

OBJECTIVES

You will have mastered the material in this chapter when you can:

- Create, modify, and program a TextBox object

- Use code to place data in the Text property of a Label object

- Use the AcceptButton and CancelButton properties

- Understand and declare String and Numeric variables

- Use assignment statements to place data in variables

- Use literals and constants in coding statements

- Understand scope rules for variables

- Convert string and numeric data

- Understand and use arithmetic operators and arithmetic operations

- Format and display numeric data as a string

- Create a form load event

- Create a concatenated string

- Debug a program

Introduction

In the Latte Selection program you developed in Chapter 2 and Chapter 3, you clicked buttons in the user interface to trigger events, but you did not enter data. In many applications, users must enter data that the program then uses in its processing.

When processing data entered by a user, a common requirement is to perform arithmetic operations on the data to generate useful output. Arithmetic operations include adding, subtracting, multiplying, and dividing numeric data.

To illustrate user data input and arithmetic operations, the application in this chapter allows the user to specify a number of bikes to rent from a beach bike rental program. The application then calculates the total cost of renting the bikes. The user interface for the program is shown in Figure 4-1.

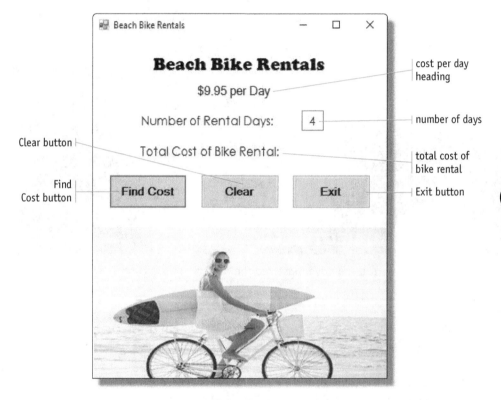

FIGURE 4-1

iStockphoto.com/Wavebreakmedia

In Figure 4-1, the user entered 4 as the number of days to rent the beach bike while on vacation. The minimum rental time is 1 day. When the user clicks the Find Cost button, the program multiplies 4 (days) by the cost per bike rental for a day ($9.95) and then displays the result as the total cost of the rental for a single bike. When the user clicks the Clear button, the values for the number of days and the total cost of the bike rental are cleared so the next user can enter a value. Clicking the Exit button closes the window and ends the program.

To create this application, the developer must understand how to perform the following processes, among others:

1. Define a text box for data entry
2. Define a label to hold the results of arithmetic operations
3. Convert data in a text box to data that can be used for arithmetic operations
4. Perform arithmetic operations on data entered by a user

The following pages describe the tools and techniques required to create the program shown in Figure 4-1.

Design the User Interface

As you have learned in Chapter 2 and Chapter 3, the next step after completing the program requirements document for an application is to define the graphical user interface. In this chapter, three new elements are introduced:

- TextBox objects
- Labels intended for variable text property values
- Accept buttons

Each of these elements is described in the following sections.

TextBox Objects

A **TextBox object** allows users to enter data into a program. In Figure 4-2, the user can enter a value into the text box.

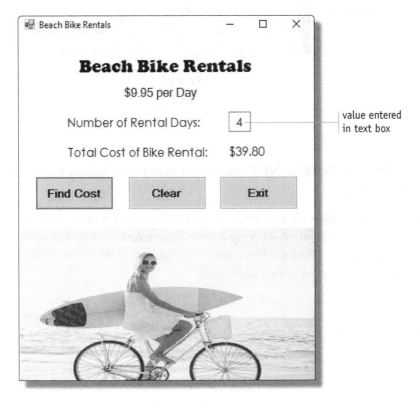

value entered in text box

FIGURE 4-2

iStockphoto.com/Wavebreakmedia

In Figure 4-2, the TextBox object is placed on the Windows Form object. A TextBox object automatically allows the user to enter data in the text box. To place a TextBox object on the Windows Form object, you can complete the following steps. (Note that the examples in this chapter illustrate new objects in the user interface. Portions of the user interface have already been completed for you. You should not expect to *click along* with these examples unless you create all the elements or follow the steps using an unformatted user interface.)

STEP 1　With Visual Studio open, the Beach Bike Rentals Windows Classic Desktop application created, and the frmBike.vb [Design] tabbed page visible, point to the TextBox .NET component in the Toolbox.

The TextBox .NET component is highlighted in the Toolbox (Figure 4-3).

TextBox .NET component

FIGURE 4-3

iStockphoto.com/Wavebreakmedia

STEP 2　Drag the TextBox .NET component onto the Windows Form object at the desired location.

While you drag, the pointer changes to indicate a TextBox object will be placed on the Windows Form object (Figure 4-4). Snap lines indicate where the TextBox object aligns with other objects on the Windows Form object. In Figure 4-4, the bottom of the TextBox object aligns with the bottom of the Label object.

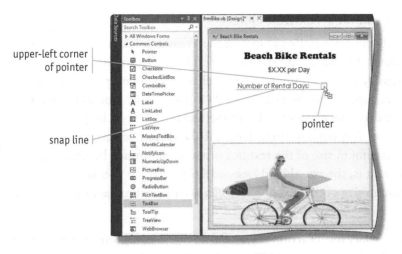

FIGURE 4-4

iStockphoto.com/Wavebreakmedia

STEP 3 When the upper-left corner of the pointer is located where you want to place the TextBox object's upper-left corner, release the TextBox object.

Visual Studio places the TextBox object at the location identified by the pointer (Figure 4-5). The default size of the TextBox object is 100 pixels wide by 20 pixels high. Notice that by default the TextBox object contains no text. You can change that by entering text in the Text property of the TextBox object.

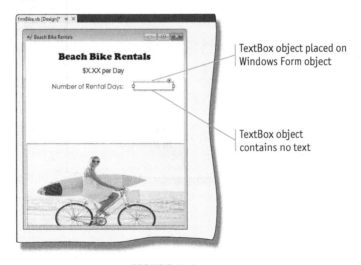

FIGURE 4-5

iStockphoto.com/Wavebreakmedia

As you have learned, whenever you place an object on the Windows Form object, you must name the object. When naming a TextBox object, the prefix should be txt. Therefore, the name of the TextBox object in Figure 4-5 could be txtNumberOfDays.

Size and Position a TextBox Object

To properly place a TextBox object on the Windows Form object, you need to know the minimum and maximum size of the text box. The minimum size normally is determined by the maximum number of characters the user will enter into the text box. For example, if the user can enter 99 in the sample program as the maximum number of days, the minimum size of the text box must be large enough to display two numbers. Although it can be larger, it should not be smaller.

The maximum size of the text box often is determined by the design of the user interface; that is, the size should *look and feel good* in the user interface. To determine the minimum size of the text box, you can use the technique in the following steps:

STEP 1   Select the TextBox object. Select the (Name) property and name the TextBox object `txtNumberOfDays`. Scroll in the Properties window until the Text property is visible and then click the right column for the Text property.

The TextBox object is selected, as shown by the thick border and sizing handles (Figure 4-6). The TextBox object is named txtNumberOfDays. The Text property for the TextBox object is highlighted and the insertion point indicates you can enter text for the Text property.

iStockphoto.com/Wavebreakmedia

FIGURE 4-6

STEP 2   Using the Properties window, change the Font property to the correct font and font size. For this application, change the font to Century Gothic and change the font size to 12. Type the maximum number of characters the user normally will enter into the text box and then press the ENTER key. Programmers often use the digit 8 in this situation because it is wider than other digits. This example uses the value 88 because two digits is the maximum number the user normally will enter for the number of days.

When the value is entered in the Text property of the TextBox object, the value is displayed in the TextBox object (Figure 4-7).

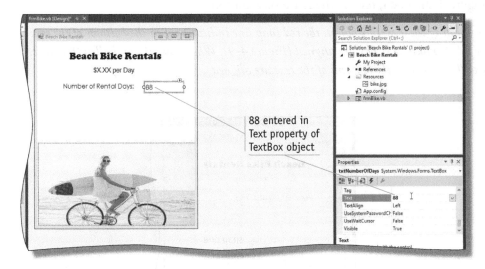

FIGURE 4-7

iStockphoto.com/Wavebreakmedia

STEP 3   Drag the right edge of the TextBox object and resize it to be slightly wider than the 88 entry.

As you drag, the size of the TextBox object changes (Figure 4-8). When you release the TextBox object, the text box will be resized.

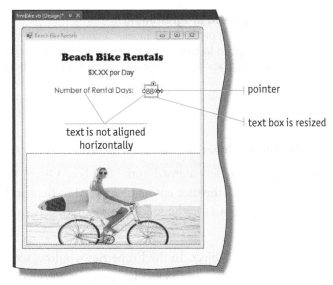

FIGURE 4-8

iStockphoto.com/Wavebreakmedia

STEP 4   To horizontally align the text in the label and the text in the text box, drag the text box up until a red snap line indicates the bottoms of the text are aligned (Figure 4-9). Then, release the left mouse button.

As you drag the TextBox object, the red snap line indicates when the bottoms of the text in the label and the text box are aligned (Figure 4-9). When you release the TextBox object, it will be placed so the bottoms of the text are aligned.

FIGURE 4-9
iStockphoto.com/Wavebreakmedia

Align Text in a TextBox Object

In Figure 4-9, the numbers are left-aligned in the text box. Often, the user interface will be more useful if the value the user enters is centered in the text box. To align the text in a TextBox object, you can use the following method:

STEP 1   Select the TextBox object. In the Properties window, scroll until the TextAlign property is visible, click the TextAlign property in the left column, and then click the list arrow in the right column of the TextAlign property.

The TextAlign property list contains the values Left, Right, and Center (Figure 4-10).

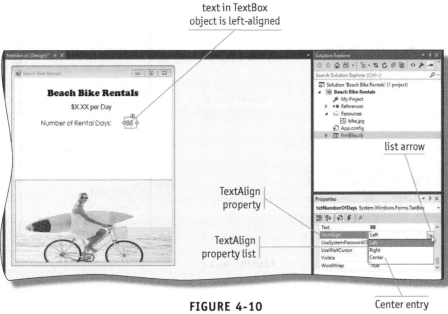

FIGURE 4-10

iStockphoto.com/Wavebreakmedia

STEP 2 Click Center in the TextAlign property list.

The text in the TextBox object is centered (Figure 4-11). When a user enters data in the text box, the data also will be centered.

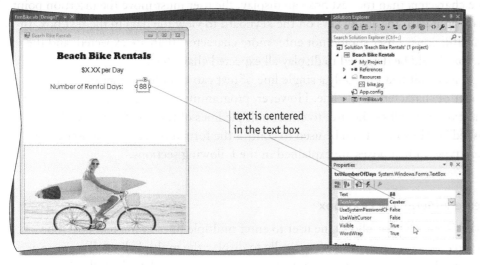

FIGURE 4-11

iStockphoto.com/Wavebreakmedia

STEP 3 Because the TextBox object is sized properly, remove the digits in the TextBox object. Select the characters 88 in the Text property, press the DELETE key, and then press the ENTER key.

The TextBox object contains no text and is ready for use in the user interface (Figure 4-12).

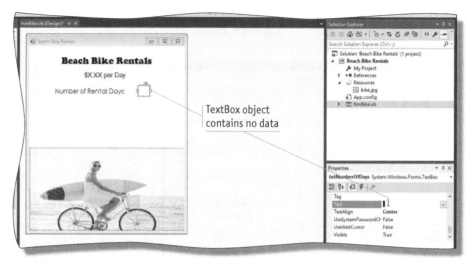

FIGURE 4-12

Enter Data in a TextBox Object

When the program is executed, the user can enter data in the text box. Users can enter letters, numbers, and other characters. If the user enters more characters than the text box can display, the characters that have already been entered scroll to the left and no longer are visible. A text box does not contain a scroll bar, so if a user enters more characters than the text box can display, the user must move the insertion point left or right with the arrow keys on the keyboard to view the data in the text box. In most situations, a user should not enter more characters than are expected, and the text box should be designed to display all expected characters.

In a default text box, only a single line of text can be entered regardless of the number of characters in the line. However, programmers can select a special option for a text box to allow the user to enter multiple lines of text. Additionally, the MaskedTextBox object can be used to control the format of data that a user enters. These types of text boxes are explained in the following sections.

Create a MultiLine Text Box

A MultiLine text box allows the user to enter multiple lines in the text box. The TextBox object must be resized vertically to display the multiple lines. To create a TextBox object that can accept multiple lines, you can complete the following steps:

STEP 1   Select the TextBox object, click the Action tag, and then point to the MultiLine check box.

The TextBox Tasks list is displayed with the MultiLine check box (Figure 4-13). When you click the MultiLine check box, the TextBox object will be able to accept multiple lines.

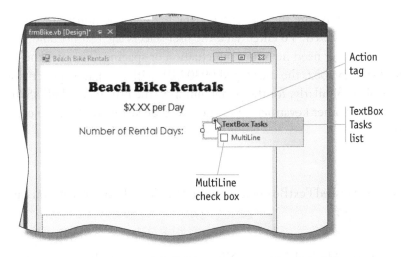

FIGURE 4-13

iStockphoto.com/Wavebreakmedia

STEP 2   Click the MultiLine check box.

The text box is enabled to accept multiple lines.

In addition to enabling multiple lines, you should increase the vertical size of the TextBox object so the multiple lines will be visible when the user enters them.

Create a MaskedTextBox Object

The MaskedTextBox object allows you to specify the data format of the value typed into the text box. Using the MaskedTextBox object removes confusion about which format should be used for data the user enters. The term *mask* refers to a predefined layout for the data. Figure 4-14 shows three examples of the MaskedTextBox used for the Short date input mask, the Phone number input mask, and the Social Security number input mask.

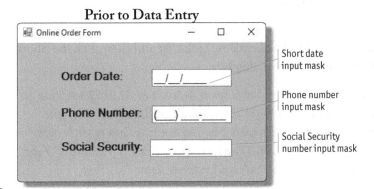

FIGURE 4-14

In Figure 4-14, before the user enters data, the mask demonstrates the format of the data to be entered. To enter data, the user selects the text box and then types data into it. The user need not enter punctuation or spacing. To enter the date in the Order Date text box, the user typed 09302018 with no spaces, punctuation, or other keystrokes. Similarly, for the phone number, the user typed 4345557600, again with no spaces or other keystrokes. For the Social Security number, the user typed 999999999.

To place a MaskedTextBox object on the Windows Form object, you can complete the following steps:

STEP 1   Drag a MaskedTextBox .NET component from the Toolbox to the Windows Form object. Then, click the Action tag on the TextBox object and point to the Set Mask command.

The MaskedTextBox object is placed on the Windows Form object (Figure 4-15). When the Action tag is clicked, the MaskedTextBox Tasks list is displayed. The Set Mask command is the only command in the list.

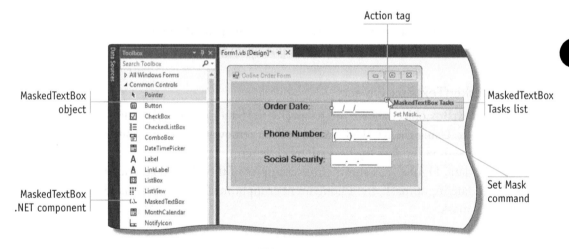

FIGURE 4-15

STEP 2   Click Set Mask on the MaskedTextBox Tasks list and then click the Short date mask description in the Input Mask dialog box.

Visual Studio displays the Input Mask dialog box (Figure 4-16). The Mask Description column contains all the masks that can be used for the MaskedTextBox object. The Short date mask description is highlighted. In the Preview box, you can type data to see how the mask will perform when it is used in the MaskedTextBox object. The Use Validating Type check box is selected to verify that the user entered valid numeric data.

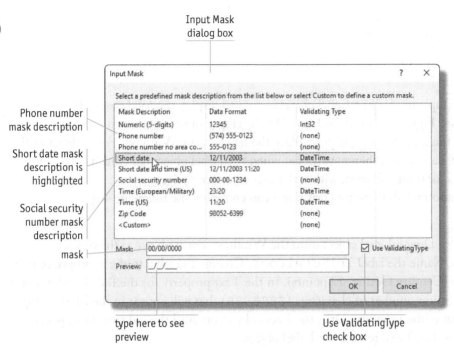

Input Mask
dialog box

Phone number
mask description

Short date mask
description is
highlighted

Social security
number mask
description

mask

type here to see
preview

Use ValidatingType
check box

FIGURE 4-16

STEP 3 Click the OK button in the Input Mask dialog box and then click anywhere in the Windows Form object.

The mask is placed in the MaskedTextBox object (Figure 4-17).

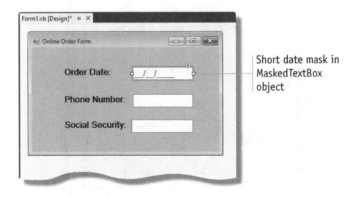

Short date mask in
MaskedTextBox
object

FIGURE 4-17

You can use the same technique to place the phone number and Social Security number in the MaskedTextBox.

Label Objects

In the sample program, a Label object is used to display the total cost of the bike rental (see Figure 4-1 on page 148). The developer must accomplish two tasks to prepare the label for this purpose: place the label on the Windows Form object in the correct location, and then ensure that when the Label object contains its maximum value, its location will work within the user interface design.

To accomplish these two tasks, you can complete the following step:

STEP 1   Drag a Label object onto the Windows Form object to the correct location. Name the label lblTotalCost. Change the label to the appropriate font and size (Century Gothic, 12 points). In the Text property for the Label object, enter the maximum number of characters ($888.88) that will appear in the label during execution of the program. Drag the Label object up until the red snap line appears (Figure 4-18). Then release the Label object.

The properly sized characters appear in the label. The label is aligned (Figure 4-18).

FIGURE 4-18

iStockphoto.com/Wavebreakmedia

When program execution begins, the label that will contain the total cost of the bike rental should be blank. In Figure 4-18, however, it contains the value in the Text property of the Label object ($888.88). If the Text property in a Label object is set to hold no content, it will not be displayed in the Windows Form object during the design phase, which makes the Label object difficult to work with in Design mode. Therefore, most designers place a value in the Text property of the Label object and leave it there during user interface design. Then, when the program begins, the label Text property will be set to blank. You will learn to perform this task later in the chapter.

Accept Button in Form Properties

Computer users often press the ENTER key to enter data in a text box and cause processing to occur. For instance, in the sample program for this chapter, users might prefer to type the number of rental days and press the ENTER key instead of typing the number and clicking the Find Cost button.

You can assign a button to be an Accept button in the user interface, which means the program will carry out the event handler processing associated with the button if the user clicks it or presses the ENTER key. To assign the Find Cost button as the Accept button, you can complete the following steps:

STEP 1   After the Button objects are added, click a blank area in the Windows Form object to select it. Scroll in the Properties window until the AcceptButton property is visible. Click the AcceptButton property name in the left column and then click the AcceptButton property list arrow in the right column.

The AcceptButton property list displays the names of the Button objects on the selected Windows Form object (Figure 4–19). Any of these buttons can be specified as the Accept button.

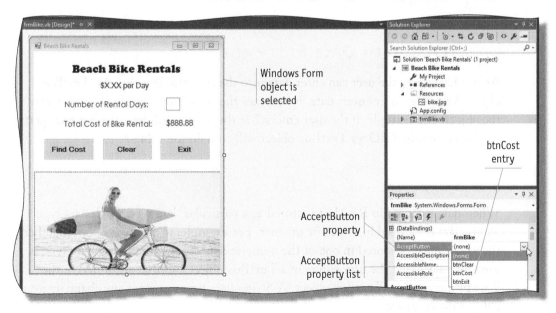

FIGURE 4-19

STEP 2   Click btnCost in the AcceptButton property list.

The btnCost Button object is designated as the Accept button. When the program is running, the user can press the ENTER key after entering data to execute the event handler processing for the Find Cost button. Notice the border of the Find Cost button displays a blue edge to identify that the AcceptButton property is set.

Cancel Button in Form Properties

In the same manner as the Accept button, you can designate a Cancel button for the Windows Form object. When the user presses the ESC key, the event handler processing will be executed for the button identified as the Cancel button. In the sample program, the Cancel button will be used to clear the text box and the total cost of bikes rented and to place the insertion point in the text box. Thus, it performs the same activity that occurs when the user clicks the Clear button. To specify the Cancel button for the sample program, you complete the following steps:

Step 1:   Click a blank area in the Windows Form object to select it.
Step 2:   Click the CancelButton property name in the left column of the Properties window for the Windows Form object, and then click the CancelButton list arrow.
Step 3:   Click the button name (btnClear) in the CancelButton property list.

When the program is executed, the user can press the ESC key to perform the same processing as when the Clear button is clicked.

Introduction to Data Entry and Data Types

As you have seen, the user can enter data into the program by using the TextBox object. When the user enters data, it becomes the value stored in the Text property of the object. For example, if the user enters 7 as the number of days, the Text property for the txtNumberOfDays TextBox object will contain the value 7.

String Data Type

When data is stored in RAM, it is stored as a particular data type. Each data type allows data to be used in a specific manner. For example, to add two values together, the values must be stored in one of the numeric data types. The **String** data type is used for values that the user enters in a TextBox object and that are stored in the Text property of the TextBox object. A String data type can store any character available on the computer.

When the user enters data into a TextBox object, it is good programming style to copy the entered value from the Text property of the TextBox object to a String variable. A **variable** is a named location in RAM where data is stored. A **String variable** is a named location in RAM that can store a string value. Thus, a person's name, a dollar amount, a phone number, or the number of bikes rented can be stored in a String variable.

The programmer defines a variable during the coding of the program. The statement in Figure 4-20 defines a string.

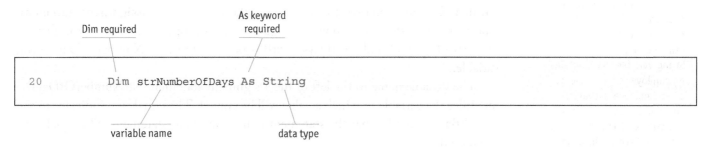

FIGURE 4-20

To begin the statement, the keyword Dim is required. This keyword stands for *variable dimension*. It indicates to the Visual Basic compiler that the entries after Dim are defining a variable.

The next entry is the variable name. Every variable must have a name so it can be referenced in other statements within the program. By convention, every String variable name begins with the letters str followed by a descriptive name. The name in Figure 4-20 (strNumberOfDays) indicates a String variable that will contain the number of days entered by the user.

The keyword As must follow the name of the variable, as shown in Figure 4-20. If it is not included, a compilation error will occur. Following the word As is the declaration for the variable's data type. In Figure 4-20, the data type is specified as String.

As a result of the statement in Figure 4-20, when the program is compiled, the Visual Basic compiler will allocate an area in RAM that is reserved to contain the value in the string.

The general format to define a variable is shown in Figure 4-21.

VARIABLE NAME RULES

Variable names in Visual Basic must follow a few simple rules. The name must begin with a letter or an underline symbol (_). The name can contain letters, numbers, and the underline symbol. It cannot contain spaces or other special characters. Reserved words in Visual Basic cannot be used for variable names; reserved words appear in blue in the code window.

General Format: Define a Variable	
Dim VariableName As DataType	
EXAMPLE	*RESULT*
Dim strNumberOfDays	String variable
Dim intNumberOfDays	Integer variable
decTotalCost As Decimal	Decimal variable

FIGURE 4-21

The Integer and Decimal variables defined as examples in Figure 4-21 are numeric variables. You will learn about numeric variables shortly.

Assignment Statements

When a variable is defined as shown in Figure 4-20, the variable does not contain any data. One method used to place data in the variable is an **assignment statement**. The assignment statement shown in Figure 4-22 will copy the data from the Text property of the txtNumberOfDays TextBox object into the strNumberOfDays String variable.

The variable name to the left of the assignment statement (strNumberOfDays) identifies the variable to which a value will be copied. The equal sign indicates to the Visual Basic compiler that the statement is an assignment statement. The equal sign is required.

The value to the right of the equal sign will be copied to the variable to the left of the equal sign. In Figure 4-22, the value in the Text property of the txtNumberOfDays TextBox object will be copied to the strNumberOfDays variable.

To enter the definition of the strNumberOfDays variable and then enter the assignment statement in Figure 4-22 using IntelliSense, you can complete the following steps:

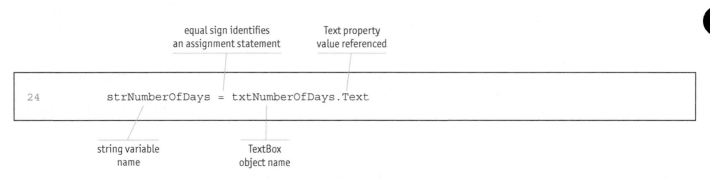

```
                equal sign identifies              Text property
                an assignment statement            value referenced


24          strNumberOfDays = txtNumberOfDays.Text



          string variable                 TextBox
          name                            object name
```

FIGURE 4-22

STEP 1 With Visual Studio open to the code window and the insertion point located in the desired column, type Dim followed by a space. Then, type the name of the String variable you want to define, strNumberOfDays.

The Dim keyword and the String name you typed are displayed in the code window (Figure 4-23). Notice that Dim is blue to indicate it is a keyword. The green curly line indicates that the keyword has not been assigned a value in the program.

name of
String variable

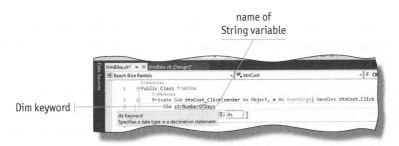

Dim keyword

FIGURE 4-23

STEP 2 Press the SPACEBAR, type the word As, and then press the SPACEBAR again.

The letters you typed are entered. When you typed the space following the word As, Intel-liSense displayed a list (Figure 4-24). The list contains all the allowable entries that can follow the As keyword. To define a String variable, the correct entry is String.

As keyword

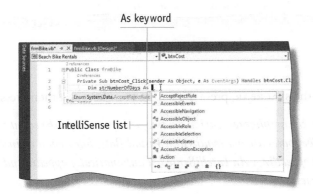

IntelliSense list

FIGURE 4-24

STEP 3 Because the correct entry is String, type str and press the ENTER key.

IntelliSense highlights String in the list. The Dim statement is entered (Figure 4-25). The green squiggly underline indicates the variable is not referenced within the program. Visual Studio will remove the underline when the variable is used in an assignment statement or other statement.

variable not
referenced

Dim statement
is complete

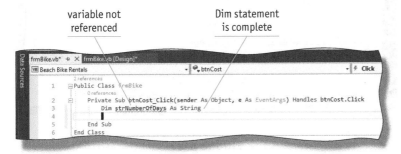

FIGURE 4-25

STEP 4   To begin the assignment statement, type `strn`. IntelliSense displays the only variable name that starts with the letters strn, which is the String variable strNumberOfDays.

IntelliSense displays a list of allowable entries for the statement (Figure 4-26). Whenever you want to reference a variable name in a statement, you can type the first few letters of the name to have IntelliSense display a list of allowable entries. The variable name strNumberOfDays is highlighted because you typed strn.

strn typed   IntelliSense list

FIGURE 4-26

STEP 5   Press the SPACEBAR, press the EQUAL SIGN key, and then press the SPACEBAR.

IntelliSense enters the highlighted variable name, the spaces, and the equal sign you typed (Figure 4-27). The spaces are not required in Visual Basic but should be included in the statement for ease of reading. An IntelliSense list automatically appears and displays the possible valid entries.

IntelliSense entered the variable name   equal sign and spaces

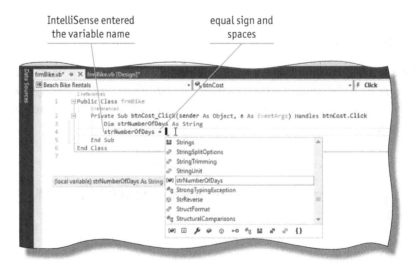

FIGURE 4-27

STEP 6   Type `txt` to display the IntelliSense list of Form objects, and then type `n` to identify the txtNumberOfDays TextBox object in the IntelliSense list.

The IntelliSense list contains the valid entries for the statement; in this case, only one object has the prefix of txt. The TextBox object txtNumberOfDays is highlighted in the list (Figure 4-28).

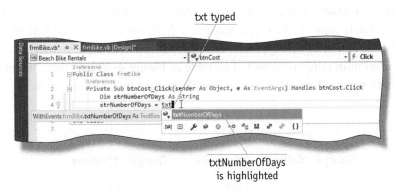

FIGURE 4-28

STEP 7   Press the PERIOD key. If necessary, type `te` to highlight the Text entry in the IntelliSense list. Press the ENTER key.

After the dot operator (period) and the txtNumberOfDays object name are entered, Visual Studio displays the IntelliSense list. When you typed te, the Text entry was highlighted in the IntelliSense list. The assignment statement is entered (Figure 4-29). When the statement is executed, the value in the Text property of the txtNumberOfDays TextBox object will be copied to the location in memory identified by the strNumberOfDays variable name. Notice also that the green squiggly lines in the Dim statement are removed because the variable now is referenced in a statement.

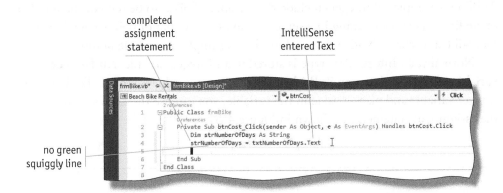

FIGURE 4-29

For any variable you define within a program, you can use the method shown in the previous steps to declare a variable name and include it in assignment statements. IntelliSense works the same with each variable name, regardless of the variable type.

> **HEADS UP**
>
> IntelliSense has different rules for entering object names and variable names into a Visual Basic statement. To enter the name of an object that has been defined in the user interface, type the prefix. To enter a variable name you have declared in the program, type the first few letters of the variable name. In each case, IntelliSense will display a list of the allowable entries.

Numeric Data Types

As you will recall, the String data type can contain any character that can be entered or stored on a computer. String data types, however, cannot be used in arithmetic operations. A **numeric data type** must be used in arithmetic operations. To multiply two values, for example, the values must be stored in one of the numeric data types.

Visual Basic allows a variety of numeric data types depending on the need of the application. Each numeric data type requires a different amount of RAM to store the numeric value, and each data type can contain a different form of numeric data and a different maximum range of values. The table in Figure 4-30 lists three widely used numeric data types. These data types are explained in the following sections.

Data Type	Sample Value	Memory Allocation	Range of Values
Integer	48	4 bytes	−2,147,483,648 to +2,147,483,647
Decimal	3.14519	16 bytes	Decimal values that may have up to 28 significant digits
Double	5.3452307 or 673.6529	8 bytes	−1.79769313486232e308 to +1.79769313486232e308

FIGURE 4-30

Integer Data Type

An **Integer data type** holds a nondecimal whole number in Visual Basic. As you can see from Figure 4-30, an Integer data type can store a value that is greater or less than 2 billion. Examples of integers include the number of bikes to be rented, the number of credit hours you are taking in a semester, and the number of points your favorite football team scored. Notice that each of these examples is a whole number.

Normally, an Integer data type is stored in an Integer variable. An **Integer variable** identifies a location in RAM where an integer value is stored. To define an Integer variable and place a value in the variable, you can use the Dim statement and the assignment statement, as shown in Figure 4-31.

```
        Dim intNumberOfDays As Integer
        intNumberOfDays = 4
```

FIGURE 4-31

The Dim statement in Figure 4-31 is similar to the Dim statement used to define the String variable (Figure 4-24 on page 165), except that the variable name begins with the prefix int and the word Integer follows the word As. Four bytes of RAM will be reserved for any value that is stored in the intNumberOfDays Integer variable as a result of the Dim statement in Figure 4-31.

The definition in Figure 4-31 will not place a value in the intNumberOfDays variable. To place a value in the variable, you can use an assignment statement. Enter the intNumberOfDays variable that will hold the value on the left side of the equal sign, and enter the value to be placed in the variable (4) on the right side of the equal sign. When the statement is executed, the value 4 will be copied to the RAM location identified by the variable name intNumberOfDays.

You also can place an initial value in the variable. For example, to define an Integer variable to hold the number of credit hours you are taking and to place the value 12 in that variable, you could write the Dim statement in Figure 4-32.

value placed in
intCreditHours
Integer variable

```
9          Dim intCreditHours As Integer = 12
```

FIGURE 4-32

The statement in Figure 4-32 defines the Integer variable named intCreditHours. The equal sign after the word *Integer* indicates to the Visual Basic compiler that the value to the right of the equal sign should be placed in the variable. The value 12 will be placed in the intCreditHours Integer variable when the program is compiled.

Decimal Data Type

A **Decimal data type** accurately represents large or very precise decimal numbers. It is ideal for use in the accounting and scientific fields to ensure that numbers keep their precision and are not subject to rounding errors. The Decimal data type can be accurate to 28 significant digits. (Significant digits are those that contribute to the precision of a number.) Often, Decimal data types are used to store dollar amounts. For example, to define the Decimal variable for the total cost of the bike rental in the sample program, you can use the statement in Figure 4-33.

```
22         Dim decTotalCost As Decimal
```

FIGURE 4-33

The Dim statement is used to define the Decimal variable. The dec prefix is used for all Decimal variable names. When the compiler processes the statement in Figure 4-33, 16 bytes of RAM will be reserved for a value to be placed in the decTotalCost variable. Initially, no value will be present in the variable unless you specify a value, as shown in Figure 4-32. You can use an assignment statement to place data into the decTotalCost variable.

Double Data Type

A **Double data type** can represent huge positive numbers and very small negative numbers that can include values to the right of the decimal point. Sometimes, a Double data type is said to represent floating-point numbers, which means the decimal point can be anywhere within the number. The Dim statement in Figure 4-34 declares a Double variable that could be used in a tax application.

```
13          Dim dblTaxRate As Double
14          dblTaxRate = 0.07875
```

FIGURE 4-34

In Figure 4-34, the dblTaxRate Double variable is declared and then the assignment statement places the value 0.07875 in the memory location identified by the variable name. Note that a Double variable begins with the dbl prefix.

Other Data Types

Visual Basic supports other data types that are used for more specialized situations. Two widely used data types are Char and Boolean (Figure 4-35).

Data Type	Sample Value	Memory Allocation	Range of Values
Char	A single character such as ? or M	2 bytes	Any single character
Boolean	True or False	2 bytes	True or False

FIGURE 4-35

Char Data Type

The **Char data type** represents a single keystroke such as a letter of the alphabet, a punctuation mark, or a symbol. The prefix for a Char variable name is chr. When you assign a value to a Char variable, you must place quotation marks around the value. For example, in Figure 4-36, the value A is assigned to the chrTopGrade Char variable.

```
16          Dim chrTopGrade As Char
17          chrTopGrade = "A"
```

FIGURE 4-36

The value A in the assignment statement has quotation marks around it. In addition, Visual Studio displays the letter and the quotation marks in red text, indicating they are not Visual Basic keywords, variable names, or object names. In fact, the value is called a literal. You will learn more about literals shortly.

Visual Studio allows 65,534 different characters in a program. These characters consist of numbers, letters, and punctuation symbols. In addition, a wide variety of technical characters, mathematical symbols, and worldwide textual characters are available, which allows developers to work in almost every known language, including Korean (Figure 4-37). These characters are represented by a coding system called Unicode. To learn more about Unicode, visit www.unicode.org.

유니코드에 대해 ?

어떤 플랫폼,
어떤 프로그램,
어떤 언어에도 상관없이
유니코드는 모든 문자에 대해 고유 번호를 제공합니다.

FIGURE 4-37

Even though you can assign a number to a Char variable, it cannot be used in arithmetic operations. A number to be used in an arithmetic operation must be assigned a numeric variable.

Boolean Data Type

A Boolean data variable can contain a value that Visual Basic interprets as either true or false. A Boolean variable name begins with the bln prefix. If a variable in your program should represent whether a condition is true or not true, then the variable should be Boolean. In Figure 4-38, a Boolean variable called blnFullTimeStudent is declared and then the assignment statement sets the Boolean variable to True.

```
19        Dim blnFullTimeStudent As Boolean
20        blnFullTimeStudent = True
```

FIGURE 4-38

In Figure 4-38, the Dim statement is used to declare the blnFullTimeStudent Boolean variable. The assignment statement sets the Boolean variable to True. This variable can be checked in the program to determine whether it is true or false, and appropriate processing can occur as a result.

Miscellaneous Data Types

Visual Basic has several other data types that are used less often than the ones you have seen so far. These data types are summarized in the table in Figure 4-39.

Data Type	Sample Value	Memory Allocation	Range of Values
Byte	A whole number such as 7	1 bytes	0 to 255
Date	April 22, 2014	8 bytes	Dates and times
Long	A whole number such as 342,534,538	8 bytes	−9,223,372,036,854,775,808 through +9,223,372,036,854,775,807
Object	Holds a reference	4 bytes	A memory address
Short	A whole number such as 16,546	2 bytes	−32,786 through 32,767
Single	A number such as 312,672.3274	4 bytes	−3.4028235E+38 through 1.401298E−45 for negative values; and from 1.401298E−45 through 3.4028235E+38 for positive values

FIGURE 4-39

As a review, the prefixes for each of the data type variable names are shown in Figure 4-40.

Data Type	Prefix
String	str
Integer	int
Decimal	dec
Double	dbl
Char	chr
Boolean	bln
Byte	byt
Date	dtm
Long	lng
Short	shr
Single	sng

FIGURE 4-40

Literals

When an assignment statement includes a value like the one in Figure 4-34 on page 170 or Figure 4-36 on page 171, the value is called a **literal** because it literally is the value required by the assignment statement. It is not a variable. The Visual Basic compiler determines the data type of the value you use for a literal based on the value itself. For example, if you type *Chicago*, the compiler treats the literal as a String data type, and if you type 49.327, the compiler treats the literal as a Double data type. The table in Figure 4-41 displays the default literal types as determined by the Visual Basic compiler.

Standard Literal Form	Default Data Type	Example
Numeric, no fractional part	Integer	104
Numeric, no fractional part, too large for Integer data type	Long	3987925494
Numeric, fractional part	Double	0.99 8.625
Enclosed within double quotes	String	"Bre Pauley"
Enclosed within number signs	Date	#3/17/2017 3:30 PM#

FIGURE 4-41

Forced Literal Types

Sometimes you might want a literal to be a different data type than the Visual Basic default type. For example, you may want to assign the number 9.95 to a Decimal data variable to take advantage of the precision of the Decimal data type. As you can see in Figure 4-41, Visual Basic will consider the value 9.95 a Double data type by default. To define the literal as a Decimal literal, you must use a special character to force Visual Basic to use a data type other than the default. Specifically, you place the literal-type character at the end of the literal value. The table in Figure 4-42 shows the available literal-type characters and examples of their use.

Literal-Type Character	Data Type	Example
S	Short	Dim shoAge As Short shoAge = 40S
I	Integer	Dim intHeight as Integer intHeight = 76I
D	Decimal	Dim decPricePerDay As Decimal decPricePerDay = 9.95D
R	Double	Dim dblWeight As Double dblWeight = 8491R
C	Char	Dim chrNumberOfDays As Char chrNumberOfDays = "7"C

FIGURE 4-42

In the first example, the value 40 will be processed by Visual Basic as a Short data type literal, even though the value would be considered an Integer value by default. In the second example, the literal-type character confirms that the value should be treated as an Integer data type. In the third example, the value 9.95 will be processed as a Decimal data type, even though it would be considered a Double data type by default. In the next example, the value 8491 would be considered an Integer data value by default, but because the R literal-type character is used, Visual Basic will treat it as a Double data type. In the final example, the value 7 will be treated as a Char data type.

Constants

Recall that a variable identifies a location in memory where a value can be stored. By its nature, the value in a variable can be changed by statements within the program. For instance, in the sample program in this chapter, one user might request 4 bike rentals and another user might request 12 bike rentals for a large group; the value in the strNumberOfDays variable can change based on the user's needs. In some instances, however, you might not want the value to be changed. For example, the cost of renting a bike in the sample program is $9.95 per day. This value will not change, regardless of how many bikes were rented.

When a value will remain the same throughout the execution of the program, you should assign a meaningful name to a value. A **constant** contains one permanent value throughout the execution of the program. It cannot be changed by any statement within the program. To define a constant value, you can use the code in Figure 4-43.

```
12      Const _cdecPricePerDay As Decimal = 9.95D
```

FIGURE 4-43

The following rules apply to a constant:

1. The declaration of a constant begins with the letters Const, not the letters Dim.
2. You must assign the value to be contained in the constant on the same line as its definition. In Figure 4-43, the value 9.95D is assigned to the constant on the same line as the Const definition.
3. You cannot attempt to change the value of the constant anywhere in the program. If you do, you will produce a compiler error.
4. The letter c often is placed before the constant name to identify it throughout the program as a variable that cannot be changed.
5. Other than the letter c, constant names are formed using the same rules and techniques as other variable names.

Using a named constant instead of a literal provides significant advantages:

6. The program becomes easier to read because the value is identified by the name. For example, instead of using the value 9.95D in a literal, you can use it in a constant called _cdecPricePerDay. This variable name describes the use of the value 9.95D and makes the program easier to read.
7. If you discover that a value must be changed in the code, it is much easier and more reliable to change the value one time in the constant as opposed to changing every occurrence of the value in a literal.

Reference a Variable

You learned earlier that when a variable is declared, it is underlined with a green squiggly line until it is referenced in a statement. This feature of Visual Basic is intended to ensure that you do not declare a variable and then forget to use it. It also helps ensure that you do not waste memory by declaring an unnecessary variable.

When using a variable in a program, it is mandatory that you define the variable before using the variable name in a statement. For example, the statements in Figure 4-44 *will cause an error* because the variable is used in an assignment statement before it is declared.

```
25          strNumberOfDays = txtNumberOfDays.Text
26          Dim strNumberOfDays As String
```

FIGURE 4-44

In the code in Figure 4-44, the variable strNumberOfDays is referenced in an assignment statement (line 25) before it is defined (line 26). This creates a compile error. The Visual Basic IDE indicates a compile error with a the blue squiggly line. In this case, the compile error occurs with the variable name strNumberOfDays on line 25. If you attempt to compile the statements on lines 25 and 26, you will receive a build error. Always define a variable before it is used in a statement.

Scope of Variables

When you declare a variable in Visual Basic, you not only declare the data type of the variable but also implicitly define its scope. The **scope of a variable** specifies where the variable can be referenced in a Visual Basic statement within the program. In larger programs with multiple classes and forms, scope becomes critical, but it is important that you understand the concept at this point.

You declare a variable in a region within a program. For instance, in the sample program in this chapter, you can declare a variable in the click event handler for the Find Cost button. You could declare another variable in the click event handler for the Clear button. Scope determines where each of these variables can be referenced and used in the Visual Basic program. *The rule is: A variable can be referenced only within the region of the program where it is defined.* A region in the programs you have seen thus far in the book is the code between the Sub statement and the End Sub statement in the event handlers. The code between the Sub statement and the End Sub statement is a **procedure**.

Therefore, if you declare a variable within the click event handler for the Find Cost button, that variable cannot be referenced in the click event handler for the Clear button, and vice versa. A variable that can be referenced only within the region of the program where it is defined is called a **local variable**. This variable is defined in one region of the program and cannot be changed by a statement in another region of the program.

In addition, when a variable is defined in a procedure and the procedure ends, the values of the local variables within the procedure are destroyed. Thus, local variables have a certain **lifetime** in the program. They are only *alive* from the time the procedure begins until it ends. If the procedure is executed again, the value the variable once contained no longer is present. One execution of the procedure is a variable's lifetime. Therefore, if a user clicks the Find Cost button, the values in the variables are valid until the click event is completed. When the user clicks the Find Cost button again, all values from the first click are gone.

You can also define variables that can be used in multiple regions of a Visual Basic program. These variables are called **global variables**. In most programs, local variables should be used because they cause fewer errors than global variables.

Understanding the scope of a variable is important when developing a program. You will learn more about the scope of variables later in this chapter and throughout this book.

Convert Variable Data

Variables used in arithmetic statements in a Visual Basic program must be numeric. String variables cannot be used in an arithmetic statement. If you attempt to use them, you will create a compilation error.

A user often enters data in a text box. Data in the Text property of a TextBox object is treated as String data. Because String data cannot be used in an arithmetic statement, the String data entered by a user must be converted to numeric data before it can be used in an arithmetic statement.

For instance, in the sample program in this chapter, the user enters the number of days to rent bikes. Before this number can be used in an arithmetic statement to determine the total cost of bike rentals, the value must be converted to an Integer data type.

Visual Basic includes several procedures that allow you to convert one data type to another data type. You will recall that a procedure is a prewritten set of code that can be called by a statement in the Visual Basic program. When the procedure is called, it performs a particular task. In this case, the task is to convert the String value the user entered into an Integer data type that can be used in an arithmetic operation. One procedure that converts a String data type to an Integer data type is named ToInt32. The number 32 in the procedure name identifies that the representation of the integer will require 32 bits or 4 bytes, which is the amount of memory required for the Integer data type. The procedure is in the Convert class, which is available in a Visual Studio 2017 class library.

Use a Procedure

When you need to use a procedure to accomplish a task in your program, you must understand what the procedure does and how to code the procedure call in a program statement. A procedure can operate in one of two ways: It can perform its task and return a value, or it can perform its task without returning a value. You will recall in the Chapter 3 sample program that the Close() procedure closed the window and ended the program. The procedure performed its task but did not return a value. A procedure of this type is called a **Sub procedure**.

In the Beach Bike Rentals program in this chapter, the requirement is to convert the String value for the number of bikes the user enters into an Integer data type. Then, it can be used in an arithmetic operation. Therefore, the procedure must return a value (the Integer value for the number of days). A procedure that returns a value is called a **Function procedure**, or a **function**.

In addition, a procedure might require data to be passed to it when called in order to carry out its processing. In the sample program in this chapter, the Function procedure to convert a String variable to an Integer variable first must be able to access the String variable. Therefore, in the statement that calls the Function procedure, the variable name for the String variable to be converted must be passed to the procedure. A value is passed to a procedure through the use of an argument.

An **argument** identifies a value required by a procedure. To pass the argument to the procedure, include its name within parentheses following the name of the procedure in the calling statement. For example, to pass the value stored in the strNumberOfDays variable to the ToInt32 procedure, you could use the statement in Figure 4-45.

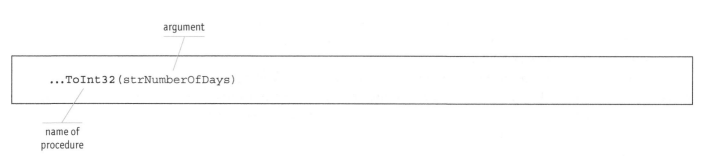

FIGURE 4-45

The name of the procedure is ToInt32. The argument is strNumberOfDays, which is the String variable that contains the value to be converted to an Integer data type by the ToInt32 procedure. Notice that the argument is enclosed within parentheses.

Every procedure is part of a class in Visual Basic. You will recall from Chapter 1 that a **class** is a named grouping of program code. When the calling statement must call a procedure, it first must identify the class that contains the procedure. Thus, in Figure 4-45 the calling statement is incomplete because the class name is not included. The class that contains the ToInt32 procedure is the Convert class. To complete the procedure call statement, the class must be added, as shown in Figure 4-46.

FIGURE 4-46

In Figure 4-46, the class name Convert begins the procedure call. A dot operator separates the class name from the procedure name (ToInt32). The argument (strNumberOfDays) within the parentheses completes the procedure call.

When a Function procedure returns a value, such as the ToInt32 procedure that returns an integer value, the returned value essentially replaces the Function procedure call in the assignment statement. In Figure 4-47, you can see that when the processing is completed within the Function procedure, the integer value is substituted for the procedure call in the assignment statement.

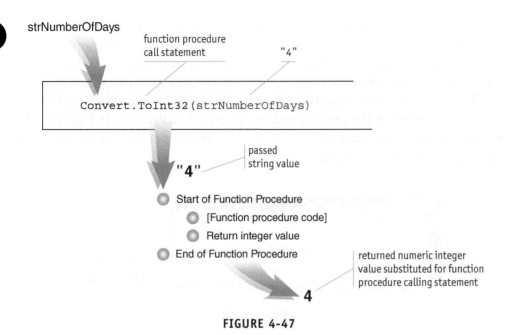

strNumberOfDays

function procedure
call statement   "4"

```
Convert.ToInt32(strNumberOfDays)
```

"4"   passed
string value

● Start of Function Procedure
  ● [Function procedure code]
  ● Return integer value
● End of Function Procedure   returned numeric integer
value substituted for function
procedure calling statement

4

FIGURE 4-47

Figure 4-48 shows the complete assignment statement to convert the String data type in the strNumberOfDays variable to an Integer data type and place it in the intNumberOfDays variable.

The intNumberOfDays variable name to the left of the equal sign identifies the Integer variable where the converted value will be copied. The equal sign in the assignment statement is required. As a result of the assignment statement in Figure 4-48, the ToInt32 Function procedure in the Convert class will convert the value in the strNumberOfDays String variable to an integer value. The assignment statement will place that integer value in the intNumberOfDays variable.

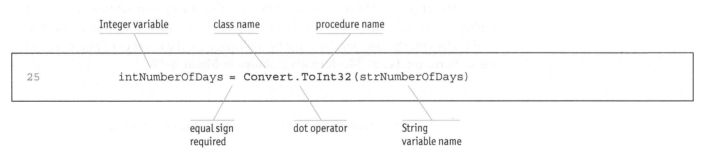

Integer variable   class name   procedure name

```
25        intNumberOfDays = Convert.ToInt32(strNumberOfDays)
```

equal sign   dot operator   String
required   variable name

FIGURE 4-48

The use of Function procedures and arguments with procedure calls is common when programming in Visual Basic. You will encounter many examples of Function procedure calls throughout this book.

Option Strict On

In the previous section, you saw an example of how to explicitly change a value from one data type to another. By default, Visual Basic will automatically convert data types if the one on the right side of the equal sign in an assignment statement is different from the one on the left side of the equal sign. Quite often, however, the automatic conversion can introduce errors and produce an incorrect converted value. Therefore, allowing automatic conversion typically is not a good programming style.

To prevent automatic conversion of values, the developer must insert the Option Strict On statement in the program prior to any event handler code. In Figure 4-49, the Option Strict On statement is shown just after the introductory comments in the sample program for this chapter.

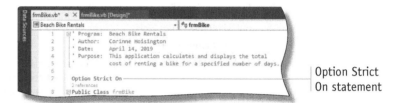

FIGURE 4-49

The Option Strict On statement explicitly prevents any default data type conversions that would cause data loss and prevents any conversion between numeric types and strings. Therefore, you must write explicit conversion statements to convert from one data type to another. This approach minimizes potential errors that can occur from data conversion.

Arithmetic Operations

The ability to perform arithmetic operations on numeric data is fundamental to computer programs. Many programs require arithmetic operations to add, subtract, multiply, and divide numeric data. For example, in the Beach Bike Rentals program in this chapter, the cost per day must be multiplied by the number of rental days to calculate the total cost. The formula is shown in Figure 4-50.

Total Cost of Bikes = Number of Days times Price per Day

FIGURE 4-50

An assignment statement is used in Visual Basic 2017 to perform the arithmetic operation shown in Figure 4-50. The statements used in the sample program and a depiction of the operation are shown in Figure 4-51.

In the code in Figure 4-51, the variable strNumberOfDays is assigned the user's entered value by the assignment statement on line 23. (See Figure 4-20 on page 163 for a detailed explanation of this statement.) The statement on line 24 converts the value in the strNumberOfDays variable to an integer and copies it to the

```
18
19    Dim strNumberOfDays As String
20    Dim intNumberOfDays As Integer
21    Dim decTotalCost As Decimal
22
23    strNumberOfDays = txtNumberOfDays.Text
24    intNumberOfDays = Convert.ToInt32(strNumberOfDays)
25    decTotalCost = intNumberOfDays * _cdecPricePerDay
26    lblTotalCost.Text = decTotalCost.ToString("C")
```

FIGURE 4-51

intNumberOfDays variable. (See Figure 4-48 on page 179 for an explanation of this statement.)

The statement on line 25 multiplies the integer value in the intNumberOfDays variable by the constant value in the _cdecPricePerDay variable, and then copies the result to the decTotalCost variable. For example, if the user enters 4 as the number of rental days, the value 4 is multiplied by 9.95 (the value in the _cdecPricePerDay variable), and the result (39.80) is copied to the decTotalCost variable.

Arithmetic Operators

The asterisk (*) is an important element on the right side of the equal sign in the assignment statement on line 25. This asterisk is the multiplication **arithmetic operator**. Whenever the compiler encounters this operator, the value to the left of the operator is multiplied by the value to the right of the operator, and these values are replaced in the assignment statement by the product of the two numbers. Thus, in Figure 4-51 on page 181, the arithmetic expression intNumberOfDays * _cdecPricePerDay is replaced by the value 39.80. Then, the assignment statement places the value 39.80 in the decTotalCost variable.

The multiplication arithmetic operator is only one of the arithmetic operators available in Visual Basic 2017. The table in Figure 4-52 lists the arithmetic operators in Visual Basic 2017, describes their use, and provides an example of their use.

Arithmetic Operator	Use	Assignment Statement Showing Use
+	Addition	decTotal = decPrice + decTax
−	Subtraction	decCost = decRegularPrice − decDiscount
*	Multiplication	decTax = decItemPrice * decTaxRate
/	Division	decClassAverage = decTotalScores / intNumberOfStudents
^	Exponentiation	intSquareArea = intSquareSide ^ 2
\	Integer Division	intResult = 13 \ 5
Mod	Modulus Arithmetic (remainder)	intRemainder = 13 Mod 5

FIGURE 4-52

The arithmetic operators shown in Figure 4-52 are explained in the following paragraphs:

Addition

The **addition arithmetic operator** (+) adds the numeric values immediately to the left and right of the operator and replaces the arithmetic expression in the assignment statement. For example, in Figure 4-53, the value in the decPrice variable is added to the value in the decTax variable.

arithmetic expression

```
40                 decTotal = decPrice + decTax
```

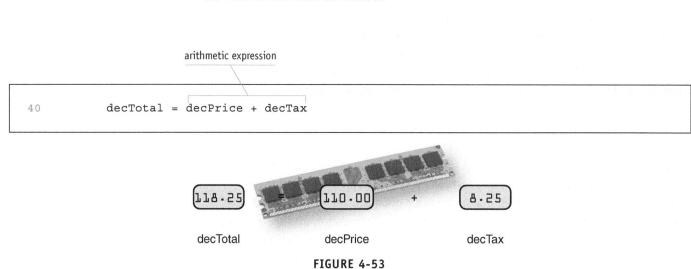

decTotal   decPrice   decTax

FIGURE 4-53

iStockphoto.com/Tpopova

In Figure 4-53, the arithmetic expression (decPrice + decTax) is evaluated, and then the assignment statement copies the sum to the decTotal variable in RAM.

An arithmetic expression that uses the addition operator can contain more than two numeric values to be added. For example, in Figure 4-54, three variables are used in the arithmetic expression.

```
47        decTotalPay = decRegularPay + decOvertimePay + decBonusPay
```

FIGURE 4-54

In Figure 4-54, the value in decRegularPay is added to the value in decOvertimePay. The result then is added to decBonusPay, and that sum is copied to the decTotalPay variable. Visual Basic imposes no limit on the number of variables in an arithmetic expression.

In addition to variables, arithmetic expressions can contain literals. The assignment statement in Figure 4-55 uses a literal.

```
53          decTicketCost = decInternetTicketCost + 10.25
```

FIGURE 4-55

In Figure 4-55, the value 10.25 is added to the value in the decInternetTicket-Cost variable, and that sum is placed in the decTicketCost variable. Generally, literals should not be used in arithmetic expressions unless you know that the value will not change. For example, if the extra cost for the ticket could change in the future, good program design would dictate that the value be placed in a variable (perhaps even a constant).

Subtraction

To subtract one value from another in an assignment statement, Visual Basic 2017 uses the **subtraction arithmetic operator** (–), as shown in Figure 4-56.

```
59          decNetProfit = decRevenue - decCosts
```

FIGURE 4-56

In Figure 4-56, the value in the decCosts variable is subtracted from the value in the decRevenue variable. The result then is copied into the decNetProfit variable. If the value in decCosts is greater than the value in decRevenue, the value placed in the decNetProfit variable will be negative.

Use Arithmetic Results

After an arithmetic operation has been performed using an assignment statement, the values used in the operation and the resulting answer can be used in subsequent arithmetic operations or for other purposes within the program. For example, the result of one operation can be used in a subsequent calculation (Figure 4-57).

```
67          decComputerCost = decMonitorCost + decSystemUnitCost
68          decNetComputerCost = decComputerCost - decSystemDiscount
```

FIGURE 4-57

In Figure 4-57, the statement on line 67 determines the computer cost by adding the costs of the monitor and the system unit. The statement on line 68 calculates the net computer cost by subtracting the system discount from the computer cost calculated on line 67. Whenever a value is stored in a variable, it can be used in other statements within the program.

Multiplication

Multiplication is accomplished through the use of an assignment statement and the multiplication operator (*), as shown in Figure 4-58.

```
74          intLandPlotArea = intLandPlotLength * intLandPlotWidth
```

FIGURE 4-58

In Figure 4-58, the value in the intLandPlotLength variable is multiplied by the value in the intLandPlotWidth variable. The product of the multiplication is placed in the intLandPlotArea variable.

If two positive numbers are multiplied, the answer is positive. If two negative numbers are multiplied, the answer is positive. If one positive number and one negative number are multiplied, the answer is negative.

When two numbers are multiplied, you must be aware of the size of the result. The largest number of digits that can appear as a result of multiplication is the sum of the number of digits in the values being multiplied. If the product is greater than the value that can be stored in the variable to the left of the assignment statement, an overflow error can occur and the program will be ended.

How should I test my program to make sure it works properly?
When you allow user input, be sure to test every possible entry by the user. If a decimal value is entered instead of an expected integer value, your program may stop functioning. As you learn more about coding in the next chapters, error validation will become an important part of developing your program.

Division

Visual Basic 2017 provides three arithmetic operators for division and related calculations: the slash (/), the backslash (\), and the MOD operator.

You use the slash for normal division. For example, in Figure 4-59, the value in the decTestScores variable is divided by 3 to obtain the average test score.

```
decAverageTestScore = decTestScores / 3
```

FIGURE 4-59

You use the backslash (\) for integer division. With integer division, the quotient returned from the division operation is an integer. If the division operation produces a quotient with a remainder, the remainder is dropped, or truncated. The examples in Figure 4-60 illustrate the use of the integer division arithmetic operator.

WATCH OUT FOR

The divisor is the number to the right of the division operator. Make sure the divisor is not zero. If you attempt to divide by zero, your program will be ended with an error.

Division Operation	Result
12\5	2
25\4	6
30\7	4

FIGURE 4-60

Notice in each example in Figure 4-60 that the result is a whole number with the remainder truncated.

The MOD operator divides the number to the left of the operator by the number to the right of the operator and returns an integer value that is the remainder of the division operation. Integer division and the MOD operator often are used together, as shown in Figure 4-61.

```
86        intHours = intTotalNumberOfMinutes \ 60
87        intMinutes = intTotalNumberOfMinutes Mod 60
```

FIGURE 4-61

In Figure 4-61, the operation on line 86 will return only the integer value of the division. For example, if the intTotalNumberOfMinutes variable contains 150, a result of 2 (2 = 150\60) will be placed in the intHours variable. The operation on line 87 will place the remainder in the intMinutes variable. The remainder in the example is 30; 150 divided by 60 is 2, with a remainder of 30.

Exponentiation

Exponentiation means raising a number to a power. It is accomplished in Visual Basic 2017 using the exponentiation arithmetic operator (^), as shown in Figure 4-62.

exponentiation
arithmetic operator

```
92              intCubeArea = intLengthOfCubeSide ^ 3
```

FIGURE 4-62

In Figure 4-62, the arithmetic expression is the same as intLengthOfCubeSide * intLengthOfCubeSide* intLengthOfCubeSide. Therefore, the value is cubed and copied to the intCubeArea variable.

The exponent used in the operation can be a fraction. If so, the root is taken (Figure 4-63).

```
94              intLengthOfCubeSide = intCubeArea ^ (1 / 3)
```

FIGURE 4-63

In Figure 4-63, the cube root of the value in the intCubeArea variable is calculated and the result is copied to the intLengthOfCubeSide variable. Thus, if the area of the cube is 64, the value calculated for the length of the cube side would be 4 (4 * 4 * 4 = 64). The fractional exponent can never be negative, and it must be placed within parentheses.

Multiple Operations

A single assignment statement can contain multiple arithmetic operations. In Figure 4-64, the addition and subtraction operators are used to calculate the new balance in a savings account by adding the deposits to the old balance and subtracting withdrawals.

```
101         decNewBalance = decOldBalance + decDeposits - decWithdrawals
```

FIGURE 4-64

When the assignment statement is executed in Figure 4-64, the value in the decOldBalance variable is added to the value in the decDeposits variable. Then, the value in the decWithdrawals variable is subtracted from that sum and the result is copied to the decNewBalance variable.

Notice in Figure 4-64 that the calculations proceed from left to right in the arithmetic expression.

Hierarchy of Operations

When multiple operations are included in a single assignment statement, the sequence for performing the calculations is determined by the following rules:

1. Exponentiation ($\wedge$) is performed first.
2. Multiplication (*) and division (/) are performed next.
3. Integer division (\\) is next.
4. MOD then occurs.
5. Addition (+) and subtraction (–) are performed last.
6. Within each of the preceding five steps, calculations are performed from left to right.

As a result of this predetermined sequence, an arithmetic expression such as decBonus + decHours * decHourlyRate would result in the product of decHours * decHourlyRate being added to decBonus.

An arithmetic expression such as decGrade1 + decGrade2 / 2 would cause the value in the decGrade2 variable to be divided by 2 and then the quotient to be added to the value in decGrade1 because division is performed before addition. However, this calculation probably was not intended. Instead, the intent probably was to add the values in decGrade1 and decGrade2 and then divide the sum by 2. To force certain operations to be performed before others, you can use parentheses. Any arithmetic expression within parentheses is evaluated before expressions outside the parentheses, as shown in Figure 4-65.

```
108          decAverageGrade = (decGrade1 + decGrade2) / 2
```

FIGURE 4-65

In Figure 4-65, the addition operation is inside the parentheses, so it will be completed before the division operation. Therefore, the result of the arithmetic expression is that the value in decGrade1 is added to the value in decGrade2. That sum then is divided by 2 and the quotient is copied to the decAverageGrade variable.

If you want to make the sequence of operations explicitly clear, you can use parentheses around multiple arithmetic operations in an arithmetic expression even if the predetermined sequence of operations will produce the correct answer.

Display Numeric Output Data

As you have learned, the result of an arithmetic expression is a numeric value that typically is stored in a numeric variable. To display the numeric data as information in a graphical user interface, usually the data must be placed in the Text property of a

Label object or a TextBox object. The Text property of these objects, however, requires that the data be a String data type. Therefore, to display a numeric value in a label or a text box, the numeric data must be converted to a String data type.

Each of the numeric data types provides a function called ToString that converts data from a numeric data type to the String data type. The general format of the function call for a Decimal numeric variable is shown in Figure 4-66.

IN THE REAL WORLD

You know that a procedure is a collection of code that a program can call to perform a particular function, such as converting data stored in a numeric data type to data stored as a String data type. In some programming languages, a procedure is called a method. Therefore, as you search the index or other areas in Visual Studio Help, you might find the word *method* used. Just remember that the terms *method* and *procedure* are virtually synonymous.

General Format: ToString Function

```
decVariable.ToString()
```

FIGURE 4-66

The statement shown in Figure 4-66 consists of the name of the Decimal variable that contains data to be converted, the dot operator (.), and the name of the function (ToString). Notice that the function name is followed immediately by closed parentheses, which indicates to the Visual Basic compiler that ToString is a procedure name. When the function call is executed, the value returned by the ToString function replaces the call.

The function call normally is contained within an assignment statement to assign the returned string value to the Text property of a Label or TextBox object. The example in Figure 4-67 shows the assignment statement to convert the numeric value in the decTemperature variable to a String value that then is placed in the Text property of the lblTemperature Label object.

name of decimal variable

ToString function call

```
118        lblTemperature.Text = decTemperature.ToString()
```

FIGURE 4-67

In Figure 4-67, the name of the Decimal variable (decTemperature) is followed by the dot operator and then the name of the function (ToString) with the required parentheses. When the statement on line 118 is executed, the ToString function is called. It converts the numeric value in the decTemperature variable to a String data type and returns the String data. The assignment statement then copies the returned String data to the Text property of the Temperature Label object.

Format Specifications for the ToString Function

In the example in Figure 4-67, the conversion from numeric value to String value is a straight conversion, which means the value is returned but not formatted in any manner. For example, if the numeric value in the Decimal variable was 47.235, then the same value was returned as a String value.

The ToString function, however, can convert numeric data to String data using a specified format. For example, the value 2317.49 could be returned as $2,317.49. The returned value is in the form of dollars and cents, or currency. To identify the format for the numeric data to be returned by the ToString function, the **format specifier** must be included as an argument in the parentheses following the ToString function name. The table in Figure 4-68 on page 189 identifies the commonly used format specifiers; in the examples, the value in the numeric field is 8976.43561.

In Figure 4-68, each format specifier is used as an argument within parentheses. The argument must be included in the quotation marks on each side of the format specifier, as shown. The letter for the format specifier can be uppercase or lowercase.

Format Specifier	Format	Description	Output from the Function
General(G)	ToString("G")	Displays the number as is	8976.43561
Currency(C)	ToString("C")	Displays the number with a dollar sign, a thousands separator (comma), 2 digits to the right of the decimal and negative numbers in parentheses	$8,976.44
Fixed(F)	ToString("F")	Displays the number with 2 digits to the right of the decimal and a minus sign for negative numbers	8976.44
Number(N)	ToString("N")	Displays a number with a thousands separator, 2 digits to the right of the decimal and a minus sign for negative numbers	8,976.44
Percent(P)	ToString("P")	Displays the number multiplied by 100 with a % sign, a thousands separator, 2 digits to the right of the decimal and a minus sign for negative numbers	897,643.56%
Scientific(E)	ToString("E")	Displays the number in E-notation and a minus sign for negative numbers	8.976436E+03

FIGURE 4-68

Precision Specifier

Each format specifier has a default number of digits that will be returned to the right of the decimal point. You can use a precision specifier, however, to override this default number. The **precision specifier** is a number included within the quotation marks in the function call that identifies the number of positions that should be returned to the right of the decimal point. The examples in Figure 4-69 illustrate the use of the precision specifier; assume that the value in the decNumericValue variable is 8976.43561.

Statement	Copied to Text Property of lblOutput Label Object
lblOutput = decNumericValue.ToString("C2")	$8,976.44
lblOutput = decNumericValue.ToString("C3")	$8,976.436
lblOutput = decNumericValue.ToString("F1")	8976.4
lblOutput = decNumericValue.ToString("N4")	8,976.4356
lblOutput = decNumericValue.ToString("P0")	897,644%

FIGURE 4-69

As you can see, the precision specifier identifies the number of digits that should be displayed to the right of the decimal point in the string returned from the ToString function. Notice that if the precision specifier is 0, no digits are returned to the right of the decimal point.

As with all conversions, when the number of positions to the right of the decimal point in the returned string is less than the number of digits to the right of the decimal point in the numeric value being converted, the returned value is rounded to the specified number of decimal places.

Clear the Form — Clear Procedure and Focus Procedure

Earlier in this chapter, you learned that when the user clicks the Clear button in the Beach Bike Rentals program (see Figure 4-1 on page 148), the event handler for the Clear button must clear the results from the window and allow the user to enter the next number of rental days. To clear the results, the Clear button event handler must complete the following tasks:

1. Clear the Text property of the TextBox object
2. Clear the Text property of the Label object that displays the total cost of the bikes rented
3. Set the focus on the TextBox object, which means placing the insertion point in the text box

You will learn to accomplish these tasks in the following sections.

Clear Procedure

The Clear procedure clears any data in the Text property of a TextBox object. The general format of the Clear procedure is shown in Figure 4-70.

General Format: Clear Procedure
`txtTextboxName.Clear()`
EXAMPLE: `txtNumberOfDays.Clear()`

FIGURE 4-70

When the Clear procedure is executed, the Text property is cleared of data. As with every procedure call, the name of the procedure must be followed by parentheses.

Clear the Text Property of a Label

The Clear procedure cannot be used with a Label object. Instead, to clear the Text property of a Label object, you must write an assignment statement that assigns a null length string to the Text property. A null length string has no length, which means it is a string with no characters. A null length string is represented by two quotation marks with no character between them (""). To assign a null length string to the Text property, you can use the statement shown in Figure 4-71.

```
39          lblTotalCost.Text = ""
```

FIGURE 4-71

In Figure 4-71, the null length string represented by the two empty quotation marks is assigned to the Text property of the lblTotalCost Label object. As a result of the assignment statement, the Text property is cleared.

Set the Focus

When the focus is on a TextBox object, the insertion point is located in the text box (Figure 4-72).

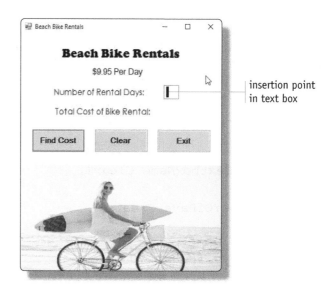

FIGURE 4-72

iStockphoto.com/Wavebreakmedia

When the user clicks a button or other item in the graphical user interface, the focus shifts to that item. Therefore, to place the focus on a text box, the user can click it. However, the programmer can use the Focus procedure to place the focus on a text box automatically without requiring the user to click it first, thus making it easier for the user to enter data in the text box (Figure 4-73).

object name   Focus procedure name

```
48              txtNumberOfDays.Focus()
```

FIGURE 4-73

As with most procedure calls, the name of the object begins the statement, followed immediately by the dot operator (period). The name of the procedure (Focus) follows the dot operator. When the statement on line 48 is executed, the focus is placed on the txtNumberOfDays TextBox object, which means the insertion point is placed in the text box.

Form Load Event

In the sample programs in Chapter 3 and this chapter, you have seen that an event can occur when the user clicks a button. The user's action triggers the code to execute in the event handler for the button click. For example, in the Beach Bike Rentals program in this chapter, the user clicks the Find Cost button and the event handler code responds by multiplying the number of days the bike is rented by the price per day and displaying the result (see Figure 4-1 on page 148).

Clicking a button is not the only action that can trigger an event. For example, a form load event occurs each time a program is started and the Windows Form object is loaded into computer memory. For the program in this chapter, a form load event occurs when the program starts and the Beach Bike Rentals form is loaded. In some programs, an event handler is not written for this particular event and no processing occurs. In the Beach Bike Rentals program, however, a form loading event handler is required. This event handler completes the following tasks:

1. Displays the cost per day per bike heading
2. Clears the placeholder from the lblTotalCost Text property
3. Sets the focus on the txtNumberOfDays text box

Concatenation, Class Scope, and Debugging

To complete the chapter project, you need to use two new programming techniques: concatenation and assigning a variable so it has class scope. Finally, you need to debug the program by checking for errors common in programs that accept user entries.

Concatenation

In the Beach Bike Rentals program, the lblCostHeading Label object displays the cost per day. In the user interface design, the lblCostHeading Label contains placeholder information for the label, but does not contain the actual cost per day (Figure 4-74).

lblCostHeading label does not contain actual cost per bike

FIGURE 4-74
iStockphoto.com/Wavebreakmedia

In Figure 4-74, the programmer had two reasons for not placing the actual rental cost in the label during the design phase. First, in the original implementation of the program, the cost per day is $9.95. In the future, however, the cost might change for a holiday or permanently over time. Generally, data that might change should be placed in the Text property of a Label object during execution time, not at design time. Therefore, the cost per bike should be placed in the label by the form load event handler when the form opens. Second, the cost per bike is used in two places in the program — in the label and when the actual calculation is performed to determine the total cost (see Figure 4-51 on page 181). Instead of using the numeric value of 9.95 several times within the program, the value should be assigned to a variable. If the value must be changed in the future, only one change to the variable is necessary. For example, if the price per daily bike rental changes to $12.95, the price can be changed in the price per day variable and then it will be correct for all uses of the variable. To illustrate, the variable for the price per day is shown in Figure 4-75.

```
12      Const _cdecPricePerDay As Decimal = 9.95D
```

FIGURE 4-75

HEADS UP

In some instances, it is better to continue a line of code in the code window on a second line so that the entire line can be read without scrolling. To continue a line of code on a subsequent line, place a space in the statement and then place an underscore (_) character in the line of code. The underscore character indicates to the Visual Basic compiler that the line of code continues on the next line (Figure 4-76).

As you can see, the price per day is declared as a constant that cannot be changed during program execution. If the price changes in the future, the developer can make one change to this declaration and all elements of the program that use the value will be correct.

To create the heading for the Beach Bike Rentals program, the value in the variable declared in Figure 4-75 must be combined with the words *per Day* and the result must be placed in the Text property of the lblCostHeading Label object. The process of joining two different values into a single string is called **concatenation**. When you use concatenation, the values being concatenated must be String data types. Note in Figure 4-75 that the _cdecPricePerDay variable is a Decimal data type. Therefore, it must be changed to a String data type before being joined with the words in the heading.

The statement in Figure 4-76 converts the Decimal data type to a String data type, concatenates (or joins) the two strings together, and then places the result in the Text property of the lblCostHeading Label object.

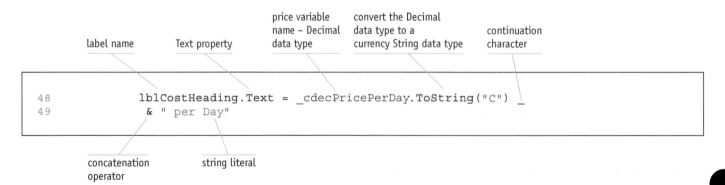

FIGURE 4-76

In Figure 4-76, the string generated to the right of the equal sign will be placed in the Text property of the lblCostHeading Label object. The first entry to the right of the equal sign is the price variable name (Figure 4-75). Following the dot operator is the ToString procedure name, followed by the currency argument within parentheses. Remember that the ToString procedure converts a numeric value to a String data type. When the currency argument ("C") is used, the String value returned is in a currency format.

Following the conversion statement is the **concatenation operator (&)**. When the Visual Basic compiler encounters this operator, the string to the left of the operator is joined with the String data to the right of the operator to create a single concatenated string. The resulting string then is placed in the Text property of the lblCostHeading Label object.

The process that occurs to the right of the equal sign is illustrated in Figure 4-77.

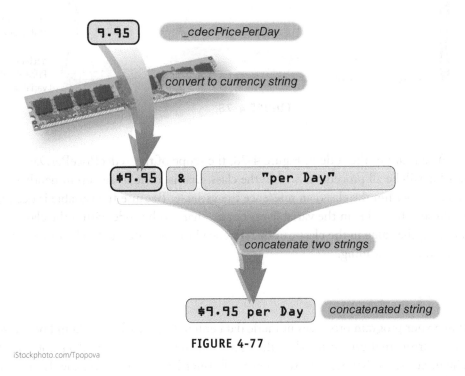

FIGURE 4-77

iStockphoto.com/Tpopova

As Figure 4-77 shows, to obtain the concatenated string, the Decimal value in the _cdecPricePerDay Decimal variable is converted to a currency String data type. Then, that value is combined with the string literal to create the concatenated string. In the assignment statement in Figure 4-76 on page 194, the concatenated string is assigned to the Text property of the lblCostHeading Label object.

Class Scope

Remember that when you declare a variable, you also define its scope. The scope of a variable identifies where within the program the variable can be referenced. For example, if a variable is declared within an event handler procedure, the variable can be referenced only within that procedure.

Sometimes, a variable must be referenced in multiple event handlers. In the Beach Bike Rentals program, the value in the _cdecPricePerDay variable is referenced in the Find Cost button event handler when the total cost is calculated (Figure 4-51 on page 181). The value also is referenced in the form load event when the heading is displayed (Figure 4-76 on page 194). Because the variable is referenced in two different event-handling procedures, it must be defined at the class level instead of the procedure (event handler) level. This means that the variable must be declared in the code before the first procedure in the program. As shown in Figure 4-78, the declaration of the _cdecPricePerDay variable follows the class definition statement but appears before the first event handler procedure.

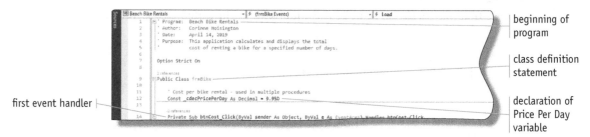

FIGURE 4-78

As a result of the code in Figure 4-78, the scope of the _cdecPricePerDay variable will be all procedures within the class; that is, code in any event handler procedure within the class can reference the variable. Because the variable is declared a constant, the value in the variable cannot be changed by code within the class; however, the value in the class can be referenced to calculate the total cost and to create the cost heading.

Debug Your Program

When your program processes numeric data entered by a user, you should be aware of several errors that can occur when the user enters data the program does not expect. The three errors that occur most often are Format Exceptions, Overflow Exceptions, and Divide By Zero Exceptions.

A **Format Exception** occurs when the user enters data that a statement within the program cannot process properly. In the Beach Bike Rentals program, the user must enter a numeric value for the number of bikes to rent. When the user clicks the Find Cost button, the program converts the entered value to an integer and then uses the numeric value in the calculation (Figure 4-48 on page 179). If the user enters a nonnumeric value, such as ab (Figure 4-79a), the conversion process cannot take place because the argument passed to the Convert class is not a numeric value. In this situation, a Format Exception error is recognized and the error box in Figure 4-79b is displayed.

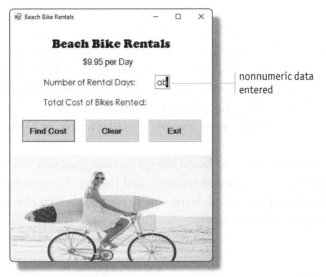

nonnumeric data
entered

FIGURE 4-79a
iStockphoto.com/Wavebreakmedia

statement that
caused the exception

```
19        Dim strNumberOfDays As String
20        Dim intNumberOfDays As Integer
21        Dim decTotalCost As Decimal
22
23        strNumberOfDays = txtNumberOfDays.Text
24        intNumberOfDays = Convert.ToInt32(strNumberOfDays) ⊗
25        decTotalCost = intNumberOfDays * _cdecPricePerDay
26        lblTotalCost.Text = decTotalCost.ToString("C")
27    End Sub
28
      0 references
29 ⊟  Private Sub btnClear_Click(ByVal sender As Object, ByV
30        ' This event handler is executed when the user cli
31        ' Clear button. It clears the number of days text
32        ' and the Text property of the Total Cost label.
```

Exception Unhandled   ⚓ ✕

System.FormatException: 'Input string was not in a correct format.'

Details... | Copy

▸ Exception Settings

troubleshooting
tips

FIGURE 4-79b

In Figure 4-79a, the user entered the value ab and then clicked the Find Cost button. When control was passed to the ToInt32 procedure to convert the String value in the text box to an integer, the Format Exception was triggered because the value in the strNumberOfDays variable was not numeric. When an exception occurs, the execution of the program is terminated. With Visual Studio running, click the Stop Debugging button on the Standard toolbar.

An **Overflow Exception** occurs when the user enters a value greater than the maximum value the statement can process. For example, in the Beach Bike Rentals program, if the user enters a value in the text box that is too large for the ToInt32 procedure to convert, an Overflow Exception occurs.

An Overflow Exception also can occur when a calculation creates a value larger than a procedure can process. For example, if two large but valid numbers are multiplied, the product of the multiplication might be too large to process.

The third type of common error is the **Divide By Zero Exception**. It is not possible to divide by zero, so if your program contains a division operation and the divisor is zero, the Divide By Zero Exception will occur.

Whenever an exception occurs, a window similar to that in Figure 4-79b will be displayed.

To avoid exceptions, which should always be your goal, you can use certain techniques for editing the data and ensuring that the user has entered valid data. In Chapter 5 and Chapter 6, you will learn how to write code that checks user input to ensure that exceptions do not occur.

Program Design

As you have learned, the requirements document identifies the purpose of the program being developed, the application title, the procedures to be followed when using the program, any required equations and calculations, any conditions within the program that must be tested, notes and restrictions that must be followed by the program, and any other comments that would be helpful to understanding the problem. The requirements document for the Beach Bike Rentals application is shown in Figure 4-80.

REQUIREMENTS DOCUMENT

Date:	April 14, 2019
Date Submitted:	
Application Title:	Beach Bike Rentals
Purpose:	The Beach Bike Rentals program allows the user to enter the number of days they intend to rent a bike. The program calculates the total cost of the bike rental based on a price of $9.95 per day.
Program Procedures:	In a Windows Classic Desktop application, the user enters the number of days to rent a bike. The program calculates the total cost of the bike rental. The user can clear the values on the screen and enter a new value for the number of days the bike is rented.

FIGURE 4-80 (continues)

Algorithms, Processing, and Conditions:	1. The user must be able to enter the number of days the bike is to be rented.
	2. The user can initiate the calculation and display the total cost of the bike rented.
	3. The application computes the total cost by multiplying the number of days by the cost per day ($9.95).
	4. The total cost of the bike rental is displayed as a currency value.
	5. The user should be able to clear the value entered for the number of days and the total cost of bike rental.
	6. The user should be provided with a button to exit the program.
Notes and Restrictions:	n/a
Comments:	A graphic should depict a bike rental image. A graphic named bike is available on CengageBrain.com.

FIGURE 4-80 (continued)

The Use Case Definition for the Beach Bike Rentals program is shown in Figure 4-81.

USE CASE DEFINITION

1. The Windows Classic Desktop application opens with a text box in which the user can enter the number of days a bike is rented. The user interface includes the text box, an area to display the total cost of the bike rental, a Find Cost button, a Clear button, and an Exit button.
2. The user enters the number of days the bike is rented.
3. The user clicks the Find Cost button.
4. The program displays the total cost of the bike rental.
5. The user clicks the Clear button to clear the Number of Rental Days text box and remove the Total Cost of the Bike Rental amount.
6. The user can repeat Steps 2 through 5.
7. The user clicks the Exit button to end the application.

FIGURE 4-81

Event-Planning Document

You will recall that the event-planning document is a table that specifies which objects in the user interface will cause events, the action taken by the user to trigger each event, and the event processing that must occur. The event-planning document for the Beach Bike Rentals program is shown in Figure 4-82.

EVENT-PLANNING DOCUMENT

Program Name: Beach Bike Rentals	Developer: Corinne Hoisington	Object: frmBikes	Date: April 14, 2019
OBJECT	EVENT TRIGGER	EVENT PROCESSING	
btnCost	Click	Assign data entered in text box to a String variable Convert entered data to numeric integer Find total cost of bike rental (number of days * price per day) Display total cost of bikes rental	
btnClear	Click	Clear Number of Rental Days text box Clear Total Cost of Bike Rental label text Set focus on Number of Rental Days text box	
btnExit	Click	Close the window and end the program	
frmBike	Load	Display heading with price per bike rental Clear the placement digits for Total Cost of Bike Rental Label object Set focus on Number of Rental Days text box	

FIGURE 4-82

Code the Program

You are now ready to code the program by entering Visual Basic statements to accomplish the tasks specified in the event-planning document. You also will implement the logic to carry out the required processing.

Guided Program Development

To design the user interface for the Beach Bike Rentals program and enter the code required to process each event in the program, complete the following steps:

NOTE TO THE LEARNER

In the following activity, you should complete the tasks within the specified steps. Each of the tasks is accompanied by a Hint Screen. The purpose of the Hint Screen is to indicate where you should perform the activity in the Visual Studio window and to remind you which method to use. If you need further help completing a step, refer to the figure identified by *ref:*.

Phase 1: Create the User Interface Mockup

1

- **Create a Windows Classic Desktop Application** Open Visual Studio and then click the New Project button on the Standard toolbar. If necessary, click Windows Classic Desktop in the left pane of the New Project window, click Windows Forms App in the center pane, and then type Beach Bike Rentals in the Name text box.

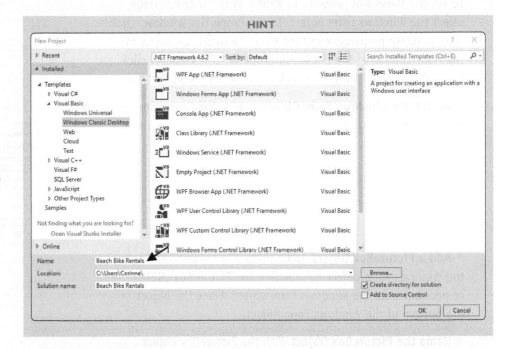

- **Display the Toolbox** Click the OK button in the New Project window, and then ensure that the Toolbox is displayed in the Visual Studio window. If it is not, click View on the menu bar and then click Toolbox. If necessary, click the triangle next to the Common Controls category name and then click the Auto Hide button to display the tools.

- **Name the Windows Form Object** In the Solution Explorer window, right-click the Form1.vb form file name and select Rename. Type frmBike.vb and then press the ENTER key.

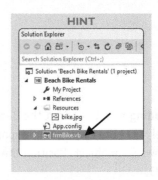

- **Change the Title on the Title Bar** To change the title on the Windows Form object, click the form, scroll in the Properties window until the Text property is displayed, double-click in the right column of the Text property, type Beach Bike Rentals, and then press the ENTER key.

(continues)

● **Set the BackColor Property for the Windows Form Object**
To set the BackColor property to White for the user interface,
select the Windows Form object. In the Properties window, click
the BackColor property, and then click the BackColor arrow in
the right column of the BackColor property. If necessary, click
the Web tab. Scroll and then click White in the BackColor list.

● **Resize the Windows Form Object** Change the Size property
of the form to 420,500.

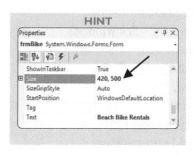

● **Add a PictureBox Object** Add a PictureBox object to
the Windows Form object by dragging the PictureBox .NET
component onto the Windows Form object. Place the object in
the bottom of the Windows Form object.

● **Name the PictureBox Object** With the PictureBox object
selected, scroll in the Properties window until the (Name)
property is visible. Double-click in the right column of the
(Name) property, type picBikes, and then press the ENTER key.

● **Resize the PictureBox Object** With the picBikes PictureBox
object still selected, click to the right of the Size property and
change it to 407,206.

● **Add a Heading Label** To insert the Beach Bike Rentals
heading label, drag the Label .NET component from the Toolbox
to the Windows Form object. Position the Label object as shown
in Figure 4-83.

● **Name the Label Object** Name the Label object lblHeading
by scrolling to the (Name) property in the Properties window,
double-clicking the (Name) property in the right column, typing
lblHeading, and then pressing the ENTER key.

- **Change the Text of the Label Object** With the lblHeading Label object selected, scroll until the Text property is visible, double-click in the right column of the Text property, type `Beach Bike Rentals`, and then press the ENTER key.

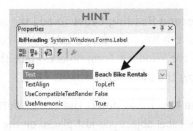

- **Change the Heading Font, Font Style, and Size** To make the heading stand out on the Windows form, its font should be larger and more prominent. To change the font to Cooper Black, its style to Black, and its size to 18, select the Label object and then scroll in the Properties window until the Font property is visible. Click the Font property in the right column, and then click the ellipsis button. In the Font dialog box, scroll if necessary, click Cooper Black (or a similar font) in the Font list, click Black in the Font style list, and then click 18 in the Size list. Click the OK button in the Font dialog box.

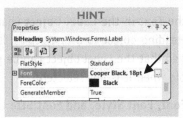

- **Horizontally Center the Label Object** The Label object should be centered horizontally in the form. Click Format on the menu bar, point to Center in Form on the Format menu, and then click Horizontally on the Center in Form submenu.

The PictureBox object and the Label object are placed on the resized Windows Form object (Figure 4-83). The font and font size for the Label object are appropriate for a heading in the window.

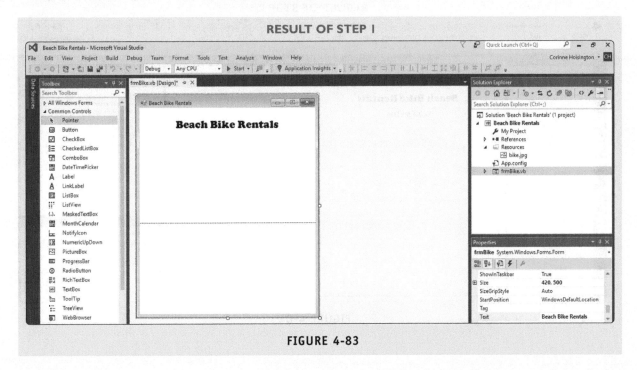

FIGURE 4-83

(continues)

2

- **Add a Second Heading Label** To add the second heading label required for the window, drag a Label .NET component from the Toolbox to the Windows Form object. Place the second Label object below the lblHeading object.

- **Name the New Label Object** Use `lblCostHeading` as the name of the Label object you just placed on the Windows Form object.

- **Change the Text in the Label Object** Change the text in the lblCostHeading object to `$X.XX per Day`. This text is a placeholder so that the Label object can be properly aligned and will be visible when it is not selected.

- **Set the Font, Font Style, and Font Size** Use the Font property and ellipsis button in the Properties window to display the Font dialog box, and then change the font to Microsoft Sans Serif, the style to Regular, and the size to 12 points for the lblCostHeading Label object.

HINT

- **Center-Align the Label Object** Select the lblCostHeading label, click Format on the menu bar, point to Center in Form, and then click Horizontally.

The PictureBox object and the Label objects are properly aligned in the Windows Form object (Figure 4-84).

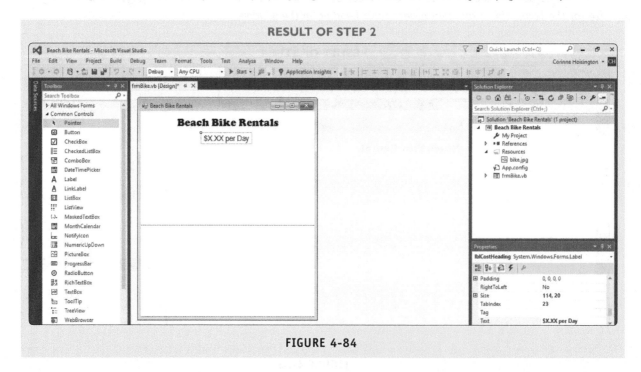

RESULT OF STEP 2

FIGURE 4-84

3

● **Add a Label for the Number of Rental Days** Add the Label object for the number of rental days by dragging it from the Toolbox. Place it below the two other Label objects.

● **Change the Name, Enter Text, and Change the Font for the Number of Rental Days Label** Using techniques you have learned previously, change the name of the Label object to lblNumberOfDays. In the Text property, enter Number of Rental Days:. Using the Font property in the Properties window, change the font to Century Gothic, Regular style, and 12-point size.

● **Add a TextBox Object for the Number of Rental Days** Drag a TextBox object to the Windows Form object. Name the TextBox object txtNumberOfDays *(ref: Figure 4-3)*.

HINT

● **Enter Data into the Text Property** As you learned in this chapter, even though the TextBox object will not contain text when the program begins, size it properly by entering text in the Text property of the TextBox object. Select the TextBox object, and then in the Properties window, change the Text property to 88 *(ref: Figure 4-7)*.

● **Change the Font and Size of the TextBox Object** Using the Properties window, change the font for the TextBox object to Century Gothic, Regular style, and 12-point size. Drag the right border of the TextBox object so the numbers fit properly in the text box *(ref: Figure 4-8)*.

● **Align the Resized TextBox Object** To realign the resized TextBox object, drag it up until the red snap line indicates the text in the TextBox object is bottom-aligned with the label *(ref: Figure 4-9)*.

● **Center-Align Text in the TextBox Object** To center-align the text in the TextBox object, select the TextBox object, scroll in the Properties window until the TextAlign property is visible, click the list arrow in the right column of the TextAlign property, and then click Center in the TextAlign property list *(ref: Figure 4-10)*.

(continues)

● **Remove Text from the TextBox Object** Because the TextBox object is sized properly, remove the digits from the TextBox object by selecting them in the Text property of the object and then pressing the DELETE key *(ref: Figure 4-12)*.

● **Add the Total Cost of Bikes Rented Label Objects** A label that reports the total cost of the bikes rented must be displayed as the Text property of a Label object. A second label actually identifies the total cost. Drag two labels onto the Windows Form object and place them on the same horizontal line using the blue snap lines. Vertically align the left side of the left label with the label above it. Vertically align the left side of the right label with the text box above it. Name the Label object on the left lblTotalLabel. Name the label on the right lblTotalCost *(ref: Figure 4-18)*.

● **Enter Text for the Labels and Change the Font** Select the lblTotalLabel Label object and then double-click the right column of the Text property for the label. Type Total Cost of Bike Rental: and then press the ENTER key. Select the lblTotalCost Label object and then double-click the right column of the Text property for the label. Enter the value $888.88 to represent the widest expected value for the label. With the right label selected, hold down the CTRL key and then click the left label. With both labels selected, change the font to Century Gothic, Regular style, 12-point size. Select the lblNumberOfDays, txtNumberOfDays, lblTotalLabel, and lblTotalCost Label objects and Center in Form horizontally (Format menu) to center the four objects across the form.

● **Add Buttons** Three buttons are required for the user interface: the Find Cost button, the Clear button, and the Exit button. Drag three buttons onto the Windows Form object below the labels. Use blue snap lines to horizontally align the tops of the buttons. Using the (Name) property for each button, name the first button btnCost, the second button btnClear, and the third button btnExit.

● **Change the Button Text and the Font Style** Using the Text property for each button, change the text for the btnCost Button object to Find Cost and the text for the btnClear button to Clear. Change the text for the btnExit button to Exit. Select all three buttons by clicking the Find Cost button, holding down the ctrl key, and then clicking the other two buttons. Next, click the Font property, click the ellipsis button in the right column of the Font property, and then change the font style to Bold and size 11 in the Font dialog box.

HINT

Beach Bike Rentals

Beach Bike Rentals

$X.XX per Day

Number of Rental Days:

Total Cost of Bike Rental: $888.88

- **Change Button Size** The btnCost button does not display the entire Text property, so it must be enlarged. Drag the right border of the btnCost button until the entire Text property is visible.

- **Change the Size of the Other Buttons** Click the btnCost button first, and then hold down the CTRL key and click the other two buttons to select all three buttons. Make these buttons the same size by clicking Format on the menu bar, pointing to Make Same Size on the Format menu, and clicking Both on the Make Same Size submenu.

- **Space and Center the Buttons** With all three buttons selected, display the Format menu, point to Horizontal Spacing on the Format menu, and then click Make Equal on the Horizontal Spacing submenu. Display the Format menu, point to Center in Form on the Format menu, and then click Horizontally on the Center in Form submenu to center all three buttons horizontally in the Windows Form object.

The mockup for the user interface is complete (Figure 4-85).

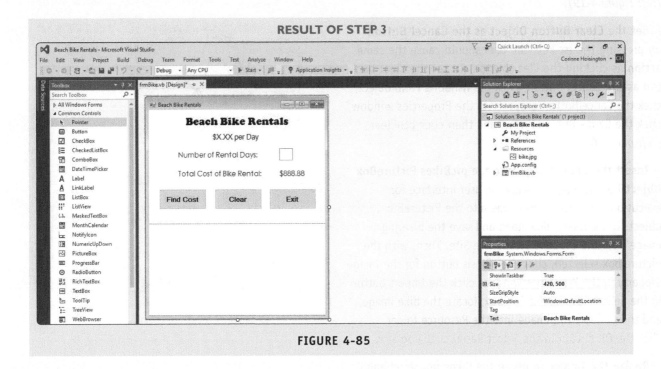

RESULT OF STEP 3

FIGURE 4-85

(continues)

Phase 2: Fine-Tune the User Interface

4

- **Set the BackColor for the Button Objects** To set the BackColor to Gold for the button objects, select all three buttons. Click the BackColor property in the Properties window, and then click the BackColor arrow in the right column of the BackColor property. Click the Web tab, if necessary. Scroll as required and then click Gold in the BackColor list.

- **Set the Find Cost Button Object as the Accept Button** When the user enters the number of days to rent a bike, she should be able to calculate the total cost by clicking the Find Cost button or by pressing the ENTER key. To assign the Find Cost button as the Accept button, first select the Windows Form object by clicking anywhere in the window except on another object. Scroll in the Properties window until the AcceptButton property is visible, click the AcceptButton property, click the AcceptButton property arrow, and then click btnCost *(ref: Figure 4-19)*.

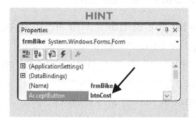

- **Set the Clear Button Object as the Cancel Button** By pressing the ESC key, the user should cause the same action as clicking the Clear button. To set the Clear button as the Cancel button, click the Windows Form object, click the CancelButton property in the Properties window, click the CancelButton arrow, and then click btnClear *(ref: page 162)*.

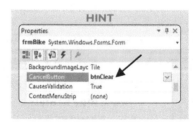

- **Insert the Bikes Image into the picBikes PictureBox Object** The last step to ready the user interface for execution is to insert the image into the PictureBox object. If necessary, download and save the bike.jpg image from the Student Companion Site. Then, with the picture box selected, click the ellipsis button for the Image property in the Properties window, click the Import button in the Select Resource dialog box, locate the bike image, and then import the image into the Resource folder. Click the OK button in the Select Resource dialog box.

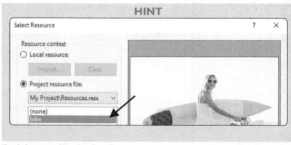

iStockphoto.com/Wavebreakmedia

- **Resize the Image** To resize the Bikes image, change the SizeMode property. With the picBikes PictureBox object selected, click the SizeMode property in the Properties window, click the SizeMode arrow in the right column, and then click StretchImage.

The user interface is complete (Figure 4-86).

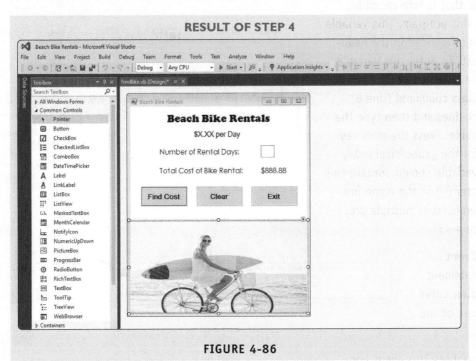

RESULT OF STEP 4

FIGURE 4-86

iStockphoto.com/Wavebreakmedia

Phase 3: Code the Application

5

● **Code the Comments** Double-click the
btnCost Button object on the frmBike
Windows Form object to open the code
window and create the btnCost_Click
event handler. Click the Close button on
the Toolbox title bar to close the Toolbox.
Click at the beginning of the first words,
Public Class frmBike, and press the ENTER
key to create a blank line. Press the
UP ARROW key and then insert the first four
standard comments. Insert the Option
Strict On command at the beginning of
the code to turn on strict type checking
(ref: Figure 4-49).

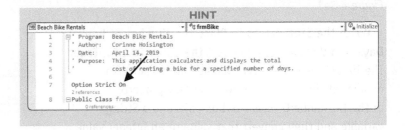

HINT

```
1    ' Program:   Beach Bike Rentals
2    ' Author:    Corinne Hoisington
3    ' Date:      April 14, 2019
4    ' Purpose:   This application calculates and displays the total
5    '            cost of renting a bike for a specified number of days.
6
7    Option Strict On
       2 references
8   ⊟Public Class frmBike
       0 references
```

(continues)

- **Enter the _cdecPricePerDay Class Variable** The next
step is to enter the class variable that is referenced in
more than one event handler in this program. This variable
contains the price per day and is referenced in the heading and to calculate the total cost. To enter this variable,
press the DOWN ARROW key until the insertion point is on the
blank line following the Public Class command (line 8).
Press the ENTER key to add a blank line, and then type the
comment that identifies the variable. Press the ENTER key
and then write the declaration for the _cdecPricePerDay
variable. The constant Decimal variable should contain the
value 9.95. The underline character (_) in the name indicates a class variable that is referenced in multiple procedures within the class *(ref: Figure 4-43)*.

- **Comment the btnCost Click Event
Handler** Following the Private statement
for the btnCost_Click event handler, enter
a comment to describe the purpose of the
btnCost_Click event.

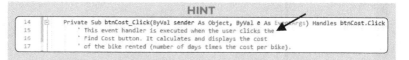

- **Declare and Initialize the Variables** This event handler requires three variables: (1) strNumberOfDays, which
holds the number of rental days entered by the user;
(2) intNumberOfDays, which holds the integer value for the
number of days entered by the user; and (3) decTotalCost,
which holds the calculated total cost of the bike rental.
Declare these three variables *(ref: Figure 4-20, Figure 4-31,
Figure 4-34)*.

- **Write the Statements to Place the Number of Rental
Days in a Variable and Convert the Value to an Integer**
The first steps in the event handler are to move the
number of the days value from the Text property
of the txtNumberOfDays TextBox object to a String
variable and then convert that value to an integer value.
Using IntelliSense, write the code to complete these steps
(ref: Figure 4-26, Figure 4-48).

- **Find the Total Cost of the Bike Rented** To calculate
the total cost of the bike rented and place the result
in the decTotalCost variable, multiply the number of
days by the price per day. Using IntelliSense, write the
statement to perform this calculation *(ref: Figure 4-51)*.

● **Convert the Decimal Total Cost of the Bike Rental to a String Currency Value and Place It in the Text Property of the lblTotalCost Label Object** After calculating the total cost of the bike rental, the result must be converted from a Decimal value to a currency String value so it can be displayed as the value in the Text property of a Label object. Write the statement to perform this conversion and place the converted value in the Text property of the lblTotalCost Label object.

The coding for the btnCost_Click event handler is complete (Figure 4-87).

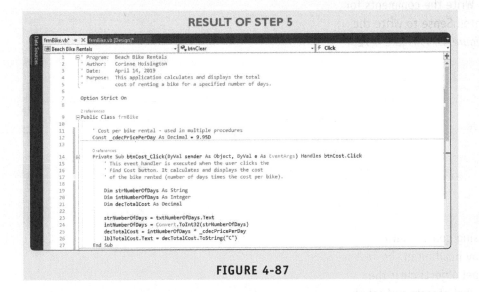

RESULT OF STEP 5

FIGURE 4-87

6

● **Run the Application** After you enter code, you should run the application to ensure it is working properly. Run the Beach Bike Rentals application by clicking the Start button on the Standard toolbar. Enter 2 for the Number of Rental Days and then click the Find Cost button. The Total Cost of the Bike Rental should be $19.90. Enter 10 for the Number of Rental Days and then press the ENTER key.

When the number of rental days is 10, the total cost of the beach bike rental is $99.50 (Figure 4-88).

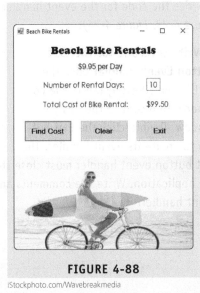

FIGURE 4-88

iStockphoto.com/Wavebreakmedia

(continues)

● **Write the Code for the Clear Button Event Handler** Click the frmBike.vb [Design] tab in the code window to return to the design window. Double-click the Clear button to create the event handler for the Clear button. The Clear button event handler must accomplish the following tasks: Clear the txtNumberOfDays text box; clear the value in the Text property of the lblTotalCost Label object; and set the focus to the txtNumberOfDays text box. Write the comments for the event handler and then use IntelliSense to write the code for the event handler *(ref: Figure 4-71, Figure 4-72, Figure 4-73).*

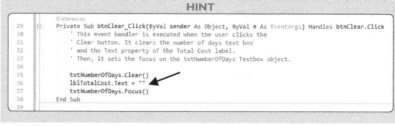

```
        0 references
29 ⊟    Private Sub btnClear_Click(ByVal sender As Object, ByVal e As EventArgs) Handles btnClear.Click
30          ' This event handler is executed when the user clicks the
31          ' Clear button. It clears the number of days text box
32          ' and the Text property of the Total Cost label.
33          ' Then, it sets the focus on the txtNumberOfDays Textbox object.
34
35          txtNumberOfDays.Clear()
36          lblTotalCost.Text = ""
37          txtNumberOfDays.Focus()
38      End Sub
39
```

● **Write the Code for the Form Load Event Handler** Click the frmBike.vb [Design] tab in the code window to return to the design window. Double-click the Windows Form object to create the event handler for the Form Load event. The Form Load event handler must accomplish the following tasks: Using concatenation, create and display the Price per Day heading in the Text property of the lblCostHeading Label object; clear the Text property of the lblTotalCost Label object; and set the focus to the txtNumberOfDays TextBox object. Write the comments for the event handler and then use IntelliSense to write the code for the event handler *(ref: Figure 4-71, Figure 4-73, Figure 4-76).*

```
39
        0 references
40 ⊟    Private Sub frmDigitalDownloads_Load(ByVal sender As Object, ByVal e As EventArgs) Handles MyBase.Load
41          ' This event handler is executed when the form is loaded.
42          ' It displays the cost heading, clears the Text property of the
43          ' Total Cost label, and sets the focus on
44          ' the txtNumberOfDays Textbox object.
45
46          lblCostHeading.Text = _cdecPricePerDay.ToString("C") & " per Day"
47          lblTotalCost.Text = ""
48          txtNumberOfDays.Focus()
49      End Sub
50
```

● **Write the Code for the Exit Button Event Handler** Click the frmBike.vb [Design] tab in the code window to return to the design window. Double-click the Exit button to create its event handler. The Exit button event handler must close the window and end the application. Write the comments and code for this event handler.

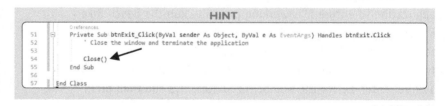

```
        0 references
51 ⊟    Private Sub btnExit_Click(ByVal sender As Object, ByVal e As EventArgs) Handles btnExit.Click
52          ' Close the window and terminate the application
53
54          Close()
55      End Sub
56
57  End Class
```

The coding is complete for the Clear button event handler, the Form load event handler, and the Exit button event handler (Figure 4-89).

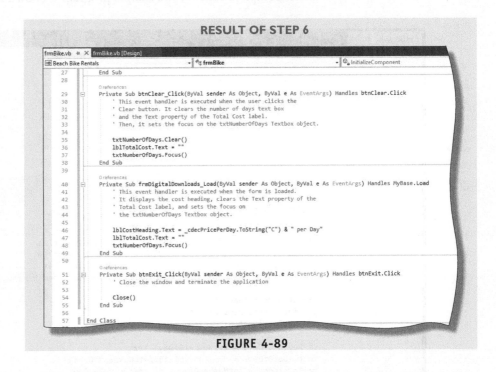

RESULT OF STEP 6

```
frmBike.vb  ⊞ ×  frmBike.vb [Design]
VB Beach Bike Rentals                          frmBike                              InitializeComponent
27          End Sub
28
     0 references
29    Private Sub btnClear_Click(ByVal sender As Object, ByVal e As EventArgs) Handles btnClear.Click
30          ' This event handler is executed when the user clicks the
31          ' Clear button. It clears the number of days text box
32          ' and the Text property of the Total Cost label.
33          ' Then, it sets the focus on the txtNumberOfDays Textbox object.
34
35          txtNumberOfDays.Clear()
36          lblTotalCost.Text = ""
37          txtNumberOfDays.Focus()
38    End Sub
39
     0 references
40    Private Sub frmDigitalDownloads_Load(ByVal sender As Object, ByVal e As EventArgs) Handles MyBase.Load
41          ' This event handler is executed when the form is loaded.
42          ' It displays the cost heading, clears the Text property of the
43          ' Total Cost label, and sets the focus on
44          ' the txtNumberOfDays Textbox object.
45
46          lblCostHeading.Text = _cdecPricePerDay.ToString("C") & " per Day"
47          lblTotalCost.Text = ""
48          txtNumberOfDays.Focus()
49    End Sub
50
     0 references
51    Private Sub btnExit_Click(ByVal sender As Object, ByVal e As EventArgs) Handles btnExit.Click
52          ' Close the window and terminate the application
53
54          Close()
55    End Sub
56
57   End Class
```

FIGURE 4-89

● **Test the Program** After finishing the coding, you should test the program to ensure it works properly. Run the Beach Bike Rentals application by clicking the Start button on the Standard toolbar. Enter 2 for the Number of Rental Days and then click the Find Cost button. The Total Cost of Bike Rental should be $19.90. Click the Clear button to clear the text box and the label that contains the total cost of the bike rental. Enter 5 for the Number of Rental Days and then press the ENTER key. The Total Cost of Bike Rental should be $49.75. Press the ESC key to clear the text box and the label that contains the total cost of the bike rental. Enter other values to test the program completely.

The program runs properly.

(continues)

Code Listing

The complete code for the sample program is shown in Figure 4-90.

```vb
frmBike.vb   ⊣  ×
[VB] Beach Bike Rentals                                            ▼   ⌖ frmBike
 1    ⊟ ' Program:   Beach Bike Rentals
 2      ' Author:    Corinne Hoisington
 3      ' Date:      April 14, 2019
 4      ' Purpose:   This application calculates and displays the total
 5      '            cost of renting a bike for a specified number of days.
 6
 7      Option Strict On
 8
      2 references
 9    ⊟ Public Class frmBike
10
11          ' Cost per bike rental - used in multiple procedures
12          Const _cdecPricePerDay As Decimal = 9.95D
13
      0 references
14    ⊟     Private Sub btnCost_Click(ByVal sender As Object, ByVal e As EventArgs) Handles btnCost.Click
15              ' This event handler is executed when the user clicks the
16              ' Find Cost button. It calculates and displays the cost
17              ' of the bike rented (number of days times the cost per bike).
18
19              Dim strNumberOfDays As String
20              Dim intNumberOfDays As Integer
21              Dim decTotalCost As Decimal
22
23              strNumberOfDays = txtNumberOfDays.Text
24              intNumberOfDays = Convert.ToInt32(strNumberOfDays)
25              decTotalCost = intNumberOfDays * _cdecPricePerDay
26              lblTotalCost.Text = decTotalCost.ToString("C")
27          End Sub
28
      0 references
29    ⊟     Private Sub btnClear_Click(ByVal sender As Object, ByVal e As EventArgs) Handles btnClear.Click
30              ' This event handler is executed when the user clicks the
31              ' Clear button. It clears the number of days text box
32              ' and the Text property of the Total Cost label.
33              ' Then, it sets the focus on the txtNumberOfDays Textbox object.
34
35              txtNumberOfDays.Clear()
36              lblTotalCost.Text = ""
37              txtNumberOfDays.Focus()
38          End Sub
39
      0 references
40    ⊟     Private Sub frmDigitalDownloads_Load(ByVal sender As Object, ByVal e As EventArgs) Handles MyBase.Load
41              ' This event handler is executed when the form is loaded.
42              ' It displays the cost heading, clears the Text property of the
43              ' Total Cost label, and sets the focus on
44              ' the txtNumberOfDays Textbox object.
45
46              lblCostHeading.Text = _cdecPricePerDay.ToString("C") & " per Day"
47              lblTotalCost.Text = ""
48              txtNumberOfDays.Focus()
49          End Sub
50
      0 references
51    ⊟     Private Sub btnExit_Click(ByVal sender As Object, ByVal e As EventArgs) Handles btnExit.Click
52              ' Close the window and terminate the application
53
54              Close()
55          End Sub
56
57      End Class
58
```

FIGURE 4-90

Knowledge Check

1. Which data type should an ampersand (&) symbol be assigned?

2. Write a Dim statement for each of the following variables using the variable type and variable name that would be best for each value.

   a. The population of Alaska

   b. The smallest data type you can use for the age of a child

   c. A constant for the first initial of your first name

   d. The minimum wage

   e. The name of the street where you live

   f. The answer to a true/false question

3. Determine whether each of the following variable names is valid or invalid. Explain the error in each invalid variable name.

   a. #samtechnow

   b. first_Input_Value

   c. Orange-is-new-black

   d. 3CPO

   e. Close

   f. Name Of Cortana

   g. _cdecPi

4. List the steps that specify how you would perfectly align a group of TextBox objects along their left edges.

5. Which data type is best for currency amounts?

6. Explain the hierarchy for the order of operations.

7. What is the solution to each of the following arithmetic expressions?

   a. 6 + 7 * 2 - 1

   b. 48 / 6 * 2^2

   c. 40 - 6 ^ 2 / 3

   d. 74 Mod 9

   e. 9 \ 4 * 3

   f. 2 ^ 3 * (8 - 5)

   g. (15 Mod 2) + 5 * 3

(continues)

8. What is the difference between a method and a procedure?

9. What is the difference between a variable and a literal?

10. Correct the following statements:

   a. `Dim itHeight As Integr`

   b. `Dim dblDiscountAmount A Dbl`

   c. `Constant _cstrCollege As Sentence = "PVCC"`

   d. `Dim strSenatorName As Number`

   e. `strLastName = 'Prof. J Starks'`

   f. `1.5 * decPay = decOverTimePayRate`

11. Write a statement that sets the focus on the txtSeafood TextBox object.

12. Write a statement that removes the contents of the txtPrince TextBox object.

13. Write a statement that blanks the Text property of the lblEligibilityAge Label object.

14. Write a statement to convert the value in the String variable strNeckSize to an integer value and place the integer value in a variable named intNeckSize.

15. Write a statement to convert the value in the String variable strHourlyPay to a Decimal value and place the Decimal value in a variable named decGross.

16. Write a statement to close a form that currently is open.

17. Write a statement that declares a constant named _cdecInsuranceDeductible as a Decimal data type and set its value to 500.00.

18. Which Windows Form property allows the user to press the ESC key while the form is active and activate a button's event handler?

19. What is a local variable? How does its scope differ from that of a global variable?

20. When the following statements are executed, what would be displayed in the lblHourlyWage Label object
```
decHourlyWage = 13.837
lblHourlyWage.Text = decHourlyWage.ToString("C")
```

1. Fix the following code:
```
Option Strict
Dim intDistance As Integer
intDistance = 17.5
```

2. Fix the following code:
```
Dim dblRegularPay As Double
Dim dblOvertimePay As Double
```

```
intRegularPay = 783.87
intOvertimePay = 105.92
lbl.TotalPay = (dblRegularPay + dblOvertimePay).ToString ('C')
```

3. Analyze the code and then correct it.

```
Dim strCity as String = "Miami"
Dim strState as Double = "Florida"
Dim strLocation as String
strLoc = strCity + strState
```

Program Analysis

1. What will occur when the user clicks the btnSlope Button in the following code?

```
Private Sub btnSlope_Click(ByVal sender As System.Object, ByVal e As System.
EventArgs) Handles btnSlope.Click
  Dim decRise As Decimal
  Dim decRun As Decimal
  Dim decSlope As Decimal
  decRise = 12.3D
  decRun = 2.1D
  decSlope = decRise / decRun
  lblSlope.Text = "The Line Slope is" & decSlope.ToString("F1")
End Sub
```

2. How would the number .0456 be displayed if the format specifier ("P") is used in a Convert.ToString statement?

3. How would the number 3746.35555 be displayed if the format specifier ("F3") is used in a Convert.ToString statement?

4. If you want the user to enter her phone number with the area code, which .NET component would be best to use on the Windows Form object?

5. Using the format specifier with the ToString procedure, write the statement that would display:

a. The value in the decDvdCost variable with a dollar sign and two places to the right of the decimal point in a label named lblDvd

b. The value in the decWithholdingTaxRate variable with a percent sign and one place to the right of the decimal point in a label named lblWithholdingTaxRate

c. The value in the decOilRevenue variable with commas as needed, two places to the right of the decimal point, and no dollar sign in a label called lblOilRevenue

(continues)

6. Write a single line of code to declare a variable decWindSpeed as a Decimal data type and assign it the value 25.47. Use a forced literal to ensure that the compiler views this number as a Decimal data type.

7. What would the values of these variables be at the end of the code that follows?

   a. intParts

   b. intBoxes

   c. intLeftovers

```
Dim intParts As Integer
Dim intBoxes As Integer
Dim intLeftovers As Integer
intParts = 78
intPartsPerBox = 8
intBoxes = intParts \ intPartsPerBox
intLeftovers = intParts Mod intBoxes
```

8. Are the following statements written correctly? If not, how should they be written?
```
Dim dblPay as Double
lblPay.Text = dblPay.ToString("C2")
```

9. For a Button object named btnCalories, write the click event handler to implement the following requirements and calculate the number of calories burned during a run:

   a. Declare variables named strMilesRan, decCaloriesConsumed, and decMilesRan.

   b. Declare a constant named _cdecCaloriesBurnedPerHour and assign it the value 700. (Assume you burn 700 calories for every mile you run.)

   c. Allow the user to enter the number of miles she ran today.

   d. Convert the number of miles to a Decimal data type.

   e. Calculate the number of calories the user burned during her run.

   f. Display the result rounded to zero decimal places in a label named lblCaloriesBurned.

10. What would the output be when the user clicks the btnDrivingAge Button?
```
Private Sub btnDrivingAge_Click(ByVal sender As System.Object, ByVal e As
System.EventArgs) Handles btnDrivingAge.Click
  Dim intPresentAge As Integer
  Const cintDrivingAge As Integer = 16
  Dim intYearsToDrive As Integer
  intPresentAge = 13
  intYearsToDrive = cintDrivingAge - intPresentAge
  lblYearsLeft.Text = intYearsToDrive.ToString() & " year(s) until you can
  drive."
End Sub
```

Complete one or more of the following case programming assignments. Submit the program and materials you create to your instructor. The level of difficulty is indicated for each assignment.

●	= Easiest
● ●	= Intermediate
● ● ●	= Challenging

1   AIRBNB RESERVATIONS

Design a Windows Classic Desktop application and write the code that will execute according to the program requirements in Figure 4-91 and the Use Case Definition in Figure 4-92. Before writing the code, create an event-planning document for each event in the program. The completed program is shown in Figure 4-93.

REQUIREMENTS DOCUMENT

Date: October 19, 2018

Date Submitted:

Application Title: Airbnb Reservations

Purpose: This Windows Classic Desktop application allows a user to calculate the cost of an Airbnb stay for an apartment in Orlando, Florida.

Program Procedures: From a window on the screen, the user chooses the number of nights to stay at the Orlando Airbnb; the total cost of the accommodations is displayed.

Algorithms, Processing, and Conditions:
1. The user must be able to enter the number of nights.
2. A picture of an Airbnb app will be displayed throughout the entire process.
3. After entering the number of nights needed, the user clicks the Display Cost button.
4. One night of accommodations costs $79 for the full apartment each night; the total cost will be displayed in currency format.

Notes and Restrictions:
1. The user can use a Clear button to clear the number of nights entered and the total cost and then enter another number of nights.
2. An Exit button should end the application.
3. The cost per night can vary, so the program should allow a different price to be placed in any headings and be used in any calculations.

Comments: The picture is named airbnb and is available on CengageBrain.com.

FIGURE 4-91

(continues)

Airbnb Reservations

USE CASE DEFINITION

1. The Windows Classic Desktop application opens.
2. The user enters the number of nights.
3. The user clicks the Display Cost button.
4. The program displays the total cost for the Airbnb stay.
5. The user can click the Clear button and repeat Steps 2 through 4.
6. The user exits the program by clicking the Exit button.

FIGURE 4-92

FIGURE 4-93

iStockphoto.com/GoodLifeStudio

2 ● SEATTLE WALKING TOUR

Design a Windows Classic Desktop application and write the code that will execute according to the program requirements in Figure 4-94 and the Use Case Definition in Figure 4-95. Before writing the code, create an event-planning document for each event in the program. The completed program is shown in Figure 4-96.

REQUIREMENTS DOCUMENT

Date:	February 19, 2018
Date Submitted:	
Application Title:	Seattle Walking Tour
Purpose:	This Windows Classic Desktop application computes the cost of a Seattle walking tour.
Program Procedures:	From a window on the screen, the user enters the number of tickets needed for a three-hour walking tour of the waterfront of Seattle. The program calculates and displays the cost of the tickets with an additional cost of $1.99 for booking using the app.
Algorithms, Processing, and Conditions:	1. The user must be able to enter the number of tickets for the Seattle Walking Tour. 2. The title of the program and an image of Seattle's skyline will be displayed throughout the entire process. 3. After entering the number of tickets, the user clicks the Display Cost button. 4. Each tour ticket is $14.99. 5. A one-time booking fee of $1.99 is charged regardless of the number of tickets purchased as a convenience charge of booking through the app. 6. The program displays the cost including the booking fee in currency format.
Notes and Restrictions:	1. The user can clear the number of tickets and make another entry. 2. An Exit button should end the application.
Comments:	The Seattle image is named seattle and is available on CengageBrain.com.

FIGURE 4-94

(continues)

Seattle Walking Tour

USE CASE DEFINITION

1. The Windows Classic Desktop application opens.
2. The user enters the number of tour tickets needed.
3. The user clicks the Display Cost button.
4. The program displays the total cost of the Seattle Walking Tour tickets.
5. The user can click the Clear button and repeat Steps 2 through 4.
6. The user exits the program by clicking the Exit button.

FIGURE 4-95

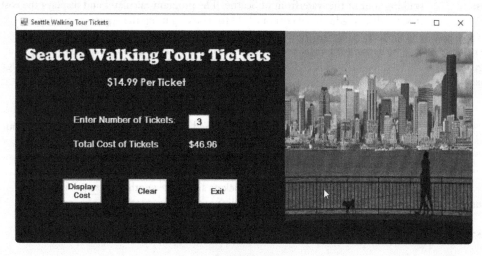

FIGURE 4-96

iStockphoto.com/LoweStock

3

DRIVERLESS UBER CAR

Design a Windows Classic Desktop application and write the code that will execute according to the program requirements in Figure 4-97. Before designing the user interface, create a Use Case Definition. Before writing the code, create an event-planning document for each event in the program.

REQUIREMENTS DOCUMENT

Date:	October 20, 2018
Date Submitted:	
Application Title:	Driverless Uber Car
Purpose:	This Windows Classic Desktop application calculates the cost of a driverless Uber car fare.
Program Procedures:	From a window on the screen, a user enters the number of miles to the destination. The program displays the flat rate per mile and the total cost of the Uber fare.
Algorithms, Processing, and Conditions:	1. The user must be able to enter the number of miles to her destination.
	2. A picture of a driverless Uber car will be displayed throughout the entire process.
	3. After entering the number of miles driven, the user clicks the Display Fare button.
	4. The cost per mile is $1.80 and a flat rate of $2.80 is charged at pickup.
	5. The total cost for the fare is displayed using the currency format.
Notes and Restrictions:	1. The user can clear the miles entered by clicking a Clear button. The user can then can enter another mileage amount.
	2. An Exit button should end the application.
Comments:	Locate an image for the app at Google or Bing images.

FIGURE 4-97

4 •• PAYROLL CALCULATOR

Design a Windows Classic Desktop application and write the code that will execute according to the program requirements in Figure 4-98. Before designing the user interface, create a Use Case Definition. Before writing the code, create an event-planning document for each event in the program.

REQUIREMENTS DOCUMENT

Date:	January 4, 2018
Date Submitted:	
Application Title:	Payroll Calculator
Purpose:	This Windows Classic Desktop application will compute and display the FICA tax, federal tax, and state tax for a two-week pay period.
Program Procedures:	From a window on the screen, the user enters her gross pay check for two weeks. The program estimates the FICA tax, federal tax, and state tax for a two week pay cycle.
Algorithms, Processing, and Conditions:	1. Users must be able to enter their biweekly income. 2. The FICA tax (7.65%), federal tax (22%), and state income tax (4%) are computed. 3. The tax amounts should be displayed on separate lines and in currency format, two places past the decimal point. 4. The net pay should be displayed after the tax amounts have been deducted.
Notes and Restrictions:	1. The user can clear the income and taxes and then enter new data. 2. The user can use an Exit button to exit the application.
Comments:	The designer should design the user interface, including the graphic and words displayed.

FIGURE 4-98

Case Programming Assignments

5 ●●● ICE SKATING RINK

Create a requirements document and a Use Case Definition document and then design a Windows application based on the case project shown in Figure 4-99. Before writing the code, create an event-planning document for each event in the program.

> Your local town is placing an indoor ice skating rink in the city center. Create a Windows application that allows you to compute how much cubic feet of ice that the ice rink will hold. The Windows application should request the length, width, and average depth (for example, most ice rinks have a depth of 2 feet of ice). The program then determines the volume of the playground in cubic feet of ice needed (volume = length * width * depth). Allow the user to enter values with decimal places. The user should be able to clear all entries and then reenter data. To exit the program, the user should be able to click a button.

FIGURE 4-99

Case Programming Assignments

6 ●●● FITNESS TRACKER APP

Create a requirements document and a Use Case Definition document and then design a Windows application based on the case project shown in Figure 4-100. Before writing the code, create an event-planning document for each event in the program.

> A fitness tracker app company has asked you to write a Windows application that its users can use to determine the total number of hours someone has exercised during their lifetimes, assuming they exercise an average of 2.5 hours per week. All users should enter their first name, their birth date, and the current date. For both dates, ask for the month, day, and year separately in numeric form. To calculate the number of hours exercised, assume 365 days per year and 30 days per month. The program must display the user's name and the number of hours the user has exercised in his or her lifetime. The user can click a Clear button to clear all entries and results. An Exit button must be available to exit the application.

FIGURE 4-100

CHAPTER 5

Decision Structures

OBJECTIVES

You will have mastered the material in this chapter when you can:

- Use the GroupBox object

- Place RadioButton objects in applications

- Display a message box

- Make decisions using If . . . Then statements

- Make decisions using If . . . Then . . . Else statements

- Make decisions using nested If statements

- Make decisions using logical operators

- Make decisions using Case statements

- Insert code snippets

- Test input to ensure a value is numeric

Introduction

Developers can code Visual Basic applications to make decisions based on the input of users or other conditions that occur. Decision making is one of the fundamental activities of a computer program. In this chapter, you will learn to write decision-making statements in Visual Basic 2017.

Visual Basic allows you to test conditions and perform different operations depending on the results. You can test whether a condition is true or false and change the flow of what happens in a program based on the user's input.

The sample program in this chapter is called the Decking Cost Calculator application. It is written for homeowners and decking contractors who want to compare the costs of three different decking options for materials. The application compares the cost of pressure-treated lumber, redwood, and composite decking.

The application asks the user to enter the number of square feet for the decking required and the desired decking material. The application then computes the cost of the decking based on a rate of $2.35 per square foot for pressure-treated lumber, $7.75 per square foot for redwood, and $8.50 per square foot for composite. Figure 5-1 shows the user interface for the application.

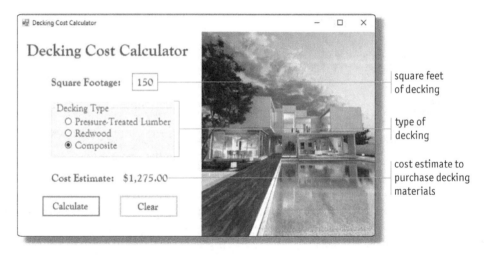

FIGURE 5-1

Franck Boston/Shutterstock.com

In Figure 5-1, the Decking Cost Calculator Windows application displays the text "Decking Cost Calculator" in the title bar. The square footage that the user enters in the TextBox object includes all decking materials for the job. The user chooses the decking type by selecting one of the following radio buttons: Pressure-Treated Lumber, Redwood, or Composite. After the user enters the number of square feet of decking and selects a type of building material, the user clicks the Calculate button to obtain the cost estimate. The calculation is the square feet multiplied by the cost of the selected decking. The cost estimate is displayed in currency format. In the example in Figure 5-1, the user entered 150 square feet for the deck size and selected Composite. After the user clicked the Calculate button, the application displayed a cost of $1275.00 (150 × $8.50).

Clicking the Clear button clears the square footage, resets the radio button selection to Pressure-Treated Lumber, which is the least expensive decking type, and clears the calculation result.

Checking the validity of data the user entered is a requirement of the sample program in this chapter. In Chapter 4, you learned that if you enter nonnumeric data and attempt to use it in a calculation, the program will be terminated. To check for invalid data, the Decking Cost Calculator application ensures that the user enters a numeric value greater than zero in the Square Footage TextBox object. A warning appears if the user leaves the TextBox blank or does not enter a valid number. Figure 5-2 displays the Input Error dialog box, called a Message Box, which directs the user to enter the square footage for the decking.

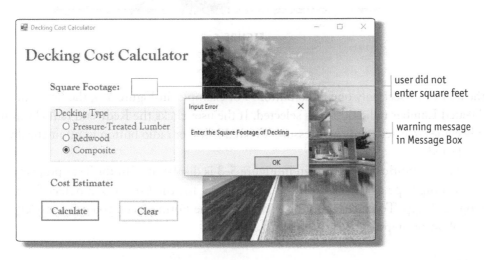

FIGURE 5-2

Franck Boston/Shutterstock.com

Checking input data for validity is an important task in Visual Basic programs. You will learn several data validation techniques in this chapter.

User Interface Design

The user interface for the Decking Cost Calculator application includes three new objects: a GroupBox, RadioButtons, and Message Boxes. The Message Boxes appear when the user enters a negative number or a nonnumeric value.

Use the GroupBox Object

The Decking Cost Calculator Form object requires a GroupBox object and RadioButton objects (Figure 5-3).

A **GroupBox** object associates items as a group, allowing the user to select one item from the group. It also includes caption text. RadioButton objects allow the user to make choices. In Figure 5-3, the GroupBox object groups the radio buttons for selecting the decking type. When RadioButton objects are contained in a group box,

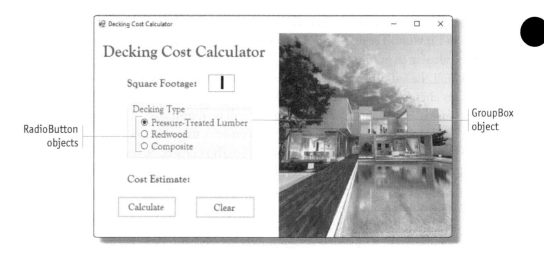

FIGURE 5-3

Franck Boston/Shutterstock.com

the user can select only one radio button. For example, in Figure 5-3, the Pressure-Treated Lumber radio button is selected. If the user clicks the Redwood radio button, it becomes selected, and the Pressure-Treated Lumber radio button is automatically deselected.

The GroupBox object shown in Figure 5-3 is displayed with the Text property of DeckingType as the caption text. The prefix for the GroupBox object (Name) property is grp. To place a GroupBox object on the Form object, you can complete the following steps:

STEP 1   Drag the GroupBox object from the Containers category of the Toolbox to the approximate location where you want to place the GroupBox object on the Form object.

The pointer changes when you place it over the Form object (Figure 5-4). The GroupBox object will be placed on the form at the location of the outline in the pointer.

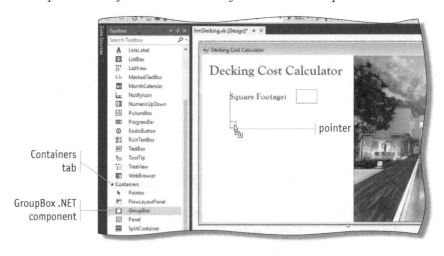

FIGURE 5-4

Franck Boston/Shutterstock.com

STEP 2   When the pointer is in the correct location, release the object. With the GroupBox object selected, scroll in the Properties window to the (Name) property. Double-click in the right column of the (Name) property and then enter the name `grpDeckType`. Double-click in the right column of the Text property to change the caption of the GroupBox object. Enter the text `Decking Type`. Change the BackColor property to the color AliceBlue and the ForeColor to Sienna. Click the right column of the Size property for the GroupBox object and enter `244, 106` as the size.

The name you entered is displayed in the (Name) property in the Properties window, the caption Decking Type is displayed, the background color is changed, and the object is resized (Figure 5-5).

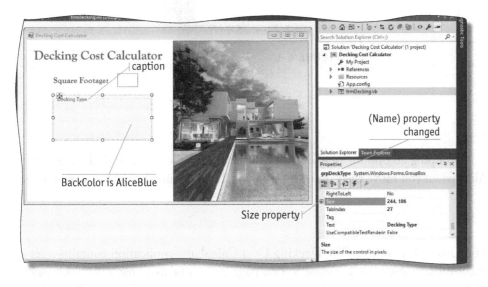

FIGURE 5-5

STEP 3   Change the Font property to Goudy Old Style, Regular, 14 points.

If you want to move the GroupBox to another location on the form, place the pointer over the drag box on the border of the GroupBox object and then drag it to the desired location. The Font property is set to Goudy Old Style (Figure 5-6).

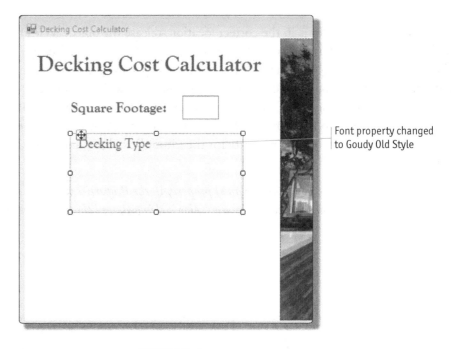

FIGURE 5-6

Grouping all options in a GroupBox object gives the user a logical visual cue. Also, when you move the GroupBox object, all its contained objects move as well.

Add the RadioButton Objects

The GroupBox object in the Decking Cost Calculator application contains a set of RadioButton objects (see Figure 5-3 on page 230). The user may select only one type of decking: pressure-treated lumber, redwood, or composite. To place RadioButton objects within the GroupBox object, you can complete the following steps:

STEP 1 Drag one RadioButton object from the Toolbox to the GroupBox object. Drag a second RadioButton object from the Toolbox into the GroupBox object, and use blue snap lines to align and separate the RadioButton objects vertically.

The second RadioButton object is aligned vertically with a blue snap line, which separates it vertically from the first RadioButton object (Figure 5-7).

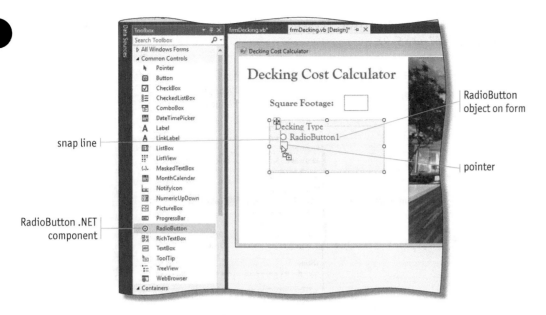

FIGURE 5-7

Franck Boston/Shutterstock.com

STEP 2   Release the RadioButton object to place it within the GroupBox object. Using the same technique, add a third RadioButton object.

Three RadioButton objects are placed on the form and aligned within the GroupBox object (Figure 5-8).

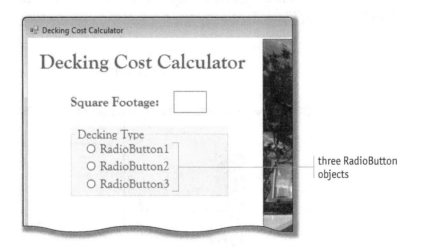

FIGURE 5-8

Franck Boston/Shutterstock.com

STEP 3   Name the RadioButton objects by selecting them one at a time, double-clicking in the right column of the (Name) property in the Properties window, and entering the name. The names for the radio buttons, from top to bottom, should be `radLumber`, `radRedwood`, and `radComposite`.

The (Name) property is selected. The names radLumber, radRedwood, and radComposite are entered (Figure 5-9).

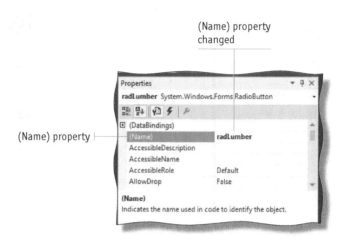

FIGURE 5-9

STEP 4   Change the Text property for each RadioButton object by double-clicking the right column of the Text property and typing `Pressure-Treated Lumber` for the first RadioButton, `Redwood` for the second RadioButton, and `Composite` for the third RadioButton.

The Text property is changed to the types of decking available: Pressure-Treated Lumber, Redwood, and Composite (Figure 5-10).

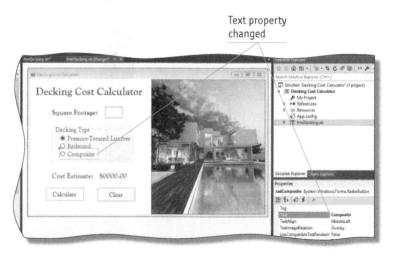

FIGURE 5-10

Franck Boston/Shutterstock.com

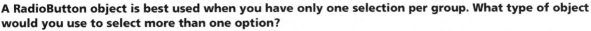

A RadioButton object is best used when you have only one selection per group. What type of object would you use to select more than one option?
CheckBox objects are used with lists of options in which the user may select any number of choices. In other words, each CheckBox object is independent of all other CheckBox objects in the list, so checking one box does not uncheck the others.

Use the Checked Property of RadioButton Objects

The RadioButton objects in the Decking Cost Calculator application allow the user to select one decking type. When the user selects Composite, as shown in Figure 5-11, the radio button is selected, and the small circle in the radio button is shaded. When the Composite radio button is selected, its Checked property changes from False (unselected) to True (selected).

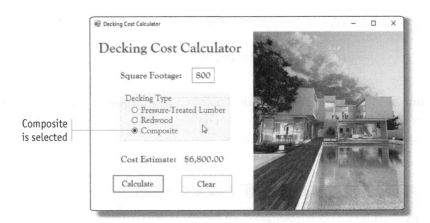

Composite
is selected

FIGURE 5-11

Franck Boston/Shutterstock.com

During design time, you usually set the Checked property to True for the most commonly selected radio button to save the user from having to select it. In the Decking Cost Calculator application, homeowners select Pressure-Treated Lumber most often due to the reduced cost. To cause the radLumber RadioButton object to appear selected (shaded) when the program begins, you change the Checked property for the radLumber RadioButton object from False to True (Figure 5-12).

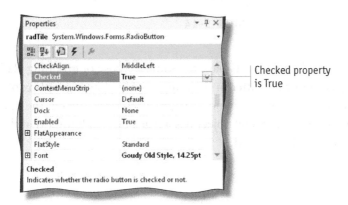

Checked property
is True

FIGURE 5-12

The Panel object in a Windows application works like a GroupBox object. For Windows applications, Visual Basic provides four additional container objects: Flow-LayoutPanel, SplitContainer, TabControl, and TableLayoutPanel. The GroupBox object is used most often; it provides several options that are not available with the Panel object. Figure 5-13 shows the differences between the GroupBox and Panel objects.

Option	GroupBox Object	Panel Object
Have a caption	Yes	No
Have scroll bars	Yes	No
Display a labeled border	Yes	No

FIGURE 5-13

Figure 5-14 shows the Visual Basic Toolbox and a GroupBox object and Panel object in a Windows Form. Notice in the Toolbox that the GroupBox and Panel objects are in a category called Containers.

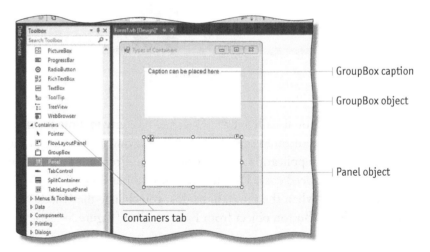

FIGURE 5-14

GroupBox and Panel objects have the same purpose of grouping RadioButtons and other objects, but they differ in their appearance. The GroupBox object in Figure 5-14 displays a border around its edges, with a text area in the upper-left portion for a caption. The Panel object has a black dashed border that does not appear when the application is executed.

Related sets of RadioButtons should be placed in separate container objects so that the user can select one radio button from each group. Always place the container object on the form first, and then drag the RadioButton objects into the container object.

The Course Sign-Up example in Figure 5-15 displays a Windows application that allows the user to sign up for a technology course. Notice the two separate groups of RadioButton objects. In the Choose Course Level GroupBox object, the user should select a course level. In the Choose Semester GroupBox object, the user should identify the semester for the course. As you can see, the user selects one radio button from the left group and one radio button from the right group.

FIGURE 5-15

Display a Message Box

In the Decking Cost Calculator application, a message box, also called a dialog box, opens if the user does not enter the square footage of the decking correctly. The dialog box displays an error message if the user omits the square footage or enters nonnumeric data (Figure 5-16).

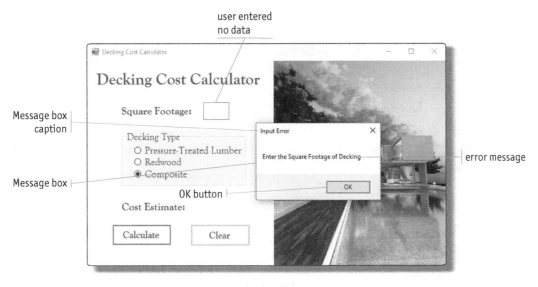

FIGURE 5-16

Franck Boston/Shutterstock.com

If the user enters a negative number for the square footage of the decking, a message box appears and indicates that a positive number is necessary (Figure 5-17).

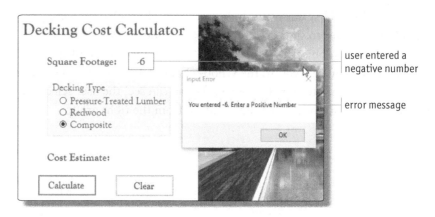

FIGURE 5-17

Franck Boston/Shutterstock.com

This message box reminds the user to enter the square footage of the decking as a positive number. A message box must be closed before the application can continue. The user can continue the application by clicking the OK button in the message box.

In Visual Basic, the message in a message box window is displayed using a procedure named Show, which is found in the MessageBox class. The syntax for the statement that displays a message in a message box is shown in Figure 5-18.

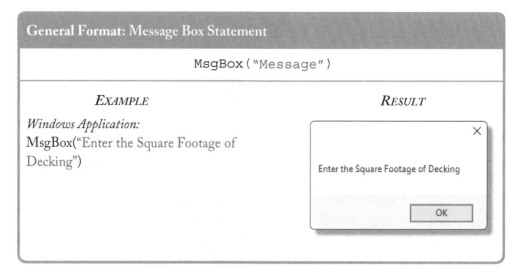

FIGURE 5-18

The string message shown in the parentheses will appear in the message box when the code is executed. The string message is considered an argument of the procedure. You will recall that an argument is a value passed to a procedure. The first argument for the MsgBox command contains the message to be printed in the message box window during execution.

The example in Figure 5-19 illustrates the code that could be used in the Calculate button click event handler. This code could be executed if the user clicks the Calculate button without entering a numeric value in the Square Footage text box (Figure 5-16 on page 237).

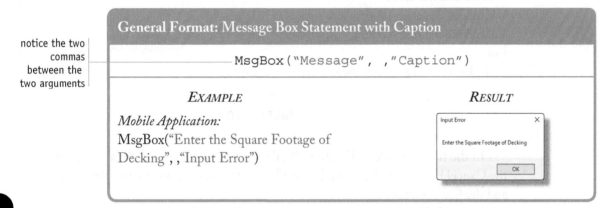

notice the two commas between the two arguments

General Format: Message Box Statement with Caption

MsgBox("Message", ,"Caption")

EXAMPLE

Mobile Application:
MsgBox("Enter the Square Footage of Decking", ,"Input Error")

RESULT

FIGURE 5-19

Display Message Box Captions

A message box can be displayed during execution with a variety of arguments. For example, by using the syntax shown in Figure 5-19, a message box can display a message and a caption in the title bar (two arguments with two commas between the arguments).

The title bar in the example in Figure 5-19 displays a caption and the message box displays a message. In many applications, the caption is used to give further information to the user.

Message Box Buttons

The general format for changing the button command from OK to another button type is shown in Figure 5-20. The button entry can be a command or a value representing a command.

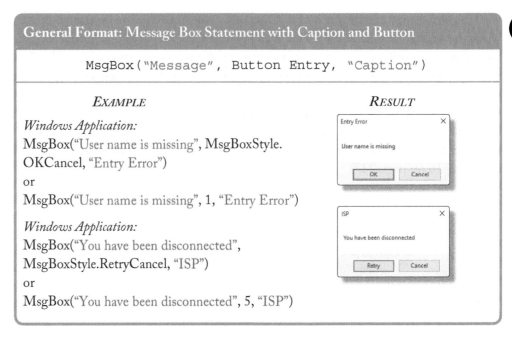

General Format: Message Box Statement with Caption and Button

```
MsgBox("Message", Button Entry, "Caption")
```

EXAMPLE	RESULT

Windows Application:
MsgBox("User name is missing", MsgBoxStyle.
OKCancel, "Entry Error")
or
MsgBox("User name is missing", 1, "Entry Error")

Windows Application:
MsgBox("You have been disconnected",
MsgBoxStyle.RetryCancel, "ISP")
or
MsgBox("You have been disconnected", 5, "ISP")

FIGURE 5-20

In the first example in Figure 5-20, the buttons specified are the OK button and the Cancel button. In the second example, the buttons shown are the Retry button and the Cancel button.

Figure 5-21 shows all the possible entries that can be placed in the Button Entry portion of the argument passed to the Show procedure.

MsgBoxButtons Arguments	Value	Use
MsgBoxStyle.OKOnly	0	Displays an OK button — default setting
MsgBoxStyle.OKCancel	1	Displays an OK and Cancel button
MsgBoxStyle.AbortRetryIgnore	2	After a failing situation, the user can choose to Abort, Retry, or Ignore
MsgBoxStyle.YesNoCancel	3	Displays Yes, No, and Cancel buttons
MsgBoxStyle.YesNo	4	Displays Yes and No buttons
MsgBoxStyle.RetryCancel	5	After an error occurs, the user can choose to Retry or Cancel

FIGURE 5-21

Message Box Icons

In the button entry portion of the argument (the second argument), you can add a message box icon (Figure 5-22). The word "or" connects the button entry to the icon entry.

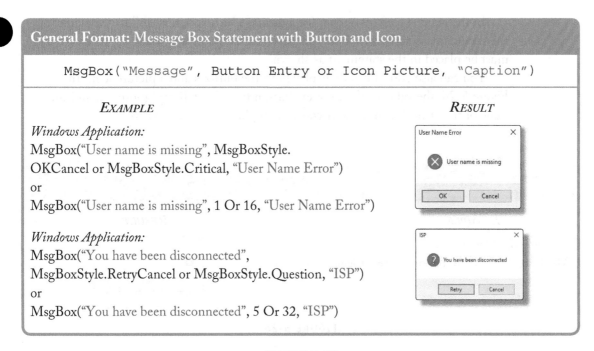

General Format: Message Box Statement with Button and Icon

```
MsgBox("Message", Button Entry or Icon Picture, "Caption")
```

EXAMPLE	RESULT

Windows Application:
MsgBox("User name is missing", MsgBoxStyle.
OKCancel or MsgBoxStyle.Critical, "User Name Error")
or
MsgBox("User name is missing", 1 Or 16, "User Name Error")

Windows Application:
MsgBox("You have been disconnected",
MsgBoxStyle.RetryCancel or MsgBoxStyle.Question, "ISP")
or
MsgBox("You have been disconnected", 5 Or 32, "ISP")

FIGURE 5-22

The picture icon represents the MsgBoxStyle that can be displayed as a graphic icon in the message box. Both examples in Figure 5-22 show an icon added to the message box.

The picture icon in the second argument can contain any of the entries shown in Figure 5-23.

MsgBoxStyle Icons	Value	Icon	Use
MsgBoxStyle.Critical	16		Alerts the user to an error
MsgBoxStyle.Question	32		Displays a question mark
MsgBoxStyle.Exclamation	48		Alerts the user to a possible problem
MsgBoxStyle.Information	64		Displays an information icon

FIGURE 5-23

In the general formats shown for a message box, you must follow the syntax of the statements exactly, which means the commas, quotation marks, and parentheses must be placed in the statement as shown.

You can also add values to display both the buttons and a picture icon. In Figure 5-24, the value of the message button type AbortRetryIgnore is 2 and the value of the critical icon is 16. If you add 16 plus 2, the result is 18.

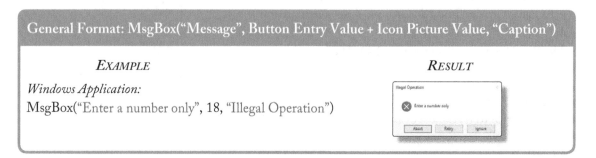

General Format: MsgBox("Message", Button Entry Value + Icon Picture Value, "Caption")

EXAMPLE	RESULT
Windows Application: MsgBox("Enter a number only", 18, "Illegal Operation")	

FIGURE 5-24

Message Box IntelliSense

When you enter the code for a message box, IntelliSense can assist you. For example, the message box you create in the following steps contains a message, caption, and buttons. To use IntelliSense to enter the code, you can complete the following steps:

STEP 1   In the code window, inside the event handler you are coding, type msg to display MsgBox in the IntelliSense list.

IntelliSense displays a list of the allowable entries (Figure 5-25). When you type msg, MsgBox is selected in the IntelliSense list.

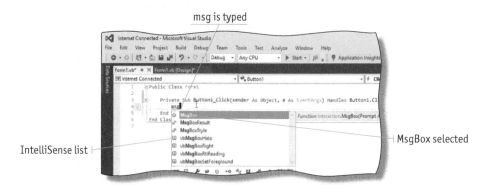

FIGURE 5-25

STEP 2   Press the TAB key to select MsgBox in the IntelliSense list. Type the following text: ("You have been disconnected from the Internet", m)

The first argument for the message box is entered (Figure 5-26). IntelliSense displays a list of allowable entries for the second argument.

first MsgBox argument entered

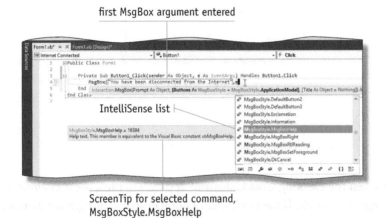

ScreenTip for selected command,
MsgBoxStyle.MsgBoxHelp

FIGURE 5-26

STEP 3   Select the MsgBoxStyle.AbortRetryIgnore argument by pressing the up arrow until the correct argument is highlighted. Type a comma, then type "ISP" and a right parenthesis.

The MsgBoxStyle.AbortRetryIgnore argument is selected. Next, the comma and the caption "ISP" are entered with a right parenthesis (Figure 5-27).

Start button

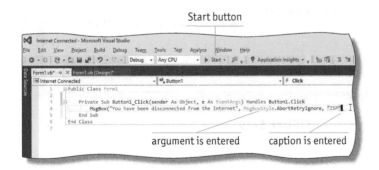

argument is entered   caption is entered

FIGURE 5-27

STEP 4   Click the Start button on the Standard toolbar.

The application runs, displaying the message box that shows the message, buttons, and caption (Figure 5-28).

FIGURE 5-28

String Concatenation

Recall that when the Decking Cost Calculator application runs, the user enters the square footage of the deck. If the user enters a number that is not greater than zero, such as –6, a message box displays "You entered –6. Enter a Positive Number", as shown in Figure 5-29.

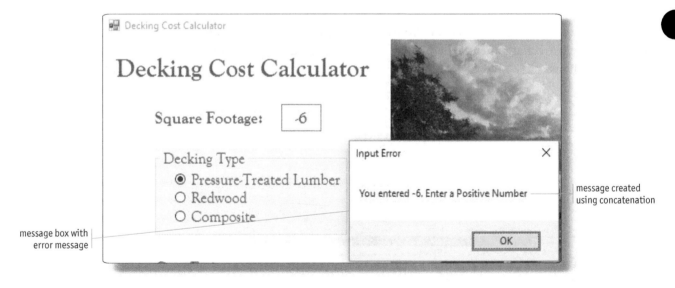

FIGURE 5-29

Franck Boston/Shutterstock.com

To create the message in the message box, you can use concatenation, which you learned about in Chapter 4. In Figure 5-29, the string message is constructed by joining a string ("You entered"), a variable named decFootage that contains the entered square footage (which must be converted to a string), and a string for the final part of the message (". Enter a Positive Number"). The code in Figure 5-30 creates the message box.

```
41              MsgBox("You entered " & decFootage.ToString() & ". Enter a Positive Number", , "Input Error")
```

FIGURE 5-30

You will recall that the operator to concatenate strings is the ampersand (&). When the statement is executed, the three string elements are joined together (concatenated) to form the one string that is displayed in the message box.

Make Decisions with Conditional Statements

In the Decking Cost Calculator application, users can select one of three types of decking: pressure-treated lumber, redwood, or composite. The price per square foot is based on the user's choice of decking. To select the decking type, the user must click one of three radio buttons titled Pressure-Treated Lumber, Redwood, and Composite. Then, based on the choice, the application uses a different decking cost.

Visual Basic uses decision structures to deal with the different conditions that occur based on the values entered into an application. A **decision structure** is one of the three fundamental control structures used in computer programming. For example, if the user clicks the Redwood radio button, the decking cost is set to $7.75 per square foot. The statement that tests the radio button is called a **conditional statement**. The condition to check is whether the Redwood radio button is selected. If so, the decking cost is set to $7.75. The cost of the decking only includes the materials and not the installation.

When a condition is tested in a Visual Basic program, the condition is either true or false. For example, when checking to determine if the Redwood radio button is selected, the condition can be either true (the button is checked) or false (is not checked). All conditional statements result in the tested condition being either true or false.

To implement a conditional statement and the statements that are executed when a condition is true or false, Visual Basic uses the If statement and its variety of formats. You will learn about the If statement in the following sections.

> **HEADS UP**
>
> In older versions of Visual Basic, the plus (+) sign was used to concatenate strings instead of the ampersand (&) symbol. The + sign still functions for concatenation, but it can be confusing because it looks like the plus sign used in addition. You should always use the ampersand.

Use the If . . . Then Statement

In the sample program, an If . . . Then statement is used to determine the cost of the decking. The simplest form of the If . . . Then statement is shown in Figure 5-31.

```
5           If condition Then
6               Statement(s) executed when condition is true
7           End If
8
```

FIGURE 5-31

In Figure 5-31, when the condition tested in the If statement on line 5 is true, the statement(s) between the If and the End If keywords will be executed. If the condition is not true, no statements between the If and End If keywords will be executed, and program execution will continue with the statement(s) after the End If statement.

Visual Basic automatically indents statements to be executed when a condition is true or not true to indicate which lines of code are within the conditional If . . . Then structure. This is why the statement on line 6 in Figure 5-31 on the previous page is indented. The End If keywords terminate the If . . . Then block of code. After executing the If . . . Then block, execution continues with any statements that follow the closing End If statement.

Relational Operators

In Figure 5-31, the condition portion of the If . . . Then statement means a condition is tested to determine if it is true or false. The conditions that can be tested are as follows:

1. Is one value equal to another value?
2. Is one value not equal to another value?
3. Is one value greater than another value?
4. Is one value less than another value?
5. Is one value greater than or equal to another value?
6. Is one value less than or equal to another value?

To test these conditions, Visual Basic provides relational operators that are used within the conditional statement to express the relationship being tested. Figure 5-32 shows these relational operators.

Relational Operator		Meaning	Example	Resulting Condition
1	=	Equal to	8 = 8	True
2	<>	Not equal to	6 <> 6	False
3	>	Greater than	7 > 9	False
4	<	Less than	4 < 6	True
5	> =	Greater than or equal to	3 > = 3	True
6	< =	Less than or equal to	7 < = 5	False

FIGURE 5-32

A condition tested using a relational operator is evaluated as true or false. Example 1 tests whether 8 is equal to 8. Because they are equal, the resulting condition is true. Example 2 tests whether 6 is not equal to 6. Because they are equal, the resulting condition is false. Similarly, Example 5 tests whether 3 is greater than or equal to 3. Because they are equal, the resulting condition is true.

As an example of using a relational operator, consider the following problem in which an If statement is used to determine if someone is old enough to vote. If the value in the intAge variable is greater than or equal to 18, then the person is old enough to vote. If not, the person is not old enough to vote. The If . . . Then statement to test this condition is shown in Figure 5-33.

```
8           If intAge >= 18 Then
9                 lblVotingEligibility.Text = "You are old enough to vote"
10          End If
```

FIGURE 5-33

In Figure 5-33, if the value in the intAge variable is greater than or equal to 18, the string value "You are old enough to vote" is assigned to the Text property of the lblVotingEligibility Label object. If not, then no processing occurs based on the conditional statement, and any statement(s) following the End If keywords will be executed.

You can see in Figure 5-33 that several keywords are required in an If . . . Then statement. The word If must be the first item. Next, the condition(s) to be tested are stated, followed by the word Then. This keyword is required in an If statement.

The End If keywords follow the statements to be executed when the condition is true. This entry is also required. It signals to the Visual Basic compiler that the statements following it must be executed regardless of the result of the conditional statement; that is, the End If keywords are the last element within the If block, and no subsequent statements depend on the If block for execution.

To enter the If . . . Then statement shown in Figure 5-33, you can complete the following steps:

STEP 1 With the insertion point in the correct location in the code, type if and then press the SPACEBAR.

The statement begins with the word If (Figure 5-34). The If command is displayed in blue because it is a Visual Basic keyword. You can type uppercase or lowercase letters.

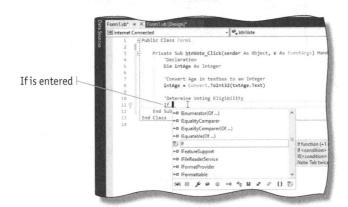

FIGURE 5-34

HEADS UP

Always place the words If and Then on the same programming line. If you use IntelliSense, this is done automatically for you. The End If statement, which terminates the decision structure, also should be on a line by itself.

STEP 2   Type `inta` to select the variable named intAge in the IntelliSense list. Type `>=18` as the condition to be tested. Press the ENTER key.

The If . . . Then statement is entered in the code window (Figure 5-35). When the ENTER key is pressed, Visual Basic adds the keyword Then to the end of the If statement line of code and inserts spaces between the elements of the statement for ease of reading. In addition, Visual Basic inserts the End If keywords following a blank line. Notice the keywords Then and End If are capitalized and displayed in blue.

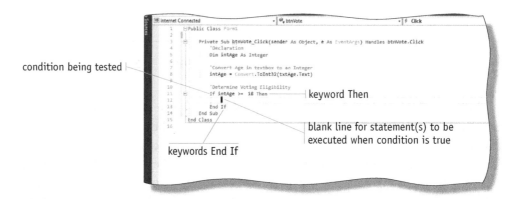

FIGURE 5-35

STEP 3   On the blank line (line 12 in Figure 5-35), enter the statement that should be executed when the condition is true. To place the message "You are old enough to vote" in the Text property of the lblVotingEligibility Label object, insert the code shown in Figure 5-33 on the previous page. Remember to use IntelliSense to reference the lblVotingEligibility Label object.

The resulting statement is entered between the If and End If keywords (Figure 5-36). Notice that Visual Basic automatically indents the line for ease of reading. The blank line allows you to enter more statements. If you have no further statements, you can press the delete key to delete the blank line in the If . . . Then statement.

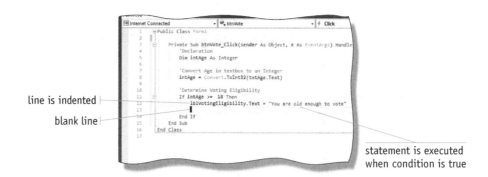

FIGURE 5-36

Compare Strings

You also can write an If . . . Then statement to compare string values using the relational operators shown in Figure 5-32 on page 246. A string value comparison compares each character in two strings, starting with the first character in each string. For example, in the two strings in Figure 5-37, the comparison begins with the first character (a) in each string. Because the characters are equal, the comparison continues with the second character in each string, which is b. Because these characters are equal, the comparison continues with the third character in each string, c. Because all three characters are equal, the strings are considered equal, and the resulting condition from the If statement is true.

```
13          Dim String1 As String = "abc"
14          Dim String2 As String = "abc"
15
16          If String1 = String2 Then
17                  lblStringTest.Text = "Equal"
18          End If
```

FIGURE 5-37

All characters found in strings, including letters, numbers, and special characters, are in a sequence based on how the characters are coded internally on the computer. In Visual Studio 2017, characters are stored and sequenced in Unicode, which is a coding methodology that can accommodate more than 60,000 characters. Appendix A shows the Unicode sequence for the standard keyboard characters. You will find that numbers have lower Unicode values than uppercase letters and uppercase letters have lower values than lowercase letters.

Using the If . . . Then statement, the following comparisons produce the following resulting conditions:

Example 1:

```
Dim String1 As String = "Powder"
Dim String2 As String = "Power"

If String1 < String2 Then
```

Resulting Condition: True because in the fourth character position, the letter d is less than the letter e.

Example 2:

```
Dim String1 As String = "6"
Dim String2 As String = "T"

If String1 < String2 Then
```

Resulting Condition: True because in a string comparison, a number is less than an uppercase letter.

CRITICAL THINKING

How do you determine if this statement is true or false: If #hashtag < @samtechnow Then? By using Appendix A, you can see the # symbol is assigned to the Unicode decimal value of 35 and the @ symbol is assigned to the Unicode decimal value of 64. The value of the # symbol is less than that of the @ symbol, making this statement true. To keep up with the latest technology, follow the author Corinne Hoisington on Twitter at @samtechnow.

Example 3:

```
Dim String1 As String = "12"
Dim String2 As String = "9"

If String1 < String2 Then
```

Resulting Condition: True because in a string comparison, the characters in the first position of the string are compared first. Because the value 1 in String1 is less than the value 9 in String2, the entire value in String1 is considered less than the value in String2.

Example 4:

```
Dim String1 As String = "anchor"
Dim String2 As String = "Anchorline"

If String1 > String2 Then
```

Resulting Condition: True because a lowercase letter (the a in the first position of String1) is considered greater than an uppercase letter (the A in the first position of String2).

Compare Different Data Types

Every type of data available in Visual Basic can be compared. Different numeric types can be compared to each other using an If statement. A single string character can be compared to a Char data type. The following examples illustrate some of the allowable comparisons.

Example 1: Decimal compared to Double

```
If decQuarterlySales > dblSalesQuota Then
```

If decQuarterlySales = 110,324.54 and dblSalesQuota = 112,435.54, the condition is false.

Example 2: Decimal compared to Integer

```
If decTirePressureReading > intTirePressureMaximum Then
```

If decTirePressureReading = 30.21 and intTirePressure-Maximum = 30, the condition is true.

Example 3: Double compared to Integer

```
If dblCurrentTemperature >= intHeatDanger Then
```

If dblCurrentTemperature = 94.543 and intHeatDanger = 98, the condition is false.

Example 4: String compared to Char

```
If strChemistryGrade < chrPassingGrade Then
```

If strChemistryGrade = "B" and chrPassingGrade = "C", the condition is true.

Visual Basic allows comparisons between most data types. If you are unsure whether a comparison can be made, write an If statement to ensure that the comparison is working properly.

Use the If . . . Then . . . Else Statement

An If . . . Then statement executes a set of instructions if a condition is true. If the condition is false, the instructions between the If statement and the End If statement are not executed and program execution continues with the statement(s) following the End If statement.

In many applications, the logic requires one set of instructions to be executed if a condition is true and another set of instructions to be executed if a condition is false. For example, a program requirement could specify that if a student's test score is 70 or greater, the message "You passed the examination" should be displayed, while if the test score is less than 70, the message "You failed the examination" should be displayed.

To execute one set of instructions if a condition is true and another set of instructions if the condition is false, you can use the If . . . Then . . . Else statement. Figure 5-38 illustrates the syntax of the If . . . Then . . . Else statement.

```
16        If condition Then
17            Statement(s) executed if condition is true
18        Else
19            Statement(s) executed if condition is false
20        End If
```

FIGURE 5-38

If the condition tested by the If statement is true, the statement(s) between the Then keyword and the Else keyword will be executed. If the condition tested is false, the statement(s) between the Else keyword and the End If keywords will be executed.

The example in Figure 5-39 shows the use of the If . . . Then . . . Else statement to calculate student fees by testing the student's status.

statement is executed if
student is a graduate

```
27        If strStudentStatus = "Graduate" Then
28            decStudentFees = decGraduateFee * intNumberOfUnits
29        Else
30            decStudentFees = decUndergraduateFee * intNumberOfUnits
31        End If
```

statement is executed if
student is not a graduate

FIGURE 5-39

If the student is in graduate school, the student fees are calculated by multiplying the graduate fee by the number of units. If the student is not a graduate student, the student fees are calculated by multiplying the undergraduate fee by the number of units. Notice that a student cannot be both an undergraduate and a graduate student, so either the statement following the Then keyword will be executed or the statement following the Else keyword will be executed.

Compare to an Arithmetic Expression

An If statement can compare an arithmetic expression to a constant or other data type. For example, in Figure 5-40, the withdrawals from a bank account are compared to the value obtained by adding the current balance to deposits and then subtracting account charges.

```
41          If decWithdrawals > decCurrentBalance + decDeposits - decAccountCharges Then
42              lblAccountStatus.Text = "Overdrawn"
43          Else
44              lblAccountStatus.Text = "Balance is Positive"
45          End If
```

FIGURE 5-40

In Figure 5-40, if the value in the decWithdrawals variable is greater than the current balance plus the deposits minus the account charges, the Text property of the lblAccountStatus Label object is set to Overdrawn. If the value in decWithdrawals is less than or equal to the value from the arithmetic expression, the message "Balance is Positive" is placed in the Text property of the lblAccountStatus Label object. Notice that the arithmetic expression is evaluated prior to the comparison. If the condition is true, the statement between the Then and Else keywords is executed. If the condition is false, the statement between the Else and End If keywords is executed.

Use the If . . . Then . . . ElseIf Statement

Complex logic problems might require a more complex structure than the If . . . Then . . . Else logic structure. For example, consider the following logical problem that must be solved in a computer program:

An online store charges a shipping fee based on the dollar amount of the order being shipped. The rules are as follows:

1. If the order amount is above $500, the shipping cost is $30.
2. If the order amount is more than $400 and not greater than $500, the shipping cost is $25.
3. If the order amount is more than $200 and not greater than $400, the shipping cost is $20.
4. If the order amount is equal to or less than $200, the shipping cost is $15.

When one of the conditions is found to be true, the rest of the conditions are not tested because the correct condition has been found. To solve this problem, you should think this way:

1. If the order amount is greater than $500.00, then the shipping cost is $30.00, and no more processing is needed to determine the shipping cost.
2. If, however, the order amount is not greater than $500.00, you must check further to see if it is greater than $400.00 (400.01 through 500.00). If so, the shipping cost is $25.00.
3. If the order amount is not greater than $400.00, the next step is to check whether it is greater than $200.00. In other words, check within the range of $201.00 to $400.00. If this is true, the shipping cost is $20.00.
4. If none of the above is true, then the order amount must be less than or equal to $200. In this case, the shipping cost is $15.00.

As you can see, a simple If . . . Then . . . Else statement could not solve this logic problem because the structure tests only a single condition and specifies the processing based on whether the condition is true or false. For a problem in which multiple conditions must be tested, the If . . . Then . . . ElseIf statement might be appropriate. The general format of the If . . . Then . . . ElseIf statement is shown in Figure 5-41.

```
105        If decOrderAmount > 500D Then
106            Statement(s) executed if condition is true
107        ElseIf decOrderAmount > 400D Then
108            Statement(s) executed if condition is true
109        ElseIf decOrderAmount > 200D Then
110            Statement(s) executed if condition is true
111        ElseIf decOrderAmount > 0D Then
112            Statement(s) executed if condition is true
113        End If
```

FIGURE 5-41

Once a condition is true in the code in Figure 5-41 on the previous page, Visual Basic bypasses the rest of the ElseIf statements. For example, assume the order amount is $455. The first condition tests whether the order amount is greater than 500. The first condition would test false because 455 is not greater than 500.

Next, the ElseIf entry will test whether 455 is greater than 400. Because the value 455 is greater than 400, the condition is true and the statement(s) on line 108 will be executed. The remaining ElseIf statements will not be evaluated because the true condition has been found.

Separate If . . . Then statements are not used in the example in Figure 5-41 because each condition would have to be tested even though a condition had already been found to be true. When using an If . . . Then . . . ElseIf statement, any remaining conditions are not tested after a condition is found to be true, making the process faster and more efficient.

HEADS UP

When testing conditions like those in the example in Figure 5-41, make sure that you do not leave a number out of the range of numbers being tested. For example, if one ElseIf statement tests decOrderAmount > 400.00 and the next ElseIf statement tests < 400.00, the value 400.00 has not been tested and the program will not properly process the value 400.00.

You may want to include a trailing Else statement at the end of an If . . . Then . . . ElseIf conditional statement to handle a condition that does not meet any of the previous conditions tested. In the example in Figure 5-42, the code is determining whether the user is eligible for Social Security benefits. If the user's age is greater than or equal to 65, the user receives full benefits. If the user's age is between 0 and 65, the user is not eligible for benefits.

```
115        If intAge >= 65 Then
116            lblSocialSecurity.Text = "Full Benefits"
117        ElseIf intAge > 0 Then
118            lblSocialSecurity.Text = "Not Eligible for Benefits"
119        Else
120            lblSocialSecurity.Text = "Invalid Age"
121        End If
```

FIGURE 5-42

In Figure 5-42, the statement on line 120 that follows the trailing Else statement on line 119 is executed if the number in the intAge variable does not meet the conditions stated in the previous If statements. For example, if the intAge variable contains a negative value such as −12, the Text property of the lblSocialSecurity Label object will be set to "Invalid Age."

At times, more than one decision has to be made to determine what processing must occur. For example, if one condition is true, a second condition may need to be tested before the correct code is executed. To test a second condition only after determining that a first condition is true (or false), you must place an If statement within another If statement. When you place one If statement within another one, the inner If statement is said to be nested within the outer If Statement. The syntax of a nested If statement is shown in Figure 5-43.

In Figure 5-43, if the first condition tested is true, the statements following the keyword Then are executed. The statement to be executed when the first condition is true is another If statement (line 124) that tests the second condition. This second If statement is said to be a nested If statement or an inner If statement. If the second condition is true, the program executes the statement(s) on line 125 following the keyword Then for the first inner If statement. If the second condition is not true, the program executes the statement(s) on line 127 following the keyword Else for the first inner If statement. The End If entry (line 128) follows the first inner If statement, indicating the end of the effect of the first inner If statement.

nested If
statement –
(first inner
If statement)

```
123        If first condition Then
124              ┌ If second condition Then
125              │     Statement(s) executed if condition 1 is true and condition 2 is true
126              │ Else
127              │     Statement(s) executed if condition 1 is true and condition 2 is false
128              └ End If ─────────────┤ end of first inner If statement
129           Else
130              ┌ If third condition Then
131              │     Statement(s) executed if condition 1 is false and condition 3 is true
132              │ Else
133              │     Statement(s) executed if condition 1 is false and condition 3 is false
134              └ End If ─────────────┤ end of second inner If statement
135           End If
```

nested If   end of first If statement
statement –
(second inner
If statement)

FIGURE 5-43

If the first condition is not true, then the program executes the statements following the keyword Else on line 129 for the first If statement. The statement to be executed when the first condition is not true is an If statement that tests the third condition (line 130). If the third condition is true, the program executes the statement(s) on line 131 following the Then keyword of the second inner If statement. Finally, if the second inner If statement that tests the third condition is false, the statements on line 133 are executed.

To illustrate a nested If statement, assume a college has the following admissions policy: If an applying student has a GPA (grade point average) greater than 3.5 and a score greater than 1000 on the SAT college entrance exam, then that student is granted admission. If an applying student has a GPA greater than 3.5 but an SAT score of 1000 or lower, the student is advised to retake the SAT exam. If an applying student has a GPA of 3.5 or lower but an SAT score greater than 1200, the student is granted probationary admission, which means she must achieve a 2.5 GPA in the first semester of college. If an applying student has a GPA of 3.5 or lower and an SAT score of 1200 or lower, the student is denied admission. The nested If statement to process this admission policy is shown in Figure 5-44.

Notice in Figure 5-44 that the test for greater than 1000 on the SAT (line 141) must take place only after the test for a GPA greater than 3.5 (line 140), because the test for greater than 1000 is required only after the program determines that the GPA is greater than 3.5. Therefore, a nested If statement is required. In addition, the test for greater than 1200 (line 147) should occur only after the program determines that

CRITICAL THINKING

Does every If statement need an End If coordinating statement?
Yes. Multiple nested If statements can be confusing to confirm that you have the correct number of End If statements. If you have 9 If statements, double-check that the code also contains 9 End If statements. Aligning each If statement with its coordinating End If statement helps you keep track of the nested statements.

```
140            If decGPA > 3.5D Then
141                If intSatScore > 1000 Then
142                    lblAdmissionStatus.Text = "You have earned admission"
143                Else
144                    lblAdmissionStatus.Text = "Retake the SAT exam"
145                End If
146            Else
147                If intSatScore > 1200 Then
148                    lblAdmissionStatus.Text = "You have earned probationary admission"
149                Else
150                    lblAdmissionStatus.Text = "You have been denied admission"
151                End If
152            End If
```

FIGURE 5-44

the GPA is 3.5 or lower. As you can see, you should use a nested If statement when a condition must be tested only after another condition has been tested.

Other Nested If Configurations

You can use nested If statements in a variety of forms. Assume, for example, that a school's admissions policy is as follows: If an applying student has a GPA greater than 3.5 and an SAT score greater than 1100, then that student is granted admission. If an applying student has a GPA greater than 3.5 but an SAT score of 1100 or lower, the student is advised to retake the SAT exam. If an applying student has a GPA of 3.5 or lower, the student is denied admission. The nested If statement in Figure 5-45 solves this logic problem.

```
154            If decGPA > 3.5D Then
155                If intSatScore > 1100 Then
156                    lblAdmissionStatus.Text = "You have earned admission"
157                Else
158                    lblAdmissionStatus.Text = "Retake the SAT exam"
159                End If
160            Else
161                lblAdmissionStatus.Text = "You have been denied admission"
162            End If
```

FIGURE 5-45

In Figure 5-45, if the GPA is greater than 3.5, then the first inner If statement on line 155 is executed to determine if the SAT score is greater than 1100. If so, the person has earned admission. If not, the person is advised to retake the SAT exam. If the GPA is not greater than 3.5, the student is denied admission. Notice that an If statement does not follow the Else keyword on line 160. An inner If statement need not follow both the If and the Else keywords.

Sometimes, after a condition is found to be true, a statement must be executed before the inner If statement is executed. For example, assume that if a student's GPA is greater than 3.5, then the student should be informed that her GPA is acceptable for admission. The code in Figure 5-46 implements this condition.

```
164        If decGPA > 3.5D Then
165            lblGPAStatus.Text = "Your GPA is acceptable"
166            If intSatScore > 1100 Then
167                lblAdmissionStatus.Text = "You have earned admission"
168            Else
169                lblAdmissionStatus.Text = "Retake the SAT exam"
170            End If
171        Else
172            lblGPAStatus.Text = "Your GPA is not acceptable"
173            lblAdmissionStatus.Text = "You have been denied admission"
174        End If
```

FIGURE 5-46

On line 165 in Figure 5-46, the message "Your GPA is acceptable" is assigned to the Text property of the lblGPAStatus Label object before checking the SAT score. As you can see, after the first condition has been tested, one or more statements can be executed prior to executing the inner If statement. This holds true for the Else portion of the If statement as well.

Match If, Else, and End If Entries

When you write a nested If statement, the inner If statement must be fully contained within the outer If statement. To accomplish this, you must ensure that each Else entry has a corresponding If entry, and an inner If statement must be terminated with an End If entry before either the Else entry or the End If entry for the outer If statement. If you code the nested If statement incorrectly, one or more of its entries will be shown with a blue squiggly line, indicating an error in the structure of the statement.

You also must place the correct executing statements with the If and Else statements within the nested If statement. For example, in Figure 5-47, the code is incorrect because the statements following the Else statements have been switched.

```
164        If decGPA > 3.5D Then
165            lblGPAStatus.Text = "Your GPA is acceptable"
166            If intSatScore > 1100 Then
167                lblAdmissionStatus.Text = "You have earned admission"
168            Else
169                lblAdmissionStatus.Text = "You have been denied admission"
170            End If
171        Else
172            lblGPAStatus Text = "Your GPA is not acceptable"
173            lblAdmissionStatus.Text = "Retake the SAT exam"          incorrect
174        End If                                                        statements
```

FIGURE 5-47

You must be precise when placing the executing statements in the nested If statement. It is easy to miscode a nested If statement.

Nest Three or More Levels of If Statements

If statements are not limited to two levels of nesting. Three or more levels can be included in a nested If statement, although the statement can become difficult to understand and code. If more than two levels are required to solve a logic problem, great care must be taken to prevent errors such as the one shown in Figure 5-47.

Test the Status of a RadioButton Object in Code

In the Decking Cost Calculator application, the user selects one RadioButton in the GroupBox object to select the decking type. The code must check each RadioButton to determine if it has been selected by the user. When the user selects a radio button, its Checked property is changed from False to True. In addition, the Checked property for other RadioButton objects in the GroupBox object is set to False. This Checked property can be tested in an If statement to determine if the RadioButton object has been selected.

To test the status of the Checked property for the radLumber RadioButton object, a programmer can write the general statement shown in Figure 5-48.

```
237        If radLumber.Checked Then
238            Statement(s) to be executed if radio button is checked
239        End If
```

FIGURE 5-48

Notice in Figure 5-48 that the RadioButton property is not compared using a relational operator. Instead, when a program tests a property that can contain only True or False, only the property must be specified in the If statement. When the property contains True, then the If statement is considered true, and when the property contains False, then the If statement is considered false.

Test Radio Buttons with the If . . . Then . . . ElseIf Statement

When a program contains multiple RadioButton objects in a Panel object or a GroupBox object, only one of the radio buttons can be selected. The If . . . Then . . . ElseIf statement is used to check multiple radio buttons because once the checked radio button is detected, checking the remaining radio buttons is unnecessary.

In the Decking Cost Calculator application, the user clicks one of three radio buttons (Pressure-Treated Lumber, Redwood, or Composite) to select the type of decking used. When using an If . . . Then . . . ElseIf statement to check the status of the radio buttons, the most likely choice should be checked first. Thus, the fewest number of tests are performed. Therefore, the first If statement should test the status of the Pressure-Treated Lumber radio button (radLumber). If the radLumber button is checked, the Cost Per Square Foot should be set to the value in the decLumberCost variable, which is 2.35. No further testing should be done (Figure 5-49).

```
27        If decFootage > 0 Then
28            ' Determine cost per square foot
29            If radLumber.Checked Then
30                decCostPerSquareFoot = decLumberCost
31            ElseIf radRedwood.Checked Then
32                decCostPerSquareFoot = decRedwoodCost
33            ElseIf radComposite.Checked Then
34                decCostPerSquareFoot = decCompositeCost
35            End If
36            ' Calculate and display the cost estimate
37            decCostEstimate = decFootage * decCostPerSquareFoot
38            lblCostEstimate.Text = decCostEstimate.ToString("C")
39        Else
```

FIGURE 5-49

If the radLumber button is not checked, then the radRedwood button should be tested. If radRedwood is checked, the Cost Per Square Foot should be set to the value in the decRedwoodCost variable (7.75), and no further testing should be done. If the radRedwood button is not checked, then the radComposite button should be tested. If the other two buttons are not checked, then the radComposite button must be checked because one of the three must be checked. The Cost Per Square Foot will be set to the value in the decCompositeCost variable (8.50).

As you learned earlier, during design time, you can set the Checked property to True for the most frequently selected RadioButton to save the user from having to select it. In the Decking Cost Calculator application, after the Cost Per Square Foot has been determined and the Cost Estimate has been calculated, the user can click the Clear button to clear the Square Footage text box, clear the Cost Estimate, and reset the radio buttons so that the Pressure-Treated Lumber button is selected. The code to reset the radio buttons is shown in Figure 5-50.

```
62        radLumber.Checked = True
63        radRedwood.Checked = False
64        radComposite.Checked = False
```

FIGURE 5-50

In Figure 5-50, the Checked property for the radLumber RadioButton object is set to True using the same method you have seen in previous chapters for setting an object property. Similarly, the Checked property for the other two RadioButton objects is set to False. As a result of these statements, the Pressure-Treated Lumber radio button will be selected in the user interface, and the Redwood and Composite radio buttons will not be selected.

Block-Level Scope

In Chapter 4, you learned that the scope of a variable is defined by where it is declared within a program. For example, if a variable is declared within an event handler, then only code within that event handler can reference the variable. Code in one event handler within a program cannot reference a variable declared in another event handler.

Within an event handler, an If . . . Then . . . Else statement is considered a block of code. To review, this statement is the code beginning with the If keyword and ending with the corresponding Else keyword or the code beginning with the Else keyword and ending with the End If keywords. Variables can be declared within the block of code, but they can be referenced only within the block of code where they are declared. For example, variables defined within an If . . . Then block of code fall out of scope (cannot be referenced) outside that block of code. To illustrate this concept, the code in Figure 5-51 shows a variable named intYears declared within an If . . . Then block of code.

```
11          If intAge < 18 Then
12              Dim intYears As Integer
13              intYears = 18 - intAge
14              lblMessage.Text = "You can vote in " & intYears & " years(s)."
15          Else
16              lblMessage.Text = "You can vote!"
17          End If
```

FIGURE 5-51

On line 12 in Figure 5-51, the variable intYears is declared as an Integer variable. On line 13, the variable is used in an arithmetic statement to receive the result of the calculation 18 − intAge, which determines the number of years less than 18 that is stored in intAge. The result in intYears is concatenated with literals in the statement on line 14. The intYears variable can be referenced in any statement between the If keyword and the Else keyword. It cannot be referenced anywhere else in the program, not even in the Else portion of the If statement. When a statement referencing the intYears variable is written outside the area between the If keyword and the Else keyword, a compilation error will occur and the program will not compile and execute.

Although the scope of the intYears variable in Figure 5-51 is between the If keyword on line 11 and the Else keyword on line 15, you should realize that the variable itself perseveres during the execution of the event handler procedure. Therefore, if the If statement in Figure 5-51 is executed a second time, the value in the intYears variable will be the same as when the If statement was completed the first time. To avoid unexpected results when the If statement is executed the second time, you should initialize block variables at the beginning of the block. In Figure 5-51, the statement on line 13 sets the value in the intYears variable immediately after it is declared, which is a good programming technique.

Use Logical Operators

The If statements you have seen thus far test a single condition. In many cases, more than one condition must be true or one of several conditions must be true to execute the statements in the Then portion of the If . . . Then . . . Else statement. When more than one condition is included in an If . . . Then . . . Else statement, the conditions are called a **compound condition**. For example, consider the following business traveling rule: "If the flight costs less than $300 and the hotel is less than $120.00 per night, the business trip is approved." In this case, both conditions — flight less than $300 *and* hotel less than $120.00 per night — must be true for the trip to be approved. If either condition is not true, then the business trip is not approved.

To create an If statement that processes the business traveling rule, you must use a **logical operator**. The most common set of logical operators are listed in Figure 5-52.

Logical Operator	Meaning
And	All conditions tested in the If statement must be true
Or	One condition tested in the If statement must be true
Not	Negates a condition

FIGURE 5-52

For the business traveling rule, you should use the And logical operator.

Use the And Logical Operator

The **And logical operator** allows you to combine two or more conditions into a compound condition that can be tested with an If statement. If any of the conditions stated in the compound condition is false, the compound condition is considered false, and the statements following the Else portion of the If statement will be executed. The code in Figure 5-53 uses the And logical operator to implement the business traveling rule.

```
137        If decFlightCost < 300D And decHotelCost < 120D Then
138            lblTripMessage.Text = "Your business trip is approved"
139        Else
140            lblTripMessage.Text = "Your business trip is denied"
141        End If
```

FIGURE 5-53

In Figure 5-53, both conditions in the compound condition (flight cost less than 300 and hotel cost less than 120) must be true for the business trip to be approved. If one of the conditions is false, then the compound condition is considered false and the If statement would return a false indication. For example, if the flight cost is 300 or more, the trip will not be approved regardless of the hotel cost. Similarly, if the hotel cost is 120 or more, the trip will not be approved regardless of the flight cost. This process is illustrated in Figure 5-54.

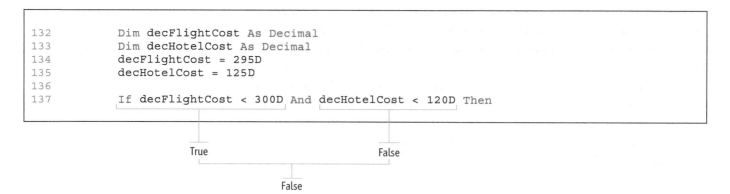

```
132          Dim decFlightCost As Decimal
133          Dim decHotelCost As Decimal
134          decFlightCost = 295D
135          decHotelCost = 125D
136
137          If decFlightCost < 300D And decHotelCost < 120D Then
```

FIGURE 5-54

In Figure 5-54, the flight cost is 295, so it is less than 300 and the first part of the compound condition is true. Following the And logical operator, the hotel cost (125) is not less than 120. Therefore, the second part of the compound condition is false. When either condition is false with the And logical operator, the If statement considers the compound condition to be false. The result of the If statement in Figure 5-54 is that the compound condition is considered to be false.

Use the Or Logical Operator

When the **Or logical operator** is used to connect two or more conditions, the compound condition is true if any tested condition is true. Even if four conditional statements are included in the compound condition, only one conditional statement in the compound condition must be true for the entire statement to be considered true.

As an example, assume a college requires each student to have either at least a 3.5 GPA or at least a 1080 score on the SAT exam to be accepted for enrollment. If the student meets one or both conditions, the student is accepted. The If statement in Figure 5-55, which uses the Or logical operator, will solve this problem.

```
147          If decGPA >= 3.5D Or intSATScore >= 1080 Then
148              lblAcceptance.Text = "You have been accepted"
149          Else
150              lblAcceptance.Text = "You are not accepted"
151          End If
```

FIGURE 5-55

In Figure 5-55, if the decGPA is 3.2 but the intSATScore is 1130, the compound condition would be considered true because at least one of its conditions (intSATScore >= 1080) is true (Figure 5-56).

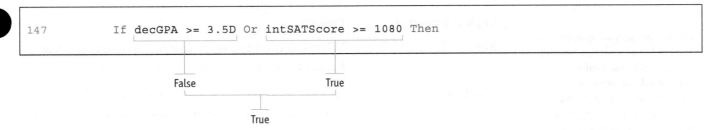

```
147        If decGPA >= 3.5D Or intSATScore >= 1080 Then
```

False   True

True

FIGURE 5-56

Use the Not Logical Operator

The **Not logical operator** allows you to state conditions that are best expressed in
a negative way. In essence, the Not logical operator reverses the logical value of a
condition on which it operates. For example, if a shoe store sells shoes under size 14
from its showroom but requires special orders for larger sizes, the code could use the
Not logical operator shown in Figure 5-57 to negate the condition in the statement.

```
155        If Not decShoeSize >= 14 Then
156            lblOrderPolicy.Text = "Showroom shoe style available"
157        Else
158            lblOrderPolicy.Text = "Special order needed"
159        End If
```

FIGURE 5-57

The statement in Figure 5-57 works, but the use of the Not logical operator
makes the If statement somewhat difficult to understand. Generally, a statement
that avoids using the Not logical operator is more easily understood. For example,
the code in Figure 5-58 accomplishes the same task as the code in Figure 5-57 and is
easier to understand.

```
162        If decShoeSize < 14 Then
163            lblOrderPolicy.Text = "Showroom shoe style available"
164        Else
165            lblOrderPolicy.Text = "Special order needed"
166        End If
```

FIGURE 5-58

Other Logical Operators

The Visual Basic programming language provides three other logical operators, as
shown in Figure 5-59.

Logical Operator	Meaning
Xor	When one condition in the compound condition is true, but not both, the compound condition is true
AndAlso	As soon as a condition is found to be false, no further conditions are tested and the compound condition is false
OrElse	As soon as a condition is found to be true, no further conditions are tested and the compound condition is true

FIGURE 5-59

Order of Operations for Logical Operators

You can combine more than one logical operator in the same If . . . Then statement. In an If statement, arithmetic operators are evaluated first, relational operators are evaluated next, and logical operators are evaluated last. The order of operations for logical operators is shown in Figure 5-60.

Logical Operator	Order
Not	Highest Precedence
And, AndAlso	Next Precedence
Or, OrElse, Xor	Last Precedence

FIGURE 5-60

In most cases, if a developer uses multiple relational or logical operators in an If statement, the order of precedence should be established through the use of parentheses to clarify the sequence of evaluation. As in arithmetic expressions, conditional expressions within parentheses are evaluated before conditional expressions outside parentheses.

Select Case Statement

In some programming applications, different operations can occur based on the value in a single field. For example, in Figure 5-61, the user enters the number of the

FIGURE 5-61

day in the week and the program displays the name of the day. The program must evaluate the number of the day value and display the name of the correct day.

In Figure 5-61, if the number of the day is 1, then the value Monday should be displayed. If the number of the day is 2, then the value Tuesday should be displayed, and so on. If the number of the day is 6 or 7, then the value Weekend should be displayed. If the user does not enter a value of 1 through 7, the user should be prompted to do so.

To solve this problem, a series of If . . . Then . . . ElseIf statements could be used, but an easier and clearer way to solve the problem is to use the Select Case statement.

When using a Select Case statement, the value in a single field, such as the day number, is evaluated. Based on the value in the field, a distinct action is taken. In this case, the name of the day is displayed.

A general example of the Select Case statement is shown in Figure 5-62.

```
168        Select Case Test Expression
169            Case First Expression
170                Statement(s) for First Case
171            Case Second Expression
172                Statement(s) for Second Case
173            Case Third Expression
174                Statement(s) for Third Case
175            Case Else
176                Statement(s) for when the Case Conditions do not match the
177                    test expressions above
178        End Select
```

FIGURE 5-62

The code for the Determine Day of Week application is shown in Figure 5-63.

```
13        Select Case intDayNumber
14            Case 1
15                lblDayOfWeek.Text = "Monday"
16            Case 2
17                lblDayOfWeek.Text = "Tuesday"
18            Case 3
19                lblDayOfWeek.Text = "Wednesday"
20            Case 4
21                lblDayOfWeek.Text = "Thursday"
22            Case 5
23                lblDayOfWeek.Text = "Friday"
24            Case 6
25                lblDayOfWeek.Text = "Weekend"
26            Case 7
27                lblDayOfWeek.Text = "Weekend"
28            Case Else
29                lblDayOfWeek.Text = "Enter 1 through 7"
30        End Select
```

FIGURE 5-63

The Select Case statement begins with the Select Case command. The test expression specifies the value or variable to be tested in the Select Case statement. In Figure 5-63, the variable is intDayNumber. So, when the Select Case statement is executed, each of the cases will be compared to the value in the intDayNumber variable.

Each Case statement specifies the value for which the test expression is checked. For example, the first Case statement on line 14 in Figure 5-63 specifies the value 1. If the value in the variable intDayNumber is equal to 1, the program executes the statement following the first Case statement up to the second Case statement (line 16). In Figure 5-63, the assignment statement on line 15 that sets the Text property of lblDayOfWeek to Monday is executed if the value in intDayNumber is equal to 1. More than one statement can follow a Case statement.

If the expression following the first Case statement is not true, then the next Case statement is evaluated. In Figure 5-63, the Case statement on line 16 checks if the value in intDayNumber is equal to 2. If so, the Text property of lblDayOfWeek is set to Tuesday. This process continues through the remainder of the Case statements.

The Case Else statement on line 28 is an optional entry that includes all conditions not specifically tested in the other Case statements. In Figure 5-63, if the value in the intDayNumber variable is not equal to 1 through 7, then the statement following the Case Else statement is executed. While not required, good programming practice dictates that the Case Else statement should be used so that all cases are accounted for and the program performs a specific action regardless of the value found in the test expression.

The End Select statement is required to end the Select Case statement. When you enter the Select Case statement in Visual Studio 2017, IntelliSense automatically includes the End Select statement.

Select Case Test Expressions

The example in Figure 5-63 on the previous page used an integer as the test expression value, but a value of any data type can be used in the test expression. For example, the test expression in Figure 5-64 uses the Text property of the txtStudentMajor TextBox object as a string value.

```
217        Select Case txtStudentMajor.Text
218            Case "Accounting"
219                lblDepartment.Text = "Business"
220            Case "Marketing"
221                lblDepartment.Text = "Business"
222            Case "Electrical Engineering"
223                lblDepartment.Text = "Engineering"
224            Case "Biochemistry"
225                lblDepartment.Text = "Chemistry"
226            Case "Shakespearean Literature"
227                lblDepartment.Text = "English"
228            Case "Web Design and E-Commerce"
229                lblDepartment.Text = "CIS"
230            Case Else
231                lblDepartment.Text = "Other"
232        End Select
```

FIGURE 5-64

In Figure 5-64, the Select Case statement is used to test the value in the Text property of the txtStudentMajor TextBox object and move the corresponding department name to the Text property of the lblDepartment object. The Case statements specify the values to be tested in the text box. The use of a string for the Select Case statement works in the same manner as other data types.

Use Relational Operators in a Select Case Statement

You can use relational operators in a Select Case statement, but you must use the keyword Is with the relational operator. For example, in Figure 5-41 on page 253, an If . . . Then . . . ElseIf statement was used to determine the shipping cost. That same processing could be accomplished using a Select Case statement, as shown in Figure 5-65.

```
191         Select Case decOrderAmount
192             Case Is > 500D
193                 decShippingCost = 30D
194             Case Is > 400D
195                 decShippingCost = 25D
196             Case Is > 200D
197                 decShippingCost = 20D
198             Case Is > 0D
199                 decShippingCost = 15D
200             Case Else
201                 decShippingCost = 0D
202         End Select
203
```

FIGURE 5-65

Use Ranges in Select Case Statements

Another way to specify values in a Select Case statement is to use ranges. In Figure 5-66, the Case statements illustrate testing for six different conditions.

```
224         Select Case intGradeLevel
225             Case 1 To 3
226                 lblGradeLevelExam.Text = "Early elementary"
227             Case 4 To 6
228                 lblGradeLevelExam.Text = "Late elementary"
229             Case 7 To 8
230                 lblGradeLevelExam.Text = "Middle school"
231             Case 9 To 10
232                 lblGradeLevelExam.Text = "Early high school"
233             Case 11
234                 lblGradeLevelExam.Text = "Late high school"
235             Case 12
236                 lblGradeLevelExam.Text = "Final exam"
237             Case Else
238                 lblGradeLevelExam.Text = "Invalid grade level"
239         End Select
```

FIGURE 5-66

As you can see, a range of values is specified in a Case statement by stating the beginning value, the word To, and then the ending value in the range. The Case statements will test the value in the intGradeLevel variable, and the appropriate statements will be executed.

You also can write Case statements so that more than one distinct value is tested. In Figure 5-67, the Case statement tests the individual values of 1, 3, 8, 11, and 17 against the value specified in the intDepartmentNumber variable.

```
230        Select Case intDepartmentNumber
231            Case 1, 3, 8, 11, 17
232
```

FIGURE 5-67

Notice in Figure 5-67 that each value in the Case statement is separated by a comma. The code in Figure 5-68 shows a combination of the two techniques, using both commas and a To statement.

```
234        Select Case intDepartmentNumber
235            Case 2, 4, 7, 12 To 16, 22
```

FIGURE 5-68

Select Which Decision Structure to Use

In some instances, you might need to determine if you should use the Select Case statement or the If . . . Then . . . ElseIf statement to solve a problem. Generally, the Select Case statement is most useful when more than two or three values must be tested for a given variable. For example, in Figure 5-64 on page 266, six different values are checked in the Text property of the txtStudentMajor TextBox object. This is a perfect example of when to use the Select Case statement.

The If . . . Then . . . ElseIf statement is more flexible because more than one variable can be used in the comparison. Programmers can also use compound conditions with the And, Or, and Not logical operators.

Use Code Snippets

Visual Basic includes a library of almost 500 pieces of code, called IntelliSense **code snippets**, that you can insert into an application. Each snippet consists of a complete programming task such as an If . . . Then . . . Else decision structure, sending an email message, or drawing a circle. Inserting these commonly used pieces of code is an effective way to enhance productivity. You also can create your own snippets and add them to the library.

In addition to inserting snippets in your program, you can display a code snippet to ensure that you understand the syntax and requirements for a given type of statement. To insert and display a code snippet for the If . . . Then . . . Else statement, you can complete the following steps:

STEP 1 Right-click the line in the code window where you want to insert the snippet.

Visual Studio displays a shortcut menu (Figure 5-69). It is important to right-click the code window in the exact location where you want the code snippet to appear. If you right-click outside this location, the shortcut menu might list customized choices for the wrong area of code. In addition, if you click in the wrong place, the snippet will be positioned in the incorrect location in your program.

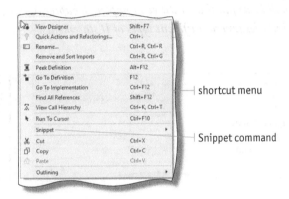

FIGURE 5-69

STEP 2 Click Snippet on the shortcut menu. Click Insert Snippet.

Visual Studio displays a menu of folders that contain snippets (Figure 5-70). The code snippets in each folder correspond to their folder titles.

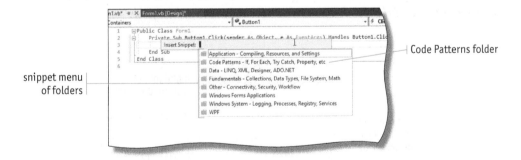

FIGURE 5-70

STEP 3 Double-click the folder named Code Patterns - If, For Each, Try Catch, Property, etc., which contains commonly used code such as the If . . . Then . . . Else statement.

Visual Studio displays a menu of folders for code patterns (Figure 5-71).

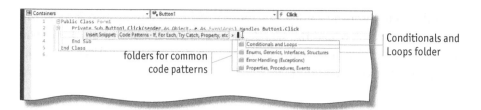

FIGURE 5-71

STEP 4   Double-click the Conditionals and Loops folder because an If . . . Then . . . Else statement is a conditional statement.

Visual Studio displays the list of Conditionals and Loops code snippets (Figure 5-72). Some of these statements will be unfamiliar until you complete Chapter 6, but you can see that the list of code snippets includes several different types of If statements.

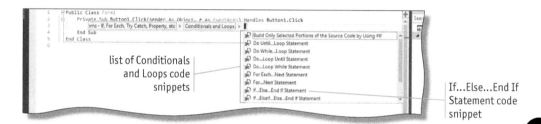

FIGURE 5-72

STEP 5   Double-click the If . . . Else . . . End If Statement code snippet.

The If . . . Else . . . End If Statement code snippet is inserted into the code on the line selected in Step 1 (Figure 5-73). The highlighted text must be replaced by the condition(s) to be tested in the If statement. The programmer must add the code to be executed when the condition is true and the code to be executed when the condition is false.

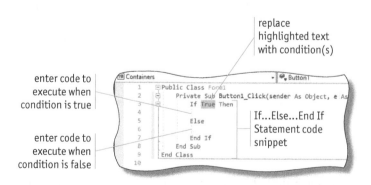

FIGURE 5-73

You must modify the code snippet shown in Figure 5-73 for the code to work properly. You may find that modifying a complicated code snippet is more work than using IntelliSense to enter the statement.

Code snippets are also helpful for learning or reviewing the format and syntax of a statement. For example, if you want to review the syntax of an If . . . Then . . . ElseIf statement, you could insert the statement into the code window and examine it. You could then either click the Undo button to remove the statement, or you could comment out the snippet code and keep it for your review. In many cases when checking syntax, reviewing a snippet is faster and clearer than consulting Visual Basic help.

Validate Data

Since the first days of computers, the phrase "garbage in, garbage out" has described the fact that allowing incorrect input data into a program produces incorrect output. Developers should anticipate that users will enter invalid data. Therefore, they must write code that prevents the invalid data from being used in the program to produce invalid output.

For example, in the Decking Cost Calculator application, the user is asked to enter the number of square feet for the decking. If the user enters a negative number or a letter or even leaves the text box blank, the program should inform the user of the input error and allow the user to reenter a proper value. If the program attempts to process invalid data, unexpected errors can occur, which is not the way a program should respond to invalid input data.

To properly check the square footage value entered by the user, two tests must be performed. First, the program must check the value to ensure it is numeric. Second, the numeric value entered by the user must be checked to ensure it is greater than zero. These tests are explained in the following sections.

Test Input to Determine If the Value Is Numeric

In the Decking Cost Calculator application, if no check is performed on the input data and the user accidentally enters a nonnumeric character such as an "a" or does not enter a value at all, the program will fail when Visual Basic attempts to convert that value to a number. An exception (error) screen will open, and the program will close. Therefore, the program must check the value entered by the user to ensure it is numeric. In addition, if the user enters a nonnumeric value, the program should inform the user of the error and request a valid numeric value.

The Visual Basic **IsNumeric function** can check the input value to determine if it can be converted into a numeric value such as an Integer or Decimal data type. If so, it returns a True Boolean value. If the value is not recognized as a numeric value, the IsNumeric function returns a False Boolean value.

For example, the IsNumeric function can check the value in the Text property of the Square Footage text box. If the user enters a letter such as "a" in the text box, the IsNumeric function will return a False Boolean value because the letter "a" is not numeric.

Because the IsNumeric function returns a Boolean value (True or False), it can be placed within an If statement as the condition to be tested. If the returned value is True, the condition in the If statement is considered true. If the returned value is False, the condition in the If statement is considered false. The code in Figure 5-74 uses an If statement to determine if the Text property of the txtFootage TextBox object is numeric.

IsNumeric   argument for
function   IsNumeric function

```
24      If IsNumeric(txtFootage.Text) Then
 :          Statement(s) executed when condition is true
39      Else
40          'Display MessageBox if user entered nonnumeric value
41          MsgBox("Enter the Square Footage of Decking", , "Input Error")
42          txtFootage.Text = ""
43          txtFootage.Focus()
44      End If
```

FIGURE 5-74

In Figure 5-74, the If statement on line 24 calls the IsNumeric function. The Text property of the txtFootage TextBox object is the argument for the IsNumeric function. As a result of this specification, the IsNumeric function will analyze the data in the Text property of the txtFootage TextBox object. If the data can be converted to a numeric data type, then the function will return a Boolean value of True. If the data cannot be converted to a numeric data type, the function will return a Boolean value of False.

Once the function has returned a Boolean value, the If statement tests the Boolean value. If it is true, the value in the Text property of the txtFootage Text-Box object is numeric, and the appropriate statements are executed. If the condition is false, meaning the value is not numeric, the statements on lines 41-43 are executed. The statement on line 41 displays a message box telling the user to enter the square footage of the decking (see Figure 5-2 on page 229). The caption of the message box is "Input Error". The statement on line 42 clears the Text property. The statement on line 43 sets the focus on the text box so the user can reenter the value.

Check for a Positive Number

If the condition in Figure 5-74 on the previous page is true, the value in the Text property must be converted to a Decimal data type. Then, the program checks to ensure that the entered value is greater than zero. These statements are shown in Figure 5-75.

```
22
23            ' Did user enter a numeric value?
24        If IsNumeric(txtFootage.Text) Then
25            decFootage = Convert.ToDecimal(txtFootage.Text)
26            ' Is Square Footage greater than zero
27            If decFootage > 0 Then
28                ' Determine cost per square foot
29                If radLumber.Checked Then
30                    decCostPerSquareFoot = decLumberCost
31                ElseIf radRedwood.Checked Then
32                    decCostPerSquareFoot = decRedwoodCost
33                ElseIf radComposite.Checked Then
34                    decCostPerSquareFoot = decCompositeCost
35                End If
36                ' Calculate and display the cost estimate
37                decCostEstimate = decFootage * decCostPerSquareFoot
38                lblCostEstimate.Text = decCostEstimate.ToString("C")
39            Else
40                ' Display error message if user entered a negative value
41                MsgBox("You entered " & decFootage.ToString() & ". Enter a Positive Number", , "Input Error")
42                txtFootage.Text = ""
43                txtFootage.Focus()
44            End If
45        Else
46            ' Display error message if user entered a nonnumeric value
47            MsgBox("Enter the Square Footage of Decking", , "Input Error")
48            txtFootage.Text = ""
49            txtFootage.Focus()
50        End If
51    End Sub
52
```

FIGURE 5-75

When the value in the Text property is numeric, it is converted to a Decimal value (line 25). On line 27, the Decimal value is compared to zero. If it is greater than zero, then the processing for a true statement is executed. If the value is not greater than zero, a message box is displayed to inform the user that an invalid entry was made (see Figure 5-29 on page 244). The user then can enter a valid value.

The process of validating input data is fundamental to programming when using a graphical user interface. A well-designed program must ensure that the user enters valid data.

Program Design

As you have learned, the requirements document identifies the purpose of the program being developed, the application title, the procedures to be followed when using the program, any required equations and calculations, any conditions that must be tested, notes and restrictions that must be followed by the program, and any other comments that would be helpful in understanding the problem. The requirements document for the Decking Cost Calculator application is shown in Figure 5-76. The Use Case Definition document is shown in Figure 5-77.

CRITICAL THINKING

Why is it so important to check that each input value is valid? As devices become smaller and more mobile, data validation is more important because it is so easy to accidentally enter incorrect characters with your touch keyboard. Developers cannot have their programs and apps crash each time someone makes an erroneous keystroke. Keep in mind that your instructor will test each of your programs with all kinds of keyboard input to verify that your program will not fail.

REQUIREMENTS DOCUMENT

Date:	January 29, 2019
Date Submitted:	
Application Title:	Decking Cost Calculator
Purpose:	This application calculates the estimated cost of decking for a job bid or homeowner installation.
Program Procedures:	The user should enter the square footage of decking needed and select the type of decking. The estimated cost for the decking job will be displayed.

Algorithms, Processing, and Conditions:

1. The user must be able to enter the number of square feet of decking.
2. The user must be able to select one of three decking types: pressure-treated lumber, redwood, or composite.
3. The user can initiate the calculation and display the cost estimate for the decking.
4. The application computes the cost estimate of the decking based on the number of square feet and the cost of the decking. Pressure-treated lumber costs $2.35 per square foot of decking, redwood costs $7.75 per square foot, and composite costs $8.50 per square foot without the cost of installation.
5. The estimate calculation is square footage * cost per square foot.
6. The cost estimate is displayed in currency format.
7. The user should be able to clear the square footage entered, reset the decking type to pressure-treated lumber, and clear the cost estimate.

Notes and Restrictions:

1. If the user enters a nonnumeric value for the square footage or leaves the TextBox object empty, the user should be advised and asked for a valid entry.
2. If the user enters a negative number for the square footage, the user should be advised and asked for a valid entry.

Comments: The title of the Windows Form should be Decking Cost Calculator.

FIGURE 5-76

USE CASE DEFINITION

1. The window opens and displays the Decking Cost Calculator, a text box requesting the number of square feet for the decking, radio buttons to select the decking type, and two buttons labeled Calculate and Clear.
2. The user enters the square footage and selects one of the decking types.
3. The user clicks the Calculate button.
4. The user will be warned if a nonnumeric value is entered, the text box is left empty, or a negative number is entered.
5. The program displays the cost estimate for the decking materials cost.
6. The user clicks the Clear button to clear the Square Footage text box, set the decking choice to Pressure-Treated Lumber, and erase the cost estimate.
7. The user clicks the Close button to exit the application.

FIGURE 5-77

Event-Planning Document

You will recall that the event-planning document is a table that specifies which objects in the user interface will cause events, the action taken by the user to trigger each event, and the event processing that must occur. The event-planning document for the Decking Cost Calculator application is shown in Figure 5-78.

Event-Planning Document

Program Name: Decking Cost Calculator	Developer: Corinne Hoisington	Object: frmDecking	Date: January 29, 2019
OBJECT	**EVENT TRIGGER**	**EVENT PROCESSING**	
btnCalculate	Click	Ensure data entered is numeric Display error message if data is not numeric or text box is empty Convert data entered to numeric Ensure data entered is greater than zero Display error message if data is not greater than zero Assign decking cost per foot based on type of decking selection Calculate cost (square footage* cost per square foot) Display cost	
btnClear	Click	Clear input text box Clear cost estimate Set the Pressure-Treated Lumber radio button to checked Clear the Redwood radio button Clear the Composite radio button Set focus on input text box	
frmDecking	Load	Set focus on input text box Clear the placement zeros for cost	

FIGURE 5-78

Design and Code the Program

After identifying the events and tasks within the events, the developer is ready to create the program. As you have learned, creating the program means designing the user interface and then entering Visual Basic statements to accomplish the tasks specified in the event-planning document. As the developer enters the code, she also will implement the logic to carry out the required processing.

NOTE TO THE LEARNER

In the following activity, you should complete the tasks within the specified steps. Each of the tasks is accompanied by a Hint Screen. The purpose of the Hint Screen is to indicate where you should perform the activity in the Visual Studio window and to remind you which method to use. If you need further help completing a step, refer to the figure identified by *ref:*.

To design the user interface for the Decking Cost Calculator application and enter the code required to process each event in the program, complete the steps on the next few pages.

Guided Program Development

Phase 1: Design the Form

1

● **Create a Windows Application** Open Visual Studio. Create a new Visual Basic Windows Application project by completing the following: Click the New Project button on the Standard toolbar; click Windows Classic Desktop in the left pane; select Windows Forms App; name the project by entering Decking Cost Calculator in the Name text box; then click the OK button in the New Project window.

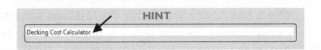

● **Name the Form** In the Solution Explorer pane, right-click Form1.vb and then click Rename. Type frmDecking.vb and then press the ENTER key. Click the Yes button to automatically change the form (Name) in the Properties window.

● **Change the Size Property** In the Properties window, change the Size property to 720, 431.

● **Change the BackColor Property** In the Properties window, change the BackColor property to White.

● **Change the Text on the Title Bar** To change the text on the title bar, click the form, scroll down the Properties window until the Text property is displayed, double-click the right column of the Text property, type Decking Cost Calculator, and then press the ENTER key.

● **Add a Heading Label** Drag a label onto the form and name the label lblHeading. Set the Text property for the Label object to Decking Cost Calculator. Set the font to Goudy Old Style, Bold, 24 points.

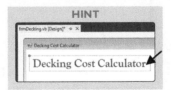

● **Add a Label** Drag a second label onto the frmDecking Form object and name the label lblSquareFeet. Set the Text property of the Label object to Square Footage:. Set the font to Goudy Old Style, Bold, 16 points.

(continues)

● **Add a TextBox Object** Drag a TextBox object onto the
form. Using snap lines, align the top of the TextBox object
with the top of the second Label object. Name the TextBox
object `txtFootage`. Change the TextAlign property to
Center. Change the font to Goudy Old Style, Bold, 16 points.
Reduce the width of the TextBox object to closely resemble
the one in Figure 5-79. Center the Label object and the
TextBox object horizontally below the title label.

*A title Label object is displayed on the first line of the form. A Label object and TextBox object occupy the second
line of the frmDecking Form object (Figure 5-79). They are centered horizontally below the title label.*

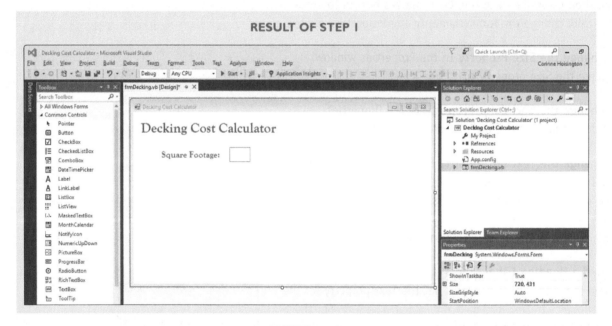

RESULT OF STEP I

FIGURE 5-79

• **Add a GroupBox** Drag a GroupBox object from the Containers category of the Toolbox to the frmDecking Form object. Name the GroupBox grpDeckType. Change the Text property to Decking Type. Set the size of the GroupBox object to 244, 106. Change the BackColor of the GroupBox object to AliceBlue. Center the GroupBox object horizontally below the title label object, and change the font to Goudy Old Style, Regular, 14 points (*ref: Figure 5-4*).

HINT

• **Add Radio Buttons** Place three RadioButton objects on the GroupBox object. Name the first RadioButton radLumber and change its Text property to Pressure-Treated Lumber. Name the second RadioButton radRedwood and change its Text property to Redwood. Name the third RadioButton radComposite and change its Text property to Composite. If necessary, select the three RadioButtons and change the font to Goudy Old Style, Regular, 14 points (*ref: Figure 5-7*).

• **Set Radio Button Properties** Click the radLumber RadioButton object and change its Checked property from False to True. Pressure-treated lumber is the decking most commonly used by homeowners (*ref: Figure 5-12*).

The group box and radio buttons are included on the frmDecking Form object (Figure 5-80). The radLumber radio button is selected because it is the most widely use decking type.

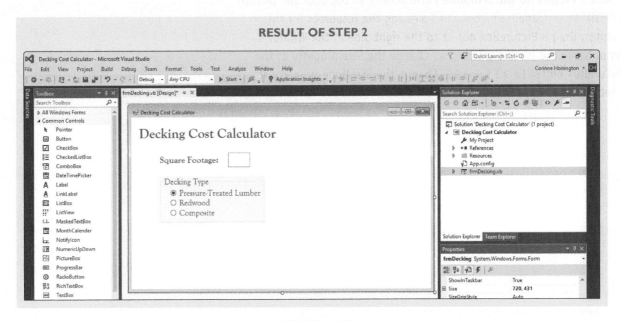

RESULT OF STEP 2

FIGURE 5-80

(continues)

3

- **Add Estimate and Cost Labels** Drag two more Label objects onto the form below the GroupBox object. Align these labels by their tops using snap lines. Name the first label lblCost, change its Text property to Cost Estimate: , and resize the Label object to view the text. Name the second label lblCostEstimate and set its Text property to $0000.00. These placement zeros allow you to view the Label object when it is not selected. The placement zeros will be cleared using code when the form is loaded. Change the font for both Label objects to Goudy Old Style, Bold, 16 points. Horizontally center the labels as a unit below the title label.

- **Add Calculate and Clear Buttons** Drag two Button objects onto the form. Align the tops of the Button objects using snap lines. Name the left Button object btnCalculate and change its Text property to Calculate. Name the right Button object btnClear and change its Text property to Clear. Change the font for these two buttons to Goudy Old Style, Bold, 14 points. Change the size of each button to 116, 41. Change the BackColor property for each button to White.

- **Change the ForeColor Property** Select every object and change the ForeColor property to Sienna.

- **Add a Picture to the Windows Form** Download the deck.jpg picture by visiting CengageBrain.com and accessing the resources for this chapter. Drag a PictureBox object to the right side of the Windows Form. Name the picture picDeck. Change the Size property of the PictureBox object to 338, 390. Change the SizeMode property to StretchImage.

The user interface is complete (Figure 5-81).

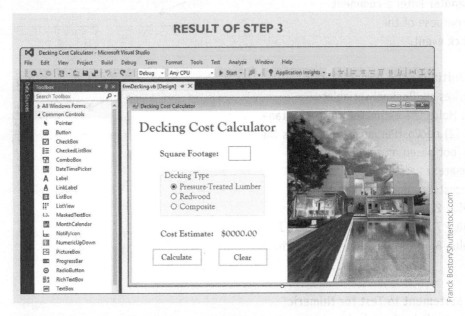

FIGURE 5-81

Phase 2: Code the Application

● **Code the Comments** Double-click the btnCalculate Button object on the frmDecking Form object to open the code window and create the btnCalculate_Click event handler. Close the Toolbox. Click before the first words, Public Class frmDecking, and then press the ENTER key to create a blank line. Insert the first four standard comments. Insert the Option Strict On command at the beginning of the code to turn on strict-type checking.

HINT

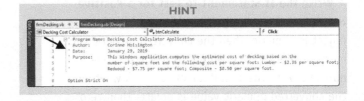

(continues)

● **Add Comments to the btnCalculate
_Click Event Handler** Enter a comment
to describe the purpose of the
btnCalculate_Click event.

● **Declare and Initialize the Variables** This
application requires six Decimal variables:
(1) decFootage: Holds the estimated square footage
of the decking; (2) decCostPerSquareFoot: Holds the
cost per square foot based on the decking type;
(3) decCostEstimate: Is assigned the calculated
final estimated cost; (4) decLumberCost: Is
assigned the value 2.35; (5) decRedwoodCost: Is
assigned the value 7.75; (6) decCompositeCost: Is
assigned the value 8.50. Declare and initialize these
six variables.

● **Write the If Statement to Test for Numeric
Data** When the user clicks the Calculate button, the
program must first ensure that the user entered a
valid numeric value in the txtFootage TextBox
object. If the user has entered a valid numeric
value, the value must be converted from a string
value into a Decimal data type. Write the If
statement and conversion statement required for
this process (*ref: Figure 5-74*).

● **Write the If Statement to Test for a Positive
Number** If the value in the txtFootage TextBox
object is numeric, then the converted numeric value
must be checked to ensure that it is a positive
number. Write the If statement to check whether
the converted numeric value is greater than zero
(*ref: Figure 5-75*).

● **Write the If Statement to Determine the Cost Per Square Foot** When the value is greater than zero, the cost per square foot is determined by checking the status of the RadioButton objects and placing the appropriate cost per square foot in the decCostPerSquareFoot variable. Using the If . . . Then . . . ElseIf structure, write the statements to identify the checked radio button and place the appropriate cost in the decCostPerSquareFoot variable (*ref: Figure 5-49*).

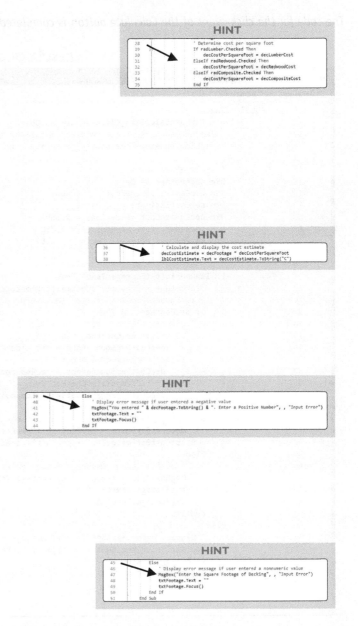

HINT
```
28          ' Determine cost per square foot
29          If radLumber.Checked Then
30              decCostPerSquareFoot = decLumberCost
31          ElseIf radRedwood.Checked Then
32              decCostPerSquareFoot = decRedwoodCost
33          ElseIf radComposite.Checked Then
34              decCostPerSquareFoot = decCompositeCost
35          End If
```

● **Calculate and Display the Cost Estimate** The next step is to calculate the cost estimate by multiplying the value in the decCostPerSquareFoot variable by the square footage. Next, display the cost estimate in the cost estimate label. Write the statements to calculate and display the cost estimate in the currency format.

HINT
```
36          ' Calculate and display the cost estimate
37          decCostEstimate = decFootage * decCostPerSquareFoot
38          lblCostEstimate.Text = decCostEstimate.ToString("C")
```

● **Display a Message Box If the Value Entered Is Not Greater Than Zero** After the processing is finished for the true portion of the If statements, the Else portion of the If statements must be written. Write the code to display the message box that contains the error message when the user enters a value that is not greater than zero (*ref: Figure 5-30*).

HINT
```
39      Else
40          ' Display error message if user entered a negative value
41          MsgBox("You entered " & decFootage.ToString() & ". Enter a Positive Number", , "Input Error")
42          txtFootage.Text = ""
43          txtFootage.Focus()
44      End If
```

● **Display an Error Message If the Value Entered Is Not Numeric** Write the Else portion of the If statement to display an error message if the value entered by the user is not numeric (*ref: Figure 5-74*).

HINT
```
45      Else
46          ' Display error message if user entered a nonnumeric value
47          MsgBox("Enter the Square Footage of Decking", , "Input Error")
48          txtFootage.Text = ""
49          txtFootage.Focus()
50      End If
51  End Sub
```

(continues)

The code for the click event of the Calculate button is completed (Figure 5-82).

RESULT OF STEP 4

frmDecking.vb   ⊔ ✕

VB Decking Cost Calculator   ▾ ● btnCalculate

```vb
10  Public Class frmDecking
11      Private Sub btnCalculate_Click(sender As Object, e As EventArgs) Handles btnCalculate.Click
12          ' The btnCalculate event handler calculates the estimated cost of
13          ' decking based on the square footage and the decking type.
14
15          ' Declaration Section
16          Dim decFootage As Decimal
17          Dim decCostPerSquareFoot As Decimal
18          Dim decCostEstimate As Decimal
19          Dim decLumberCost As Decimal = 2.35D
20          Dim decRedwoodCost As Decimal = 7.75D
21          Dim decCompositeCost As Decimal = 8.5D
22
23          ' Did user enter a numeric value?
24          If IsNumeric(txtFootage.Text) Then
25              decFootage = Convert.ToDecimal(txtFootage.Text)
26              ' Is Square Footage greater than zero
27              If decFootage > 0 Then
28                  ' Determine cost per square foot
29                  If radLumber.Checked Then
30                      decCostPerSquareFoot = decLumberCost
31                  ElseIf radRedwood.Checked Then
32                      decCostPerSquareFoot = decRedwoodCost
33                  ElseIf radComposite.Checked Then
34                      decCostPerSquareFoot = decCompositeCost
35                  End If
36                  ' Calculate and display the cost estimate
37                  decCostEstimate = decFootage * decCostPerSquareFoot
38                  lblCostEstimate.Text = decCostEstimate.ToString("C")
39              Else
40                  ' Display error message if user entered a negative value
41                  MsgBox("You entered " & decFootage.ToString() & ". Enter a Positive Number", , "Input Error")
42                  txtFootage.Text = ""
43                  txtFootage.Focus()
44              End If
45          Else
46              ' Display error message if user entered a nonnumeric value
47              MsgBox("Enter the Square Footage of Decking", , "Input Error")
48              txtFootage.Text = ""
49              txtFootage.Focus()
50          End If
51      End Sub
52
```

FIGURE 5-82

5

● **Create the Clear Button Click Event Handler** The Clear button click event includes the following processing: (1) clear the txtFootage Text property; (2) clear the lblCostEstimate Text property; (3) set the radLumber Checked property to True; (4) set the radRedwood and radComposite Checked properties to False; (5) set the focus in the txtFootage text box. To enter this code, click the frmDecking.vb [Design] tab and then double-click the Clear button. Using IntelliSense, enter the required code.

```
HINT
53    Private Sub btnClear_Click(sender As Object, e As EventArgs) Handles btnClear.Click
54        ' This event handler is executed when the user clicks the Clear button. It
55        ' clears the square footage text box and the cost estimate label, resets the radio
56        ' buttons with Lumber selected, and sets the focus to the square footage text box.
57
58        txtFootage.Clear()
59        lblCostEstimate.Text = ""
60        radLumber.Checked = True
61        radRedwood.Checked = False
62        radComposite.Checked = False
63        txtFootage.Focus()
64    End Sub
```

● **Create the Form Load Event Handler** When the frmDecking Form object loads, the following processing should occur: (1) the focus is in the txtFootage text box; (2) the lblCostEstimate Text property is set to null. Click the frmDecking.vb [Design] tab to return to Design view and then double-click the form. Enter the code for the form load event handler.

```
HINT
66    Private Sub frmDecking_Load(sender As Object, e As EventArgs) Handles MyBase.Load
67        ' This event handler is executed when the form is loaded at the start of
68        ' the program. It sets the focus to the square footage text box and
69        ' clears the cost estimate label.
70
71        txtFootage.Focus()
72        lblCostEstimate.Text = ""
73    End Sub
74 End Class
```

6

● **Run the Application** After you have completed the code, you should run the application to ensure that it works properly.

● **Test the Application** Test the application with the following data: (1) square footage 250, decking type Pressure-Treated Lumber; (2) square footage 210, decking type Composite; (3) square footage 170, decking type Redwood; (4) square footage Fifteen (use this word), decking type Composite; (5) square footage -800, decking type Pressure-Treated Lumber; (6) use other values to thoroughly test the program. After each test, click the Clear button before entering new data.

● **Close the Program** After testing the application, close the window by clicking the Close button in the title bar of the window.

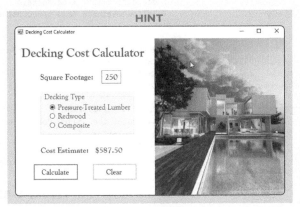

HINT

Code Listing

The complete code for the sample program is shown in Figure 5-83.

```vb
frmDecking.vb + X

VB Decking Cost Calculator                                    ▼ ⨍ (frmDecking Events)

 1    ' Program Name: Decking Cost Calculator Application
 2    ' Author:       Corinne Hoisington
 3    ' Date:         January 29, 2019
 4    ' Purpose:      This Windows application computes the estimated cost of decking based on the
 5    '               number of square feet and the following cost per square foot: Lumber - $2.35 per square foot;
 6    '               Redwood - $7.75 per square foot; Composite - $8.50 per square foot.
 7
 8    Option Strict On
 9
10    Public Class frmDecking
11        Private Sub btnCalculate_Click(sender As Object, e As EventArgs) Handles btnCalculate.Click
12            ' The btnCalculate event handler calculates the estimated cost of
13            ' decking based on the square footage and the decking type.
14
15            ' Declaration Section
16            Dim decFootage As Decimal
17            Dim decCostPerSquareFoot As Decimal
18            Dim decCostEstimate As Decimal
19            Dim decLumberCost As Decimal = 2.35D
20            Dim decRedwoodCost As Decimal = 7.75D
21            Dim decCompositeCost As Decimal = 8.5D
22
23            ' Did user enter a numeric value?
24            If IsNumeric(txtFootage.Text) Then
25                decFootage = Convert.ToDecimal(txtFootage.Text)
26                ' Is Square Footage greater than zero
27                If decFootage > 0 Then
28                    ' Determine cost per square foot
29                    If radLumber.Checked Then
30                        decCostPerSquareFoot = decLumberCost
31                    ElseIf radRedwood.Checked Then
32                        decCostPerSquareFoot = decRedwoodCost
33                    ElseIf radComposite.Checked Then
34                        decCostPerSquareFoot = decCompositeCost
35                    End If
36                    ' Calculate and display the cost estimate
37                    decCostEstimate = decFootage * decCostPerSquareFoot
38                    lblCostEstimate.Text = decCostEstimate.ToString("C")
39                Else
40                    ' Display error message if user entered a negative value
41                    MsgBox("You entered " & decFootage.ToString() & ". Enter a Positive Number", , "Input Error")
42                    txtFootage.Text = ""
43                    txtFootage.Focus()
44                End If
45            Else
46                ' Display error message if user entered a nonnumeric value
47                MsgBox("Enter the Square Footage of Decking", , "Input Error")
48                txtFootage.Text = ""
49                txtFootage.Focus()
50            End If
51        End Sub
```

FIGURE 5-83 (continues)

```
52
53    Private Sub btnClear_Click(sender As Object, e As EventArgs) Handles btnClear.Click
54        ' This event handler is executed when the user clicks the Clear button. It
55        ' clears the square footage text box and the cost estimate label, resets the radio
56        ' buttons with Lumber selected, and sets the focus to the square footage text box.
57
58        txtFootage.Clear()
59        lblCostEstimate.Text = ""
60        radLumber.Checked = True
61        radRedwood.Checked = False
62        radComposite.Checked = False
63        txtFootage.Focus()
64    End Sub
65
66    Private Sub frmDecking_Load(sender As Object, e As EventArgs) Handles MyBase.Load
67        ' This event handler is executed when the form is loaded at the start of
68        ' the program. It sets the focus to the square footage text box and
69        ' clears the cost estimate label.
70
71        txtFootage.Focus()
72        lblCostEstimate.Text = ""
73    End Sub
74 End Class
75
```

FIGURE 5-83 (continued)

Summary

In this chapter, you have learned to make decisions based on the user's input.

1. If a form opens and the first of three RadioButtons is checked within a GroupBox object, what happens to the first RadioButton object when you click the second RadioButton object?

2. Write an If . . . Then statement that tests whether the value in the variable intRow is between 1 and 8. If the number is in that range, set the Text property for the lblCabin Label object to "First Class."

3. Name the six relational operators and state the purpose of each operator.

4. Write an If . . . Then . . . Else statement that assigns 70 to a variable named intSpeed if strInterstate is equal to "I40." Otherwise, assign 60 to intSpeed.

5. List the three most common logical operators and explain their meaning.

6. Rewrite the following line of code without a Not logical operator but keep the same logical processing:

   ```
   If Not decHoloLens <= 429.99 Then
   ```

7. The intent of the following statement is to check whether the radBusTicket RadioButton object is checked. What is the error in the statement? Rewrite the statement so it is correct.

   ```
   If radBusTicket = Checked Then
   ```

8. The intent of the following statement is to check whether the value in the intGrade variable is less than 0 or greater than 100. What is the error in the statement? Rewrite the statement so it is correct.

   ```
   If intGrade < 0 And intGrade > 100 Then
   ```

9. What is the most commonly used container object?

10. One of the most common mistakes when writing an If statement is writing one similar to this statement. Fix this statement.

    ```
    If decShoeSize > 5.5 and < 10.0 Then
    ```

11. What is the prefix for a RadioButton object and a GroupBox object?

12. Write a statement that opens a dialog box with the title "Escape Room" and the message "Group Size of Booking."

13. What is the difference between a Panel object and a GroupBox object?

14. What is the difference between the Or logical operator and the Xor logical operator?

15. Write a data validation statement that would check to ensure that the value in the intAge variable is between 1 and 115. If the age is not valid, display an error message box that states the age is invalid.

16. How many radio buttons in a group can be selected at one time?

17. Using the concatenation operator (&), write a statement that would create the compound word "reunion" from the following two strings: strClass1 = "re" and strClass2 = "union." Assign the compound word to the strCompound string variable.

18. Write a statement that would clear the radio button named radDrake.

19. Write a Select Case statement using the fewest Case statements possible to display the number of days in each month. The user enters the number of the month, such as 8, which is converted to an integer and assigned to the intMonth variable. The Select Case statement should display a message box that states the number of days in the month, such as "31 Days."

20. Which logical operator has the highest precedence in the order of operations?

Debugging Exercises

1. Explain how the two statements shown in Figure 5-84 are evaluated.

```
If strAirline = "Jet Green" AndAlso strHotel = "Homeland Suites" Then

    If strAirline = "Jet Green" And strHotel = "Homeland Suites" Then
```

FIGURE 5-84

2. Identify the error in the code shown in Figure 5-85 and explain how to correct the code.

```
If dblCommission >= 2500 Then
    Dim intBonus As Integer
    intBonus = 500
Else
    intBonus = 0
End If
```

FIGURE 5-85

3. The Select Case statement shown in Figure 5-86 contains one or more errors. Identify the error(s) and rewrite the statements correctly.

```
Select Case intNumberOfSeats
    Case > 5000
        strVenueType = "Stadium"
    Case > 2000
        strVenueType = "Amphitheater"
    Case > 1000
        strVenueType = "Auditorium"
    Case > 200
        strVenueType = "Theater"
    Case > 0
        strVenueType = "Club"
    Else Case
        strVenueType = "Error"
Select End
```

FIGURE 5-86

(continues)

Debugging Exercises *continued*

4. The Select Case statement shown in Figure 5-87 contains one or more errors. Identify the error(s) and rewrite the statements correctly.

```
Select Case charFlightCode
       Case 'F', 'A'
              lblFare.Text = 'First Class'
       Case 'B', 'Q'
              lblFare.Text = 'Business Class'
       Case 'Y', 'S', 'M'
              lblFare.Text = 'Full Fare Economy'
       Case 'K', 'C'
              lblFare.Text = 'Preferred Economy'
       Case 'U', 'J', 'P', 'G'
              lblFare.Text = 'Economy'
       Else
              lblFare.Text = 'Unknown'
End Select
```

FIGURE 5-87

5. The If . . . Then . . . Else statement shown in Figure 5-88 contains one or more errors. Identify the error(s) and rewrite the statements correctly.

```
If strShippingMethod = "Overnite" Then
    If strDeliveryTime = "Morning" Then
        decDeliveryCost = 29.00D
    Else
        decDeliveryCost = 24.00D
Else
    If strShippingMethod = "Two Days" Then
        decDeliveryCost = 14.00D
    Else
        decDeliveryCost = 4.00D
End If
```

FIGURE 5-88

Program Analysis

1. Write an If . . . Then decision structure to compare the two numbers in the decDeveloperPay and decWebDesignerPay variables. Display a message box that states decDeveloperPay is greater than decWebDesignerPay.

2. Write an If statement that displays the message box "A Day's Drive" if the value in the variable decMiles is within the range from 300 to 599.

3. Write an If . . . Then . . . Else statement that checks the value in the variable chrGender for the value M (Male) or F (Female) and assigns the information shown in Figure 5-89 to lblCollegeExpectation.Text based on the gender. If the variable chrGender contains a value other than M or F, assign the message "Invalid Gender" to lblCollegeExpectation.Text.

Gender	College Expectation
Male	75% plan to graduate from college
Female	85% plan to graduate from college

FIGURE 5-89

4. Write a Select Case statement that tests the user's age in a variable named intAge and assigns the generation name of that age group to the variable strGeneration, according to the information shown in Figure 5-90.

Age Group	Generation Name
50 and above	Baby Boomers
39–49	Generation X
18–38	Generation Y
Below 18	Millennials

FIGURE 5-90

5. Rewrite the Select Case statement shown in Figure 5-91 as an If . . . Then . . . Else statement.

```
Select Case chrDepartment
    Case "B", "b"
        strDept = "Baby / Infant Clothing"
    Case "T", "t"
        strDept = "Technology"
End Select
```

FIGURE 5-91

(continues)

6. In each of the following examples, is the condition True or False?

    a. "CVCC" >= "GRCC"

    b. "G" >= "g"

    c. "Nerdy" < "Nerd"

    d. "Cool" <> "cool"

    e. "50" >= "Fifty"

    f. ("Paris" < "Barcelona") And ("Amsterdam" <= "Prague")

    g. ("Ford" > "Chevrolet") Or ("Toyota" < "Honda")

    h. 3 ^ 2 <= 3 * 4

    i. Not ("CNN" >= "ABC")

    j. Not ("Tim" > "Tom") And Not ("Great" <> "great")

Complete one or more of the following case programming assignments. Submit the program and materials you create to your instructor. The level of difficulty is indicated for each assignment.

●	= Easiest
●●	= Intermediate
●●●	= Challenging

1 ●

PLANETARY WEIGHT

Design a Windows Classic Desktop application and write the code that will execute according to the program requirements in Figure 5-92. Before writing the code, create a Use Case Definition, as shown in Figure 5-93. Before writing the code, create an event-planning document for each event in the program. The completed Form object and other objects in the user interface are shown in Figure 5-94 on the next page.

REQUIREMENTS DOCUMENT

Date:	May 6, 2019
Date Submitted:	
Application Title:	Planetary Weight Application
Purpose:	This Windows Classic Desktop application calculates a user's weight in pounds and kilograms on Venus or on Mars.
Program Procedures:	The user enters her weight in pounds and selects either Venus or Mars. The application will determine the user's weight on Venus or Mars in pounds and kilograms.
Algorithms, Processing, and Conditions:	1. The user must be able to enter her weight in pounds and indicate that she wants to see her equivalent weight on Venus or Mars.
	2. One pound on Earth is equivalent to 0.907 pounds on Venus. One pound on Earth is equivalent to 0.377 pounds on Mars.
	3. One pound is equivalent to 0.454 kilograms.
	4. The user must be able to initiate the calculation and the display of her weight on Venus or Mars.
	5. The user must be able to clear her input and the results.
Notes and Restrictions:	1. If the user's weight entry is blank or nonnumeric, the user should be advised and asked for a valid entry.
	2. The results should be displayed one place past the decimal point.
Comments:	Obtain an image for this program from CengageBrain.com. The name of the image file is planets.

FIGURE 5-92

(continues)

PLanetary Weight

USE CASE DEFINITION

1. The Windows Classic Desktop application window opens.
2. The user enters a weight in pounds and selects whether to convert it to the equivalent weight on Venus or Mars.
3. The user clicks the Display button to display the selected weight.
4. The user clears the input and the result by clicking the Clear button.
5. If desired, the user repeats the process.

FIGURE 5-93

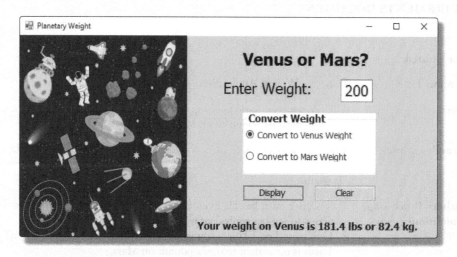

FIGURE 5-94

iStockphoto.com/Askold Romanov

2 COMIC CONVENTION

Design a Windows Classic Desktop application and write the code that will execute according to the program requirements in Figure 5-95 and the Use Case Definition in Figure 5-96. Before writing the code, create an event-planning document for each event in the program. The completed Form object and other objects in the user interface are shown in Figure 5-97.

REQUIREMENTS DOCUMENT

Date:	May 11, 2019
Date Submitted:	
Application Title:	Comic Convention
Purpose:	This Windows Classic Desktop application computes the registration cost of attending a Comic Convention.
Program Procedures:	The user enters the size of the group attending the Comic Convention. The application computes the registration cost for the group based on badge type.

Algorithms, Processing, and Conditions:

1. A user must be able to enter the size of the group and select the desired badge type. The user can select the following badge types:
   - Convention + Superhero Experience ($380)
   - Convention + Autographs ($275)
   - Convention ($209)
2. The user must be able to initiate the registration calculation and the display of the registration cost.
3. The user must be able to clear the entries and results.

Notes and Restrictions:

1. If the user enters a nonnumeric value for the group size or does not enter a group size, the user should be advised and asked for a valid entry.
2. If the user enters a negative group size, the user should be advised and asked for a valid entry.
3. If the value entered is greater than 20, the user should be advised and asked for a valid entry.
4. The registration cost should be displayed in currency format.

Comments:

Obtain an image for this program from CengageBrain.com. The name of the image file is comic.

FIGURE 5-95

(continues)

Comic Convention

USE CASE DEFINITION

1. The Windows Classic Desktop application window opens.
2. The user enters the group size and selects the type of convention badge.
3. The user clicks the Calculate button.
4. The program displays the cost of the convention tickets using currency format.
5. A MsgBox appears and displays a warning if the user enters a negative number for the group size.
6. A MsgBox appears and displays a warning if the user enters a value for the group size that exceeds 20.
7. The user can clear the input and the results by clicking the Clear button.

FIGURE 5-96

FIGURE 5-97

3 ●●
LONDON TUBE TICKETS

Design a Windows Classic Desktop application and write the code that will execute according to the program requirements in Figure 5-98. Before designing the user interface, create a Use Case Definition. Before writing the code, create an event-planning document for each event in the program.

REQUIREMENTS DOCUMENT

Date:	May 6, 2019
Date Submitted:	
Application Title:	London Tube Tickets
Purpose:	This Windows Classic Desktop application calculates the cost of tickets on the London Tube.
Program Procedures:	The user should enter the number of tickets and the zones of intended travel. The ticket cost will be computed and displayed for the entered number of tickets in U.S. dollars. The single-fare adult ticket costs in British pounds are as follows: • Zones 1-3: £4.90 • Zones 1-5: £5.90 • Zones 1-6: £6.00
Algorithms, Processing, and Conditions:	1. The user must enter the number of single-fare tickets. 2. Based on the zones covered, the ticket cost is calculated and then converted to U.S. dollars using the conversion at the website xe.com. 3. The user should be able to clear the number of single-fare tickets, the number of zones, and the cost of the tickets in U.S. dollars.
Notes and Restrictions:	1. If the user enters a nonnumeric value for the number of single-fare tickets, the user should be advised and asked for a valid entry. 2. If the user enters a negative number of tickets or does not enter a number, the user should be advised and asked for a valid entry. 3. The default ticket type is Zones 1–3.
Comments:	n/a

FIGURE 5-98

4

●●
BUILDING PLANS CONVERSION

Design a Windows Classic Desktop application and write the code that will execute according to the program requirements in Figure 5-99. Before designing the user interface, create a Use Case Definition. Before writing the code, create an event-planning document for each event in the program.

REQUIREMENTS DOCUMENT

Date:	May 6, 2019
Date Submitted:	
Application Title:	Building Plans Conversion
Purpose:	This Windows Classic Desktop application converts inches to meters or from meters to inches when building plans need to be converted between Imperial and Metric systems.
Program Procedures:	The user enters the number of inches or meters to be converted and selects either Imperial to Metric or Metric to Imperial.
Algorithms, Processing, and Conditions:	1. The user must be able to enter the measurement to be converted in inches or meters. 2. One inch is equivalent to 0.0254 meters. One meter is equivalent to 39.37008 inches. 3. The user must be able to initiate the calculation and the display of the conversion. 4. The user must be able to clear her input and the results.
Notes and Restrictions:	1. If the user's entry is blank or nonnumeric, the user should be advised and asked for a valid entry. 2. The results should be displayed three places past the decimal point.
Comments:	n/a

FIGURE 5-99

Case Programming Assignments

5 ●●● BROADWAY TICKET GROUP DISCOUNT

Based on the case project shown in Figure 5-100, create a requirements document and a Use Case Definition document and then design a Windows application. Before writing the code, create an event-planning document for each event in the program.

To create a perfect evening for your group, the Broadway Ticket Group Discount Program offers a discount based on group size for excellent orchestra seating. The following table specifies the cost per person. Write this program using Case statements for the total cost of the tickets sold as a group. Do not accept requests for negative values or 100+ tickets.

Group Size	Broadway Tickets per Person
1-8	$249
9-12	$219
13-24	$199
25-99	$169

FIGURE 5-100

Case Programming Assignments

6 ●●● PARTY PLATTERS

Based on the case project shown in Figure 5-101, create a requirements document and a Use Case Definition document and then design a Windows application. Before writing the code, create an event-planning document for each event in the program.

> A local grocery store offers party platters made to order. The grocery store has asked you to create a Windows application that allows customers to enter their orders on a flat-screen computer. Create an application that allows the user to select one of five party platters. Create and display a list of platters of your own choice, along with a display of prices for each platter using radio buttons. A second radio button group should request if the customer will pre-pay or pay upon order pickup. The grocery store has a loyalty program that deducts 5 percent of the total order cost for every 10 points a customer has earned. Allow users to enter their total number of loyalty points and compute the cost of their order. Customers cannot receive money back if their loyalty points exceed the full cost of their order.

FIGURE 5-101

CHAPTER 6

Loop Structures

OBJECTIVES

You will have mastered the material in this chapter when you can:

- Add a MenuStrip object

- Use the InputBox function

- Display data using the ListBox object

- Add a Background Image

- Understand the use of counters and accumulators

- Understand the use of compound operators

- Repeat a process using a For… Next loop

- Repeat a process using a Do loop

- Avoid infinite loops

- Prime a loop

- Validate data

- Create a nested loop

- Select the best type of loop

- Debug using DataTips at breakpoints

- Publish a finished application using ClickOnce technology

Introduction

In Chapter 5, you learned about the decision structure, one of the major control structures used in computer programming. In this chapter, you will learn another major structure called the **looping structure**, or the **iteration structure**.

A fundamental process in a computer program is to repeat a series of instructions either while a condition is true (or not true) or until a condition is true (or not true). For example, if a company is processing electronic pay checks for 5,000 employees, it can use the same set of instructions to post an electronic deposit for each employee, varying only the name of the employee and amount paid for each check. This process would continue until all checks are deposited. Unique check deposit instructions for each employee in the company are not required.

The process of repeating a set of instructions while a condition is true or until a condition is true is called **looping**. When the program is executing those instructions, it is said to be in a loop. Another term for looping is **iteration**.

The programming project in this chapter uses a loop to obtain input data and produce output information. A large company challenged groups of eight employees to form weight loss fitness teams. The Human Resource department requested a Windows application that determines the average weight loss for each team. This application, called the Fitness Challenge application, computes the average weight loss for up to eight team members who enter the total number of pounds they lost during their weight loss challenge. The application uses a loop to request and display the weight loss amounts of the team members. The application then displays the average weight loss by the fitness team (Figure 6-1).

File menu

Enter Weight Loss button

eight weight loss values entered

average weight loss for the team

FIGURE 6-1

iStockphoto.com/udra

Figure 6-1 shows eight values the user entered in a list. After the user enters the weight loss values, the application calculates the average weight loss of the entire team.

When the Fitness Challenge application begins, the main window shows no weight loss values (Figure 6-2).

no weight loss values entered

FIGURE 6-2

iStockphoto.com/udra

When the user clicks the Enter Weight Loss button, the Weight Loss dialog box opens (Figure 6-3), allowing the user to enter the weight loss of the first team member. This dialog box is called an **input box**.

user enters weight loss amount here

FIGURE 6-3

After entering the first weight loss value, the user clicks the OK button in the Weight Loss dialog box. The application lists the weight loss value in the main window and then displays the input box again, requesting the next team member's weight loss. This process repeats for up to eight team members and is implemented using a loop in the program. When the user is entering weight loss values, the program is said to be in a loop. The loop is terminated when the user enters the weight loss for the eighth team member or clicks the Cancel button in the Weight Loss dialog box. After the loop is terminated, the Fitness Challenge application displays the average weight loss for the team, as shown in Figure 6-1 on page 302.

The Fitness Challenge application has several other features. Figure 6-1 shows a menu bar containing the File menu at the top of the window. The File menu contains the Clear command, which clears the list and the average weight loss, and the Exit command, which closes the window and ends the application. In this chapter, you will learn to design and code a menu.

In addition, the application contains input validation. For example, if a user enters a nonnumeric or negative value for the weight loss, the application requests the weight loss amount again, until the user enters a reasonable value.

Finally, the application displays the average weight loss to one decimal place, such as 11.2 lbs.

User Interface Design

The user interface for the Fitness Challenge application includes three new elements: a menu, an input box, and a list for the weight loss values. The menu and the list of team member weight loss values are objects placed on the Windows Form object. The input box is created through the use of a function call in the program code. Each of these items is explained in the following sections.

Insert a MenuStrip Object

A **menu bar** is a strip across the top of a window that contains one or more menu names. A **menu** is a group of commands, or items, presented in a list. In the sample program, a File menu is created in the application window (Figure 6-4).

FIGURE 6-4

When the user clicks File on the menu bar during program execution, a menu appears with two commands: Clear and Exit. The user clicks the Clear menu command to clear the entered weight values and the results. Clicking the Exit menu command ends the application. An advantage of a menu is that it conserves space instead of cluttering the form with objects such as buttons.

Using Visual Studio 2017, you can place menus at the top of a Windows Form using the MenuStrip object. To place a MenuStrip object on a Windows Form, you can complete the following steps:

STEP 1   With a Windows Form object open in the Visual Studio window, scroll in the Toolbox to display the Menus & Toolbars category. If the category is not open, click the expand icon (the right-pointing triangle) next to the Menus & Toolbars category name. Drag the MenuStrip .NET component to the Windows Form object.

The pointer changes when you place it over the Windows Form object (Figure 6-5).

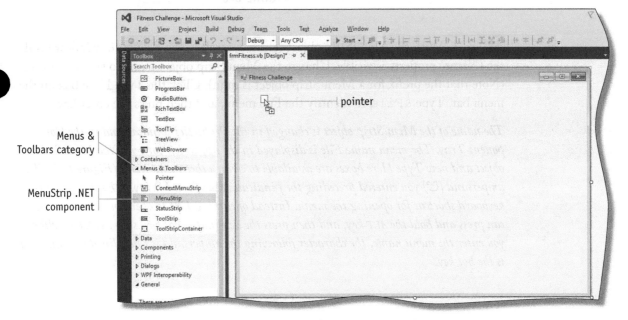

FIGURE 6-5

STEP 2   Release the object.

Visual Studio places the MenuStrip object at the top of the form regardless of where you released the object (Figure 6-6). The Component Tray, which is displayed below the form, organizes nongraphical Toolbox objects. It displays the MenuStrip1 object name.

Type Here box

menu strip

Component
Tray

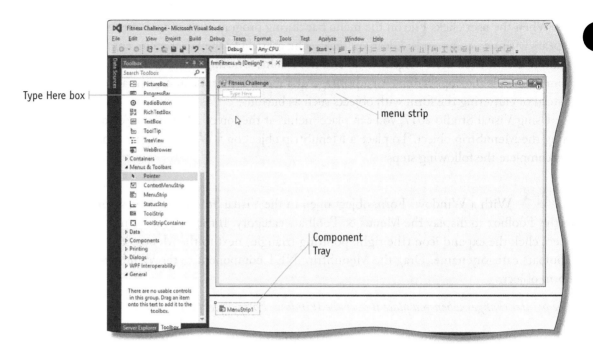

FIGURE 6-6

STEP 3   With the MenuStrip object selected, scroll in the Properties window until
the (Name) property is visible. Change the MenuStrip object name to `mnuFitness`.
(Note that the prefix for a MenuStrip object is mnu). Click the Type Here box on the
menu bar. Type `&File` to identify the File menu, and then press the enter key.

*The name of the MenuStrip object is changed in the Properties window and in the Com-
ponent Tray. The menu name File is displayed in the upper-left corner of the MenuStrip
object and new Type Here boxes are available to create other menu items (Figure 6-7). The
ampersand (&) you entered preceding the f indicates that f is a hot key. A hot key provides a
keyboard shortcut for opening the menu. Instead of clicking File to open the menu, the user
can press and hold the ALT key, and then press the designated hot key, such as ALT+F. After
you enter the menu name, the character following the ampersand is underlined to indicate it
is the hot key.*

File menu
name

F is
underlined

new Type Here
boxes

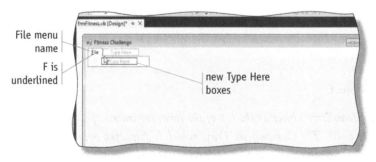

FIGURE 6-7

STEP 4   Click File in the MenuStrip object to select it, scroll in the Properties window to the (Name) property, and then change the name to `mnuFile`. To add a menu item to the File menu, click the Type Here box below the File menu name. Type `&Clear` and then press ENTER to create a new menu item named Clear with c as the hot key.

The name of the File menu is displayed in the (Name) property in the Properties window. The Clear menu item is displayed below the File menu (Figure 6-8). After you press the ENTER key, the character following the ampersand is underlined to indicate it is the hot key.

Clear menu item

C is underlined

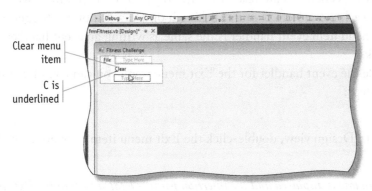

FIGURE 6-8

STEP 5   On the File menu, click Clear to select it, scroll in the Properties window until the (Name) property is visible, and then change the name to `mnuClear`.

The mnuClear name is displayed in the (Name) property in the Properties window (Figure 6-9).

(Name) property

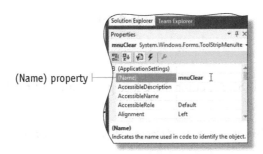

FIGURE 6-9

The letter representing a hot key appears underlined in the menu name, as shown in Figure 6-8. The first letter often is used for the hot key, but not always. For example, in the chapter project, the File menu includes the Exit item (see Figure 6-4 on page 304). The hot key typically used for the Exit item is the letter x. When entering the Exit menu item on the File menu, the developer can type E&xit, which assigns the letter following the & (x) as the hot key.

When assigning menu item hot keys, you should be aware that they are not case-sensitive. Therefore, you should not assign "T" to one menu item and "t" to another.

Event Handlers for Menu Items

Recall that the design of the user interface occurs before you write the code for event handlers. When you are ready to write code, however, you must write an event handler for each menu item because clicking it or using its hot key triggers an event. Writing a menu item event handler is the same as writing an event handler for a button click.

To code the event handler for the Exit menu item, you can complete the following steps:

STEP 1   In Design view, double-click the Exit menu item to open the code window.

The code window is displayed and the insertion point is located within the Exit item click event handler (Figure 6-10). When the user clicks the Exit item on the File menu, the code in the event handler will be executed.

FIGURE 6-10

STEP 2   Using IntelliSense, enter the Close procedure call to close the window and exit the application.

When executed, the Close procedure will close the window and the program (Figure 6-11).

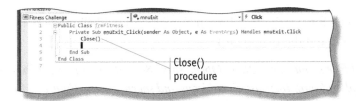

FIGURE 6-11

Insert Standard Items for a Menu

Developers often customize the MenuStrip object for the specific needs of an application. In addition, Visual Basic 2017 contains an **Action Tag** that allows you to create a full standard menu bar commonly provided in Windows programs, with File, Edit, Tools, and Help menus. In Visual Basic 2017, an Action Tag appears in the upper-right corner of many objects, including a MenuStrip. Action Tags provide a way for you to specify a set of actions, called **smart actions**, for an object as you design a form. For example, to insert a full standard menu, you can complete the following steps:

STEP 1 With a new Windows Form object open, drag the MenuStrip .NET component onto the Windows Form object. Click the Action Tag on the MenuStrip object.

The MenuStrip Tasks menu opens (Figure 6-12).

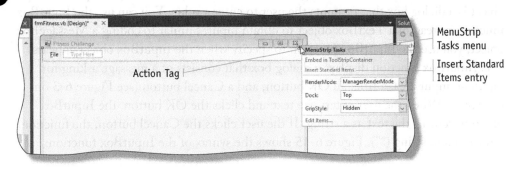

FIGURE 6-12

STEP 2 Click Insert Standard Items on the MenuStrip Tasks menu.

The MenuStrip object contains four menu names: File, Edit, Tools, and Help (Figure 6-13). These are the standard menus found in many Windows applications. Each menu contains the items typically listed on the menus.

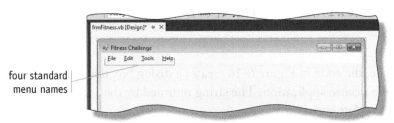

FIGURE 6-13

STEP 3   Click File on the menu bar to view the individual menu items, their associated icons, and their shortcut keys.

The standard File menu items (New, Open, Save, Save As, Print, Print Preview, and Exit) are displayed with their associated icons and shortcut keys (Figure 6-14). The other menus also contain standard items. You can code an event handler for each menu item by double-clicking the item.

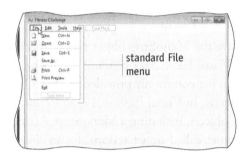

FIGURE 6-14

Use the InputBox Function

To calculate a team's weight loss, the Fitness Challenge application uses an InputBox object in which users enter the weight loss of each team member. The InputBox object is a dialog box that prompts the user to enter a value. You can use the InputBox function instead of a TextBox object to obtain input. Similar to coding a MessageBox object, you use the InputBox function to specify when the InputBox object appears. The InputBox function displays a dialog box that consists of a message asking for input, an input area, a title, an OK button, and a Cancel button (see Figure 6-3 on page 303). When the user enters the text and clicks the OK button, the InputBox function returns the text as a string. If the user clicks the Cancel button, the function returns a null string (""). Figure 6-15 shows the syntax of the InputBox function:

General Format: InputBox Function

```
strVariableName = InputBox("Question to Prompt User",
                        "Title Bar")
```

FIGURE 6-15

For example, the code in Figure 6-16 creates a dialog box that requests the user's age for a driver's license application. The string returned by the InputBox function is assigned to the strAge variable.

```
5          Dim strAge As String
6
7          strAge = InputBox("Please enter your age", "Driver's License Agency")
```

FIGURE 6-16

When the application runs, the InputBox object in Figure 6-17 opens, requesting that the user enter his or her age.

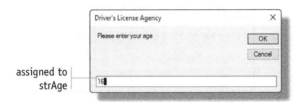

assigned to
strAge

FIGURE 6-17

The InputBox object returns all data entered as a string, which then can be converted to the appropriate data type.

Display a Default Value in an InputBox Object

The InputBox object can be assigned a default value. For example, if a college application for admission requests the student's home state and the college or university is located in Ohio, the most likely state, Ohio, can be the default value in the InputBox, as shown in Figure 6-18.

default value

FIGURE 6-18

The code to produce this input box is shown in Figure 6-19.

```
9          Dim strState As String
10
11         strState = InputBox("Please enter the state in which you reside:", _
12             "College Application", "Ohio")
```

FIGURE 6-19

As you can see, the third argument for the InputBox function call is the default value that is placed in the input box. It must be a String value and follow the syntax shown in Figure 6-19.

Create the InputBox Object for Fitness Challenge Application

The Fitness Challenge application uses an InputBox object that requests the weight loss amounts of team members numbered 1–8, as shown in Figure 6-20.

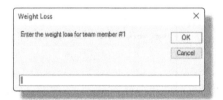

FIGURE 6-20

The code for the Weight Loss InputBox is shown in Figure 6-21. Notice that the prompt message for the user is assigned to the strInputMessage variable, and the title bar text (Weight Loss) is assigned to the strInputHeading variable.

```
15        Dim strWeightLoss As String
16        Dim strInputMessage As String = "Enter the weight loss for team member #"
17        Dim strInputHeading As String = "Weight Loss"
18        Dim intNumberOfEntries As Integer = 1
19
20        strWeightLoss = InputBox(strInputMessage & intNumberOfEntries, strInputHeading, " ")
21
```

FIGURE 6-21

The variable intNumberOfEntries identifies the team member's number. It is included in the prompt message through the use of concatenation. The variable intNumberOfEntries is incremented later in the code so that it refers to the correct team member each time the InputBox function call is executed.

In Figure 6-21, the default value is specified as a space (" "). When the input box is displayed, a space will be selected in the input area. This space is required so that if a user clicks the OK button without entering any data, the InputBox will not return a null character (" "), which indicates the user clicked the Cancel button. This normally is a good programming practice.

When the user clicks the Cancel button in an input box and the InputBox function returns a null character, the program can test for the null character to determine further processing.

Display Data Using the ListBox Object

In the Fitness Challenge application, the user enters weight loss values into the InputBox object, and the application displays the weight loss values in a list box (see Figure 6-1 on page 302). To create such a list, you use the ListBox object provided in the Visual Basic Toolbox. A ListBox object displays a group of values, called items, with one item per line. To add a ListBox object to a Windows Form object, you can complete the following steps:

STEP 1 Drag the ListBox object from the Toolbox to where you want to place the ListBox object on the Windows Form object. When the pointer is in the correct location, release the object.

The ListBox object is placed on the form (Figure 6-22).

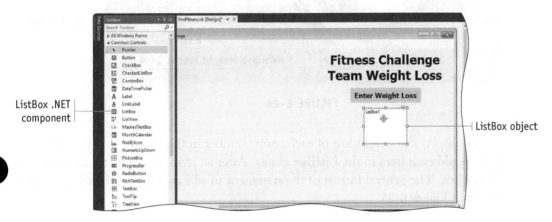

FIGURE 6-22

STEP 2 With the ListBox object selected, scroll in the Properties window to the (Name) property. Name the ListBox object `lstWeightLoss`.

The name you entered is displayed in the (Name) property in the Properties window (Figure 6-23). Notice a ListBox object name begins with lst (be sure to use a lowercase letter l, not the number one).

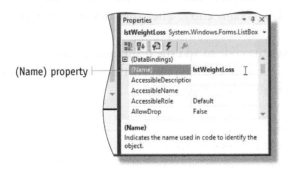

FIGURE 6-23

After placing a ListBox object on the Windows Form object, you can adjust the size by dragging the size handles. Be sure to resize the ListBox so that it is large enough to hold the application data. The ListBox object for the Fitness Challenge application is designed to be wide enough to hold three digits and a decimal point and long enough to hold eight numbers (Figure 6-24).

FIGURE 6-24

iStockphoto.com/udra

To display the weight loss of each team member in the list box, you must write code to add each item to the ListBox object. After an item is added, it is displayed in the list box. The general format of the statement to add an item to a ListBox object is shown in Figure 6-25.

General Format: Adding Items to a ListBox Object

```
lstListBoxName.Items.Add(Variable Name)
```

FIGURE 6-25

In Figure 6-25, the Add procedure will add the item contained in the variable identified by the Variable Name entry. The syntax for the statement must be followed precisely.

Figure 6-26 shows the code to add the team member weight loss values to the lstWeightLoss ListBox object and then display the weight loss of each team member (decWeightLoss) in the ListBox object.

```
45    lstWeightLoss.Items.Add(decWeightLoss)
```

FIGURE 6-26

If the number of items exceeds the number that can be displayed in the designated length of the ListBox object, a scroll bar automatically is added to the ListBox object, as shown in Figure 6-27.

FIGURE 6-27

iStockphoto.com/udra

To clear the items in a ListBox object, the Clear method works as it does for the TextBox object. The syntax of the statement to clear the ListBox is shown in Figure 6-28.

> **General Format:** Clear the ListBox Object
>
> ```
> lstListBoxName.Items.Clear()
> ```

FIGURE 6-28

In the Fitness Challenge application, the user can select the Clear menu item to clear the form. The code in Figure 6-29 removes the items from the lstWeightLoss ListBox.

```
81        lstWeightLoss.Items.Clear()
```

FIGURE 6-29

Can I control where the InputBox appears on the screen?

To control the position of the InputBox, you can add an optional X position and Y position representing the upper-left edge of the dialog box. The syntax of the InputBox with sample X and Y positions is as follows:

myValue = InputBox(message, title, defaultValue, 150, 100)

The 150 pixels represents the X position (horizontal) and the 100 pixels represents the Y position (vertical).

Add ListBox Items during Design

The Fitness Challenge application allows the user to add items to the ListBox object during program execution, but you can also add items to a ListBox object while designing the form. Adding items to the ListBox object during the design phase allows the user to select an item from the ListBox object during execution. For example, in an application to select a favorite clothing store, you can add items to a ListBox object named lstStores during the form design by completing the following steps:

STEP 1   Assume the lstStores ListBox object already has been placed and named on the Windows Form object. Select the ListBox object on the Windows Form object and then click the Items property in the Properties window.

The Items property in the Properties window is selected. An ellipsis button appears to the right of the (Collection) entry (Figure 6–30).

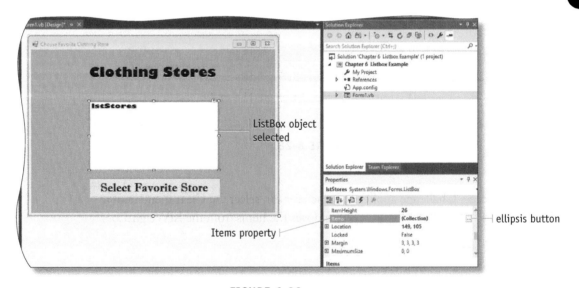

FIGURE 6-30

STEP 2   Click the ellipsis button in the right column of the Items property.

The String Collection Editor window opens, allowing you to enter items that will be displayed in the lstStores ListBox object (Figure 6–31).

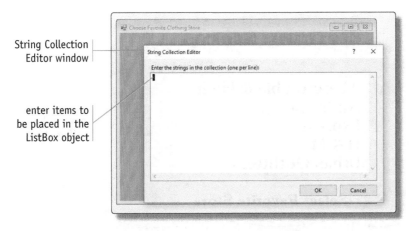

String Collection
Editor window

enter items to
be placed in the
ListBox object

FIGURE 6-31

STEP 3   Click the String Collection Editor window. Type the following items to represent popular retail stores, and then press ENTER at the end of each line:

```
Abercrombie & Fitch
Anthropologie
Express
H & M
Urban Outfitters
```

The items representing favorite retail stores appear in the String Collection Editor window on separate lines (Figure 6-32).

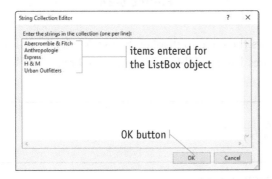

items entered for
the ListBox object

OK button

FIGURE 6-32

STEP 4   Click the OK button.

The Windows Form object displays the stores in the lstStores ListBox object (Figure 6-33). The user can select one of the items in the ListBox object during execution.

FIGURE 6-33

Use the SelectedItem Property

The SelectedItem property identifies which item in the ListBox is selected. An assignment statement assigns that property to a variable, as shown in Figure 6-34.

> **General Format: Assign the Selected Item in a ListBox Object**
>
> ```
> StrVariableName = lstListBoxName.selectedItem
> ```

FIGURE 6-34

Figure 6-35 shows the code to display the user's selection of his or her favorite store from the lstStores ListBox object in a message box.

```
5        MsgBox("Your favorite store is "_
6        &lstStores.SelectedItem & ".")
```

FIGURE 6-35

Add a Background Image

In addition to using background colors to design the Windows Form object, you may want to place a background image on the form itself. Background images are commonly displayed in your Facebook header and in mobile apps such as clouds in the background of the Weather Channel app. The **BackgroundImage** property of the Form object can set the background image to an imported image. The **Background ImageLayout** property can be used to control the appearance of the image on the form. By default the background image repeats the same picture in a tile pattern, but the BackgroundImageLayout property can be changed to Center, Stretch, or Zoom.

To change the background image on the form, you can complete the following steps, which assumes that you have downloaded the health image file from the CengageBrain site.

STEP 1 Click the Form object. In the Properties window, click the ellipsis button of the BackgroundImage property. Click the Import button and open the file location of the health image file. Click health.jpg and click the Open button.

The Select Resource window displays the imported background image file named health.jpg (Figure 6-36).

Select Resource dialog box

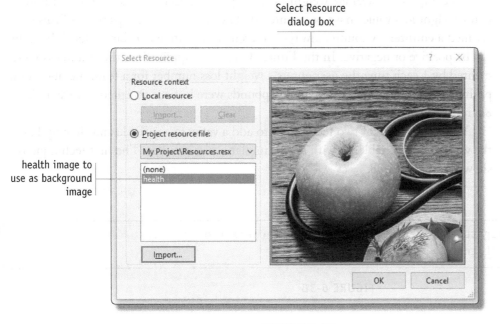

health image to use as background image

FIGURE 6-36

iStockphoto.com/udra

STEP 2 Click the OK button.

The background image health.jpg is displayed in the frmFitness form (Figure 6-37).

health image displayed in background

FIGURE 6-37

iStockphoto.com/udra

After the user enters the weight loss values of up to eight team members, the Fitness Challenge application calculates the average weight loss (see Figure 6-1 on page 302). The formula to calculate the average weight loss is: (total of all weight loss values entered) / (number of team members). For example, if the total of all the weight loss values entered is 145.2 and weight loss values were entered for eight team members, the average weight loss is 18.2 pounds.

To calculate the average, the program must add the weight loss of each team member to a variable. The variable that contains an accumulated value such as the total of all the weight loss values is called an **accumulator**.

To compute the average weight loss, the program must also keep track of how many weight loss values have been entered. The variable that keeps track of this value is called a **counter**. A counter always is incremented with a constant value. This value can be positive or negative. In the Fitness Challenge application, the counter is incremented by 1 each time the user enters a weight loss number for a team member. Only positive values that indicate how many pounds were lost are accepted; for example, 8.3 represents 8.3 pounds lost.

You can use one of two techniques to add a value to a variable and then update the value in the variable, as with an accumulator or a counter. The first technique is shown in Figure 6-38.

```
26        decTotalWeightLoss = decTotalWeightLoss + decWeightLoss
27        intNumberOfEntries = intNumberOfEntries + 1
```

FIGURE 6-38

CRITICAL THINKING

Why are accumulators typically found within a loop?
An accumulator calculates a running total. For example, at a basketball game, a three-point shot adds three points to the present score, so an accumulator of score += 3 adds three points to the existing score. The repetition of the game allows many three pointers to be scored, so each time the scorekeeper clicks the three-point button, the loop repeats and the score code statement within the loop accumulates three more points in its value.

On line 26 in Figure 6-38, the value in the decTotalWeightLoss variable is added to the value in the decWeightLoss variable and the result is stored in the decTotalWeightLoss variable. This statement accumulates the weight loss values in the decTotalWeightLoss accumulator. The statement in line 27 increments the number of entries counter by 1. The effect is that the value in the number of entries counter is increased by 1 each time the statement is executed.

A second method for accomplishing this task is to use a shortcut mathematical operator called a **compound operator** that allows you to add, subtract, multiply, divide, use modulus or exponents, or concatenate strings, storing the result in the same variable. An assignment statement that includes a compound operator begins with the variable that will contain the accumulated value, such as an accumulator or a counter, followed by the compound operator. A compound operator consists of an arithmetic operator and an equal sign. The last element in the assignment statement is the variable or literal containing the value to be used in the calculation.

An assignment statement using a compound operator such as:

```
intNumberOfEntries += 1
```

is the same as:

```
intNumberOfEntries = intNumberOfEntries + 1
```

The += compound operator adds the value of the right operand to the value of the left operand and stores the result in the left operand's variable. Similarly, the statement:

```
decTotalWeightLoss += decWeightLoss
```

is the same as:

```
decTotalWeightLoss = decTotalWeightLoss + decWeightLoss
```

The table in Figure 6-39 shows an example of compound operators used in code. Assume that intResult = 24, decResult = 24, and strSample = "tree".

Operation	Example with Single Operators	Example with Compound Operator	Result
Addition	intResult = intResult + 1	intResult + = 1	intResult = 25
Subtraction	intResult = intResult − 3	intResult − = 3	intResult = 21
Multiplication	intResult = intResult * 2	intResult * = 2	intResult = 48
Decimal Division	decResult = decResult / 5	decResult / = 5	decResult = 4.8
Integer Division	intResult = intResult \ 5	intResult \ = 5	intResult = 4
Exponents	intResult = intResult ^ 2	intResult ^ = 2	intResult = 576
Concatenate	strSample = strSample & "house"	strSample & = "house"	strSample = "tree house"

FIGURE 6-39

Developers often use compound operators in Visual Basic coding. The coding example in Figure 6-40 uses several compound operators and a MsgBox object. When the following code is executed, the result shown in the MsgBox object is "Final Result = 2."

```
30          Dim intTotal As Integer
31          intTotal = 7
32          intTotal += 6
33          intTotal *= 2
34          intTotal /= 13
35          MsgBox("Final Result = " & intTotal.ToString(), , "Compound Operators")
```

FIGURE 6-40

Compound operators can also be used to connect two strings with the concatenation operator (&). The code in Figure 6-41 creates the phrase "To err is human!" in a MsgBox object by using compound operators to concatenate the strPhrase variable. Each compound operator joins another word to the end of the phrase assigned to the strPhrase variable.

```
30          Dim strPhrase As String
31          strPhrase = "To err"
32          strPhrase &= " is "
33          strPhrase &= "human!"
34          MsgBox(strPhrase, , "Compound Operators")
```

FIGURE 6-41

Use Loops to Perform Repetitive Tasks

In the Fitness Challenge application, the user enters weight loss values in an InputBox for up to eight team members. The repetitive process of entering eight weight loss values can be coded within a loop to simplify the task with fewer lines of code. Unlike If…Then statements that execute only once, loops repeat multiple times.

Each repetition of the loop is called an iteration. An iteration is a single execution of a set of instructions that are to be repeated.

Loops are powerful structures that repeat a section of code a certain number of times or until a particular condition is met. Visual Basic has two main types of loops: For...Next loops and Do loops.

Repeat a Process Using the For...Next Loop

You can use a For...Next loop when a section of code should be executed an exact number of times. The syntax of a For...Next loop is shown in Figure 6-42.

General Format: For...Next loop

```
For Control Variable = Beginning Numeric Value To Ending
                       Numeric Value

   ' Body of the Loop

Next
```

FIGURE 6-42

In Figure 6-42, the For...Next loop begins with the keyword For. Following this keyword is the control variable, which is the numeric variable that keeps track of the number of iterations the loop completes. To begin the loop, the For statement places the beginning numeric value in the control variable. The program then executes the code between the For and Next statements, which is called the body of the loop.

Upon reaching the Next statement, the program returns to the For statement and increments the value of the control variable. This process continues until the value in the control variable is greater than the ending numeric value. The program then executes the statement(s) that follows the Next command.

Figure 6-43 shows a For...Next loop designed to execute four times. The control value is a variable named intNumber.

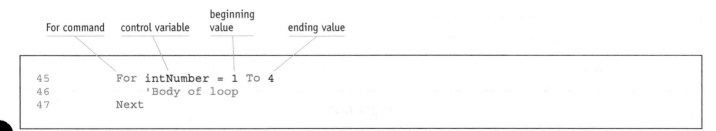

FIGURE 6-43

The first line in Figure 6-43 specifies that the control variable (intNumber) is assigned the value 1 because the literal 1 is the beginning value. Then the program executes the body of the loop. When the program encounters the Next statement, control returns to the For statement where, by default, the value 1 is added to the control variable. The code in the body of the loop is executed again. This process continues until the value in the control variable is greater than the ending value, which is 4 in this example. Then the program executes the statement(s) that follow the Next command. A loop never ends in the middle of the loop. The comparison is made to the upper limit of the For statement, and when the value exceeds the upper limit, the loop terminates. The table in Figure 6-44 illustrates the looping process.

Loop Iteration	Value of intNumber	Process
1	intNumber = 1	Executes the code inside the loop
2	intNumber = 2	Executes the code inside the loop
3	intNumber = 3	Executes the code inside the loop
4	intNumber = 4	Executes the code inside the loop
5 (exits the loop)	intNumber = 5	The control variable value exceeds the ending value, so the application exits the For...Next loop. This means the statement(s) following the Next command are executed.

FIGURE 6-44

Include a Step Value in a For...Next Loop

A Step value is the value in a For...Next loop that is added to or subtracted from the beginning value on each iteration of the loop. If you do not include a Step value in the For statement, as shown in Figure 6-45, by default the value in the control variable is incremented by 1 after each iteration of the loop.

Step value

```
49        For intNumber = 1 To 99 Step 2
50            ' Body of loop
51        Next
```

FIGURE 6-45

In Figure 6-45, a Step value of 2 has been added to the For statement. The control variable intNumber is set to the initial value of 1, and the lines of code in the body of the loop are executed. After the first iteration of the loop, the Step value is added to the control variable, changing the value in the control variable to 3 (1 + 2 = 3). The For loop will continue until the value in intNumber is greater than 99.

The Step value can be negative. If so, the value in the control variable is decreased on each iteration of the loop. To exit the loop, you must specify an ending value that is less than the beginning value, as shown in Figure 6-46.

negative
Step value

```
55          For intCount = 25 To -10 Step -5
56              ' Body of loop
57          Next
```

FIGURE 6-46

In the first iteration of the For...Next loop in Figure 6-46, the control variable value is 25. The value in the intCount control variable is decreased by 5 each time the loop repeats. This repetition continues until the value in intCount is less than –10. Then the loop ends.

You can also assign decimal values to the control variable in a For...Next loop. For example, the For loop in Figure 6-47 has a starting value of 3.1. The loop ends when the value in the control variable is greater than 4.5. The Step value is 0.1, which means the value in decNumber increments by 0.1 on each pass through the loop.

decimal
Step value

```
61          For decNumber = 3.1 To 4.5 Step 0.1
62              ' Body of loop
63          Next
```

FIGURE 6-47

A For...Next loop can also include variables and mathematical expressions, as shown in Figure 6-48.

```
69            For intNumber = intBegin To (intEnd * 2) Step intIncrement
70                'Body of loop
71            Next
```

FIGURE 6-48

In Figure 6-48, the intNumber control variable is initialized with the value in the intBegin variable. Each time the Next statement is encountered and control is returned to the For statement, the value in intNumber is incremented by the value in the intIncrement variable. The loop continues until the value in intNumber is greater than the product of the value in intEnd times 2.

Use IntelliSense to Enter the For...Next Loop Code

Suppose an application is designed to have a list box that displays the population growth for Alaska during the next six years. Assume that the current population of Alaska is 675,000 people and is expected to grow at 5 percent per year for the next six years. The code in Figure 6-49 accomplishes this processing.

```
4      Dim intAlaskaPopulation As Integer = 675000
5      Dim intYears As Integer
6
7      For intYears = 1 To 6
8          intAlaskaPopulation += (intAlaskaPopulation * 0.05)
9          lstGrowth.Items.Add("Year " & intYears & " Population " & intAlaskaPopulation)
10
11     Next
```

FIGURE 6-49

To use IntelliSense to enter the code shown in Figure 6-49, you can complete the following steps, which assume a lstGrowth ListBox object has been defined on a Windows Form object.

STEP 1   In the code window, type Dim intAlaskaPopulation As Integer = 675000 and then press the ENTER key. Type Dim intYears As Integer and then press the ENTER key two times. Type for and a space to open an IntelliSense list.

When you press the SPACEBAR, For is capitalized because it is a reserved word (Figure 6-50).

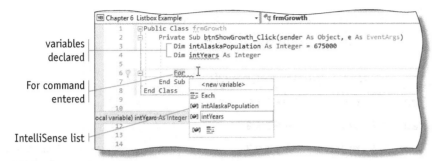

FIGURE 6-50

STEP 2 Type the first four letters of the intYears variable name (intY) to select intYears in the IntelliSense list. Type = 1 to 6 and then press the ENTER key to specify the beginning value and ending value for the loop.

Visual Basic automatically inserts the Next statement in the code (Figure 6-51). For, To, and Next are blue to indicate they are keywords.

```
 1  Public Class frmGrowth
 2      Private Sub btnShowGrowth_Click(sender As Object, e As EventArgs)
 3          Dim intAlaskaPopulation As Integer = 675000
 4          Dim intYears As Integer
 5
 6          For intYears = 1 To 6          | For statement entered
 7                                          | line indented
 8          Next                            |
 9      End Sub                             | Next statement
10  End Class                               | entered automatically
11
12
13
14
15
```

FIGURE 6-51

STEP 3 Use IntelliSense to select the appropriate variables. Enter the two new lines shown in Figure 6-52.

Each line of code automatically is indented between the For and Next statements (Figure 6-52).

```
 1  Public Class frmGrowth
 2      Private Sub btnShowGrowth_Click(sender As Object, e As EventArgs) Handles btnShowGrowth.Click
 3          Dim intAlaskaPopulation As Integer = 675000
 4          Dim intYears As Integer
 5
 6          For intYears = 1 To 6
 7              intAlaskaPopulation += (intAlaskaPopulation * 0.05)
 8              lstGrowth.Items.Add("Year " & intYears & " Population " & intAlaskaPopulation)
 9
10          Next
11      End Sub
12  End Class
13
```

statements in body of loop

FIGURE 6-52

STEP 4 Run the program to see the results of the loop.

The loop calculates and displays the Alaskan population growth for six years based on 5 percent growth per year (Figure 6-53).

IN THE REAL WORLD

It is best to indent the body of the loop to clearly display what is being repeated. When you use IntelliSense to enter the loop, Visual Basic automatically indents the code properly. When other developers read the code, it is easy to identify the indented portion as the loop body.

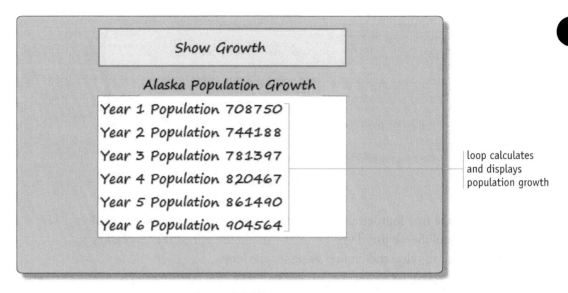

loop calculates
and displays
population growth

FIGURE 6-53

Handle User Input in a For...Next Loop

The beginning, ending, and Step values used in a For...Next loop can vary based
on user input. For example, the Squared Values application shown in Figure 6-54
displays the squared values of a range of numbers the user enters. The user enters the
beginning (minimum) and ending (maximum) range of values and then clicks the
Calculate Values button to view the squares of the numbers in the range.

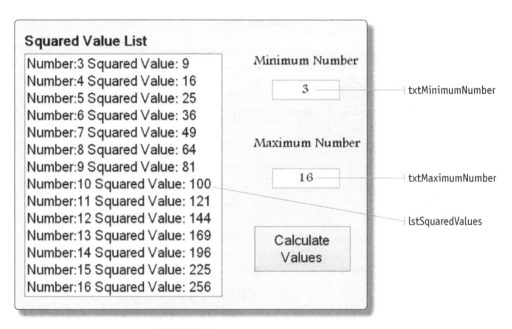

FIGURE 6-54

The code for the Squared Values application is shown in Figure 6-55.

```
5      Dim intCount As Integer
6      Dim intBegin As Integer
7      Dim intEnd As Integer
8
9      intBegin = Convert.ToInt32(txtMinimumNumber.Text)
10     intEnd = Convert.ToInt32(txtMaximumNumber.Text)
11
12     For intCount = intBegin To intEnd
13         lstSquaredValues.Items.Add("Number: " & intCount & " Squared Value: " & (intCount ^ 2))
14     Next
15
16   End Sub
```

FIGURE 6-55

On line 9 in Figure 6-55, the minimum value the user entered is converted to an integer and placed in the intBegin variable. Similarly, on line 10, the maximum value the user entered is converted to an integer and assigned to the intEnd variable. On line 12, the value in intBegin is used as the beginning value in the For...Next loop, and the value in intEnd is used as the ending value. As you can see, the number of iterations for the loop is determined by values the user entered.

Within the loop, the value in intCount begins with the value in intBegin and is incremented by the default value of 1 each time through the loop. The application calculates the squared value from the number in intCount. As a result, the application calculates the squared values for all numbers beginning with the minimum number and ending with the maximum number.

Repeat a Process Using a Do Loop

You use a For...Next loop to repeat a process an exact number of times. In many applications, however, a loop should be repeated until a certain condition changes. For example, in the Fitness Challenge application, the user repeats the process of entering a weight loss value eight times and then stops entering values by clicking the Cancel button. The loop in the Fitness Challenge application continues until one of two conditions becomes true: either the count of the weight loss values entered reaches 8 or the user clicks the Cancel button on the InputBox object.

In a **Do loop**, the body of the loop is executed while or until a condition is true or false. The Do loop uses a condition similar to an If...Then decision structure to determine whether it should continue looping. In this way, you can use a Do loop to execute a body of statements an indefinite number of times. In the Fitness Challenge application, a Do loop can run an indefinite number of times because the user can end the loop at any time by clicking the Cancel button.

Visual Basic 2017 provides two types of Do loops: the Do While loop and the Do Until loop. Both Do loops execute statements repeatedly until a specified condition becomes true or false. Each loop examines a condition to determine whether the condition is true. The **Do While loop** executes as long as the condition is true. It is stated as, "Do the loop processing while the condition is true."

The **Do Until loop** executes until the condition becomes true. It is stated as, "Do the loop processing until a condition is true."

Do loops are either top-controlled or bottom-controlled, depending on whether the condition is tested before the loop begins or after the body of the loop has executed one time. A **top-controlled loop** is tested before the loop is entered. A top-controlled loop is also called a pre-test. The body of a top-controlled loop might not be executed at all because the condition being tested might be true before any processing in the loop occurs.

Bottom-controlled loops test the condition at the bottom of the loop, also called a post test, so the body of a bottom-controlled loop is executed at least once. Visual Basic provides top-controlled and bottom-controlled Do While and Do Until loops, meaning it can execute four types of Do loops.

Top-Controlled Do While Loops

You use a top-controlled Do While loop if you want the body of the loop to repeat as long as a condition remains true. Figure 6-56 shows the syntax of a top-controlled Do While loop.

General Format: Do While Loop (Top-Controlled)

```
Do While condition
    ' Body of loop
Loop
```

FIGURE 6-56

A top-controlled Do While loop begins with the keywords Do While. Next, the condition is specified. The condition is expressed using the same relational operators that are available with the If statements that you learned in Chapter 5. Any condition that can be specified in an If statement can be specified in a Do While condition. The condition can compare numeric values or string values.

The body of the loop contains the instructions that are executed as long as the condition is true. The Loop keyword indicates the end of the loop. Visual Basic inserts it automatically when you enter the Do While keywords.

A statement within the body of the Do While loop must cause the condition to change at some point so the loop ends. For example, consider the following statement:

```
Do While strColor = "Red"
```

The loop continues to process as long as the value in the strColor variable remains Red. Based on the processing in the body of the loop, at some point the value in the strColor variable must be changed from Red. If not, the loop will not end. A loop that does not end is called an **infinite loop**.

The code in Figure 6-57 is an example of a top-controlled Do While loop. It continues to add 1 to the variable intScore while intScore is less than 5. It is considered a top-controlled loop because the condition is checked at the top of the loop.

```
17          Dim intScore As Integer = 0
18          Do While intScore < 5
19              intScore += 1
20          Loop
```

FIGURE 6-57

The loop in Figure 6-57 begins by testing whether intScore is less than 5. Because intScore starts with the value 0, the condition tested is true: 0 is less than 5. Next, the variable intScore is incremented by 1, and the loop repeats. The table in Figure 6-58 displays the values that are assigned to intScore each time the condition is checked in the code in Figure 6-57.

Loop Iteration	Value of intScore	Result of Condition Tested
1	intScore = 0	True
2	intScore = 1	True
3	intScore = 2	True
4	intScore = 3	True
5	intScore = 4	True
6	intScore = 5	False

FIGURE 6-58

The loop in Figure 6-57 is executed five times because intScore is less than 5 during five iterations of the loop. As shown in Figure 6-57, if the value in the variable intScore is 5 or greater when the Do While statement is first executed, the body of the loop never will be executed because the condition is not true prior to the first iteration of the loop.

Enter a Do Loop Using IntelliSense

To use IntelliSense to enter the Do While loop shown in Figure 6-57, you can complete the following steps:

STEP 1   In the code window, enter the intScore variable declaration and then press the ENTER key. Type Do While and a space to display an IntelliSense list. Type ints to highlight intScore in the list.

The words Do While appear in blue because they are Visual Basic keywords (Figure 6-59). The IntelliSense list contains the valid entries and the intScore variable name is highlighted.

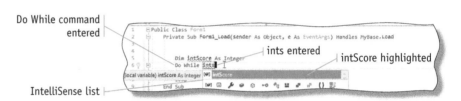

Do While command entered

ints entered

intScore highlighted

IntelliSense list

FIGURE 6-59

STEP 2   Type < 5 and then press the ENTER key.

Visual Basic automatically inserts the intScore variable name and the characters you typed (Figure 6-60). The keyword Loop is also inserted and the insertion point is located inside the loop, ready to enter the body of the loop.

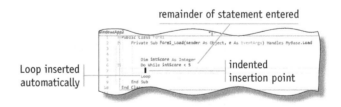

remainder of statement entered

Loop inserted automatically

indented insertion point

FIGURE 6-60

STEP 3   Type ints to highlight the intScore variable. Complete the statement by typing += 1 and then pressing the ENTER key. Press the DELETE key to delete the blank line.

The statement automatically is indented between the Do While and Loop statements (Figure 6-61). The intScore += 1 statement uses a compound operator to increment the intScore variable.

FIGURE 6-61

Bottom-Controlled Do While Loops

You can write a Do While loop in which the condition is tested at the bottom of the loop. A bottom-controlled loop works the same way as the top-controlled Do While loop except that the body of the loop is executed before the condition is checked the first time, guaranteeing that at least one iteration of a loop will be completed. The bottom-controlled Do While loop has the syntax shown in Figure 6-62.

General Format: Do While Loop (Bottom-controlled)

```
Do

            ' Loop Body

Loop While condition
```

FIGURE 6-62

In Figure 6-62, the word Do appears on its own line at the beginning of the loop. The loop body follows, and the Loop While statement is the last statement in the loop. The Loop While statement contains the condition that is tested to determine if the loop should be terminated. Because the While condition is in the last statement of the loop, the body of the loop is executed one time regardless of the status of the condition.

The code in Figure 6-63 is an example of a bottom-controlled Do While loop.

```
22        Dim intScore As Integer = 0
23        Do
24            intScore = intScore + 1
25        Loop While intScore < 5
```

FIGURE 6-63

The body of the Do loop in Figure 6-63 is executed one time before the condition in the Loop While statement is checked. The variable intScore begins with the initial value of 0 and is incremented in the body of the loop, changing the value to 1. The condition is then tested and found to be true because 1 < 5. The loop repeats and the value of intScore increases, as shown in Figure 6-64.

Loop Iteration	Value of intScore at Start of the Loop	Value of intScore When Checked	Result of Condition Tested
1	intScore = 0	intScore = 1	True
2	intScore = 1	intScore = 2	True
3	intScore = 2	intScore = 3	True
4	intScore = 3	intScore = 4	True
5	intScore = 4	intScore = 5	False

FIGURE 6-64

The body of the loop in Figure 6-63 is executed four times because intScore is less than 5 during five iterations of the loop.

Use Do Until Loops

A loop similar to a Do While loop is called a Do Until loop. The Do Until loop allows you to specify that an action repeats until a condition becomes true. When the condition in a Do Until loop becomes true, the loop ends.

Top-Controlled Do Until Loops

A Do Until loop can be both top-controlled and bottom-controlled. The syntax of the top-controlled Do Until loop is shown in Figure 6-65.

General Format: Do Until Loop (Top-Controlled)

```
Do Until condition

          ' Loop Body

Loop
```

FIGURE 6-65

A top-controlled Do Until loop begins with the keywords Do Until. Next, as with the Do While top-controlled loop, the condition is specified. The condition is expressed using the same relational operators that are available with If statements. Any condition that can be specified in an If statement can be specified in a Do Until condition. The condition can compare numeric values or string values.

The Do Until loop example shown in Figure 6-66 displays a parking meter application that computes the number of minutes a user can purchase based on the cost of 25 cents for each 15 minutes of parking. If the user only has 88 cents in pocket change, for example, the application computes how many minutes of parking time 88 cents will purchase.

```
 4          Dim decAmount As Decimal = 0.88
 5          Dim intQuarters As Integer = 0
 6          Dim intTime As Integer = 15
 7          Dim intParkingTime As Integer
 8
 9          Do Until decAmount < 0.25
10              intQuarters += 1
11              decAmount -= 0.25
12          Loop
13          intParkingTime = intQuarters * intTime
14          lblParkingTime.Text = "Parking Time: " &
15                              intParkingTime.ToString() & " minutes"
```

FIGURE 6-66

In the code example in Figure 6-66, the application checks the Do Until loop condition before executing the body of the loop. The first time the condition is tested, the expression decAmount < 0.25 is false because the decAmount variable contains 0.88. The body of the loop is executed because the Do Until statement specifies that the loop continues until the value in decAmount is less than 0.25. When the body of the loop is executed, it adds 1 to intQuarters to count the number of quarters the user has for the parking meter, and then subtracts 0.25 from decAmount because a quarter is worth 25 cents. Because decAmount is first assigned the value 0.88, the loop executes three times (decAmount = 0.88, decAmount = 0.63, and decAmount = 0.38) and stops when decAmount becomes less than 0.25. The lblParkingTime Label object displays the text "Parking Time: 45 minutes."

Bottom-Controlled Do Until Loops

The last of the four Do loops is the bottom-controlled Do Until loop. This Do Until loop checks the condition after the body of the loop is executed. The loop continues until the condition becomes true. The syntax of the bottom-controlled Do Until loop is shown in Figure 6-67.

General Format: Do Until Loop (Botttom-Controlled)

```
Do
            ' Loop Body
Loop Until condition
```

FIGURE 6-67

In Figure 6-67, the bottom-controlled Do Until loop begins with the word Do. The body of the loop is executed one time regardless of the condition being tested. The Loop Until statement checks the condition. The loop will be repeated until the condition is true.

CRITICAL THINKING

In a payroll program, should I use a For loop or Do While loop to repeat the process of entering the hours for each employee every two weeks? Typically a Do While loop is the better option because the number of employees fluctuates. If you do not know the exact number of iterations, it is best to use the Do While loop structure.

Other Loop Considerations

Other considerations when using loops are creating user input loops, avoiding infinite loops, priming a loop, validating data with a loop, creating a nested loop, and selecting the best type of loop.

User Input Loops

Do loops often are written to end when the user enters a certain value or performs a certain action such as clicking the Cancel button in an input box. The developer determines the value or action. For example, a Do Until loop might accumulate the total of all the entered test scores until the user clicks the Cancel button in the input box. If the user clicks the Cancel button, the InputBox function returns a null string that is assigned to the strTestGrade variable. The Do Until statement tests the string. If it contains a null character, the loop is terminated.

Avoid Infinite Loops

Recall that an infinite loop is a loop that never ends. It happens when the condition specified to end the loop never occurs. If the loop does not end, it repeats until the program is interrupted. Figure 6-68 shows an example of an infinite loop.

```
        Dim intProblem = 0
        Do While intProblem <= 5
            Box.Show("This loop will not end", "Infinite Loop")
        Loop
```

FIGURE 6-68

The Do While loop in Figure 6-68 never ends because the value in the variable intProblem is never changed from its initial value of zero. Because the value in intProblem never exceeds 5, the condition in the Do While loop (intProblem <= 5) never becomes false. The processing in a loop eventually must change the condition being tested in the Do While loop so the loop will terminate. When working in Visual Basic 2017, you can interrupt an infinite loop by clicking the Stop Debugging button on the Standard toolbar.

How do I know which type of loop to use?

All loops have the same basic function of repeating certain lines of a program. Some loops are best suited under certain conditions. For example, if you want to check the condition before the loop is run, use a top-controlled loop. Often the type of loop you use is just programmer preference.

CONSIDER THIS

Prime the Loop

As you have learned, a top-controlled loop tests a condition prior to beginning the loop. In most cases, the value to test must be set before the condition is tested the first time in the Do While or Do Until statement. Starting a loop with a preset value in the variable(s) tested in the condition is called **priming the loop**. You have seen this in previous examples, such as in Figure 6-66 on page 306, where the value in decAmount is set before the condition is tested the first time.

In some applications, the loop is primed with a value the user enters or an action the user takes. For example, in the Fitness Challenge application, the user enters the weight loss value for each team member (up to eight values) or clicks the Cancel button in the input box. Prior to executing the Do Until statement the first time in the Do Until loop that processes the data the user enters, the InputBox function must be executed to obtain an initial value. Then, the Do Until statement can test the action taken by the user (enter a value and click the Cancel button). The coding to implement this processing is shown in Figure 6-69.

```
30          Dim strCancelClicked As String = ""
31          Dim intMaxNumberOfEntries As Integer = 8
32          Dim intNumberOfEntries As Integer = 1
   ⋮
38          strWeightLoss = InputBox(strInputMessage & intNumberOfEntries, strInputHeading, " ")
39
40          Do Until intNumberOfEntries > intMaxNumberOfEntries Or strWeightLoss = strCancelClicked
   ⋮
47                  intNumberOfEntries += 1
   ⋮
56              If intNumberOfEntries <= intMaxNumberOfEntries Then
57                  strWeightLoss = InputBox(strInputMessage & intNumberOfEntries, strInputHeading, " ")
58              End If
59
60          Loop
```

FIGURE 6-69

In the Do Until loop shown in Figure 6-69, the Do Until statement on line 40 tests two conditions: Is the value in the intNumberOfEntries variable greater than the value in the intMaxNumberOfEntries variable or is the value in the strWeightLoss variable equal to the value in the strCancelClicked variable, which is a null character (see line 30)? If either condition is true, the body of the loop is not executed.

The Do Until loop must have two primed variables: the intNumberOfEntries variable and the strWeightLoss variable. The intNumberOfEntries variable is initialized to 1 on line 32. The strWeightLoss variable is initialized by the InputBox function call on line 38. In this function call, the user either entered a value or clicked the Cancel button. If the user clicked the Cancel button, the body of the loop should not be entered.

To continue the loop, the processing within the body of the loop eventually must change one of the conditions being tested in the Do Until statement or the loop never terminates. In the sample program, the conditions being tested are whether the user entered eight weight loss values or clicked the Cancel button. Therefore, within the loop, the variable containing intNumberOfEntries must be incremented when the user enters a valid weight loss value. The user then must be able to enter more weight loss values or click the Cancel button. On line 47 in Figure 6-69, the value in intNumberOfEntries is incremented by 1 each time the user enters a valid weight loss value. In addition, the statement on line 57 displays an input box that allows the user to enter a new value or click the Cancel button as long as the number of valid entries is not greater than the maximum number of entries.

Validate Data

As you learned in Chapter 5, you must test the data a user enters to ensure it is accurate and that its use in other programming statements, such as converting string data to numeric data, will not cause a program exception. When using an input box, the data should be checked using the IsNumeric function and If statements, as discussed in Chapter 5. If the data is not valid, the user must be notified of the error and an input box displayed to allow the user to enter valid data.

For example, if the user enters nonnumeric data, the input box in Figure 6-70 should be displayed.

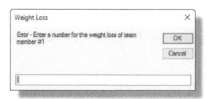

FIGURE 6-70

Similarly, if the user enters a negative number, the message in Figure 6-71 should be displayed in an input box.

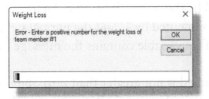

FIGURE 6-71

When error checking is performed within a loop and the user is asked to enter data in an input box, the body of the loop must be executed each time the user enters data, regardless of whether the data is valid or invalid. If the user enters valid data, then the data is processed according to the needs of the program.

If the user enters invalid data, an error message is displayed and the user is given the opportunity to enter valid data in the input box. The coding for the Fitness Challenge application that accomplishes these tasks is shown in Figure 6-72.

```vb
33          ' clicks the Cancel button or the Close button in the InputBox
34          strWeightLoss = InputBox(strInputMessage & intNumberOfEntries, strInputHeading, " ")
35
36          Do Until intNumberOfEntries > intMaxNumberOfEntries Or strWeightLoss = strCancelClicked
37              If IsNumeric(strWeightLoss) Then
38                  decWeightLoss = Convert.ToDecimal(strWeightLoss)
39                  If decWeightLoss > 0 Then
40                      lstWeightLoss.Items.Add(decWeightLoss)
41                      decTotalWeightLoss += decWeightLoss
42                      intNumberOfEntries += 1
43                      strInputMessage = strNormalMessage
44                  Else
45                      strInputMessage = strNegativeError
46                  End If
47              Else
48                  strInputMessage = strNonNumericError
49              End If
50              If intNumberOfEntries <= intMaxNumberOfEntries Then
51                  strWeightLoss = InputBox(strInputMessage & intNumberOfEntries, strInputHeading, " ")
52              End If
53          Loop
```

FIGURE 6-72

In Figure 6-72, the loop is primed by the InputBox function call on line 34. The Do Until statement on line 36 checks the two conditions—if the value in the intNumberOfEntries counter is greater than the maximum number of entries or if the user clicks the Cancel button. In either case, the body of the loop is not executed.

When the body of the loop is executed, the application checks the data the user entered to verify it is numeric. If it is numeric, the value is converted to a Decimal data type and then is checked to ensure it is greater than zero (line 39). If it is greater than zero, it is added to the lstWeightLoss ListBox object, the decTotalWeightLoss accumulator is incremented by the weight loss value the user entered, the intNumberOfEntries counter is incremented by 1, and the normal message is moved to the strInputMessage variable. This variable contains the message that is displayed in the input box (see line 34).

If the value the user entered is not greater than zero, the statement following the Else statement on line 45 moves the value in the strNegativeError variable to the strInputMessage variable so that the next time the InputBox function is called, the message will indicate an error, as shown in Figure 6-71.

If the value the user entered was not numeric (as tested by the statement on line 37), the statement on line 48 moves the value in the strNonNumericError variable to the strInputMessage variable so that the next time the InputBox function is called, the message will indicate a nonnumeric error, as shown in Figure 6-70.

On lines 50 and 51, as long as the number of entries is not greater than the maximum number of entries, the InputBox function is called. The message that is displayed in the input box depends on whether an error occurred. The Do Until statement on line 36 is executed and the process begins again.

Create a Nested Loop

In Chapter 5, you learned to nest If...Then...Else statements within each other. Loops can also be nested. You can place any type of loop within any other type of loop under the following conditions: Interior loops must be completely contained inside the outer loop and must have a different control variable. The example in Figure 6-73 uses a nested For loop to display a list of the weeks in the first quarter of the year (13 weeks) along with the days in each week. The outer For...Next loop counts from 1 to 13 for the 13 weeks, and the inner For...Next loop counts from 1 to 7 for the days in each of the 13 weeks.

The code in Figure 6-73 displays the output shown in Figure 6-74.

```
6       Dim intOuterCount As Integer ' Counts the first 13 weeks in a quarter
7       Dim intInnerCount As Integer ' Counts the 7 days in a week
8       For intOuterCount = 1 To 13 ' For weeks in the 1st quarter of the year
9           For intInnerCount = 1 To 7 ' For the 7 days in a week
10              lstDays.Items.Add("Week: " & intOuterCount.ToString() _
11                              & " Day: " & intInnerCount.ToString())
12          Next
13      Next
```

FIGURE 6-73

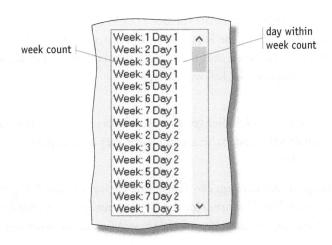

week count

day within
week count

FIGURE 6-74

Select the Best Loop

When writing a program, you might have to make a decision regarding which loop structure to use. For...Next loops are best when the number of repetitions is fixed. Do loops are best when the condition to enter or exit the loop needs to be re-evaluated continually. When deciding which loop to use, keep the following considerations in mind:

1. Use a Do loop if the number of repetitions is unknown and is based on a condition changing; a For...Next loop is best if the exact number of repetitions is fixed.
2. If a loop condition must be tested before the body of the loop is executed, use a top-controlled Do While or Do Until loop. If the instructions within a loop must be executed one time regardless of the status of a condition, use a bottom-controlled Do While or Do Until loop.
3. Use the keyword While if you want to continue execution of the loop while the condition is true. Use the keyword Until if you want to continue execution until the condition is true.

Use a DataTip with Breakpoints

As programs become longer and more complex, the likelihood of errors increases, and you need to carefully find and remove these errors. Resolving defects in code is called **debugging**. When you debug a program, you collect information and find out what is wrong with the code in the program. You then fix that code.

A good way to collect information is to pause the execution of the code where a possible error could occur. One way to pause execution is to use breakpoints. **Breakpoints** are stop points placed in the code to tell the Visual Studio 2017 debugger where and when to pause the execution of the application. During this pause, the program is in break mode. While in break mode, you can examine the values in all variables that are within the scope of execution through the use of **DataTips**. In the Fitness Challenge application, you can insert a breakpoint in the

assignment statement that increments the decTotalWeightLoss accumulator to view
its value after each iteration of the loop as the user enters each weight loss value.
To set a breakpoint in your code and then check the data at the breakpoint using
DataTips, you can complete the following steps:

STEP 1 With the Fitness Challenge application open in the code window, click
line 41, which contains the code where you want to set a breakpoint, and then click
Debug on the menu bar.

The Debug menu opens that contains the Toggle Breakpoint command (Figure 6-75).
Setting a breakpoint on line 41 means that the program will pause at that line during
execution so that the values in variables within the scope of execution can be examined.

FIGURE 6-75

STEP 2 Click Toggle Breakpoint on the submenu.

A breakpoint is set on line 41, which is the line in the Do Until loop that adds the
weight loss value the user entered to the weight loss accumulator — decTotalWeightLoss
(Figure 6-76). The breakpoint is identified by the red bullet to the left of the line numbers
and the highlight effect on the code.

FIGURE 6-76

STEP 3 To run and test the program with the breakpoint, click the Start button on the Standard toolbar.

The program starts and the Fitness Challenge window opens (Figure 6-77).

Start changes to Continue

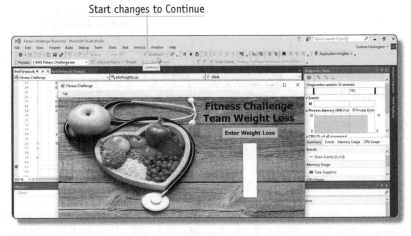

FIGURE 6-77

iStockphoto.com/udra

STEP 4 Click the Enter Weight Loss button. Type 3 . 4 as the weight loss amount of the first team member.

The Weight Loss input box contains 3.4 as the weight loss amount of the first team member (Figure 6-78).

3.4 entered in Weight Loss input box

FIGURE 6-78

iStockphoto.com/udra

STEP 5 Click the OK button in the input box.

The program executes the lines of code in the event handler until reaching the breakpoint, where it pauses execution on the accumulator line (Figure 6-79). The application is now in break mode. Notice the breakpoint line is highlighted in yellow.

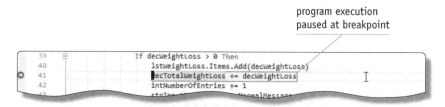

program execution
paused at breakpoint

```
39      If decWeightLoss > 0 Then
40          lstWeightLoss.Items.Add(decWeightLoss)
41          decTotalWeightLoss += decWeightLoss
42          intNumberOfEntries += 1
```

FIGURE 6-79

STEP 6 Point to the variable decWeightLoss on line 41.

A DataTip appears, displaying the value of the decWeightLoss variable when execution was paused (Figure 6-80). The value is 3.4 because the user entered this value in Step 4. It is a Decimal value (3.4D) because the statement in line 38 converted the value the user entered to a Decimal value.

pointer on
decWeightLoss
variable

DataTip displays
the value in the
decWeightLoss
variable

FIGURE 6-80

STEP 7 You can view the value in any other variable within execution scope by pointing to that variable. To illustrate, point to the variable decTotalWeightLoss on line 41.

The value in the decTotalWeightLoss variable is displayed (Figure 6-81). The value is zero, which means the assignment statement on line 41 has not yet been executed. When a breakpoint is set, the program pauses before executing the statement that contains the breakpoint.

pointer on
decTotalWeightLoss
variable

DataTip displays
the value in the
decTotalWeightLoss
variable

FIGURE 6-81

STEP 8 Continue the program by clicking the Continue button on the Standard toolbar. Notice that the Continue button is the same as the Start button.

The program continues by opening the next InputBox function, where the user can enter the weight loss value for the next team member. The program runs until it again reaches the breakpoint, where it pauses so you can point to any variable to view its present value in a DataTip (Figure 6-82).

Continue
button

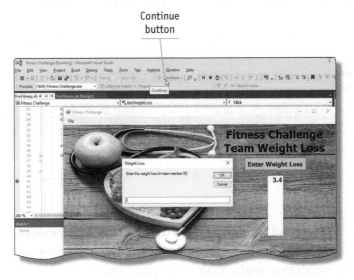

FIGURE 6-82

iStockphoto.com/udra

The preceding example illustrated the use of one breakpoint, but you can include multiple breakpoints in a program if they will be useful. Sometimes, breakpoints before and after an instruction that you suspect is in error can pinpoint the problem. Breakpoints can also be configured with conditions and actions to improve your debugging experience. For example, a breakpoint can be configured to stop after a coding situation has been reached a certain amount of times or a tracepoint can print a message to the output window to track a particular value.

To remove a breakpoint, you can complete the following steps:

STEP 1   Click the statement containing the breakpoint, and then point to the red bullet representing the breakpoint.

The pointer is located on the Breakpoint entry bullet (Figure 6-83).

Breakpoint bullet

```
                              If decWeightLoss > 0 Then
                                  lstWeightLoss.Items.Add(decWeightLoss)
     41                           decTotalWeightLoss += decWeightLoss
location: frmFitness.vb, line 41 character 21 ('Fitness_Challenge.frmFitness.btnWeightLoss_Click(Object, System.EventArgs)')
     43                                  strInputMessage = strNormalMessage
```

FIGURE 6-83

STEP 2   Click the red bullet breakpoint.

The breakpoint is removed when you click the red bullet (Figure 6-84).

breakpoint is
removed, but
variable is
highlighted

```
35
36       Do Until intNumberOfEntries > intMaxNumberOfEntries Or strWeightLoss = strCancelClicked
37           If IsNumeric(strWeightLoss) Then
38               decWeightLoss = Convert.ToDecimal(strWeightLoss)
39               If decWeightLoss > 0 Then
40                   lstWeightLoss.Items.Add(decWeightLoss)
41                   decTotalWeightLoss += decWeightLoss
42                   intNumberOfEntries += 1
43                   strInputMessage = strNormalMessage
44               Else
45                   strInputMessage = strNegativeError
46               End If
```

FIGURE 6-84

Using breakpoints and DataTips allows you to examine any variables during the execution of the program. By moving step by step through the program, normally you can identify any errors that might occur in the program.

Publish an Application with ClickOnce Deployment

After an application is completely debugged and working properly, you can deploy the project. Deploying a project means placing an executable version of the program on your hard disk (which then can be placed on CD, DVD, or in the cloud), on a web server, or on a network server.

You probably have purchased software on a CD or DVD or downloaded software from a cloud-based site. To install the application on your computer, you insert the CD or DVD into your computer and then follow the setup instructions. The version of the program you receive on the CD or DVD is the deployed version of the program.

When programming using Visual Basic 2017, you can create a deployed program by using **ClickOnce Deployment**. The deployed version of the program you create can be installed and executed on any computer that has the .NET framework installed. The computer does not need Visual Studio 2017 installed to run the program.

To publish the Fitness Challenge application using ClickOnce Deployment, you can complete the following steps:

STEP 1 With the Fitness Challenge application open, click Build on the menu bar.

The Build menu is displayed (Figure 6-85).

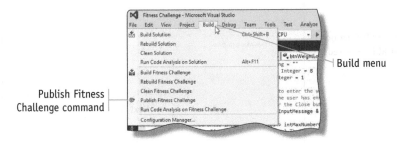

FIGURE 6-85

STEP 2 Click Publish Fitness Challenge on the Build menu.

The Publish Wizard starts (Figure 6-86). The first Publish Wizard dialog box asks where you want to publish the application. The application can be published to a web server, a network, or as a setup file on a hard disk or USB drive for burning on a CD or DVD. This dialog box includes publish\ as the default location, which you can change to a file location.

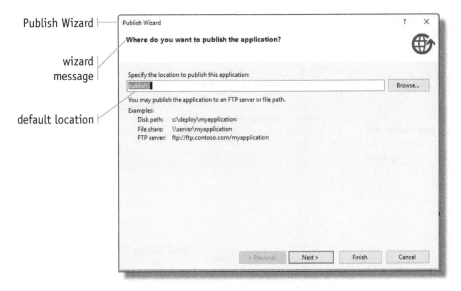

FIGURE 6-86

STEP 3   Change the default location from publish\ to a file location. To publish to a USB drive, type the drive letter. In this example, enter D: for a USB drive. Click the Next button.

The Publish Wizard dialog box requests where you want to publish the application. The Fitness Challenge application will be saved to the USB drive, which is drive D: in this example. The wizard next asks how users will install the application (Figure 6-87).

From a CD-ROM or
DVD-ROM selected

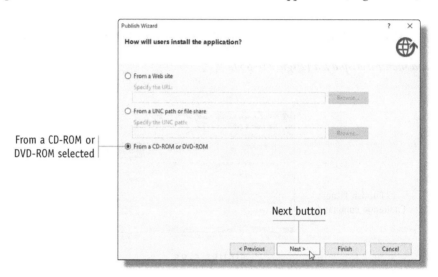

FIGURE 6-87

STEP 4   If necessary, click the From a CD-ROM or DVD-ROM radio button, and then click the Next button.

Visual Basic displays a Publish Wizard dialog box that asks, "Where will the application check for updates?" (Figure 6-88). You can select and enter a location or indicate that the application will not check for updates. Generally, when an application will be deployed to a CD, DVD, or USB drive, the application will not check for updates. If the application is deployed to a web server or network server, then it might check for updates before being executed on the user's computer.

application will
not check for
updates

FIGURE 6-88

STEP 5 If necessary, click the "The application will not check for updates" option button, and then click the Next button.

The Ready to Publish! window is displayed (Figure 6-89). Notice the message in this window—when the program is installed on the user's machine, a shortcut for the program will be added to the user's computer, and the program can be deleted using the Add/Remove Programs function in the Control Panel.

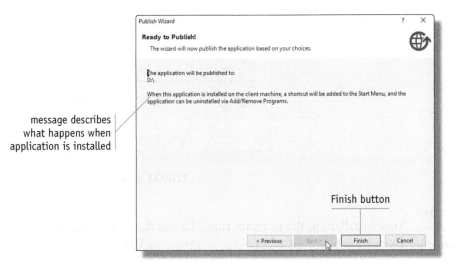

message describes
what happens when
application is installed

Finish button

FIGURE 6-89

STEP 6 Click the Finish button.

The Visual Basic window displays several messages indicating that the application is being published. The last message is "Publish succeeded" and the USB drive dialog box opens. The installation files are placed on the USB drive, and the user can double-click the setup file to begin the installation (Figure 6-90).

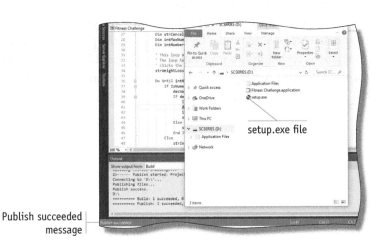

setup.exe file

Publish succeeded
message

FIGURE 6-90

STEP 7 To install the application, double-click the setup file.

After the user double-clicks the setup file, the application is installed on the local computer. During installation, Windows might display the dialog box shown in Figure 6-91. This dialog box is intended to protect you from installing programs that might harm your computer. Because you know the source of this program, you can click the Install button to continue installing the program.

Application Install – Security Warning dialog box

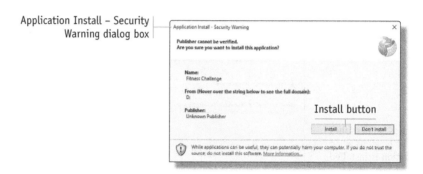

FIGURE 6-91

STEP 8 After installation, the program runs. To run the installed application again, click the Search box, type `Fitness`, and then click the Fitness Challenge icon.

Program Design

As you have learned, the requirements document identifies the purpose of the program being developed, the application title, the procedures to be followed when using the program, any required equations and calculations, any conditions that must be tested, notes and restrictions that must be followed by the program, and any other comments that would be helpful to understanding the problem. The requirements document for the Fitness Challenge application is shown in Figure 6-92.

REQUIREMENTS DOCUMENT

Date:	September 30, 2019
Date Submitted:	
Application Title:	Fitness Challenge Application
Purpose:	This application finds the average weight loss of a team of eight employees.
Program Procedures:	In a Windows Classic Desktop application, the user enters the weight loss amounts of eight employees as positive numbers to compute the average weight loss for the entire team.

Algorithms, Processing, and Conditions:

1. The user must be able to enter each of eight weight loss values in pounds after clicking the Enter Weight Loss button.
2. Each weight loss value is validated to confirm it is numeric and greater than zero.
3. Each weight loss value is displayed in a ListBox object.
4. After the user enters eight weight loss values or clicks the Cancel button in an input box, the program calculates and displays the average weight loss for the team.
5. A menu bar includes the File menu, which contains Clear and Exit items. The Clear menu item clears the result and the weight loss values. The Exit menu item closes the application.

Notes and Restrictions:

1. If a nonnumeric or negative value is entered for the weight loss, the program should display an error message and ask the user to re-enter the value.
2. If the user clicks the Cancel button before entering any weight loss values, a message should indicate no weight loss values were entered. An average is not calculated when no weight loss values are entered.

Comments:

1. The picture shown in the window can be found on CengageBrain.com. The name of the picture is health.
2. The average weight loss should be formatted as a Decimal value with one decimal place.

FIGURE 6-92

The Use Case Definition shown in Figure 6-93 specifies the procedures the user will follow to use this application.

USE CASE DEFINITION

1. The Windows application opens, displaying the Fitness Challenge title, a ListBox object to hold the numeric entries, and a Button object that allows the user to begin entering up to eight weight loss values.
2. A menu bar displays the File menu, which has two menu items: Clear and Exit.
3. In an InputBox object, the user enters up to eight values representing the number of pounds lost, such as 3.2 pounds.
4. The program asks the user for the weight loss value again if a value is nonnumeric or negative.
5. The user ends data entry by entering eight values or by clicking the Cancel button in the InputBox object.
6. The program calculates the average weight loss for the values the user entered.
7. In a Label object, the program displays the average weight loss as a Decimal value with one decimal place.
8. The user can clear the input and the results by clicking the Clear menu item, and can then repeat Steps 3 through 7.
9. The user clicks Exit on the File menu to close the application.

FIGURE 6-93

Event Planning Document

You will recall that the event planning document is a table that specifies which objects in the user interface will cause events, the action taken by the user to trigger each event, and the event processing that must occur. The event planning document for the Fitness Challenge application is shown in Figure 6-94.

EVENT PLANNING DOCUMENT

Program Name:	Developer:	Object:	Date:
Fitness Challenge Application	Corinne Hoisington	frmFitness	September 30, 2019

OBJECT	EVENT TRIGGER	EVENT PROCESSING
btnWeightLoss	Click	Display an InputBox object to obtain each team member's weight loss up to eight times or until the user clicks the Cancel button
		Check if strWeightLoss is numeric
		If the weight loss value is numeric, convert strWeightLoss to a Decimal value
		If strWeightLoss is numeric, check whether the value is positive
		If the weight loss value is positive:
		Display the value in lstWeightLoss
		Accumulate the total of the weight loss values in decTotalWeightLoss
		Update the number of entries
		Set the InputBox message to the normal message
		If the value entered is not numeric, display an error message in the input box
		If the value entered is not positive, display an error message in the input box
		After all weight loss values are entered, change the Visible property of lblAverageLoss to true
		If one or more weight loss values are entered: Calculate the average weight loss in decAverageLoss Display the average weight loss in lblAverageLoss
		If no values are entered: Display the text "No weight loss value entered" Disable the btnWeightLoss Button
mnuClear	Click	Clear the lstWeightLoss ListBox
		Change the Visible property of lblAverageLoss to False
		Enable the btnWeightLoss Button
mnuExit	Click	Exit the application

FIGURE 6-94

Design and Code the Program

After identifying the events and tasks within the events, the developer is ready to create the program. As you have learned, creating the program means designing the user interface and then entering Visual Basic statements to accomplish the tasks specified in the event planning document. As the developer enters the code, she will also implement the logic to carry out the required processing.

Guided Program Development

To design the user interface for the Fitness Challenge application and enter the code required to process each event in the program, complete the steps on the following pages:

NOTE TO THE LEARNER

In the following activity, you should complete the tasks within the specified steps. Each of the tasks is accompanied by a Hint Screen. The purpose of the Hint Screen is to indicate where you should perform the activity in the Visual Studio window and to remind you which method to use. If you need further help completing a step, refer to the figure identified by *ref:*.

Guided Program Development

Phase 1: Design the Form

1

- **Create a Windows Application** Open Visual Studio and then close the Start page. Create a new Visual Basic Windows Forms App project by clicking the New Project button on the Standard toolbar, selecting Windows Classic Desktop as the project type, selecting Windows Forms App in the center pane, naming the project Fitness Challenge in the Name text box, and then clicking the OK button in the New Project window.

- **Display the Toolbox** Ensure that the Toolbox is displayed in the Visual Studio window and that the Common Controls are accessible.

- **Name the Windows Form Object** In the Solution Explorer window, right-click Form1.vb, click Rename, and then rename the form frmFitness.

- **Change the Text on the Title Bar for the Windows Form Object** Change the title bar text of the Windows Form object to Fitness Challenge.

- **Change the Size of the Form Object** Resize the Form object by changing the Size property to 883, 477.

- **Add the MenuStrip Object** Drag a MenuStrip object from the Menus & Toolbars category of the Toolbox to the Windows Form object. The MenuStrip snaps into place below the title bar. Name the MenuStrip object mnuFitness in the Properties window. Click the Type Here box on the MenuStrip object, type &File, and then press the ENTER key. The ampersand creates a hot key for the letter F. Name the File menu item mnuFile (ref: Figure 6-5).

- **Add Menu Items** The next step is to add two menu items to the File menu. Click the Type Here box below the word File, and then enter &Clear. Name the Clear menu item mnu-Clear. Click the Type Here box below the Clear menu item, and then enter E&xit to make the "x" in Exit the hot key. Name the Exit menu item mnuExit (ref: Figure 6-10).

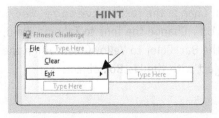

(continues)

● **Add the Title Label Object** Drag a Label .NET component
onto the Windows Form object. Name the label lblTitle.
Enter the text for this label as Fitness Challenge Team
Weight Loss on two lines. (*Hint:* Click the Text property list
arrow in the Properties window to enter a label with multiple
lines. Press the ENTER key to move to a new line.) Choose
Tahoma as the font, Bold as the font style, and 26 points as the
size. Change the TextAlign property to MiddleCenter by clicking the TextAlign list arrow and then clicking the Center block.
Change the Location property of the lblTitle Label object to
505, 33.

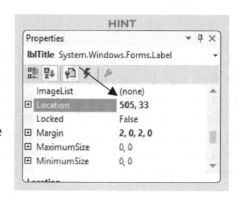

● **Add the Enter Weight Loss Button Object** Drag a Button
object onto the Windows Form object below the title label.
Name the Button btnWeightLoss. Change the text of
the button to Enter Weight Loss. Change the font to
14-point, Bold, and Tahoma. Change the BackColor property
to YellowGreen. Resize the Button object to view the complete
text. Align the centers of the Button object with the title
Label object.

● **Add the ListBox Object for the Team Members' Weight
Loss** To add the ListBox object that displays the team members'
weight loss, drag a ListBox object onto the Windows Form
object below the Button object. Name the ListBox lst-
WeightLoss. Change the font of the text in the ListBox
object to 14-point, Bold, and Tahoma. Resize the ListBox to the
width of four characters because the top weight loss of a team
member could reach an amount such as 46.3 pounds. Lengthen
the ListBox object to display eight numbers. The Size property
for the ListBox object in the sample program is 50, 188. Change
the RightToLeft property to Yes to right-align the numeric values. Align the centers of the ListBox object with the Button
object (*ref: Figure 6-22*).

● **Add the Result Label** To add the label where the average
weight loss message is displayed, drag a Label object onto the
Windows Form object. Name the Label object lblAvera-
geLoss. Change the text to Average weight loss is
XX.X lbs. Change the font to Tahoma, Bold, and 18-point.
Change the BackColor to YellowGreen. Align the centers of the
Label object with the ListBox object.

The user interface mockup is complete (Figure 6-95).

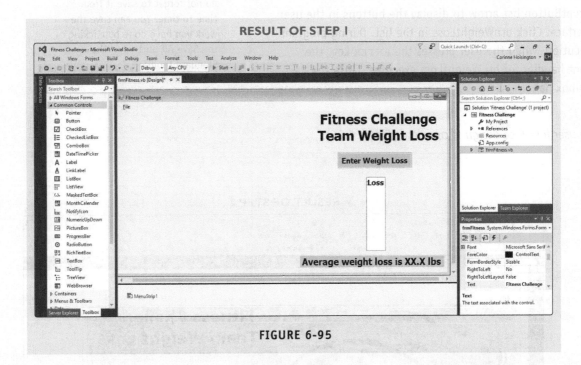

FIGURE 6-95

Phase 2: Fine-Tune the User Interface

2

● **Change the BackgroundImage Property of the Windows Form Object** Select the Windows Form object and then click the ellipsis button on the BackgroundImage property. Click the Import button and navigate to the health image. Click the OK button. Change the BackgroundImageLayout property to Stretch.

● **Change the Visible Property for the Average Weight Loss Label** Select the lblAverageLoss Label object and change its Visible property to False because the Label object is not displayed until the average weight loss is calculated.

(continues)

● **Make the Enter Weight Loss Button the Accept Button** Click the background of the Windows Form object to select it. In the Properties window, click the AcceptButton list arrow to display the buttons in the user interface. Click btnWeightLoss in the list. During program execution, when the user presses the ENTER key, the event handler for btnWeightLoss executes. Close the Toolbox pane.

The user interface design is complete (Figure 6-96).

FIGURE 6-96

iStockphoto.com/udra

Phase 3: Code the Program

3

● **Enter the Comments for the Enter Weight Loss Button Event Handler** Double-click the btnWeightLoss Button object on the Windows Form object to open the button event handler. Insert the first four standard comments at the top of the code window. Insert the command `Option Strict On` at the beginning of the code to turn on strict type checking.

HINT

● **Comment on the btnWeightLoss_Click Event Handler** Enter a comment to describe the purpose of the btnWeightLoss_Click event handler.

HINT

● **Declare and Initialize the Variables to Calculate the Average Weight Loss** Four variables are used to calculate the average weight loss (besides the team member count). These variables are: 1) strWeightLoss: Is assigned the value from the InputBox function call; 2) decWeightLoss: Is assigned the converted team member weight loss; 3) decAverageLoss: Contains the calculated average weight loss; 4) decTotalWeightLoss: The accumulator used to collect the total weight loss values entered by a user. Declare and initialize these four variables.

HINT

● **Declare and Initialize the Variables Used with the InputBox Function Call** Five variables contain messages used in the input box to obtain the team members' weight loss. These variables are: 1) strInputMessage: Is used in the function call to contain the message displayed in the input box; 2) strInputHeading: Contains the message displayed in the title bar of the input box; 3) strNormalMessage: The normal message that appears in the input box when no error has occurred; 4) strNonNumericError: The message that appears in the input box when the user has entered a nonnumeric value; 5) strNegativeError: The message that appears in the input box when the user has entered zero or a negative number. Declare and initialize these five variables.

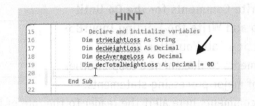

HINT

(continues)

● **Declare and Initialize Variables Used in the Loop Processing** Three variables are used for processing the loop in the program. These variables are: 1) strCancelClicked: This variable contains a null string and is used to determine if the user tapped or clicked the Cancel button in the input box; 2) intMaxNumberOfEntries: Contains the maximum number of entries for team member weight losses (program requirements state the maximum number is eight); 3) intNumberOfEntries: The counter for the valid number of team member weight loss values entered by the user. This variable is used to determine when the maximum number of entries has been made and to act as the divisor when calculating the average weight loss per team member.

```
HINT
28      'Declare and initialize loop variables
29
30      Dim strCancelClicked As String = ""
31      Dim intMaxNumberOfEntries As Integer = 8
32      Dim intNumberOfEntries As Integer = 1
```

● **Write Comments for the Do Until Loop and Write the Priming InputBox Function Call** You often can use comments to document a loop or other set of major processing statements.
The comments here alert the reader to the role of the Do Until loop. The priming InputBox function call obtains the first team members' weight loss or allows the user to click the Cancel button. The normal message is displayed. The space at the end of the argument list places a space in the input box so if the user clicks the OK button without entering any data, the command will not be treated the same as clicking the Cancel button *(ref: Figure 6-70).*

```
HINT
30
31      ' This loop allows the user to enter the weight loss of up to 8 team members.
32      ' The loop terminates when the user has entered 8 weight loss vales or the user
33      ' clicks the Cancel button or the Close button in the InputBox
34      strWeightLoss = InputBox(strInputMessage & intNumberOfEntries, strInputHeading, " ")
35
```

● **Code the Do Until Loop** Because the application requests the weight loss values of up to eight team members, the Do Until loop should continue until eight weight losses are entered or until the user clicks the Cancel or Close button in the input box. Enter the Do Until loop using IntelliSense *(ref: Figure 6-63, Figure 6-69).*

```
HINT
36      Do Until intNumberOfEntries > intMaxNumberOfEntries Or strWeightLoss = strCancelClicked
```

● **Validate That the Entry Is a Number** The first process in the Do Until loop is to validate that the team member weight loss entered by the user is a numeric value. Enter the If...Then statement to test if the value in the strWeightLoss variable is numeric.

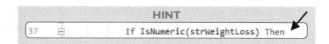

```
HINT
37      If IsNumeric(strWeightLoss) Then
```

- **Convert the Value Entered from a String to the Decimal Data Type** If the user entered a numeric value, the next step is to convert the string value the user entered to a Decimal data type. Using IntelliSense, enter the code to convert the value in the strWeightLoss variable from the String to the Decimal data type and place the result in the decWeightLoss variable.

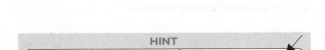

```
HINT
38                    decWeightLoss = Convert.ToDecimal(strWeightLoss)
```

- **Validate That the Entered Value Is a Positive Number** After the value is converted, the program must validate that the number is positive. Write the If...Then statement to test whether the value in the decWeightLoss variable is greater than zero.

```
HINT
39            If decWeightLoss > 0 Then
```

- **Perform the Processing When the User Enters a Valid Weight Loss** After ensuring the weight loss entered by the user is valid, the next steps are to perform the processing for valid weight loss. Four steps are required: 1) Add the weight loss as an item to the lstWeightLoss ListBox object *(ref: Figure 6-26)*; 2) Add the weight loss the user entered to the decTotalWeightLoss accumulator *(ref: Figure 6-38)*. The accumulated weight loss is used to calculate the average weight loss; 3) Increment the intNumberOfEntries counter by 1 because the user entered a valid weight loss *(ref: Figure 6-38)*. This value is used as the divisor to determine the average weight loss, and as one of the indicators that the loop should be terminated; 4) Because the user entered a valid weight loss, the normal message should appear the next time the input box is displayed. Therefore, the normal message should be moved to the strInputMessage variable. Using IntelliSense, enter the code for these four activities.

```
HINT
40            lstWeightLoss.Items.Add(decWeightLoss)
41            decTotalWeightLoss += decWeightLoss
42            intNumberOfEntries += 1
43            strInputMessage = strNormalMessage
```

- **Assign an Error Message If the User Entered a Negative Weight Loss** If the user entered a negative weight loss, the next input box should display the negative number error message *(ref: Figure 6-71)*. Following the Else statement for the If statement that checks for a number greater than zero, enter the assignment statement that places the value in the strNegativeError variable in the strInputMessage variable.

```
HINT
44            Else
45                strInputMessage = strNegativeError
46            End If
```

(continues)

- **Assign an Error Message If the User Enters a Nonnumeric Weight Loss** If the user enters a nonnumeric weight loss, the next input box should show the nonnumeric error message *(ref: Figure 6-70)*. Following the Else Statement for the If statement that checks for numeric data, enter the assignment statement that places the value in the strNonNumericError variable in the strInputMessage variable.

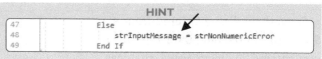

```
HINT
47          Else
48              strInputMessage = strNonNumericError
49          End If
```

- **Code the InputBox Function Call** The first InputBox function call was placed before the Do Until loop to prime the loop. To continue the process after the first value is entered, another InputBox function is needed as the last statement inside the loop to request subsequent values. This statement should be executed only if the maximum number of entries has not been exceeded. So, an If structure is required to determine if the maximum number of entries has been reached. If not, the InputBox function call is executed *(ref: Figure 6-72)*.

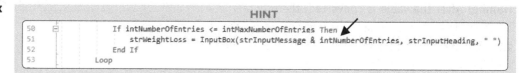

```
HINT
50      If intNumberOfEntries <= intMaxNumberOfEntries Then
51          strWeightLoss = InputBox(strInputMessage & intNumberOfEntries, strInputHeading, " ")
52      End If
53  Loop
```

The coding for the variables and Do Until loop that processes the data in the program is complete (Figure 6-97). Examine the code in Figure 6-97 to understand the loop processing. The priming of the loop, by both setting the value in the intNumberOfEntries variable (line 29) and calling the InputBox function (line 34), is critical for proper execution of the loop. Increasing the loop counter when a valid entry is made (line 42) also is fundamental in the loop processing because testing this counter is one way the Do Until loop can be terminated. Also, using variables for messages instead of literals in the actual code demonstrates how professional programs are coded. You should follow these examples in your programming.

RESULT OF STEP 6

```
30
31          ' This loop allows the user to enter the weight loss of up to 8 team members.
32          ' The loop terminates when the user has entered 8 weight loss vales or the user
33          ' clicks the Cancel button or the Close button in the InputBox
34          strWeightLoss = InputBox(strInputMessage & intNumberOfEntries, strInputHeading, " ")
35
36          Do Until intNumberOfEntries > intMaxNumberOfEntries Or strWeightLoss = strCancelClicked
37              If IsNumeric(strWeightLoss) Then
38                  decWeightLoss = Convert.ToDecimal(strWeightLoss)
39                  If decWeightLoss > 0 Then
40                      lstWeightLoss.Items.Add(decWeightLoss)
41                      decTotalWeightLoss += decWeightLoss
42                      intNumberOfEntries += 1
43                      strInputMessage = strNormalMessage
44                  Else
45                      strInputMessage = strNegativeError
46                  End If
47              Else
48                  strInputMessage = strNonNumericError
49              End If
50              If intNumberOfEntries <= intMaxNumberOfEntries Then
51                  strWeightLoss = InputBox(strInputMessage & intNumberOfEntries, strInputHeading, " ")
52              End If
53          Loop
54
```

FIGURE 6-97

4

● **Set the Result Label's Visible Property** When you finish the Do Until loop, you must complete three tasks to finish the Enter Weight Loss button click event handler: 1) Make the label that will contain the average weight loss visible; 2) Calculate and display the average weight loss; 3) Disable the Enter Weight Loss button. If at least one weight loss value has been entered using IntelliSense, write the code to create the If statement and make the lblAverageLoss label visible.

HINT

```
55          'Calculates and displays average team weight loss
56          If intNumberOfEntries > 1 Then
57              lblAverageLoss.Visible = True
58              decAverageLoss = decTotalWeightLoss / (intNumberOfEntries - 1)
59              lblAverageLoss.Text = "Average weight loss is " &
60                  decAverageLoss.ToString("F1") & " lbs"
61          Else
62              MsgBox("No weight loss value entered")
63          End If
```

(continues)

● **Calculate the Average Weight Loss**
To calculate the average of the weight loss values the user entered, the value in the decTotalWeightLoss variable (accumulator) must be divided by the number of team members entered (counter). At the end of the loop shown in Figure 6-97, the value in the intNumberOfEntries variable always will be one greater than the actual number of team members entered, so the total weight loss must be divided by the value in intNumberOfEntries minus 1. This calculation should occur only if one or more team members weight loss values were entered, so an If statement must be used to check whether the value in the intNumberOfEntries variable is greater than 1. If so, the average weight loss is calculated; if not, the "No weight loss value entered" message should be displayed using a MsgBox. Using IntelliSense, write the code to perform this processing.

```
                                          HINT
58              decAverageLoss = decTotalWeightLoss / (intNumberOfEntries - 1)
59              lblAverageLoss.Text = "Average weight loss is " &
60                  decAverageLoss.ToString("F1") & " lbs"
61          Else
62              MsgBox("No weight loss value entered")
63          End If
```

● **Change the Enter Weight Loss Button Enabled Property to False** After the average weight loss is calculated and displayed, the Enabled property of the btnWeightLoss button is set to False to dim the button. Using IntelliSense, write the code to accomplish this processing.

The code for the btnWeightLoss button click event handler is completed (Figure 6-98).

RESULT OF STEP 6

```
54
55              'Calculates and displays average team weight loss
56          If intNumberOfEntries > 1 Then
57              lblAverageLoss.Visible = True
58              decAverageLoss = decTotalWeightLoss / (intNumberOfEntries - 1)
59              lblAverageLoss.Text = "Average weight loss is " &
60                  decAverageLoss.ToString("F1") & " lbs"
61          Else
62              MsgBox("No weight loss value entered")
63          End If
64
65              ' Disables the Weight Loss button
66          btnWeightLoss.Enabled = False
67      End Sub
```

FIGURE 6-98

5

● **Run the Program** After coding a major section of the program, you should run the program to ensure it is working properly. Click the Start button on the Standard toolbar to run the Fitness Challenge application. Click the Enter Weight Loss button and then enter the weight loss of eight team members. Verify the weight losses are displayed properly and the average weight loss is correct. Close the program by clicking the Close button. Run the program again, click the Enter Weight Loss button, enter the weight loss for four team members, enter a nonnumeric weight loss, enter a weight loss that is less than zero, and then click the Cancel button in the input box. Ensure that the weight loss values are displayed properly, the average weight loss is correct, and the error messages are displayed properly in the input box. Close the program. Run the program again, click the Enter Weight Loss button, and then click the Cancel button in the input box. Ensure that the "No weight loss value entered" message is displayed. Close the program and then run it as many times as necessary to ensure the program is working properly. If the program does not run properly, consider setting a breakpoint and checking the values in the variables *(ref: Figure 6-76)*.

iStockphoto.com/udra

6

● **Enter the Code for the Clear Menu Item Click Event** Click the frmFitness.vb [Design] tab in the code window to display the design window. Click File on the MenuStrip object, and then double-click the Clear menu item to open the Clear click event handler in the code window. The Clear click event handler must perform three tasks: 1) Clear the lstWeightLoss list box; 2) Hide the average weight loss Label object; 3) Enable the Enter Weight Loss Button object. Using IntelliSense, write the code for these three tasks.

```
HINT
68
69    Private Sub mnuClear_Click(sender As Object, e As EventArgs) Handles mnuClear.Click
70        ' The mnuClear click event clears the ListBox object and hides
71        ' the average weight loss label. It also enables the Weight Loss button
72
73        lstWeightLoss.Items.Clear()
74        lblAverageLoss.Visible = False
75        btnWeightLoss.Enabled = True
76    End Sub
77
```

(continues)

• **Enter the Code for the Exit Menu Item Click Event** Return to
the design window. Double-click the Exit menu item. In the code
window, enter a Close procedure call that will close the window and
exit the program.

*The code for the Clear menu item click event and the Exit menu item click event is completed (Figure 6-99). The code
for the program is also completed.*

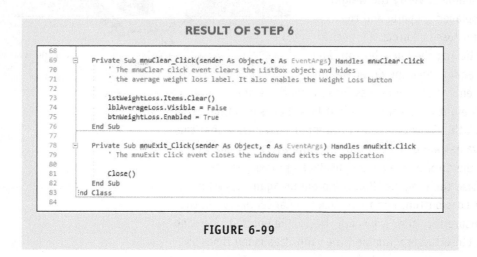

RESULT OF STEP 6

```
68
69  ⊟    Private Sub mnuClear_Click(sender As Object, e As EventArgs) Handles mnuClear.Click
70           ' The mnuClear click event clears the ListBox object and hides
71           ' the average weight loss label. It also enables the Weight Loss button
72
73           lstWeightLoss.Items.Clear()
74           lblAverageLoss.Visible = False
75           btnWeightLoss.Enabled = True
76       End Sub
77
78  ⊟    Private Sub mnuExit_Click(sender As Object, e As EventArgs) Handles mnuExit.Click
79           ' The mnuExit click event closes the window and exits the application
80
81           Close()
82       End Sub
83   End Class
84
```

FIGURE 6-99

7

• **Publish the Fitness Challenge Application** After completing the
program, you can publish it using ClickOnce deployment so it can
be installed on multiple computers. To open the Publish Wizard and
begin the deployment process, click Build on the menu bar and then
click Publish Fitness Challenge on the Build menu *(ref: Figure 6-86)*.

• **Select the Publish File Location** The Publish Wizard dialog box
asks where you want to publish the application. Change the default
location to the same file location that you used to save your Windows
application by clicking the Browse button and then selecting the
drive. For example, select the D: drive, a USB drive. After selecting
the drive, click the Next button in the Publish Wizard dialog box
(ref: Figure 6-86).

- **Select How Users Will Install the Application** In the next Publish Wizard dialog box, select the option that lets users install the application from a CD-ROM or DVD-ROM. Then, click the Next button *(ref: Figure 6-87)*.

- **Indicate the Application Will Not Check for Updates** Click the "The application will not check for updates" radio button to indicate no updates will be checked. This is the normal selection when programs are placed on CDs or DVDs. Then, click the Next button in the Publish Wizard dialog box *(ref: Figure 6-88)*.

- **View the Summary Window** The Publish Wizard summary is displayed. Click the Finish button to publish the application *(ref: Figure 6-89)*.

- **View the Installation Files** After the publishing succeeds, a folder is created with the installation files that could be placed on a CD, DVD, or other computer *(ref: Figure 6-90)*.

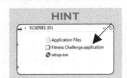

HINT

Code Listing

The complete code for the sample program is shown in Figure 6-100.

```vb
┌ Fitness Challenge

frmFitness.vb ⊕ ✕

VB Fitness Challenge                                        ▾  ⚙ frmFitness

   1    ☐ ' Program Name: Fitness Challenge
   2      ' Author:        Corinne Hoisington
   3      ' Date:          September 30, 2019
   4      ' Purpose:       The Fitness Challenge program enters the weight loss
   5      '                loss from team members for a fitness challenge. It displays each
   6      '                weight loss value. After all weight loss values have been entered,
   7      '                it displays the average weight loss for the team.
   8
   9      Option Strict On
  10    ☐ Public Class frmFitness
  11    ☐     Private Sub btnWeightLoss_Click(sender As Object, e As EventArgs) Handles btnWeightLoss.Click
  12              ' The btnWeightLoss_Click event accepts and displays up to 8 weight loss values
  13              ' and then calculates and displays the average weight loss for the team
  14
  15              ' Declare and initialize variables
  16              Dim strWeightLoss As String
  17              Dim decWeightLoss As Decimal
  18              Dim decAverageLoss As Decimal
  19              Dim decTotalWeightLoss As Decimal = 0D
  20              Dim strInputMessage As String = "Enter the weight loss for team member #"
  21              Dim strInputHeading As String = "Weight Loss"
  22              Dim strNormalMessage As String = "Enter the weight loss for team member #"
  23              Dim strNonNumericError As String = "Error - Enter a number for the weight loss of team member #"
  24              Dim strNegativeError As String = "Error - Enter a positive number for the weight loss of team member #"
  25
  26              'Declare and initialize loop variables
  27              Dim strCancelClicked As String = ""
  28              Dim intMaxNumberOfEntries As Integer = 8
  29              Dim intNumberOfEntries As Integer = 1
  30
  31              ' This loop allows the user to enter the weight loss of up to 8 team members.
  32              ' The loop terminates when the user has entered 8 weight loss vales or the user
  33              ' clicks the Cancel button or the Close button in the InputBox
  34              strWeightLoss = InputBox(strInputMessage & intNumberOfEntries, strInputHeading, " ")
  35
  36    ☐         Do Until intNumberOfEntries > intMaxNumberOfEntries Or strWeightLoss = strCancelClicked
  37    ☐             If IsNumeric(strWeightLoss) Then
  38                       decWeightLoss = Convert.ToDecimal(strWeightLoss)
  39    ☐                 If decWeightLoss > 0 Then
  40                           lstWeightLoss.Items.Add(decWeightLoss)
  41                           decTotalWeightLoss += decWeightLoss
  42                           intNumberOfEntries += 1
  43                           strInputMessage = strNormalMessage
  44                       Else
  45                           strInputMessage = strNegativeError
  46                       End If
  47                   Else
  48                       strInputMessage = strNonNumericError
  49                   End If
  50    ☐             If intNumberOfEntries <= intMaxNumberOfEntries Then
  51                       strWeightLoss = InputBox(strInputMessage & intNumberOfEntries, strInputHeading, " ")
  52                   End If
  53              Loop
```

FIGURE 6-100 (continues)

```
54
55          'Calculates and displays average team weight loss
56          If intNumberOfEntries > 1 Then
57              lblAverageLoss.Visible = True
58              decAverageLoss = decTotalWeightLoss / (intNumberOfEntries - 1)
59              lblAverageLoss.Text = "Average weight loss is " &
60                  decAverageLoss.ToString("F1") & " lbs"
61          Else
62              MsgBox("No weight loss value entered")
63          End If
64
65          ' Disables the Weight Loss button
66          btnWeightLoss.Enabled = False
67      End Sub
68
69      Private Sub mnuClear_Click(sender As Object, e As EventArgs) Handles mnuClear.Click
70          ' The mnuClear click event clears the ListBox object and hides
71          ' the average weight loss label. It also enables the Weight Loss button
72
73          lstWeightLoss.Items.Clear()
74          lblAverageLoss.Visible = False
75          btnWeightLoss.Enabled = True
76      End Sub
77
78      Private Sub mnuExit_Click(sender As Object, e As EventArgs) Handles mnuExit.Click
79          ' The mnuExit click event closes the window and exits the application
80
81          Close()
82      End Sub
83  End Class
84
```

FIGURE 6-100 (continued)

Summary

In this chapter you have learned to design and write code to implement loops and to create menus, list boxes, and an input box.

1. Write a statement that displays the default value of $5.49 in the input box shown in Figure 6-101 and assigns the return value from the InputBox function to a variable named decPizzaSlice with the message Cost of Pizza Slice with the title Giordano's Pizza.

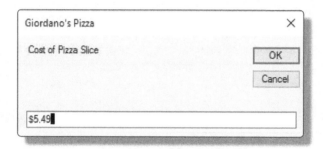

FIGURE 6-101

2. Write compound operators for the following equations:

   a. intStrike = intStrike+ 10

   b. dblCube = dblCube ^ 3

   c. strDog = strDog & "Treat"

   d. decOvertime = decOvertime *1.5

3. Write For...Next loops that calculate the sum of the following ranges and assign their sum to a variable named intSum:

   a. The first 50 numbers starting with 0

   b. The even numbers beginning at 10 and ending with 100

   c. The numbers 20, 30, 40, 50, 60, 70 and 80

4. Find the error(s) in the following For...Next header statements:

   a. For intCounter = "1" To "19"

   b. For strNumber = 98 To 71 Step 2

   c. For intValue = 12 To 52 Step –4

5. Explain the purpose of placing an ampersand before or within a MenuStrip item.

6. Write a command to add a list of precipitation types to a ListBox object named lstWater.

7. Write the command to clear a ListBox object named lstWinners.

8. What is the name of the property that displays an image as the background of a Form object?

9. What is the name of the property that can be used to stretch the background image of the Form object?

10. Using a compound operator, write an assignment statement to decrease the value in intCounter by 6.7.

11. Write a top-controlled Do Until loop with an empty body that would continue until intValue is less than 19.

12. Write a bottom-controlled Do While loop with an empty body that continues while the user enters "Yes" into the strContinue variable.

13. Write a Do While loop to validate that the user enters a nonzero integer into an input box for a variable named intDenominator.

14. Is the For...Next loop top-controlled or bottom-controlled?

15. Write the code for an infinite Do Until loop with the variable intForever.

16. Which loop should be used if you know the required number of times the loop will be executed?

17. What is the fewest number of times a top-controlled Do Until loop is executed?

18. Write a data validation Do loop to check that the variable intValidAge entered from an input box is between 1 and 118.

19. A loop inside another loop is called a _____ _____.

20. When you insert standard items in a MenuStrip object, what File menu items are automatically created by default?

1. The loop shown in Figure 6-102 should repeat 10 times. If it will not repeat 10 times, change the code so it will.

```
7        For intRepeat = 20 To 10
8            MsgBox("The value is " & intRepeat.ToString("C0"))
9        Next
```

FIGURE 6-102

(continues)

2. What output does the code shown in Figure 6-103 produce? How would you change the code to produce a list box containing the values 12–22?

```
15          intRate = 12
16          Do While intRate <= 10
17              lstDisplay.Items.Add(intRate)
18              intRate += 1
19          Loop
```

FIGURE 6-103

3. What is the output of the code shown in Figure 6-104?

```
5           Dim intAdd As Integer
6           Dim intOuterLoop As Integer
7           Dim intInnerLoop As Integer
8
9           intAdd = 0
10          For intOuterLoop = 1 To 8
11              For intInnerLoop = 3 To 7
12                  intAdd += 1
13              Next
14          Next
            MsgBox.Show("The final value is " & intAdd.ToString())
```

FIGURE 6-104

4. What is the output of the code shown in Figure 6-105?

```
33          Dim intValue As Integer
34
35          intValue = 2
36          Do While intValue <= 9
37              lstDisplay.Items.Add(intValue & " " & intValue ^ 3)
38              intValue += 2
39          Loop
```

FIGURE 6-105

5. Fix the errors in the loop shown in Figure 6-106.

```
41          Dim intStart As Integer = 8
42
43          Loop
44          intStart = +4
45          Do While intStart < 24
```

FIGURE 6-106

6. What is the output of the code shown in Figure 6-107?

```
53          intCount = 40
54          Do Until intCount < 26
55              intCount -= 2
56              lstCount.Items.Add(intCount)
57          Loop
```

FIGURE 6-107

Program Analysis

1. What is the value of lblResult after the code shown in Figure 6-108 is executed?

```
73          Dim intCounter As Integer = -15
74
75          Do While intCount < 25
76              intCount += 5
77              lblResult.Text &= intCount.ToString() & " "
78          Loop
```

FIGURE 6-108

2. What is the value of lblResult after the code shown in Figure 6-109 is executed?

```
80          Dim intCountIt As Integer
81
82          intCountIt = 6
83          Do
84              intCountIt += 3
85              lblResult.Text &= intCountIt.ToString() & " "
86          Loop Until intCountIt = 21
```

FIGURE 6-109

3. Rewrite the top-controlled Do While loop shown in Figure 6-110 as a top-controlled Do Until loop.

```
88          Dim intQuantity As Integer
89
90          intQuantity = -5
91          Do While intQuantity < 30
92              intQuantity += 5
93          Loop
```

FIGURE 6-110

(continues)

4. Convert the Do loop shown in Figure 6-111 to a For...Next loop.

```
 95          Dim intIncrease As Integer
 96
 97          intIncrease = 10
 98          Do While intIncrease < 40
 99              lstDisplay.Items.Add(intIncrease)
100              intIncrease += 2
101          Loop
```

FIGURE 6-111

5. How many times will the inner statement inside the nested loop in Figure 6-112 be executed?

```
103          For intOuterLoop = 3 To 5
104              For intInnerLoop = 6 To 10
105                  lstDays.Items.Add("Value: " & intOuterLoop.ToString() & _
106                      " Count: " & intInnerLoop.ToString())
107              Next
108          Next
```

FIGURE 6-112

6. Write a For...Next loop that adds the odd numbers 1 through 49 and assigns their sum to the variable intSum. The program should start with the lines shown in Figure 6-113 (use the variables shown in lines 120–123 in your code).

```
120          Dim intLoopValue As Integer
121          Dim intStartvalue As Integer
122          Dim intEndvalue As Integer
123          Dim intSum As Integer
124
125          intStartvalue = 1
126          intEndvalue = 49
127          intSum = 0
```

FIGURE 6-113

Complete one or more of the following case programming assignments. Submit the program and materials you create to your instructor. The level of difficulty is indicated for each case programming assignment.

●	= Easiest
● ●	= Intermediate
● ● ●	= Challenging

1

MOST RAINFALL IN THE USA

Design a Windows application and write the code that will execute according to the program requirements shown in Figure 6-114. Before writing the code, create an event planning document for each event in the program. The Use Case Definition document is shown in Figure 6-115 on the following page. The completed user interface is shown in Figure 6-116 on the following page.

REQUIREMENTS DOCUMENT

Date:	March 17, 2019
Date Submitted:	
Application Title:	Most Rainfall in the USA
Purpose:	This Windows Classic Desktop application is written for Kauai, Hawaii, the rainiest location in the United States, to compute the average monthly amount of rainfall per year.
Program Procedures:	In a Windows application, the user enters up to 12 values representing the number of inches of rain each month to compute the average rainfall in a given number of months or a full year.
Algorithms, Processing, and Conditions:	1. In an InputBox object, the user enters up to 12 amounts of rainfall per month in inches.
	2. Each amount of rainfall per month is displayed in the ListBox object.
	3. After 12 entries of rainfall values are entered, the average rainfall is calculated and displayed.
	4. A File menu contains a Clear and an Exit option. The Clear menu item clears the average rainfall and the 12 values representing the amount of rainfall per month in Kauai. The Exit menu item closes the application.
	5. If the user clicks the Cancel button in the input box before entering 12 values, compute the average amount of rainfall entered.
	6. If the user clicks the Cancel button before entering any rainfall values, display a message indicating the user did not enter a value.
Notes and Restrictions:	1. Nonnumeric values should not be accepted.
	2. Negative values should not be accepted.
	3. The average rainfall should be rounded to the nearest tenth of an inch.
Comments:	1. The application allows decimal entries.
	2. Obtain a background image for this program from CengageBrain.com. The name of the image file is hawaii.

FIGURE 6-114

(continues)

Most Rainfall in the USA

USE CASE DEFINITION

1. The Windows application opens with the heading "Most Rainfall in US - Kauai," a ListBox object that displays the monthly rainfall amounts, an image, and a Button object that allows the user to begin entering their rainfall amounts in inches.
2. A menu bar displays the File menu, which has two menu items: Clear and Exit.
3. The user enters up to 12 monthly values in an InputBox object, with each value representing the number of inches of rainfall per month in Kauai.
4. The program asks the user for the rainfall amount again if the value is a negative number or the entry is a nonnumeric value.
5. The program displays the average inches of rainfall rounded to one decimal place.
6. The user can clear the input and the result by clicking the Clear menu item, and then can repeat Steps 3–5. If the user clicks the Cancel button in the input box, the average for the values entered is calculated. If the user did not enter any values, the program displays an appropriate message.
7. The user clicks the Exit menu item to close the application.

FIGURE 6-115

FIGURE 6-116

iStockphoto.com/EllenSmile

2

INTERNET SPEED TEST SURVEY

Design a Windows application and write the code that will execute according to the program requirements shown in Figure 6-117. Before writing the code, create an event planning document for each event in the program. The Use Case Definition document is shown in Figure 6-118 on the following page. The completed user interface is shown in Figure 6-119 on the following page.

REQUIREMENTS DOCUMENT

Date:	July 31, 2019
Date Submitted:	
Application Title:	Internet Speed Test Survey
Purpose:	This Windows Classic Desktop application finds the average speed of a home Internet connection (see speedtest.net to measure your own connection's download speed).
Program Procedures:	To test the average speed of an Internet service provider with their local customers, a Windows application will compute the average Internet download speed. The application allows the user to enter up to 10 download speeds. The average speed is displayed in Mbps (Megabits per second).
Algorithms, Processing, and Conditions:	1. The user clicks the Enter Internet Speed button to enter their Internet speed in Mbps.
	2. Each speed is displayed in a ListBox object with a scroll bar that appears when the number of values exceeds the given space.
	3. After 10 values have been entered, the average is displayed.
	4. If the user clicks the Cancel button before entering any time values, display an appropriate message.
Notes and Restrictions:	1. The result should include two places after the decimal point.
	2. Nonnumeric values should not be accepted.
	3. Negative numbers should not be accepted.
Comments:	1. The application allows decimal entries.
	2. Obtain a background image for this program from CengageBrain.com. The name of the image file is speed.

FIGURE 6-117

Internet Speed Test Survey

USE CASE DEFINITION

1. The Windows application opens, displaying Internet Speed Test Survey as the heading, a ListBox object with a scroll bar as needed that will display the Internet download speed of each home user tested at speedtest.net, and a Button object that allows the user to enter their download speed in Mbps.
2. In an InputBox object, the user enters up to 10 values representing the Internet speed of their home connection.
3. The program asks the user for the Internet speed again if the value is a negative or nonnumeric value.
4. The program displays the average time to two decimal places.
5. If the user clicks the Cancel button in the input box before entering 10 time values, the program uses the number of seconds entered for calculations. If the user enters no values, an appropriate message is displayed.

FIGURE 6-118

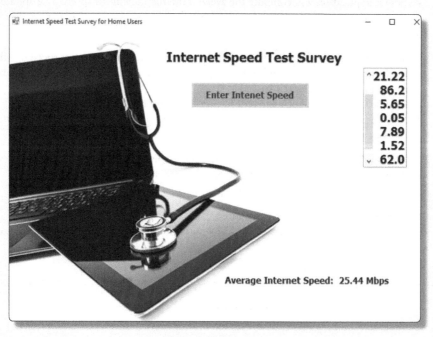

iStockphoto.com/PhotoBylove

FIGURE 6-119

3 •• SOFTBALL SCOREBOARD

Design a Windows application and write the code that will execute according to the program requirements shown in Figure 6-120. Before writing the code, create an event planning document for each event in the program.

REQUIREMENTS DOCUMENT

Date:	November 3, 2019
Date Submitted:	
Application Title:	Softball Scoreboard
Purpose:	This application calculates the score of each inning during a softball game for one team.
Program Procedures:	In a Windows Classic Desktop application, the user enters the score of each inning to display the total on the scoreboard after the seven innings in a regulation softball game.
Algorithms, Processing, and Conditions:	1. The user clicks the Enter Score button in an InputBox object to enter a score after each inning of the game. 2. The number of runs and the running score is displayed in a ListBox after each inning. 3. The total final score is displayed after the seventh inning. 4. A File menu contains a Clear and an Exit option. The Clear menu item clears the result and the number of runs. The Exit menu item closes the application.
Notes and Restrictions:	1. Nonnumeric values should not be accepted. 2. A negative value should not be accepted.
Comments:	Locate an appropriate image online. This image should be placed as a background image and stretched across the Form object.

FIGURE 6-120

4

PENNY OR NICKEL CHALLENAGE

Design a Windows application and write the code that will execute according to the program requirements shown in Figure 6-121. Before writing the code, create an event planning document for each event in the program. Create a Use Case Definition document for the application.

REQUIREMENTS DOCUMENT

Date:	June 21, 2019
Date Submitted:	
Application Title:	Penny or Nickel Challenge
Purpose:	This Windows Classic Desktop application finds the amount of your monthly pay if you are paid a penny or nickel for the first workday and the pay is doubled each subsequent workday. New employees are paid a penny for the first workday and experienced employees are paid a nickel for the first day.
Program Procedures:	The user enters the number of workdays in a monthly pay period and the pay for the first day. The program calculates and displays the amount of pay for the pay period.
Algorithms, Processing, and Conditions:	1. The user enters the number of days in the pay period.
	2. The user selects a RadioButton object to indicate the pay amount for the first day: a penny or a nickel.
	3. After the user enters the number of days and pay for the first day, the total amount earned is calculated and displayed.
	4. A File menu contains a Clear and an Exit option. The Clear menu item clears the result and the RadioButton object. The Exit menu item closes the application.
Notes and Restrictions:	1. Nonnumeric values should not be accepted.
	2. Negative values should not be accepted.
	3. The minimum number of workdays in the pay period is 10 days. The maximum number of workdays in a pay period is 22 days.
	4. A background image should be located online and displayed on the form.
Comments:	n/a

FIGURE 6-121

Case Programming Assignments

5

●●●

FACTORIAL CALCULATOR

Create a requirements document and a Use Case Definition document and design a Windows application based on the case project shown in Figure 6-122:

Most calculators have an operation called a "factorial," which is shown on a calculator key as an exclamation point. For example, 5! (5 factorial) multiplies 5 * 4 * 3 * 2 * 1 to calculate the result of 120. Request that the user select a number from 1 to 12 and display all the factorials up to the value, including that value. Using loops to compute the factorial, display the following factorials in a ListBox object. The application should have a single background image and menus. Publish the application.

1! 1

2! 2

3! 6

4! 24

5! 120

…

12! 479001600

FIGURE 6-122

Case Programming Assignments

6 ●●● HOME DOWN PAYMENT

Create a requirements document and a Use Case Definition document and design a Windows application based on the case project shown in Figure 6-123:

> Write a Windows application that allows you to enter the amount of money you would like to place as a down payment on a home, the interest rate, and a number of years. For example, if you hope to buy a home in five years with a down payment, would the principal of $17,000 grow over five years at 4 percent interest to a down payment of $20,000? Display a ListBox object for each year and the amount of money in the account at the end of that year. Determine whether you have saved enough money for the home example. Nonnumeric and negative values should not be accepted. Publish the application. *Hint*: The formula for compound interest for one year is: Amount = Principal * (1 + Rate). For 5 years of compound interest, this formula should be executed 5 times with the principal increasing to the new amount each year. The application should have a single background image and menus.

FIGURE 6-123

Using Procedures and Exception Handling

OBJECTIVES

You will have mastered the material in this chapter when you can:

- Create a splash screen

- Pause the splash screen

- Add a ComboBox object to a Windows form

- Write code for a SelectedIndexChanged event

- Understand procedures

- Code a Sub procedure

- Pass an argument to a procedure by value

- Pass an argument to a procedure by reference

- Code a Function procedure to return a value

- Create a class-level variable

- Catch an exception using a Try-Catch block

- Determine the order of exceptions in a Try-Catch block

Introduction

The programs you have written thus far in this course were relatively small applications. Most real-world software, however, solves more expansive problems. As an application grows, it is important to divide each facet of a problem into separate sections of code called **procedures**. By using the principle of divide and conquer to create procedures, the code becomes more manageable.

In previous programs you have learned about data verification to ensure the user enters valid data before the data is processed. To expand your knowledge of data verification, you need to understand exception handling using Try-Catch blocks, which can check for any error a user might commit. By managing exceptions using Try-Catch blocks, you build high-quality, robust applications.

Finally, one way to make your programs more professional is to display a splash screen while the full program opens. In this chapter, you will learn to design and write procedures, include Try-Catch blocks in your program, and create a splash screen.

Chapter Project

The sample program in this chapter displays two Windows forms and is more complex than previous applications. An international company has requested a Windows application that provides pricing information for scuba diving expeditions. The Oceanic Scuba Expeditions company promises to provide the highest reef fish diversity in the world. Travel to such places as Australia, Belize, and Fiji where you scuba dive into the most beautiful reefs on the planet. Your dive team can consist of two to six PADI certified scuba divers. The purpose of the application is to display the pricing information for scuba expeditions at worldwide locations. The Scuba Expeditions application offers scuba tours in Australia, Belize, and Fiji. Each location specializes in a different type of underwater experience. Figure 7-1 shows the available scuba adventures, the length of each dive, and the cost.

Location	Scuba Dive	Dive Length (Multiple Tanks)	Cost
Australia	Great Barrier Reef	8 hours	$350 USD
	Tiger Shark	6 hours	$200
	Fathom Chasm	4 hours	$125
Belize	Great Blue Chasm	8 hours	$200 USD
	Rainbow Reef	6 hours	$150
Fiji	Fathom Chasm	8 hours	$280 USD
	Namena Sunken Ship	6 hours	$225
	Tiger Shark	4 hours	$200

FIGURE 7-1

The program begins with an opening screen called a splash screen. In Figure 7-2, the splash screen displays the company name and image logo for approximately five seconds.

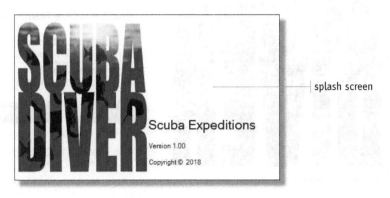

splash screen

FIGURE 7-2

iStockphoto.com/KeithBishop

After the splash screen closes, the main form of the application opens and requests that the user select the scuba dive location. When the user clicks the ComboBox arrow, the three dive locations of Australia, Belize, and Fiji appear in the drop-down list, as shown in Figure 7-3.

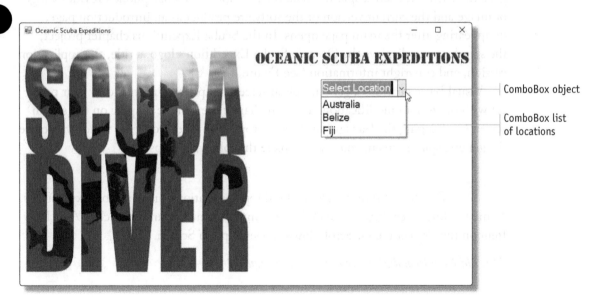

ComboBox object

ComboBox list of locations

FIGURE 7-3

iStockphoto.com/KeithBishop

After the user selects the dive location, the Windows form displays form controls that request the number of guests in the team and the type of dive trip. The user enters the number of guests on the dive team, selects the scuba dive she wants, and then clicks the Find Team Cost button. As shown in Figure 7-4, the program displays the cost and length of the scuba expedition.

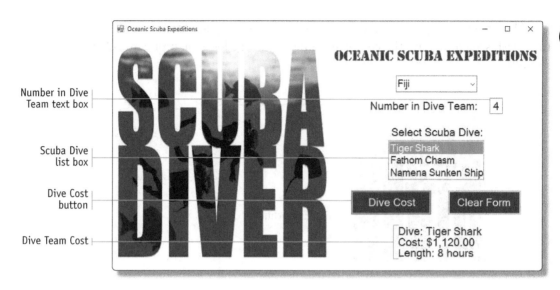

Number in Dive
Team text box

Scuba Dive
list box

Dive Cost
button

Dive Team Cost

FIGURE 7-4

iStockphoto.com/KeithBishop

Create a Splash Screen

A **splash screen** is an opening screen that appears as an application is loading, signaling that the program is about to start and displaying an image and information to engage the user. Typically a splash screen on a computer or smartphone provides a logo or image and the current version of the software product as an introduction page, disappearing after the main page opens. In the Scuba Expeditions chapter project, the splash screen displays the Oceanic Scuba Expedition's logo, a title, the application version, and copyright information (see Figure 7-2).

Visual Basic provides a generic splash screen template you can add to your project with or without modification. You can change the generic graphic on the splash screen by changing the BackgroundImage property on the Properties window. To use the generic splash screen, you can complete the following steps:

STEP 1   Create a Windows Classic Desktop application named Scuba Expeditions. Name the form `frmScuba`. Click Project on the menu bar and then click Add New Item on the Project menu. Scroll down to view Splash Screen.

The Add New Item dialog box is displayed (Figure 7-5).

Add New Item dialog box

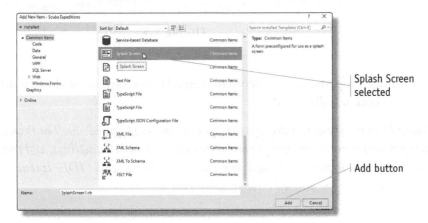

FIGURE 7-5

STEP 2 In the Add New Item dialog box, select Splash Screen in the center pane.

The Splash Screen template is selected (Figure 7-6).

Splash Screen
selected

Add button

FIGURE 7-6

STEP 3 Click the Add button in the Add New Item dialog box.

A form preconfigured by Visual Studio as a splash screen opens as a new tab named Splash-Screen1.vb[Design] in the Design window (Figure 7-7). The splash screen can be customized with different graphics and text to suit an application.

tab for Splash
Screen form

click to select
Splash Screen
form

preconfigured
Splash Screen

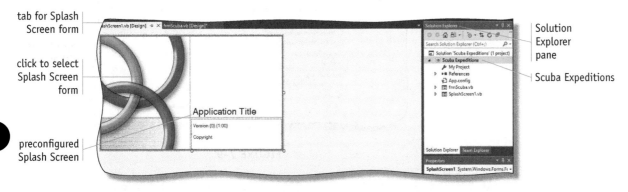

Solution
Explorer
pane

Scuba Expeditions

FIGURE 7-7

STEP 4 Click the left side of the splash screen form to select it. To set the application to display the splash screen first, right-click Scuba Expeditions in the Solution Explorer.

The splash screen form is selected (Figure 7-8). A shortcut menu opens.

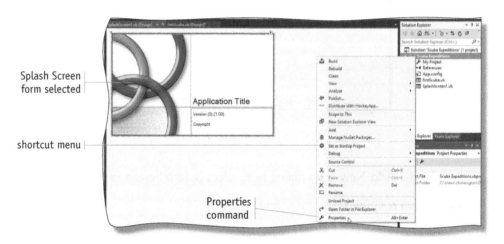

Splash Screen form selected

shortcut menu

Properties command

FIGURE 7-8

STEP 5 Click Properties on the shortcut menu. If necessary, scroll down until the Splash screen option is displayed.

The Project Designer opens and displays the Application tab (Figure 7-9). The Project Designer provides a central location for managing project properties, settings, and resources. The Project Designer appears as a single window in the Visual Studio IDE. It contains a number of pages that are accessed through tabs on the left.

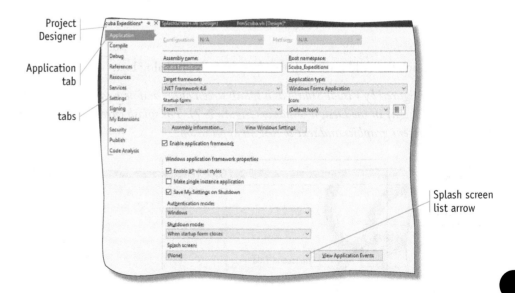

Project Designer

Application tab

tabs

Splash screen list arrow

FIGURE 7-9

STEP 6 In the Windows application framework properties section, click the Splash screen list arrow, and then click SplashScreen1 to select it as the splash screen used for the project.

SplashScreen1 is selected in the Splash screen list (Figure 7-10).

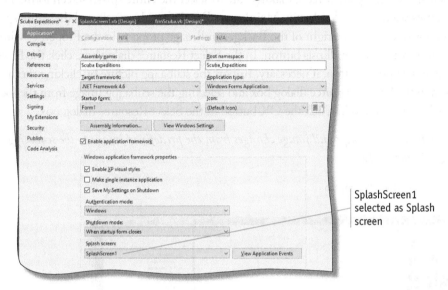

SplashScreen1
selected as Splash
screen

FIGURE 7-10

STEP 7 Scroll up and click the Assembly Information button on the Project Designer to open the Assembly Information dialog box. To customize the splash screen, if necessary, change the copyright to the present year. The title can be changed if needed and the numbers in the File version boxes can be changed as you update the application.

The copyright year is changed. The text on the splash screen form will not change until the application runs (Figure 7-11).

FIGURE 7-11

STEP 8 Click the OK button on the Assembly Information dialog box. Close the Scuba Expeditions* Project Designer window. To change the predefined image, first make sure you have the scuba.jpg picture (available on CengageBrain.com) and that you stored the image in a location you remember. Then, click the SplashScreen1.vb [Design] tab. Click the left side of the splash screen, making sure to select the entire splash screen form. The Properties window should identify MainLayoutPanel if you have selected the entire splash screen form. Click to the right of the BackgroundImage property in the Properties window, and then click the ellipsis button. In the Select Resource dialog box, click the Project resource file option button, if necessary. Import the scuba.jpg picture by clicking the Import button in the Select Resource dialog box and selecting the scuba.jpg image from the location where you stored it. Click the OK button in the Select Resource dialog box.

The splash screen background image changes from the predefined image to the scuba.jpg image (Figure 7-12).

SplashScreen1.vb [Design] tab

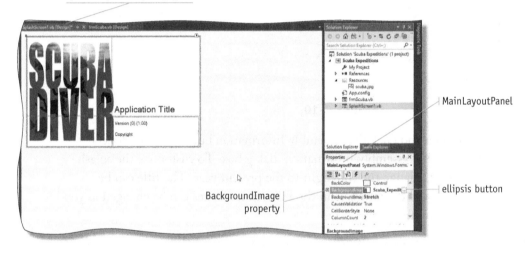

MainLayoutPanel

BackgroundImage property

ellipsis button

FIGURE 7-12

iStockphoto.com/KeithBishop

STEP 9 Run the application by clicking the Start button on the Standard toolbar.

The application begins to run. The splash screen appears for a moment and immediately closes (Figure 7-13). The amount of time the splash screen is displayed is based on the time needed to open the main form.

FIGURE 7-13

iStockphoto.com/KeithBishop

Pause the Splash Screen

The user needs enough time to read the splash screen before it closes and the main form opens. To pause the splash screen for a specific time period, you can call the Sleep procedure. In fact, you can pause the execution of any application by calling the Thread.Sleep procedure. The Sleep procedure uses an integer value that determines how long the application should pause. To pause the splash screen, you can complete the following steps:

STEP 1 After the splash screen opens, the application executes any code in the form load event handler. To display the splash screen for five seconds, you insert code that calls the Sleep procedure in the form load event handler. To open the code window and the form load event handler, double-click the background of the frmScuba Windows Form object in the Design window.

The frmScuba_Load event handler opens in the code window (Figure 7-14).

frmScuba_Load
event handler

FIGURE 7-14

STEP 2 Click inside the frmScuba_Load event handler. Type `Threading.` (with an ending period) to have IntelliSense display a list of possible entries. If necessary, type `T` to select Thread from the IntelliSense list. Type `.S` to select Sleep from the IntelliSense list. Type `(5000).`

The call for the Sleep procedure is entered (Figure 7-15). When the program runs and the frmScuba_Load event is executed, the Sleep procedure suspends the execution of the application for 5000 milliseconds (5 seconds). This means that while the splash screen is displayed, the form will not be loaded for five seconds. You can increase the number of milliseconds if you want a longer pause.

Sleep procedure call   5000 milliseconds

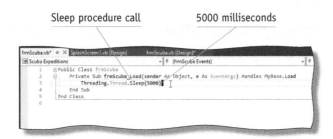

FIGURE 7-15

Add a ComboBox Object

The Scuba Expeditions sample program requires a new type of object, called a ComboBox object, to determine which dive the user will select for their scuba expedition (Figure 7-16).

FIGURE 7-16

A ComboBox object consists of two parts. The top part is a text box that allows the user to enter text. The second part is a list box; when the user clicks the arrow, the list box displays a list of items from which the user can select one item. To save space on a form, you can use a ComboBox object because the full list is not displayed until the user clicks the list arrow. The prefix for the ComboBox object (Name) property is cbo. To place a ComboBox object on a Windows Form object, you can complete the following steps:

STEP 1   Drag the ComboBox .NET component from the Common Controls category of the Toolbox to the approximate location where you want to place the ComboBox object.

The ComboBox object is placed on the Windows Form object (Figure 7-17).

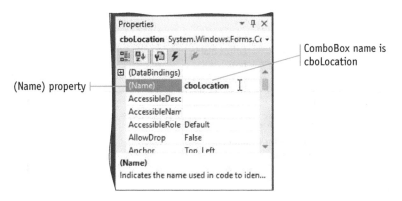

FIGURE 7-17

iStockphoto.com/KeithBishop

STEP 2 With the ComboBox object selected, scroll in the Properties window to the (Name) property. Double-click in the right column of the (Name) property, and then enter the name cboLocation.

The name you entered is displayed in the (Name) property in the Properties window (Figure 7-18).

FIGURE 7-18

STEP 3 In the Properties window, scroll to the Text property. Click to the right of the Text property and enter Select Location: to specify the text that appears in the combo box. Change the text size to 14. Resize the ComboBox object as needed to display the data in the box.

The Text property is changed to the instructions to select a scuba location (Figure 7-19).

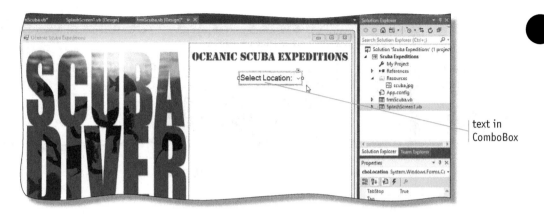

FIGURE 7-19

STEP 4 In the Properties window, scroll to the Items property, and then click to the right of the Items property on the word (Collection). Click the ellipsis button. The String Collection Editor dialog box opens. Enter the scuba diving locations `Australia` (press ENTER), `Belize` (press ENTER), and `Fiji`.

The three items for the ComboBox list are shown in the String Collection Editor dialog box (Figure 7-20).

FIGURE 7-20

STEP 5 In the String Collection Editor dialog box, click the OK button. Click the Start button on the Standard toolbar to run the application. Click the list arrow on the right side of the ComboBox object to view the contents. You can select a choice from the list.

The list in the ComboBox object contains the names previously entered in the String Collection Editor dialog box (Figure 7–21). The user can select one of the items in the list.

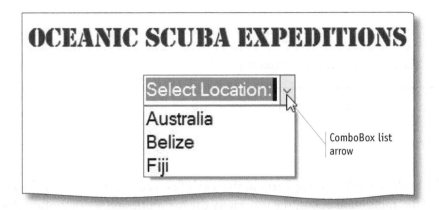

FIGURE 7-21

Determine the ComboBox Selected Index

To determine the cost of the scuba trip selected in the Scuba Expeditions sample program, the user first selects the location from the ComboBox object list. Code for the program must determine both that a value was selected and which one was selected. When the user selects an item in the ComboBox object list, the **SelectedIndex** property of the ComboBox object is assigned a number that represents the selected item. These numbers are a zero-based index, which means it begins with zero. For example, if the user selects Australia, as shown in Figure 7-22, the index of 0 is the SelectedIndex for the ComboBox object. This index number can be assigned to an Integer data type variable.

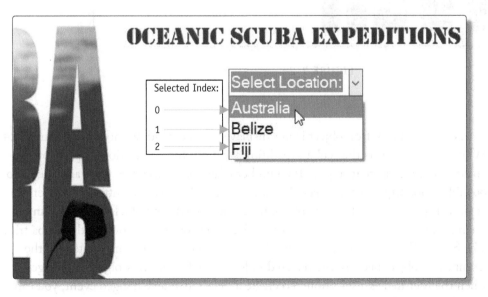

FIGURE 7-22

If the user has not made a selection, the SelectedIndex property is set to 21. To assign the item that the user selects using the SelectedIndex property, you can use a statement as shown in Figure 7-23.

```
32          intLocationChoice = cboLocation.SelectedIndex()
```

FIGURE 7-23

Handle SelectedIndexChanged Events

In the Scuba Expeditions application, the user's first action is to select the location. When the application opens, the user views the main title and a ComboBox object named cboLocation, as shown in Figure 7-24.

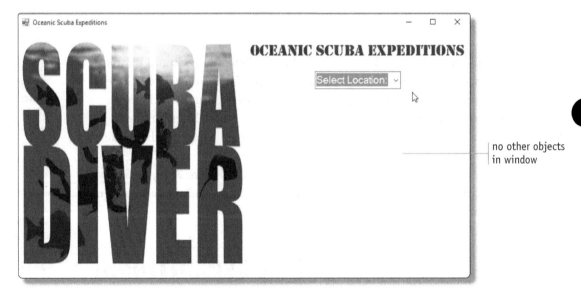

no other objects in window

FIGURE 7-24

iStockphoto.com/KeithBishop

Notice that a Button object is not displayed in the window shown in Figure 7-24. When the user selects the scuba expedition location, the application displays other objects on the form that request the number of people in the dive team and the list of possible scuba trips for the selected location. Instead of using a button click event to begin this process, another type of event handler called the **SelectedIndexChanged** event handler is executed when the user selects the country location of the scuba trip. The SelectedIndexChanged event is triggered by the user selecting an item in the ComboBox object because the selected index in the ComboBox object is changed when the user makes a selection. To create a SelectedIndexChanged event, you can complete the following steps:

STEP 1   Select the ComboBox object named cboLocation on the Windows Form object.

The cboLocation ComboBox object is selected on the form (Figure 7-25).

ComboBox object selected

FIGURE 7-25

STEP 2   Double-click the ComboBox object, and then close the Toolbox.

The code window is opened and the code generated by Visual Studio for the SelectedIndexChanged event handler is displayed (Figure 7-26). Within the event handler, you can write any code that should be executed when the user makes a selection in the cboLocation ComboBox object.

cboLocation_SelectedIndexChanged event handler

FIGURE 7-26

By executing an event handler when the user selects a particular item in the cboLocation ComboBox object, the program works efficiently without multiple user clicks. Many objects, such as the ListBox and DropDownList objects, can be used in the same manner as the ComboBox object with a SelectedIndexChanged event handler.

Procedures

The Scuba Expeditions application is a larger and more complex program than those in previous chapters. Because the code for each event handler will be long, you should divide the code into smaller parts, each of which completes a specific task for the event handler. It is easier to deal with a larger program if you can focus on code that accomplishes a single task.

When a program is broken into manageable parts, each part is called a **procedure**. A procedure is a named set of code that performs a given task. In previous programs you have called procedures, such as the Clear procedure and the ToString procedure that have been written by the developers of Visual Studio. In the Scuba Expeditions program in this chapter, you will both write and call procedures.

Visual Basic provides two types of procedures: Sub procedures and Function procedures. The following sections explain these two types of procedures and how to code them.

How is breaking my programs into procedures like taking a detour on a highway?
A Sub procedure call is like a detour on the highway. After the Sub procedure is completed, control returns to the calling procedure. It is much easier to debug a smaller set of statements in a procedure than in a large program.

Code a Sub Procedure

A **Sub procedure** is a procedure that completes its task but does not return any data to the calling procedure. A Sub procedure in Visual Basic 2017 is defined by using the Sub keyword. A **Sub** procedure is the series of Visual Basic statements enclosed by the Sub and End Sub statements. Each time the Sub procedure is called, its statements are executed, starting with the first executable statement after the Sub statement and ending with the first End Sub statement. A Sub procedure is called with a statement consisting of the procedure name and a set of parentheses in the form of a **procedure call**, as shown in Figure 7-27.

General Format: Procedure Call

The procedure call is made:

```
ProcedureName ()
```

The **procedure declaration** that begins the Sub procedure has the form:

```
Private Sub ProcedureName ()

    ' Line(s) of code

End Sub
```

FIGURE 7-27

In the Scuba Expeditions application, users can select the scuba dive trip for each location. Based on the user's selection of a dive location, the ListBox object in Figure 7-28 is filled with the various scuba dive trips that are available. For example, if the user selects Australia, dive trips such as the Great Barrier Reef, Tiger Shark, and Fathom Chasm are displayed in the ListBox object.

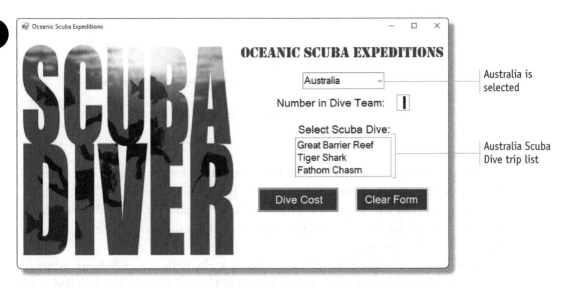

FIGURE 7-28

iStockphoto.com/KeithBishop

The items in the ListBox object are different based on the scuba expedition location selected. Figure 7-29 shows the code in the SelectedIndexChanged event handler that calls a Sub procedure to fill in the items in the ListBox object based on the location selected by the user.

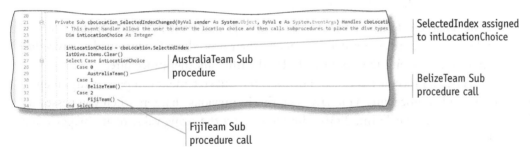

FIGURE 7-29

In Figure 7-29, the selected index for the cboLocation ComboBox is assigned to the Integer variable named intLocationChoice. Then, in the Select Case statement, the appropriate Sub procedure is called based on the location the user selected. When the selected index is equal to zero, the user selected the first item in the ComboBox list, which is Australia, so the AustraliaTeam Sub procedure is called. Notice that the name of the Sub procedure is specified with open and closed parentheses. As you learned previously, the Visual Basic compiler recognizes a procedure call by the parentheses.

The AustraliaTeam Sub procedure code is shown in Figure 7-30.

```
52
53  ⊟       Private Sub AustraliaTeam()
54                  ' This procedure fills in the possible dive types offered in Australia
55                  lstDive.Items.Add(_strDive1)
56                  lstDive.Items.Add(_strDive2)
57                  lstDive.Items.Add(_strDive3)
58          End Sub
```

FIGURE 7-30

In the code shown in Figure 7-30, the string values for the types of dive types available in Australia are added as items in the lstDive ListBox object. Notice that the String variables contain an underscore as the first character. You will recall that this designation identifies the variables as class variables that can be referenced in any procedure within the class.

In Figure 7-29, if the SelectedIndex value is 1, the BelizeTeam Sub procedure is called, and if the SelectedIndex value is 2, the FijiTeam Sub procedure is called. Each Sub procedure adds items to the lstDive ListBox object, depending on what dive types are available for each location.

A Sub procedure call may be used within a loop, If statements, or even Select Case statements, as shown in Figure 7-29. When a Sub procedure is called, the program gives control to the called Sub procedure and executes the lines of code within it. After the Sub procedure has completed its execution, program control returns to the calling procedure and program execution resumes in the calling procedure.

Pass Arguments

Earlier chapters defined and used the term *scope* and explained that variables declared within a procedure are limited in scope to their procedure. Code outside a procedure cannot interact with the variables declared within another procedure.

When a procedure is called, however, the call statement can pass an argument to the called procedure. You have seen this in previous chapters when you passed a string value to the ToInt32 procedure to convert the string value to an integer value (Figure 7-31).

procedure call   argument

```
117           intTeamSize = Convert.ToInt32(txtTeam.Text)
```

FIGURE 7-31

In Figure 7-31, the argument is contained within parentheses. In this example, the argument is the Text property of the txtTeam TextBox object.

In many applications, passing variables to another procedure is essential because the called procedure requires the value(s) in order to complete its processing. For example, in Figure 7-32, the btnDaysOfWeek_Click event determines whether a certain day of the week is part of the work week or the weekend. When the Weekday Sub procedure is called, a variable named intNumericDayOfWeek is passed to the Weekday Sub procedure because it must know the numeric day in order to perform its processing.

```
20      Private Sub btnDaysOfWeek_Click(ByVal sender As System.Object, ByVal e As System. ↙
        EventArgs) Handles btnDaysOfWeek.Click
21          Dim intNumericDayOfWeek As Integer
22
23          intNumericDayOfWeek = Convert.ToInt32(txtDay.Text)
24          Weekday(intNumericDayOfWeek)
25          MsgBox("Have a Great Week!", "Goodbye")
26      End Sub
27
28      Private Sub Weekday(ByVal intDay As Integer)
29          If intDay = 1 Or intDay = 7 Then
30              lblDisplayDay.Text = "Weekend"
31          End If
32          If intDay >= 2 And intDay <= 6 Then
33              lblDisplayDay.Text = "Weekday"
34          End If
35      End Sub
```

FIGURE 7-32

In Figure 7-32, the variable named intNumericDayOfWeek is passed to the Weekday Sub procedure by the calling statement on line 24. The value in the intNumericDayOfWeek variable should be 1 for Sunday, 2 for Monday, 3 for Tuesday, 4 for Wednesday, 5 for Thursday, 6 for Friday, and 7 for Saturday.

When a value is passed to a Sub procedure, its declaration, which identifies the name of the Sub procedure, must also contain an entry that defines the argument for use within the Sub procedure. In the Weekday Sub procedure in Figure 7-32, the parentheses following the Sub procedure name on line 28 contain the command ByVal intDay as Integer. This entry defines an Integer variable name (intDay) for use within the Sub procedure.

Visual Basic treats variables passed from a calling procedure to a called procedure in one of two ways: ByVal or ByRef. The following sections explain these two methods.

Pass Arguments by Value (ByVal)

When an argument is passed ByVal, it means the Sub procedure has access to the value of the passed argument but does not actually reference the variable declared in the calling procedure. Instead, the value is copied into a variable whose name is specified in the Sub procedure declaration statement. For example, in Figure 7-32 the argument is passed ByVal, so the value in intNumericDayOfWeek is copied to the variable defined in the procedure declaration of the called Sub procedure (intDay).

The intDay variable contains the value passed from the calling procedure only as long as the called Sub procedure has processing control. When the Sub procedure has completed processing and passes control back to the calling procedure, the variable is lost. If the Sub procedure is called again, the variable is created again as a new variable with no preexisting value. So, you can consider the variable defined in the Sub procedure declaration as a temporary variable that exists only during processing within the Sub procedure when the argument is passed ByVal.

The temporary variable can be given any name, including the name of the variable in the calling procedure, but most developers use different names to avoid confusion. Notice that the name used in the calling procedure is intNumericDayOfWeek and the name used in the Sub procedure for the temporary variable is intDay.

When the argument is passed ByVal, the Sub procedure code can change the value in the temporary variable and use it in any manner required. The original value of the variable in the calling procedure is not affected because the value is copied into the temporary Sub procedure variable and the variable in the calling procedure is never referenced in the Sub procedure.

ByVal is the default option for all passed arguments. The keyword ByVal is added automatically if you do not enter it when you code the Sub procedure declaration.

The code in Figure 7-33 illustrates the fact that the Sub procedure can change the passed value, but that value is not changed in the calling procedure when the value is passed ByVal.

```
22      Private Sub btnShowMessages Click(ByVal sender As System.Object, ByVal e As System.↙
        EventArgs) Handles btnShowMessages.Click
23          Dim strMessage As String
24
25          strMessage = "The Original Welcome Message"
26          MsgBox(strMessage, ,"First Message")
27          DisplayMessage(strMessage)
28          MsgBox(strMessage, ,"Fourth Message")
29      End Sub
30
31      Private Sub DisplayMessage(ByVal strShowMessage As String)
32          MsgBox(strShowMessage, ,"Second Message")
33          strShowMessage = "The Changed Welcome Message"
34          MsgBox(strShowMessage, ,"Third Message")
35      End Sub
36  End Class
```

FIGURE 7-33

The output for the code in Figure 7-33 is shown in Figure 7-34.

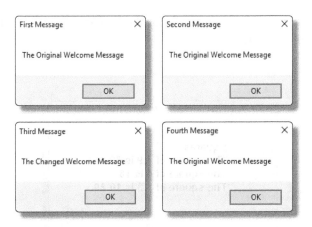

FIGURE 7-34

Figure 7-34 shows that the DisplayMessage Sub procedure in Figure 7-33 changed the message. The third message box displays this changed message: "The Changed Welcome Message." When the Sub procedure is finished and control is passed back to the calling procedure, however, the value in the strMessage variable is passed to the Sub procedure but is not changed, as shown in the Fourth Message window.

You can call the same Sub procedure repeatedly, as shown in Figure 7-35. The Sub procedure DisplayMessage is called once and the Square Sub procedure is called three times. Notice that either literals or variables can be passed to a Sub procedure.

```
23      Private Sub btnSquare_Click(ByVal sender As System.Object, ByVal e As System.
        EventArgs) Handles btnSquare.Click
24
25          Dim decNum As Decimal
26
27          decNum = 3.3
28          DisplayMessage()
29          Square(7.9)
30          Square(4.0)
31          Square(decNum)
32
33      End Sub
34
35      Private Sub Square(ByVal decValue As Decimal)
36          lstResult.Items.Add("The square of " & decValue & " is " & _
37          (decValue * decValue))
38
39      End Sub
40
41      Private Sub DisplayMessage()
42          lstResult.Items.Add("Squares:")
43      End Sub
```

FIGURE 7-35

After executing the code in Figure 7-35, the ListBox object would contain the values shown in Figure 7-36.

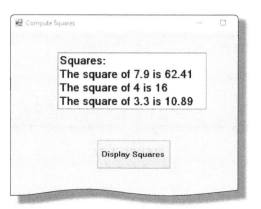

FIGURE 7-36

Pass Arguments by Reference (ByRef)

When an argument is passed ByVal, it means the Sub procedure has access to the value of the passed argument but does not actually reference the variable declared in the calling procedure. Instead, the value is copied into a variable whose name is specified in the Sub procedure declaration statement. As Figure 7-32 on page 401 shows, because the argument is passed ByVal, the value in intNumericDayOfWeek is copied to the variable defined in the procedure declaration of the called Sub procedure (intDay).

Passing a value by reference allows code in the Sub procedure to modify the contents of the variable that is being passed because when you use ByRef, you are passing a reference to the variable that holds the value instead of the value itself, as when you use ByVal. Thus, if a Sub procedure changes the value of a variable passed ByRef, the original variable in the calling procedure is changed. You should select the option to pass a variable by reference if you intend to change the original value when it is passed to the Sub procedure.

In the code example in Figure 7-37, the calling procedure assigns the value Vincent Van Gogh to the strFavoriteArtist variable (line 49) and then passes the variable ByRef (line 55).

The Sub procedure changes the value of the passed variable to Paul Cezanne (line 58). Because the variable is passed by reference (ByRef), the value in the variable that is passed from the calling procedure is changed to Paul Cezanne. In the output shown in Figure 7-38, the changed value is displayed in the fourth message box when the btnDisplayMessage_Click event displays the last message box (line 52).

WATCH OUT FOR

Passing ByVal means the Sub procedure *cannot* change the original value. Passing ByRef means the Sub procedure *can* change the original value.

```
46      Private Sub btnDisplayMessage_Click(ByVal sender As System.Object, ByVal e As        ↙
        System.EventArgs) Handles btnDisplayMessage.Click
47          Dim strFavoriteArtist As String
48
49          strFavoriteArtist = "Vincent Van Gogh"
50          MsgBox("Favorite Artist is " & strFavoriteArtist, , "First Message")
51          DisplayMessage(strFavoriteArtist)
52          MsgBox("Favorite Artist is now " & strFavoriteArtist, , "Fourth Message")
53      End Sub
54
55      Private Sub DisplayMessage(ByRef strshowArtist As String)
56          MsgBox("Favorite Artist is " & strshowArtist, , "Second Message")
57          ' The artist name is changed
58          strshowArtist = "Paul Cezanne "
59          MsgBox("Favorite Artist is " & strshowArtist, , "Third Message")
60      End Sub
61 End Class
```

FIGURE 7-37

FIGURE 7-38

Pass Multiple Arguments

You can pass as many arguments as needed to a Sub procedure. If you have more than one argument, the variables are passed in the same order in which they appear in the procedure call statement.

Function Procedures

A **Function procedure** is similar to a Sub procedure except that a Function procedure returns a single value to the calling procedure. Just like a Sub procedure, you can pass variables to the Function procedure using ByVal and ByRef. A Function procedure uses the keyword Function (instead of the keyword Sub) in the procedure declaration.

You must also specify a return data type in the procedure declaration to define the type of variable that is being returned to the calling procedure by the Function procedure. The Function procedure call has the syntax shown in Figure 7-39.

General Format: Function Procedure Call

The procedure call is made:

```
VariableName = FunctionProcedureName()
```

The **procedure declaration** that begins the Function procedure has the form:

```
Private Function FunctionProcedureName () as DataType

    ' Line(s) of code

    Return VariableName

End Function
```

FIGURE 7-39

HEADS UP

You can exclude the receiving variable in the procedure call if you use the value immediately, as in lblResult.Text = "Price: " & FindPrice(intValue).ToString().

The Private keyword is optional in the Function procedure declaration. If it is omitted, the default option is Public, which means any code in any class can reference the Function procedure. In many instances, Public access is not desirable, so the Private access modifier is used.

In the Function procedure call statement in Figure 7-39, the FunctionProcedure-Name on the right side of the assignment statement is replaced by the value that is returned from the Function procedure. That value then is assigned to the variable on the left side of the equal sign.

The Function procedure is different in appearance from a Sub procedure in the following ways:

- The Function procedure call has a receiving variable that is assigned the returned value from the Function procedure.
- The data type of the return value is listed in the procedure declaration.
- The keyword Return is used in the Function procedure to return a single value.

A Function procedure can pass only one value back to the calling procedure. The coding example in Figure 7-40 determines the gas mileage of a vehicle by dividing the number of miles driven by the number of gallons of gas used. The ComputeGasMileage Function procedure returns one value representing the gas mileage (Return statement on line 87). When the gas mileage value is returned, it is assigned to the receiving variable decMilesPerGallon (line 76 in the btnCompute_ Click event).

```
69    Private Sub btnCompute_Click(ByVal sender As System.Object, ByVal e As System.    ↙
      EventArgs) Handles btnCompute.Click
70        Dim decMiles As Decimal
71        Dim decGallons As Decimal
72        Dim decMilesPerGallon As Decimal
73
74        decMiles = Convert.ToDecimal(txtMiles.Text)
75        decGallons = Convert.ToDecimal(txtGallons.Text)
76        decMilesPerGallon = ComputeGasMileage(decMiles, decGallons)
77        MsgBox("You are getting " & decMilesPerGallon.ToString("F1") & " miles per    ↙
      gallon", , "MPG")
78
79    End Sub
80
81    Function ComputeGasMileage(ByVal decMiles As Decimal, ByVal decGallons As Decimal)
      As Decimal
82        Dim decMileage As Decimal
83
84        decMileage = decMiles / decGallons
85        ' The following statement returns control to the calling
86        ' procedure and returns the value in the decMileage variable.
87        Return decMileage
88
89    End Function
```

FIGURE 7-40

When writing a Function procedure, do not place any lines of its code after the Return statement because control returns to the calling procedure when the Return statement is executed.

It is best to use a Function procedure when you plan to return a value from a called procedure. In the Scuba Expeditions chapter project, a Function procedure returns the final cost of the selected dive type, as shown in Figure 7-41.

Calling Procedure

```
94          Select Case intLocationChoice
95              Case 0
96                  decTotalCost = AustraliaDiveCost(intDiveChoice, intTeamSize, intLength)
```

FIGURE 7-41a

Called Procedure

```
156     Private Function AustraliaDiveCost(ByVal intDive As Integer, ByVal intTeam As Integer, ByRef intTime As Integer) As Decimal
157         ' This function calculates the cost of the dive team in Australia
158         Dim decTeamCost As Decimal
159         Dim decFinalCost As Decimal
160         Dim decAustraliaDive1 As Decimal = 359D
161         Dim decAustraliaDive2 As Decimal = 200D
162         Dim decAustraliaDive3 As Decimal = 125D
163
164         Select Case intDive
165             Case 0
166                 decTeamCost = decAustraliaDive1
167                 intTime = _intEightHour
168             Case 1
169                 decTeamCost = decAustraliaDive2
170                 intTime = _intSixHour
171             Case 2
172                 decTeamCost = decAustraliaDive3
173                 intTime = _intFourHour
174         End Select
175         decFinalCost = decTeamCost * intTeam
176         Return decFinalCost
177     End Function
```

FIGURE 7-41b

WATCH OUT FOR

If you need to return more than one variable to the calling procedure, use ByRef. You can only return one value using the Return keyword.

In Figure 7-41, the function call on line 156 calls the AustraliaDiveCost Function procedure. The arguments include the integer value of the user's dive choice in the list box (intDive), the integer value of the number in the team (intTeam), and a variable to contain the amount of time of the chosen dive expedition (intTime).

In the called Function procedure, the dive and team size are passed ByVal. The length of the expedition in hours is passed ByRef. Therefore, when the Function procedure changes a value in the dive expedition time, a change is made in the passed variable.

You can use Sub procedures and Function procedures in any Visual Basic application, including Windows Classic Desktop applications, Web applications, and Windows Store applications.

Create a Private Class-Level Variable

In previous programs within this book, you have defined class-level variables for use in multiple procedures or event handlers within the class. In those programs, the variable was declared using the Dim statement. You will recall that a class-level variable is defined within the class but outside any procedure. When a class-level variable is declared using the Dim statement, it can be referenced by any code within any procedure within the class.

It cannot, however, be referenced by any code outside the class. (In larger projects, multiple classes can be created.) When a class-level variable cannot be referenced outside the class in which it is declared, the variable is said to have Private access. Generally, it is a good programming practice to limit the scope of a class-level variable to the class in which it is declared.

By default, a class-level variable declared using the Dim statement has Private access. You can also declare class-level variables by using the Private keyword instead of the Dim keyword. The class-level variables used in the Scuba Expeditions program in this chapter are shown in Figure 7-42.

```
8    Public Class frmScuba
9
10        ' Class variables
11        Private _intFourHour As Integer = 4
12        Private _intSixHour As Integer = 6
13        Private _intEightHour As Integer = 8
14        Private _strDive1 As String = "Great Barrier Reef"
15        Private _strDive2 As String = "Tiger Shark"
16        Private _strDive3 As String = "Fathom Chasm"
17        Private _strDive4 As String = "Great Blue Chasm"
18        Private _strDive5 As String = "Rainbow Reef"
19        Private _strDive6 As String = "Namena Sunken Ship"
```

FIGURE 7-42

As you can see in Figure 7-42, each of the variables is declared using the Private keyword. All of the variables will have Private access, which means code in any procedure within the class can reference the variables but code in another class cannot.

Exception Handling

In previous programs in this book, you have learned how to ensure that users enter valid data, which is an essential task. You have used loops and If statements to check the values entered by users to ensure that the data does not cause an exception within the program.

Visual Basic provides another tool you can use to detect exceptions and take corrective action. This tool is called the **Try-Catch** set of statements. The Try keyword means "Try to execute this code." The Catch keyword means "Catch errors here." A Try-Catch block includes a statement or statements that are executed in the Try block and the statements that are executed in the Catch block(s) when an exception occurs. The format of the Try-Catch block is shown in Figure 7-43.

General Format: Try-Catch block

```
Try

          'Try Block of Code – Executable statement(s) that may generate an exception.
Catch (filter for possible exceptions)

          'Catch Block of Code for handling the exception
[Optional: Additional Catch blocks]

[Optional Finally]

          'Optional statements that will always execute before finishing the Try block
End Try
```

FIGURE 7-43

To illustrate the use of a Try-Catch block, assume the value in one variable is being divided by the value in another variable. As you will recall, it is invalid to divide by zero. If a program tries to divide by zero, a DivideByZero exception will occur. Therefore, the division operation should be placed in a Try block and the Catch block should be set for a divide by zero exception. If the exception occurs, the code in Figure 7-44 will open a message box stating that an attempt was made to divide by zero.

```
 91        Dim decNumerator As Decimal
 92        Dim decDenominator As Decimal
 93        Dim decDivision As Decimal
 94
 95        decNumerator = Convert.ToDecimal(txtNum.Text)
 96        decDenominator = Convert.ToDecimal(txtDen.Text)
 97        Try
 98            decDivision = decNumerator / decDenominator
 99        Catch Exception As DivideByZeroException
100            MsgBox("Attempt to divide by zero")
101        End Try
102
103    End Sub
104 End Class
```

FIGURE 7-44

In Figure 7-44, the division operation occurs in the statement on line 98. Note that the division operation is within the Try-Catch block, as defined by the Try keyword on line 97, the Catch keyword on line 99, and the End Try statement on line

101. You can define the particular class of exception in a Catch block by mentioning the name of the exception with the Catch keyword. In Figure 7-44, DivideByZero-Exception is included to catch the specific exception. If the value in decDenominator is zero when the division operation occurs, the code in the Catch block will display a message box with an error message. More importantly, the program will not be terminated. A Try-Catch block allows the program to handle exceptions elegantly so that the program does not abruptly end.

Different types of exceptions can occur. Figure 7-45 identifies some of the possible exceptions.

Exception Type	Condition when Exception Occurs	Code Example
ArgumentNullException	A variable that has no value is passed to a procedure	`Dim strTerm As String` `1stDisplay.Items.Add(strTerm)`
DivideByZeroException	A value is divided by zero	`intResult = intNum / 0`
FormatException	A variable is converted to another type that is not possible	`strTerm = "Code"` `intValue = Convert.ToInt32(strTerm)`
NullReferenceException	A procedure is called when the result is not possible	`Dim strTerm As String` `intValue = strTerm.Length`
OverflowException	A value exceeds its assigned data type	`Dim intCost As Integer` `intCost = 58 ^ 4000000000`
SystemException	Generic	`Catches all other exceptions`

FIGURE 7-45

Figure 7-46 shows another example of a Try-Catch block, in which a very large number assigned to the variable intBaseValue is squared within a Try-Catch block. Notice that when the value intBaseValue is squared, the result will exceed the range for an Integer data type, causing an OverflowException. When the exception occurs within the Try block, the Catch block is called to deal with the OverflowException.

```
105        Dim intBaseValue As Integer
106        Dim intSquaredValue As Integer
107
108        intBaseValue = 50000000
109        Try
110            intSquaredValue = intBaseValue ^ 2
111        Catch Exception As OverflowException
112            'This catch block detects an overflow of the range of the data type
113            MsgBox("The value exceeds the range of the data type", , "Error")
114        End Try
```

FIGURE 7-46

Multiple Catch blocks can be defined for a single Try block, in which each Catch block will catch a particular class of exception. This approach is useful when you want to state which type of error occurred and tell users the mistake they made. It is best to order exceptions in Catch blocks from the most specific to the least specific. In other words, the Catch block that is most likely to be needed for the most common exception should appear first in a series of Catch statements. If an exception occurs during the execution of the Try block, Visual Basic examines each Catch statement within the Try-Catch block until it finds one whose condition matches that error. If a match is found, control transfers to the first line of code in the Catch block. If no matching Catch statement is found, the search proceeds to the next Catch statement in the Try-Catch block. This process continues through the entire code block until a matching Catch block is found in the current procedure. If no match is found, an exception occurs that stops the program.

In the Scuba Expeditions application, you need to validate the variable that is assigned the value of the number in the team. You want to make sure that the user enters a number, not a letter or other symbol, and that the number is from 2 to 6 divers. The code in Figure 7-47 displays a Try-Catch block used within a Function procedure named ValidateNumberInTeam. It uses three Catch blocks.

```vb
108
109    Private Function ValidateNumberInTeam() As Boolean
110        ' This procedure validates the value entered for the dive team size
111        Dim intTeamSize As Integer
112        Dim blnValidityCheck As Boolean = False
113        Dim strNumberInTeamMessage As String = "Please enter the number of people in your dive team (2-6)"
114        Dim strMessageBoxTitle As String = "Error"
115
116        Try
117            intTeamSize = Convert.ToInt32(txtTeam.Text)
118            If intTeamSize >= 2 And intTeamSize <= 6 Then
119                blnValidityCheck = True
120            Else
121                MsgBox(strNumberInTeamMessage, , strMessageBoxTitle)
122                txtTeam.Focus()
123                txtTeam.Clear()
124            End If
125        Catch Exception As FormatException
126            MsgBox(strNumberInTeamMessage, , strMessageBoxTitle)
127            txtTeam.Focus()
128            txtTeam.Clear()
129        Catch Exception As OverflowException
130            MsgBox(strNumberInTeamMessage, , strMessageBoxTitle)
131            txtTeam.Focus()
132            txtTeam.Clear()
133        Catch Exception As SystemException
134            MsgBox(strNumberInTeamMessage, , strMessageBoxTitle)
135            txtTeam.Focus()
136            txtTeam.Clear()
137        End Try
138        Return blnValidityCheck
139    End Function
```

FIGURE 7-47

The Boolean variable blnValidityCheck (line 112 in the code in Figure 7-47) is initially set to false, but it is set to true if an exception is not thrown (line 119); in other words, the Catch block is not executed if an exception is not thrown. This Boolean variable set to True then is returned to the calling procedure (line 138), which can continue its processing.

If an exception is thrown when the value in the Text property of the txtTeam TextBox is converted to an integer (line 117), the statements below the Convert. ToInt32 statement will not be executed because control is passed to the appropriate Catch statement. The processing in each of the Catch blocks displays a message box with an error message, places the focus on the text box where the user enters the number in the team, and clears the text box.

When the processing in the Try-Catch block is complete, the Return statement on line 138 returns the value of the Boolean variable. If the data was valid, the Boolean variable contains the True value. If the data was not valid, the variable contains False because it initially was set to False (line 112) and its value was not changed by the Catch block processing.

An optional portion of the Try-Catch block is the Finally statement. The code in the Finally section always executes last, regardless of whether the code in the Catch blocks has been executed. Place cleanup code, such as code that closes files, in the Finally section. Code in the Finally section always is executed, no matter what happens in the Try-Catch blocks.

CRITICAL THINKING

Can Try-Catch statements be used for any other purpose than error checking?
Yes. Many developers code Try-Catch statements to alert a database administrator or trigger other actions when users do not enter an expected entry. For example, a call center taking sales orders may need to alert the warehouse if a large number of orders is getting "stuck" in high volume processing.

Program Design

As you have learned, the requirements document identifies the purpose of the program being developed, the application title, the procedures to be followed when using the program, any required equations and calculations, any conditions that must be tested, notes and restrictions that must be followed by the program, and any other comments that would be helpful to understanding the problem. The requirements document for the Scuba Expeditions application is shown in Figure 7-48.

REQUIREMENTS DOCUMENT

Date:	June 22, 2019
Date Submitted:	
Application Title:	Scuba Expeditions Application
Purpose:	This Windows Classic Desktop application allows a customer to view scuba expeditions available in various locations around the world.
Program Procedures:	The user can select a location and scuba dive trip for a group and find out pricing information.
Algorithms, Processing, and Conditions:	1. The user first selects the scuba dive location with the application title displayed. No other objects are displayed at this point. 2. When the user selects a location, the following items are displayed in the window: the Number in Dive Team text box, a custom list of the available scuba dives for the chosen location, a button to find the dive team cost of the selected dive trip, and a button to clear the form. 3. The user enters the number of the dive team size. 4. From the custom list of scuba dives that are available for the chosen location, the user selects a scuba dive trip. 5. The total dive team price of the scuba dive is displayed.
Notes and Restrictions:	1. Validate numeric input with Try-Catch blocks. 2. Use multiple procedures to break the application into manageable sections.
Comments:	1. The picture shown in the window is available on CengageBrain.com. The name of the picture is scuba. 2. A splash screen is shown for approximately five seconds before the main window is displayed with a logo image and current year.

FIGURE 7-48

The Use Case Definition for the application is shown in Figure 7-49.

USE CASE DEFINITION

1. A splash screen welcomes the user for approximately five seconds.
2. The user selects a location.
3. The program displays a text box for the number of people in the dive team and a list of available scuba dives for the selected location.
4. The user enters the number of people in the team, selects a scuba dive, and clicks the Dive Cost button.
5. The program identifies the scuba dive, calculates and displays the scuba dive cost for the dive team, and specifies the length of the dive in hours.
6. The user can change any of the entries (location choice, number in dive team, and scuba dive) and click the Dive Cost button to recalculate the dive cost.
7. The user can clear the form by clicking the Clear Form button.

FIGURE 7-49

Figure 7-50 contains information about available dives for each location, the dive lengths, and the dive trip costs.

Location	Scuba Dive	Dive Length (Multiple Tanks)	Cost
Australia	Great Barrier Reef	8 hours	$350 USD
	Tiger Shark	6 hours	$200
	Fathom Chasm	4 hours	$125
Belize	Great Blue Chasm	8 hours	$200 USD
	Rainbow Reef	6 hours	$150
Fiji	Fathom Chasm	8 hours	$280 USD
	Namena Sunken Ship	6 hours	$225
	Tiger Shark	4 hours	$200

FIGURE 7-50

As noted previously, larger programs often should be divided into procedures that perform specific tasks within the program. The goal of using procedures is to make the program easier to read, understand, and debug. The final result is a program that is more reliable and easier to maintain.

The developer must determine what code should be placed in a procedure. Several rules are important to follow when creating procedures in a program; otherwise, the use of procedures might make the program more difficult and more confusing. These rules include the following:

- The Sub procedure or the Function procedure should perform a single, defined task, such as checking the validity of a specific user input or calculating the cost of a dive type. Procedures that perform multiple tasks tend to become large and difficult to design and code.
- A Sub procedure or a Function procedure must perform reasonably substantial processing. It makes little sense to place a procedure call statement in a calling procedure and have the called procedure contain one or two program statements. In such cases, it would be easier and clearer just to place the statements in the calling procedure.
- When deciding whether a set of programming steps should be placed in a Sub procedure or a Function procedure, ask yourself the following questions: (1) Will the program be easier to read and understand if the code is placed in a separate procedure? (2) Does the proposed code perform a single task and does this task require more than three or four programming statements? (3) Can the Sub procedure or Function procedure perform its processing by receiving data as arguments and by returning data either using the Return statement or by using ByRef arguments?

If the answers to these questions are *yes*, then the code is a good candidate for a procedure within your program.

In the Scuba Expeditions application, four event handlers are required: (1) Selected Index Change: This event handler is executed when the user selects a scuba expedition location from a combo box; (2) Dive Cost Button: This event handler is executed when the user clicks the btnDiveCost Button object; (3) Clear Button: This event handler is executed when the user clicks the btnClear Button object; (4) frmScuba Load Event: This event handler is executed when the Windows Form object is loaded.

Within each event handler, the event planning document is used to identify the tasks that must be accomplished. As each of the tasks is identified, you should ask the preceding questions. If it appears that the task should be accomplished in a procedure, the procedure must be included in the event planning document.

You will recall that the event planning document is a table that specifies which objects in the user interface will cause events, the action taken by the user to trigger each event, and the event processing that must occur. The event planning document for the program in this chapter must specify two forms and the events that occur for objects on each form. In addition, the tasks that must be accomplished for each event must be identified and decisions must be made for whether the tasks will be accomplished in a Sub or Function procedure. The event planning document for the Scuba Expeditions Trip Selection program is shown in Figure 7-51 and Figure 7-52.

EVENT PLANNING DOCUMENT

Program Name: Scuba Expeditions	Developer: Corinne Hoisington	Object: SplashScreen1	Date: June 22, 2019
OBJECT	EVENT TRIGGER	EVENT PROCESSING	
SplashScreen1_Load	Load	An opening splash screen appears with the company name, version number, and year of copyright	

FIGURE 7-51

EVENT PLANNING DOCUMENT

Program Name: Scuba Expeditions	Developer: Corinne Hoisington	Object: frmScuba	Date: June 22, 2019
OBJECT	EVENT TRIGGER	EVENT PROCESSING	
cboLocation_SelectedIndexChanged	Select Index	Assign location selection to an Integer SUB (AustraliaTeam(), BelizeTeam(), FijiTeam()): Based on the dive type, display a list of the available scuba dives in each location Change Visible property to True for all objects on the form Clear the labels that provide dive information Set the focus on the Number in Dive Team text box	
AustraliaTeam()	Sub procedure call	Display list of available scuba dives (Great Barrier Reef, Tiger Shark, Fathom Chasm) in list box	
BelizeTeam()	Sub procedure call	Display list of available dive types (Great Blue Chasm and Rainbow Reef) in list box	
FijiTeam()	Sub procedure call	Display list of available dive types (Fathom Chasm, Namena Sunken Ship, and Tiger Shark) in list box	

FIGURE 7-52 (continues)

Program Name: Scuba Expeditions	Developer: Corinne Hoisington	Object: frmScuba	Date: June 22, 2019
OBJECT	**EVENT TRIGGER**	**EVENT PROCESSING**	

btnDiveCost	Click	FUNCTION (ValidateNumberInTeam): Validate that the value in the Number in Dive Team text box is valid
		FUNCTION (ValidateDiveSelection): Ensure that the user has selected a dive type in the list box
		If the number in the team is valid and a dive type is selected:
		    Convert number in dive team to an integer
		    Change selected dive type index to integer
		    FUNCTION(AustraliaDiveCost,
		        BelizeDiveCost, FijiDiveCost):
		        Calculate cost based on dive choice
		        Display dive, cost, and length
		Else display error message	

ValidateNumberInTeam()	Function procedure call	Set Boolean indicator to False
		Convert number in team to integer
		If conversion valid
		    If number > = 2 and < = 6
		        Set Boolean indicator to True for valid number
		If conversion not valid
		    Catch format, overflow, and system exceptions
		    Display error message boxes
		    Place focus in Number in Team text box
		    Clear Number in Dive Team text box
		Return Boolean indicator	

ValidateDiveSelection()	Function procedure call	Convert dive type selection index to integer
		If conversion successful
		    Place selected item string in ByRef variable
		    Set Boolean validity indicator to True
		Else Display error message box
		    Set Boolean validity indicator to False
		Return dive type selected index integer	

AustraliaDiveCost()	Function procedure call	If dive type selected is GreatBarrier Reef
		    Set cost to Australia Great Barrier Reef for one person
		    Set length to eight hours
		If dive type selected is Tiger Shark
		    Set cost to Australia Tiger Shark for one person
		    Set length to six hours
		If dive type selected is Fathom Chasm
		    Set cost to Australia Fathom Chasm for one person
		    Set length to four hours
		Calculate cost of scuba expedition: cost * number in team
		Return cost of scuba expedition	

FIGURE 7-52 (continues)

Program Name: Scuba Expeditions	Developer: Corinne Hoisington	Object: frmScuba	Date: June 22, 2019
OBJECT	**EVENT TRIGGER**	**EVENT PROCESSING**	
BelizeDiveCost()	Function procedure call	If dive type selected is Great Blue Chasm 　　Set cost to Belize Great Blue Chasm dive type for one person 　　Set length to eight hours If dive type selected is Rainbow Reef 　　Set cost to Belize Rainbow Reef for one person 　　Set length to six hours Calculate cost of scuba expedition: cost * number in team Return cost of scuba expedition	
FijiDiveCost()	Function procedure call	If dive type selected is Fathom Chasm 　　Set cost to Fiji Fathom Chasm for one person 　　Set length to eight hours If dive type selected is Namena Sunken Ship 　　Set cost to Fiji Namena Sunken Ship for one person 　　Set length to six hours If dive type selected is Tiger Shark 　　Set cost to Fiji Tiger Shark for one person 　　Set length to four hours Calculate cost of scuba expedition: cost * number in team Return cost of scuba expedition	
btnClear	Click	Set Select Location cboLocation text to "Select Location" Clear text box, list, and labels Hide all objects except Select Location Listbox	
frmScuba_Load	Load	Set sleeping period to 5000 milliseconds	

FIGURE 7-52 (continued)

Design and Code the Program

After identifying the events and tasks within the events, the developer is ready to create the program. As you have learned, creating the program means designing the user interface and then entering Visual Basic statements to accomplish the tasks specified in the event planning document. As the developer enters the code, she will also implement the logic to carry out the required processing.

Guided Program Development

To design the user interface for the Scuba Expeditions application and enter the code required to process each event in the program, complete the steps on the following pages:

NOTE TO THE LEARNER

In the following activity, you should complete the tasks within the specified steps. Each of the tasks is accompanied by a Hint Screen. The purpose of the Hint Screen is to indicate where you should perform the activity in the Visual Studio window and to remind you which method to use. If you need further help completing a step, refer to the figure identified by *ref:*.

1

- **Create a New Windows Project** Open Visual Studio and then close the Start page. Click the New Project button on the Standard toolbar. Begin a Windows Classic Desktop Forms App project and name the project Scuba Expeditions. Name the Form object frmScuba.vb.

- **Add a New Item to the Project** Click Project on the menu bar and then click Add New Item on the Project menu *(ref: Figure 7-5)*.

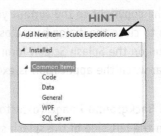

HINT

Add New Item - Scuba Expeditions

◢ Installed

◢ Common Items
   Code
   Data
   General
   WPF
   SQL Server

- **Select Splash Screen as the New Item** Scroll down and select the Splash Screen template. Click the Add button *(ref: Figure 7-6)*.

HINT

SplashScreen1.vb [Design]   ⊕ ✕ frmScuba.vb [Design]*

Application Title

Version {0}.{1:00}

Copyright

- **Select the Generic Splash Screen** When the generic splash screen opens, click the left side of the screen to select it *(ref: Figure 7-7)*.

- **Prepare to Set the Contents of the Splash Screen** Right-click the application name Scuba Expeditions in the Solution Explorer, and then click Properties on the shortcut menu to open the Project Designer window *(ref: Figure 7-8)*

- **Set the Splash Screen** On the Application tab, scroll down and click the Splash screen list arrow to change the setting of (None) to SplashScreen1 *(ref: Figure 7-10)*.

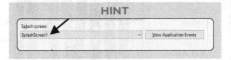

HINT

Splash screen:

SplashScreen1   ∨   View Application Events

(continues)

● **Add Text to the Splash Screen** To change the text of the splash screen, click the Assembly Information button in the Project Designer window *(ref: Figure 7-11)*.

● **Set the Assembly Information** In the Assembly Information dialog box, change the copyright to the current year *(ref: Figure 7-11)*. Click the OK button to close the dialog box. Close the Properties window. The information on the Splash Screen form does not change. The changes appear when the application is executed.

● **Change the Background Image** To customize the picture, click the background on the left side of the splash screen and select the BackgroundImage property in the Properties window. Click the ellipsis button *(ref: Figure 7-12)*.

● **Select the Project Resource File** The Select Resource dialog box opens. Click the Project resource file option button, if necessary, and ensure that the Resources.resx file is selected.

● **Select an Image File** Click Import and select the image file scuba.jpg, which is provided with your data files and is available on CengageBrain.com. Click the OK button in the Select Resource dialog box.

The splash screen is designed (Figure 7-53).

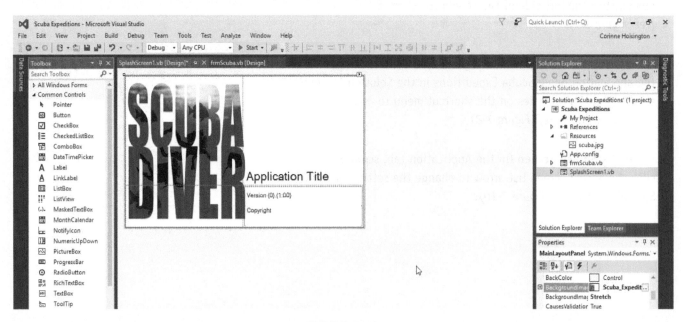

FIGURE 7-53

2

● **Resize the Windows Form Object** Resize the Windows
Form object frmScuba to (870, 490) to view the entire
image.

● **Assign a Title to the Form Object** With the Windows
Form object selected, change its Text property to Oceanic
Scuba Expeditions.

● **Add a Background Image** With the Windows Form object
selected, click the ellipsis button for the BackgroundImage
property. Select the scuba image in the Select Resource
dialog box. Click the OK button in the Select Resource dialog
box. Change the BackgroundImageLayout to the Stretch
property.

● **Add a Panel Object** Drag a Panel object from the
Containers category of the Toolbox to the portion of the
Windows Form object not covered by the image. Resize the
Panel object so it covers the white space where no image
is displayed.

HINT

iStockphoto.com/KeithBishop

● **Change the Panel Object's BackColor to Transparent**
In the BackColor property for the Panel object, click the
BackColor property arrow, click the Web tab if necessary,
and then click Transparent on the Web palette. Making
the panel transparent allows all the objects placed on the
Windows Form object to be visible but allows you to center
and align objects within the Panel object instead of the
entire Windows Form object.

HINT

(continues)

● **Add a Label and a ComboBox Object** Add a Label object on the right side of the Form object. Change the Text property to Oceanic Scuba Expeditions. Name the Label object lblTitle. Change the font property to Stencil, 22 points. Change the FontColor property of the Label object to MidnightBlue in the Web palette. The location of the Label object can be (2, 17). Add a ComboBox object below the Label object. The location is (130, 72). Name the ComboBox object cboLocation. Change the Text property to Select Location:. Change the font size to 14 points *(ref: Figure 7-19)*.

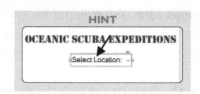

● **Add the Locations in the Items Property** Enter the following locations in the Items property of the ComboBox object: Australia, Belize, and Fiji on separate lines *(ref: Figure 7-20)*.

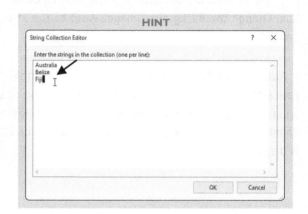

● **Add a Label Object** Drag a Label object from the Toolbox to the Form object. Place the Label object at location (74, 118) within the Panel object. Change the Text property to Number in Dive Team:. Name the Label object lblTeam. Change the font size to 16 points.

● **Add a TextBox Object for the Number in Team** Drag a TextBox object from the Toolbox to the Panel object on the Windows Form object. Place the TextBox object at location (316, 115). Resize the TextBox object to fit the length of approximately two numbers. Name the TextBox object txtTeam. Change the font size to 16 points.

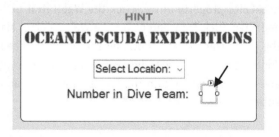

- **Add the Select Dive Label Object** Drag a Label object from the Toolbox to the Windows Form object. The location is (116, 169). Change the Text property to Select Scuba Dive:. Name the Label object lblSelect. Change the font size to 16 points.

- **Add the Dive ListBox Object** Drag a ListBox object from the Toolbox to the Windows Form object. The location is (123, 197). Name the ListBox lstDive. Change the font size to 14 points.

- **Add the Dive Cost Button Object** Drag a Button object from the Toolbox to the Windows Form object. The location is (41, 293). Name the Button object btnDiveCost and change the Text property to Dive Cost. Resize the button until the text is visible. Change the BackColor property to MidnightBlue and the ForeColor property to White.

- **Add the Clear Button Object** Drag another Button object from the Toolbox to the Windows Form object. The location is (233, 293). Name the Button object btnClear and change the Text property to Clear Form. Change the BackColor property to MidnightBlue and the ForeColor property to White. Make the buttons the same size and centered in the Panel.

- **Add a Label Object for the Dive Trip** Drag a Label object from the Toolbox to the Windows Form object. The location is (130, 360). Name the Label object lblScubaDive. Enter 12 Xs for the Text property. Change the Font to size 16.

- **Add a Label Object for the Cost** Drag a Label object from the Toolbox to the Windows Form object. The location is (130, 381). Name this Label object lblCost. Enter 12 Xs for the Text property. Change the Font to size 16.

(continues)

● **Add a Label Object for the Dive Length** Drag a Label object from the Toolbox to the Windows Form object. The location is (130, 402). Name this Label object lblLength. Enter 12 Xs for the Text property. Change the Font to size 16.

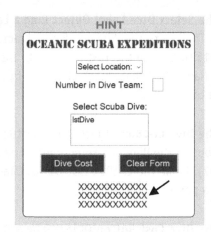

● **Set the Visible Properties** Change the Visible property to False for the following objects: lblTeam, txtTeam, lblSelect, lstDive, btnDiveCost, btnClear, lblScubaDive, lblCost, and lblLength. These objects are not displayed until the scuba dive is selected.

● **Set the Accept Button** Click the background of the Windows Form object on its title bar and change the AcceptButton property of the Button object to btnDiveCost.

● **Set the Cancel Button** Click the background of the Windows Form object on its title bar and change the CancelButton property of the Button object to btnClear. Close the Toolbox.

The Form object frmScuba is designed (Figure 7-54).

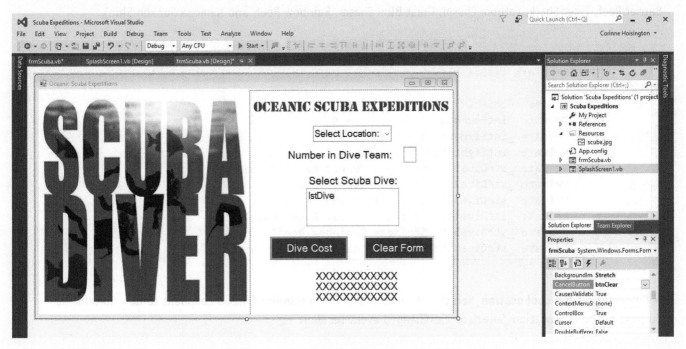

FIGURE 7-54

iStockphoto.com/KeithBishop

3

• **Code the Comments** Double-click the cboLocation ComboBox object on the frmScuba.vb [Design] tab to open the code window and create the cboLocation_SelectedIndexChanged event handler. Close the Toolbox. Click before the first word in Public Class frmScuba, and then press the ENTER key to create a blank line. Insert the first four standard comments. Insert the Option Strict On command following the comments to turn on strict type checking.

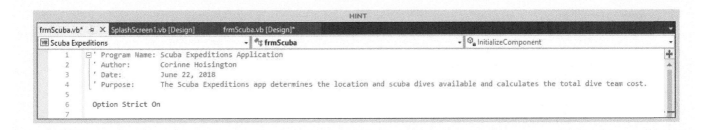

(continues)

● **Enter the Class Variables** Following the Public Class header line, enter the class variables required for the program. These class variables are (1) the length of each scuba dive; (2) the scuba dive trips available (Great Barrier Reef, Tiger Shark, Fathom Chasm, Great Blue Chasm, Rainbow Reef, and Namena Sunken Ship).

HINT

```
 8    ⊟Public Class frmScuba
 9
10          ' Class variables
11          Private _intFourHour As Integer = 4
12          Private _intSixHour As Integer = 6
13          Private _intEightHour As Integer = 8
14          Private _strDive1 As String = "Great Barrier Reef"
15          Private _strDive2 As String = "Tiger Shark"
16          Private _strDive3 As String = "Fathom Chasm"
17          Private _strDive4 As String = "Great Blue Chasm"
18          Private _strDive5 As String = "Rainbow Reef"
19          Private _strDive6 As String = "Namena Sunken Ship"
```

● **Comment on the cboLocation_SelectedIndexChanged Event Handler** Enter a comment to describe the purpose of the cboLocation_SelectedIndexChanged event handler.

HINT

```
21   ⊟    Private Sub cboLocation_SelectedIndexChanged(ByVal sender As System.Object, ByVal e As System.EventArgs) Handles cboLocation.SelectedIndexChanged
22              ' This event handler allows the user to enter the location choice and then calls subprocedures to place the dive types in the list.
23              Dim intLocationChoice As Integer
```

● **Code the Sub Procedure Calls to Place the Appropriate Scuba Dive Trips in the List Box** When the user selects a location in the cboLocation ComboBox object, the SelectedIndexChanged event is triggered. In that event handler, the scuba dive indicated by the selected index must be changed to an integer. Then, based on that integer, the appropriate Sub procedure is called to place the available scuba dives in the lstDive list box. Write the code to obtain the selected index integer, clear the lstDive ListBox object of any previous entries, and then call the appropriate Sub procedure *(ref: Figure 7-29)*.

HINT

```
21   ⊟    Private Sub cboLocation_SelectedIndexChanged(ByVal sender As System.Object, ByVal e As System.EventArgs) Handles cboLocation.SelectedIndexChanged
22              ' This event handler allows the user to enter the location choice and then calls subprocedures to place the dive types in the list.
23              Dim intLocationChoice As Integer
24
25              intLocationChoice = cboLocation.SelectedIndex
26              lstDive.Items.Clear()
27   ⊟          Select Case intLocationChoice
28                  Case 0
29                      AustraliaTeam()
30                  Case 1
31                      BelizeTeam()
32                  Case 2
33                      FijiTeam()
34              End Select
```

• **Set the Visibility and Focus** After the user selects the dive location from the ComboBox object and the event handler calls the Sub procedures to load the ListBox object with the correct dive trips, the objects on the Windows Form object must become visible. In addition, the Label objects for the dive trip, cost, and length must be cleared of the Xs placed in them during design. Finally, the focus should be set on the txtTeam TextBox object. Enter the code to complete this processing.

HINT

```
35            ' Make items visible in the window
36            lblTeam.Visible = True
37            txtTeam.Visible = True
38            lblSelect.Visible = True
39            lstDive.Visible = True
40            btnDiveCost.Visible = True
41            btnClear.Visible = True
42            lblScubaDive.Visible = True
43            lblCost.Visible = True
44            lblLength.Visible = True
45            ' Clear the labels
46            lblScubaDive.Text = ""
47            lblCost.Text = ""
48            lblLength.Text = ""
49            ' Set focus on number in dive team text box
50            txtTeam.Focus()
51        End Sub
```

• **Code the Sub Procedures for Australia Dive Type Options** After the first event handler is completed, the Sub procedures called by the event handler should be written. The event handler that handles the cboLocation_ SelectedIndexChanged event calls three Sub procedures. Code the first referenced Sub procedure, which is called AustraliaTeam. To do so, click below the End Sub statement for the event handler, press the enter key to insert a blank line, and then write the Sub procedure declaration. It begins with the word Private, followed by the word Sub and then the name of the Sub procedure. Press the enter key, write a comment that explains the purpose of the Sub procedure, and then write the statements that put the Australia dive trips in the lstDive ListBox object *(ref: Figure 7-30)*.

HINT

```
53    □   Private Sub AustraliaTeam()
54            ' This procedure fills in the possible dive types offered in Australia
55            lstDive.Items.Add(_strDive1)
56            lstDive.Items.Add(_strDive2)
57            lstDive.Items.Add(_strDive3)
58        End Sub
```

(continues)

● **Code the Sub Procedures for the Belize and Fiji Scuba Expedition Options** In a similar manner, write the code for the Belize and Fiji Sub procedures that place the appropriate scuba expeditions in the lstDive ListBox object.

HINT

```
59
60    ⊟    Private Sub BelizeTeam()
61              'This procedure fills in the possible dive types offered in Belize
62              lstDive.Items.Add(_strDive4)
63              lstDive.Items.Add(_strDive5)
64         End Sub
65
66    ⊟    Private Sub FijiTeam()
67              'This procedure fills in the possible dive types offered in Fiji
68              lstDive.Items.Add(_strDive2)
69              lstDive.Items.Add(_strDive3)
70              lstDive.Items.Add(_strDive6)
71         End Sub
72
```

● **Initialize the btnDiveCost_Click Event and Write the Event Handler Variables** Click the frmScuba.vb [Design] tab and then double-click the Dive Cost button to create the event handler for the button click event. The first step is to write a comment describing the purpose of the event handler. Then, code the variable declarations for the variables required in the event handler. These variables include (1) integer variables for the dive team size, scuba dive choice, and length (duration in hours) of scuba dive; (2) Boolean variables to indicate the validity of the number in the dive team and the scuba dive selection; (3) a String variable to contain the name of the selected scuba dive; (4) a Decimal variable to contain the total cost of the selected scuba dive. Write the code to create and initialize these variables.

HINT

```
73    ⊟    Private Sub btnDiveCost_Click(ByVal sender As System.Object, ByVal e As System.EventArgs) Handles btnDiveCost.Click
74              ' This button event handler determines the cost of scuba expeditions and
75              ' displays the size of the dive team, the cost, and the length of the dive
76
77              Dim intTeamSize As Integer
78              Dim blnNumberInTeamIsValid As Boolean = False
79              Dim blnDiveIsSelected As Boolean = False
80              Dim intDiveChoice As Integer
81              Dim strSelectedTeam As String = ""
82              Dim intLocationChoice As Integer
83              Dim intLength As Integer = 0
84              Dim decTotalCost As Decimal
```

- **Validate the User Input** The next steps are to call two Function procedures. The first procedure verifies that the value entered in the txtTeam TextBox object is valid, and the second verifies that a scuba dive trip was selected. Write the two Function calls for these Function procedures. The ValidateNumberInTeam Function procedure returns a Boolean value indicating whether the number entered is valid (True) or not valid (False). The ValidateDiveSelection Function procedure returns the number of the dive type selected by the user. It also sets a Boolean value in the blnDive Boolean variable to indicate if a dive type has been selected (True) or not selected (False). This value is set because the blnDiveIsSelected variable is passed to the Function procedure ByRef.

	HINT
86	`' Call a function to ensure the number of people in the dive team is valid`
87	`blnNumberInTeamIsValid = ValidateNumberInTeam()`
88	`' Call a function to ensure a scuba dive was selected`
89	`intDiveChoice = ValidateDiveSelection(blnDiveIsSelected, strSelectedTeam)`

- **Code the Rest of the btnDiveCost_Click Event** Upon return from the procedure calls, the btnDiveCost_Click event handler must determine whether the number of people in a dive team is valid and that a scuba dive trip was selected. If both are true, the Text property of the txtTeam TextBox is converted to an integer value named intTeamSize. The Function procedures are passed three variables that are needed in the procedures. The variables intDiveChoice and intTeamSize are passed by value because the values are not changed in the Function procedures. The variable intLength type is passed by reference because the value is changed in the Function procedures. The value returned from the Function procedures as the total cost of the dive type is assigned to the variable decTotalCost. After the Function procedures are called, the event handler displays the selected dive trip, cost, and length. Write the code to implement this processing.

	HINT
90	`' If number of people and the dive trip are valid, calculate the cost`
91	`If (blnNumberInTeamIsValid And blnDiveIsSelected) Then`
92	`    intTeamSize = Convert.ToInt32(txtTeam.Text)`
93	`    intLocationChoice = cboLocation.SelectedIndex`
94	`    Select Case intLocationChoice`
95	`        Case 0`
96	`            decTotalCost = AustraliaDiveCost(intDiveChoice, intTeamSize, intLength)`
97	`        Case 1`
98	`            decTotalCost = BelizeDiveCost(intDiveChoice, intTeamSize, intLength)`
99	`        Case 2`
100	`            decTotalCost = FijiDiveCost(intDiveChoice, intTeamSize, intLength)`
101	`    End Select`
102	`    ' Display the cost of the scuba dive`
103	`    lblScubaDive.Text = "Dive: " & strSelectedTeam`
104	`    lblCost.Text = "Cost: " & decTotalCost.ToString("C")`
105	`    lblLength.Text = "Length: " & intLength.ToString() & " hours"`
106	`End If`
107	`End Sub`

(continues)

● **Code the ValidateNumberInTeam Function Procedure** The next step is to code the ValidateNumberInTeam Function procedure. Click below the btnDiveCost_Click event handler and enter the Function procedure declaration. The Function procedure returns a Boolean value that indicates whether the user entered a valid number. The value must be an integer that is greater than or equal to 2 and less than or equal to 6 because the scuba expeditions are limited to dive teams with two to six people. A Try-Catch block is used for the conversion to an integer operation to catch any invalid data the user entered. Multiple Catch blocks are used to catch specific exceptions. If an exception occurs, the error message is displayed in a message box, the focus is placed on the txtTeam TextBox object, and the value in the TextBox object is cleared. Write the code for this Function procedure *(ref: Figure 7-47)*.

```
                                         HINT
109        Private Function ValidateNumberInTeam() As Boolean
110            ' This procedure validates the value entered for the dive team size
111            Dim intTeamSize As Integer
112            Dim blnValidityCheck As Boolean = False
113            Dim strNumberInTeamMessage As String = "Please enter the number of people in your dive team (2-6)"
114            Dim strMessageBoxTitle As String = "Error"
115
116            Try
117                intTeamSize = Convert.ToInt32(txtTeam.Text)
118                If intTeamSize >= 2 And intTeamSize <= 6 Then
119                    blnValidityCheck = True
120                Else
121                    MsgBox(strNumberInTeamMessage, , strMessageBoxTitle)
122                    txtTeam.Focus()
123                    txtTeam.Clear()
124                End If
125            Catch Exception As FormatException
126                MsgBox(strNumberInTeamMessage, , strMessageBoxTitle)
127                txtTeam.Focus()
128                txtTeam.Clear()
129            Catch Exception As OverflowException
130                MsgBox(strNumberInTeamMessage, , strMessageBoxTitle)
131                txtTeam.Focus()
132                txtTeam.Clear()
133            Catch Exception As SystemException
134                MsgBox(strNumberInTeamMessage, , strMessageBoxTitle)
135                txtTeam.Focus()
136                txtTeam.Clear()
137            End Try
138            Return blnValidityCheck
139        End Function
```

● **Code the ValidateDiveSelection Function Procedure** Click below the ValidateNumberInTeam function and enter the ValidateDiveSelection Function procedure declaration. This Function procedure ensures that the user selected a dive trip from the lstDive ListBox object and then returns an integer value for the list selection to the calling procedure. To determine if a scuba dive trip was selected, the procedure uses a Try-Catch block to convert the selected index value to an integer. If the conversion is successful, a choice was made and the choice is returned. In addition, a Boolean variable in the calling procedure is set to True because the variable was passed ByRef. If the selected index is not converted, the user did not make a choice; an error message box is displayed and the Boolean variable is set to False. One Catch block is used because the only error that uses the ListBox object occurs if the user does not select a scuba dive trip.

```
                                       HINT
141  ⊟     Private Function ValidateDiveSelection(ByRef blnDive As Boolean, ByRef strDive As String) As Integer
142             ' This function ensures the user selected a dive type
143          Dim intDiveTyoe As Integer
144  ⊟     Try
145                 intDiveTyoe = Convert.ToInt32(lstDive.SelectedIndex)
146                 strDive = lstDive.SelectedItem.ToString()
147                 blnDive = True
148          Catch Exception As SystemException
149                 ' Detects if a dive type is not selected
150                 MsgBox("Select a Dive Type", , "Error")
151                 blnDive = False
152          End Try
153          Return intDiveTyoe
154       End Function
```

● **Code the AustraliaDiveCost Function Procedure to Find the Cost of an Australia Scuba Expedition**
Click below the ValidateDiveSelection Function procedure and enter the AustraliaDiveCost Function procedure
declaration. The purpose of this Function procedure is to determine the cost of an Australia scuba dive trip. Three
variables are passed to the function. Two are passed ByVal: the scuba dive selection and the dive team size. Dive
length is passed ByRef. The AustraliaDiveCost Function procedure uses the scuba dive selection and dive team size
to determine the cost of the dive trip based on published rates (*ref: Figure 7-50*). It also changes the values in the
dive length field for use in the calling procedure. Write the code for the AustraliaDiveCost Function procedure.

```
                                       HINT
Private Function AustraliaDiveCost(ByVal intDive As Integer, ByVal intTeam As Integer, ByRef intTime As Integer) As Decimal
    ' This function calculates the cost of the dive team in Australia
    Dim decTeamCost As Decimal
    Dim decFinalCost As Decimal
    Dim decAustraliaDive1 As Decimal = 359D
    Dim decAustraliaDive2 As Decimal = 200D
    Dim decAustraliaDive3 As Decimal = 125D

    Select Case intDive
        Case 0
            decTeamCost = decAustraliaDive1
            intTime = _intEightHour
        Case 1
            decTeamCost = decAustraliaDive2
            intTime = _intSixHour
        Case 2
            decTeamCost = decAustraliaDive3
            intTime = _intFourHour
    End Select
    decFinalCost = decTeamCost * intTeam
    Return decFinalCost
```

● **Code the BelizeDiveCost Function Procedure to Find the Cost of a Belize Scuba Expedition** Click below the
AustraliaDiveCost Function procedure and enter the BelizeDiveCost Function procedure declaration. The purpose
of this Function procedure is to determine the cost of a Belize scuba dive trip. It uses the same three passed
variables as the AustraliaDiveCost Function procedure. It also uses similar logic and returns the same values.
Write the code for the BelizeDiveCost Function procedure.

(continues)

```
                                        HINT
178
179  ⊟   Private Function BelizeDiveCost(ByVal intDive As Integer, ByVal intTeam As Integer, ByRef intTime As Integer) As Decimal
180           ' This function calculates the cost of the dive team in Belize
181           Dim decTeamCost As Decimal
182           Dim decFinalCost As Decimal
183           Dim decBelizeDive4 As Decimal = 200D
184           Dim decBelizeDive5 As Decimal = 150D
185
186  ⊟        Select Case intDive
187               Case 0
188                   decTeamCost = decBelizeDive4
189                   intTime = _intEightHour
190               Case 1
191                   decTeamCost = decBelizeDive5
192                   intTime = _intSixHour
193           End Select
194           decFinalCost = decTeamCost * intTeam
195           Return decFinalCost
196       End Function
```

● **Code the FijiDiveCost Function Procedure to Find the Cost of a Fiji Scuba Expedition** Click below the BelizeDiveCost Function procedure and enter the FijiDiveCost Function procedure declaration. The purpose of this Function procedure is to determine the cost of a Fiji scuba dive trip. It uses the same three passed variables as the BelizeDiveCost Function procedure. It also uses similar logic and returns the same values. Write the code for the FijiDiveCost Function procedure.

```
                                        HINT
198  ⊟   Private Function FijiDiveCost(ByVal intDive As Integer, ByVal intTeam As Integer, ByRef intTime As Integer) As Decimal
199           ' This function calculates the cost of the dive team in Fiji
200           Dim decTeamCost As Decimal
201           Dim decFinalCost As Decimal
202           Dim decFijiDive2 As Decimal = 280D
203           Dim decFijiDive3 As Decimal = 225D
204           Dim decFijiDive6 As Decimal = 200D
205
206  ⊟        Select Case intDive
207               Case 0
208                   decTeamCost = decFijiDive2
209                   intTime = _intEightHour
210               Case 1
211                   decTeamCost = decFijiDive3
212                   intTime = _intSixHour
213               Case 2
214                   decTeamCost = decFijiDive6
215                   intTime = _intFourHour
216           End Select
217           decFinalCost = decTeamCost * intTeam
218           Return decFinalCost
219       End Function
```

● **Code the Clear Button Click Event** After the Function procedures that are called from the btnDiveCost_Click event handler have been coded, the next step is to write the code for the Clear Button click event handler. This event handler must reset the Windows Form object and objects on the form to look the same as when the program starts. This includes resetting the message in the cboLocation ComboBox object, clearing the Number in Dive Team text box and the dive type list box, blanking the labels that display the results, and removing all the objects from view except the cboLocation ComboBox object. Display the Design window and then double-click the btnClear object to open the btnClear_Click event handler. Write the code for the event handler.

HINT

```
Private Sub btnClear_Click(ByVal sender As System.Object, ByVal e As System.EventArgs) Handles btnClear.Click
    ' This event handler clears the form and resets the form for reuse when the user clicks the Clear button.
    cboLocation.Text = "Select Location"
    txtTeam.Clear()
    lstDive.Items.Clear()
    lblScubaDive.Text = ""
    lblCost.Text = ""
    lblLength.Text = ""
    lblTeam.Visible = False
    txtTeam.Visible = False
    lblSelect.Visible = False
    lstDive.Visible = False
    btnDiveCost.Visible = False
    btnClear.Visible = False
    lblScubaDive.Visible = False
    lblCost.Visible = False
    lblLength.Visible = False
End Sub
```

● **Code the frmScuba_Load Event** The last bit of code to write for the Scuba Expeditions program is the event handler for the frmScuba load event. You will recall that when the application begins, a splash screen opens first. To display the splash screen longer than the default time, you must add a sleep timer. Return to the frmScuba.vb [Design] window and double-click the Windows Form object. Assuming that you want the splash screen to be displayed for 5 seconds, code the statement to delay program execution for 5000 milliseconds (*ref: Figure 7-15*).

HINT

```
240    Private Sub frmScuba_Load(sender As Object, e As EventArgs) Handles MyBase.Load
241        ' Hold the splash screen for 5 seconds
242        Threading.Thread.Sleep(5000)
243    End Sub
244 End Class
```

(continues)

Code Listing

The complete code for the sample program is shown in Figure 7-55.

```vbnet
1    ' Program Name:  Scuba Expeditions Application
2    ' Author:        Corinne Hoisington
3    ' Date:          June 22, 2018
4    ' Purpose:       The Scuba Expeditions app determines the location and scuba dives available and calculates the total dive team cost.
5
6    Option Strict On
7
8    Public Class frmScuba
9
10       ' Class variables
11       Private _intFourHour As Integer = 4
12       Private _intSixHour As Integer = 6
13       Private _intEightHour As Integer = 8
14       Private _strDive1 As String = "Great Barrier Reef"
15       Private _strDive2 As String = "Tiger Shark"
16       Private _strDive3 As String = "Fathom Chasm"
17       Private _strDive4 As String = "Great Blue Chasm"
18       Private _strDive5 As String = "Rainbow Reef"
19       Private _strDive6 As String = "Namena Sunken Ship"
20
21       Private Sub cboLocation_SelectedIndexChanged(ByVal sender As System.Object, ByVal e As System.EventArgs) Handles cboLocation.SelectedIndexChanged
22          ' This event handler allows the user to enter the location choice and then calls subprocedures to place the dive types in the list.
23          Dim intLocationChoice As Integer
24
25          intLocationChoice = cboLocation.SelectedIndex
26          lstDive.Items.Clear()
27          Select Case intLocationChoice
28             Case 0
29                AustraliaTeam()
30             Case 1
31                BelizeTeam()
32             Case 2
33                FijiTeam()
34          End Select
35          ' Make items visible in the window
36          lblTeam.Visible = True
37          txtTeam.Visible = True
38          lblSelect.Visible = True
39          lstDive.Visible = True
40          btnDiveCost.Visible = True
41          btnClear.Visible = True
42          lblScubaDive.Visible = True
43          lblCost.Visible = True
44          lblLength.Visible = True
45          ' Clear the labels
46          lblScubaDive.Text = ""
47          lblCost.Text = ""
48          lblLength.Text = ""
49          ' Set focus on number in dive team text box
50          txtTeam.Focus()
51       End Sub
52
53       Private Sub AustraliaTeam()
54          ' This procedure fills in the possible dive types offered in Australia
55          lstDive.Items.Add(_strDive1)
56          lstDive.Items.Add(_strDive2)
57          lstDive.Items.Add(_strDive3)
58       End Sub
59
60       Private Sub BelizeTeam()
61          'This procedure fills in the possible dive types offered in Belize
62          lstDive.Items.Add(_strDive4)
63          lstDive.Items.Add(_strDive5)
64       End Sub
65
66       Private Sub FijiTeam()
67          'This procedure fills in the possible dive types offered in Fiji
68          lstDive.Items.Add(_strDive2)
69          lstDive.Items.Add(_strDive3)
70          lstDive.Items.Add(_strDive6)
71       End Sub
```

FIGURE 7-55 (continues)

```vbnet
72
73    Private Sub btnDiveCost_Click(ByVal sender As System.Object, ByVal e As System.EventArgs) Handles btnDiveCost.Click
74        ' This button event handler determines the cost of scuba expeditions and
75        ' displays the size of the dive team, the cost, and the length of the dive
76
77        Dim intTeamSize As Integer
78        Dim blnNumberInTeamIsValid As Boolean = False
79        Dim blnDiveIsSelected As Boolean = False
80        Dim intDiveChoice As Integer
81        Dim strSelectedTeam As String = ""
82        Dim intLocationChoice As Integer
83        Dim intLength As Integer = 0
84        Dim decTotalCost As Decimal
85
86        ' Call a function to ensure the number of people in the dive team is valid
87        blnNumberInTeamIsValid = ValidateNumberInTeam()
88        ' Call a function to ensure a scuba dive was selected
89        intDiveChoice = ValidateDiveSelection(blnDiveIsSelected, strSelectedTeam)
90        ' If number of people and the dive trip are valid, calculate the cost
91        If (blnNumberInTeamIsValid And blnDiveIsSelected) Then
92            intTeamSize = Convert.ToInt32(txtTeam.Text)
93            intLocationChoice = cboLocation.SelectedIndex
94            Select Case intLocationChoice
95                Case 0
96                    decTotalCost = AustraliaDiveCost(intDiveChoice, intTeamSize, intLength)
97                Case 1
98                    decTotalCost = BelizeDiveCost(intDiveChoice, intTeamSize, intLength)
99                Case 2
100                   decTotalCost = FijiDiveCost(intDiveChoice, intTeamSize, intLength)
101           End Select
102           ' Display the cost of the scuba dive
103           lblScubaDive.Text = "Dive: " & strSelectedTeam
104           lblCost.Text = "Cost: " & decTotalCost.ToString("C")
105           lblLength.Text = "Length: " & intLength.ToString() & " hours"
106       End If
107   End Sub
108
109   Private Function ValidateNumberInTeam() As Boolean
110       ' This procedure validates the value entered for the dive team size
111       Dim intTeamSize As Integer
112       Dim blnValidityCheck As Boolean = False
113       Dim strNumberInTeamMessage As String = "Please enter the number of people in your dive team (2-6)"
114       Dim strMessageBoxTitle As String = "Error"
115
116       Try
117           intTeamSize = Convert.ToInt32(txtTeam.Text)
118           If intTeamSize >= 2 And intTeamSize <= 6 Then
119               blnValidityCheck = True
120           Else
121               MsgBox(strNumberInTeamMessage, , strMessageBoxTitle)
122               txtTeam.Focus()
123               txtTeam.Clear()
124           End If
125       Catch Exception As FormatException
126           MsgBox(strNumberInTeamMessage, , strMessageBoxTitle)
127           txtTeam.Focus()
128           txtTeam.Clear()
129       Catch Exception As OverflowException
130           MsgBox(strNumberInTeamMessage, , strMessageBoxTitle)
131           txtTeam.Focus()
132           txtTeam.Clear()
133       Catch Exception As SystemException
134           MsgBox(strNumberInTeamMessage, , strMessageBoxTitle)
135           txtTeam.Focus()
136           txtTeam.Clear()
137       End Try
138       Return blnValidityCheck
139   End Function
140
```

FIGURE 7-55 (continues)

```
141   Private Function ValidateDiveSelection(ByRef blnDive As Boolean, ByRef strDive As String) As Integer
142       ' This function ensures the user selected a dive type
143       Dim intDiveTyoe As Integer
144       Try
145           intDiveTyoe = Convert.ToInt32(lstDive.SelectedIndex)
146           strDive = lstDive.SelectedItem.ToString()
147           blnDive = True
148       Catch Exception As SystemException
149           ' Detects if a dive type is not selected
150           MsgBox("Select a Dive Type", , "Error")
151           blnDive = False
152       End Try
153       Return intDiveTyoe
154   End Function
155
156   Private Function AustraliaDiveCost(ByVal intDive As Integer, ByVal intTeam As Integer, ByRef intTime As Integer) As Decimal
157       ' This function calculates the cost of the dive team in Australia
158       Dim decTeamCost As Decimal
159       Dim decFinalCost As Decimal
160       Dim decAustraliaDive1 As Decimal = 359D
161       Dim decAustraliaDive2 As Decimal = 200D
162       Dim decAustraliaDive3 As Decimal = 125D
163
164       Select Case intDive
165           Case 0
166               decTeamCost = decAustraliaDive1
167               intTime = _intEightHour
168           Case 1
169               decTeamCost = decAustraliaDive2
170               intTime = _intSixHour
171           Case 2
172               decTeamCost = decAustraliaDive3
173               intTime = _intFourHour
174       End Select
175       decFinalCost = decTeamCost * intTeam
176       Return decFinalCost
177   End Function
178
179   Private Function BelizeDiveCost(ByVal intDive As Integer, ByVal intTeam As Integer, ByRef intTime As Integer) As Decimal
180       ' This function calculates the cost of the dive team in Belize
181       Dim decTeamCost As Decimal
182       Dim decFinalCost As Decimal
183       Dim decBelizeDive4 As Decimal = 200D
184       Dim decBelizeDive5 As Decimal = 150D
185
186       Select Case intDive
187           Case 0
188               decTeamCost = decBelizeDive4
189               intTime = _intEightHour
190           Case 1
191               decTeamCost = decBelizeDive5
192               intTime = _intSixHour
193       End Select
194       decFinalCost = decTeamCost * intTeam
195       Return decFinalCost
196   End Function
197
198   Private Function FijiDiveCost(ByVal intDive As Integer, ByVal intTeam As Integer, ByRef intTime As Integer) As Decimal
199       ' This function calculates the cost of the dive team in Fiji
200       Dim decTeamCost As Decimal
201       Dim decFinalCost As Decimal
202       Dim decFijiDive2 As Decimal = 200D
203       Dim decFijiDive3 As Decimal = 225D
204       Dim decFijiDive6 As Decimal = 200D
205
206       Select Case intDive
207           Case 0
208               decTeamCost = decFijiDive2
209               intTime = _intEightHour
210           Case 1
211               decTeamCost = decFijiDive3
212               intTime = _intSixHour
213           Case 2
214               decTeamCost = decFijiDive6
215               intTime = _intFourHour
216       End Select
217       decFinalCost = decTeamCost * intTeam
218       Return decFinalCost
219   End Function
```

FIGURE 7-55 (continues)

```vbnet
220
221     Private Sub btnClear_Click(ByVal sender As System.Object, ByVal e As System.EventArgs) Handles btnClear.Click
222         ' This event handler clears the form and resets the form for reuse when the user clicks the Clear button.
223         cboLocation.Text = "Select Location"
224         txtTeam.Clear()
225         lstDive.Items.Clear()
226         lblScubaDive.Text = ""
227         lblCost.Text = ""
228         lblLength.Text = ""
229         lblTeam.Visible = False
230         txtTeam.Visible = False
231         lblSelect.Visible = False
232         lstDive.Visible = False
233         btnDiveCost.Visible = False
234         btnClear.Visible = False
235         lblScubaDive.Visible = False
236         lblCost.Visible = False
237         lblLength.Visible = False
238     End Sub
239
240     Private Sub frmScuba_Load(sender As Object, e As EventArgs) Handles MyBase.Load
241         ' Hold the splash screen for 5 seconds
242         Threading.Thread.Sleep(5000)
243     End Sub
244 End Class
```

FIGURE 7-55 (continued)

1. What is the name of the screen that displays a logo and version number of an application allowing the program to load?

2. Name the two types of procedures.

3. Write the line of code that would display frmSplash1 for approximately six seconds.

4. What is the difference between passing by value and passing by reference?

5. What is the fewest number of arguments you can pass to a Sub procedure?

6. What section of code performs a specific task and returns a value?

7. What section of code performs a specific task and does not return a value?

8. If a variable intPlatform is assigned the value 4 in a Sub procedure, what is the value of intPlatform when the variable is placed outside of the Sub procedure if it is not passed out of the procedure?

9. How many values can a Function procedure return?

10. Write a Return statement that returns the variable intCricketScore.

11. Write the Visual Basic statements declaring a Sub procedure called Elevator that receives one variable called intFloors. The variable intFloors will be changed in the procedure. Write only the first and last lines of the Sub procedure.

12. When multiple arguments are passed to a procedure, the order is not important. True or false?

13. If you want a copy of a variable passed to a procedure, which way should you pass it?

14. You must have a Return statement in a Sub procedure. True or false?

15. You cannot have a Return statement in a Function procedure. True or false?

16. Which type of exception would be detected if you used the conversion command Convert.ToInt32 to convert a non-integer value?

17. Which type of exception would be detected if you used the conversion command Convert.ToDecimal to try to convert an ampersand?

18. If you enter a number that is too large for the data type, which type of exception would be detected?

19. When deciding whether a set of programming steps should be placed in a Sub procedure or a Function procedure, what are three questions you should ask?

1. Fix the code:

```
Private Sub btnCyberMonday_Tap(ByVal sender As System.Object, ByVal e As
System.EventArgs) Handles btnCyberMonday.Tap
    Dim decPurchase As Decimal
    Dim intCount As Decimal

        decPurchase = Convert.ToDecimal(txtCost.Txt)
        Inventory(decPurchase$, intCount)
End Sub

Private Sub Inventory(ByVal purchase, ByVal count)
        count +=4
        shop *=. 0.7
End Sub
```

2. Fix the code:

```
Private Sub btnSoftball_Click(ByVal sender As System.Object, ByVal e As
System.EventArgs) Handles btnSoftball.Click
        Dim decHits As Decimal = 210
        Dim decTimesAtBat As Decimal = 428
        Dim decBattingAverage As Decimal

        decBattingAverage = BattingAverage(decHits, decTimesAtBat)
        lblHits.Text = "The batting average is " &
        decBattingAverage.ToString()
End Sub

Private Function BattingAverage(ByVal decHitsCount As Decimal, ByVal
decNumberAtBat)
        Dim decAverageAtBat As Decimal
        decAverageAtBat = decHitsCount / decNumberAtBat
End Function
```

3. Fix the code:

```
Private Sub btnMileage_Click(ByVal sender As System.Object, ByVal e As
System.EventArgs) Handles btnMileage.Click
        Dim intMiles As Decimal = 323.2D
        Dim decGallons As Decimal = 13.8D
        Dim decMilesPer As Decimal

        decMilesPer = Compute(decMiles, decGallons)
        lblDisplays.Text = "Your MPG is " & decMiles.ToString()
End Sub
```

(continues)

```
Private Sub Compute(ByVal decM As Decimal, ByVal decG) As Decimal
        Dim decMPG As Decimal
        decMPG = decM / decG
        Return MilesPerGallon

End Function
```

Program Analysis

1. What is the output of the following code?

```
Private Sub btnFives_Click(ByVal sender As System.Object, ByVal e As
System.EventArgs) Handles btnFives.Click
        Dim intCount As Integer
        For intCount = 1 To 5
            CalculateFives(intCount)
        Next
End Sub

Private Sub CalculateFives(ByVal intCountValue As Integer)
        Dim intResult As Integer
        intResult = intCountValue ^ 3
        lstAnswer.Items.Add(intResult.ToString())
End Sub
```

2. What is the output of the following code?

```
Private Sub btnJoke_Click(ByVal sender As System.Object, ByVal e As System.
EventArgs) Handles btnJoke.Click
        DisplayRiddle()
        DisplayAnswer()
End Sub

Private Sub DisplayAnswer()
        lblAnswer.Text = " Yesterday, Today, and Tomorrow."
End Sub

Private Sub DisplayRiddle()
        lblRiddle.Text = " Can you name three consecutive days without
        using the words Monday, Tuesday, Wednesday, Thursday, Friday,
        Saturday, or Sunday?"
End Sub
```

Program Analysis *continued*

3. The following program contains the procedure declaration. Write the Function call statement that assigns the returned value to intTriple and passes a variable named intValue.

```
Private Function Cube(ByVal intNum As Integer) As Integer
        Return intNum * intNum * intNum
End Function
```

4. A program converts and validates a value entered as the population of a city. Write a statement that passes the variable intBase to a procedure and assigns the return value to a variable named intSolution. Write the code that would declare a variable named intPopulation as an Integer. Allow the user to enter the population of her city in a TextBox object named txtCityPopulation. Convert the value to an integer within a Try block. Write a Try-Catch block with an overflow Catch block first, a format exception Catch block second, and a generic exception last. Each Catch block should display a message box that explains the problem with the user's input.

5. Write the code for a Sub procedure named FindHeight that will calculate a person's height in inches when given the feet and inches. For example, a person who is 5'10" is 70 inches tall. Display the result in a message box.

Complete one or more of the following case programming assignments. Submit the program and materials you create to your instructor. The level of difficulty is indicated for each case programming assignment.

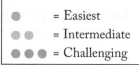

● = Easiest
●● = Intermediate
●●● = Challenging

1 ●
IMAX THEATRE

Design a Windows Classic Desktop application and write the code that will execute according to the program requirements in Figure 7-56 and the Use Case Definition in Figure 7-57 on the next page. Before writing the code, create an event planning document for each event in the program. The completed Windows Form object and other objects for the user interface are shown in Figure 7-58.

REQUIREMENTS DOCUMENT

Date:	June 21, 2019
Date Submitted:	
Application Title:	IMAX Theatre
Purpose:	This Windows Classic Desktop application computes the cost of matinee and evening tickets with varying base and data plans.
Program Procedures:	Allow the user to select from the Matinee ($16) or the Evening ($27) showing, request the number of tickets needed, and compute the cost of the tickets.
Algorithms, Processing, and Conditions:	1. The user is asked to select one of two IMAX tickets from a ComboBox object (Matinee $16 or Evening $27). The other objects are not visible until the user selects this option.
	2. The user is asked to enter the number of tickets.
	3. The value entered for the number of tickets is sent to another procedure to be validated.
	4. One of two Function procedures will be called for the type of tickets to compute and pass back the cost of the total ticket cost.
Notes and Restrictions:	1. A Clear Form button should clear the form.
	2. A Try-Catch block in a separate procedure will validate the input.
Comments:	1. A splash screen begins this application for four seconds.
	2. Obtain an image for this program from CengageBrain.com. The name of the picture for the application is named imax.

FIGURE 7-56

IMAX Theatre

USE CASE DEFINITION

1. The user views the opening splash screen for approximately four seconds.
2. The user selects the type of IMAX ticket and enters the number of tickets needed.
3. The user clicks the Ticket Cost button.
4. The user views the cost of the tickets.

FIGURE 7-57

FIGURE 7-58a

iStockphoto.com/SunflowerEY

FIGURE 7-58b

iStockphoto.com/SunflowerEY

2   KARAOKE MUSIC NIGHT

Design a Windows Classic Desktop application and write the code that will execute according to the program requirements in Figure 7-59 and the Use Case Definition in Figure 7-60 on page 447. Before writing the code, create an event planning document for each event in the program. The completed Windows Form object and other objects in the user interface are shown in Figure 7-61 on page 447.

REQUIREMENTS DOCUMENT

Date:	August 11, 2019
Date Submitted:	
Application Title:	Karaoke Music Night
Purpose:	This Windows Classic Desktop application computes either the customized evening cost of an open microphone costing $2.99 per song or renting a private karaoke room for $8.99 an hour.
Program Procedures:	The user can select singing karaoke per song or renting a private karaoke room for a group by the hour.
Algorithms, Processing, and Conditions:	1. The user first selects whether to compute the cost of each karaoke song or a rental karaoke room by the hour. 2. After the user selects an option, display the necessary objects based on the selection. If the user selects number of songs ($2.99 per song), request the number of karaoke songs. If the user chooses the private karaoke room ($8.99 per hour), request the number of rental hours. 3. Based on the cost of $2.99 per song or $8.99 per hour for the private karaoke room, calculate the cost of the number of songs or hourly rental. Use separate procedures to make the two calculations. 4. Display the total cost result of the calculation on the form.
Notes and Restrictions:	1. A Clear Form button should clear the form. 2. The data the user enters should be validated in Try-Catch blocks in separate procedures as needed.
Comments:	1. The application should begin with a splash screen that appears for approximately three seconds. 2. Obtain images for this program from CengageBrain.com. The name of the picture for the Windows form and the picture on the splash screen is karaoke.

FIGURE 7-59

Karaoke Music Night

USE CASE DEFINITION

1. The user views the opening splash screen for three seconds.
2. The user selects whether to purchase songs by the hour or rent a private karaoke room.
3. The user enters the number of songs or hours based on their initial selection.
4. The user clicks the Total Cost button to display the final cost.

FIGURE 7-60

FIGURE 7-61a

iStockphoto.com/Annykos

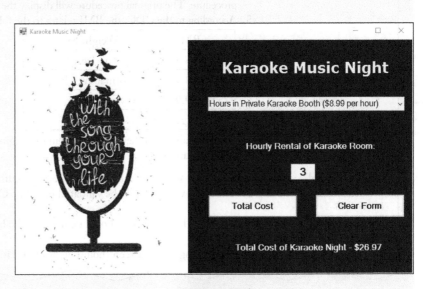

iStockphoto.com/Annykos

FIGURE 7-61b

3

BODY MASS INDEX (BMI) CALCULATOR WITH CDC CHART

Design a Windows Classic Desktop application and write the code that will execute according to the program requirements in Figure 7-62. Before designing the user interface, create a Use Case Definition. Before writing the code, create an event planning document for each event in the program.

REQUIREMENTS DOCUMENT

Date:	October 19, 2019
Date Submitted:	
Application Title:	Body Mass Index (BMI) Calculator with CDC Chart
Purpose:	This Windows Classic Desktop application allows the user to enter a height and weight and computes the user's body mass index. An interpretation according to CDC standards is displayed correlating to the BMI value.
Program Procedures:	The user will enter a height and weight using either the imperial or metric system.
Algorithms, Processing, and Conditions:	1. The user first views a Windows application that displays a title, a BMI graphic, a ListBox object to select the imperial or metric system, and labels to enter information for the user's height and weight.
	2. When the user selects imperial or metric and the height and weight, the Compute BMI button can be selected.
	3. A Sub procedure should be called to handle the imperial and metric BMI calculations using the following formulas:
	BMI = (Weight in Pounds / (Height in Inches * Height in Inches)) * 703
	BMI = Weight in Kilograms / (Height in Meters * Height in Meters)
	4. Two Function procedures should be called based on the system selected. Each Function procedure will calculate the BMI and return the Decimal value to the calling procedure. The original procedure will display the result.
	5. According to the CDC, the BMI relates to the following interpretations:

BMI	Weight Status
Below 18.5	Underweight
18.5 – 24.9	Normal Weight
25.0 – 29.9	Overweight
30.0 and Above	Obese

Display a label with the weight status in the original procedure based on the BMI/Weight Status chart.

Notes and Restrictions:	1. The result should be calculated to the hundredths place.
	2. The input values should be validated by a Try-Catch block.
Comments:	1. An image from the web should be used for the background BMI graphic on both forms.
	2. An opening splash screen should be displayed for two seconds.

FIGURE 7-62

4 UBER, SUBWAY, OR BUS COMMUTE

Design a Windows Classic Desktop application and write the code that will execute according to the program requirements in Figure 7-63. Before designing the user interface, create a Use Case Definition. Before writing the code, create an event planning document for each event in the program.

REQUIREMENTS DOCUMENT

Date:	March 12, 2019
Date Submitted:	
Application Title:	Uber, Subway, or Bus Commute
Purpose:	This Windows Classic Desktop application computes the yearly cost of commuting to work via Uber car service, subway, or bus.
Program Procedures:	The user selects how she commutes to work and then answers questions based on that response to compute the cost of traveling to and from work for one year in a city.
Algorithms, Processing, and Conditions:	1. The user first views a Windows application with a title and a ComboBox object that asks how she commutes—Uber, subway, or bus. The other objects on the form are not visible at this point.
	2. After the user selects the mode of travel, the questions related to that type of travel are displayed immediately.
	3. The following customized questions are displayed based on the user's choice:
	• Uber: Daily round trip cost using Uber, days worked per month. When you compute the Uber cost, increase the cost by 20 percent to cover surge pricing. Surge pricing is when fares temporarily increase to encourage more Uber drivers to get on the road and head to areas of the city where demand for rides is high.
	• Subway: Round trip transit fare and days worked per month.
	• Bus: Round trip transit fare and days worked per month.
	4. After the values have been validated, calculate the cost of commuting for one year for the selected choice.
Notes and Restrictions:	All values that the user enters should be validated.
Comments:	1. The background picture shown should be selected from pictures available on the web.
	2. Each portion of the program should be performed in separate functions and procedures.
	3. A splash screen should open the application for five seconds.

FIGURE 7-63

SAVE AS YOU GO REWARDS

Create a requirements document and a Use Case Definition document and then design a Windows application based on the case project description in Figure 7-64. Before writing the code, create an event planning document for each event in the program.

Many banks offer a Save as You Go reward savings program that transfers $1 into your vacation savings account each time you make a debit card purchase or pay bills online using your bank account. The bank wants you to write a Windows application that customers can use to check their balance on their rewards account by requesting the number of transactions (debit card purchases and online bills paid) or requesting a withdrawal from the vacation rewards account. The application should allow the user to enter a starting balance and indicate whether the account has a monthly interest rate of zero or more. Validate the beginning balance and interest rate to verify that the numbers are possible. Allow the user to enter the number of debit card purchases and bills paid online ($1 added for each transaction). Customers can also make withdrawals to use their vacation reward cash. Also, calculate the interest for one month and add the interest amount to the final balance. Users can add multiple rewards and withdrawals and continue until indicating that they are finished making transactions. The interest will be added to the final balance after the transactions are completed. Data validation is needed for all input. An opening splash screen will be displayed as well.

FIGURE 7-64

Case Programming Assignments

6 ●●● AIRLINES PASSENGER GROWTH

Create a requirements document and a Use Case Definition document and then design a Windows application based on the case project description in Figure 7-65. Before writing the code, create an event planning document for each event in the program.

> An international travel provider would like you to create a Windows application that will display the global growth of airline passengers. As of 2017, 3.8 billion passengers travelled on the world's commercial airlines. The airline passenger market is growing at 6.9 percent per year. Based on this growth rate, create a Sub procedure that calculates and displays the next 10 years of growth in a ListBox object. Also, create a Function procedure that allows the user to enter a year from the next 10 years and then passes back that year's airline passenger number projection. Validate all entries. An opening splash screen will be displayed as well.

FIGURE 7-65

CHAPTER 8

Using Arrays and File Handling

OBJECTIVES

You will have mastered the material in this chapter when you can:

- Initialize an array

- Initialize an array with default values

- Access array elements using a loop

- Use ReDim to resize an array

- Determine the number of elements in an array using the Length command

- Use the For Each loop

- Initialize two-dimensional arrays

- Read a text file

- Write to a text file

- Calculate depreciation

- Use multiple Form objects

- Access variable objects on other forms

Introduction

You can use Visual Basic to create applications for small businesses or multinational corporations. As programming applications grow in size, the role of organizing, storing, and retrieving large amounts of data becomes vital. This chapter explains how to develop applications that can keep data for later processing, including sorting, calculating, and display.

Chapter Project

In the sample chapter project, a burger food truck named Chef Shack requires a Windows application to compute the depreciation of its food truck, point of sale register, storage freezers, office computer, and picnic tables. Depreciation is an accounting term that describes the decline in value of a physical asset over a certain period of time. Most assets lose value due to use, aging, obsolescence, and impairment. Depreciation is an estimate of this declining value and is used for determining taxes and other financial purposes.

Chef Shack sells fresh grilled grass-fed beef and veggie burgers. The company cannot depreciate the cost of its food, but it can claim the depreciated value of its physical assets, such as the point of sale register and other food truck equipment. Each inventory item is assigned a four-character identifying code. A table that lists these items and associated codes is stored in a text file, which is kept on a storage medium such as a USB drive or cloud computing drive.

When the Windows application for Chef Shack starts, it opens the text file and fills the Select Inventory Item ListBox object with the item numbers. Before calculating depreciation, the user selects an item and a depreciation method, as shown in Figure 8-1.

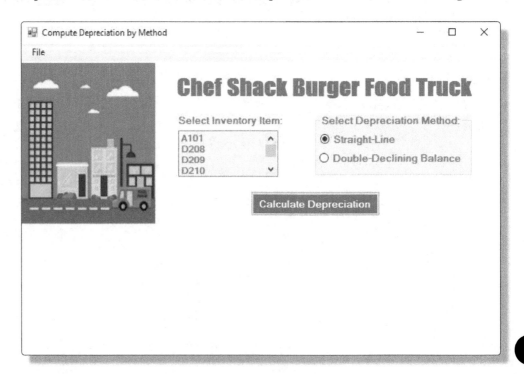

ipayo/Shutterstock.com

FIGURE 8-1

In Figure 8-1, the user clicks the list box arrow to display the items in inventory. After selecting an item, the user can click a radio button to select either the Straight-Line or the Double-Declining Balance depreciation method.

In straight-line depreciation, the asset is depreciated by the same amount each year for the life of the asset. In double-declining depreciation, the depreciation is accelerated.

After selecting an item number and a method of depreciation, the user clicks the Calculate Depreciation button. The Windows form then displays the product name, the quantity in inventory, and the amount the item is worth over the next five years due to depreciation, as shown in Figure 8-2.

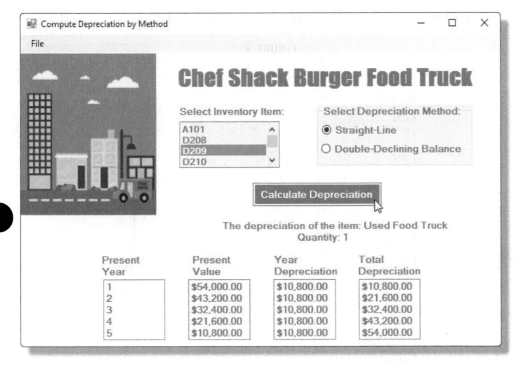

FIGURE 8-2

Chef Shack purchased the items shown in Figure 8-3 in its first year of business.

Each item in Figure 8-3 is depreciated each year for tax reasons. The Internal Revenue Service allows depreciation deductions for five years because the average useful life of these types of items is five years. The items in Figure 8-3 are stored in a text file named inventory.txt. Figure 8-4 shows this file in Notepad. The Windows application opens the inventory.txt text file and reads the information for use in the program. In this case the text file is stored on an USB drive named D: drive.

The Chef Shack Depreciation application also contains a File menu that displays the following menu items: Display Inventory, Clear, and Exit (Figure 8-5).

Inventory Item	Item Number	Initial Cost	Quantity
Point of Sale Registers	A101	599.99	1
Outside Signage	D208	49.99	5
Used Food Truck	D209	54000.00	1
Storage Freezers	D210	799.99	3
Stove	D211	1959.99	2
Office Computers	E101	529.99	1
Picnic Tables	F310	345.00	8
Refrigerators	F311	829.99	2

FIGURE 8-3

FIGURE 8-4

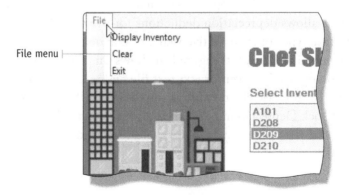

FIGURE 8-5

When the user clicks the Display Inventory menu item, the application opens a second Windows Form object that shows the items in inventory in sorted alphabetical order (Figure 8-6).

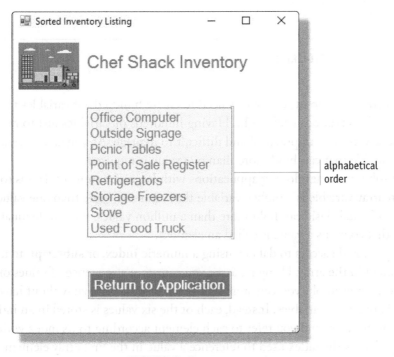

FIGURE 8-6

Ipayo/Shutterstock.com

Introduction to Arrays

After completing Chapters 1 through 7 in this book, you know how to create the user interface for the chapter project, which involves Button, ListBox, Label, and RadioButton objects. The challenge in this chapter is to write code that adds data to the form efficiently and accurately. To do so, you must understand arrays and file handling. The next section provides background on arrays.

Arrays

Every application you have developed thus far involved a limited number of variables and data, but in professional programming projects, applications deal with much larger sets of data that need numerous variables. You have learned that data type variables can store only one value at a time. Therefore, you have not used data types that contain more than one memory location to store more than one value at a time. If you changed a variable's value, the previous value was erased because a typical variable can store only one value at a time. For example, if you wanted to create an application that recorded dinner reservations at a restaurant for named groups with different numbers of people in the groups, you would need a unique variable name for each reservation, as shown in Figure 8-7.

```
5              Dim intBakerReservation As Integer = 4
6              Dim intLopezReservation As Integer = 5
7              Dim intBuckReservation As Integer = 12
8              Dim intChanReservation As Integer = 2
9              Dim intTirrellReservation As Integer = 8
```

FIGURE 8-7

For a large restaurant, you would need to create hundreds of variables to hold hundreds of reservations each night. Having hundreds of variables just to record each night's reservations is impractical and difficult to manage. As you can see, a different kind of variable that can hold more than one value is required.

The solution to developing applications with larger amounts of data is to use an array. An array variable is simply a variable that can store more than one value. In fact, an array in Visual Basic can hold more than a million values. Each individual item in an array that contains a value is called an element.

Arrays provide access to data by using a numeric **index**, or **subscript**, to identify each element in the array. Using an array, you can store a sequence of values of similar data types. For example, you can store six values of type Decimal without having to declare six different variables. Instead, each of the six values is stored in an individual element of the array, and you refer to each element according to its index within the array. Zero is the index used to reference a value in the first array element. Each subsequent element is referenced by an increasing index value, as shown in Figure 8-8.

decShoeSize(0)	decShoeSize(1)	decShoeSize(2)	decShoeSize(3)	decShoeSize(4)	decShoeSize(5)
9.0	11.5	6.0	7.5	13.0	8.0

FIGURE 8-8

CRITICAL THINKING

Can an array be used in a Visual Basic program to extract and display values from a database like Microsoft Access or Oracle?
Typically, if you are storing a large amount of values, a database is the best option for organizing and retrieving information. Later in this text, values from a database will be retrieved and processed using a VB program.

In Figure 8-8, an array named decShoeSize holds six shoe sizes. Each shoe size is stored in an array element, and each element is assigned a unique index. The first value (9.0) is stored in the element with the index of 0. The element is identified by the term decShoeSize(0), which is pronounced "decShoeSize sub zero." The second shoe size (11.5) is stored in the second element of the array, which is referenced as decShoeSize(1). The same scheme is used for all elements in the array.

Initialize an Array

To declare an array in a program, you must include an array declaration statement, which states the name of the array, how many items it can store, and what sort of data it can store. To initialize or declare an array, just as in declaring any other variable, you must reserve the amount of memory that will be needed to store the array. The syntax for declaring an array begins with the word Dim (Figure 8-9).

> **General Format: Define an Array**
>
> ```
> Dim intReservations(300) as Integer
> ```
>
> intReservations assigns the array name.
>
> 300 is the index or subscript reserving the amount of memory needed – it is the highest numbered index.
>
> Integer determines the data type of the entire array.

FIGURE 8-9

The statement in Figure 8-9 declares intReservations as an array of integer variables that holds 301 elements. The first array element is intReservations(0), then intReservations(1), and so on to the last element in the array, intReservations(300). All arrays in Visual Basic 2017 are zero based, meaning that the index of the first element is zero and the indexes increase sequentially by 1. You must specify the number of array elements by indicating the upper-bound index of the array. The upper-bound number specifies the index of the last element of the array. Setting the size of an array is called dimensioning the array.

If you know the values to be placed in each element in the array, you can declare an array by assigning values to each element, as shown in Figure 8-10.

```
13          Dim strNames() As String = {"Baker", "Lopez", "Buck", "Chan", "Tirrell"}
14          Dim intReservations() As Integer = {4, 5, 12, 2, 8}
```

FIGURE 8-10

The data to be placed in each element is contained within curly brackets. An array can be any data type. In Figure 8-10, the first array is a String data type and the second array is an Integer data type. strNames() is an array of String variables that contains five names, with Baker stored in strNames(0), Lopez in strNames(1), and so on. intReservations() is an array of Integer variables that contains five values, with 4 stored in intReservations(0), 5 in intReservations(1), and so on.

These two arrays are **parallel arrays**. Parallel arrays store related data in two or more arrays. The information for one reservation includes strNames(0) for the Baker reservation and the number of people associated with it (4) in intReservations(0). The same subscript is used for the corresponding array elements, as shown in Figure 8-11 and Figure 8-12, which illustrate the arrays created by the code in Figure 8-10.

strNames(0)	strNames(1)	strNames(2)	strNames(3)	strNames(4)
Baker	Lopez	Buck	Chan	Tirrell

FIGURE 8-11

intReservations(0)	intReservations(1)	intReservations(2)	intReservations(3)	intReservations(4)
4	5	12	2	8

FIGURE 8-12

Visual Basic determines the size of the array by counting the number of items within the curly brackets. In this case, each array has five elements, and each element has an index number ranging from 0 to 4. The upper-bound index is 4, which specifies the last element of the array. When a number is not used in the declaration statement to state the size of the array, the array is **implicitly sized**, meaning that the number of values is determined at execution. Instead of stating the size, you list the values stored in the array.

Another way to declare an array is to specify its upper-bound index and assign each item of the array one by one, as shown in Figure 8-13. Each sport is assigned to a different element of the strAthlete() array.

HEADS UP

When declaring an implicitly sized array, do not place an upper-bound index in the parentheses following the array name in the declaration. If you do, an error will occur when the array is assigned elements.

```
17          Dim strAthlete(5) As String
18
19          strAthlete(0) = "Football"
20          strAthlete(1) = "Soccer"
21          strAthlete(2) = "Lacrosse"
22          strAthlete(3) = "Baseball"
23          strAthlete(4) = "Tennis"
24          strAthlete(5) = "Hockey"
```

FIGURE 8-13

Initialize an Array with Default Values

When you initialize an array but do not assign values immediately, each element is assigned a default value. The table in Figure 8-14 shows the default value assigned to each data type.

Data Type	Default Value
All numeric data types	0
String data type	Null
Boolean data type	False

FIGURE 8-14

After the array has been initialized, specific values can be assigned to each element, replacing the default value for each item. You can assign explicit values to the first few elements of the array and allow its remaining elements to be assigned to the default values automatically.

Access Array Elements Using a Loop

Because an array can contain multiple elements, in code you can use a loop to reference each element of an array. Loops can save valuable time when processing a large array because you don't have to write code for each array element. For example, if you were recording the lowest temperature for each day during the month of January to use in later calculations, the code in Figure 8-15 would allow the user to enter all 31 temperatures.

```
26        Dim intDailyTempJanuary(31) As Integer
27        Dim strTemp As String
28        Dim intDays As Integer
29
30        For intDays = 0 To 30
31            strTemp = InputBox("Enter the lowest temperature on January " _
32                & intDays + 1, "Obtain Temperatures")
33            intDailyTempJanuary(intDays) = Convert.ToInt32(strTemp)
34        Next
```

FIGURE 8-15

The array intDailyTempJanuary can hold the low temperature for each of the 31 days in January by using the elements referenced by the subscripts of 0 to 30. The loop counts from 0 to 30 using the variable intDays. The first time through the loop, the temperature obtained in an InputBox is assigned to a String named strTemp. Then, the value in strTemp is converted to an integer and assigned to the element intDailyTempJanuary(0). On each subsequent pass through the loop, the temperature obtained is placed in the next element, moving from intDailyTempJanuary(1) to intDailyTempJanuary(2) and so on until the final value for January 31 is assigned to the array element intDailyTempJanuary(30).

By using a loop in this manner, the program can process items in a large array with a few simple lines.

Array Boundaries

The Visual Basic compiler determines if each subscript is within the boundaries set when you initialized the array. For example, if you initialize an array to contain 31 elements but attempt to reference an element outside that boundary, as shown in Figure 8-16, an exception is produced when the code is executed.

```
37          Dim intDailyTempJanuary(30) As Integer
38          Dim strTemp As String
39          Dim intDays As Integer
40
41          For intDays = 0 To 31
42              strTemp = InputBox("Enter the lowest temperature on January " _
43                  & intDays + 1, "Obtain Temperatures")
44              intDailyTempJanuary(intDays) = Convert.ToInt32(strTemp)
45          Next
```

FIGURE 8-16

The exception occurs when the loop tries to reference an element with the subscript 31. This element does not exist because the array contains 31 elements with an upper-bound index of 30. (Remember that an array's elements always are numbered beginning with zero.) The exception created by the code in Figure 8-16 is an IndexOutOfRangeException (Figure 8-17). A Try-Catch statement can catch this exception, but it is best to stay within the array boundaries of zero and the upper-bound array subscript.

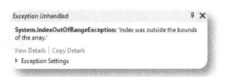

FIGURE 8-17

Upper-Bound Index Constant

An array can use a constant value to represent its upper-bound index. By using a constant, the size of several arrays can be specified quickly; as you will learn in the next section, they also can be changed quickly. In Figure 8-18, the arrays strFirstNames() and strLastNames() are sized to hold 41 elements (the indexes are from 0 to 40).

```
Const intUpperBound As Integer = 40
Dim strFirstNames(intUpperBound) As String
Dim strLastNames(intUpperBound) As String
```

FIGURE 8-18

Reinitialize an Array

Although you usually set the number of elements in an array when you declare it, you can alter the size of the array later in the code. Every array in Visual Basic is considered **dynamic**, which means that you can resize it at run time. When you change the number of elements in an existing array, you redimension it. The **ReDim** statement assigns a new array size to the specified array variable. You use a ReDim statement to change the number of elements in an array. The code in Figure 8-19 reinitializes the strEmployees array.

HEADS UP

If you redimension an array to a smaller size and use the Preserve command, you still will lose the items between the original upper-bound array size and the new upper-bound size.

```
Dim strEmployees(50) As String
' Later in the code
ReDim strEmployees(65)
```

FIGURE 8-19

The strEmployees array originally is sized to hold 51 values, but is reinitialized later in the code to hold 66 values. When you use the ReDim statement to redimension the array, all the data contained in the array is lost. If you want to preserve the existing data, you can use the keyword **Preserve**, as shown in Figure 8-20. Preserve resizes the array and retains the data in the elements from 0 through 50.

```
Dim strEmployees(50) As String
' Later in the code
ReDim Preserve strEmployees(65)
```

FIGURE 8-20

Use the Length Property

The Length property of an array contains the number of elements in an array. The code shown in Figure 8-21 displays 51 as the array size.

```
59          Dim strBranchOffices(50) As String
60
61          lblArraySize.Text = "The array size is " & (strBranchOffices.Length)
```

FIGURE 8-21

You can use the Length property in a loop to determine the exact number of iterations needed to cycle through each element in the array. Using the Length property can prevent the program from throwing the IndexOutOfRange exception. In the code in Figure 8-22, the For loop uses the Length property to determine the number of loop iterations.

```
63          Dim intYear(99) As Integer
64          Dim intCount As Integer
65
66          ' Assigns the years from 2001 to 2100 to the elements in the table
67          For intCount = 0 To (intYear.Length - 1)
68              intYear(intCount) = 2001 + intCount
69          Next
```

FIGURE 8-22

In the code in Figure 8-22, intYear.Length is equal to 100 (elements 0 through 99), one more than the array's upper-bound index number. In the For loop, the loop count will run from 0 through 99 (intYear.Length − 1), which means the loop will be executed 100 times, once for each element in the array.

Because an array can be resized anytime, the Length property is useful when you are unsure of an array's size.

Use Arrays

Arrays can be useful in many situations, such as when dealing with large amounts of data and finding totals and averages. For example, the code in Figure 8-23 computes the total yearly income and average yearly income for 10 employees in the warehouse department.

```
71          Dim intYearlySalary(9) As Integer
72          Dim intNumberOfEmployees As Integer
73          Dim intAdd As Integer
74          Dim intTotal As Integer
75
76          ' Allows the user to enter the 10 yearly salaries
77          For intNumberOfEmployees = 0 To (intYearlySalary.Length - 1)
78              intYearlySalary(intNumberOfEmployees) = _
79                  InputBox("Enter Salary #" & intNumberOfEmployees + 1, _
80                  "Warehouse Dept.")
81          Next
82
83          ' Finds the total amount of salaries entered
84          For intAdd = 0 To (intYearlySalary.Length - 1)
85              intTotal += intYearlySalary(intAdd)
86          Next
87
88          lblDisplayTotalSalary.Text = intTotal.ToString("C2")
89          lblDisplayAverageSalary.Text =_
90          (intTotal / intYearlySalary.Length).ToString("C2")
```

FIGURE 8-23

The reason the value accumulated in the intTotal variable is divided by the Length property is that the intYearlySalary array contains 10 elements. To find the average, you add all the numbers and divide by the number of elements. The line of code that finds the average (line 89) is outside of the loop because the average should be determined once, not repeatedly within the loop.

In the chapter project, the Items property of the lstInventoryId ListBox object must be filled with the inventory item numbers. The inventory item numbers are contained in the _strItemId array. The code in Figure 8-24 places the inventory item numbers in the Items property of the ListBox object. The Length property of the _strItemId array is used to determine the number of iterations in the For loop.

```
43          ' The ListBox object is filled with the Inventory IDs
44          For intFill = 0 To (_strItemId.Length - 1)
45              lstInventoryId.Items.Add(_strItemId(intFill))
46          Next
```

FIGURE 8-24

On line 44, the For loop begins with the intFill variable containing the value 0, which references the first element in the _strItemId array. On each pass through the loop, the value in intFill is incremented by 1 so it references the next element in the array. The loop terminates when the value in intFill is greater than the length of the array minus 1. Recall that the length of the array counts from 1 but the subscript counts from 0. Therefore, the length of the array minus 1 references the last element in the array.

The result of the code in Figure 8-24 is shown in Figure 8-25.

item numbers in ListBox object

FIGURE 8-25

Ipayo/Shutterstock.com

When I use an array in code, I can refer to multiple values by the same name. Does this make my code shorter?

Arrays can shorten and simplify your code, allowing you to create loops that deal efficiently with any number of elements.

The For Each Loop

Recall from earlier chapters that a loop repeats a process. A special loop designed specifically for arrays is called a For Each loop. The loop syntax is shown in Figure 8-26.

General Format: For Each

For Each *Control Variable Name* in *Array Name*

```
' Lines of Code
```

Next

For Each — This type of loop iterates through an array until the array reaches the last element.

Control Variable Name — This variable will contain each individual element of the array without a subscript as the loop is processed. During the first iteration of the loop, the first element in the array is assigned to the control variable.

Array Name( ) — The name of the array that the loop cycles through. The array must be initialized first.

Next — This statement continues the loop to its next iteration.

FIGURE 8-26

A For Each loop cycles through each array element until the end of the array. In Figure 8-27, each element in the array is assigned to the variable strPioneer as the For Each loop is executed. The For Each loop does not require the program to keep track of the subscript for each element, and it stops when the loop has processed every element in the array.

Because each element in the array is assigned to the control variable, the elements and the variable must be the same data type. For example, in Figure 8-27, the array elements and the control variable are both Strings.

```
93      Private Sub btnHistory_Click(ByVal sender As System.Object, ByVal e As System.    ↙
        EventArgs) Handles btnHistory.Click
94
95          Dim strFamousComputerPioneers() As String = {"Pascal", _
96              "Babbage", "Ada", "Aiken", "Jobs"}
97          Dim strHeading As String = "Computer Pioneers:"
98          Dim strPioneer As String
99
100         lstPioneers.Items.Add(strHeading)
101         lstPioneers.Items.Add("")
102
103         For Each strPioneer In strFamousComputerPioneers
104             lstPioneers.Items.Add(strPioneer)
105         Next
106
107     End Sub
```

FIGURE 8-27

When the loop begins, the first element of the strFamousComputerPioneers array is placed in the strPioneer variable and the body of the loop is executed. In the body of the loop, the value in strPioneer is added to the Items property of the lstPioneers ListBox object. On the second iteration of the loop, the second element of the array is placed in the strPioneer variable and the body of the loop is executed again. This looping continues until all elements within the array have been processed.

After the loop processing is complete, the lstPioneers ListBox object displays the output shown in Figure 8-28.

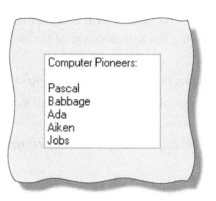

Computer Pioneers:

Pascal
Babbage
Ada
Aiken
Jobs

FIGURE 8-28

Scope of Arrays

The scope of an array declared within a procedure is local to that procedure, but an array can be declared as a class-level variable. As with other variables, an array declared as a class-level variable is visible to all procedures within the class. For example, in the chapter project, multiple procedures will use the contents of the arrays that hold the inventory information for Chef Shack. Therefore, these arrays should be declared as class-level arrays, as shown in Figure 8-29. Later in the chapter, the scope of these variables will be changed so that other classes can access the variables.

```
 9     Public Class frmDepreciation
10
11     ' Class Level Private variables
12     Private _intLifeOfItems As Integer = 5
13     Private _intSizeOfArray As Integer = 7
14     Private _strInventoryItem(_intSizeOfArray) As String
15     Private _strItemId(_intSizeOfArray) As String
16     Private _decInitialPrice(_intSizeOfArray) As Decimal
17     Private _intQuantity(_intSizeOfArray) As Integer
```

FIGURE 8-29

The arrays in Figure 8-29 can be referenced in any procedure following the declaration within the class. Notice that the size of the arrays is determined by the value in the _intSizeOfArray variable, which is declared on line 13.

Pass an Array

An array can be passed as an argument to a Sub procedure or a Function procedure. For example, if you need to find the sum of a salesperson's commissions, you can pass the array that holds the commission amounts to a Sub procedure. The Sub procedure named ComputeDisplayTotal in Figure 8-30 accepts a Decimal array. The For Each loop in this Sub procedure accumulates the sum of the commission amounts.

```
109     Private Sub btnCommission_Click(ByVal sender As System.Object, ByVal e As System. ↙
        EventArgs) Handles btnCommission.Click
110
111         Dim decCommissionAmounts() As Decimal = {1345.99, 7800.16, _
112             5699.99, 3928.09, 1829.45}
113
114         ComputeDisplayTotal(decCommissionAmounts)
115
116     End Sub
117
118     Private Sub ComputeDisplayTotal(ByVal decValueOfCommission() As Decimal)
119
120         Dim decAmount As Decimal
121         Dim decTotal As Decimal = 0
122
123         For Each decAmount In decValueOfCommission
124             decTotal += decAmount
125         Next
126
127         lblTotalCommission.Text = "The Total Commission is " _
128             & decTotal.ToString("C")
129     End Sub
```

FIGURE 8-30

Notice that the array is passed using the ByVal keyword, but with arrays ByVal has a different meaning. Arrays can be passed by value or by reference; however, the ByVal keyword does not restrict a Sub procedure or Function procedure from changing the array's elements. Whether you pass an array by value or by reference, the original array can be accessed and modified within the Sub or Function procedure. When passing arrays using ByVal, the array is not duplicated. If you change the value of any array element in a procedure, the original array is changed.

In Figure 8-31, the decCommissionAmounts array is defined on line 133. The third element is given the value 5699.99. On line 147 in the ChangeValue Sub procedure, the third element in the array, referenced as decValueOfCommission(2), is changed. When the array is displayed in the btnCommission_Click event (line 131), the third element has been changed (see Figure 8-32).

```
131     Private Sub btnCommission_Click(ByVal sender As System.Object, ByVal e As System. ↙
        EventArgs) Handles btnCommission.Click
132
133         Dim decCommissionAmounts() As Decimal = {1345.99, 7800.16, _
134             5699.99, 3928.09, 1829.45}
135         Dim decDisplay As Decimal
136
137         ChangeValue(decCommissionAmounts)
138
139         For Each decDisplay In decCommissionAmounts
140             lstDisplay.Items.Add(decDisplay.ToString("C"))
141         Next
142
143     End Sub
144
145     Private Sub ChangeValue(ByVal decValueOfCommission() As Decimal)
146
147         decValueOfCommission(2) = 4599.99
148
149     End Sub
```

FIGURE 8-31

FIGURE 8-32

Sort an Array

The data in an array often is sorted for an organized display. For example, the telephone white pages are sorted by last name, which makes it easier to search for and locate friends and family members. To sort array contents in Visual Basic, you use a procedure named **Sort**. When the Sort procedure is applied to an array, the lowest value is placed in the first element in the array with an index of zero, the next lowest value is placed in the second element, and so on until the largest value is stored in the highest element of the array. The syntax for the Sort procedure is shown in Figure 8-33.

General Format: Sort Procedure
Array.Sort (ArrayName)
Coding Example: Dim intAges() as Integer = {16, 64, 41, 8, 19, 81, 23} Array.Sort(intAges)
After the sort executes, the values in the array are in the order 8, 16, 19, 23, 41, 64, and 81.

FIGURE 8-33

In the Chef Shack Inventory Depreciation application, the array _strInventory-Item is declared as a class-level private variable that contains String data, as shown in Figure 8-34. Later the variable will be changed to public to be accessed by a second class. The size of the array is specified by the value in the _intSizeOfArray variable.

```
13      Private _intSizeOfArray As Integer = 7
14      Private _strInventoryItem(_intSizeOfArray) As String
```

FIGURE 8-34

The array is filled with data from a text file in another procedure. The inventory items in the text file are not sorted, but the items should be sorted before being displayed in a ListBox object. Therefore, the array is sorted using the Array.Sort procedure, as shown in Figure 8-35. After sorting, a For Each loop displays the elements in the array in ascending alphabetic (A to Z) order, as shown in Figure 8-36.

```
11          Dim strItem As String
12
13          ' Sorts the _strInventoryItem array
14          Array.Sort(frmDepreciation._strInventoryItem)
15
16          ' Displays the _strInventoryItem array
17          For Each strItem In frmDepreciation._strInventoryItem
18              lstDisplay.Items.Add(strItem)
19          Next
```

FIGURE 8-35

ascending alphabetical sequence

FIGURE 8-36

Ipayo/Shutterstock.com

Search an Array

Arrays provide an excellent way to store and process information. Suppose an array holds 5,000 student names in alphabetical order. If you searched for one name in that array, the search could take some time. One search approach is to begin with the first name in index zero and evaluate each name until you find a match. Searching each element in an array is called a sequential search. Theoretically, you might have to search 5,000 names before you find a match or discover that the name is not even in the array. For these reasons, a sequential search is not the most efficient way of searching for an element.

If an array is large and requires many repeated searches, you need a more efficient search approach. The BinarySearch method searches a sorted array for a value using a binary search algorithm, which searches an array by repeatedly dividing the search interval in half. In an array with the contents shown in Figure 8-37, you could quickly find the value 405 using the BinarySearch method.

searching for this value

```
165             Dim intCalories() As Integer = {35, 45, 75, 110, 145, 160, 195, 405, 435}
```

FIGURE 8-37

The steps for the BinarySearch method are:

1. Determine the halfway point of the array, which is the number 145 in Figure 8-37. Compare that value first: 145 is less than 405.
2. If the first comparison is not equal to the number being searched, determine whether the value of the search number is less than the middle value. If the search value is less, narrow the search interval to the lower half of the array. Otherwise, narrow the search to the upper half of the array. The search value 405 is greater than the middle value 145, so the process narrows the search to the upper half of the array, which contains 160, 195, 405, and 435.
3. Repeatedly check each interval until the value is found or until the halving process evaluates the entire element list of the array.

The BinarySearch procedure returns the matching index value if the element is found. If the array does not contain the specified value, the method returns a negative integer. The BinarySearch procedure syntax is shown in Figure 8-38.

General Format: BinarySearch Procedure

```
intValue = Array.BinarySearch(arrayname, value)
```

If intValue returns a positive number or zero, a match was found at the subscript number equal to intValue.

If intValue returns a negative number, a match was not found.

FIGURE 8-38

As another example, a user enters the number of calories to consume, and the code in Figure 8-39 determines if the number of calories is found in the intCalories() array. The code also displays the food item index location if it finds a match with the number of calories entered. If the number of calories is not found, a message reports that the food item is not found.

```
165          Dim intCalories() As Integer = {35, 45, 75, 110, 145, 160, _
166              195, 405, 435}
167          Dim strFoods() As String = {"Carrots", "Kiwi", "Egg", "Orange", _
168              "Cola", "Taco", "Yogurt", "Apple Pie Slice", "Raisins"}
169          Dim intSelection As Integer
170          Dim intIndexLocation As Integer
171
172          intSelection = Convert.ToInt32(txtCalories.Text)
173          intIndexLocation = Array.BinarySearch(intCalories, intSelection)
174          If intIndexLocation >= 0 Then
175              lblLocation.Text = "The search item is found in subscript number " _
176                  & intIndexLocation
177              lblFood.Text = strFoods(intIndexLocation)
178          Else
179              lblLocation.Text = "The food item not found"
180          End If
```

FIGURE 8-39

If the calorie value of 405 is entered into the txtCalories TextBox object, the message "The search item is found in subscript number 7" is displayed in lblLocation. The second Label object displays Apple Pie Slice.

Create a Two-Dimensional Array

An array that has a single index or subscript is called a one-dimensional array, but arrays can be multidimensional and hold complex information. An array that has two dimensions has two subscripts. A **two-dimensional array** holds data that is arranged in rows and columns, as shown in Figure 8-40. In other words, two-dimensional arrays store the elements of tables. The array intVal is initialized with three rows and four columns in Figure 8-41 (recall that the values in parentheses specify the highest numbered element).

```
182         Dim intVal(2, 3) As Integer
```

FIGURE 8-40

	column 0	column 1	column 2	column 3
row 0	intVal(0,0)	intVal(0,1)	intVal(0,2)	intVal(0,3)
row 1	intVal(1,0)	intVal(1,1)	intVal(1,2)	intVal(1,3)
row 2	intVal(2,0)	intVal(2,1)	intVal(2,2)	intVal(2,3)

FIGURE 8-41

The table in Figure 8-42 shows the four busiest airports in the United States. The numbers are represented in millions, and identify the number of passengers traveling through each airport each year, according to the Bureau of Transportation Services. The table shows that Atlanta is the busiest airport in the United States, with over 34 million passengers flying through the airport each year. The table has four rows and two columns.

	column 0 2017	column 1 2016	
Atlanta	35	34	**row(0)**
Chicago	28	27	**row(1)**
Dallas	24	23	**row(2)**
Los Angeles	20	19	**row(3)**

FIGURE 8-42

The array declared to hold the contents of the busiest airport table is the same as a one-dimensional array, except for the two subscripts that hold the row and column index values. The declaration statement in Figure 8-43 initializes an array with four rows (0, 1, 2, 3) and two columns (0, 1) named intPassengers.

```
184          Dim intPassengers(3, 1) As Integer
```

FIGURE 8-43

After the array has been initialized, users can enter the values into a TextBox object from the table information or the program can assign the values by using an implicitly sized array, such as the one shown in Figure 8-44.

```
192          Dim intPassengers(,) As Integer = {{35, 34}, {28, 27}, {24, 23}, _
193              {20, 19}}
```

FIGURE 8-44

In the code shown in Figure 8-45, the array representing the busiest U.S. airports is totaled by column to find the number of passengers who flew through the four airports in each of the two years. A nested loop is used to total the two columns of the two-dimensional array. The outer loop controls the column index and the inner loop controls the row index of the array.

```
192            Dim intPassengers(,) As Integer = {{35, 34}, {28, 27}, {24, 23}, _
193                {20, 19}}
194            Dim intTotalColumn As Integer = 0
195            Dim intCol As Integer
196            Dim intRow As Integer
197
198            For intCol = 0 To 1
199                'Resets the total to 0
200                intTotalColumn = 0
201                For intRow = 0 To 3
202                    intTotalColumn += intPassengers(intRow, intCol)
203                Next
204                MsgBox("The Sum of Column #" & intCol + 1 & " is " _
205                    & intTotalColumn.ToString & " million.")
206            Next
```

FIGURE 8-45

The output for the airport program is shown in Figure 8-46 and Figure 8-47.

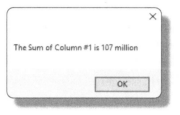

FIGURE 8-46

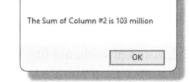

FIGURE 8-47

File Handling

In the applications you created in this book so far, the information entered has originated from assigning data to variables or asking the user to enter data in objects on the form. In many business applications, entering information can be time consuming if you must enter data for thousands of items. To process data more efficiently, many developers use text files to store and access information for use within an application. Text files have a .txt extension. The Windows operating system provides a basic text editor called Notepad that allows you to save files with the .txt extension. A simple text file is called a sequential file.

For example, in the chapter project, Chef Shack's inventory is stored in a text file. By gaining access to that information, the depreciation program can manipulate the data and compute the depreciation for items in the inventory. The text file is available at CengageBrain.com. Visual Basic can access many types of files, including text files, as discussed in this chapter, or various types of databases, which are covered in Chapter 10.

With Visual Basic 2017, the System.IO (input/output) namespace in the .NET Framework provides several classes for working with text files, binary files, directories, and byte streams. The System.IO namespace allows you to create, copy, move, and delete files. The file handler supports all types of data, including both string and numeric data types. The most commonly used classes are FileStream, BinaryReader, BinaryWriter, StreamReader, and StreamWriter.

CONSIDER THIS

Can I read other types of files besides a text file created in Notepad?

The code in this chapter deals specifically with text files created in a text editor such as Notepad, but the System.IO namespace in the .NET Framework provides several classes for working with text files, binary files, directories, and byte streams.

Read a Text File

To open a text file, you need an object available in the System.IO called a **StreamReader**. As its name suggests, this object reads streams of text. You create a StreamReader to provide access to standard input and output files.

To read a file, a variable object is first created for a data type called StreamReader. The prefix for an object is obj in the format used in Figure 8-48.

```
24          Dim objReader As IO.StreamReader
```

FIGURE 8-48

After the object variable is declared, an If statement in the form IO.File.Exists("*filename*") determines if the file is available, as shown in Figure 8-49. The command IO.File.OpenText("*filename*") opens the text file and assigns it to the object variable objReader.

```
31          If IO.File.Exists("e:\inventory.txt") = True Then
32              objReader = IO.File.OpenText("e:\inventory.txt")
33          Else
34              MsgBox("The file is not available. Restart the program when the  ↙
        file is available",,"Error")
35              Close()
36          End If
```

FIGURE 8-49

To read each line of the text file, you use a ReadLine procedure. The first line of data in the text file is assigned to the first element in the array _strInventoryItem (see Figure 8-50).

```
35          _strInventoryItem(intCount) = objReader.ReadLine()
```

FIGURE 8-50

To determine whether the end of the file has been reached, use the Peek procedure of the StreamReader object. The Peek procedure reads the next character in the file without changing position. If the end of the file is reached, the Peek procedure returns the value of −1. You can use a Do While loop to determine if all the lines in the file have been read. When the Peek procedure reaches the end of the file and returns a −1, the Do While loop ends, as shown in Figure 8-51.

```
34          Do While objReader.Peek <> -1
35              _strInventoryItem(intCount) = objReader.ReadLine()
36              _strItemId(intCount) = objReader.ReadLine()
37              _decInitialPrice(intCount) = Convert.ToDecimal(objReader.ReadLine())
38              _intQuantity(intCount) = Convert.ToInt32(objReader.ReadLine())
39              intCount += 1
40          Loop
```

FIGURE 8-51

```
40          objReader.Close()
```

FIGURE 8-52

The Chef Shack application opens and reads a file named inventory.txt. To read data from a text file, you can complete the following steps:

STEP 1   Open the code window by clicking the View Code button on the Solution Explorer toolbar. Click inside the frmDepreciation_Load event. Initialize the variables. Assign an object variable to the IO.StreamReader object. Type Dim objReader As IO to initialize the StreamReader object. An IntelliSense window opens. Select StreamReader. Press ENTER. Finish declaring the rest of the variable names.

The code window opens and the insertion point appears in the frmDepreciation_Load event handler. After the objReader object variable is initialized in the IO namespace, IntelliSense opens a listing of IO procedures. The variables are initialized (Figure 8-53).

```
19    Private Sub frmDepreciation_Load(ByVal sender As System.Object, ByVal e As System.EventArgs) Handles MyBase.Load
20        ' The frmDepreciation load event reads the inventory text file and
21        ' fills the Listbox object with the inventory items
22
23        ' Initialize an instance of the StreamReader object and declare variables
24        Dim objReader As IO.StreamReader
25        Dim intCount As Integer = 0
26        Dim intFill As Integer
27
28    End Sub
```

FIGURE 8-53

STEP 2   Verify that the inventory.txt data file is available by typing `If IO.` to open an IntelliSense window. Complete the rest of the line using IntelliSense, as shown in Figure 8-54. Assign the objReader variable by typing `objR` and then pressing CTRL+SPACEBAR to complete the variable name. Type `= IO.` to open an IntelliSense window. Type `F`.

The If statement confirms that the data file exists. The objReader is assigned to open the inventory.txt file (Figure 8-54).

IntelliSense list ——

FIGURE 8-54

STEP 3   Select File by typing a period and then select OpenText from the IntelliSense list. Type `("d:\inventory.txt")` to access the inventory text file from the USB drive (drive D).

The inventory.txt file is opened on the USB drive (Figure 8-55).

FIGURE 8-55

STEP 4   To read each line of the text file, insert a Do While loop that continues until the Peek procedure returns the value of –1. Specify that the ReadLine() procedure reads each line of the text file. Use the variable intCount to determine the index of each array element.

The code is entered to read inventory item names, item IDs, initial price, and quantity from the text file and assign them to class module-level array variables until the last item of the file is read (Figure 8-56). Notice a variable has been assigned the path of the text file.

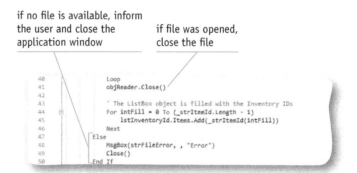

```
30        ' Verify the file exists
31    ⊟   If IO.File.Exists(strLocationAndNameOfFile) Then
32            objReader = IO.File.OpenText(strLocationAndNameOfFile)
33            ' Read the file line by line until the file is completed
34    ⊟       Do While objReader.Peek <> -1
35                _strInventoryItem(intCount) = objReader.ReadLine()
36                _strItemId(intCount) = objReader.ReadLine()
37                _decInitialPrice(intCount) = Convert.ToDecimal(objReader.ReadLine())
38                _intQuantity(intCount) = Convert.ToInt32(objReader.ReadLine())
39                intCount += 1
40            Loop
41            objReader.Close()
```

read each line of the text file into the appropriate array element

FIGURE 8-56

STEP 5   After the data file has been read, close the file. Insert an Else statement that informs the user if the file cannot be opened and then closes the application.

The object variable objReader file is closed and the Else statement informs the user if the file is not available (Figure 8-57).

if no file is available, inform the user and close the application window

if file was opened, close the file

```
40            Loop
41            objReader.Close()
42
43            ' The ListBox object is filled with the Inventory IDs
44    ⊟       For intFill = 0 To (_strItemId.Length - 1)
45                lstInventoryId.Items.Add(_strItemId(intFill))
46            Next
47        Else
48            MsgBox(strFileError, , "Error")
49            Close()
50        End If
```

FIGURE 8-57

CONSIDER THIS

Do I have to access a text file stored on a USB drive?
The text file can be stored on any local computer path or network path. When you select a file using File Explorer, Windows 10 has a feature called Copy path that allows you to copy the path where the file is stored. You can then paste that path into your code.

Write to a Text File

Writing to a text file is similar to reading a text file. The System.IO namespace also includes the StreamWriter, which is used to write a stream of text to a file. The following example writes a file of users with their names and logon passwords to a new text file named NewAccounts.txt. Each name and password is written to a separate line in the file. The btnCreateAccount_Click event creates a text file with the new customer information, as shown in Figure 8-58. The Notepad text file named NewAccounts.txt is displayed in Figure 8-59.

```
53      Private Sub btnCreateAccount_Click(ByVal sender As System.Object, ByVal e As System↙
        .EventArgs) Handles btnCreateAccount.Click
54          ' Initialize Variables
55          Dim strCustomerName(5) As String
56          Dim strPassword(5) As String
57          Dim objWriter As New IO.StreamWriter("e:\NewAccounts.txt")
58          Dim intCount As Integer
59
60          For intCount = 0 To (strCustomerName.Length - 1)
61              strCustomerName(intCount) = InputBox("Please enter your name:", "Login    ↙
        Information")
62              strPassword(intCount) = InputBox("Please enter a password:", "Password    ↙
        Information")
63              If IO.File.Exists("e:\NewAccounts.txt") Then
64                  ' Write the file line by line until the file is completed
65                  objWriter.WriteLine(strCustomerName(intCount))
66                  objWriter.WriteLine(strPassword(intCount))
67              Else
68                  MsgBox("The file is not available. Restart the program when      ↙
        the file is available",,"Error")
69                  Close()
70              End If
71          Next
72
73          ' The file is closed
74          objWriter.Close()
75
76      End Sub
```

FIGURE 8-58

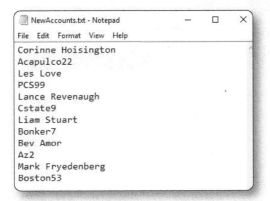

FIGURE 8-59

Compute Depreciation

Depreciation is the decrease in property value and the reduction in the balance sheet value of a company asset to reflect its age and prolonged use. The U.S. Internal Revenue Service states that the life of office equipment is five years for depreciation purposes. The two common ways of computing depreciation are the straight-line method and the double-declining balance method.

The simplest and most common method, straight-line depreciation, is calculated by dividing the purchase or acquisition price of an asset by the total number of productive years it can reasonably be expected to benefit the company. This value is called the life of the asset. In the chapter project, each asset in the inventory file has a life of five years. Figure 8-60 shows the formula for computing straight-line depreciation.

```
95          decStraightDepreciation = _decInitialPrice(intItemId) / _intLifeOfItems
```

FIGURE 8-60

To calculate the depreciation for storage freezers in the Chef Shack program, you can use the straight-line depreciation method shown in Figure 8-61.

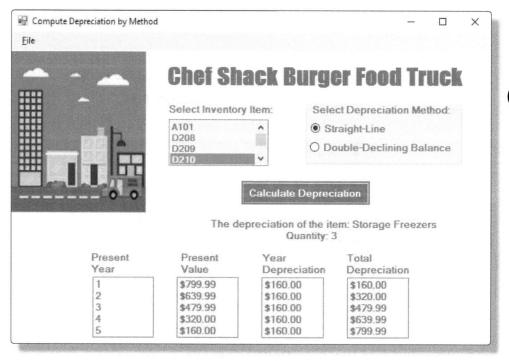

FIGURE 8-61

Ipayo/Shutterstock.com

The double-declining balance depreciation method is like the straight-line method doubled. To use the double-declining balance method, first calculate depreciation using the formula in Figure 8-62. Notice that the price is doubled and divided by the item's life in years. After that asset is depreciated for the first year, subtract the depreciation amount from the initial price for the next year. The resulting value after subtracting the depreciation is used in the formula for each subsequent year.

```
124         ' The loop repeats for the life of the items
125         For intDoublePresentYear = 1 To _intLifeOfItems
126             ' The formula for double-declining depreciation inside the loop to repeat the process
127             decDoubleDepreciation = (decDoublePresentYearValue * 2D) / _intLifeOfItems
128             ' Accumulates the total of depreciation
129             decDoubleTotal += decDoubleDepreciation
130             ' Displays the depreciation amounts
131         Next
        End Sub
```

FIGURE 8-62

To calculate the depreciation for outside signage in the Chef Shack program, you can use the double-declining balance depreciation method shown in Figure 8-63.

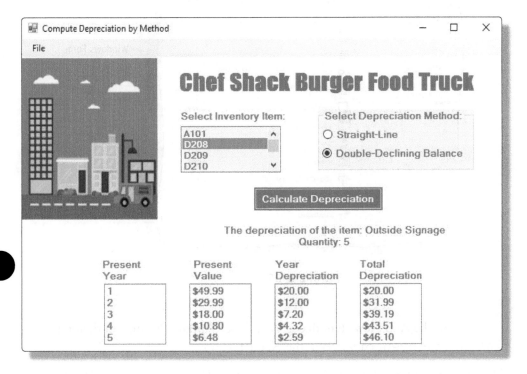

FIGURE 8-63

Ipayo/Shutterstock.com

Use Multiple Form Objects

As program applications become larger, more than one Windows Form object often is needed to display information. Each Windows Form object in your program (Figure 8-64) is associated with a file displayed in the Solution Explorer. For example, the code stored in the frmDepreciation.vb file is displayed in the code window when you click the frmDepreciation.vb tab in the design window.

FIGURE 8-64

Visual Basic 2017 allows you to add multiple Windows Form objects to an application. To add a second Windows Form object to an application, you can complete the following steps:

STEP 1   Click Project on the menu bar, and then click Add Windows Form.

The Add New Item dialog box opens (Figure 8-65).

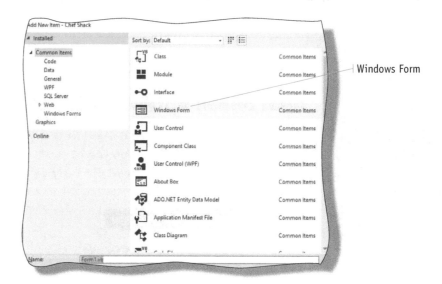

FIGURE 8-65

STEP 2   In the Add New Item dialog box, click Windows Form, and then type `frmDisplayInventory.vb` in the Name text box.

A Windows Form is selected to add as a new item to the Depreciation project. The form is named frmDisplayInventory.vb (Figure 8-66).

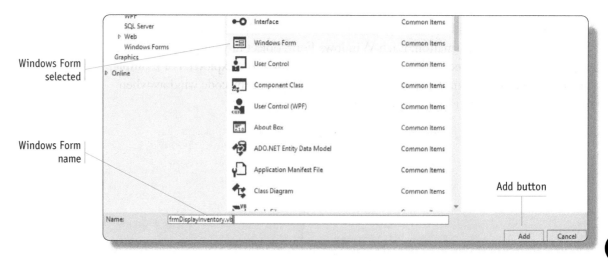

FIGURE 8-66

STEP 3   Click the Add button in the Add New Item dialog box. A second Form object named frmDisplayInventory.vb opens in the Visual Basic 2017 window. In the Properties window, change the Text property of the frmDisplayInventory object to Sorted Inventory Listing.

The second Form object opens and its Text property is changed (Figure 8-67).

properties of
new Windows
Form object

new Windows
Form object

Text property
changed

FIGURE 8-67

Choose a Startup Object

Every application begins executing a project by displaying the object designated as the **Startup** object. For the depreciation application, the default Startup object is frmDepreciation.vb. However, you can change the Startup object if you want a different Form object to open first. To begin, right-click the project name in Solution Explorer and then click Properties on the shortcut menu. Click the Application tab shown in Figure 8-68, click the Startup form list arrow, and then click the object you want to open when the application starts.

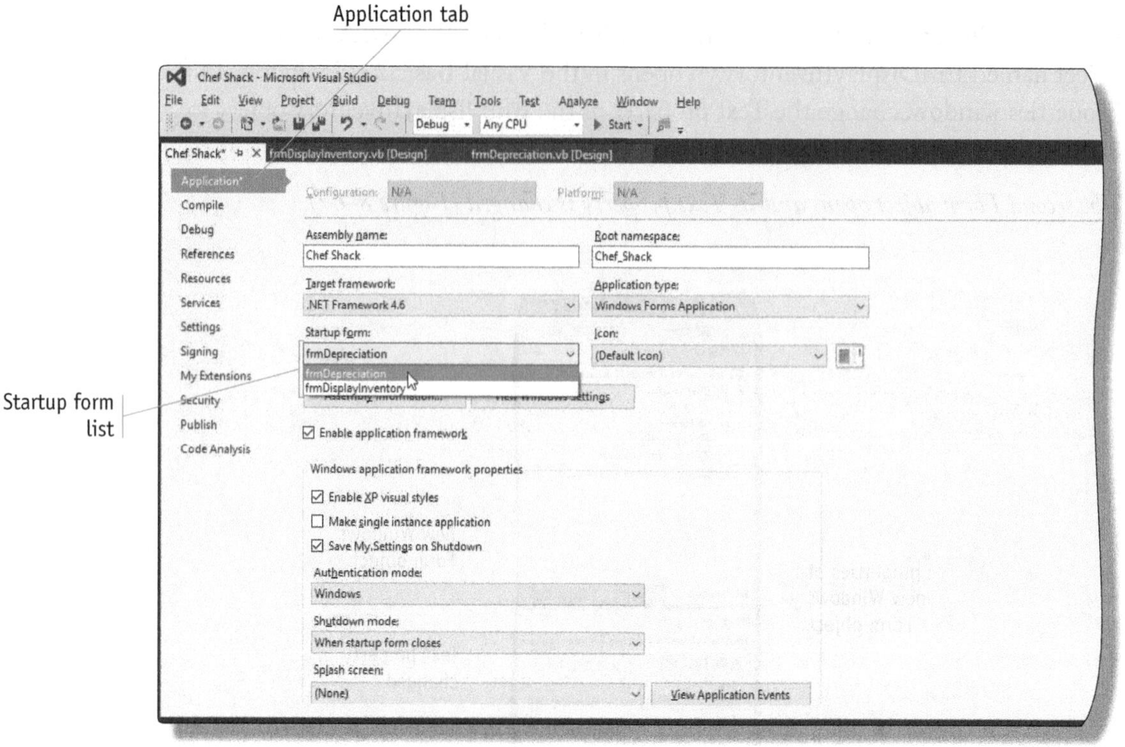

Application tab

FIGURE 8-68

Create an Instance of a Windows Form Object

Now that you have multiple Windows Form objects in the application, you must write code that opens the Form objects as needed. As you create each Form object, code associated with the Form object creates a class declaration. Figure 8-69 displays the code.

```
96  Public Class frmDepreciation
97
98  End Class
```

FIGURE 8-69

The class frmDepreciation holds the object's properties and the procedures for that class. To display a second or subsequent form, the initial step is to create an **instance** of the Windows Form object. An instance is an object variable that references the second form's class name to access the object's procedures and properties. For example, in the code for the chapter project shown in Figure 8-70, the mnuDisplay_Click event opens when the user clicks the Display Inventory menu item. The click event declares an instance of the second form, which is named frmDisplayInventory. The object variable frmSecond references the instance of the Form object frmDisplayInventory.

```
158    Private Sub mnuDisplay_Click(ByVal sender As System.Object, ByVal e As System.EventArgs) Handles mnuDisplay.Click
159         ' The mnuDisplay click event creates an instance of the frmDisplayInventory
160         Dim frmSecond As New frmDisplayInventory
```

FIGURE 8-70

After the instance of the Form object is created, another statement must be written to display the instance of the second form. When creating multiple Windows Form objects, Visual Basic allows you to generate two types of forms: **modal** and **modeless**. A modal form retains the input focus while open, and the user cannot switch between Form objects until the first form is closed. You create a modal form with the ShowDialog procedure. In the code example in Figure 8-71, the second Form object, named frmSecond, is displayed using the ShowDialog procedure. The line preceding the ShowDialog() procedure hides the first form using the **Hide** procedure. The Hide procedure removes the first form from the user's screen so that it does not cover up the information it references.

HEADS UP

Command lines placed after the ShowDialog method call are not executed until the second Form object is closed.

```
162         'Hide this form and show the Display Inventory form
163         Hide()
164         frmSecond.ShowDialog()
```

FIGURE 8-71

The second method used when displaying multiple forms is referred to as a modeless Form object. A modeless form allows you to switch the input focus to another window. The first form stays open when you switch to another form, and lets you use the two forms at the same time. For example, a modeless form is useful for a help window that displays instructions. You create a modeless Form object with the Show procedure, as shown in Figure 8-72. A Hide method is not necessary because both Form objects are displayed at the same time.

IN THE REAL WORLD

Modeless forms are used more often than modal forms in Windows applications.

```
91         frmSecond.Show()
```

FIGURE 8-72

Access Variables on Other Forms

When you create multiple Form objects, you might need to access the variable objects used in one form when you are working in another form. In the chapter project, the user can click the Display Inventory menu item to open a second Form object that displays the sorted inventory items. The second form needs to reference the array initialized in the first form's code. You control the availability of a variable by specifying its access level, or access specifier. The access level determines what code has permission to read or write to a variable. To access a variable object on a different form, you can declare a class module-level variable with an access specifier other than Private. The access specifier Private determines that the variable can be used only with the class in which it is declared. For example, the variable _intLifeOfItems declared in Figure 8-73 can be accessed only within the class frmDepreciation because it has the access specifier Private.

```
10    ☐Public Class frmDepreciation
11          ' Class Level Private variables
12          Private _intLifeOfItems As Integer = 5
```

FIGURE 8-73

If you want to declare a variable object that can be used in the class where it is declared and in different classes within other Form objects, the variable can be declared using the access specifier Public Shared. A Public Shared variable is shared by all instances of a Form's class. In the chapter project, if you initialize the array of inventory items with the access specifier Public Shared in the frmDepreciation class, as shown in Figure 8-74, the Integer _intSizeOfArray and the array _strInventoryItem are now accessible in the second form. By using the Public Shared access specifier, the variable's values are shared across all objects in the depreciation application.

```
13          Public Shared _intSizeOfArray As Integer = 7
14          Public Shared _strInventoryItem(_intSizeOfArray)
```

FIGURE 8-74

After the variables are initialized with the access specifier Public Shared, they can be used within a different class on more than one form. To access the shared variable on another form, specify the name of the originating Form object followed by the name of the variable object. In the chapter project, a second Form object named frmDisplayInventory accesses the _strInventoryItem array. To access the array in the second form, the array name must begin with the originating form, frmDepreciation. The originating Form object and the variable name are separated by the dot operator, as shown in Figure 8-75. The array is sorted and displayed on the second Form object.

```
8     Private Sub frmDisplayInventory_Load(ByVal sender As System.Object, ByVal e As System.EventArgs) Handles MyBase.Load
9          ' The frmDisplayInventory load event is a second forms that
10         ' displays the sorted inventory items
11
12         Dim strItem As String                                    originating
13                                                                   form name
14         ' Sorts the _strInventoryItem array
15         Array.Sort(frmDepreciation._strInventoryItem)
16
17         ' Displays the _strInventoryItem array
18         For Each strItem In frmDepreciation._strInventoryItem
19             lstDisplay.Items.Add(strItem)
20         Next
21     End Sub
```

dot operator   variable name

FIGURE 8-75

HEADS UP

In applications that include multiple forms, it is best to declare every variable as Private unless the variable is used in multiple Form objects.

When you type frmDepreciation and the dot operator, IntelliSense displays the names of the shared variables from that Form object (see Figure 8-76).

originating form name   shared variable name   IntelliSense list

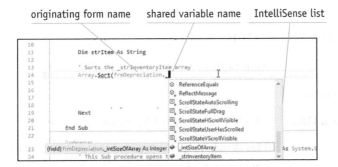

FIGURE 8-76

After the second form opens, the user can click the Return to Application button (Figure 8-77) to close the second Form object and return to the first Form object, frmDepreciation. The code in Figure 8-78 is executed when the Return to Application button is tapped or clicked. An instance of the first form, frmFirst, is created for frmDepreciation. The second form is hidden and the first form is opened again.

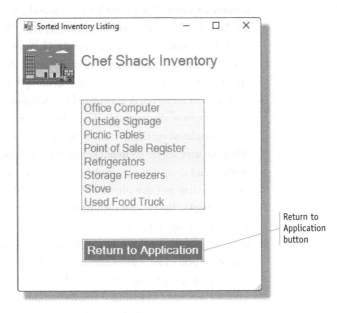

FIGURE 8-77

```
22
23    Private Sub btnReturn_Click(ByVal sender As System.Object, ByVal e As System.EventArgs) Handles btnReturn.Click
24        ' This Sub procedure opens the first form
25        Dim frmFirst As New frmDepreciation
26
27        Hide()
28        frmFirst.ShowDialog()
29    End Sub
```

FIGURE 8-78

Program Design

The requirements document for the Chef Shack Inventory Depreciation application is shown in Figure 8-79, and the Use Case Definition document is shown in Figure 8-80.

REQUIREMENTS DOCUMENT

Date:	April 14, 2019
Date Submitted:	
Application Title:	Chef Shack Inventory Depreciation Application
Purpose:	This Windows application opens an inventory data file and computes item depreciation based on the straight-line and double-declining balance methods.
Program Procedures:	A Windows application opens the inventory text file so that the user can select an item and the type of depreciation method. The depreciation is calculated for the five-year life of the inventory item.

Algorithms, Processing, and Conditions:

1. The user first views a Windows application that includes the following: a title; a File menu that includes Display Inventory, Clear, and Exit commands; a ListBox object that displays the inventory item IDs filled from the inventory text file; and a GroupBox object with two RadioButton objects that provide options for straight-line and double-declining balance depreciation methods. A Calculate Depreciation Button object is also available. The Chef Shack logo is displayed on the left side of the Form object.

2. After the user selects an item ID and the depreciation method and then clicks the Button object, the selected inventory item and quantity are displayed. ListBox objects display the present year, present value, year depreciation, and total depreciation.

3. If the user selects the Display Inventory menu item, a second Form object opens and displays the sorted inventory items list. The first Form object closes. The second Form object provides a Return to Application Button object to reopen the first Form object.

4. The user can select the Clear menu item to clear and reset the first Form object. The user can select the Exit menu item to close the application.

Notes and Restrictions:	The inventory.txt file is located on the USB drive (D:).
Comments:	The image shown in the window should be a picture available on the Cengage site named truck.jpg.

FIGURE 8-79

USE CASE DEFINITION

1. The user selects the inventory item ID and the type of depreciation.
2. The user clicks the Calculate Depreciation button to display the selected inventory item and quantity below the button.
3. The depreciation values are displayed for the present year, present value, year depreciation, and total depreciation.
4. The user clicks the Display Inventory menu item to view the sorted inventory items.
5. The user clicks the Clear menu item to clear and reset the form.
6. The user clicks the Exit menu item to close the application.

FIGURE 8-80

Design the Program Processing Objects

The event planning documents for the Chef Shack Inventor Depreciation application are shown in Figure 8-81 and Figure 8-82.

EVENT PLANNING DOCUMENT

Program Name: Depreciation	Developer: Corinne Hoisington	Object: frmDepreciation	Date: April 14, 2019
OBJECT	**EVENT TRIGGER**	**EVENT PROCESSING**	
frmDepreciation_Load	Load	Open the inventory.txt file from the USB drive; use If ... Else statements to handle possible errors when opening the file Assign each line of the text file to array variables Continue to read the text file until all items are assigned If the text file is not available, display a message Fill the ListBox object with the array of inventory item IDs	
btnCalculateDepreciation	Click	If the ListBox object and one RadioButton object are selected, call the appropriate Sub procedure based on the depreciation method selected If neither object is selected, display a message reminding the user to make a selection	

FIGURE 8-81 (continues)

EVENT PLANNING DOCUMENT

Program Name: Depreciation	Developer: Corinne Hoisington	Object: frmDepreciation	Date: April 14, 2019
OBJECT	**EVENT TRIGGER**	**EVENT PROCESSING**	
StraightLineDepreciation	Called Sub procedure	Make objects visible to display results by calling the MakeObjectsVisible Sub procedure Display the inventory item selected and the quantity of that item Calculate the straight-line depreciation based on the following formula: initial price / life of the item in years Assign the initial price to the present year value In a loop that repeats five times due to the assigned life of the item, accumulate the total depreciation Display the present years in a ListBox object Display the present values in a ListBox object Display the year depreciation in a ListBox object Display the total depreciation in a ListBox object	
DoubleDecliningDepreciation	Called Sub procedure	Show objects needed for results by calling the MakeObjectsVisible Sub procedure Display the inventory item selected and the quantity of that item Assign the initial price to the present year value In a loop that repeats five times due to the assigned life of the item, calculate the double-declining balance depreciation based on the following formula: initial price × 2 / life of the item in years Accumulate the total depreciation Display the present years in a ListBox object Display the present values in a ListBox object Display the year depreciation in a ListBox object Display the total depreciation in a ListBox object	
MakeObjectsVisible	Called Sub procedure	Change the Visible property of the result objects to true Clear the ListBox objects	
mnuDisplay	Click	Create an instance of the second Form object Hide the first Form object Show the second Form object	
mnuClear	Click	Reset the ListBox SelectedIndex property to −1, clearing the user's selection Set the Checked property of the RadioButton objects to false, clearing the user's selection Change the Visible property of all the result objects to false Clear all the ListBox objects	
mnuExit	Click	Close the application	

FIGURE 8-81 (continued)

EVENT PLANNING DOCUMENT

Program Name: ChefShack Inventory Depreciation	Developer: Corinne Hoisington	Object: frmDisplayInventory	Date: April 14, 2019
OBJECT	**EVENT TRIGGER**	**EVENT PROCESSING**	
frmDisplayInventory_Load	Load	Sort the inventory item array Display the inventory item array in sorted order in a ListBox object	
btnReturn	Click	Hide the second Form object Open the first Form object	

FIGURE 8-82

Guided Program Development

To design the user interface for the Chef Shack Inventory Depreciation application and enter the code required to process each event in the program, complete the steps in this section.

NOTE TO THE LEARNER

In the following activity, you should complete the tasks within the specified steps. Each of the tasks is accompanied by a Hint Screen. The purpose of the Hint Screen is to indicate where you should perform the activity in the Visual Studio window and to remind you which method to use. If you need further help completing a step, refer to the figure identified by *ref:*.

Guided Program Development

Phase I: Design the Form

1

• **Create a New Windows Project** Open Visual Studio and then close the Start page. Click the New Project button on the Standard toolbar. Begin a Windows Forms App project and name the project Depreciation.

• **Name the Form Object** Select the Form object. Change the (Name) property of the Form object to frmDepreciation.

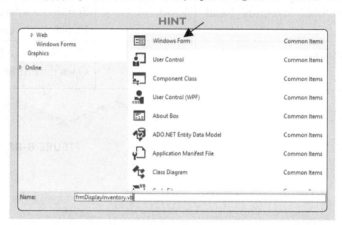

• **Assign a Title to the Form Object** Open the main Form object. Select the Form object and change the Text property to Compute Depreciation by Method.

• **Create the User Interface** Using the skills you have acquired in this course, create the user interface for the frmDepreciation Windows Form object, as shown in Figure 8-83a and Figure 8-83b.

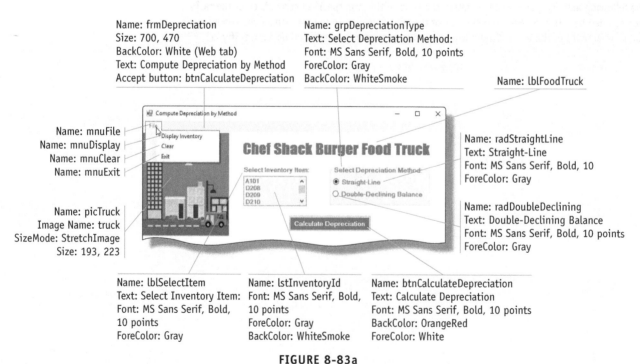

Name: frmDepreciation
Size: 700, 470
BackColor: White (Web tab)
Text: Compute Depreciation by Method
Accept button: btnCalculateDepreciation

Name: grpDepreciationType
Text: Select Depreciation Method:
Font: MS Sans Serif, Bold, 10 points
ForeColor: Gray
BackColor: WhiteSmoke

Name: lblFoodTruck

Name: mnuFile
Name: mnuDisplay
Name: mnuClear
Name: mnuExit

Name: radStraightLine
Text: Straight-Line
Font: MS Sans Serif, Bold, 10
ForeColor: Gray

Name: radDoubleDeclining
Text: Double-Declining Balance
Font: MS Sans Serif, Bold, 10 points
ForeColor: Gray

Name: picTruck
Image Name: truck
SizeMode: StretchImage
Size: 193, 223

Name: lblSelectItem
Text: Select Inventory Item:
Font: MS Sans Serif, Bold, 10 points
ForeColor: Gray

Name: lstInventoryId
Font: MS Sans Serif, Bold, 10 points
ForeColor: Gray
BackColor: WhiteSmoke

Name: btnCalculateDepreciation
Text: Calculate Depreciation
Font: MS Sans Serif, Bold, 10 points
BackColor: OrangeRed
ForeColor: White

FIGURE 8-83a

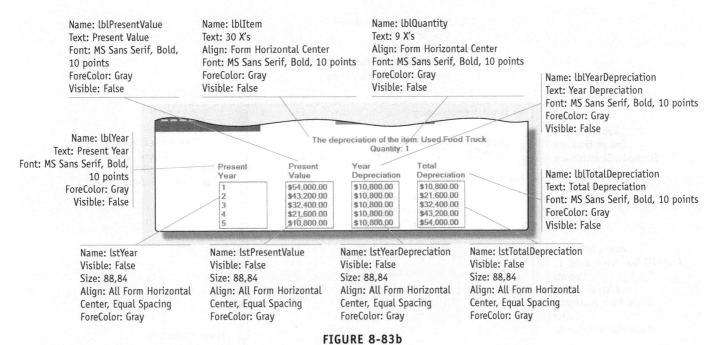

Name: lblPresentValue
Text: Present Value
Font: MS Sans Serif, Bold, 10 points
ForeColor: Gray
Visible: False

Name: lblItem
Text: 30 X's
Align: Form Horizontal Center
Font: MS Sans Serif, Bold, 10 points
ForeColor: Gray
Visible: False

Name: lblQuantity
Text: 9 X's
Align: Form Horizontal Center
Font: MS Sans Serif, Bold, 10 points
ForeColor: Gray
Visible: False

Name: lblYearDepreciation
Text: Year Depreciation
Font: MS Sans Serif, Bold, 10 points
ForeColor: Gray
Visible: False

Name: lblYear
Text: Present Year
Font: MS Sans Serif, Bold, 10 points
ForeColor: Gray
Visible: False

Name: lblTotalDepreciation
Text: Total Depreciation
Font: MS Sans Serif, Bold, 10 points
ForeColor: Gray
Visible: False

Name: lstYear
Visible: False
Size: 88,84
Align: All Form Horizontal Center, Equal Spacing
ForeColor: Gray

Name: lstPresentValue
Visible: False
Size: 88,84
Align: All Form Horizontal Center, Equal Spacing
ForeColor: Gray

Name: lstYearDepreciation
Visible: False
Size: 88,84
Align: All Form Horizontal Center, Equal Spacing
ForeColor: Gray

Name: lstTotalDepreciation
Visible: False
Size: 88,84
Align: All Form Horizontal Center, Equal Spacing
ForeColor: Gray

FIGURE 8-83b

2

- **Add a Second Form Object** Click Project on the menu bar, and then click Add Windows Form. In the Add New Item dialog box, click Windows Form. Name the Windows Form object `frmDisplayInventory.vb`. Click the Add button *(ref: Figure 8-66)*.

- **Assign a Title to the Form Object** Open the frmDisplayInventory.vb object. Select the Form object and change the Text property to `Sorted Inventory Listing`.

- **Create the User Interface for the Windows Form Object** Using the skills you have learned in this course, create the user interface for the frmDisplayInventory Windows Form object, as shown in Figure 8-84.

(continues)

Name: frmDisplayInventory
Size: 387, 419
BackColor: White
AcceptButton: btnReturn
Text: Sorted Inventory Listing

Name: picTruck
Image: truck.jpg
SizeMode: StretchImage
Size: 79, 59

Name: lblTitle2
Text: Chef Shack Inventory
Font: MS Sans Serif, 17 points
ForeColor: OrangeRed
Align: Form Horizontal Center

Name: lstDisplay
Font: MS Sans Serif, Bold, 12 points
ForeColor: Gray
Align: Form Horizontal Center
BackColor:WhiteSmoke

Name: btnReturn
Text: Return to Application
Font: MS Sans Serif, Bold, 12 points
BackColor: OrangeRed
ForeColor: White
Align: Form Horizontal Center

FIGURE 8-84

Phase 2: Code the Application

3

• **Code the Comments** Click the View Code button to begin coding the application in frmDepreciation.vb. Type the first four standard comments at the top of the code window. Insert the command Option Strict On at the beginning of the code to turn on strict type checking.

HINT

```
frmDepreciation.vb  ⊟ ×  frmDisplayInventory.vb [Design]        frmDepreciation.vb [Design]
VB Chef Shack                                    ▾  frmDepreciation                           ▾  InitializeCompo
     1   ⊟'  Program Name:  Chef Shack Food Truck Depreciation Windows Application
     2    '  Author:         Corinne Hoisington
     3    '  Date:           April 14, 2019
     4    '  Purpose:        The Chef Shack Inventory Windows Application determines
     5    '                  the depreciation based on a 5 year life of items in inventory
     6    '                  using the straight-line and double-declining balance methods.
     7
     8       Option Strict On
     9
    10   ⊟Public Class frmDepreciation
    11
```

• **Initialize the Variables** Enter the comment shown in the corresponding Hint Screen and initialize the class module-level variables in the code window within the frmDepreciation class *(ref: Figure 8-29)*.

HINT

```
     9
    10   ⊟Public Class frmDepreciation
    11        ' Class Level Private variables
    12        Private _intLifeOfItems As Integer = 5
    13        Public Shared _intSizeOfArray As Integer = 7
    14        Public Shared _strInventoryItem(_intSizeOfArray) As String
    15        Private _strItemId(_intSizeOfArray) As String
    16        Private _decInitialPrice(_intSizeOfArray) As Decimal
    17        Private _intQuantity(_intSizeOfArray) As Integer
    18
```

• **Code the frmDepreciation Load Event** To initialize the variables of this event, type the comments and code shown in the corresponding Hint Screen.

HINT

```
    19   ⊟    Private Sub frmDepreciation_Load(ByVal sender As System.Object, ByVal e As System.EventArgs) Handles MyBase.Load
    20            ' The frmDepreciation load event reads the inventory text file and
    21            ' fills the Listbox object with the inventory items
    22
    23            ' Initialize an instance of the StreamReader object and declare variables
    24            Dim objReader As IO.StreamReader
    25            Dim strLocationAndNameOfFile As String = "d:\inventory.txt"
    26            Dim intCount As Integer = 0
    27            Dim intFill As Integer
    28            Dim strFileError As String = "The file is not available. Restart when the file is available."
```

(continues)

● **Code the If … Else Statements** Inside the frmDepreciation_Load event, after the variables are initialized, insert an If statement that validates whether the inventory.txt file exists. The inventory file is opened from the USB drive and assigned to the instance of the StreamReader named objReader. The Do While loop continues to read each item in the file until the file is completed (Peek < > –1). Each line of the file is read and assigned to a unique array subscript by the ReadLine command. The counter intCount increments after each iteration of the loop to increase the subscript number *(ref: Figures 8-54, 8-55, 8-56)*.

HINT

```
29
30              ' Verify the file exists
31         If IO.File.Exists(strLocationAndNameOfFile) Then
32              objReader = IO.File.OpenText(strLocationAndNameOfFile)
33              ' Read the file line by line until the file is completed
34         Do While objReader.Peek <> -1
35              _strInventoryItem(intCount) = objReader.ReadLine()
36              _strItemId(intCount) = objReader.ReadLine()
37              _decInitialPrice(intCount) = Convert.ToDecimal(objReader.ReadLine())
38              _intQuantity(intCount) = Convert.ToInt32(objReader.ReadLine())
39              intCount += 1
40         Loop
```

● **Fill the ListBox Object** Inside the frmDepreciation load event, a For loop counts from the beginning of the array at the index of 0 until the end of the array is reached. The statement within the loop fills the inventory IDs in the lstInventoryId ListBox object. Because the file might not be found, include an Else statement to inform the user if the file is not available and close the application.

HINT

```
41              objReader.Close()
42
43              ' The ListBox object is filled with the Inventory IDs
44         For intFill = 0 To (_strItemId.Length - 1)
45              lstInventoryId.Items.Add(_strItemId(intFill))
46         Next
47         Else
48              MsgBox(strFileError, , "Error")
49              Close()
50         End If
51     End Sub
```

• **Code the btnCalculateDepreciation_Click Event** Click the frmDepreciation.vb [Design] tab. Double-click the Calculate Depreciation Button object. The btnCalculateDepreciation_Click event opens. If the lstInventoryId ListBox and one of the RadioButton objects have been selected by the user, one of the depreciation methods is called. A message box is displayed to remind the user to select one of the objects if they are left blank.

HINT

```
52
53    Private Sub btnCalculateDepreciation_Click(ByVal sender As System.Object, ByVal e As System.EventArgs) Handles btnCalculateDepreciation.Click
54        ' The btnCalculateDepreciation click event calls the depreciation Sub procedures
55        ' Declare variables
56        Dim intSelectedItemId As Integer
57        Dim strMissingSelection As String = "Missing Selection"
58        Dim strSelectDepreciationError As String = "Select a Depreciation Method"
59        Dim strSelectInventoryItemIDError As String = "Select an Inventory Item ID"
60
61        ' If the ListBox and a Depreciation RadioButton object are selected,
62        ' call the depreciation procedures
63        If lstInventoryId.SelectedIndex >= 0 Then
64            intSelectedItemId = lstInventoryId.SelectedIndex
65            If radStraightLine.Checked Then
66                StraightLineDepreciation(intSelectedItemId)
67            ElseIf radDoubleDeclining.Checked Then
68                DoubleDecliningDepreciation(intSelectedItemId)
69            Else
70                MsgBox(strSelectDepreciationError, , strMissingSelection)
71            End If
72        Else
73            MsgBox(strSelectInventoryItemIDError, , strMissingSelection)
74        End If
75    End Sub
```

(continues)

● **Code the StraightLineDepreciation Sub Procedure** Begin a new Sub procedure that calculates the depreciation when the straight-line method is selected. The result objects are displayed in the MakeObjectsVisible Sub procedure. The cost of straight-line depreciation is calculated and displayed in the ListBox objects on the Form object *(ref: Figure 8-60)*.

HINT

```vbnet
77      Private Sub StraightLineDepreciation(ByVal intItemId As Integer)
78          'This Sub procedure computes and displays the straight line depreciation for the item selected
79          ' Declare variables
80          Dim intStraightPresentYear As Integer
81          Dim decStraightPresentYearValue As Decimal = 0
82          Dim decStraightDepreciation As Decimal
83          Dim decStraightTotal As Decimal
84          Dim strDepreciationItem As String = "The depreciation of the item: "
85          Dim strQuantityMessage As String = "Quantity: "
86
87          ' The procedure MakeObjectsVisible is called to display the Form objects
88          MakeObjectsVisible()
89          ' Display the item and quantity of the selected item
90          lblItem.Text = strDepreciationItem & _strInventoryItem(intItemId)
91          lblQuantity.Text = strQuantityMessage & _intQuantity(intItemId).ToString()
92          ' The formula for straight-line depreciation
93          decStraightDepreciation = _decInitialPrice(intItemId) / _intLifeOfItems
94          decStraightPresentYearValue = _decInitialPrice(intItemId)
95
96          ' The loop repeats for the life of the items
97          For intStraightPresentYear = 1 To _intLifeOfItems
98              ' Accumulates the total of depreciation
99              decStraightTotal += decStraightDepreciation
100             ' Displays the depreciation amounts
101             lstYear.Items.Add(intStraightPresentYear.ToString())
102             lstPresentValue.Items.Add(decStraightPresentYearValue.ToString("C"))
103             lstYearDepreciation.Items.Add(decStraightDepreciation.ToString("C"))
104             lstTotalDepreciation.Items.Add(decStraightTotal.ToString("C"))
105             decStraightPresentYearValue -= decStraightDepreciation
106         Next
107     End Sub
```

● **Code the DoubleDecliningDepreciation Sub Procedure** Begin a new Sub procedure that calculates the depreciation when the double-declining balance method is selected. The result objects are displayed in the MakeObjectsVisible Sub procedure. The cost of double-declining balance depreciation is calculated and displayed in the ListBox objects on the Form object *(ref: Figure 8-62)*.

HINT

```
108
109    Private Sub DoubleDecliningDepreciation(ByVal intItemId As Integer)
110        ' This Sub procedure computes and displays the double declining
111        ' balance depreciation for the item selected
112        Dim intDoublePresentYear As Integer
113        Dim decDoublePresentYearValue As Decimal = 0
114        Dim decDoubleDepreciation As Decimal
115        Dim decDoubleTotal As Decimal
116
117        ' The procedure MakeObjectsVisible is called to display the Form objects
118        MakeObjectsVisible()
119        ' Display the item and quantity of the selected item
120        lblItem.Text = "The depreciation of the item: " & _strInventoryItem(intItemId)
121        lblQuantity.Text = "Quantity: " & _intQuantity(intItemId).ToString()
122        decDoublePresentYearValue = _decInitialPrice(intItemId)
123
124        ' The loop repeats for the life of the items
125        For intDoublePresentYear = 1 To _intLifeOfItems
126            ' The formula for double-declining depreciation inside the loop to repeat the process
127            decDoubleDepreciation = (decDoublePresentYearValue * 2D) / _intLifeOfItems
128            ' Accumulates the total of depreciation
129            decDoubleTotal += decDoubleDepreciation
130            ' Displays the depreciation amounts
131            lstYear.Items.Add(intDoublePresentYear.ToString())
132            lstPresentValue.Items.Add(decDoublePresentYearValue.ToString("C"))
133            lstYearDepreciation.Items.Add(decDoubleDepreciation.ToString("C"))
134            lstTotalDepreciation.Items.Add(decDoubleTotal.ToString("C"))
135            decDoublePresentYearValue -= decDoubleDepreciation
136        Next
137    End Sub
```

(continues)

● **Code the MakeObjectsVisible Sub Procedure** The Form objects that display the results are made visible. The ListBox objects are also cleared.

HINT

```
116
117            ' The procedure MakeObjectsVisible is called to display the Form objects
118            MakeObjectsVisible()
119            ' Display the item and quantity of the selected item
120            lblItem.Text = "The depreciation of the item: " & _strInventoryItem(intItemId)
121            lblQuantity.Text = "Quantity: " & _intQuantity(intItemId).ToString()
122            decDoublePresentYearValue = _decInitialPrice(intItemId)
123
124            ' The loop repeats for the life of the items
125            For intDoublePresentYear = 1 To _intLifeOfItems
126                ' The formula for double-declining depreciation inside the loop to repeat the process
127                decDoubleDepreciation = (decDoublePresentYearValue * 2D) / _intLifeOfItems
128                ' Accumulates the total of depreciation
129                decDoubleTotal += decDoubleDepreciation
130                ' Displays the depreciation amounts
131                lstYear.Items.Add(intDoublePresentYear.ToString())
132                lstPresentValue.Items.Add(decDoublePresentYearValue.ToString("C"))
133                lstYearDepreciation.Items.Add(decDoubleDepreciation.ToString("C"))
134                lstTotalDepreciation.Items.Add(decDoubleTotal.ToString("C"))
135                decDoublePresentYearValue -= decDoubleDepreciation
136            Next
137        End Sub
```

● **Code the mnuDisplay_Click Event** An instance of the second Form object, frmDisplayInventory, is named frmSecond. The first form is hidden and the second form is opened *(ref: Figure 8-70 and Figure 8-71)*.

HINT

```
157
158    Private Sub mnuDisplay_Click(ByVal sender As System.Object, ByVal e As System.EventArgs) Handles mnuDisplay.Click
159        ' The mnuDisplay click event creates an instance of the frmDisplayInventory
160        Dim frmSecond As New frmDisplayInventory
161
162        'Hide this form and show the Display Inventory form
163        Hide()
164        frmSecond.ShowDialog()
165    End Sub
166
```

● **Code the mnuClear_Click Event** The mnuClear_Click event clears the Form object for the next set of inputs.

HINT

```
166
167   Private Sub mnuClear_Click(ByVal sender As System.Object, ByVal e As System.EventArgs) Handles mnuClear.Click
168       ' The mnuClear click event clears and resets the form
169       lstInventoryId.SelectedIndex = -1
170       radStraightLine.Checked = False
171       radDoubleDeclining.Checked = False
172       lblItem.Visible = False
173       lblQuantity.Visible = False
174       lblYear.Visible = False
175       lstYear.Visible = False
176       lstYear.Items.Clear()
177       lblPresentValue.Visible = False
178       lstPresentValue.Visible = False
179       lstPresentValue.Items.Clear()
180       lblYearDepreciation.Visible = False
181       lstYearDepreciation.Visible = False
182       lstYearDepreciation.Items.Clear()
183       lblTotalDepreciation.Visible = False
184       lstTotalDepreciation.Visible = False
185       lstTotalDepreciation.Items.Clear()
186   End Sub
```

● **Code the mnuExit_Click Event** The mnuExit_Click event closes the application.

HINT

```
187
188   Private Sub mnuExit_Click(ByVal sender As System.Object, ByVal e As System.EventArgs) Handles mnuExit.Click
189       ' The mnuExit click event closes the application
190       Application.Exit()
191   End Sub
192
193   End Class
```

(continues)

The frmDepreciation code is completed (Figure 8-85).

FIGURE 8-85 (continues)

```
53    Private Sub btnCalculateDepreciation_Click(ByVal sender As System.Object, ByVal e As System.EventArgs) Handles btnCalculateDepreciation.Click
54        ' The btnCalculateDepreciation click event calls the depreciation Sub procedures
55        ' Declare variables
56        Dim intSelectedItemId As Integer
57        Dim strMissingSelection As String = "Missing Selection"
58        Dim strSelectDepreciationError As String = "Select a Depreciation Method"
59        Dim strSelectInventoryItemIDError As String = "Select an Inventory Item ID"
60
61        ' If the ListBox and a Depreciation RadioButton object are selected,
62        ' call the depreciation procedures
63        If lstInventoryId.SelectedIndex >= 0 Then
64            intSelectedItemId = lstInventoryId.SelectedIndex
65            If radStraightLine.Checked Then
66                StraightLineDepreciation(intSelectedItemId)
67            ElseIf radDoubleDeclining.Checked Then
68                DoubleDecliningDepreciation(intSelectedItemId)
69            Else
70                MsgBox(strSelectDepreciationError, , strMissingSelection)
71            End If
72        Else
73            MsgBox(strSelectInventoryItemIDError, , strMissingSelection)
74        End If
75    End Sub
76
77    Private Sub StraightLineDepreciation(ByVal intItemId As Integer)
78        'This Sub procedure computes and displays the straight line depreciation for the item selected
79        ' Declare variables
80        Dim intStraightPresentYear As Integer
81        Dim decStraightPresentYearValue As Decimal = 0
82        Dim decStraightDepreciation As Decimal
83        Dim decStraightTotal As Decimal
84        Dim strDepreciationItem As String = "The depreciation of the item: "
85        Dim strQuantityMessage As String = "Quantity: "
86
87        ' The procedure MakeObjectsVisible is called to display the Form objects
88        MakeObjectsVisible()
89        ' Display the item and quantity of the selected item
90        lblItem.Text = strDepreciationItem & _strInventoryItem(intItemId)
91        lblQuantity.Text = strQuantityMessage & _intQuantity(intItemId).ToString()
92        ' The formula for straight-line depreciation
93        decStraightDepreciation = _decInitialPrice(intItemId) / _intLifeOfItems
94        decStraightPresentYearValue = _decInitialPrice(intItemId)
95
96        ' The loop repeats for the life of the items
97        For intStraightPresentYear = 1 To _intLifeOfItems
98            ' Accumulates the total of depreciation
99            decStraightTotal += decStraightDepreciation
100           ' Displays the depreciation amounts
101           lstYear.Items.Add(intStraightPresentYear.ToString())
102           lstPresentValue.Items.Add(decStraightPresentYearValue.ToString("C"))
103           lstYearDepreciation.Items.Add(decStraightDepreciation.ToString("C"))
104           lstTotalDepreciation.Items.Add(decStraightTotal.ToString("C"))
105           decStraightPresentYearValue -= decStraightDepreciation
106       Next
107    End Sub
108
```

FIGURE 8-85 (continues)

(continues)

```
109    Private Sub DoubleDecliningDepreciation(ByVal intItemId As Integer)
110        ' This Sub procedure computes and displays the double declining
111        ' balance depreciation for the item selected
112        Dim intDoublePresentYear As Integer
113        Dim decDoublePresentYearValue As Decimal = 0
114        Dim decDoubleDepreciation As Decimal
115        Dim decDoubleTotal As Decimal
116
117        ' The procedure MakeObjectsVisible is called to display the Form objects
118        MakeObjectsVisible()
119        ' Display the item and quantity of the selected item
120        lblItem.Text = "The depreciation of the item: " & _strInventoryItem(intItemId)
121        lblQuantity.Text = "Quantity: " & _intQuantity(intItemId).ToString()
122        decDoublePresentYearValue = _decInitialPrice(intItemId)
123
124        ' The loop repeats for the life of the items
125        For intDoublePresentYear = 1 To _intLifeOfItems
126            ' The formula for double-declining depreciation inside the loop to repeat the process
127            decDoubleDepreciation = (decDoublePresentYearValue * 2D) / _intLifeOfItems
128            ' Accumulates the total of depreciation
129            decDoubleTotal += decDoubleDepreciation
130            ' Displays the depreciation amounts
131            lstYear.Items.Add(intDoublePresentYear.ToString())
132            lstPresentValue.Items.Add(decDoublePresentYearValue.ToString("C"))
133            lstYearDepreciation.Items.Add(decDoubleDepreciation.ToString("C"))
134            lstTotalDepreciation.Items.Add(decDoubleTotal.ToString("C"))
135            decDoublePresentYearValue -= decDoubleDepreciation
136        Next
137    End Sub
138
139    Private Sub MakeObjectsVisible()
140        ' This procedure displays the objects showing the results
141        lblItem.Visible = True
142        lblQuantity.Visible = True
143        lblYear.Visible = True
144        lstYear.Visible = True
145        lblPresentValue.Visible = True
146        lstPresentValue.Visible = True
147        lblYearDepreciation.Visible = True
148        lstYearDepreciation.Visible = True
149        lblTotalDepreciation.Visible = True
150        lstTotalDepreciation.Visible = True
151        ' The previous data is removed
152        lstYear.Items.Clear()
153        lstPresentValue.Items.Clear()
154        lstYearDepreciation.Items.Clear()
155        lstTotalDepreciation.Items.Clear()
156    End Sub
157
158    Private Sub mnuDisplay_Click(ByVal sender As System.Object, ByVal e As System.EventArgs) Handles mnuDisplay
159        ' The mnuDisplay click event creates an instance of the frmDisplayInventory
160        Dim frmSecond As New frmDisplayInventory
161
162        'Hide this form and show the Display Inventory form
163        Hide()
164        frmSecond.ShowDialog()
165    End Sub
166
```

FIGURE 8-85 (continues)

```
167    Private Sub mnuClear_Click(ByVal sender As System.Object, ByVal e As System.EventArgs) Handles mnuClear.Click
168        ' The mnuClear click event clears and resets the form
169        lstInventoryId.SelectedIndex = -1
170        radStraightLine.Checked = False
171        radDoubleDeclining.Checked = False
172        lblItem.Visible = False
173        lblQuantity.Visible = False
174        lblYear.Visible = False
175        lstYear.Visible = False
176        lstYear.Items.Clear()
177        lblPresentValue.Visible = False
178        lstPresentValue.Visible = False
179        lstPresentValue.Items.Clear()
180        lblYearDepreciation.Visible = False
181        lstYearDepreciation.Visible = False
182        lstYearDepreciation.Items.Clear()
183        lblTotalDepreciation.Visible = False
184        lstTotalDepreciation.Visible = False
185        lstTotalDepreciation.Items.Clear()
186    End Sub
187
188    Private Sub mnuExit_Click(ByVal sender As System.Object, ByVal e As System.EventArgs) Handles mnuExit.Click
189        ' The mnuExit click event closes the application
190        Application.Exit()
191    End Sub
192
193 End Class
194
```

FIGURE 8-85 (continued)

4

● **Code the Comments for the Second Form, frmDisplayInventory** Click the frmDisplayInventory tab to
return to Design view. Double-click the Form object to open the code window. Code the comments for the form
processing. Code the Option Strict On statement.

HINT

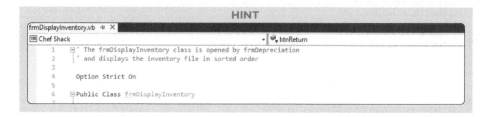

```
frmDisplayInventory.vb ⊞ ✕
VB Chef Shack                                                    ▾  btnReturn
    1    ⊟ ' The frmDisplayInventory class is opened by frmDepreciation
    2      ' and displays the inventory file in sorted order
    3
    4        Option Strict On
    5
    6    ⊟ Public Class frmDisplayInventory
    7
```

● **Code the frmDisplayInventory_Load Event** The _strInventoryItem array is sorted. The For Each loop
starts at the beginning element and continues until the last item is displayed in the ListBox object
(ref: Figure 8-35).

HINT

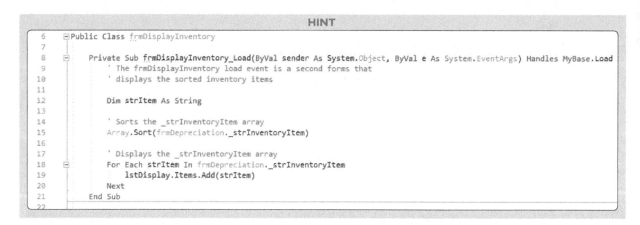

```
    6    ⊟ Public Class frmDisplayInventory
    7
    8    ⊟     Private Sub frmDisplayInventory_Load(ByVal sender As System.Object, ByVal e As System.EventArgs) Handles MyBase.Load
    9              ' The frmDisplayInventory load event is a second forms that
   10              ' displays the sorted inventory items
   11
   12            Dim strItem As String
   13
   14            ' Sorts the _strInventoryItem array
   15            Array.Sort(frmDepreciation._strInventoryItem)
   16
   17            ' Displays the _strInventoryItem array
   18    ⊟         For Each strItem In frmDepreciation._strInventoryItem
   19                  lstDisplay.Items.Add(strItem)
   20              Next
   21          End Sub
   22
```

● **Code the btnReturn_Click Event** Click the frmDisplayInventory [Design]* tab. Double-click the Return to Application button. Inside the btnReturn Click event, create an instance of the frmDepreciation Form object named frmFirst. Hide the second form and open the first form.

HINT

```
23   Private Sub btnReturn_Click(ByVal sender As System.Object, ByVal e As System.EventArgs) Handles btnReturn.Click
24       ' This Sub procedure opens the first form
25       Dim frmFirst As New frmDepreciation
26
27       Hide()
28       frmFirst.ShowDialog()
29   End Sub
30
31 End Class
```

The frmDisplayInventory code is completed (Figure 8-86).

RESULT OF STEP 4

```
1   ' The frmDisplayInventory class is opened by frmDepreciation
2   ' and displays the inventory file in sorted order
3
4   Option Strict On
5
6   Public Class frmDisplayInventory
7
8       Private Sub frmDisplayInventory_Load(ByVal sender As System.Object, ByVal e As System.EventArgs) Handles MyBase.Load
9           ' The frmDisplayInventory load event is a second forms that
10          ' displays the sorted inventory items
11
12          Dim strItem As String
13
14          ' Sorts the _strInventoryItem array
15          Array.Sort(frmDepreciation._strInventoryItem)
16
17          ' Displays the _strInventoryItem array
18          For Each strItem In frmDepreciation._strInventoryItem
19              lstDisplay.Items.Add(strItem)
20          Next
21      End Sub
22
23      Private Sub btnReturn_Click(ByVal sender As System.Object, ByVal e As System.EventArgs) Handles btnReturn.Click
24          ' This Sub procedure opens the first form
25          Dim frmFirst As New frmDepreciation
26
27          Hide()
28          frmFirst.ShowDialog()
29      End Sub
30
31  End Class
```

FIGURE 8-86

Summary

In this chapter you have learned to create a Windows application using arrays and data files.

Knowledge Check

1. Using implicit sizing, assign the integers 2, 3, 5, 7, 11, and 13 to an array named intPrimeNumbers.

2. What is the upper-bound index of an array whose size is 52?

3. Write a statement that assigns the length of an array named strBroadwayPlay to a variable named intSignCount.

4. Write a line of code that initializes an array named intEven with the first five even numbers, starting with 0.

5. Answer the following questions about the following initialized array: Dim strSeafood(8) as String

   a. Assign Oysters to the first array location. What is the index number?

   b. Assign Lobster to the fourth location in the array. What would the assignment statement look like?

   c. What value does strSeafood.Length have?

   d. How many types of seafood can this array hold?

   e. What would happen if you assigned strSeafood(9) = "Red Snapper"?

6. Can you have a Boolean data type array?

7. Write a line of code that assigns the values Jon Snow, Tyrion Lannister, and Cersei to the elements in the array strGameOfThrones().

8. Which of the three main characters in question 7 would be assigned to strGameOfThrones(1)?

9. What is the lower index of an array?

10. Write a statement that assigns the length of an array named intMovieTimes to intSpan.

11. Write a statement that assigns the elements shown in Figure 8-87 to a two-dimensional array with implicit sizing named intPinNumbers.

1659	2916	9876	3928
1117	9665	5397	4488
1211	0767	2956	2041

FIGURE 8-87

12. How many elements can be stored in the array in Figure 8-88?

```
Dim decRoomSize(4, 6) As Decimal
```

FIGURE 8-88

13. Write a statement that assigns the value 16.7 to the last item in the array in question 12.

14. Write a statement that assigns the first line of an opened text file to the first element in an array named strHobbit.

15. Write a statement that opens a text file named d:\accesscodes.txt and assigns the instance of the StreamReader to objReader.

16. Write a Sort statement to sort an array named strZipCodes.

17. If a binary search returns a negative value, what does that mean?

(continues)

18. What is the default value of the elements in an array called intTopSpeed()?

19. Write the statement that hides the Windows Form object that is currently open in an application.

20. Write the statement that would initialize the variable intFinalExam as a Public Shared class-level variable that can be accessed in other Windows Form objects.

Debugging Exercises

1. Correct the lines of code in Figure 8-89.

```
Dim intJellyBeans() As Integer = (23, 77, 89, 124, 25)
ReDim intJellyBeans(10) As Integer
```

FIGURE 8-89

2. Correct the line of code in Figure 8-90.

```
Dim strHighwayNumbers() As String = {95, 81, 605, 5}
```

FIGURE 8-90

3. Rewrite the code shown in Figure 8-91 to fix any errors.

```
Dim strFriends(4) = {"Brea", "Eric", "Daniel", "Ryan", "Brittany"}
```

FIGURE 8-91

4. What exception would be produced by the code shown in Figure 8-92?

```
Dim intPlaneType(300) As Integer
Dim intCount As Integer

For intCount = 0 To 301
        intPlaneType(intCount)=767

Next
```

FIGURE 8-92

5. Rewrite the code in Figure 8-93 to read each line of a text file into an array named strFordModel.

```
Do While objReader.Peek = -1
        strFordModel(intCount) = objReader.ReadLine()
        intCount += 1

Loop
```

FIGURE 8-93

Debugging Exercises *continued*

6. Rewrite the statement in Figure 8-94 to fix the error.

```
Dim intEvenNumbers(4),(8) As Integer
```

FIGURE 8-94

Program Analysis

1. What is the output of the code shown in Figure 8-95?

```
Private Sub btnSuperHero_Click(ByVal sender As System.Object, ByVal e As
System.EventArgs) Handles btnSuperHero.Click

      Dim strName() As String = {"Wonder Woman", "Superman", "Spiderman",
"Green Lantern", "Batman"}

      Array.Sort(strName)
      lblFavorite.Text = "My favorite super hero is " & strName(3)

End Sub
```

FIGURE 8-95

2. What are the values for every element by subscript in the array when the code in Figure 8-96 has been executed?

```
Dim intJellyBeans() As Integer = {23, 77, 89, 124, 25}
intJellyBeans(3) = 59
ReDim intJellyBeans(6)
intJellyBeans(2) = 24
```

FIGURE 8-96

3. What are the values for every element by subscript in the array when the code in Figure 8-97 has been executed?

```
Dim intJellyBeans() As Integer = {23, 77, 89, 124, 25}
intJellyBeans(3) = 59
ReDim Preserve intJellyBeans(6)
intJellyBeans(2) = 24
```

FIGURE 8-97

(continues)

4. Write a For Each loop that displays every element of an array named strSongNames in a ListBox named lstDisplay. The loop variable is named strPlay.

5. Write a section of code that declares an array named strStocksOwned initialized with the values in the table in Figure 8-98. Sort the array. Write the contents of the sorted array to a new file named d:\stockportfolio.txt. Close the file when the file has been created with the stock names.

Stocks Owned
Microsoft
Cisco
Coca-Cola
Disney
Exxon
Merck

FIGURE 8-98

6. Write a For Next loop using the Length command that computes the sum of an array named decMaySales. After the loop, display the average in a Label object named lblAverage with the currency format. Use Length in the formula that computes the average.

7. What is the output of the code shown in Figure 8-99?

```
Dim intDoubleArray(3, 2) As Integer
Dim strDisplay As String = " "
Dim intOuter As Integer
Dim intInner As Integer

For intOuter = 0 To 3
    For intInner = 0 To 2
        intDoubleArray(intOuter, intInner) = intOuter + intInner
        strDisplay &= intDoubleArray(intOuter, intInner) & " "
    Next
Next
txtValues.Text = strDisplay
```

FIGURE 8-99

8. Write the code to implicitly size an array named strDay and to determine the day of the week (such as Monday) if the user enters the number 1 into a TextBox object named txtDayOfWeek and the number is converted to an Integer variable named intDay. The day of the week is displayed in a Label object named lblFullDay.

Complete one or more of the following case programming assignments. Submit the program and materials you create to your instructor. The level of difficulty is indicated for each case programming assignment.

●	= Easiest
●●	= Intermediate
●●●	= Challenging

1

SMART HOME MONTHLY ELECTRIC SAVINGS

Design a Windows Desktop application and write the code that will execute according to the program requirements in Figure 8-100 and the Use Case Definition in Figure 8-101. Before writing the code, create an event-planning document for each event in the program. The completed program is shown in Figure 8-102.

REQUIREMENTS DOCUMENT

Date:	April 2, 2019
Date Submitted:	
Application Title:	Smart Home Monthly Electric Savings
Purpose:	This Windows application opens a text file that lists the monthly savings of a smart home's electric bill in comparison to a previous year without smart device activation. A smart thermostat, lighting system, and water heater were installed one year ago and the text file lists the savings each month. The user selects a month read from the text file and displays that month's electric bill savings. A Button object displays the average monthly savings with the smart home devices and the month with the most significant savings.
Program Procedures:	In a Windows application, a user can view the individual monthly savings of a smart home's electric bill.
Algorithms, Processing, and Conditions:	1. The user views a Windows application that contains a title, graphic, and a ComboBox object displaying the months of the year. The ComboBox object is filled from a text file named savings.txt that is opened and read by the application from the USB drive (drive d:). The text file contains each month with the electric bill savings from that month.
	2. After the user selects the month from the ComboBox object, that month's savings is displayed and the Display Statistics button is shown. When the user clicks the button, the average monthly savings and the month with the most significant savings is displayed.
Notes and Restrictions:	The user must select a month from the ComboBox object before the Button object is displayed.
Comments:	1. The savings.txt file is available on CengageBrain.com.
	2. Obtain an image for this program from CengageBrain.com. The name of the picture on the Windows form is smarthome.

FIGURE 8-100

(continues)

Smart Home Monthly Electric Savings

USE CASE DEFINITION

1. The user selects a month to display that month's electric bill savings.
2. The user selects the Display Statistics button to display the average monthly savings and the month with the most significant savings.

FIGURE 8-101

FIGURE 8-102

Alexander Kirch/Shutterstock.com

2

APARTMENT RENTAL BY CITY

Design a Windows application and write the code that will execute according to the program requirements in Figure 8-103 and the Use Case Definition in Figure 8-104. Before writing the code, create an event planning document for each event in the program. The completed Windows application and other objects in the user interface are shown in Figure 8-105.

REQUIREMENTS DOCUMENT

Date:	August 17, 2019
Date Submitted:	
Application Title:	Apartment Rental by City
Purpose:	This Windows application uses a text file of median rental costs for a two-bedroom apartment in 10 major cities to find the average rental cost. The user can select a city to display the median rental cost for that city.
Program Procedures:	A Windows application analyzes the median apartment rental cost for 10 major cities. The user can select a city and view the average cost of an apartment rental in these cities.
Algorithms, Processing, and Conditions:	1. The application first opens a text file of information from the National Department of Housing. The file is named rentals.txt, and it lists the median apartment rental costs in the 10 most expensive U.S. cities.
	2. The user can select a city in the displayed data to view the median apartment cost for a two-bedroom apartment in that city.
	3. When the user clicks the Compute Average Rental button, the average apartment rental within the 10 cities is displayed.
	4. A File menu displays the Display Top Ten Cities and Rental Cost, Clear, and Exit menu items.
	5. The second Form object displays a Cities and Rental costs and has a button to reopen the initial Form object.
Notes and Restrictions:	Use two Sub methods to compute the average rental cost.
Comments:	1. The rentals.txt file is available on CengageBrain.com.
	2. Obtain an image for this program from CengageBrain.com. The name of the picture on the Windows form is rental.

FIGURE 8-103

(continues)

Apartment Rental by City

USE CASE DEFINITION

1. From a list box, the user selects a city from the top 10 most expensive apartment rental cities.
2. The program displays the monthly rental cost for that city.
3. The user clicks the Compute Average Rental button to view the average rental cost.
4. The user selects the Display Top Ten Cities and Rental Cost menu item to open a second form that displays the current median apartment prices in the 10 most expensive U.S. cities.
5. The user selects the Clear menu item to clear the form.
6. The user selects the Exit menu item to exit the application.

FIGURE 8-104

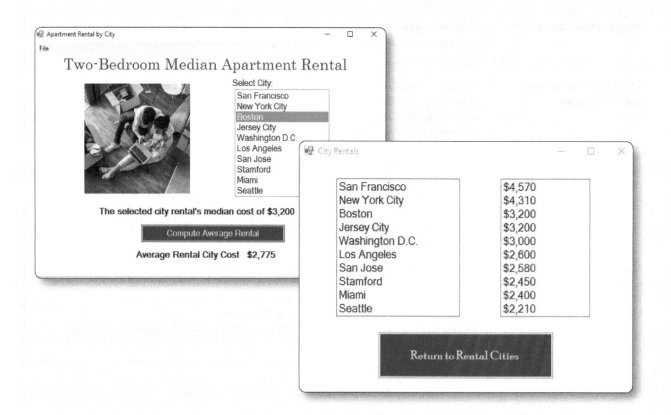

FIGURE 8-105

3
PATIENT CHOLESTEROL SCREENING

Design a Windows Desktop application and write the code that will execute according to the program requirements in Figure 8-106. Before designing the user interface, create a Use Case Definition. Before writing the code, create an event-planning document for each event in the program.

REQUIREMENTS DOCUMENT

Date:	February 14, 2019
Date Submitted:	
Application Title:	Patient Cholesterol Screening
Purpose:	This Windows application determines which patients have a cholesterol level reading that is considered too high.
Program Procedures:	In a Windows application, a text file of patient information named patient.txt is opened. The patients who have a cholesterol number above 200 are written to a second text file named consult.txt for consultation.
Algorithms, Processing, and Conditions:	1. Each day, a text file named patient.txt is opened from the USB drive. The patient.txt file contains patient names, ID numbers, and cholesterol results from a lab.
	2. An opening graphic and title are displayed as a splash screen.
	3. A File menu includes options to Display Patient Information, Clear, and Exit. Selecting the Display Patient Information option displays the contents of the patient.txt file on a second Windows Form object.
	4. The patient names and cholesterol levels are assigned to an array that holds 15 elements each.
	5. Cholesterol levels are tested to check whether the value is above the value 200.
	6. All patients who have a cholesterol screening level above 200 have their names and cholesterol results written to a text file named consult.txt on the USB drive. A nurse will contact these patients for further evaluation.
	7. The program displays the number of patients who had a cholesterol level above 200 and the average cholesterol value of today's patients.
Notes and Restrictions:	n/a
Comments:	1. The patient.txt file is available on CengageBrain.com.
	2. An appropriate image for this application should be selected from a picture available on the web.

FIGURE 8-106

DANCE BAND

Design a Windows application and write the code that will execute according to the program requirements in Figure 8-107. Before designing the user interface, create a Use Case Definition. Before writing the code, create an event planning document for each event in the program.

REQUIREMENTS DOCUMENT

Date:	March 4, 2019
Date Submitted:	
Application Title:	Dance Band
Purpose:	This Windows application opens a text file that contains song names ordered by popularity, their music genre, and the song length in minutes. The application allows a user to select a genre of music and a list of songs and their length can be displayed. The application also allows you to view all the songs that the dance band can play in order of popularity or alphabetical order.
Program Procedures:	In a Windows application, the user can select a type of music and have the appropriate songs on the playlist displayed with their song length.
Algorithms, Processing, and Conditions:	1. The application opens and reads the values from a song list named songs.txt, which includes the title, genre, and length of each song. The length of each song is listed in the format *minutes.seconds*. For example, 3.16 represents 3 minutes and 16 seconds.
	2. The user can click a drop-down list of music genres such as Rock, Country, Rap, or R&B, select a genre, and display the songs in the playlist from that genre with the play time listed for each song.
	3. The user can select the Display Song Set menu item to open a second Form object that provides a choice of displaying the playlist in the current play order or as a sorted song list. The first Form object closes. The second Form object provides a button that the user can click to return to the first Form object.
	4. The user can select the Clear menu item to clear and reset the first Form object. The user can also select the Exit menu item to close the application.
Notes and Restrictions:	n/a
Comments:	1. The songs.txt file is available on CengageBrain.com.
	2. An appropriate image for this application should be selected from a picture available on the web.

FIGURE 8-107

5

●●●

MOST POPULAR GAMES SOLD

Create a requirements document and a Use Case Definition document and then design a Windows application based on the case project shown in Figure 8-108. Before writing the code, create an event planning document for each event in the program:

If necessary, download the text file named mobile.txt from CengageBrain.com. The file contains the names of the nation's 10 top-selling mobile video games of all times and the number of paid downloads in millions. Open the text file and assign the contents to an array that identifies each game title. Display the top 10 mobile games and allow the user to select one of the mobile games and display that games number of downloads. Also, compute the total amount of downloads made by the top 10 mobile games and display the total downloads. Sort the array alphabetically by game title and display the sorted array on a second form.

FIGURE 8-108

Case Programming Assignments

6 ●●●

JOB GROWTH IN THE INFORMATION TECHNOLOGY FIELD

Create a requirements document and a Use Case Definition document and then design a Windows application based on the case project shown in Figure 8-109. Before writing the code, create an event planning document for each event in the program:

The U.S. Department of Labor has projected that the Information Technology job sector is growing. Enter the information from the following table into Notepad and save the text file.

Job Title	Jobs in 2018	Jobs Projected for 2022
Computer Developers	857,000	1,281,000
Internet Security	862,000	1,016,000
Systems Analysts	504,000	650,000
Database Administrators	119,000	154,000
Network Administrators	262,000	402,000
Web Developers	285,000	407,000

Fill a ListBox object with the job titles so that the user can select a position and see the number of available jobs for the years 2018 and 2022 on the opening form. Also calculate the changes in job numbers for each position and display the values on the opening form. On the second form show three ListBox objects with the job titles, present job numbers for 2018 and future job numbers for 2022.

FIGURE 8-109

CHAPTER 9

Creating Web Applications

OBJECTIVES

You will have mastered the material in this chapter when you can:

- Create a web application
- Build a web form using ASP.NET
- Set web form properties
- Add objects to a web form

- Add a DropDownList object
- Add a Calendar object
- Add a custom table for layout
- Validate data on web forms

- Use the <br> tag in Visual Basic code
- Use string manipulation methods in the String class

Introduction

Visual Studio allows you to create applications that can run on the web. Visual Basic 2017 includes ASP.NET technology, with which you can create a user interface and a form for a web application. A **web form** is a page displayed in a web browser, such as Microsoft Edge and Firefox, that requests data from the user. The Visual Basic tools and techniques you use will be familiar based on what you have learned thus far in this course.

A practical example of a web application developed using Visual Basic 2017 that can be delivered over the Internet is the project developed in this chapter — a glamping tent-rental website that includes a Home page and Reservations page. Glamping is a style of camping that combines glamour and the adventure of camping. This chapter project is based on a request from a camping resort called Moonbeam Glamping to create a web application for guests who want to reserve luxury tents online. The application displays a webpage welcoming guests to Moonbeam Glamping, and then displays a web form that requests the guest's first and last names, email address, tent selection(s), the number of nights the guest wants to stay, and the check-in date, as shown in Figure 9-1.

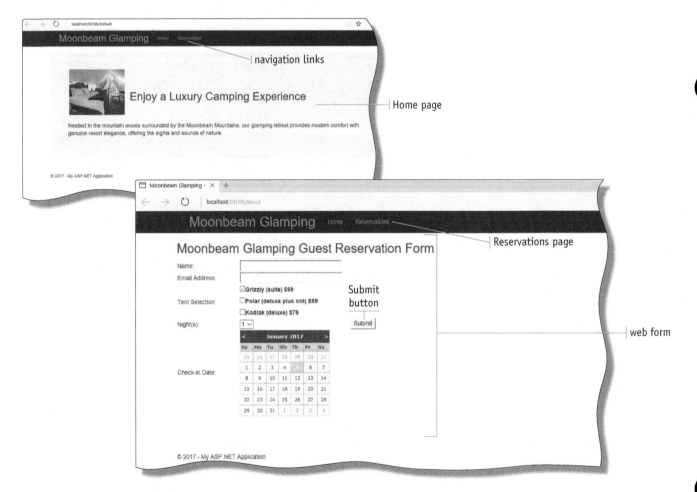

FIGURE 9-1

Chiyacat/Shutterstock.com

After the Home page is displayed in a browser, the user can click the Reservations navigation link to complete the form by entering the requested information, and then click the Submit button on the form. The application validates the information the user entered by confirming that the guest entered a name, provided an email address in the correct format, and selected a valid check-in date. If the user makes an error, a message identifies the error, as shown in Figure 9-2.

FIGURE 9-2

When the validation is complete, a reservation message is displayed that confirms the reservation information and calculates the total cost of the stay, as shown in Figure 9-3.

FIGURE 9-3

Create a Web Application

To develop a form such as the one shown in Figure 9-3 using Visual Basic, you create a web application, which is similar to creating a Windows application. When completed, a Visual Basic web application is displayed as one or more webpages in a browser.

A webpage that allows users to enter information on a web form, like the Moonbeam Glamping page in this chapter, is considered a **dynamic** webpage because the user enters data and the webpage reacts to the data. In contrast, a webpage that displays information such as text and pictures but has no interactivity is called a **static** webpage.

After a webpage is created, it is hosted (placed) on a web server. A **web server** is a computer that stores web documents and makes them available to people on the Internet. When you test your web application created using Visual Basic 2017, Visual Studio 2017 creates a temporary web server on your computer so you can view your webpage in a browser. When your webpage is ready for the world to see, it must be placed on an actual web server.

Active Server Page (ASP.NET) Platform

The ASP.NET technology used with Visual Basic 2017 creates an **active server page (ASP)**. When describing an active server page, developers speak of the server-side computer and the client-side computer. The server-side computer is the web/cloud server that contains the actual active-server page and that will deliver the page to the client-side computer via the Internet. The client-side computer (often referred to as the client) runs the web browser that requests a webpage from the web server and displays the page. Visual Basic allows you to test the webpage using any installed browser such as Microsoft Edge (for Windows 10), Internet Explorer, Firefox, Google Chrome, Safari, and phone emulators. This book displays the chapter project website in the Microsoft Edge browser. ASP.NET optimizes the development of apps that are either deployed to the cloud or run on the premises on traditional computers, tablets, or mobile devices. Mobile devices can vary in size and form layout, and their screens are much smaller than desktop monitors. That means you may need to design completely different page layouts for them.

An active server page has two primary components: the generated code component that executes on the web server and the HTML component that is interpreted and executed by a web browser.

CRITICAL THINKING

Why is it important to be able to build a webpage for both a traditional computer and a mobile device?
Mobile devices such as smartphones and tablets continue to grow in popularity as a means to access the web. Businesses want to connect to their customers on any device so it is vital to provide a great browsing experience for visitors who use those devices.

CONSIDER THIS

What is the purpose of HTML code?
Hypertext Markup Language (HTML) code is a standardized system for tagging text files to achieve font, color, graphic, and hyperlink effects on webpages displayed in browsers. You can view the HTML code on a webpage using the Microsoft Edge browser by right-clicking the page and then selecting View source.

When Visual Basic compiles an active server page using ASP.NET technology, the page contains both the server-side code that will operate on data entered by the user, such as computing the total cost of a reservation in the Moonbeam Glamping web application, and the HTML code that will display the page in a web browser on the client-side computer. When the page is requested by a browser, ASP sends the HTML code to the client requesting the webpage, where the page is displayed. The user can interact with the page by entering data or making selections, such as selecting the check-in date. When the user clicks the Submit button, as in the Moonbeam Glamping application, the data is sent to the web server, where the coding within the application is executed. For example, the application code can calculate the total tent cost and then display it on the web form.

When you develop an ASP page in Visual Basic, the work you do on the design page to create the user interface will generate the HTML code for the active server page. This code includes the HTML to format and display the page, and might include JavaScript code to perform certain processing, such as ensuring that a text box contains data.

The event handler code that you write in Visual Basic for an event, such as clicking the Submit button, is executed on the web server. When the user clicks the Submit button on the Moonbeam Glamping dynamic webpage, the control returns to the web server and the event handler code written by the developer is executed. This code can perform calculations and other processing as you have seen in previous chapters. When the event handler code changes an object displayed on the webpage, such as changing the Label object that contains the reservation message, that change immediately is displayed on the webpage.

Create a Dynamic Website Using Visual Basic

Using Visual Basic 2017 to create a dynamic website is similar to creating an interactive Windows application — you drag objects from the Toolbox and place them in a design window to build a form. Some of the web form objects are different from Windows objects because they are designed for online use. To create a Visual Basic web project for the Moonbeam Glamping application, you can complete the following steps:

STEP 1   Start Visual Studio. Click File on the menu bar and then click New Web Site.

The New Web Site dialog box opens (Figure 9-4).

New Web Site
dialog box

FIGURE 9-4

STEP 2   In the center pane, click ASP.NET Web Forms Site. Use the Web location text box to name the chapter project application glamping. As shown in Figure 9-5, the website is placed on the d: drive.

The ASP.NET website will be stored on the d: drive (Figure 9-5). The project name is lowercase because most website names use all lowercase letters.

ASP.NET Web Forms
Site selected

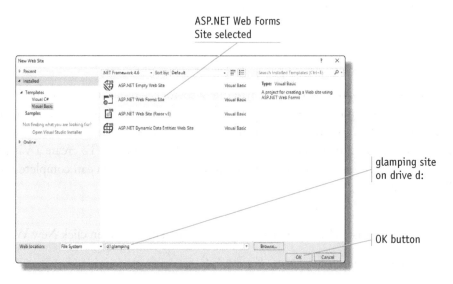

glamping site
on drive d:

OK button

FIGURE 9-5

STEP 3   Click the OK button in the New Web Site dialog box. If necessary, close the Toolbox.

The web application Design window opens (Figure 9-6). The Default.aspx page is displayed. On the scroll bar at the bottom of the page, the Design button is selected, showing that the Design window is displayed.

ScriptManager may show
Unnamed3 or another number

Default.aspx
page

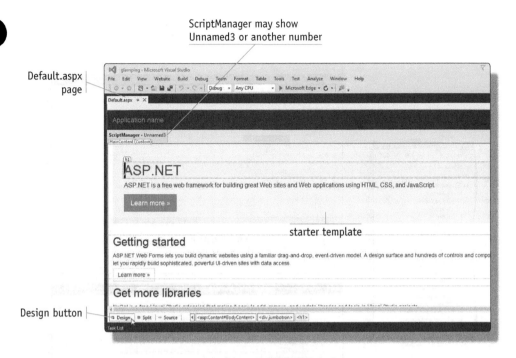

starter template

Design button

FIGURE 9-6

Use a Multipage Starter Template

Visual Basic 2017 provides a starter template to assist you in designing a webpage. The starter template allows you to create a new ASP.NET application with some layout and structure already implemented within it. When you first open the starter template, the Default.aspx page opens, but many other template pages are available with the starter template. Figure 9-7 shows the file named Site.master in the Solution Explorer. The **Site.master** file is a master page file that provides an overall layout for the site with headers, buttons, and footers. A **master page** is designed to create a consistent layout for the pages in your application. It defines the look and feel and standard behavior that you want for all of the pages in your website. If you change the color or title of the master page, all the pages in the site will reflect that same color and title. First design the master page and then customize the actual pages on the website. The website in this project has two pages. The default page (Default.aspx) serves as the Home page, which gives the traveler information about Moonbeam Glamping. The Reservations page (About.aspx) provides a reservation form that a traveler can use to make reservations.

About.aspx is the
Reservations page

Default.aspx is
the Home page

Site.master page
specifies the design
for both pages

FIGURE 9-7

Chiyacat/Shutterstock.com

Customize the Master Page

The master page specifies the layout, color, and text that are repeated on the actual
webpages displayed by the browser. A master page is basically defined as a nondis-
playing page. It contains the information about the layout of the page, which will
be used in the creation of body pages. It enables the user to create the layouts of the
pages quickly and conveniently across the entire website. To change the text on the
master page, you can complete the following steps:

STEP 1 If necessary in the Solution Explorer window, scroll down and then
double-click Site.master to open the page. Click the Design tab, if it is not already
displayed.

The Site.master page opens (Figure 9-8).

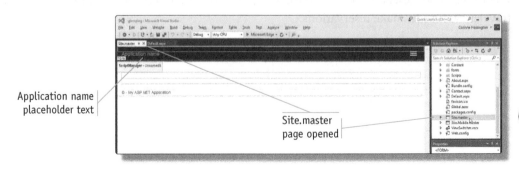

Application name
placeholder text

Site.master
page opened

FIGURE 9-8

STEP 2 Click View on the menu bar, point to Toolbars, and then click Formatting. Select the "Application name" placeholder text at the top of the Site.master page. Type Moonbeam Glamping to replace the original title. On the Formatting toolbar, click the Font Size box arrow, and then select xx-large (36 pt).

The title on the Master page changes to Moonbeam Glamping. The font size is changed (Figure 9-9).

Formatting
toolbar

Font Size
box arrow

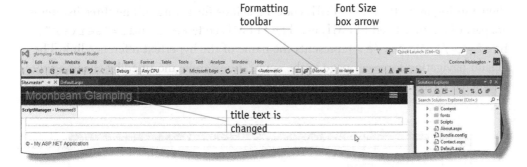

title text is
changed

FIGURE 9-9

CONSIDER THIS

Can I use the Formatting toolbar to change the color of the text or background?
Yes. When you select text within the webpage, you can change the foreground and background color using the Formatting toolbar.

Customize Navigation Links on the Master Template

The Master page has built-in navigation links that play an integral role in making your site easy to use and navigate. By default, the Master site has three links: Home, which connects to the Default.aspx page when clicked; About, which connects to the About.aspx page when clicked; and Contact, which connects to the Contact.aspx page (Figure 9-10). The chapter project has only two pages — Home and Reservations — so the Contact link should be deleted. It also would make more sense for the About link to be renamed Reservations. The site does not need a Register or Log in portion, so these default options will be deleted.

navigational links built
into the template

FIGURE 9-10

The easiest way to change the three navigational links and to delete the Register and Log in portion is to alter the HTML code. An ASP.NET application consists of HTML and Visual Basic code. A traditional or mobile web browser can read HTML files and compose them into visible webpages. In Visual Basic, the Design tab is shown by default. To view the HTML code, click the Source tab at the bottom left of the Site.master page. The highlighted lines in Figure 9-11 are responsible for displaying the three navigational links — Home, About, and Contact — as shown in Figure 9-10. The HTML code li stands for list item. The three list items are part of an unordered HTML list. The HTML code `<a runat="server" href="~/">Home</a>` represents the name of the hypertext reference link. The default navigation for every page in the application can be modified by changing the unordered navigation list element on the Site.master page.

Source HTML code

FIGURE 9-11

To delete the Contact navigational HTML link, rename the second navigational link to Reservations, and delete the Register and Log in tabs, follow these steps:

STEP 1   On the Site.master page, click the Source tab in the lower-left part of the window. Select the HTML code `<li><a runat="server" href="~/ Contact">Contact</a></li>`.

On the Source tab, the HTML list item is selected; this item creates a link to the Contact page (Figure 9-12).

```
60      <div class="navbar-collapse collapse">
61          <ul class="nav navbar-nav">
62              <li><a runat="server" href="~/">Home</a></li>
63              <li><a runat="server" href="~/About">About</a></li>
64              <li><a runat="server" href="~/Contact">Contact</a></li>
65          </ul>
66          <asp:LoginView runat="server" ViewStateMode="Disabled">
67              <AnonymousTemplate>
68                  <ul class="nav navbar-nav navbar-right">
69                      <li><a runat="server" href="~/Account/Register">Register</a></li>
70                      <li><a runat="server" href="~/Account/Login">Log in</a></li>
```

Contact list item
link selected

FIGURE 9-12

STEP 2 Press the DELETE key to delete the Contact list item line of code. Select the black text "About" in the About list item link and type Reservations to re-name the displayed text in the link.

The Contact list item link is deleted and the About text is renamed Reservations (Figure 9-13).

```
58              <a class="auto-style1" runat="server" href="~/">Moonbeam Glamping</a>
59          </div>
60      <div class="navbar-collapse collapse">
61          <ul class="nav navbar-nav">
62              <li><a runat="server" href="~/">Home</a></li>
63              <li><a runat="server" href="~/About">Reservations</a></li>
64
65          </ul>
```

text changed to
Reservations

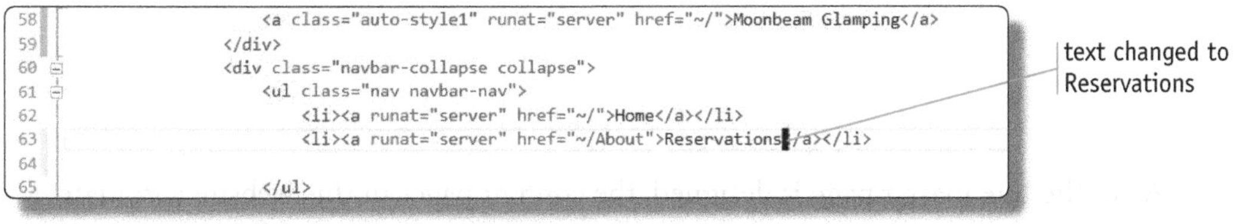

FIGURE 9-13

STEP 3 Select the following HTML code that displays Register and Log in links on the Site.master page:

```
<li><a runat="server" href="~/Account/Register">
Register</a></li>

<li><a runat="server" href="~/Account/Login"> Log in</a></li>
```

The Register and Log in list item lines of code are selected (Figure 9-14).

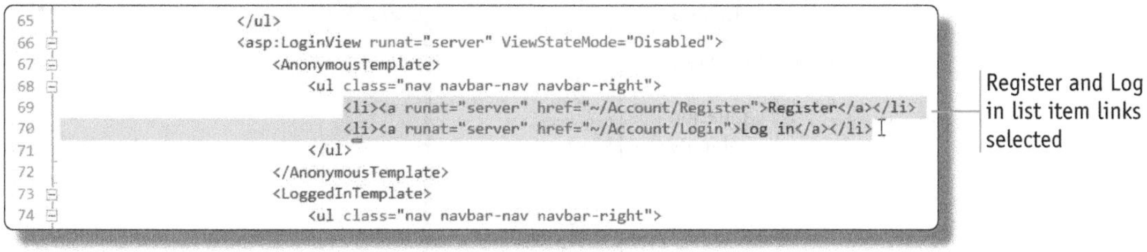

```
65          </ul>
66      <asp:LoginView runat="server" ViewStateMode="Disabled">
67          <AnonymousTemplate>
68              <ul class="nav navbar-nav navbar-right">
69                  <li><a runat="server" href="~/Account/Register">Register</a></li>
70                  <li><a runat="server" href="~/Account/Login">Log in</a></li>
71              </ul>
72          </AnonymousTemplate>
73          <LoggedInTemplate>
74              <ul class="nav navbar-nav navbar-right">
```

Register and Log
in list item links
selected

FIGURE 9-14

STEP 4   Press the DELETE key to remove the Register and Log in links from the Site.master page.

The Register and Log in tabs are deleted (Figure 9-15).

```
58              <a class="auto-style1" runat="server" href="~/">Moonbeam Glamping</a>
59          </div>
60          <div class="navbar-collapse collapse">
61              <ul class="nav navbar-nav">
62                  <li><a runat="server" href="~/">Home</a></li>
63                  <li><a runat="server" href="~/About">Reservations</a></li>
64
65              </ul>
66              <asp:LoginView runat="server" ViewStateMode="Disabled">
67                  <AnonymousTemplate>
68                      <ul class="nav navbar-nav navbar-right">
69
70                      </ul>
71                  </AnonymousTemplate>
72                  <LoggedInTemplate>
73                      <ul class="nav navbar-nav navbar-right">
74                          <li><a runat="server" href="~/Account/Manage" title="Manage your a
```

list item
links deleted

FIGURE 9-15

CRITICAL THINKING

Is it necessary to save the Site.master page to update the other customized page links?
Yes. As soon as you save the Site.master page, the title is updated on the Default, Home, and About webpages.

Customize the Default Page

After the Site.master page is designed, the content pages in this website automatically inherit the changes in the page style and navigation buttons. For example, the Default.aspx page, which serves as the Home page to the Moonbeam Glamping site, inherits the font and link changes made when the Master page was customized. The customized links are changed on the Default, Home, and About webpages.

Add Objects to the Webpage

Using Visual Studio's ASP.NET objects and code, you can create interactive web forms. You place objects on the webpage using a Toolbox similar to the one used for Windows applications, though the ASP.NET categories of tools are different. The Moonbeam Glamping application uses objects in the Standard and Validation categories of the Toolbox shown in Figure 9-16.

Toolbox

Standard category

Validation
category

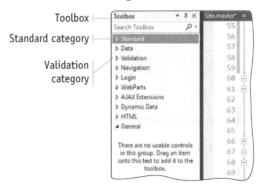

FIGURE 9-16

Toolbox objects unique to web applications include Login objects for allowing user access, Navigation objects for creating site maps, and Validation objects for checking web form input. Some Windows application objects work the same way, but have different object names in the web environment. For example, in a Windows application you use a PictureBox object to display a picture, but in an ASP.NET webpage, you use an Image object. Both the PictureBox object and the Image object place an image into the application, but the Image object needs a URL to specify where the picture resides. The Moonbeam Glamping Home page displays a picture, and a description of Moonbeam Glamping.

Add an Image Object to the Default Page

On the Moonbeam Glamping Home page (Default.aspx), an image of Moonbeam Glamping is displayed in an Image object on the left side of the page below the navigation buttons. The **Image** object is similar to the PictureBox object in a Windows application. The major difference is where the Image object is stored. Most webpages reference a picture stored on a web server connected to the Internet. On an ASP.NET web form, you do this by specifying the entire URL (web address) in the ImageUrl property of an Image object. To add an Image object that displays an image stored on a web server, you can complete the following steps:

STEP 1   Close and save the Site.master page. Open the Toolbox. If necessary, in the Solution Explorer, double-click Default.aspx. Notice that the Default.aspx page has inherited the title from the Site.master page. Select the "ASP.NET" heading in the MainContent (Custom) area, and then press the DELETE key.

The Default.aspx page opens and the MainContent heading is cleared (Figure 9-17).

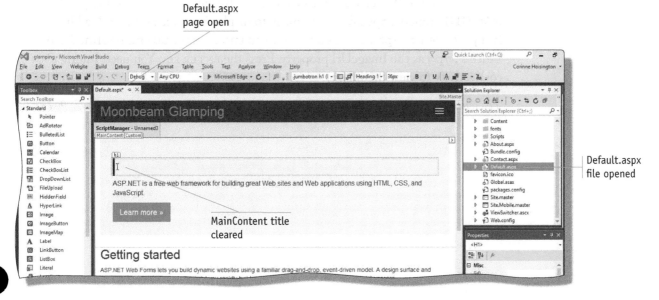

Default.aspx page open

Default.aspx file opened

MainContent title cleared

FIGURE 9-17

STEP 2   Double-click the Image object in the Standard category of the Toolbox to display it on the webpage in the MainContent area. Resize the object so that it is 175 pixels (Width property) by 150 pixels (Height property).

The Image object appears on the Default.aspx page and is resized (Figure 9-18). A placeholder appears in the Image object until you specify a URL or path to an image file.

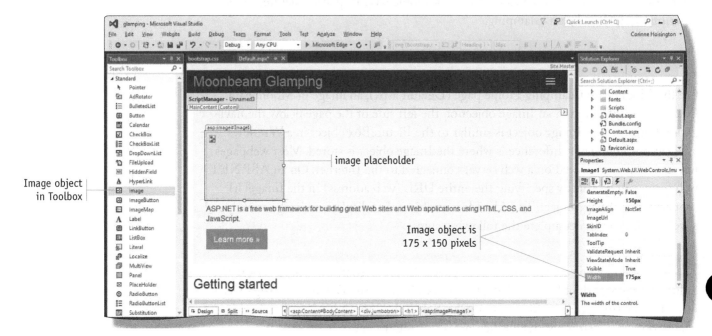

FIGURE 9-18

STEP 3   In the Properties window, name the Image object by entering `picTent` in its (ID) property. Specify which image to display by entering the web address `http://delgraphics.delmarlearning.com/CourseTechnology/ tents.jpg` as the ImageUrl property. Press the ENTER key. You need Internet connectivity to view the image.

The tents.jpg image appears in the Image object, replacing the placeholder (Figure 9-19).

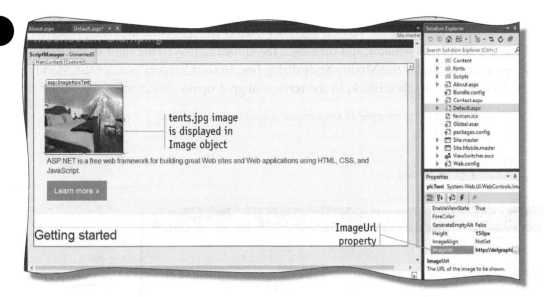

FIGURE 9-19

Enter Text Directly on the Webpage

ASP.NET allows you to enter text directly on the webpage without creating labels. You should enter text directly on the page only if the text will not be changed by coded statements. Label objects are useful if you intend to change their contents after the user makes a selection on the webpage and the web application needs to display a result. If the text is not going to change, type it directly on the page. As you type, use the SPACEBAR key to add spaces and align text, and use the ENTER key to start a new line. To enter text directly on a webpage, follow these steps:

STEP 1 Click to the right of the Image object. Add a space using the SPACE-BAR key and type Enjoy a Luxury Camping Experience directly on the Default.aspx page.

A space and the text Enjoy a Luxury Camping Experience appear to the right of the picture (Figure 9-20).

FIGURE 9-20

STEP 2   To change the vertical alignment, select the text, click the style property in the Properties window, and then click the ellipsis button to the right of the style property to display the Modify Style dialog box. In the Category pane of the Modify Style dialog box, click Block. In the vertical-align drop box, select top.

The style property is changed to top vertical alignment in the Modify Style dialog box (Figure 9-21).

Block category and top
vertical-align are selected

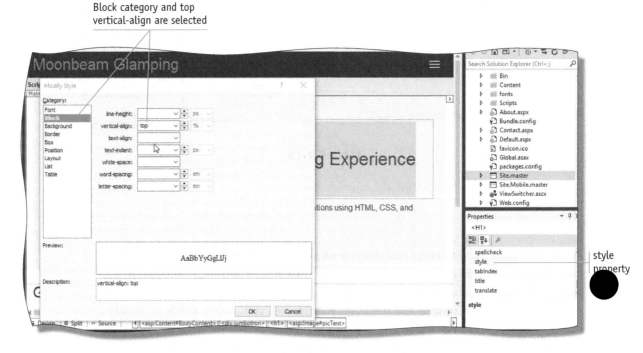

FIGURE 9-21

STEP 3   Click the OK button, and then click a blank spot to deselect the text.

The typed text is vertically aligned to the top of the MainContent area (Figure 9-22).

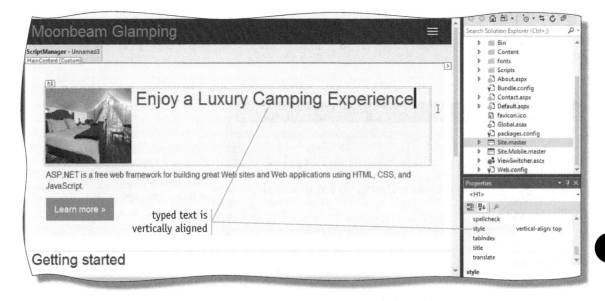

FIGURE 9-22

STEP 4   Select the text in the placeholder paragraph below the image and press the DELETE key. Change the font size to large using the Formatting toolbar. Enter the text Nestled in the mountain woods surrounded by the Moonbeam Mountains, our glamping retreat provides modern comfort with genuine resort elegance, offering the sights and sounds of nature.

The text describing Moonbeam Glamping is displayed on the page (Figure 9-23).

FIGURE 9-23

Chiyacat/Shutterstock.com

STEP 5   Delete the button and the rest of the text on the page. Do not delete the footnote © - My ASP.NET Application.

The remaining button and text on the Default.aspx page are deleted (Figure 9-24).

FIGURE 9-24

Chiyacat/Shutterstock.com

Create an ASP Web Form for the Reservations Page

Webpages are often interactive. For example, an online college application has text boxes that can be validated to be sure the information is correct. The Guest Reservation form in the chapter project will request each guest's name, email address, tent type, the number of nights, and the date of arrival.

Add a Table for Alignment on a Web Form

A table is often used to organize website content into columns. On the Reservations page (About.aspx), a table is used to simplify object placement. The Guest Reservation form includes a table with seven rows and three columns filled with TextBox objects, CheckBox objects, a DropDownList object, and a Calendar object. To add a table to the Reservations page to organize form objects, follow these steps:

STEP 1   In the Solution Explorer window, double-click About.aspx to create a web form for the Reservations page. If necessary, click the Design tab and then delete the text in the MainContent area. Click in the MainContent area and type Guest Reservation Form. Press the ENTER key. Click in the paragraph below the typed text and delete all the text below Guest Reservation Form. Click Table on the menu bar, and then click Insert Table. In the Size section of the Insert Table dialog box, change the number of Rows to 7 and the number of Columns to 3.

The Insert Table dialog box opens. The number of rows is changed to seven and the number of columns is changed to three in the About.aspx page (Figure 9-25).

FIGURE 9-25

STEP 2   Click the OK button. To resize the columns, point to a column divider until a two-sided arrow appears. Drag the divider to change the column width. As you drag, a ScreenTip shows the width of the column in pixels. Resize the first column until it is 150 px wide. Resize the second column to 250 px wide.

The table is displayed in the About.aspx page. The width of the first column is changed to 150 px and the second column width is changed to 250 px (Figure 9-26).

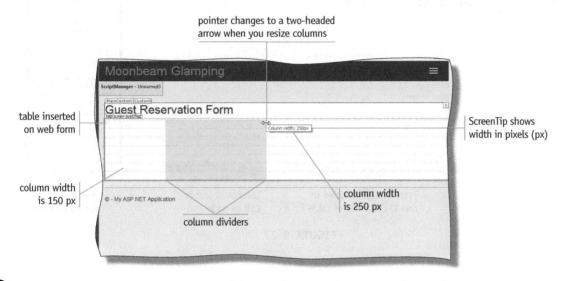

FIGURE 9-26

Add TextBox and Button Objects

Like other web form objects, TextBox and Button objects are similar to their Windows counterparts apart from a few exceptions. A TextBox object on a webpage usually is provided for data entry, allowing a user to enter a name, an address, an email address, or a zip code, for example. The Text property of a TextBox object, therefore, is blank. A Button object on a web form serves the same purpose as it does in Windows applications. Because the user generally clicks the Button object after completing the web form, the Text property for a Button object on a web form often is Submit. To name the TextBox and Button objects, you use the (ID) property. You add a Submit button to a web form the same way you add a button to a Windows application. To add a TextBox object to a web form, follow these steps:

STEP 1   On the About.aspx web form, click in the first cell of the table and type `Name:` to enter text directly into the table. Open the Toolbox, drag a TextBox object from the Toolbox to the form, and then position the TextBox object in the second cell in the first row of the table. Resize the TextBox object to a width of 250 px (Width property). Name this `TextBox` object `txtName` using the (ID) property.

Text is typed into the first cell and a TextBox object is placed inside the second cell on the top row of the table (Figure 9-27).

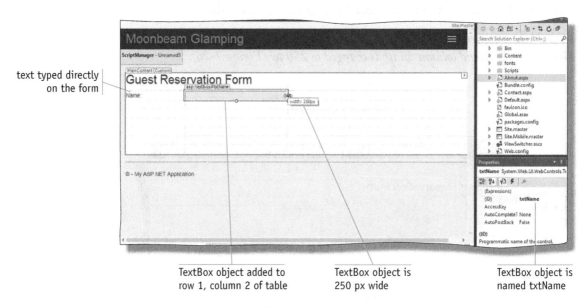

text typed directly on the form

TextBox object added to row 1, column 2 of table

TextBox object is 250 px wide

TextBox object is named txtName

FIGURE 9-27

STEP 2 In the first cell in the second row of the table, type `Email Address:` to enter text directly into the table. Drag a TextBox object from the Toolbox to the form and then position the TextBox object in the second cell in the second row in the table. Resize the TextBox object to a width of 250 px (Width property). Name this TextBox object `txtEmail` using the (ID) property.

Text is typed into the first cell and a TextBox object is placed inside the second cell on the second row of the table (Figure 9-28).

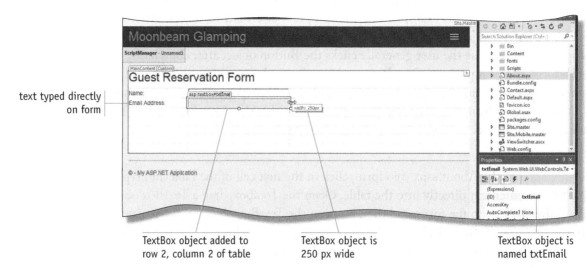

text typed directly on form

TextBox object added to row 2, column 2 of table

TextBox object is 250 px wide

TextBox object is named txtEmail

FIGURE 9-28

Add CheckBox Objects

Three CheckBox objects are used in the Guest Reservation form to determine which tent(s) the guest wants to reserve. The **CheckBox** object allows the user to choose from several options. It is similar to the RadioButton object, except the CheckBox object allows the user to pick more than one option. In contrast, the RadioButton object allows a user to choose only one option from a group of related options. The CheckBox and RadioButton objects work the same in Web, Windows, and Mobile applications.

When you name a CheckBox object, you should include the chk prefix in its (ID) property. In addition, you can specify that a check box is selected by default when a form opens. For example, because the Grizzly tent (luxury suite) is the most popular tent choice at Moonbeam Glamping, the check box for the Grizzly tent should be selected when the page first is displayed. To specify this setting, change the Checked property of the CheckBox object from False to True.

In the Moonbeam Glamping application, the user can select one or more tents based on an individual or group reservation. For example, as shown in Figure 9-29, a large family might select the Grizzly (suite) for the parents and the Kodiak (deluxe) for the teen children. RadioButton objects would not work in this example because only one RadioButton object can be selected at the same time within the same group.

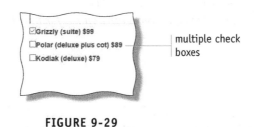

FIGURE 9-29

To place a CheckBox object on a web form, you can complete the following steps:

STEP 1 In the third row of the table, type `Tent Selection:` in the first cell. Drag the CheckBox object from the Toolbox to the web form, and then position it in the third row, second cell.

The CheckBox object is placed on the web form (Figure 9-30). The placeholder text will remain until you change the Text property. It does not, however, appear on the webpage when the page is displayed in a web browser.

CheckBox object in Toolbox

text typed directly on form

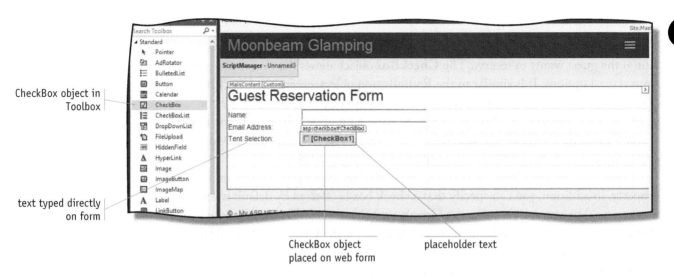

CheckBox object placed on web form

placeholder text

FIGURE 9-30

STEP 2   Name the CheckBox object by clicking to the right of its (ID) property in the Properties window and then entering `chkGrizzly`. Change the Text property of the CheckBox object to `Grizzly (suite) $99`.

The CheckBox object is named chkGrizzly in the (ID) property. After changing the Text property of chkGrizzly, the CheckBox object on the form displays the new text (Figure 9-31).

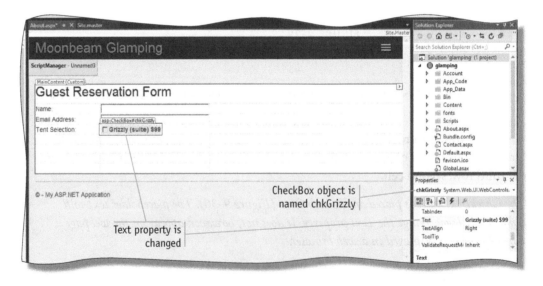

Text property is changed

CheckBox object is named chkGrizzly

FIGURE 9-31

STEP 3 At Moonbeam Glamping, the Grizzly is the most popular tent. This tent, therefore, should be checked when the form opens to save time for the user. To select the Grizzly check box, change the Checked property for the object from False to True.

The chkGrizzly CheckBox object appears with a check mark on the form, and the Checked property is set to True (Figure 9-32).

MainContent (Custom)

Guest Reservation Form

Name:
Email Address: asp:CheckBox#chkGrizzly
Tent Selection: ☑ Grizzly (suite) $99

© - My ASP.NET Application

Checked property
set to True

CheckBox object
checked

use Checked arrow
button to change
property

▷ Account
▷ App_Code
App_Data
▷ Bin
▷ Content
▷ fonts
▷ Scripts
▷ About.aspx
Bundle.config
▷ Contact.aspx
▷ Default.aspx
favicon.ico
Global.asax

Properties
chkGrizzly System.Web.UI.WebControls

CausesValidation   False
Checked   True
ClientIDMode   Inherit
CssClass
Enabled   True

Checked

FIGURE 9-32

STEP 4 In the second column, fourth and fifth rows of the table, add two more CheckBox objects named `chkPolar` and `chkKodiak`, respectively. Change the Text property of the first CheckBox object to `Polar (deluxe plus cot) $89` and the second CheckBox object to `Kodiak (deluxe) $79`.

Two CheckBox objects are added to the form (Figure 9-33).

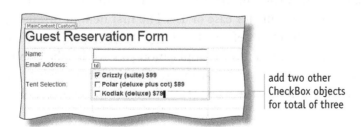

MainContent (Custom)

Guest Reservation Form

Name:
Email Address: td
                        ☑ Grizzly (suite) $99
Tent Selection: ☐ Polar (deluxe plus cot) $89
                        ☐ Kodiak (deluxe) $79

add two other
CheckBox objects
for total of three

FIGURE 9-33

Code for CheckBox Objects

After the user selects one or more CheckBox objects representing the tent selections and clicks the Submit button on the web form, control returns to the web server. On the web server, the event handler for the Submit button can evaluate which CheckBox objects are selected. The code shown in Figure 9-34 determines which CheckBox objects are selected by referring to the Checked property, in the same manner as when RadioButton objects are checked.

```
42          If chkGrizzly.Checked Then
43              decTentCost += decGrizzlyCost
44          End If
45          If chkPolar.Checked Then
46              decTentCost += decPolarCost
47          End If
48          If chkKodiak.Checked Then
49              decTentCost += decKodiakCost
50          End If
```

FIGURE 9-34

In Figure 9-34, the statement on line 42 checks the Checked property for the chkGrizzly check box. If it is checked, the Grizzly tent cost is added to the value in the decTentCost variable. Similarly, if the chkPolar check box is checked, its tent cost is added to the value in the decTentCost variable. The same is true for the chkKodiak check box. If all three check boxes are checked, the value in the decTentCost variable will be the sum of the individual tent costs for all three tents.

Add a DropDownList Object

On the Guest Reservation web form, guests can use a DropDownList object to specify the number of nights they plan to stay. The DropDownList object allows users to select one item from a predefined list. It is similar to the ListBox object used in Windows applications, except that for a DropDownList object, the list of items remains hidden until users click the list arrow button.

After adding a DropDownList object to a form and naming it, you can specify the items you want to display in the list. You often want to order these items alphabetically or numerically for ease of use. The first item in this list appears in the DropDownList object by default. The DropDownList object will not display the items in the list until you run the application and display the web form in a browser. The user must click the list arrow to view the complete list of items during execution. The prefix for the name (ID) of the DropDownList object in Visual Basic is ddl.

On the Guest Reservation form, a DropDownList object is used to determine the number of nights the guests plan to stay at the tent. To add a DropDownList object to the web form, you can complete the following steps:

STEP 1 In the sixth row of the table, type `Night(s):` in the first column. Drag the DropDownList object to the second column of the sixth row. Name the DropDownList object by clicking to the right of the (ID) property in the object's Properties window and then typing `ddlNights`.

A DropDownList object appears on the web form and is named ddlNights (Figure 9-35).

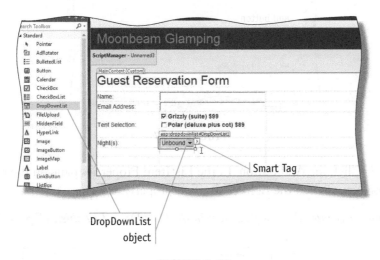

FIGURE 9-35

STEP 2 To fill the DropDownList object with list items, click the Smart Tag on the upper-right corner of the object.

The DropDownList Tasks menu opens (Figure 9-36).

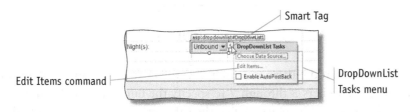

FIGURE 9-36

STEP 3   Click Edit Items on the DropDownList Tasks menu.

The ListItem Collection Editor dialog box opens (Figure 9-37).

ListItem Collection
Editor dialog box

FIGURE 9-37

STEP 4   Click the Add button. In the ListItem Properties pane on the right side of the dialog box, click to the right of the Text property and enter 1.

The number 1 is entered as the first item in the DropDownList object (Figure 9-38).

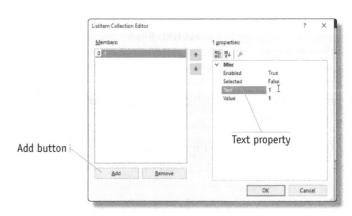

FIGURE 9-38

STEP 5   Click the Add button and enter 2 as the next Text property. Repeat this step, entering the numbers 3 through 7 to specify the number of nights users can select in the DropDownList object. Click the OK button in the ListItem Collection Editor dialog box. Resize the DropDownList object to the width of a single digit, if necessary. To view the completed DropDownList object, run the application by clicking the Start Debugging button on the Standard toolbar. If necessary, click the Reservations navigation button to open the Reservations page in the browser. Click the list arrow on the DropDownList object on the webpage.

After clicking the Start Debugging button, the browser opens. After clicking the list arrow on the DropDownList object, the list item contents appear (Figure 9-39).

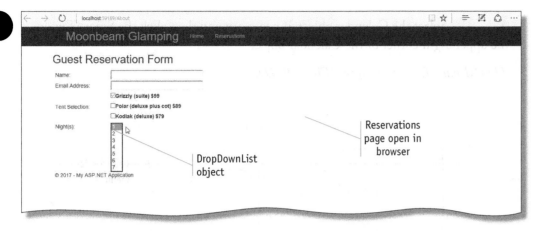

FIGURE 9-39

Add a Calendar Object

The Guest Reservation form contains a calendar that allows guests to select their arrival date. Visual Basic provides an object to manipulate months, days, and years when specifying information such as reservations, anniversaries, or bill payments. The **Calendar** object is organized by month and displays the number of days in each month as appropriate for the year. For example, March has 31 days and February includes an extra day when the year is a leap year. By default, the Calendar object displays the current month according to the system date and selects the current day when the application is executed. You can use the Calendar object in any type of Visual Studio application, including Windows and web applications. When creating a Calendar object, use the prefix cld in the name. To place the Calendar object on a web form, you can complete the following steps:

STEP 1 Close the browser window. In the last row of the table, type `Check-in Date:`. Drag the Calendar object from the Toolbox to the web form, and then position it on the form. In the (ID) property, name the Calendar object `cldArrival`.

The Calendar object is placed on the Windows form (Figure 9–40).

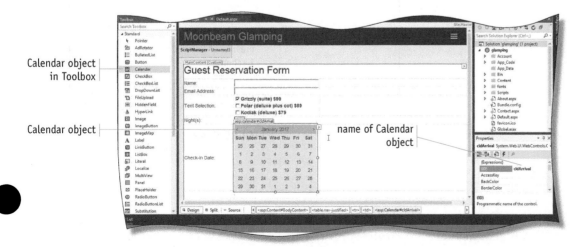

FIGURE 9-40

STEP 2   Select the Calendar object, if necessary, and then click the Smart Tag on the upper-right corner of the Calendar object.

The Calendar Tasks menu opens (Figure 9-41).

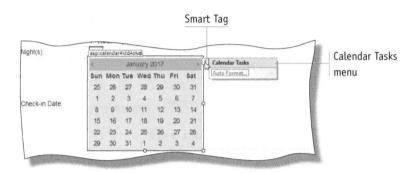

FIGURE 9-41

STEP 3   Click Auto Format on the Calendar Tasks menu. When the AutoFormat dialog box opens, click the Colorful 1 scheme in the Select a scheme list.

The AutoFormat dialog box previews the selected Colorful 1 scheme (Figure 9-42).

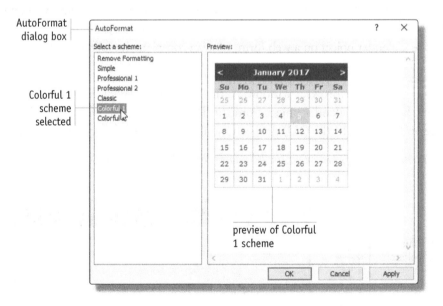

FIGURE 9-42

Specify a Web Form Title

A web form displays its title in the title bar of the browser used to view the form. Not all browsers have a title bar, but the title also appears as the title of the Main-Content area and as the tab name in the browser. You specify the title bar text for a web form using the Title property. To change the browser Title property from its default of About Us on the Reservations page to Moonbeam Glamping Guest Reservation Form, you can complete the following steps:

STEP 1   Click the OK button to close the AutoFormat dialog box. In the Properties window of the Reservations web form, click the drop-down box at the top and select DOCUMENT.

DOCUMENT is selected in the Properties window (Figure 9-43).

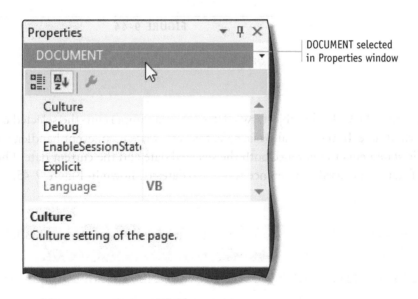

DOCUMENT selected in Properties window

FIGURE 9-43

STEP 2   In the Properties window, scroll until the Title property is visible, and then click the right column of the Title property. Enter the title Moonbeam Glamping with a blank space following the text entry. When the webpage is displayed, the Title property appears before the MainContent title.

The title Moonbeam Glamping is entered in the Title property of the Properties window. This title will be displayed in front of the MainContent title and on some browsers as the title bar or tab name of the Reservations page (Figure 9-44).

title appears before "Guest Reservation Form"

FIGURE 9-44

Code for a Calendar Object

When using the Calendar object, two dates often are important: the selected date and the current date. In the Visual Basic code that you write in an event handler, you can include statements to reference both the selected date and the current date. The format of statements used to reference these two dates is shown in Figure 9-45.

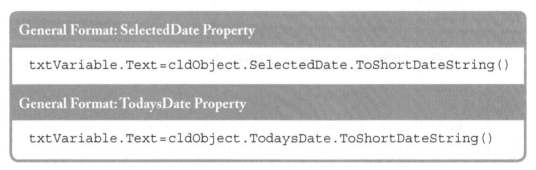

General Format: SelectedDate Property

```
txtVariable.Text=cldObject.SelectedDate.ToShortDateString()
```

General Format: TodaysDate Property

```
txtVariable.Text=cldObject.TodaysDate.ToShortDateString()
```

FIGURE 9-45

In Figure 9-45, the SelectedDate property references the date the user clicked in the Calendar object. In the general format, the ToShortDateString() procedure changes the date to a String format so it can be displayed in a TextBox object. If you are referencing only the selected date without the need to change it to a string value, the procedure is not required.

Similarly, the current date is referenced by the property TodaysDate.

The Moonbeam Glamping application should ensure that the date the user selects is equal to or greater than the current date. For a reservation date, a user cannot select a date that has already passed. One of the If statements used in the sample program to test this condition is shown in Figure 9-46.

```
If Not (chkGrizzly.Checked Or chkPolar.Checked Or chkKodiak.Checked) Then
    lblTentError.Visible = True
If cldArrival.SelectedDate < cldArrival.TodaysDate Then
    lblCalendarError.Visible = True
Else
    lblCalendarError.Visible = False
End If
```

FIGURE 9-46

In Figure 9-46, the selected date for the cldArrival Calendar object is compared to the current date (TodaysDate) for the cldArrival Calendar object. If the selected date is less than the current date, an error message is displayed; otherwise, the error message is not displayed.

If the user does not click a date on the calendar prior to clicking the Submit button and running the event handler code, the Calendar object automatically returns a date that is less than the current date. Therefore, the If statement on line 32 will detect both the case when the user selects a date less than the current date and the case when the user does not select a date.

Add Validation Controls

An important part of creating web forms is validating the data entered in the form to make sure the user has entered reasonable values. Instead of using a series of If statements or other complex code, ASP.NET provides built-in validation control objects that compare a form's objects to a set rule using little or no code. The validation control objects check input forms for errors and display messages if users enter incorrect or incomplete responses. Built-in validation control objects include Required-FieldValidator, which verifies that a required field contains data, and RangeValidator, which tests whether an entry falls within a given range.

Apply a Required Field Validator

The simplest validation control is the **RequiredFieldValidator** object, which finds a specified object to validate and determines whether the object is empty. For example, in the Moonbeam Glamping application, the user must enter her first and last name, otherwise, a reservation cannot be made. The RequiredFieldValidator object reminds the user to complete all required fields. You can customize this reminder by changing the ErrorMessage property, which often is helpful to let users know what they have done incorrectly. If the user enters a value in a field, the RequiredFieldValidator does not display an error message.

In the Moonbeam Glamping Guest Reservation form, the first object to validate is the Name TextBox object, which is named txtName. You can add a Required-FieldValidator object to the web form that tests txtName to determine if it is empty. If it is, an error message appears reminding the user to enter a name. After adding the RequiredFieldValidator object, you must specify that it validates the txtName TextBox object.

The prefix used for the RequiredFieldValidator is rfv. To validate a required TextBox object using a RequiredFieldValidator object, follow these steps:

STEP 1   In the Toolbox, hide the Standard tools by clicking the filled triangle icon next to Standard. Expand the Validation tools by clicking the open triangle icon next to Validation.

The seven Validation tools are displayed (Figure 9-47).

FIGURE 9-47

STEP 2   Drag the RequiredFieldValidator to the right of the Name TextBox object in the third column of the table.

The RequiredFieldValidator object is placed to the right of txtName (Figure 9-48).

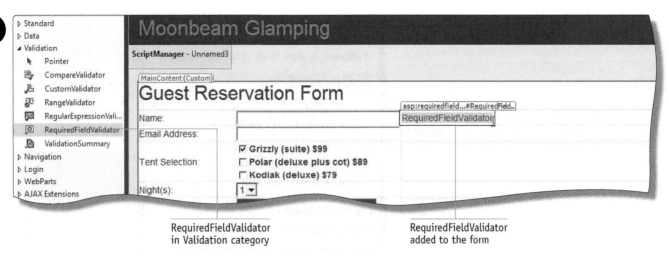

RequiredFieldValidator
in Validation category

RequiredFieldValidator
added to the form

FIGURE 9-48

STEP 3   Name the RequiredFieldValidator by typing `rfvName` in its (ID) property.

The RequiredFieldValidator object is named rfvName (Figure 9-49).

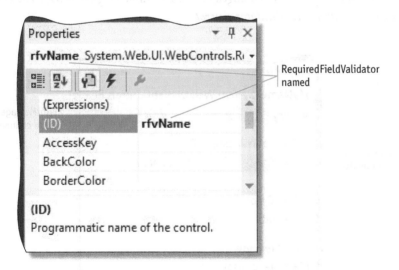

RequiredFieldValidator
named

FIGURE 9-49

STEP 4   To specify that the rfvName RequiredFieldValidator object validates the txtName TextBox object, click to the right of the ControlToValidate property in the Properties window, click the list arrow, and then select txtName.

The ControlToValidate property is set to txtName (Figure 9-50).

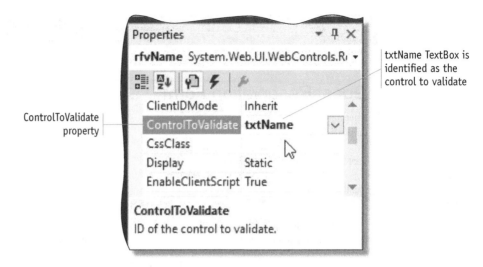

FIGURE 9-50

STEP 5   In the Properties window for the RequiredFieldValidator, change the ErrorMessage property to * Enter Name.

*The ErrorMessage property is changed to * Enter Name (Figure 9-51). The txtEmail field also uses a RequiredFieldValidator control.*

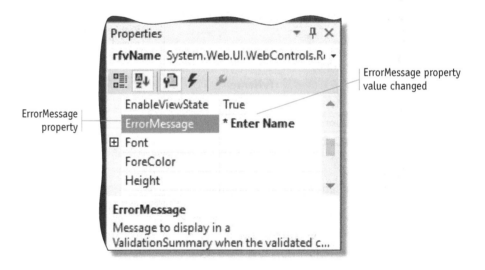

FIGURE 9-51

When the application is run on a web browser with a Submit button, the error message will be displayed if the Submit button is clicked and no text has been entered in the txtName text box.

Apply the Range Validator

Another validation control built into ASP.NET is the **RangeValidator** control, which tests whether an input value falls within a given range. If you were testing whether a number entered on a webpage was a valid day in a month, the RangeValidator control could test if the day number is between 1 and 31. The RangeValidator control uses the prefix rgv in its name, and the following five properties to complete its validation:

* The **ControlToValidate** property contains the name of the object you are validating.
* The **MinimumValue** property contains the smallest value in the range.
* The **MaximumValue** property contains the largest value in the range.
* The **Type** property matches the data type of the value, such as Integer or String.
* The **ErrorMessage** property explains to the user what value is requested.

Apply the Compare Validator

Another validation control is the **CompareValidator** object, which you use to compare an object's value with another object or a constant value. The CompareValidator control can also compare the value in one object to the value in another object. In the example shown in Figure 9-52, the user enters a password into a web form, and reenters the password to confirm that the two passwords are the same. You can use the CompareValidator control to verify that the passwords match.

FIGURE 9-52

The CompareValidator control uses three properties to complete its validation:

* The **ControlToValidate** property contains the name of the object that you are validating.
* The **ControlToCompare** property contains the name of the object that you are comparing to the ControlToValidate property.
* The **ErrorMessage** property contains a message stating that the value does not match.

In Figure 9-53, four properties are changed to apply the CompareValidator object to verify a password: (ID), ControlToCompare, ControlToValidate, and ErrorMessage. This figure also shows that the prefix for the CompareValidator object is cmv.

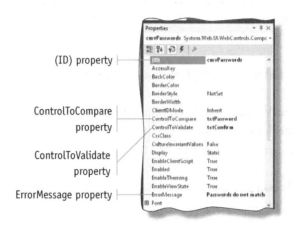

FIGURE 9-53

Apply the Regular Expression Validator

The **RegularExpressionValidator** control confirms whether the user entered data that matches standard formats, such as for a phone number, email address, URL, zip code, or Social Security number. If the user does not enter the data in the proper format, an error message is displayed. The prefix rev is used for the RegularExpressionValidator control. The control uses three properties to complete its validation:

- The **ControlToValidate** property contains the name of the object that you are validating.
- The **ErrorMessage** property contains a message stating that the value does not match the valid format.
- The **ValidationExpression** property allows the user to select the format for the object.

In the Moonbeam Glamping Guest Reservation form, the second TextBox object on the form requests the user's email address. To confirm that the information entered is a possible email address, a RegularExpressionValidator object can test the contents of the Text property of the txtEmail object and verify that it matches the format of a valid email address, which follows the format of *name@domain.com*. To incorporate a RegularExpressionValidator object in a webpage, you can complete the following steps:

STEP 1 Drag the RegularExpressionValidator object from the Toolbox to the right of the Email Address TextBox object in the table.

The RegularExpressionValidator object is placed in the table to the right of the txtEmail object (Figure 9-54).

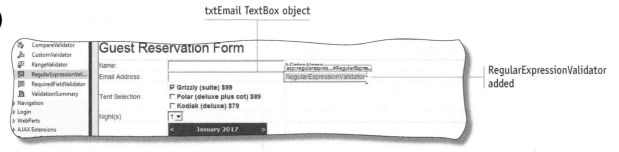

txtEmail TextBox object

RegularExpressionValidator added

FIGURE 9-54

STEP 2 Name the RegularExpressionValidator by typing `revEmail` in its (ID) property.

The RegularExpressionValidator object is named revEmail (Figure 9-55).

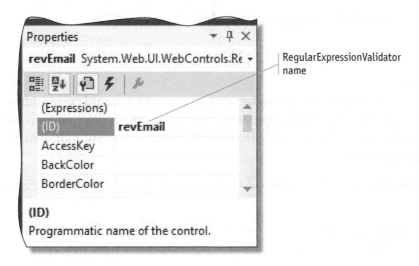

RegularExpressionValidator name

FIGURE 9-55

STEP 3 Click to the right of the ControlToValidate property, click the list arrow, and then click txtEmail.

The ControlToValidate property is set to txtEmail (Figure 9-56).

txtEmail is control to validate

ControlToValidate property

FIGURE 9-56

STEP 4   Change the ErrorMessage property to * Error Email Format.

*The ErrorMessage property is changed to * Error Email Format (Figure 9-57).*

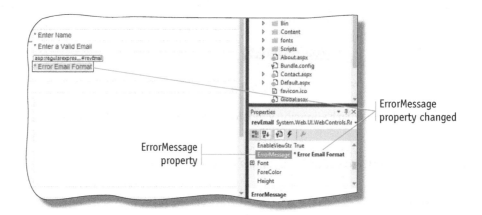

FIGURE 9-57

STEP 5   To set txtEmail to validate that it contains a standard email address, click to the right of the ValidationExpression property, and then click its ellipsis button. In the Regular Expression Editor dialog box, select Internet e-mail address in the Standard expressions list.

The Internet e-mail address is selected as the standard expression to validate (Figure 9-58).

FIGURE 9-58

STEP 6   Click the OK button in the Regular Expression Editor dialog box. Run the application by clicking the Start Debugging button on the Standard toolbar. Enter a name and an email address without an @ symbol, such as lochlan.fix. com, and then press the ENTER key.

An error message appears to the right of the Email Address TextBox object (Figure 9-59). When a valid email address is entered and the ENTER key is pressed again, the error message is removed.

FIGURE 9-59

Apply Multiple Validations

You can apply more than one type of validation control on an object to validate more than one aspect of the data. Often you may want to make a certain control required using the RequiredFieldValidator object, and to check the range using the Range-Validator object. In Figure 9-60, a RequiredFieldValidator confirms that the number of hours worked is not left blank, and the RangeValidator verifies that the number entered is between 1 and 60. Each validation control displays an error message if the object does not meet the specified criteria.

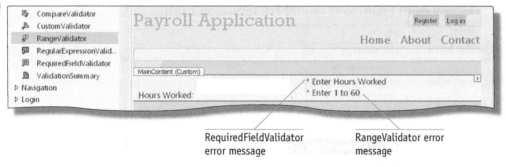

FIGURE 9-60

Display a ValidationSummary Control

Instead of validating data, the **ValidationSummary** control lets you display validation error messages in a single location, creating a clean layout for the web form. By default, each validation control displays an error message next to the object it validates. On a large or complex form, however, the error messages might interfere with data or other objects. You can use the ValidationSummary object to display all of the error messages in a different place, listing them in a blank area at the top or bottom of the form, for example, where they will appear together when the validation criteria for any control are not met.

To use a ValidationSummary object, drag the object to the location on the webpage where you want the summary to appear. The prefix used for naming the ValidationSummary object is vsm.

CONSIDER THIS

Do I have to set the ControlToValidate property for a validation summary?
The validation summary displays the error messages for all the other validation objects, so you do not have to set the ControlToValidate property. The error message displayed in this control is specified by the ErrorMessage property of each validation control. If the ErrorMessage property of the validation control is not set, no error message is displayed for that validation control.

Use the
 Tag in Visual Basic Code

One HTML tag often used when creating webpages is the **
** tag, which stands for break; it breaks the text by starting a new line. When you are creating a web form in Visual Basic, you can use the <br> tag to skip a line before starting a new one in a Label object.

In the Moonbeam Glamping chapter project, after the user enters reservation information, a confirmation message is displayed that includes details about the reservation such as the name, email address, cost of the tents, date, and number of nights (Figure 9-61).

reservation confirmation message

FIGURE 9-61

In Figure 9-61, the message consists of five lines. Based on your screen resolution, the text may wrap and you may have six lines. Each of the lines except the last line ends with the <br> tag so that the text that follows will be on the next line. The code to create the message is shown in Figure 9-62.

```
53            strMessage = "A reservation has been made for: " & "<br>" _
54                & strName & "<br>" & "Email: " & strEmail & "<br>"
55            strMessage &= "The Tent(s) cost is: " _
56                & decTentCost.ToString("C") & "<br>"
57            strMessage &= "Arrival Date: " _
58                & cldArrival.SelectedDate.ToShortDateString() _
59                & "<br>" & " for " & intNumberOfNights & " night(s)"
60            lblReservation.Text = strMessage
```

FIGURE 9-62

In Figure 9-62, the message to be displayed is built in the strMessage String variable. On line 53, the first line of the message is placed in the variable. The last item in the string is the <br> tag, which will cause the text that follows to be on the next line. Notice that the tag must be within double quotation marks because it is a string.

The statements on lines 54 and 56 also end with the <br> tag. As a result of the statements in Figure 9-62, a five-line message will be created.

Use String Manipulation Properties and Procedures in the String Class

The String class in Visual Basic has many properties and procedures that allow you to manipulate strings, which you often need to do when developing web forms. For example, you might want to find the length of the string that the user entered or convert lowercase text to uppercase. The commands discussed in this section work with ASP.NET as well as in any Windows or mobile application.

Find String Length

You can use the **Length** property to determine the number of characters in a particular string. The syntax for determining string length is shown in Figure 9-63.

General Format: Determine String Length

```
intValue = strName.Length
```

FIGURE 9-63

In the statement intLength = "Visual Basic".Length, the value placed in the intLength Integer variable would be 12 because the Length property counts spaces as well as characters, and "Visual Basic" contains 11 characters and one space. The code shown in Figure 9-64 determines if the zip code entered in the txtZipCode TextBox object has a length of five characters.

```
 8              Dim intCount As Integer
 9
10              intCount = txtZipCode.Text.Length
11              If intCount <> 5 Then
12                  lblError.Text = "You must enter 5 digits"
13              End If
14
```

FIGURE 9-64

If you enter only four digits in the zip code, as shown in Figure 9-65, a message appears reminding you to enter five digits.

FIGURE 9-65

Use the Trim Procedure

When entering information into a TextBox object, the user might accidentally add extra spaces before or after the input string. When that string is used later, the extra spaces might distort the format of the output. To prevent this, Visual Basic provides a procedure named **Trim** to remove spaces from the beginning and end of a string. The syntax for the Trim procedure is shown in Figure 9-66.

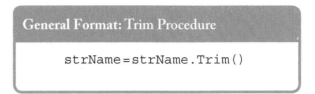

General Format: Trim Procedure

```
strName = strName.Trim()
```

FIGURE 9-66

In the Moonbeam Glamping Guest Reservation form, the user enters a name and an email address. If the user includes spaces before or after the entries, the spaces will appear in the final output. The Trim procedure shown in Figure 9-67 removes extra spaces.

```
26              ' Trim additional spaces that are entered by the user
27              strName = txtName.Text.Trim
28              strEmail = txtEmail.Text.Trim
```

FIGURE 9-67

Convert Uppercase and Lowercase Text

The **ToUpper** and **ToLower** procedures convert a string to all uppercase or all low-ercase letters, respectively. The syntax in Figure 9-68 shows how to use the ToUpper and ToLower procedures:

General Format: UpperCase and LowerCase Procedures
strName = strName.ToUpper()
strName = strName.ToLower()

FIGURE 9-68

When you compare a string, Visual Basic checks if you entered the word as speci-fied. For example, if you enter YES in response to a question, but the code accepts only yes, the If statement shown in Figure 9-69 would convert the response of YES to yes. The ToUpper() and ToLower() methods save coding time because all the possible ways to enter a response do not have to be compared.

```
87          If strAnswer.ToLower() = "yes" Then
```

FIGURE 9-69

Program Design

As you have learned, the requirements document identifies the purpose of the pro-gram being developed, the application title, the procedures to be followed when using the program, any equations and calculations required in the program, any conditions within the program that must be tested, notes and restrictions that must be followed by the program, and any other comments that would be helpful to understanding the problem. The requirements document for the Moonbeam Glamping web application is shown in Figure 9-70 and the Use Case Definition is shown in Figure 9-71.

REQUIREMENTS DOCUMENT

Date:	May 3, 2019
Date Submitted:	
Application Title:	Moonbeam Glamping
Purpose:	This web application allows the user to book a reservation at the Moonbeam Glamping website using a web form.
Program Procedures:	From a web application, the user should complete an online reservation form to enter the guest's name, email address, tent preference, number of nights, and starting date. The total cost of the stay should be calculated and displayed.

Algorithms, Processing, and Conditions:

1. The user must be able to enter the requested reservation information on a web form. The information should include the guest's name, email address, which tents the guest prefers, number of nights, and starting date of the stay. The user can select one or more tents from the following choices: Grizzly (suite) $99, Polar (deluxe plus cot) $89, and Kodiak (deluxe) $79.
2. After entering the reservation information, the user clicks the Submit button.
3. The information entered is validated.
4. The application displays the final cost of the stay.

Notes and Restrictions:

1. Data in the Name TextBox object is required.
2. Data in the Email TextBox object is validated to confirm that it is in an email address format.
3. The Calendar object is checked to confirm that a date is selected and that the selected date is not before the current date. The maximum length of stay is seven nights.

Comments: Display a picture of the tents on the web form.

FIGURE 9-70

USE CASE DEFINITION

1. The webpage opens, displaying the title Moonbeam Glamping with a picture as well as TextBox objects to enter the guest's name and email address. A Calendar object is used to select the beginning date of the reservation. A DropDownList object is used to enter the number of nights. The tent selections are entered with CheckBox objects.
2. User clicks the Submit button.
3. The data entered is checked and validated.
4. If necessary, the user makes corrections and resubmits the data.
5. The application confirms the reservation and displays the final cost of the stay.

FIGURE 9-71

Event Planning Document

You will recall that the event planning document consists of a table that specifies an object in the user interface that will cause an event, the action taken by the user to trigger the event, and the event processing that must occur. The event planning document for the Moonbeam Glamping web application is shown in Figure 9-72.

EVENT PLANNING DOCUMENT

Program Name:	Developer:	Object:	Date:
Moonbeam Glamping	Corinne Hoisington	About.aspx	May 3, 2019

OBJECT	EVENT TRIGGER	EVENT PROCESSING
btnSubmit	Click	Validate the name to confirm it is not empty
		Validate email address to confirm it is in the email address format
		Trim extra spaces from name and email data
		Clear the reservation message
		If a tent has not been selected
		Display a tent error message
		If arrival date is not valid
		Display a calendar error message
		Else
		Hide the calendar error message
		Else
		Hide the tent error message
		If arrival date is valid
		Accumulate tent costs
		Convert number of nights to Integer
		Calculate cost of tent (total tent costs * number of nights)
		Create the reservation message
		Display the reservation message
		Else
		Display calendar error message

FIGURE 9-72

Code the Program

After identifying the events and tasks within the events, you are ready to create the program. As you have learned, creating the program means designing the user interface and then entering Visual Basic statements to accomplish the tasks specified on the event planning document. As you enter the code, you also will implement the logic to carry out the required processing.

Guided Program Development

NOTE TO THE LEARNER

In the following activity, you should complete the tasks within the specified steps. Each of the tasks is accompanied by a Hint Screen. The purpose of the Hint Screen is to indicate where you should perform the activity in the Visual Studio window and to remind you which method to use. If you need further help completing a step, refer to the Figure identified by *ref:*.

Phase 1: Customize the Master and Home Pages

1

● **Begin the Web Application** Start Visual Studio, and then create a Visual Basic Web Site Application project by clicking the New Project button on the Standard toolbar, and then clicking New Web Site. In the center pane, click ASP.NET Web Forms Site, if necessary. Enter the project name glamping and store the program on the d: drive (or a network or USB drive of your choice). Click the OK button *(ref: Figure 9-4)*.

● **Display the Formatting Toolbar** Click View on the menu bar, point to Toolbars, and then click Formatting.

● **Change the Heading on the Site.master Page** In the Solution Explorer, double-click the Site.master page. On the page, select the "Application name" placeholder text and type Moonbeam Glamping. Select the typed title. On the Formatting toolbar, change the font size to xx-large *(ref: Figure 9-9)*.

● **Change the Second Navigational Link Using HTML** On the Site.master page, click the Source tab at the lower-left part of the window. Select the HTML code `<li><a runat="server" href="~/Contact">Contact</a></li>`. Press the delete key to delete the Contact list item line of code. Select the black text "About" in the About list item link and type Reservations to rename the displayed text in the link *(ref: Figures 9-12 and 9-13)*.

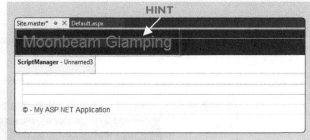

```
</div>
<div class="navbar-collapse collapse">
    <ul class="nav navbar-nav">
        <li><a runat="server" href="~/">Home</a></li>
        <li><a runat="server" href="~/About">Reservations</a></li>

    </ul>
    <asp:LoginView runat="server" ViewStateMode="Disabled">
```

● **Delete the Register and Log in Links** Select the HTML code that displays Register and Log in links on the Site.master page:

```
<li><a runat="server" href="~/Account/
Register">Register</a></li> <li><a runat="server"
href="~/Account/Login">Log in</a></li>
```

● Press the DELETE key to remove the Register and Log in links from the Site. master page.

● **Add an Image Object** Close and save the Site.master page and switch to the Default.aspx page. Delete the existing text in the title placeholder in the MainContent area. Double-click the Image object in the Standard category of the Toolbox to display it within the webpage in the MainContent area. Resize the object so that it is 175 pixels (width) by 150 pixels (height). Change its ImageUrl property to http://delgraphics.delmarlearning.com/CourseTechnology/tents.jpg *(ref: Figure 9-19)*.

(continues)

- **Type Directly on the Page** Click to the right of the Image object and type Enjoy a Luxury Camping Experience. Click the ellipsis button of the style property in the Properties window. In the Modify Style dialog box, select the Block category and then select top in the vertical-align box. Click the OK button *(ref: Figure 9-21)*.

- **Type the Paragraph** Select the text in the paragraph below the image and press the DELETE key. Change the font size to large using the Formatting toolbar. Enter the text Nestled in the mountain woods surrounded by the Moonbeam Mountains, our glamping retreat provides modern comfort with genuine resort elegance, offering the sights and sounds of nature. Delete the button and the rest of the text on the Default.aspx page. Do not delete the footnote © - My ASP.NET Application *(ref: Figure 9-23)*.

The Default.aspx webpage includes an image and typed text (Figure 9-73).

RESULT OF STEP 2

FIGURE 9-73

Phase 2: Build the Guest Reservation Web Form

3

- **Insert a Table in the Web Form** In the Solution Explorer, double-click the About.aspx file. Delete the text in the MainContent area. Type Guest Reservation Form in the MainContent area. Click Table on the menu bar, and then click Insert Table. In the Insert Table dialog box, enter 7 in the Rows text box and 3 in the Columns text box, and then click the OK button to create a table with seven rows and three columns *(ref: Figure 9-25)*.

HINT

- **Change the Size of the Table Columns** Point to the divider between the first and second columns of the table, and then drag to resize the first column to 150 pixels. Resize the second column to 250 pixels *(ref: Figure 9-26)*.

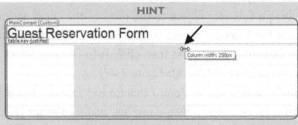
HINT

- **Enter Text and Objects in the Table**

- In the first column of the table, enter Name:, Email Address:, Tent Selection:, Night(s):, and Check-in Date: in separate rows. In the second column, drag the first TextBox object to the right of the Name title, and then name the TextBox object txtName *(ref: Figure 9-27)*.

- Drag the second TextBox object to the right of the Email Address title, and then name the TextBox object txtEmail *(ref: Figure 9-28)*.

- Drag a CheckBox object to the right of the Tent Selection text. Name the CheckBox object chkGrizzly. Change the Text property to Grizzly (suite) $99. Change the Checked property to True *(ref: Figure 9-31)*.

- Drag the second CheckBox object below the first CheckBox object, and then name the CheckBox object chkPolar. Change its Text property to Polar (deluxe plus cot) $89. Drag the third CheckBox object below the second CheckBox object, and then name the third CheckBox object chkKodiak. Change its Text property to Kodiak (deluxe) $79 *(ref: Figure 9-33)*.

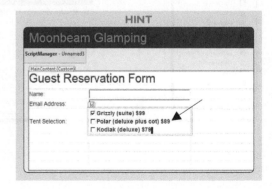
HINT

(continues)

- Drag a DropDownList object to the right of the Night(s) title. Change the name of the DropDownList object to `ddlNights`. Click the Smart Tag on the DropDownList object, and then click Edit Items. The ListItem Collection Editor dialog box opens. Click the Add button, and then enter the number 1 as the Text property. Click the Add button as necessary to add the numbers 2 through 7. After adding number 7, click the Remove button to remove the entry in the Members list, if necessary. Click the OK button *(ref: Figure 9-38)*.

- Drag a Calendar object to the right of the Check-in Date text. Name the Calendar object `cldArrival`. Click the Smart Tag on the Calendar object, and then click Auto Format. Select Colorful 1, and then click OK *(ref: Figure 9-42)*.

The Guest Reservation Form (About.aspx) includes typed text, text boxes, check boxes, a drop-down list, and a calendar (Figure 9-74).

RESULT OF STEP 3

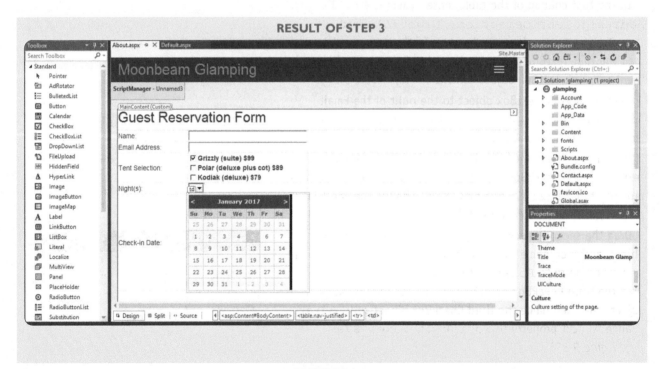

FIGURE 9-74

Phase 3: Add Validation Objects

4

- **Add the Required Validation Objects** In the Toolbox, expand the Validation controls by clicking the expand icon next to Validation *(ref: Figure 9-47).*

HEADS UP

When you run the web application, a message may appear in a dialog box that states "Debugging Not Enabled." Select the "Modify the Web. config file to enable debugging" option button, and then click OK.

- **Validate the Name TextBox Object** Drag the RequiredFieldValidator object onto the web form to the first row in the third column. Name the Validator Object rfvName. Change its ErrorMessage property to * Enter Name *(ref: Figure 9-51).*

HINT

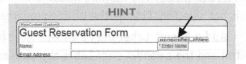

- **Select the TextBox Object to Validate** In the Properties window for the rfvName object, click the list arrow in the ControlToValidate property and then click txtName *(ref: Figure 9-50).*

- **Validate the Email TextBox Object** Drag the Required FieldValidator object onto the web form in the second row of the third column. Place the RequiredFieldValidator object to the right of the txtEmail TextBox object. Name the Validator object rfvEmail. Change its ErrorMessage property to * Enter a Valid Email. In the Properties window, click the list arrow in the ControlToValidate property and then click txtEmail.

HINT

- **Add a Regular Expression Validator for Email** Drag the RegularExpressionValidator object below the Email Address field. Name the Validator object revEmail. Change its ErrorMessage property to * Error Email Format. Click the list arrow in the ControlToValidate property, and then click txtEmail. Click the ellipsis button in the ValidationExpression property. When the Regular Expression Editor dialog box opens, select Internet e-mail address. Click the OK button *(ref: Figure 9-58).*

HINT

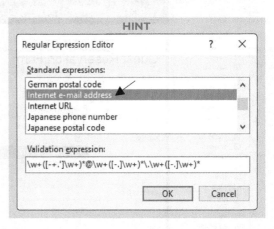

- **Add the Tent Selection Message** Drag a Label object onto the web form to the third row in the third column. Place the label in the same row as the Grizzly check box. Name the label lblTentError. Change the Text property to * Select a Tent. Set the Visible property for the label to False.

(continues)

● **Add the Submit Button** Drag a Button object to the last row of the third column to the right of the Calendar object. Change the Button object (ID) property to btnSubmit. Change the Text property to Submit. Click after the Submit button and press the ENTER key several times until the Submit button is at the top of the cell.

● **Add a Calendar Warning Label** Drag a Label object below the Submit button. Change the (ID) property of the Label object to lblCalendarError. Change the Text property to * Select a Valid Date. The warning message is displayed only if a valid date is not selected. Change the Visible property to False.

● **Add a Result Label** Drag a Label object below the Submit button and the calendar error Label object. Name the Label object lblReservation. Delete any value in the Text property. The lblReservation placeholder with the text [lblReservation] is displayed on the web form, but will not appear in the actual webpage.

● **Change the DOCUMENT Property** Click the object arrow in the Properties window and then select DOCUMENT. Type Moonbeam Glamping as the Title property.

The validation objects and messages are part of the web form (Figure 9-75).

RESULT OF STEP 4

FIGURE 9-75

Phase 4: Code the Application

5

● **Code the Comments** Close the Toolbox. Double-click the Submit button on the form to begin coding the btnSubmit_Click event in the web application. Insert the first four standard comments at the top of the code window. Insert the command Option Strict On at the beginning of the code to turn on strict type checking.

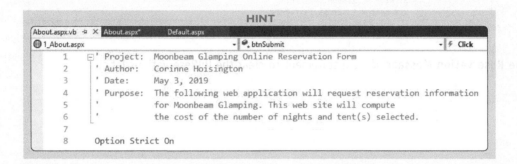

```
HINT
About.aspx.vb  ₽ ×  About.aspx*        Default.aspx
⊕ 1_About.aspx                                    ▾ ●, btnSubmit                    ▾ ⨍ Click
    1    ⊟' Project:   Moonbeam Glamping Online Reservation Form
    2      ' Author:    Corinne Hoisington
    3      ' Date:      May 3, 2019
    4      ' Purpose:   The following web application will request reservation information
    5      '               for Moonbeam Glamping. This web site will compute
    6      '               the cost of the number of nights and tent(s) selected.
    7
    8        Option Strict On
```

● **Comment on the btnSubmit Click Event** In the btnSubmit click event, enter a comment that explains the purpose of the click event.

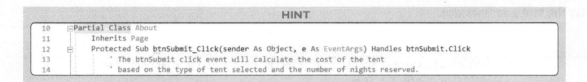

```
HINT
   10    ⊟Partial Class About
   11          Inherits Page
   12    ⊟    Protected Sub btnSubmit_Click(sender As Object, e As EventArgs) Handles btnSubmit.Click
   13              ' The btnSubmit click event will calculate the cost of the tent
   14              ' based on the type of tent selected and the number of nights reserved.
```

● **Initialize Variables** Click in the btnSubmit click event and enter the variables used in the application. These variables include String variables for the name and email address; Decimal variables that will contain the costs for the three tents and the result of the tent cost calculation; an Integer value for the number of nights the user selects from the drop-down list; and a String variable in which to compose the reservation message.

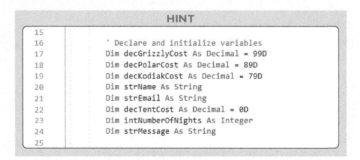

```
HINT
   15
   16              ' Declare and initialize variables
   17              Dim decGrizzlyCost As Decimal = 99D
   18              Dim decPolarCost As Decimal = 89D
   19              Dim decKodiakCost As Decimal = 79D
   20              Dim strName As String
   21              Dim strEmail As String
   22              Dim decTentCost As Decimal = 0D
   23              Dim intNumberOfNights As Integer
   24              Dim strMessage As String
   25
```

(continues)

● **Trim the TextBox Object Data** Using the Trim procedure, write the code to remove excess spaces from the data the user entered. Place the trimmed Name from the TextBox object in the strName variable and the trimmed Email address in the strEmail variable (ref: Figure 9-67).

	HINT
25	
26	' Trim additional spaces that are entered by the user
27	strName = txtName.Text.Trim
28	strEmail = txtEmail.Text.Trim

● **Clear the Reservation Message** Write a statement to clear the lblReservations label.

	HINT
29	lblReservation.Text = ""

● **Ensure a Tent Is Selected** Write an If statement that ensures a tent has been selected. The Checked property of one or more of the CheckBox objects must be true. Use the Not operator to check for all three properties. If the tent has not been selected, display the tent error message.

	HINT
30	If Not (chkGrizzly.Checked Or chkPolar.Checked Or chkKodiak.Checked) Then
31	lblTentError.Visible = True

● **Ensure a Valid Date Is Selected** Regardless of whether a valid tent was selected, the program must ensure a valid date was selected. If a tent is not selected, write an If statement that ensures the date is valid (that is, the selected date is not less than the current date). If the date is invalid, display the calendar error message; otherwise, do not display the calendar error message.

```
                                     HINT
32  ⊟           If cldArrival.SelectedDate < cldArrival.TodaysDate Then
33                  lblCalendarError.Visible = True
34              Else
35                  lblCalendarError.Visible = False
36              End If
```

● **Hide the Tent Message When a Tent Is Selected** If a tent is selected, the tent error message must be hidden; that is, the tent error message Visible property must be set to False. Write the statement to set the Visible property to False.

```
                                     HINT
37              Else
38                  lblTentError.Visible = False
```

● **Ensure a Valid Date Is Selected** When a tent has been selected, the program must ensure a valid date was selected. If a tent is selected and a valid date is selected, the data validity checking is complete and the tent cost can be calculated. Write a statement to ensure that the selected date is greater than or equal to the current date, and if the date is valid, set the Visible property for the error message to False.

```
                                 HINT
38              lblTentError.Visible = False
39  ⊟           If cldArrival.SelectedDate >= cldArrival.TodaysDate Then
40                  lblCalendarError.Visible = False
```

● **Determine the Total Tent Costs** The user can select more than one tent. For example, one tent might be for parents and another tent might be for their children. Therefore, the program must determine if each check box is checked, and if so, the tent cost per night is accumulated. Write the statements to determine if a tent check box is checked and, if so, to accumulate the tent costs in the decTentCost variable.

```
                                 HINT
41              ' Calculate the cost of the tent(s) selected by the user
42  ⊟           If chkGrizzly.Checked Then
43                  decTentCost += decGrizzlyCost
44              End If
45  ⊟           If chkPolar.Checked Then
46                  decTentCost += decPolarCost
47              End If
48  ⊟           If chkKodiak.Checked Then
49                  decTentCost += decKodiakCost
50              End If
```

(continues)

- **Calculate the Total Cost** To calculate the total cost of the stay, the number of nights selected by the user from the drop-down list must be converted from a String to an Integer. Then, the total costs (number of nights × tent cost) must be calculated. Write the statements to perform these activities.

	HINT
51	intNumberOfNights = Convert.ToInt32(ddlNights.SelectedItem.Text)
52	decTentCost = intNumberOfNights * decTentCost

- **Create the Reservation Message** Write the code to create the reservation message and place it in the strMessage String variable. Then, place the message stored in the strMessage variable in the Text property of the lblReservation Label object (ref: Figure 9-62).

	HINT
53	strMessage = "A reservation has been made for: " & " " _
54	& strName & " " & "Email: " & strEmail & " "
55	strMessage &= "The Tent(s) cost is: " _
56	& decTentCost.ToString("C") & " "
57	strMessage &= "Arrival Date: " _
58	& cldArrival.SelectedDate.ToShortDateString() _
59	& " " & " for " & intNumberOfNights & " night(s)"
60	lblReservation.Text = strMessage

- **Show the Calendar Error Message** If the user did not select a valid date for the check-in date, display the calendar error message by changing the Visible property for the error message label to True.

	HINT
61	Else
62	lblCalendarError.Visible = True
63	End If
64	End If
65	End Sub

Code Listing

The complete code for the sample program is shown in Figure 9-76.

```vbnet
1    □' Project:  Moonbeam Glamping Online Reservation Form
2     ' Author:   Corinne Hoisington
3     ' Date:     May 3, 2019
4     ' Purpose:  The following web application will request reservation information
5     '              for Moonbeam Glamping. This web site will compute
6     '              the cost of the number of nights and tent(s) selected.
7
8     Option Strict On
9
10   □Partial Class About
11        Inherits Page
12   □    Protected Sub btnSubmit_Click(sender As Object, e As EventArgs) Handles btnSubmit.Click
13            ' The btnSubmit click event will calculate the cost of the tent
14            ' based on the type of tent selected and the number of nights reserved.
15
16            ' Declare and initialize variables
17            Dim decGrizzlyCost As Decimal = 99D
18            Dim decPolarCost As Decimal = 89D
19            Dim decKodiakCost As Decimal = 79D
20            Dim strName As String
21            Dim strEmail As String
22            Dim decTentCost As Decimal = 0D
23            Dim intNumberOfNights As Integer
24            Dim strMessage As String
25
26            ' Trim additional spaces that are entered by the user
27            strName = txtName.Text.Trim
28            strEmail = txtEmail.Text.Trim
29            lblReservation.Text = ""
30   □        If Not (chkGrizzly.Checked Or chkPolar.Checked Or chkKodiak.Checked) Then
31                lblTentError.Visible = True
32   □            If cldArrival.SelectedDate < cldArrival.TodaysDate Then
33                    lblCalendarError.Visible = True
34                Else
35                    lblCalendarError.Visible = False
36                End If
37            Else
38                lblTentError.Visible = False
39   □            If cldArrival.SelectedDate >= cldArrival.TodaysDate Then
40                    lblCalendarError.Visible = False
41                    ' Calculate the cost of the tent(s) selected by the user
42   □                If chkGrizzly.Checked Then
43                        decTentCost += decGrizzlyCost
44                    End If
45   □                If chkPolar.Checked Then
46                        decTentCost += decPolarCost
47                    End If
48   □                If chkKodiak.Checked Then
49                        decTentCost += decKodiakCost
50                    End If
51                    intNumberOfNights = Convert.ToInt32(ddlNights.SelectedItem.Text)
52                    decTentCost = intNumberOfNights * decTentCost
53                    strMessage = "A reservation has been made for: " & "<br>" _
54                        & strName & "<br>" & "Email: " & strEmail & "<br>"
55                    strMessage &= "The Tent(s) cost is: " _
56                        & decTentCost.ToString("C") & "<br>"
57                    strMessage &= "Arrival Date: " _
58                        & cldArrival.SelectedDate.ToShortDateString() _
59                        & "<br>" & " for " & intNumberOfNights & " night(s)"
60                    lblReservation.Text = strMessage
61                Else
62                    lblCalendarError.Visible = True
63                End If
64            End If
65        End Sub
66   End Class
```

FIGURE 9-76

Summary

In this chapter you have learned to create an online web application using ASP.NET.

1. In an active server page, what type of computer executes the event handler code you write in Visual Basic 2017?

2. Name six locations where you can test and display a Visual Basic ASP.NET webpage.

3. Name five websites that incorporate web forms and state the purpose of each web form (such as to enter customer information for purchasing an item). Do not list any sites that were mentioned in this chapter.

4. What is the extension of an ASP webpage?

5. A webpage or website is hosted on a(n) _____ _____.

6. In a Windows application, each object has a (Name) property. In a web application, each object has a(n) _____ property, which is similar to the (Name) property.

7. A website that allows you to enter information is considered a(n) _____ webpage.

8. Write a line of code that would display the date selected by the user in the TextBox shown in Figure 9-77.

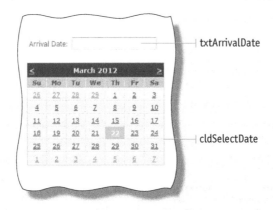

FIGURE 9-77

9. In the DropDownList object (ddlCoffee) that displays three coffee size options T, G, and V, write the lines of code that would display in a Label named lblCoffeeSize "You have selected size: Venti" if the user selects "V."

10. Explain the major difference between CheckBox and RadioButton objects.

11. What is the name of the property that assigns a message that is displayed when the object cannot be validated?

12. Which control validator checks if a value is between 42 and 64?

13. Which control validator confirms that a TextBox object is not left blank?

14. Write a line of code that would convert strTrainName to all lowercase letters.

15. Write a line of code that would assign the length of a string named strTeamMascot to the variable intSizeOfMascot.

16. Write a line of code that would display in a Label object named lblDisplayBirthday the date a user selected from a Calendar object named cldBirthdate.

17. How does the Image object in ASP.NET differ from an image in a Windows application?

18. What is the name of the page that serves as a template for the pages that are actually displayed in the browser?

19. What type of validator would you use to compare correct login text?

20. Can an object have multiple validators?

Debugging Exercises

1. What will be contained in the Text property of the lblResult Label object after executing the following code?

```
Dim strPhrase As String
strPhrase = "Everyone should know how to code a computer;"
strPhrase += " because it teaches "
strPhrase+= "you how to think."
strPhrase = strPhrase.Trim()
lblResult.Text=strPhrase
```

2. Fix the error(s) in the following line of code.

```
decRoyalTitle = strRoyalTitle(Text.StringLength)
```

3. Fix the error(s) in the following lines of code.

```
If (chkSpeedingTicket.Checked) = True Then
decTicket = 280
End If
```

4. What is the output of the following code?

```
Dim strPhrase As String
strPhrase = "Shut the front door please"
lblResult.Text= "Count =" & strPhrase.Length
```

5. Write the output that would be displayed in the Info label after the following statements are executed.

```
lblInfo.Text = "Home Address: " & "<br>" & "356 Harvard Rd" & "<br>" &
"Lynchburg, VA 24502"
```

1. Name each of the property changes that are required in the Properties window for a Range Validator in order to validate that a TextBox named txtDeductibleRange contains a value in the range 300.50 up to and including 500.00. Display an error message that states "Please enter an acceptable deductible between 300.50 and 500."

2. Write a Visual Basic statement that displays the length of a variable named strSentence in a Label object named lblStringLength.

3. Write the section of code that would display a list of services in a Label object named lblService if the user selects any of the corresponding CheckBoxes shown in Figure 9-78.

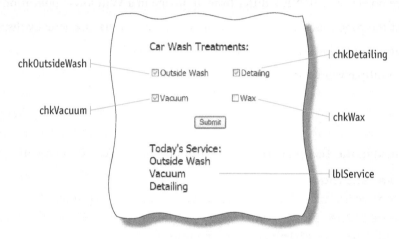

FIGURE 9-78

Complete one or more of the following case programming assignments. Submit the program and materials you create to your instructor. The level of difficulty is indicated for each case programming assignment.

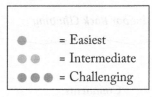

● = Easiest
●● = Intermediate
●●● = Challenging

1 ●
INDOOR ROCK CLIMBING

Design a web application for an application that allows the user to book an indoor rock climbing reservation. Write the code that will execute according to the program requirements shown in Figure 9-79 and the Use Case Definition document shown in Figure 9-80. Before writing the code, create an event planning document for each event in the program. The completed webpage is shown in Figure 9-81 on page 584.

REQUIREMENTS DOCUMENT

Date:	August 11, 2019
Date Submitted:	
Application Title:	Indoor Rock Climbing
Purpose:	This web application allows the user to book an indoor rock climbing reservation in Atlanta or Miami.
Program Procedures:	From a web application, the user completes an online booking form to select the location of the indoor rock climbing, the number of hours (1–4), and the booking date.
Algorithms, Processing, and Conditions:	1. The user must be able to enter the requested reservation information on a web form. The information should include the user's name, the city location for the indoor rock climbing (Atlanta at $23 per hour or Miami at $27 per hour), the number of hours (maximum of 4 hours), and the preferred booking date.
	2. After entering the reservation information, the user clicks the Submit button.
	3. The information entered is validated.
	4. The application displays the final cost of rock climbing at the selected location.
Notes and Restrictions:	1. Data validation controls should be used. The name text box is validated to confirm that it is not left blank.
	2. The calendar object must have a date selected that is later than the current date.
	3. Only one city can be selected.
	4. The number of hours must be 1–4 hours.
	5. A user may reserve only for one person.

FIGURE 9-79 (continues)

(continues)

Indoor Rock Climbing

Comments:	1. Display a picture of an indoor rock climber on the web form. An image URL can be located with a search engine such as Bing or Google. 2. Place the image and title on the Site.master page. Delete the navigational links to make a single page.

FIGURE 9-79 (continued)

USE CASE DEFINITION

1. The webpage opens, displaying a picture of a rock climber, one TextBox object to request a name, two RadioButton objects to select a city location, a DropDownList object displaying the number of hours (1–4 hours), a Calendar object to select the booking date, and a Submit button.
2. The user enters the information, makes the appropriate selections, and clicks the Submit button.
3. Validation controls check the data.
4. The application displays the final cost of the rock climbing.

FIGURE 9-80

FIGURE 9-81

2 PHONE SCREEN REPAIR

Design a web application and write the code that will execute according to the program requirements shown in Figure 9-82 and the Use Case Definition document in Figure 9-83. Before writing the code, create an event planning document for each event in the program. The completed webpage is shown in Figure 9-84.

REQUIREMENTS DOCUMENT

Date:	February 22, 2019
Date Submitted:	
Application Title:	Phone Screen Repair
Purpose:	This web application allows customers to request repairs for their smartphone screen.
Program Procedures:	From a web application, the user should enter her name, email address, the phone platform (using a DropDownList object with two options), and a problem description in a large TextBox object to create a repair order.
Algorithms, Processing, and Conditions:	1. The user must be able to enter information about the requested phone repair on a web form. The user will enter her first and last names, email address, phone number, the phone platform (using a DropDownList object with the choices of Android or iOS), and a problem description in a large TextBox object to create a repair order.
	2. After the information is entered, the user can click the Submit button.
	3. The information entered is validated.
	4. The application displays a repair order with the cost of the repair.
Notes and Restrictions:	1. Data validation tools should be used. The first and last name text boxes are validated to confirm that they are not left blank.
	2. The email address is checked to verify that it conforms to the proper email format.
	3. The phone number is checked to verify that it conforms to a U.S. phone number.
	4. The cost of the Android screen replacement is $79.99 and the iOS screen replacement is $99.99.
Comments:	Display a picture representing the phone repair on the web form.

FIGURE 9-82

(continues)

Phone Screen Repair

USE CASE DEFINITION

1. The webpage opens, displaying a phone screen repair form with a picture representing a broken smartphone; TextBox objects requesting the user's first and last names, email address, and phone number; phone platform DropDownList object; a TextBox object for users to describe the issue; and a Submit button.
2. The user clicks the Submit button.
3. Validation controls check the data.
4. The application displays the information that was sent to the phone repair company along with the cost.

FIGURE 9-83

FIGURE 9-84

iStockphoto.com/praetorianphoto

3

TEE TIMES FOR GOLF

Design a web application and write the code that will execute according to the program requirements shown in Figure 9-85. Before writing the code, create an event planning document for each event in the program. Create a Use Case Definition document for the application.

REQUIREMENTS DOCUMENT

Date:	January 4, 2019
Date Submitted:	
Application Title:	Golf Tee Times
Purpose:	This web application allows the user to sign up online for a golf tee time and date.
Program Procedures:	From a web application, the user should select a tee time and date.
Algorithms, Processing, and Conditions:	1. The website has two pages. The Home page provides information about the golf course. The second page allows users to sign up for a tee time.
	2. The web form should include the name of the golfer requesting the tee time, the possible times, and a calendar to select a date.
	3. After the selection is entered, the user clicks the Submit button.
	4. The information entered is validated.
Notes and Restrictions:	1. Data validation controls should be used.
	2. No optional service is required.
	3. A drop-down list control displays tee times on the half hour and hour from 8 am to 2 pm.
	4. The golf date must be later than the current date.
Comments:	Display a picture representing the golf course on the web form.

FIGURE 9-85

4 ●●
STREET TACOS

Design a web application that calculates the cost of a street taco order according to the prices listed in Figure 9-86. The Home page opens with a picture and information about the tacos that customers can order. The Order page provides an order form and displays the final price. Write the code that will execute according to the program requirements shown in Figure 9-87. Before writing the code, create an event planning document for each event in the program. Create a Use Case Definition document for the application.

Meat	Cost
Chipotle Chicken	$8.99
Pastor Pork	$9.99
Blackened Fish	$12.99
Carne Asada	$13.99
Each Extra Topping (Cheese Included)	$0.99

FIGURE 9-86

REQUIREMENTS DOCUMENT

Date:	July 24, 2019
Date Submitted:	
Application Title:	Street Tacos
Purpose:	This web application allows a customer to fill out a street taco order form.
Program Procedures:	From a web application, users should enter their name, address, and phone number. They also should select the type of taco they want to order and the toppings. The final cost of the order will be displayed.
Algorithms, Processing, and Conditions:	1. The website has two pages. The Home page promotes the street taco restaurant and lists a phone number to call when ordering. The Order page displays an order form. 2. The user must be able to enter order information for a street taco using a web form. The user will enter her first and last name, address, phone number, the type of taco meat from a DropDownList object, and at least five taco topping choices from a series of CheckBoxes. 3. After the information is entered, the user clicks the Submit button. 4. The information entered will be validated. 5. The application displays the final cost of the taco order and a message that the order will be ready in 10 minutes.
Notes and Restrictions:	1. Data validation tools should be used. The first and last name text boxes are validated to confirm that they are not left blank. 2. The phone number is checked to ensure that it conforms to a U.S. phone number.
Comments:	A picture representing street tacos will be displayed on the web form.

FIGURE 9-87

Case Programming Assignments

5 ●●● RE-CREATE AN ONLINE FORM

Create a requirements document and a Use Case Definition document, and then design a web application, based on the case project shown in Figure 9-88.

> Find an online form you would like to re-create that has varied objects such as a label, radio button, check box, text box, and drop down list objects. Use a layout similar to the existing website and include at least eight objects on the form to display your own version of the website for practice. Validate the form using validation objects as needed.

FIGURE 9-88

6 ●●●
CASTLE HOSTELS

Create a requirements document and a Use Case Definition document, and then create a web application, based on the case project shown in Figure 9-89.

A youth hostel group called Castle Hostels has requested a web application that creates an online reservation form and displays the costs of a hostel based on the number of nights and city selection. Allow users to enter their name, city selection (see table), number of nights (1-7), and calendar dates. Use validation controls. Create an opening page and reservations page with two different images.

City	Cost per Night
Edinburgh	$17
Florence	$23
Barcelona	$28

FIGURE 9-89

CHAPTER 10

Incorporating Databases with ADO.NET

OBJECTIVES

You will have mastered the material in this chapter when you can:

- Understand database files

- Connect to a database using ADO.NET

- Connect Form objects to the data source

- Bind database fields to the Windows Form object

- Access database information on a Windows Form object

- Add a record

- Delete a record

- Select records from a list

- Program beyond the Database Wizard

- Create the OleDbDataAdapter object

Introduction

As you have learned, information used in Visual Basic 2017 can originate from any source, including data entered into objects such as a TextBox, data assigned within the code, or data read from a text file. Large applications often need to connect to the data required in business today. Businesses store huge volumes of data in databases, and information technology (IT) must manage this data and perform database operations such as changes, additions, and deletions. IT must also retrieve database information for viewing and decision making. Increasingly, developers use Visual Basic 2017 to connect to databases and allow users to perform the aforementioned operations and more. Within the Visual Studio environment, applications can connect to a variety of database sources through the data access technology of ADO.NET.

Chapter Project

In the sample chapter project, the Gaming Art Commission requires a Windows application to access its Game Art & Design Competition database for video game development and design, which documents local graphic artists, the names of their submitted artwork, and the retail price of their artwork. Art from the commission is displayed online, in galleries, and in public and private collections. A prize will be awarded each year to the best gaming graphic submitted to the Gaming Art Commission. The commission provides a platform for anyone to be an artist and for any space within the community to be a venue.

The information in the Art database is stored as a Microsoft Access database. By placing the information in a simple-to-use Windows application, the staff of the Gaming Art Commission can easily view, update, and delete local graphic artists' information. By accessing the Gaming Art Windows application, the entire staff can identify local graphic artists, their exhibition locations, and the sale price of their art.

The Gaming Art Windows application loads information about local graphic artists and their works from a Microsoft Access 2016 database named Art.accdb, which is stored on a USB drive. When the Windows form opens, it displays the first record, which indicates the first artist, as shown in Figure 10-1.

Move next
button

Move last
button

FIGURE 10-1

NextMars/Shutterstock.com

The user can use the navigation toolbar at the top of the Windows form to continue through the other artists' information. The Windows form displays each of the 16 records that currently are saved in the Artist table, which was created using Microsoft Access 2016, as shown in Figure 10-2.

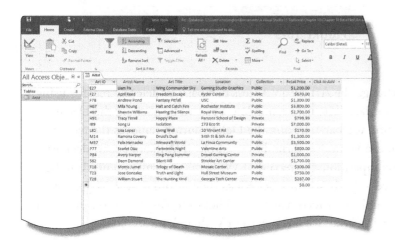

FIGURE 10-2

The Art.accdb database can also be updated to include new artists who are taking part in the Game Art & Design competition. The user can click the Add new button on the navigation toolbar at the top of the Windows form to open a blank record. Figure 10-3 shows a new record entered into the Windows form to represent a new artist named Eric Matthews. After entering the record, the user can add the record to the database by clicking the Save Data button on the navigation toolbar. The original Access database is permanently updated.

FIGURE 10-3

A user can also change the Art.accdb Access database by deleting records using the Windows form interface. The user can delete a record by clicking the Delete button on the navigation toolbar. Clicking the Delete button removes the record currently displayed in the Windows form. For example, if William Stuart decides not to be part of the competition, the record of William's information needs to be removed from the Access database. The user clicks the buttons on the navigation toolbar to access William's artist record and then clicks the Delete button shown in Figure 10-4 to permanently remove any record of William's information.

Delete
button

FIGURE 10-4

NextMars/Shutterstock.com

TextBox objects are not the only objects that can be used to display database data. In Figure 10-5, a ComboBox object is used to display the artist's name, which is stored in the Artist Name field. When a field such as Artist Name is displayed in a ComboBox object, the user can click the ComboBox arrow to display a list of values in the field. The user then can click a name in the Artist Name field list to navigate directly to the individual record for the selected artist. For example, the user can view information about artist Liam Fix by selecting his name from the ComboBox object for the Artist Name field, as shown in Figure 10-5.

FIGURE 10-5

NextMars/Shutterstock.com

The Gaming Art Commission intends to keep track of the retail price of all artwork because after the competition, several local art museums may be interested in purchasing the entire lot for their own collection. A Total Retail Value button allows the user to compute the total retail price of all graphic art records within the database. Figure 10-6 shows the Gaming Art form after the Total Retail Value button has been clicked. The artwork in the Art database currently has a total value of $27,257.00.

FIGURE 10-6

Database Files

A **database** is a collection of related information stored in a structured format. Common examples of business databases include a customer list, product information, a mailing list, or a reservation system. A database organizes data in **tables**. A table is a collection of data about a specific topic, such as a listing of local artists vying for the prize sponsored by the Gaming Art Commission. Using a separate table for each topic means that you store the data only once, which makes a database efficient and reduces data-entry errors.

The chapter project creates a user interface that accesses the data from the Gaming Art Commission's database, which is named Art.accdb. The Art database contains a table shown in Figure 10-7 that displays each local artist's information and their submissions for the Game Art & Design competition. A table structures data into rows and columns. Each row is referred to as a **record**. A record in a table contains information about a person, product, item, or other entity.

Each record in the Artist table of the Art database contains information about a local artist and their submitted art. In Figure 10-7, the selected record shows information about Liam Fix's art submission.

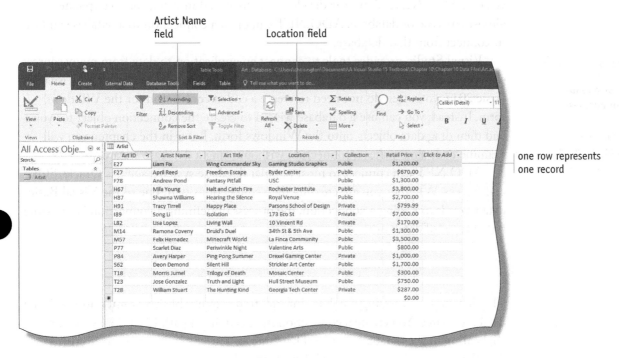

FIGURE 10-7

Each record begins with the Art ID, which is a unique number that identifies each submission in the Game Art & Design competition and can be used only once. The Art ID is contained in the Art ID field. Each column in a table is referred to as a **field**. A field contains a specific piece of data within a record. For example, in the Artist table, the column that lists the exhibition location of each artwork is the Location field. Each column in the table is a field and displays data such as the names of the artists, locations, whether the exhibition location is public or privately owned, and the retail price of the artwork.

Each table in a relational database must contain a unique value. Therefore, no two artists in the Art database are assigned the same Art ID. A unique field is an identifier that represents the **primary key** for the table. The Art ID is the primary key for the Artist table in the Art database. A primary key is used in relational databases to avoid problems such as duplicate records and conflicting values in fields.

Connect to a Database Using ADO.NET

To support databases that use Visual Basic 2017, a library called ActiveX Data Objects works within all Windows, Office, and Web applications. The current version, ADO.NET, allows the developer to create, administer, and manipulate almost any type of database. ADO.NET can open a connection to a database and can disconnect from that database.

CRITICAL THINKING

Which is the most popular database used in business today?
Go to http://db-engines.com/en/ranking to see which database is currently in the lead.

Visual Studio provides tools to connect an application to data from many sources, such as databases, web services, and objects. If you are using ADO.NET in Visual Basic 2017, you often do not need to create a coded connection for the Windows form. Instead, you can use a database wizard to create the connection object for you and then drag data objects onto the Windows form. Later in the chapter, you will examine code that makes a connection without using a database wizard.

ADO.NET can connect to most popular database systems such as Oracle, SQL, and Access. Whether you are creating data connections with one of the Visual Basic data wizards or coding a connection, the process of defining a connection is the same for all types of databases.

Establish a Database Connection

The first step in accessing database information is to establish a **connection** with the database source. You create a connection by specifying a path from the Windows application to the database source. The database source can be accessed from any digital source, such as a local hard drive, network drive, or a connection to a remote database through the Internet. To connect a Visual Basic 2017 application to data in a database, you can use the **Data Source Configuration Wizard**. After you complete the wizard, data is available in the **Data Sources window** for dragging onto a Windows form. A connection string contacts the data source and establishes a connection with the database using the Data Source Configuration Wizard. The wizard uses the Fill method to fill a DataSet object with table rows and columns from a selected table within a database. A **DataSet** object is a temporary cache storage for data retrieved from a data source. The DataSet object is a major component of the ADO.NET architecture.

For the Gaming Art chapter project, a Windows application must connect to the Access database table named Artist in the Art.accdb database. To connect to the database using the Data Source Configuration Wizard, you can complete the following steps:

STEP 1   Create a Windows application named Gaming Art. Name the form frmArt. Change the Text property to Gaming Art Commission - Game Art & Design Competition. Resize the form to a size of 670, 450. Change the BackColor property to White on the Web tab. An image from one of the local artists, named art.jpg, is available with your Data Files. Place a PictureBox object on the left side of the window. Name the PictureBox object picArt. Change the Size property to 293, 160. Using the Image property, import the art.jpg image for the PictureBox object. Change the SizeMode to StretchImage. On the right side of the form, place a Label object named lblTitle. Change the Text property to Game Design Finalists on two lines. Make the Font property Script MT, Bold, size 40, and the ForeColor property Green on the Web tab. Center-align the text. Close the Toolbox, and then click Project on the menu bar.

The Windows form is created and the Project menu is opened (Figure 10-8).

FIGURE 10-8

STEP 2   Click Add New Data Source on the Project menu.

The Data Source Configuration Wizard opens and requests the Data Source Type (Figure 10-9).

Data Source
Configuration
Wizard

Database is
source of data

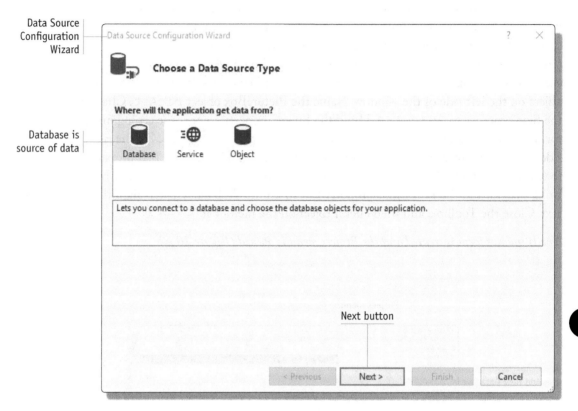

FIGURE 10-9

STEP 3 In the Choose a Data Source Type dialog box, click Database, and then click Next. In the Choose a Database Model dialog box, click Dataset, and then click Next.

After you select the Dataset option and click the Next button, the Choose Your Data Connection dialog box opens (Figure 10-10).

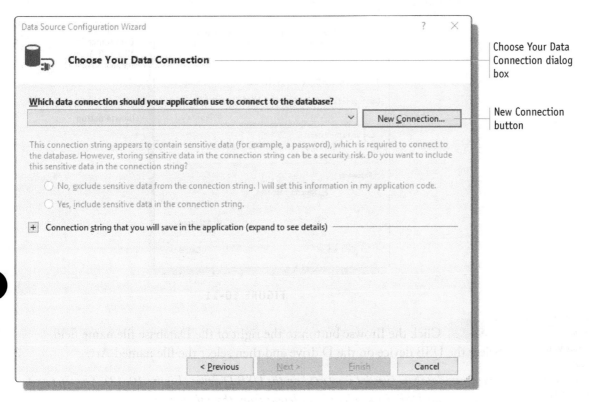

FIGURE 10-10

STEP 4   Click the New Connection button. In the Choose Data Source dialog box, select Microsoft Access Database File because the Art database is an Access database. Click the Continue button.

The Add Connection dialog box reopens (Figure 10-11). The Data source appears as Microsoft Access Database File.

FIGURE 10-11

HEADS UP

This chapter assumes that your USB drive is assigned to drive D. If your USB drive is assigned to a different drive letter, substitute that letter for "D" throughout the chapter.

STEP 5   Click the Browse button to the right of the Database file name field. Select the USB device on the D drive and then select the file named Art.

The Access database file Art is selected on the USB D drive (Figure 10-12). The files and folders on your USB drive might be different from those shown here.

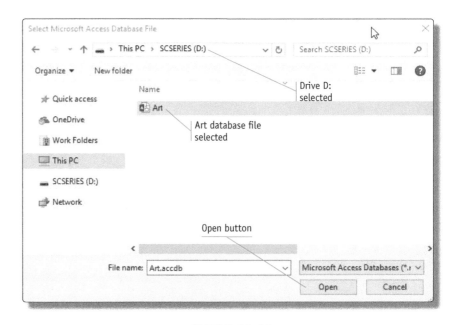

FIGURE 10-12

STEP 6 Click the Open button.

The Add Connection dialog box reopens (Figure 10-13).

Add Connection
dialog box

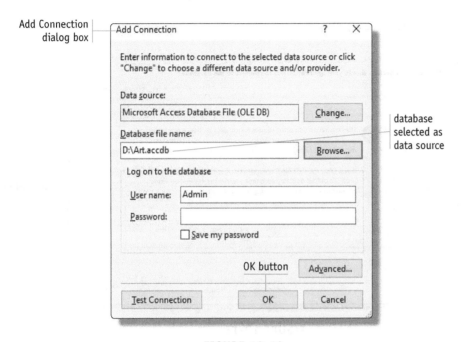

database
selected as
data source

OK button

FIGURE 10-13

STEP 7 Click the OK button in the Add Connection dialog box.

The Choose Your Data Connection dialog box opens to confirm the database file you are using (Figure 10-14).

data connection is
an Access database
file named
Art.accdb

Next button

FIGURE 10-14

STEP 8   Click the Next button.

FIGURE 10-15

A dialog box opens to remind you that the connection uses a local data file that is not in the current project (Figure 10-15). The dialog box also asks if you want to copy the file to your project. You do not want to add data and update the copied database. It is best to update the original database file.

STEP 9   Click the No button and then click the Next button. When the Choose Your Database Objects dialog box opens, select which database objects you want in the DataSet. Click the expand icon next to the Tables option. Click the Artist check box to select that table. A connection is made from the Visual Basic application to the Artist table within the Art.accdb database.

After the expand icon is clicked to display the available tables, the Artist check box is checked (Figure 10–16).

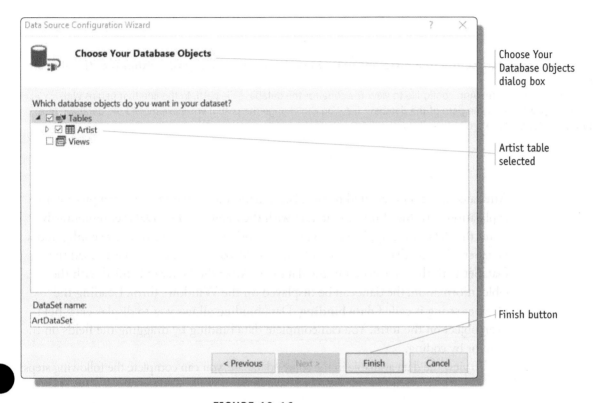

Choose Your Database Objects dialog box

Artist table selected

Finish button

FIGURE 10-16

STEP 10 Click the Finish button. Click ArtDataSet.xsd to select the DataSet.

The dialog box closes, and a connection is made to the Artist table. The Solution Explorer displays the DataSet named ArtDataSet.xsd (Figure 10–17).

ArtDataSet added to program

NextMars/Shutterstock.com

FIGURE 10-17

After a connection is established, you can design programs using the open connection and retrieve and manipulate the data accessed with the database file.

If I move my Access database file to a different path, how do I change that path within the Visual Basic application?
In the Solution Explorer, click the App.config file to view the code for the database file path. In the line that begins with connectionString, you can view the path of the database file. You can change the path if you have moved the database to a different location—for example, from drive D: to drive E:.

View Data Available in the Source Database

After a connection is created to an existing data source, the DataSet can provide the application with the ability to interact with the database. The DataSet temporarily stores the data in the application while you work with it. After you have configured a DataSet with the Data Source Configuration Wizard, the next step is to load the DataSet with the data stored in the database. After the DataSet is filled with the table information, the data can be displayed on the Windows form. Loading the DataSet string is called **data binding**. Data binding allows you to display each field as an object on the form. You can complete data binding by dragging the fields on the form or by coding.

To view the data available in the source database, you can complete the following steps:

STEP 1 In the Art project window, point to the Data Sources tab on the left side. If the Data Sources tab is not visible, click View on the menu bar, click Other Windows, and then click Data Sources.

The Data Sources tab is selected (Figure 10-18).

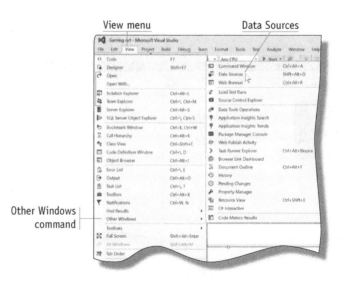

FIGURE 10-18

STEP 2 Click Data Sources to view the database sources.

A DataSet named ArtDataSet is displayed along with a connection to the Artist table (Figure 10-19).

Data Sources window

ArtDataSet

Artist table

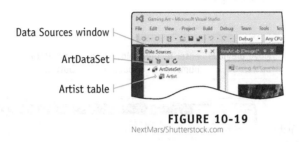

FIGURE 10-19
NextMars/Shutterstock.com

STEP 3 Click the expand icon for the Artist table to expand the list of field names within the table. Each bindable field item in the Data Sources window can be placed on the Windows Form object.

The fields of the Artist table are displayed (Figure 10-20). Each field is displayed by default with an icon that designates each database item as a TextBox object.

Data Sources window

icon identifies a field as a default TextBox object

fields in the Artist table

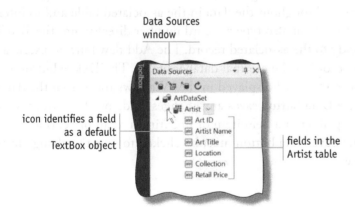

FIGURE 10-20

Bind Database Fields to the Windows Form

After a connection is created to link the database to the Windows application and the data source displays the existing field objects, you can drag the field objects to the Windows Form object. When you drag field objects from the Data Sources window, Visual Studio automatically creates a **databinding** to populate the form by binding the form object to the DataSet information.

After the first field item is placed on the Windows form, a navigation toolbar control called the **BindingNavigator** appears on the form, as shown in Figure 10-21. The BindingNavigator control consists of a ToolStrip with a series of ToolStripItem objects for most common data-related actions, such as navigating through data, adding data, and deleting data. By default, the BindingNavigator control contains the standard buttons shown in Figure 10-21.

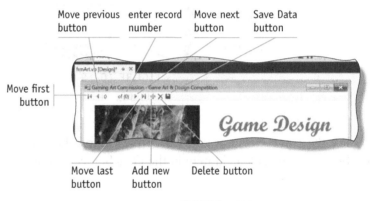

FIGURE 10-21

The first four arrow navigation buttons on the BindingNavigator control allow the user to move throughout the data in the associated table and to interact with the records. A user can also type a record number directly into the TextBox to navigate quickly to the associated record. The Add new button inserts a new row to add a new record to the original database table. The Delete button permanently deletes the current record displayed in the Windows form from the database table. The Save Data button saves any changes made on the current form, such as changing the spelling of a field item or updating a retail price. If a record is added or deleted, the Save Data button must be clicked to save the change to the original database table.

The BindingNavigator appears when the first table field is bound to the Windows form. To bind each database field to the Windows form object, follow these steps:

STEP 1 Select the Art ID field in the Data Sources window. Drag the Art ID field to the Windows Form object below the PictureBox object.

The Art ID field is placed on the Windows form (Figure 10-22). The Art ID TextBox object is now bound to the data in the table. A navigation toolbar called a Binding-Navigator control automatically is added to the top of the Windows Form object. An ArtDataSet, ArtistBindingSource, ArtistTableAdapter, TableAdapterManager, and BindingNavigator appear in the component tray and bind the database data to the Windows Form object.

FIGURE 10-22

NextMars/Shutterstock.com

STEP 2 Drag the rest of the field objects from the Data Sources window to the Windows form. Select all the field labels and field TextBox objects and change their font size to 10 points and bold. Use the formatting tools on the Format menu to equally distribute the bound objects. You can select the Label and TextBox objects separately to move them independently of each other. Use the layout shown in Figure 10-23.

All of the field objects are placed on the Windows form and are formatted to align with one another (Figure 10-23).

FIGURE 10-23

STEP 3 Run the application by clicking the Start button on the Standard toolbar to fill the Windows Form object with the data from the Artist table. Use the Move next button on the navigation toolbar to move through the records. Click the Move last button to display the last record.

The Windows form opens and the data in the first record fills the TextBox objects. The Move next button on the navigation toolbar is clicked to view records. The last record is displayed (Figure 10-24).

last record
displayed

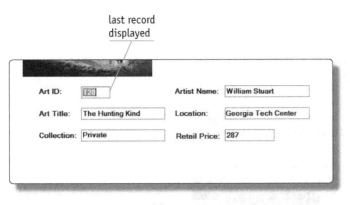

FIGURE 10-24

Add Records

By running the application, the user can view every record within the database. In the Gaming Art application, the Windows form allows the user to update the database by adding new artists. To add a new record to the database table, you can follow these steps:

STEP 1   If necessary, click the Start button on the Standard toolbar to run the Gaming Art application.

The Windows form opens, displaying the first record (Figure 10–25).

Add new
button

first record
displayed

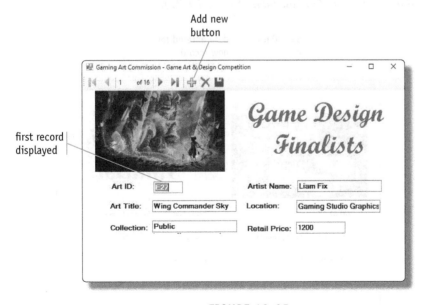

FIGURE 10-25

CRITICAL THINKING

Why not have the Gaming Art Commission simply view the database within Microsoft Access instead of creating a Visual Basic interface?

If the staff of any organization is not familiar with database technologies, it can be quite overwhelming to understand how to manipulate data with queries and reports. The front-end, database-driven Windows application is simple to navigate one record at a time, and it allows users to update and delete records via an easy interface.

WATCH OUT FOR

If you receive an InvalidOperationException error when you run this database application, go to the Download Center at www.microsoft.com/ en-us/download and then search for and install the 2007 Office System Driver: Data Connectivity Components. The 2007 drivers work for newer versions.

STEP 2   Click the Add new button to add a new record to the database table.

A blank record opens and displays 17 as the record number in the navigation toolbar (Figure 10-26).

record 17
displayed

Add new
button

FIGURE 10-26

NextMars/Shutterstock.com

STEP 3   Add a new record by typing Y77 in the Art ID field. Type the rest of the information displayed in Figure 10-27. After the record is complete, click the Save Data button on the BindingNavigator control to save the new record to the original database.

After the new record is typed into the Windows form, the Save Data button is clicked to add the record to the original database table (Figure 10-27).

Save Data
button

data entered for
new record

FIGURE 10-27

NextMars/Shutterstock.com

Delete Records

Users might need to remove information for an artist who is no longer part of the Gaming Art application. To delete an existing record from the database table, follow these steps:

STEP 1   If necessary, click the Start button on the Standard toolbar to execute the Gaming Art application.

The Windows form opens, displaying the first record (Figure 10–28).

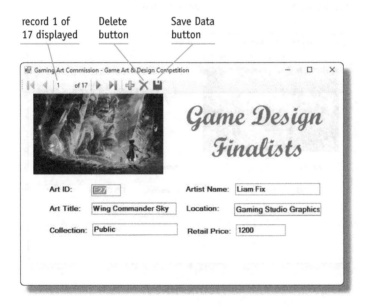

FIGURE 10-28

NextMars/Shutterstock.com

HEADS UP

In the Visual Studio design window, you can right-click any button on the BindingNavigator control to delete the button. For example, if you want the user only to read the information in the Windows form and not be able to add or delete records, you can remove the Add new and Delete buttons from the navigation toolbar.

STEP 2 Use the navigation buttons to move to Tracy Tirrell's record. Her artist record should be deleted because she has decided not to enter artwork in this year's competition. Click the Delete button on the BindingNavigator control to delete her record from the database table. Click the Save Data button to remove the record from the original database.

After the Delete button is clicked, Tracy Tirrell's record is deleted from the Windows form and Song Li's record is displayed (Figure 10-29). Notice that the database now has 16 records instead of 17 records.

16 records in
the database

one record has
been deleted

FIGURE 10-29

NextMars/Shutterstock.com

Select Records from a List

By default, the Data Sources window displays each table item as a TextBox object, but Visual Basic 2017 allows you to change the default TextBox object to another Toolbox object of your choice. In Figure 10-30, Art ID is selected in the Data Sources window, so a list arrow appears to the right of the field. When the list arrow is clicked, a listing of common Toolbox objects is displayed. The Customize option lets you select other Toolbox objects that are not already listed. For example, you can select Customize to add a MaskedTextBox instead of using the default TextBox option if you are including a phone number or zip code.

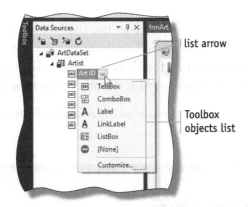

FIGURE 10-30

In Figure 10-29, the only way to navigate through the records is to use the BindingNavigator control or enter a record number. A quicker way to move directly to a particular record is to select it from a ComboBox object. For example, in Figure 10-5 on page 595, the artist's name is displayed in a ComboBox object. The user clicks the list arrow to view the items in the Artist Name list and then clicks a name. The record matching the selected artist's name is displayed immediately.

To change the Toolbox object type, you can complete the following steps:

STEP 1   Select the Artist Name Label and TextBox objects on the Windows form. Press the DELETE key to delete the Artist Name objects from the Windows form. Select the Artist Name table field in the Data Sources window and then click its list arrow.

The Artist Name objects are deleted from the Windows Form object (Figure 10–31). The Artist Name field in the Data Sources window displays a list of possible Toolbox object selections.

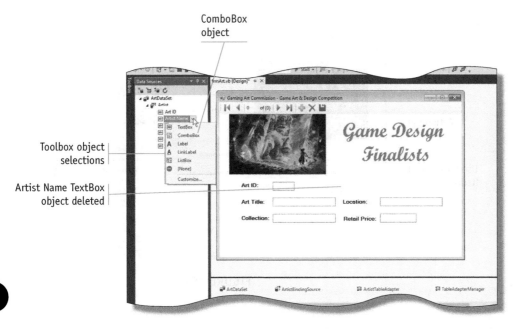

FIGURE 10-31

STEP 2 Click the ComboBox object from the Toolbox object listing for the Artist Name field. Drag the Artist Name field ComboBox object to the original location of the Artist Name TextBox object on the Windows Form object. Change the font size to 10 and bold. Align the ComboBox with the other objects on the Windows form.

The Artist Name ComboBox object is placed on the Windows Form object (Figure 10-32).

FIGURE 10-32

NextMars/Shutterstock.com

STEP 3 To fill the ComboBox object with the names of the artists, the ComboBox object must be bound to the Artist Name field. To bind the items to the ComboBox object, select the Artist Name object on the Windows form and click the Action tag on the Artist Name ComboBox object.

The ComboBox Tasks menu appears (Figure 10-33).

FIGURE 10-33

NextMars/Shutterstock.com

STEP 4   Click the Use Data Bound Items check box on the ComboBox Tasks menu. The Data Binding Mode list is displayed. Click the Data Source list arrow under Data Binding Mode, and then select ArtistBindingSource to connect the table to the ComboBox object. Next, click the Display Member list arrow and then select Artist Name. Click the Value Member list arrow and then click Artist Name in the list. Do not change the Selected Value entry.

The ComboBox object is now bound to the Artist Name field in the Artist table (Figure 10-34).

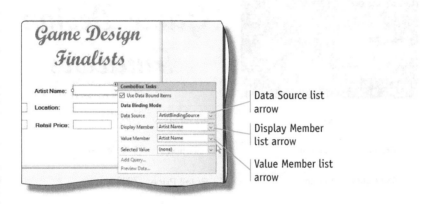

FIGURE 10-34

STEP 5   Click the Start button on the Standard toolbar to run the application. After the Windows form opens, click the list arrow on the Artist Name ComboBox object.

The Artist Name ComboBox object displays the artists' names (Figure 10-35).

FIGURE 10-35

STEP 6 Click Song Li to move directly to the record containing the information for Song Li's artwork.

The application navigates directly to the selected record (Figure 10-36).

FIGURE 10-36

Program beyond the Database Wizard

Although the Database Wizard allows you to view, update, and delete records from a database, other operations, such as calculating an average or determining how many records meet certain criteria, often need to be programmed. For example, in the chapter project, the Gaming Art Commission would like to use a Button object on the Gaming Art Windows form to compute the total retail value of the Game Art & Design collection. The Gaming Art Commission then can calculate and track the current worth of the entire Game Art & Design collection. Code must be written to handle that request.

CONSIDER THIS

Can I add a Try-Catch statement to confirm that the database is available?

In the Form Load event, you can add this code:

```
Try
      ArtistTableAdapter.Fill(ArtDataSet.Artist)
Catch
      MsgBox("The database is not on the USB drive")
End Try
```

Create the OleDbDataAdapter Object

The Database Wizard creates a bridge between the DataSet and the database that contains the data. The bridge that carries the database table information is called an **OleDbDataAdapter.**

The OleDbDataAdapter has two parts. The first part represents a set of data commands programmed using a SQL Select command. **SQL** stands for Structured Query Language, which is the language that communicates with databases. The second part of an OleDbDataAdapter is a path statement to connect to the database that fills the DataSet. The general format for the code that defines the two parts of the OleDbDataAdapter is shown in Figure 10-37.

General Format: OleDbDataAdapter

```
Dim odaName As New OleDb.OleDbDataAdapter(SQL Select command, Path statement)
```

Code:

```
'strSql is a SQL statement that selects all the fields from the Artist table
Dim strSql As String = "SELECT * FROM Artist"

' strPath provides the database type and path of the Art database
Dim strPath As String = "Provider=Microsoft.ACE.OLEDB.12.0 ;" - & "Data
Source=d:\Art.accdb"

Dim odaArtist As New OleDb.OleDbDataAdapter(strSql, strPath)
```

The SQL statement assigned to strSQL("SELECT * FROM Artist") is a query statement that requests that the entire table named Artist is opened for use by the application. The * symbol represents the wildcard symbol, which means all fields within the table are available.

The Path statement assigned to strPath("Provider=Microsoft.ACE.OLEDB.12.0 ;" & "Data Source=d:\Art.accdb") has two portions. The first portion represents the database source. Microsoft.ACE.OLEDB12.0 assigns the drivers needed to create a connection to an Access database. The second portion represents the path of where the database resides.

An instance of the OleDbDataAdapter is assigned to the variable odaArtist. The prefix oda is used for an OleDbDataAdapter.

FIGURE 10-37

Fill a DataTable Object

After the OleDbDataAdapter makes a connection to the database, a **DataTable** is needed to hold the data retrieved from that connection. The DataTable is a crucial object in the ADO.NET library. The DataSet used in the Database Wizard is a collection of DataTable objects. The DataTable is initialized using the dat prefix.

After the DataTable is initialized, it must be filled using the **Fill** command with the data from the selected table. When the DataTable is filled, the appropriate tables and columns are created for the table data. As soon as you connect to the database and fill the DataTable object, the next statement should disconnect the application from the database. To keep the maximum number of connections available, you should keep connections open only as long as necessary. By using the database in disconnected form, the system resources of the computer and network are not overloaded. To disconnect from the database, use the **Dispose** command.

The code in Figure 10-38 can be executed in a program without using the Database Wizard, or you can run the wizard to access the data. The code opens a connection to the Artist table in the Art.accdb Access database on the USB drive. A DataTable named datValue is initialized. The DataTable datValue is then filled with the data from the Artist table. The Dispose procedure closes the connection for the datValue DataTable.

```vb
20
21    Private Sub btnValue_Click(sender As Object, e As EventArgs) Handles btnValue.Click
22        ' strSql is a SQL statement that selects all the fields from the
23        ' Artist table
24
25        Dim strSql As String = "SELECT * FROM Artist"
26
27        'strPath provides the database type and path of the Art database
28        Dim strPath As String = "Provider=Microsoft.ACE.OLEDB.12.0 ;" & "Data Source=D:\Art.accdb"
29        Dim odaArtist As New OleDb.OleDbDataAdapter(strSql, strPath)
30        Dim datValue As New DataTable
31        Dim intCount As Integer
32        Dim decTotalValue As Decimal = 0D
33
34        ' The DataTable named datValue is filled with the table data
35        odaArtist.Fill(datValue)
36        'The connection to the database is disconnected
37        odaArtist.Dispose()
38        For intCount = 0 To datValue.Rows.Count - 1
39            decTotalValue += Convert.ToDecimal(datValue.Rows(intCount)("Retail Price"))
40        Next
41        lblTotalRetailValue.Visible = True
42        lblTotalRetailValue.Text = "The Total Retail Value is " & decTotalValue.ToString("C")
43    End Sub
```

FIGURE 10-38

After the DataTable is created, commands can access the data stored in its rows and columns. The number of rows or columns in the DataTable can be computed with the **Count** property. In the DataTable named datValue, the code entered with IntelliSense in Figure 10-39 determines the number of rows in the DataTable object. The Artist table contains 16 rows numbered 0 to 15.

```
46          Dim intNumberOfRows As Integer
47          intNumberOfRows = datValue.Rows.Count
```

FIGURE 10-39

The number of rows in the code in Figure 10-39 is equal to the number of records in the DataTable object. You can also compute the number of columns in a DataTable by entering the code in Figure 10-40.

```
49          Dim intNumberOfColumns As Integer
50          intNumberOfColumns = datValue.Columns.Count
```

FIGURE 10-40

The DataTable object can also be used with the Rows procedure to access individual fields within a database. For example, if you want to determine the first value in the Retail Price field for the first record, the field name "Retail Price" can be used with the DataTable Rows procedure. In Figure 10-41, the variable decFirstValue is assigned to the first record's retail price.

```
52          Dim decFirstValue As Decimal
53          decFirstValue = Convert.ToDecimal(datValue.Rows(0)("Retail Price"))
```

FIGURE 10-41

In Figure 10-41, the first argument for the Rows procedure (0) references the first row (row zero) in the data table, which is the first record in the table. The entry in the second parentheses ("Retail Price") identifies the field within the first row.

In the original database shown in Figure 10-2 on page 593, if datValue represents the DataTable for the Artist table, the first field value for the Retail Price field is assigned to decFirstValue. The value 1200.00 is assigned to the variable decFirstValue in Figure 10-41.

Using the Rows method and the field name, you can also compute the total or average value of the Game Art & Design collection for all the records in the table. In the chapter project, when the user clicks a button on the Windows Form object, the event handler for the button click computes the retail price of the Game Art & Design collection.

To code a connection with a database and compute the total value of all artwork in the collection, you can complete the following steps:

STEP 1   Download the original Access database file Art.accdb again to overwrite any data you added or deleted from the database. Open the Gaming Art Windows application. Add a Button object named `btnValue` to the Windows Form object and change the Text property to `Total Retail Value`. Change the font size to 12 and the ForeColor property to Green on the Web tab. Set the Size property for the button to `178, 28` and center the Button object horizontally across the form. Below the Button object, add a Label object named `lblTotalRetailValue` with the Text property of 23 "Xs," and then center the text. Change the font size to 12 points. Set the Visible property to False for the lblTotalRetailValue Label object because the Xs should not be displayed when the program begins.

A Button object and Label object are added to the Windows Form object (Figure 10–42).

FIGURE 10-42

STEP 2   Double-click the Total Retail Value button to create the btnValue_Click event handler. To initialize the OleDbDataAdapter, enter the code shown in Figure 10-43 inside the click event. The first variable, strSql, is assigned the SQL statement that queries all the fields in the Artist table. The second variable, strPath, is assigned the database driver for Access and the path to the Art.accdb file. The third variable, odaArtist, is an instance of the OleDbDataAdapter.

Inside the btnValue_Click event, the variables are initialized for the OleDbDataAdapter (Figure 10-43).

```
21    Private Sub btnValue_Click(sender As Object, e As EventArgs) Handles btnValue.Click
22        ' strSql1 is a SQL statement that selects all the fields from the
23        ' Artist table
24
25        Dim strSql As String = "SELECT * FROM Artist"
26
27        'strPath provides the database type and path of the Art database
28        Dim strPath As String = "Provider=Microsoft.ACE.OLEDB.12.0 ;" & "Data Source=D:\Art.accdb"
29        Dim odaArtist As New OleDb.OleDbDataAdapter(strSql, strPath)
```

FIGURE 10-43

STEP 3   After the first three variables are initialized, initialize the rest of the variables needed for the Button object event handler. An instance named datValue is initialized to represent the DataTable object. The intCount variable is used to count through a For loop. The last variable, decTotalValue, will contain the total value of the Game Art & Design collection.

The rest of the variables are initialized (Figure 10-44).

```
30        Dim datValue As New DataTable
31        Dim intCount As Integer
32        Dim decTotalValue As Decimal = 0D
```

FIGURE 10-44

STEP 4   Continuing inside the btnValue_Click event handler, enter the code shown in Figure 10-45 to fill the DataTable with the contents of the Artist table. In the next line of code, use the Dispose method to close the connection.

The DataTable is filled and the connection is disconnected (Figure 10-45).

```
34              ' The DataTable named datValue is filled with the table data
35              odaArtist.Fill(datValue)
36              'The connection to the database is disconnected
37              odaArtist.Dispose()
```

FIGURE 10-45

STEP 5   Enter the code shown in Figure 10-46 to create a For loop to increment through each record in the Artist table. Because the rows are numbered 0 to 15, the upper range is one less than the number of rows in the table, making 16 records. The value in each Retail Price field is added to the value in the decTotalValue variable.

The total Game Art & Design collection value is computed in the For loop (Figure 10-46).

```
38          For intCount = 0 To datValue.Rows.Count - 1
39              decTotalValue += Convert.ToDecimal(datValue.Rows(intCount)("Retail Price"))
40          Next
```

FIGURE 10-46

HEADS UP

You can use the process described beginning in Figure 10-42 with or without a database wizard.

CRITICAL THINKING

How could the code be changed to compute the average?
Add a formula to the code to divide the sum of the values by the number of values.

STEP 6   Enter the code shown in Figure 10-47 to display the total value of the Game Art & Design collection.

The total value of the collection is displayed (Figure 10-47).

```
41              lblTotalRetailValue.Visible = True
42              lblTotalRetailValue.Text = "The Total Retail Value is " & decTotalValue.ToString("C")
43          End Sub
44      End Class
```

FIGURE 10-47

Program Design

The requirements document for the Gaming Art application is shown in
Figure 10-48, and the Use Case Definition document is shown in Figure 10-49.

REQUIREMENTS DOCUMENT

Date:	February 22, 2019
Date Submitted:	
Application Title:	Gaming Art
Purpose:	This Windows application opens a Windows form that displays an Access database with data for local artwork. The data can be viewed, updated, and deleted. The application also computes the total value of the Game Art & Design collection.
Program Procedures:	In a Windows application, the Art Access database file is opened and the user can view, add, and delete records as needed. The user can calculate the total value of the Game Art & Design collection.
Algorithms, Processing, and Conditions:	1. The user first views a Windows application that loads an Access database table, which includes fields for the Art ID, Artist Name, Art Title, Location, Collection (public or private), and Retail Price. A navigation toolbar appears at the top of the Windows form, allowing the user to move from record to record. The Windows form also includes a title and artistic image.
	2. The user can click the Add new button on the navigation toolbar to add a new artist. The record is saved when the user clicks the Save Data button on the navigation toolbar.
	3. The user can click the Delete button on the navigation toolbar to delete an artist's record. The record is permanently deleted when the user clicks the Save Data button on the navigation toolbar.
	4. The user can click the Total Retail Value button to compute the total value of the Game Art & Design collection.
Notes and Restrictions:	The Access database named Art.accdb is located on the USB drive (the D drive).
Comments:	1. The Art.accdb file is available on CengageBrain.com.
	2. Obtain an image for this program from CengageBrain.com. The name of the picture on the Windows form is art.jpg.

FIGURE 10-48

USE CASE DEFINITION

1. The user views the Access database information about local artwork.
2. The user clicks the Add new button to add an artist and clicks the Save Data button to permanently save the new artist to the database.
3. The user clicks the Delete button to delete an artist and clicks the Save Data button to permanently delete the record from the database.
4. The user clicks the Total Retail Value button to display the total value of the Game Art & Design collection.

FIGURE 10-49

Event Planning Document

The event planning document for the Gaming Art Windows application is shown in Figure 10-50.

EVENT PLANNING DOCUMENT

Program Name: Gaming Art Windows Application	Developer: Corinne Hoisington	Object: frmArt	Date: February 22, 2019
OBJECT	**EVENT TRIGGER**	**EVENT PROCESSING**	
frmArt	Load	Fill the DataSet object using the Data Source Configuration Wizard	
btnValue	Click	Initialize the OleDbDataAdapter with the type of database and path statement Fill the data table Disconnect the database For each record in the database: Add each record's value to the total value of the collection Display the Total Retail Value of the collection	

FIGURE 10-50

Guided Program Development

Phase 1: Design the Form

1

● **Create a New Windows Project** Open Visual Studio and then close the Start page. Click the New Project button on the Standard toolbar. Begin a Windows Forms App project and name the project `Gaming Art`.

● **Name the Form Object** Select the Windows Form object. In the Solution Explorer, rename Form1.vb to `frmArt.vb`.

● **Title the Form Object** Select the Windows Form object and change the Text property to `Gaming Art Commission - Game Art & Design Competition`.

● **Build the Top Portion of the Windows Form Object** Using the skills you have learned in this course, complete the top portion of the Windows Form object. For detailed specifications, see Figure 10-8 on page 599.

The top portion of the form is completed (Figure 10-51).

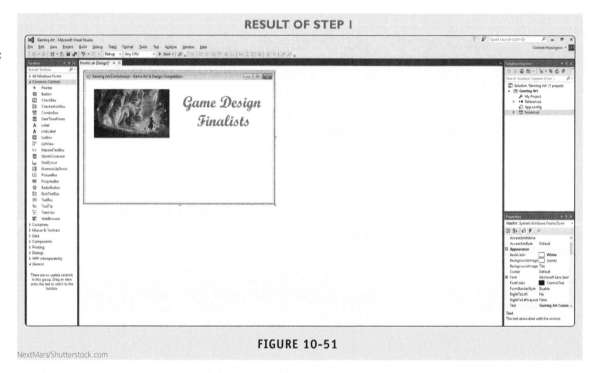

RESULT OF STEP 1

FIGURE 10-51

NextMars/Shutterstock.com

2

● **Create a Connection Using the Data Source Configuration Wizard**
In the Gaming Art project window, click Project on the menu bar, and then click Add New Data Source on the Project menu *(ref: Figure 10-8.)*

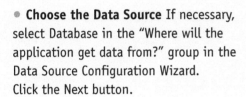

● **Choose the Data Source** If necessary, select Database in the "Where will the application get data from?" group in the Data Source Configuration Wizard. Click the Next button.

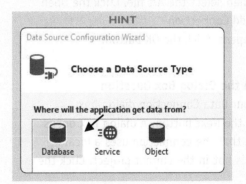

● **Add a Connection** If necessary, click Dataset in the Choose a Database Model dialog box and then click the Next button. Click the New Connection button. In the Add Connection dialog box, click the Change button to select the data source.

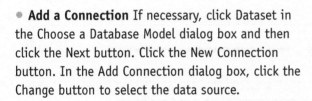

(continues)

● **Change the Data Source** In the Choose Data Source dialog box, select Microsoft Access Database File because the Art database was created in Microsoft Access.

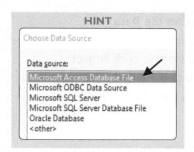

● **Select the Database File** Click the Continue button. Click the Browse button to the right of the Database file name field. Select the USB device on drive D: and then select the Art file. Click the Open button. The Add Connection dialog box reopens. Click the OK button.

● **Respond to the Dialog Box Question** The Choose Your Data Connection dialog box reopens. Click the Next button. A dialog box opens to remind you that the connection uses a local data file that is not in the current project. Click the No button.

● **Save the Connection String** The next dialog box opens and asks which connection your application should use. Click the Next button.

● **Connect to the Artist Table** The Choose Your
Database Objects dialog box opens. Click the expand icon next to the
Tables option. Click the Artist check box to select the Artist table. Click
the Finish button. Click ArtDataSet.xsd to select the DataSet.

The ArtDataSet is displayed in the Solution Explorer (Figure 10-52).

RESULT OF STEP 2

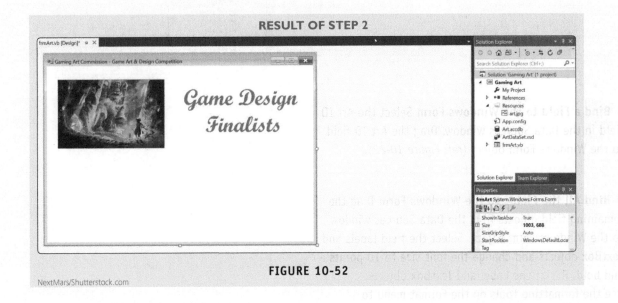

NextMars/Shutterstock.com

FIGURE 10-52

(continues)

3

- **Display the Data Sources Window** Click the View menu, click Other Windows, and then click Data Sources to display the Data Sources window. If necessary, click the Push Pin icon to pin the Data Sources window.

- **Display the Field Names** Click the expand icon next to the Artist table to expand the listing of field names within the table.

HINT

- **Bind a Field to the Windows Form** Select the Art ID field in the Data Sources window. Drag the Art ID field to the Windows Form object (*ref: Figure 10-22*).

- **Bind All the Fields to the Windows Form** Drag the remaining field objects from the Data Sources window to the Windows Form object. Select the field labels and TextBox objects and change the font size to 10 points and bold. Resize the Label and TextBox objects. Use the formatting tools on the Format menu to equally distribute the bound objects. Use the layout shown in Figure 10-53.

• **Add Button and Label Objects** Add a Button object named `btnValue` to the Windows form with the Text property changed to `Total Retail Value`. Change the font size to 12 points and the ForeColor property to Green on the Web tab. Add a Label object named `lblTotalRetailValue` with the Text property of 23 Xs. Change the font size to 12 points. Set the Visible property to False. Center the Label object on the form (see Figure 10-53 for layout).

The Windows Form object is designed (Figure 10-53).

FIGURE 10-53

NextMars/Shutterstock.com

4

• **Execute the Application to Load the Database Data** Click the Start button on the Standard toolbar to run the application. The data fills the Windows form.

• **Use the Navigation Toolbar** With the application running, navigate through the database records. Add a record, and then delete a record.

The Windows form is designed and the database is connected to the application (Figure 10-54).

FIGURE 10-54

NextMars/Shutterstock.com

(continues)

Guided Program Development *continued*

Phase 2: Code the Application

5

- **Code the Comments** Click the View Code button on the Solution Explorer toolbar to begin coding the application. Type the first four standard comments at the top of the code window.

```
HINT
frmArt.vb  -|  X  frmArt.vb [Design]
VB Gaming Art                                    ▾  btnValue                              ▾  ⚡ Click
    1     ⊟'Title:      Gaming Art Windows Application
    2      'Author:     Corinne Hoisington
    3      'Date:       February 22, 2019
    4      'Purpose:    The application displays the game design artists who have entered the Game Art &
    5      '            design competition as an interface for a Microsoft Access database.
```

- **Code the OleDbDataAdapter for the btnValue_Click Event** Notice that the Configuration Wizard created two Sub methods. Double-click the Total Retail Value button in the Design window to create the btnValue_Click event handler. To initialize the OleDbDataAdapter, enter the code shown in the adjacent Hint Screen inside the click event. The first variable, strSql, is assigned the SQL statement that queries all the fields in the Artist table. The second variable, strPath, is assigned the database driver for Access and the path to the Art.accdb file. The third variable, odaArtist, is an instance of the OleDbDataAdapter (*ref: Figure 10-43*).

```
                                        HINT
    6
    7     ⊟Public Class frmArt
    8     ⊟    Private Sub ArtistBindingNavigatorSaveItem_Click(sender As Object, e As EventArgs) Handles ArtistBindingNavigatorSaveItem.Click
    9              Me.Validate()
   10              Me.ArtistBindingSource.EndEdit()
   11              Me.TableAdapterManager.UpdateAll(Me.ArtDataSet)
   12
   13          End Sub
   14
   15     ⊟    Private Sub frmArt_Load(sender As Object, e As EventArgs) Handles MyBase.Load
   16              'TODO: This line of code loads data into the 'ArtDataSet.Artist' table. You can move, or remove it, as needed.
   17              Me.ArtistTableAdapter.Fill(Me.ArtDataSet.Artist)
   18
   19          End Sub
   20
   21     ⊟    Private Sub btnValue_Click(sender As Object, e As EventArgs) Handles btnValue.Click
   22              ' strSql is a SQL statement that selects all the fields from the
   23              ' Artist table
   24
   25              Dim strSql As String = "SELECT * FROM Artist"
   26
   27              'strPath provides the database type and path of the Art database
   28              Dim strPath As String = "Provider=Microsoft.ACE.OLEDB.12.0 ;" & "Data Source=D:\Art.accdb"
   29              Dim odaArtist As New OleDb.OleDbDataAdapter(strSql, strPath)
```

- **Fill the DataTable Object** Inside the btnValue_Click event, after initializing the OleDbDataAdapter, initialize an instance named datValue to represent the DataTable object. Declare the intCount variable for use in counting through a For loop. Initialize the last variable, decTotalValue, which will contain the total value of the Game Art & Design collection. Write the statement to fill the DataTable with the contents of the Artist table. Code the Dispose method to close the open connection.

```
   30              Dim datValue As New DataTable
   31              Dim intCount As Integer
   32              Dim decTotalValue As Decimal = 0D
   33
   34              ' The DataTable name datValue is filled with the table data
   35              odaArtist.Fill(datValue)
   36              'The connection to the database is disconnected
   37              odaArtist.Dispose()
```

● **Calculate and Display the Total Value of the Artwork** Write a For loop statement to increment the count for each record in the Artist table. Because the rows are numbered 0 to 15, the upper range is one less than the number of rows in the table, making 16 records. Write the code within the loop to add the value in each Retail Price field to the value in the decTotalValue variable. Write the code to display the total retail value of the Game Art & Design collection in the lblTotalRetailValue Label object, including the code that makes the Label object visible.

```
38          For intCount = 0 To datValue.Rows.Count - 1
39              decTotalValue += Convert.ToDecimal(datValue.Rows(intCount)("Retail Price"))
40          Next
41          lblTotalRetailValue.Visible = True
42          lblTotalRetailValue.Text = "The Total Retail Value is " & decTotalValue.ToString("C")
43      End Sub
44  End Class
```

The code is completed (Figure 10-55).

RESULT OF STEP 5

```
1   'Title:      Gaming Art Windows Application
2   'Author:     Corinne Hoisington
3   'Date:       February 22, 2019
4   'Purpose:    The application displays the game design artists who have entered the Game Art &
5   '            design competition as an interface for a Microsoft Access database.
6
7   Public Class frmArt
8       Private Sub ArtistBindingNavigatorSaveItem_Click(sender As Object, e As EventArgs) Handles ArtistBindingNavigatorSaveItem.Click
9           Me.Validate()
10          Me.ArtistBindingSource.EndEdit()
11          Me.TableAdapterManager.UpdateAll(Me.ArtDataSet)
12
13      End Sub
14
15      Private Sub frmArt_Load(sender As Object, e As EventArgs) Handles MyBase.Load
16          'TODO: This line of code loads data into the 'ArtDataSet.Artist' table. You can move, or remove it, as needed.
17          Me.ArtistTableAdapter.Fill(Me.ArtDataSet.Artist)
18
19      End Sub
20
21      Private Sub btnValue_Click(sender As Object, e As EventArgs) Handles btnValue.Click
22          ' strSql is a SQL statement that selects all the fields from the
23          ' Artist table
24
25          Dim strSql As String = "SELECT * FROM Artist"
26
27          'strPath provides the database type and path of the Art database
28          Dim strPath As String = "Provider=Microsoft.ACE.OLEDB.12.0 ;" & "Data Source=D:\Art.accdb"
29          Dim odaArtist As New OleDb.OleDbDataAdapter(strSql, strPath)
30          Dim datValue As New DataTable
31          Dim intCount As Integer
32          Dim decTotalValue As Decimal = 0D
33
34          ' The DataTable name datValue is filled with the table data
35          odaArtist.Fill(datValue)
36          'The connection to the database is disconnected
37          odaArtist.Dispose()
38          For intCount = 0 To datValue.Rows.Count - 1
39              decTotalValue += Convert.ToDecimal(datValue.Rows(intCount)("Retail Price"))
40          Next
41          lblTotalRetailValue.Visible = True
42          lblTotalRetailValue.Text = "The Total Retail Value is " & decTotalValue.ToString("C")
43      End Sub
44  End Class
45
```

FIGURE 10-55

Summary

In this chapter, you have learned to create a Windows application that uses database files and ADO.NET.

Knowledge Check

1. ADO.NET can only work with Microsoft Access databases. True or False?
2. What is the name of a unique field that must be present in each relational database?
3. Define ADO.
4. Define SQL.
5. A database can only be stored on a local computer. True or False?
6. What is a DataSet object?
7. Does a row in a database table represent a record or a field?
8. Name five types of objects that can be dragged from a data field in the Data Sources window to the Windows Form object without using the Customize option.
9. What is the object name of the navigation toolbar?
10. When you add a record to a database using the Add new button on the navigation toolbar, the record is not added to the original database. What action is needed to add the record to the original data source?
11. How many records are contained in the database table named SouthernStates, as displayed in Figure 10-56?

APPROXIMATE POPULATION OF THE SOUTHERN STATES PROJECTED FOR 2025			
AutoNumber	**State Name**	**State Capital**	**Population**
1	Florida	Tallahassee	20,066,000
2	Georgia	Atlanta	10,962,000
3	South Carolina	Columbia	4,574,000
4	North Carolina	Raleigh	9,916,000
5	Virginia	Richmond	8,165,000
6	Alabama	Montgomery	5,224,000
7	Louisiana	Baton Rouge	5,111,000
8	Tennessee	Nashville	7,249,000
9	West Virginia	Charleston	1,864,000
10	Mississippi	Jackson	3,413,000
11	Kentucky	Frankfort	4,314,000
Source: http://www.census.gov/population/projections/state/stpjpop.txt			

FIGURE 10-56

12. In the table in Figure 10-56, which field is the primary key?

13. For the table in Figure 10-56, write a statement that references the capital of Alabama and assign the value to the strCapital variable.

14. What properties under the Data Binding Mode must you set when you bind a ComboBox object to a Windows form?

15. What command disconnects a database connection?

16. What procedure places data in the DataTable?

17. Write a line of code to initialize a String variable named strCafe to a Select SQL statement that would select all the fields from a table named Java.

18. Which wildcard symbol is used in a Select statement?

19. What does the wildcard symbol mean in the Select statement?

20. Write the statement that would fill a DataTable object named datPlanets if an instance of the OleDbData-Adapter is named odaCollection.

Debugging Exercises

1. The code shown in Figure 10-57 is designed to increment through each row in a database table. Correct the error in the code.

```
For intRecordCount = 0 To datPeople.Rows.Count
    ' Processing statements
Next
```

FIGURE 10-57

2. Correct the line of code shown in Figure 10-58:

```
strNumberOfRows = datCityName.Rows.Count
```

FIGURE 10-58

3. Rewrite the code shown in Figure 10-59 correctly:

```
strNumberOfRows = Convert.ToString(datBeachName.Rows(6)(Beach))
```

FIGURE 10-59

Program Analysis

1. Write a command that assigns an Access database named tinyhouses.accdb and a path located on the D drive to a string named strConnect for use later in an instance of an OleDbDataAdapter.

2. Consider the database table named TopMalls shown in Figure 10-60. If the instance of the DataTable is named datShop, what value would the statement in Figure 10-61 assign to the variable intCount?

Mall Number	Mall	Location
304	Mall of America	Minneapolis, MN
402	King of Prussia	Philadelphia, PA
503	Sawgrass Mills	Sunrise, FL
606	The Galleria	Houston, TX
703	Via Bellagio	Las Vegas, NV
801	The Grove	Los Angeles, CA

FIGURE 10-60

```
intCount = datShop.Rows.Count
```

FIGURE 10-61

3. Using the database table in Figure 10-60, what value would be assigned to strMallName in the code in Figure 10-62?

```
strMallName = Convert.ToString(datShop.Rows(1)("Mall"))
```

FIGURE 10-62

4. Using the database table in Figure 10-60, what value would be assigned to strLocation in the code in Figure 10-63?

```
strLocation = Convert.ToString(datShop.Rows(2)("Location"))
```

FIGURE 10-63

Complete one or more of the following case programming assignments. Submit the program and materials you create to your instructor. The level of difficulty is indicated for each assignment.

● = Easiest
●● = Intermediate
●●● = Challenging

Instructor's Note: If you open a student's project that was created with a different path to the Access database, open the Solution Explorer of their program and then open the app.config file. Change the following statement's path statement to the path of your local database: `<add name="Gaming_Art.My.MySettings.ArtConnection String"connectionString="Provider=Microsoft.ACE.OLEDB.12.0;Data Source=D:\Art. accdb"providerName="System.Data.OleDb"/`

1 ●
ANTIQUE CAR COMPETITION DATABASE

Design a Windows application and write the code that will execute according to the program requirements in Figure 10-64 and the Use Case Definition in Figure 10-65. Before writing the code, create an event planning document for each event in the program. The completed Windows application and other objects in the user interface are shown in Figure 10-66.

REQUIREMENTS DOCUMENT

Date:	October 30, 2019
Date Submitted:	
Application Title:	Antique Car Competition Database
Purpose:	This Windows application opens an Access database that contains information about the top 10 finalists competing in the Antique Car Show this Saturday. The data in the database can be viewed, updated, and deleted.
Program Procedures:	In a Windows application, the Access database file is opened and the user can view, add, and delete records as needed.
Algorithms, Processing, and Conditions:	1. The user first views a Windows application that loads an Access database table named Car, which includes the Contestant ID, Car Year, Car Model, Owner Name, and Hometown. A navigation toolbar appears at the top of the Windows form, allowing the user to move from record to record. The Windows form also includes a title and an image.
	2. The user can click the Add new button on the navigation toolbar to add a car. The record is saved when the user clicks the Save Data button on the navigation toolbar.
	3. The user can click the Delete button on the navigation toolbar to delete a car. The record is permanently deleted when the user clicks the Save Data button on the navigation toolbar.
Notes and Restrictions:	The Car.accdb file is located on the USB drive (the D drive).
Comments:	1. The Car.accdb file is available on CengageBrain.com.
	2. Obtain an image for this program from CengageBrain.com. The name of the picture on the Windows form is car.

FIGURE 10-64

(continues)

Antique Car Competition Database

USE CASE DEFINITION

1. The user views the Access database, which displays the car year, model, and owner information.
2. The user clicks the Add new button to add a new car and clicks the Save Data button to save the item to the database.
3. The user clicks the Delete button to delete a car and permanently deletes the record from the database by clicking the Save Data button.

FIGURE 10-65

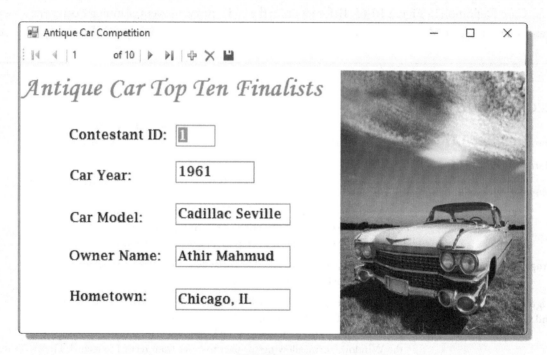

iStockphoto.com/BillPhilpot

FIGURE 10-66

2

TINY HOUSE BUILDERS DATABASE

Design a Windows application and write the code that will execute according to the program requirements in Figure 10-67 and the Use Case Definition in Figure 10-68. Before writing the code, create an event planning document for each event in the program. The completed Windows application and other objects in the user interface are shown in Figure 10-69.

REQUIREMENTS DOCUMENT

Date:	August 1, 2019
Date Submitted:	
Application Title:	Tiny House Builders Database
Purpose:	This Windows application opens an Access database in a Windows form that displays information about 13 builders of tiny houses. The data in the database can be viewed, updated, and deleted.
Program Procedures:	In a Windows application, the Access database file is opened and the user can view, add, and delete records as needed.
Algorithms, Processing, and Conditions:	1. The user first views a Windows application that loads an Access database table, which includes the builder ID, builder, tiny house specialty, email address, and whether the builder prefers to build on-site. A navigation toolbar appears at the top of the Windows form, allowing the user to move from record to record. The Windows form also includes a title and a graphic image.
	2. The user can click the Add new button on the navigation toolbar to add a new builder to the database. The record is saved when the user clicks the Save Data button on the navigation toolbar.
	3. The user can click the Delete button on the navigation toolbar to delete a builder's record. The record is permanently deleted when the user clicks the Save Data button on the navigation toolbar.
Notes and Restrictions:	The TinyHouses.accdb file is located on the USB drive (the D drive).
Comments:	1. The TinyHouses.accdb file is available on CengageBrain.com.
	2. Obtain an image for this program from CengageBrain.com. The name of the picture on the Windows form is builder.

FIGURE 10-67

(continues)

Tiny House Builders Database

USE CASE DEFINITION

1. The user views the Access database information, which displays the tiny house builders and their specialty.
2. The user clicks the Add new button to add a new builder and clicks the Save Data button to save the item to the database.
3. The user clicks the Delete button to delete a builder record and permanently deletes it from the database by clicking the Save Data button.

FIGURE 10-68

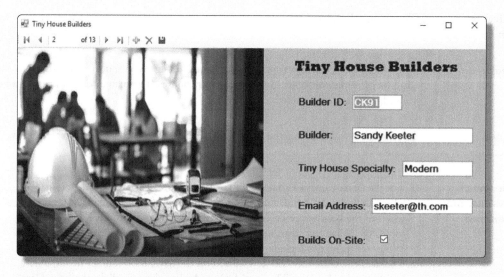

FIGURE 10-69

indypendenz/Shutterstock.com

3

YOUTH LEAGUE SOCCER TEAM DATABASE

Design a Windows application and write the code that will execute according to the program requirements in Figure 10-70. Before designing the user interface, create a Use Case Definition. Before writing the code, create an event planning document for each event in the program.

REQUIREMENTS DOCUMENT

Date:	May 13, 2019
Date Submitted:	
Application Title:	Youth League Soccer Team Database
Purpose:	This Windows application opens an Access database that displays information about 22 boys and girls (ages 12–14) who are playing in the National Youth League Soccer championship. The data in the database can be viewed, updated, and deleted in the Windows form. The application computes in three separate counts the number of team members who are 12, 13, or 14 years old, and calculates the average age of the team.
Program Procedures:	In a Windows application, the Access database file is opened and the user can view, add, and delete records as needed. You can also display the total number of players of each age (12, 13, or 14) in the database.
Algorithms, Processing, and Conditions:	1. The user first views a Windows application that loads an Access database table, which includes the player's number, first name, last name, parent's name, city, state, zip, phone, and age. A navigation toolbar appears at the top of the Windows form, allowing the user to move from record to record. The Windows form also includes a title.
	2. The user can click the Add new button on the navigation toolbar to add a new player to the team. The record is saved when the user clicks the Save Data button on the navigation toolbar.
	3. The user can click the Delete button on the navigation toolbar to delete a player. The record is permanently deleted when the user clicks the Save Data button on the navigation toolbar.
	4. The user can click the Ages Button object to compute the total number of team members who are 12, 13, or 14 years old. The user can also compute the average age of the team.
Notes and Restrictions:	The Soccer.accdb file is located on the USB drive (the D drive).
Comments:	The Soccer.accdb file is available on CengageBrain.com.

FIGURE 10-70

ONLINE DEGREES

Design a Windows application and write the code that will execute according to the program requirements in Figure 10-71. Before designing the user interface, create a Use Case Definition. Before writing the code, create an event planning document for each event in the program.

REQUIREMENTS DOCUMENT

Date:	March 9, 2019
Date Submitted:	
Application Title:	Online Degrees
Purpose:	This Windows application opens an Access database that displays information about 36 online college majors in a Windows form. The data in the database can be viewed, updated, and deleted. The application also computes the total number of students attending the college online. The user can select a major from a ComboBox list and the application will display the percentage of students participating in that major.
Program Procedures:	In a Windows application, the Access database file is opened and the user can view, add, and delete records as needed. The total student population and number of students in a particular major can also be displayed.
Algorithms, Processing, and Conditions:	1. The user first views a Windows application that loads an Access database table, which includes fields for the department, college major, and number of students in that major. A navigation toolbar appears at the top of the Windows form, allowing the user to move from record to record. The Windows form also includes a title.
	2. The user can click the Add new button on the navigation toolbar to add a new major to the online college. The record is saved when the user clicks the Save Data button on the navigation toolbar.
	3. The user can click the Delete button on the navigation toolbar to delete a major. The record is permanently deleted when the user clicks the Save Data button on the navigation toolbar.
	4. The user can click the Find Total Button object to compute the total number of students enrolled in each major.
	5. The user can select a major from a ComboBox list and the application will display the number of students at the college participating in that major.
Notes and Restrictions:	The College.accdb file is located on the USB drive (the D drive).
Comments:	1. The College.accdb file is available on CengageBrain.com.
	2. Use a graphic image you obtain from the web.

FIGURE 10-71

Case Programming Assignments

5 ●●● HEALTHY EATING

Create a requirements document and a Use Case Definition document, and then design a Windows application based on the case project shown in Figure 10-72. Before writing the code, create an event planning document for each event in the program.

A nutritionist often has patients create a food diary to see the amount of calories they consume each day. Create an Access database with the following fields: an item number as an AutoNumber field, food consumed, and number of calories. On the web, research the amount of calories each food contains. Enter calorie data into the database for all food and beverages consumed in one day (at least 12 items). Develop a Windows application that displays the Access database table of calories consumed in one day. The application will compute the total number of calories consumed. The U.S. Department of Health estimates that the average requirement for daily calorie intake is 1,940 for women and 2,550 for men. The application should ask whether the user is male or female. When the total number of calories is displayed, the percentage of calories consumed above or below the recommended daily intake should also be shown.

FIGURE 10-72

Case Programming Assignments

6 ●●● CREATE A VB INTERFACE FOR YOUR SPRING BREAK VACATION

Create a requirements document and a Use Case Definition document, and then design a Windows application based on the case project shown in Figure 10-73. Before writing the code, create an event planning document for each event in the program.

> Create an Access database with the following information about 10 of your friends who will be joining you on a vacation for spring break. Add each friend's first name, last name, address, city, state, zip, and how much each has paid toward the shared rental of the AirBnB home. Create a database application in Visual Basic that uses a ComboBox object for last names. Compute and display the total cost that has been paid for the home rental so far. Use an image and allow users to add and delete friends from the database.

FIGURE 10-73

CHAPTER 11

Multiple Classes and Inheritance

OBJECTIVES

You will have mastered the material in this chapter when you can:

- Use the TabIndex property

- Edit input, including MaskedTextBox, TextBox, and ComboBox objects

- Describe the three-tiered program structure

- Understand a class

- Create a class

- Instantiate an object

- Pass arguments when instantiating an object

- Write a class constructor

- Call a procedure in a separate class

- Code a base class and a subclass to incorporate inheritance

- Call procedures found in a base class and a subclass

- Write overridable and overrides procedures

- Create and write a comma-delimited text file

- Run the Performance Profiler

Introduction

In previous chapters, you have learned that a class is a named group of program code. Within a class such as Form1, you can define attributes, Sub procedures, and Function procedures. The classes you have used thus far have either been generated by the design feature of Visual Basic or were used from a library of classes supplied by Visual Studio 2017. In this chapter, you will define a class in code and will develop the code in the class to help complete the chapter project.

When you define classes, you have the option of using a feature called inheritance, which is common to object-oriented programming languages such as Visual Basic. Inheritance allows one class, called a subclass, to use attributes and procedures defined in another class, called a base class.

Finally, when you define your own classes, you have the opportunity to design a three-tiered structure for your program so it is more reliable, more robust, and more easily understood. The sample program in this chapter uses the three-tiered program structure.

Chapter Project

The sample chapter project features the College Registration Costs window displayed in Figure 11-1.

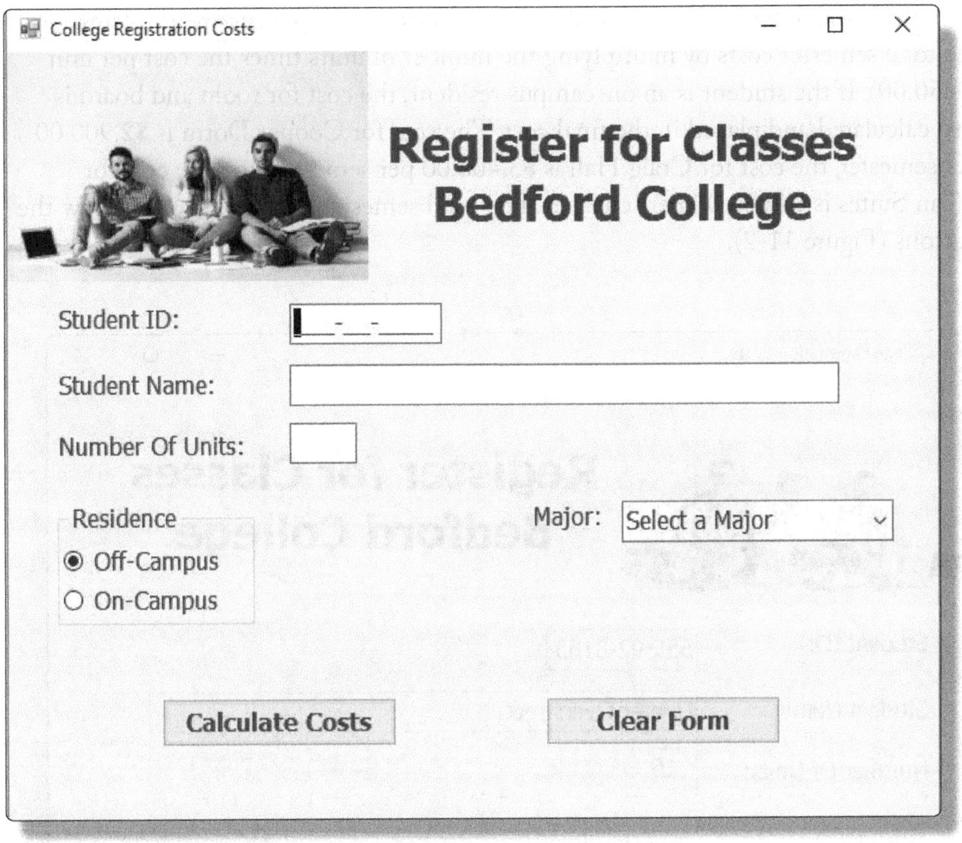

FIGURE 11-1

iStockphoto.com/mediaphotos

In the window shown in Figure 11-1, a student or a worker assisting the student enters the student ID number, the student name, and the number of units for which the student is registering. The user also identifies whether the student is living off campus or on campus, the housing and board an on-campus student is using, and the student's major.

When the user clicks the Calculate Costs button, the application calculates the total semester costs by multiplying the number of units times the cost per unit ($450.00). If the student is an on-campus resident, the cost for room and board is also calculated and placed in the final cost. The cost for Cooper Dorm is $2,900.00 per semester, the cost for Craig Hall is $3,400.00 per semester, and the cost for Julian Suites is $4,000.00 per semester. The total semester costs are shown below the buttons (Figure 11-2).

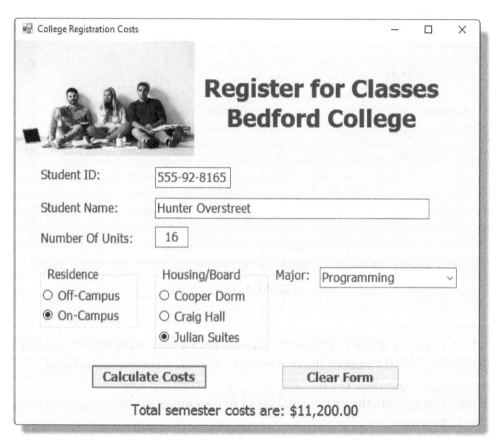

FIGURE 11-2

iStockphoto.com/mediaphotos

The user is required to enter valid values for each of the items on the registration form. If the user does not enter a value or enters an invalid value, such as a nonnumeric value in the Number of Units text box, a message box is displayed to prompt the user to enter a valid value (Figure 11-3).

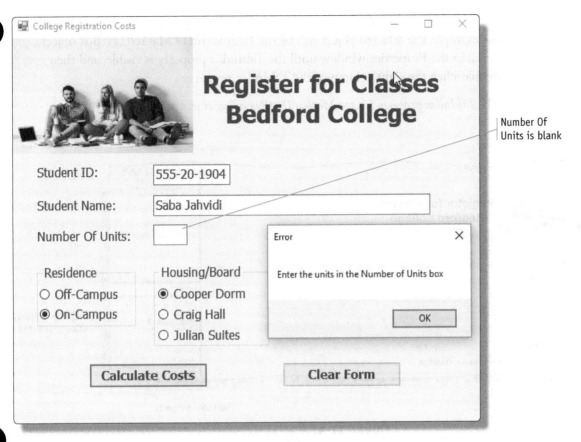

Number Of
Units is blank

FIGURE 11-3

iStockphoto.com/mediaphotos

In Figure 11-3, the user failed to enter the number of units, so the message box directs the user to enter the number.

In addition to calculating the total semester costs, this program creates a log on disk for the students whose costs have been calculated. This log is kept as a text file. The program must write records in the text file as students use the program.

Use the TabIndex Property in the User Interface

The user interface in the College Registration Costs program does not contain any objects that you have not seen in previous programs. However, the program does implement a new property that users often find useful.

When users enter data into a Windows Form object, they usually enter the data in sequence on the form. For example, in Figure 11-2, the user can enter the Student ID first, followed by the Student Name, then the Number of Units, and so on. Often, users prefer to press the tab key to move the insertion point from one object on the Windows Form object to the next. To specify the sequence of objects that will be selected when the user presses the TAB key, you use the TabIndex property. To implement the TabIndex property for the Windows Form object in Figure 11-2, you can complete the following steps:

STEP 1   Select the object that will be selected when program execution begins. In the example, the selected object will be the txtStudentID MaskedTextBox object. Scroll in the Properties window until the TabIndex property is visible, and then double-click the right column of the TabIndex property.

The TabIndex property for the MaskedTextBox object is selected (Figure 11-4).

Student ID object is selected

TabIndex property value is selected

TabIndex property

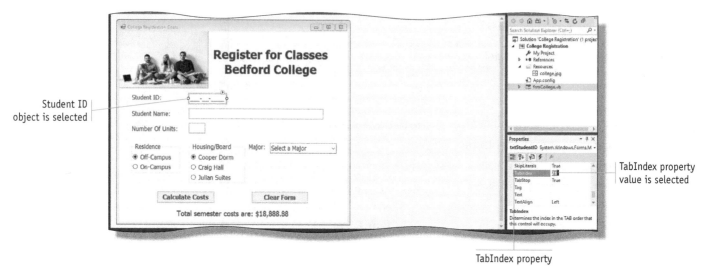

FIGURE 11-4

iStockphoto.com/mediaphotos

STEP 2   Type 1 and then press the ENTER key.

The value 1 in the TabIndex property of an object indicates that the object will be selected when the program begins execution (Figure 11-5). When program execution begins, the insertion point will be located in the txtStudentID MaskedTextBox object.

TabIndex property value changed to 1

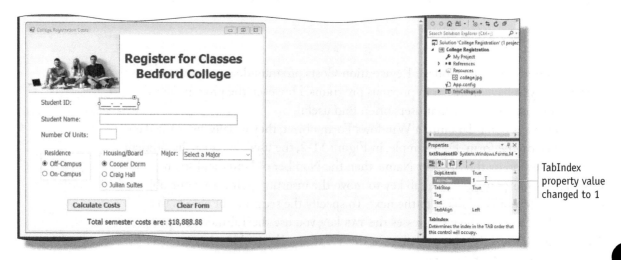

iStockphoto.com/mediaphotos

FIGURE 11-5

STEP 3   Select the object that should be selected when the user presses the tab key. In the sample program, the txtStudentName TextBox object should be selected. Double-click the right column of the TabIndex property for the txtStudentName TextBox object, type 2, and then press the ENTER key.

The TabIndex value for the txtStudentName object is set to 2 in the Properties window (Figure 11-6). When the user enters the Student ID value and presses the TAB key, the insertion point will be in the Student Name text box. Using these same techniques, you can continue to identify objects on the Windows Form object that will be selected when the user presses the TAB key.

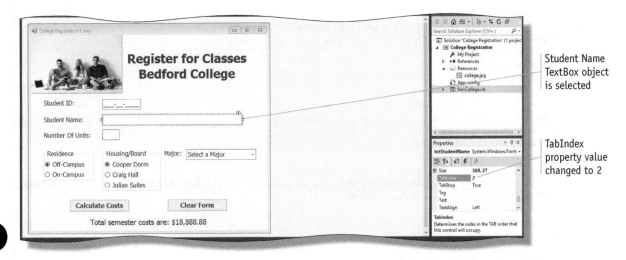

FIGURE 11-6

iStockphoto.com/mediaphotos

Edit Input Data

Like other applications in this book, the data that users enter in the College Registration Costs program must be checked to ensure its validity. When the user clicks the Calculate Costs button, the following items must be checked:

1. Student ID: The Student ID object is a masked text box, and the mask is for the Social Security number in the same layout, so the mask ensures that the user can enter only numbers. However, the Social Security mask does not ensure that the user enters all nine numbers. Therefore, a check must be included in the program to require the user to enter all nine numeric digits.

2. Student Name: The program must ensure that the user enters characters in this TextBox object. In addition, spaces cannot be entered instead of actual alphabetic characters.

3. Number of Units: The user must enter a numeric value from 1 through 24 for the number of units the student is taking.

4. Major: The user must select a major from the list in the Major ComboBox object.

The code to implement these editing requirements is shown in Figure 11-7.

```
13
14          Dim objStudent As Student
15          Dim objOnCampusStudent As OnCampusStudent
16          Dim InputError As Boolean = False
17
18          ' Is student ID entered properly
19          If txtStudentID.MaskFull = False Then
20              MsgBox("Enter your Student ID in the Student ID box", , "Error")
21              txtStudentID.Clear()
22              txtStudentID.Focus()
23              InputError = True
24              ' Is student name entered properly
25          ElseIf txtStudentName.TextLength < 1 Or txtStudentName.Text < "A" Then
26              MsgBox("Enter your name in the Student Name box", , "Error")
27              txtStudentName.Clear()
28              txtStudentName.Focus()
29              InputError = True
30              ' Is number of units entered properly
31          ElseIf Not IsNumeric(txtNumberOfUnits.Text) Then
32              MsgBox("Enter the units in the Number of Units box", , "Error")
33              txtNumberOfUnits.Clear()
34              txtNumberOfUnits.Focus()
35              InputError = True
36              ' Has 1-24 units been entered
37          ElseIf Convert.ToInt32(txtNumberOfUnits.Text) < 1 Or Convert.ToInt32(txtNumberOfUnits.Text) > 24 Then
38              MsgBox("Units must be 1 - 24", , "Error")
39              txtNumberOfUnits.Clear()
40              txtNumberOfUnits.Focus()
41              InputError = True
42              ' Has a major been selected
43          ElseIf cboMajor.SelectedIndex < 0 Then
44              MsgBox("Please select a major", , "Error")
45              cboMajor.Focus()
46              InputError = True
47          End If
```

FIGURE 11-7

In Figure 11-7, on line 16, a Boolean variable named InputError is defined and given the value False. This variable will be set to a value of True if an error is found in the editing statements. If any input area contains an error, the registration costs will not be calculated.

The editing checks are completed within an If...Else If statement. Because of the checks in this statement, each of the fields must contain valid data before the next field is checked; for example, until the Student ID field contains valid data, the Student Name field is not checked. This approach ensures that each field will contain valid data before the registration costs are calculated.

To ensure that the Student ID masked text box contains all nine numeric digits, the MaskFull property is tested, as shown in Figure 11-8.

```
18              ' Is student ID entered properly
19         □    If txtStudentID.MaskFull = False Then
20                  MsgBox("Enter your Student ID in the Student ID box", , "Error")
21                  txtStudentID.Clear()
22                  txtStudentID.Focus()
23                  InputError = True
```

FIGURE 11-8

The MaskFull property identifies whether all digits have been entered into the mask. For the Student ID, if all nine numeric digits have been entered into the masked text box, the property will be true; otherwise, the property will be false. If the MaskFull property is false, a message box will be displayed that directs the user to enter the student ID in the Student ID box. In addition, the masked text box is cleared, the focus is placed in the masked text box, and the InputError Boolean variable is set to True, indicating an error occurred.

If the Student ID field is correct, the next check is to ensure that the Student Name text box contains data. The Else…If statement to check the Student Name text box is shown in Figure 11-9.

```
24              ' Is student name entered properly
25              ElseIf txtStudentName.TextLength < 1 Or txtStudentName.Text < "A" Then
26                  MsgBox("Enter your name in the Student Name box", , "Error")
27                  txtStudentName.Clear()
28                  txtStudentName.Focus()
29                  InputError = True
```

FIGURE 11-9

The If statement tests whether the length of the data in the text box is less than 1 and whether the first character entered is less than the letter A. If the length is less than 1, no data was entered in the text box. If the first character is less than A, then either a space or a special character was entered as the first character, both of which are invalid. If either of these conditions is true, a message box appears and instructs the user to enter a student name, the text box is cleared, focus is placed back on the Student Name text box, and the InputError Boolean variable is set to True.

CRITICAL THINKING

If you compared txtStudentName.Text < "a", would that guarantee that the entry is a valid name? No. If the student entered a capital letter, the condition would be true because of the ASCII value chart (see Appendix A).

If the Student Name text box contains valid data, the Number of Units TextBox object is checked to ensure that it contains a numeric value from 1 through 24. To make this check, two If statements are required: one to check for numeric data (line 31 in Figure 11-10) and one to ensure that the value is 1 through 24 (lines 37–38 in Figure 11-10). If either of these tests finds an error, a message box is displayed again, the TextBox object is cleared, the focus is placed in the text box, and the InputError variable is set to True.

```
30              ' Is number of units entered properly
31          ElseIf Not IsNumeric(txtNumberOfUnits.Text) Then
32              MsgBox("Enter the units in the Number of Units box", , "Error")
33              txtNumberOfUnits.Clear()
34              txtNumberOfUnits.Focus()
35              InputError = True
36              ' Has 1-24 units been entered
37          ElseIf Convert.ToInt32(txtNumberOfUnits.Text) < 1 Or Convert.ToInt32(txtNumberOfUnits.Text) > 24 Then
38              MsgBox("Units must be 1 - 24", , "Error")
39              txtNumberOfUnits.Clear()
40              txtNumberOfUnits.Focus()
41              InputError = True
```

FIGURE 11-10

The last data-editing step is to ensure that the user selected a major in the Major ComboBox object (Figure 11-11).

```
42              ' Has a major been selected
43          ElseIf cboMajor.SelectedIndex < 0 Then
44              MsgBox("Please select a major", , "Error")
45              cboMajor.Focus()
46              InputError = True
47          End If
```

FIGURE 11-11

As you have learned, when testing for a selection in a ComboBox object, the SelectedIndex property will contain the value −1 if a selection has not been made and will contain the index value of the selected entry if a selection has been made. If the SelectedIndex property is less than zero, then a selection has not been made, so a message box displays an error message, the focus is placed on the ComboBox object, and the InputError Boolean variable is set to true.

If all tests are passed, the processing to compute the registration costs and other processing can occur.

Program Structure Using Classes

In previous programs, the Form class has been the basis of the program. It presented the user interface and has contained the Visual Basic statements that have processed data the user entered. In some programs, multiple procedures have been included in the class to complete the required processing.

When programs become larger and more complex, often you will divide the necessary processing into classes. This can have several benefits:

* The program is easier to read, understand, and maintain.
* A class can be used in more than one program for the same purpose. For example, the Button class that is used to create buttons in the user interface is used each time a Button object is placed on the Windows Form object.
* The processing accomplished in a class is separated from other classes, making the program easier to maintain and less prone to error.
* Variables defined in one class can be hidden from processing in other classes, so there is less likelihood of programming errors. Controlling the use of these variables (often called attributes or properties) by other classes reduces the inadvertent or purposeful inappropriate use of the attributes.

The concept of separating processing and hiding data within specific classes is called **encapsulation,** and is a major contributor to reliable and robust programs. Encapsulation is one of the fundamental principles of object-oriented programming. Encapsulation wraps related data and functions into a single entity.

Why should I use encapsulation?

* Encapsulation gives maintainability, flexibility, and extensibility to your code.

* Encapsulation provides a way to protect data from accidental corruption by keeping portions of the code in separate classes.

* Encapsulation hides information within an object.

CONSIDER THIS

When developing programs with multiple classes, a starting point for determining what classes should appear in a program is the three-tiered program structure. This structure specifies that a program is divided into three separate tiers: Presentation, Business, and Persistence (see Figure 11-12).

Presentation Tier	Business Tier	Persistence Tier
User Interface, Forms	Logic, Calculations	Data Storage (Files and Databases)

FIGURE 11-12

The **presentation tier** contains the classes that display information for the user and accept user input. In many programs, the presentation tier consists of one or more forms and the objects placed on the forms. In a Web application, the presentation tier is the web form and webpage that appear to the user. In addition, the processing in the presentation tier ensures that valid data is entered into the program for processing in the business tier.

The **business tier** contains the logic and calculations that must occur to fulfill the requirements of the program. The class(es) in the business tier generally use data entered by users and data obtained from storage to perform the logic and calculations. The business tier is named for the fact that it implements the "business rules" required for the application.

The **persistence tier**, sometimes called the **data access tier**, contains the code required to read and write data from permanent storage. Data that is stored in a file or database on disk often is called persistent data because it remains after the program ends.

When designing a program using the three-tiered approach, a primary rule is that classes in the presentation tier can communicate only with classes in the business tier. They never can communicate with classes in the persistence tier. In the same manner, classes in the persistence tier cannot communicate with classes in the presentation tier.

By following this rule, a program is much easier to maintain if changes must be made. For example, if a program currently writes data to a text file, such as in the College Registration Costs program in this chapter, and a decision is made to write the data in a database instead, only the class(es) in the persistence tier must be examined and changed. The user interface classes should have nothing to do with how data is stored. Therefore, the developer can be confident that if the correct changes are made to the persistence classes, the program will run properly regardless of the processing in the presentation classes.

Similarly, the business classes need not be concerned with how the data is obtained or stored. While the business classes will decide what data is needed and what data should be written to storage, only the persistence classes will actually read or write data.

This same thinking holds true for the separation of the business and presentation tiers. The classes in the business tier, where the logic and calculations occur, should not have to be concerned with the functionality of the user interface, nor should the user interface classes be concerned with how the data is manipulated by the business classes.

By placing classes in one of the three tiers depending on each class's function, the program becomes much easier to design, develop, and maintain.

CRITICAL THINKING

In another programming class, my instructor called the three tiers a three-layer approach. Is this the same thing?
Yes. Tiers or layers are references to the same separately constructed application. A wedding cake is said to have tiers while a birthday cake is said to have layers, but the words mean the same thing.

Sample Program Classes

The College Registration Costs program in this chapter uses the three-tiered approach. The classes in each of the tiers are as follows:

1. Presentation tier: The presentation tier contains the frmCollege class. This class displays the user interface in a Windows Form object and edits the user input data to ensure its validity.

2. Business tier: The business tier contains two classes: the Student class and the OnCampusStudent class. The Student class contains data for each registered student and calculates the registration costs for some students. The OnCampusStudent class is used for registered students who live in on-campus residence halls.

3. Persistence tier: The persistence tier consists of one class, StudentCostsFile, which creates and writes the Student Costs File.

Create a Class

The class in the presentation tier, the frmCollege class, is created when the new Windows application is started. The other classes are created using the technique shown in the following steps:

STEP 1 With Visual Studio open and a new Windows Application project started, right-click the project name in the Solution Explorer window and then point to Add on the shortcut menu.

The shortcut menu is displayed (Figure 11-13). When you point to the Add menu item, the Add submenu is also displayed.

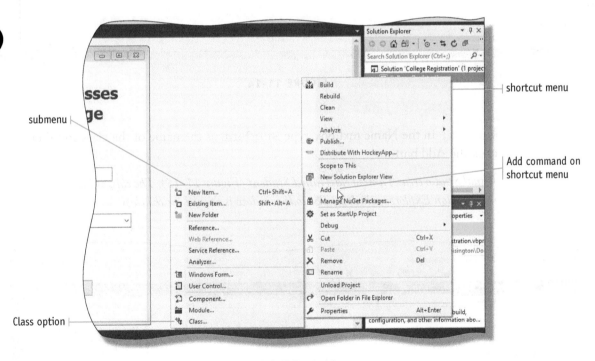

FIGURE 11-13

STEP 2 Click Class on the Add submenu.

The Add New Item dialog box is displayed (Figure 11-14). Class is selected as an installed template in the middle pane.

FIGURE 11-14

STEP 3 In the Name text box, type Student as the name of the class and then click the Add button.

Visual Studio creates a new class called Student (Figure 11-15). The class is identified in the Solution Explorer window. The code window is opened for the class.

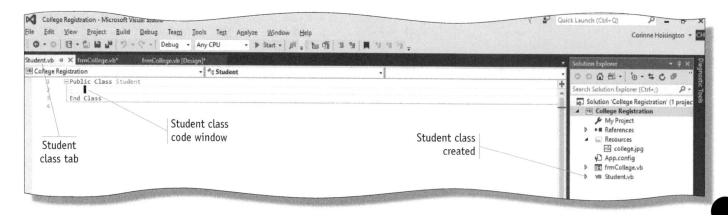

FIGURE 11-15

STEP 4   Using the same techniques, create the OnCampusStudent class and the StudentCostsFile class.

The Solution Explorer window now shows the four classes for the program: OnCampus-Student, frmCollege, Student, and StudentCostsFile (Figure 11-16). To select a class and display its code window, double-click the class name in the Solution Explorer.

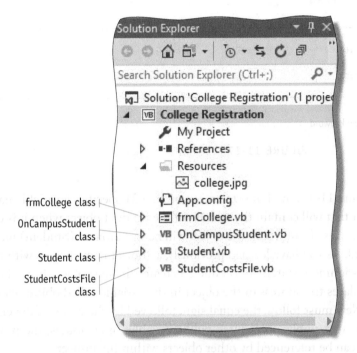

frmCollege class

OnCampusStudent class

Student class

StudentCostsFile class

FIGURE 11-16

Code Classes

After the classes have been defined, you must write the code for each class. You can write code for each class using the same techniques you have used for previous programs. Before beginning, however, you must consider how classes communicate so you can write the correct code.

Instantiate a Class and Class Communication

As you have learned, the code in a class acts as a template for an object. For example, when you drag the Button.NET component from the Toolbox to the Windows Form object, the Button object is created, or instantiated, based on the code in the Button class. Properties of the Button object, such as the text shown in the button, are processed using the code in the Button class.

Similarly, whenever you define a class in your Visual Basic program, you must instantiate an object based on that class in order for the processing within the object to take place. To instantiate an object, you can use the New statement, as shown in Figure 11-17.

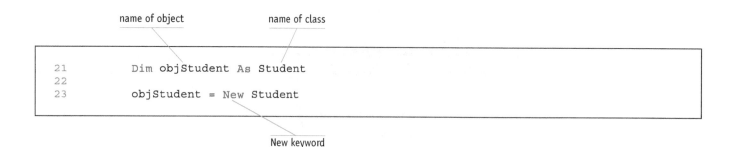

name of object   name of class

```
21          Dim objStudent As Student
22
23          objStudent = New Student
```

New keyword

FIGURE 11-17

In Figure 11-17, the Dim statement on line 21 specifies a variable named objStudent that will contain the address of the Student object when it is created. The name of the class from which the object will be instantiated (Student) must follow the As keyword. As you have learned previously, an object name begins with the prefix obj.

The assignment statement on line 23 creates the new object from the Student class and places the address of the object in the variable called objStudent. The keyword New must follow the equal sign, followed by the name of the class. Once the object is created, public procedures, public variables or attributes, and properties of the object can be referenced by other objects within the project.

A single statement can also be used to create an object, as shown in Figure 11-18.

```
25          Dim objStudent As New Student
```

FIGURE 11-18

The Dim statement on line 25 in Figure 11-18 both creates a variable to hold the address of the object (objStudent) and instantiates the object by using the keyword New followed by the name of the class.

The technique shown in Figure 11-17 is more widely used because the variable can be defined in the variables section of the code and the object is not instantiated until it is needed.

Constructors in New Instantiated Classes

When a class is instantiated into an object using the New keyword, a special procedure called a constructor is executed in the class. The **constructor** prepares the object for use in the program. The code in the constructor executes before any other code in the object. In addition to processes that are automatically completed by the constructor, the user can choose to write code for the constructor as well.

If the developer writes no code for a class constructor, Visual Basic automatically generates any processing that must be accomplished to prepare the object for use. The developer can include a constructor with no executing code, as shown in Figure 11-19.

```
 1 Public Class Student
 2
 3     Sub New()
 4         'Constructor for Student class
 5
 6         'If required, initializing statements go here
 7
 8     End Sub
 9
10 End Class
```

FIGURE 11-19

Note in Figure 11-19 that the constructor begins with the statement Sub New(). No name is required for the constructor — the New keyword identifies the Sub procedure as the constructor.

Because the code in the constructor executes before any other code in the object, it is a good location to place initializing code statements that prepare the object for execution.

Pass Arguments When Instantiating an Object

When you instantiate an object, data often must be passed to the object. For example, in the College Registration Costs program, the user enters the Student ID, Student Name, and other data into the user interface form. The Student object requires this data to calculate the registration costs and cause the StudentCostsFile object to write the required text file. If an object requires data when it is instantiated, the data can be passed as part of the instantiation code. For example, to pass the Student ID, the Student Name, the Major, and the Number of Units from the Form object to the Student object when the Student object is instantiated in the Form object, the statement in Figure 11-20 can be used.

New keyword   arguments

```
51            objStudent = New Student(txtStudentID.Text, txtStudentName.Text,
        cboMajor.SelectedItem, txtNumberOfUnits.Text)
```

FIGURE 11-20

In Figure 11-20, the assignment statement that is specified in the Form class uses the New keyword in a manner similar to that shown in Figure 11-17 on page 662, except that arguments are included within the parentheses following the New keyword. Notice that the format of the arguments for the New statement is identical to the format used when passing arguments to a procedure, as you saw in Chapter 8. In Figure 11-20, the values in the txtStudentID Text property, the txtStudentName Text property, the cboMajor.SelectedItem property, and the txtNumberOfUnits Text property are passed to the instantiated object.

In the Student class, the New statement must be written with corresponding arguments; that is, the "signature" of the instantiating statement (Figure 11-20) must be the same as the constructor heading in the class. The New statement for the Student class is shown in Figure 11-21.

```
12    Sub New(ByVal strStudentID As String, ByVal strStudentName As String, ByVal        ↙
      strMajor As String, ByVal intUnits As String)
```

FIGURE 11-21

Note in Figure 11-21 that the arguments for the New statement in the Student class match the arguments in the instantiation statement in Figure 11-20. The arguments are passed ByVal, which you recall means a copy of the value is passed to the instantiated object but the original value is not used.

Once the object is instantiated and the arguments are passed, the constructor can use the values in the arguments to set the values in variables within the class. The code in Figure 11-22 illustrates the assignment statements in the constructor to set the value of the variables defined in the Student class to the values passed from the calling object by the statement in Figure 11-21.

```
9     Public Class Student
10
11        'Class variables
12        Protected _strStudentID As String
13        Protected _strStudentName As String
14        Protected _strMajor As String
15        Protected _intUnits As Integer
16        Protected _decCost As Decimal
17        Protected _decCostPerUnit As Decimal = 450D
18
19        Dim objStudentCostsFile As StudentCostsFile
20
21        Sub New(ByVal strStudentID As String, ByVal strStudentName As String, ByVal strMajor As String, ByVal intUnits As String)
22            ' This subprocedure is a constructor for the Student class. It is called when the object is instantiated with arguments
23
24            'The following code assigns the arguments to class variables
25            _strStudentID = strStudentID
26            _strStudentName = strStudentName
27            _strMajor = strMajor
28            _intUnits = Convert.ToInt32(intUnits)
29
30        End Sub
```

FIGURE 11-22

In the constructor shown in Figure 11-22, the assignment statements on lines 25 through 28 place the values passed from the instantiation statement into the variables defined in the Student class (lines 12 through 17). When the object based on the Student class is instantiated, the constructor code ensures that the variables in the object contain data entered by the user.

Notice that the variables in the Student class are defined with Protected access. Generally, when using multiple classes within a program, variables (also called attributes) should not be available to code within other classes of the program. Classes can reference attributes within another class only if the class that contains the attributes allows it. You will learn techniques for such access later in this chapter, but attributes should usually be defined with Private access.

Call a Procedure in a Separate Class

Most of the time, separate classes in a program contain procedures that must be executed. For example, in the College Registration Costs program, the Student class must contain a procedure that calculates the registration costs. This procedure is shown in Figure 11-23.

```
15      Private _intUnits As Integer
16      Private _decCost As Decimal
17      Private _decCostPerUnit As Decimal = 450D
  .
  .
  .
32      Function ComputeCosts() As Decimal
33          ' This function computes the registration costs, and
34          ' returns the registration costs
35
36          _decCost = _intUnits * _decCostPerUnit
37
38          Return _decCost
39
40      End Function
```

FIGURE 11-23

In Figure 11-23, the ComputeCosts function in the Student class multiplies the number of units (_intUnits) times the cost per unit (_decCostPerUnit) to determine the cost (_decCost). The cost then is returned as a decimal value to the calling class by the Return statement on line 38.

You might ask why the statement on line 36 cannot be included in the Form class that calls the Student class instead of calling the ComputeCosts function in the Student class. The short answer is that it could be. However, when designing larger and more robust programs, it is important to keep the tasks of each class separate.

In this case, the presentation tier of the three-tiered structure, represented by the Form object, should have no knowledge of how student registration costs are calculated. In the sample program of this chapter, the calculation is a simple multiplication statement. In the future, the calculation of registration costs might involve multiple lookups in a database, complex calculations based on major, in-state or out-of-state residence, and so on. The presentation class(es) should have nothing to do with these processes; the Student class should be the class in the program that knows how to perform all student activities. Therefore, even when the calculation is simple, as in the sample program, these tasks should be contained within the correct class.

To call the ComputeCosts procedure in the Student object, a statement in the Form object must identify both the object and the procedure within the object. The statement on line 54 calls the ComputeCosts procedure, as shown in Figure 11-24.

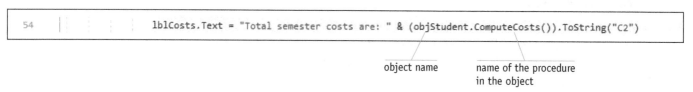

FIGURE 11-24

On line 54 in Figure 11-24, the statement objStudent.ComputeCosts() identifies the objStudent object from Figure 11-17 on page 662 and the ComputeCosts procedure from Figure 11-23 on page 665, separated by the dot operator (.). The dot operator specifies a member of a type or namespace. The statement says, "Pass control to the ComputeCosts procedure found in the objStudent object." The ComputeCosts procedure is a Function procedure, and the value returned from the procedure call is converted to a string and then assigned to the Text property of the lblCosts Label object so it can be displayed in the Windows Form object (see Figure 11-2 on page 650).

In this section, you have seen the entire process for creating a class, instantiating a class, and calling a procedure in a class. This process is fundamental when designing larger and more robust programs.

Inheritance

In the College Registration Costs program, the Student object contains student information from the Form object and performs calculations for the student. A student living on campus is a specialized student whose costs include housing and board. Therefore, the cost calculation for the on-campus student is different from that for an off-campus student. In addition, the On-Campus Student object must include Boolean indicators for the type of housing selected.

If the student lives off campus, a Student object will be instantiated, and if the student lives on campus, an On-Campus Student object will be instantiated. Because the Student and On-Campus Student objects contain some different attributes and their cost calculations are different, logically they could be separate objects. Visual Basic and other object-oriented programming languages offer an alternative, however. This alternative is inheritance.

Inheritance allows one class to inherit attributes and procedures from another class. For example, the Student object contains the Student ID, the Student Name, the Major, and the Number of Units. These same values are required for the on-campus student. In addition, the On-Campus Student object contains indicators for the housing selected. By using inheritance, the attributes of the Student object can be used by the On-Campus Student object as well. Inheritance is the ability to use all of the functionality of an existing class and extend those capabilities without rewriting the class (Figure 11-25).

Base Class

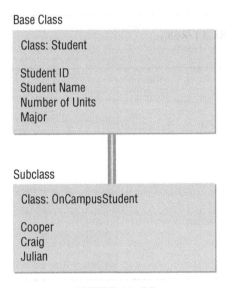

Subclass

FIGURE 11-25

In Figure 11-25, the Student class contains the Student ID, Student Name, Number of Units, and Major attributes. Because the OnCampusStudent class inherits from the Student class, the OnCampusStudent class can reference the Student ID variable in the Student class as if that variable were defined in the OnCampusStudent class. This is true of the other Student class variables as well. As you can see, the OnCampusStudent class inherits the attributes it can use from the Student class and then defines the unique attributes it requires as well.

In the example in Figure 11-25, the Student class is called the **base class**. The OnCampusStudent class is called the **subclass**. The subclass can use attributes from the base class as if those attributes were defined in the subclass.

The code for the attributes in the Student base class and the OnCampusStudent subclass is shown in Figure 11-26.

```
1    ' Class:       Student
2    ' Developer:   Corinne Hoisington
3    ' Date:        August 29, 2019
4    ' Purpose:     This business class for a registering college student calculates the semester costs for tuition. It also causes the
5    '              student costs file to be written.
6
7    Option Strict On
8
9    Public Class Student
10
11       'Class variables
12       Protected _strStudentID As String
13       Protected _strStudentName As String
14       Protected _strMajor As String
15       Protected _intUnits As Integer
16       Protected _decCost As Decimal
17       Protected _decCostPerUnit As Decimal = 450D
18
19       Dim objStudentCostsFile As StudentCostsFile
```

FIGURE 11-26a

```
1    ' Class:       OnCampusStudent
2    ' Developer:   Corinne Hoisington
3    ' Date:        August 29, 2019
4    ' Purpose:     This business class for registering an on-campus college student calculates the semester costs, including tuition
5    '              and housing. It also causes the student costs file to be written.
6
7    Option Strict On
8
9    Public Class OnCampusStudent
10       Inherits Student
11
12       ' Class variables
13       Private _Cooper As Boolean
14       Private _Craig As Boolean
15       Private _Julian As Boolean
16
17       Dim objStudentCostsFile As StudentCostsFile
```

FIGURE 11-26b

After the usual comment statements for the Student class, the variables required for the Student class are declared. You can see that the string variables for Student ID, Student Name, and Major are declared, together with an integer variable for the Number of Units. In addition, the _decCost Decimal variable will contain the result of the calculation, and _decCostPerUnit is a Decimal variable that contains the fixed cost per unit (450D) used in the calculation for semester costs.

Note that the variables in the Student class are declared with Protected access. Protected means statements in the subclasses of the base class can reference the variable as if the referencing statement were declared in the base class instead of the subclass. Statements outside the base class and the subclasses, however, cannot reference the variables.

In the OnCampusStudent subclass, the Class statement on line 9 includes the Inherits entry on line 10. This required entry indicates that the OnCampusStudent class inherits from the Student class. Any subclass must include the Inherits entry to indicate the class from which it inherits.

The three Boolean variables required in the subclass are declared, but no declarations are made for Student ID, Student Name, or the other variables declared in the Student base class. These variables can be used as if they are part of the OnCampusStudent subclass.

Why should I use inheritance?

- Inheritance provides a clear model structure that is easy to understand without much complexity.

- Inheritance enables you to create new classes that reuse, extend, and modify the behavior defined in other classes.

- Using inheritance manages code by dividing it into parent and child classes.

CONSIDER THIS

Constructors

Both the base class and the subclass must have constructors. The code for the base class constructor and the subclass constructor is shown in Figures 11-27 and 11-28.

BASE CLASS CONSTRUCTOR

```
20
21    Sub New(ByVal strStudentID As String, ByVal strStudentName As String, ByVal strMajor As String, ByVal intUnits As String)
22        ' This subprocedure is a constructor for the Student class. It is called when the object is instantiated with arguments
23
24        'The following code assigns the arguments to class variables
25        _strStudentID = strStudentID
26        _strStudentName = strStudentName
27        _strMajor = strMajor
28        _intUnits = Convert.ToInt32(intUnits)
29
30    End Sub
31
```

FIGURE 11-27

SUBCLASS CONSTRUCTOR

```
19    Sub New(ByVal StudentID As String, ByVal StudentName As String, ByVal Major As String, ByVal Units As String,
20            ByVal Cooper As Boolean, ByVal Craig As Boolean, ByVal Julian As Boolean)
21        ' This subprocedure is a constructor for the Student class. It is called when instantiated with arguments
22
23        MyBase.New(StudentID, StudentName, Major, Units)
24
25        'The following code assigns the arguments to class variables
26        _Cooper = Cooper
27        _Craig = Craig
28        _Julian = Julian
29
30    End Sub
31
```

FIGURE 11-28

In the constructor for the Student base class, the Student ID, Student Name, Major, and Number of Units are passed when the object is instantiated. The constructor places the Student ID, Student Name, and Major in string variables and converts the Number of Units to an integer.

In the constructor for the OnCampusStudent subclass, the Student ID, Student Name, Major, Number of Units, and the Boolean indicators for Cooper, Craig, and Julian are passed by the instantiating statement. The required first statement in the subclass constructor is the MyBase.New statement (line 23 in Figure 11-28). This statement calls the code in the base class (Student) constructor and executes it. Therefore, when the subclass is instantiated, both the base class and subclass constructors are executed.

In Figure 11-28, after the base class constructor is executed, the OnCampusStudent constructor places the Boolean indicators in variables so they can be tested in the class processing.

Again, it should be emphasized that the Student ID, Student Name, Major, and Number of Units variables are available to the OnCampusStudent subclass even though these variables are not declared within the class. They are available because of inheritance.

Inheritance and Procedures

When using inheritance, the subclass can use the procedures within the base class as well as its variables. Between the base class and the subclass, five different techniques can be used for referencing and calling a procedure from an outside class such as a Form class. After the base class and the subclass have been instantiated, the following techniques are available:

Base Class:

1. Call a named procedure in the base class.
   Example: `objBaseClass.RegularBaseClassFunction()`

2. Call an Overridable procedure in the base class.
   Example: `objBaseClass.OverridableBaseClassFunction()`

Subclass:

1. Call an Overridable procedure in the subclass.
   Example: `objSubClass.OverridableBaseClassFunction()`

2. Call a named procedure in the subclass.
   Example: `objSubClass.RegularSubClassFunction()`

3. Call a base class procedure in the subclass.
   Example: `objSubClass.RegularBaseClassFunction()`

Each of these methods is explained in the following sections.

Call a Named Procedure in the Base Class

A Sub procedure or a Function procedure in the base class can be called from another class in the manner you have seen previously. Thus, if a base class contains a Function procedure called RegularBaseClassFunction, another class can call the function using the statement objBaseClass.RegularBaseClassFunction(), where objBaseClass is the instantiated base class object and RegularBaseClassFunction is the name of the Function procedure.

An example of the code for this process is shown in Figure 11-29.

FORM CLASS

```
4        Dim objSubClass As SubClass
5        Dim objBaseClass As BaseClass
6
7        objSubClass = New SubClass
8        objBaseClass = New BaseClass
9
10       MsgBox(objBaseClass.RegularBaseClassFunction())
```

FIGURE 11-29a

SUBCLASS CLASS

```
3        Function RegularBaseClassFunction() As String
4            Return "Regular base class function"
5        End Function
```

FIGURE 11-29b

FIGURE 11-29c

In Figure 11-29a, the objBaseClass object is instantiated on line 8 of the Form class. The statement on line 10 in Figure 11-29a calls the RegularBaseClassFunction in the objBaseClass object. When the function returns the text value, the value is displayed in the message box in Figure 11-29c. The process shown in Figure 11-29 is the normal process for calling a procedure in another class.

Call an Overridable Procedure in a Base Class

When a procedure is written in the base class, the procedure will perform its assigned processing. Sometimes, the subclass might require basically the same task to be completed but with some differences in how it is accomplished. For example, in the College Registration Costs sample program, the Student base class procedure determines the costs by multiplying the number of units times the cost per unit. In the OnCampusStudent subclass, the costs are calculated by multiplying the number of units times the cost per unit and then adding the housing/board costs.

Even though the process accomplishes the same task of computing costs, the calculations are different. When a task is accomplished in a different manner in a base class than in a subclass, the procedure can have the same name in both the base class and the subclass, but if the procedure in the subclass is called, it overrides the procedure in the base class. If the procedure in the base class is called, it is executed as a normal procedure call, as shown in Figure 11-30.

FORM CLASS

```
4          Dim objSubClass  As SubClass
5          Dim objBaseClass  As BaseClass
6
7          objSubClass  = New SubClass
8          objBaseClass  = New BaseClass
9
10         MsgBox(objBaseClass .OverridableBaseClassFunction())
```

FIGURE 11-30a

BASE CLASS

```
7      Overridable Function OverridableBaseClassFunction() As String
8          Return "Overridable base class function"
9      End Function
```

FIGURE 11-30b

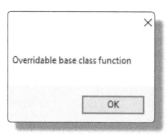

FIGURE 11-30c

Notice in Figure 11-30b that the keyword Overridable precedes the Function keyword. Overridable means a subclass can contain a procedure with the same procedure name as that in the base class. If the procedure in the subclass is called (in other words, SubClassName.ProcedureName), then it is executed even though it has the same name as the procedure in the base class. In Figure 11-30a, however, the procedure named OverridableBaseClassFunction in the base class is called from the Form class, so that procedure is executed.

Call an Overridable Procedure in a Subclass

In Figure 11-31, a call is made to the OverridableBaseClassFunction that is defined in the subclass. Notice in Figure 11-31c that the Function name in the subclass is preceded by the Overrides keyword, which indicates the function in the base class will be overridden by the function in the subclass when the latter function is called.

FORM CLASS

```
4        Dim objSubClass As SubClass
5        Dim objBaseClass As BaseClass
6
7        objSubClass = New SubClass
8        objBaseClass = New BaseClass
9
10       MsgBox(objSubClass.OverridableBaseClassFunction())
```

FIGURE 11-31a

BASE CLASS

```
7    Overridable Function OverridableBaseClassFunction() As String
8        Return "Overridable base class function"
9    End Function
```

FIGURE 11-31b

SUB CLASS

```
8    Overrides Function OverridableBaseClassFunction() As String
9        Return "Overrode the base class overridable function"
10   End Function
```

FIGURE 11-31c

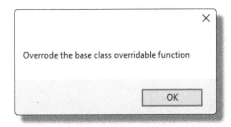

FIGURE 11-31d

In Figure 11-31b, the function defined on line 7 of the base class is called OverridableBaseClassFunction, and the name is preceded by the Overridable keyword. In Figure 11-31c, the function with the same name on line 8 of the subclass overrides the function in the base class. As a result, when the subclass function is called (line 10 of the Form class in Figure 11-31a), the subclass message appears in the message box.

Call a Named Procedure in the Subclass

As with any other public procedure in a class, a named procedure in a subclass can be called (Figure 11-32).

FORM CLASS

```
4        Dim objSubClass As SubClass
5        Dim objBaseClass As BaseClass
6
7        objSubClass = New SubClass
8        objBaseClass = New BaseClass
9
10       MsgBox(objSubClass.RegularSubClassFunction())
```

FIGURE 11-32a

SUB CLASS

```
4    Function RegularSubClassFunction() As String
5        Return "Regular subclass function"
6    End Function
```

FIGURE 11-32b

FIGURE 11-32c

The example in Figure 11-32 is a straightforward procedure call to a procedure in another class.

Call a Base Class Procedure in the Subclass

The last common procedure call involving inheritance occurs when a procedure in the base class is called by referencing the subclass, as shown in Figure 11-33.

FORM CLASS

```
4        Dim objSubClass As SubClass
5        Dim objBaseClass As BaseClass
6
7        objSubClass = New SubClass
8        objBaseClass = New BaseClass
9
10       MsgBox(objSubClass.RegularBaseClassFunction())
```

FIGURE 11-33a

BASE CLASS

```
3      Function RegularBaseClassFunction() As String
4          Return "Regular base class function"
5      End Function
```

FIGURE 11-33b

FIGURE 11-33c

In Figure 11-33 on the previous page, the procedure call statement in the Form class (line 10 in Figure 11-33a) calls a procedure that is not even in the subclass. Nonetheless, the regular base class function is executed because when a procedure is called that is not in the class specified in the call statement, Visual Basic will move up to the base class to see if the procedure is located there. If so, the procedure in the base class is executed.

Inheritance can be a relatively complex subject that has more ramifications than you have learned in this chapter. Nonetheless, this beginning knowledge of inheritance will serve you well as you continue your education in programming and development.

Persistence Classes

As you learned earlier in this chapter, the persistence tier in an application is sometimes called the data access tier. It contains classes that are involved in saving and retrieving data stored on a permanent storage medium, such as a hard disk or a USB drive. A typical persistence class is the StudentCostsFile class in the College Registration Costs sample program in this chapter. This class is concerned with performing all tasks required for the Student Costs file. In the sample program, this processing consists of writing the file as a text file and saving it on a USB drive. Other processing might be required for this file in the future, including the retrieval of the text file or converting the text file into a database file. Generally, any required processing of the Student Costs file should be carried out by the StudentCostsFile class.

To define the StudentCostsFile class, you must write comments, variables, and a constructor, as you have seen earlier in this chapter. The code to define the Student-CostsFile class is shown in Figure 11-34.

```
1     ' Class:        Student Costs File
2     ' Developer:    Corinne Hoisington
3     ' Date:         August 29, 2019
4     ' Purpose:      This class represents the Student Costs File. The WriteRecord procedure writes a comma-delimited student costs file that
5                     contains the Student ID, Student Name, Major, and Student Costs.
6
7     Option Strict On
8
9     Public Class StudentCostsFile
10
11        ' Class variables
12        Private _strStudentID As String
13        Private _strStudentName As String
14        Private _strMajor As String
15        Private _decStudentCosts As Decimal
16
17        Sub New(ByVal StudentID As String, ByVal StudentName As String, ByVal Major As String, ByVal Costs As Decimal)
18            ' This sub procedure is the constructor for the StudentCostsFile class.
19
20            ' The following code assigns the arguments to class variables
21            _strStudentID = StudentID
22            _strStudentName = StudentName
23            _strMajor = Major
24            _decStudentCosts = Costs
25
26        End Sub
```

FIGURE 11-34

In Figure 11-34, the typical comments are followed by the declaration of the variables used in the class. Notice that each of the variables is declared with Private access so they cannot be referenced by code in any other class within the program.

Following the variable declarations is the constructor procedure, as identified by the keyword New. Within the constructor, the code on lines 21–24 sets the values in the variables to the values passed to the StudentCostsFile class when it is instantiated.

Comma-Delimited Text Files

The StudentCosts file is a comma-delimited text file, which means a comma separates each field in a record in the file, as shown in Figure 11-35.

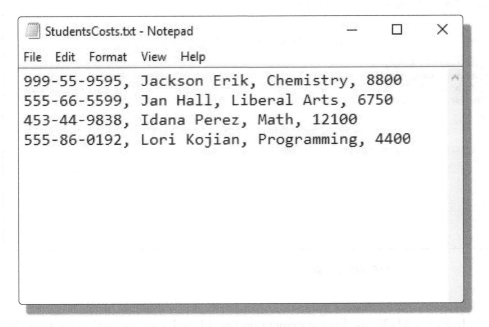

FIGURE 11-35

Notice in Figure 11-35 that a comma appears at the end of each field, but no comma is displayed at the end of the record. A comma-delimited text file is commonly used because it can be read into programs such as Microsoft Excel and Microsoft Access to import the data into the application.

In Chapter 8, you learned to use a StreamWriter to write a stream of text to a file. To create the file shown in Figure 11-35, a record that contains the Student ID, the Student Name, the Major, and the Costs must be added to the file each time new registration costs are calculated for a student. Because you do not know how many records will be placed in the file during the registration process, a StreamWriter must be created that can append, or add, records to the file. Because a record contains four fields, the first three of which are followed by a comma, a Write statement must be used so that a new line is not created in the file each time part of a record is written to the disk. The code to accomplish this processing is shown in the WriteRecord Sub procedure in Figure 11-36.

```
28      Sub WriteRecord()
29          ' This subprocedure opens the StudentCosts output text file and then writes a record in the comma-delimited file
30
31          Dim strNameandLocationOfFile As String = "d:\StudentCosts.txt"
32
33          Try
34              Dim objWriter As IO.StreamWriter = IO.File.AppendText(strNameandLocationOfFile)
35
36              objWriter.Write(_strStudentID & ",")
37              objWriter.Write(_strStudentName & ",")
38              objWriter.Write(_strMajor & ",")
39              objWriter.WriteLine(_decStudentCosts)
40              objWriter.Close()
41
42          Catch ex As Exception
43              MsgBox("No device available - program aborted", , "Error")
44              Application.Exit()
45
46          End Try
47
48      End Sub
49
50  End Class
```

FIGURE 11-36

In Figure 11-36, the Dim statement on line 34 declares a string that contains the name and location of the file to be written. A Try-Catch block is created on line 33 because if a USB drive is not located on drive D, an exception will be thrown. The Catch statement on line 42 catches the exception, displays a message box containing an error message, and exits the application.

Assuming no exception occurs, the Dim statement on line 34 declares the objWriter as an IO.StreamWriter. The identification of the IO.StreamWriter indicates that the writer will append text to the file. Appending the text means writing the next record in the file following the last record in the file; that is, the records accumulate in the file as it is written.

The Write procedure calls on lines 36–38 write the Student ID, the Student Name, and the Major in the record, each followed by a comma. The WriteLine procedure call on line 39 writes the Student Costs in the record and places a line return in the file so the next record can be written. Finally, the Close procedure call on line 40 closes the file.

Performance Profiling

As programs become larger in scope, testing the speed and performance of the code is a means of quality assurance. It involves testing software applications to ensure they will perform well on various computers without crashing or slowing the CPU speed significantly. The focus of testing your finished program before releasing it to your clients is to determine if the app responds quickly and can handle more users simultaneously running the application. Every developer should determine the **scalability** of their project, which identifies the number of users the software program can handle.

Visual Studio comes equipped with many Profiling Tools to analyze performance issues in your application. To test and graph the performance load on your CPU while a program is running, follow these steps to analyze the app using the Performance Profiler:

STEP 1 In the Standard toolbar, change the selection in the Solution Configurations drop-down box from Debug to Release.

The Release option is selected in the Solution Configurations box (Figure 11-37).

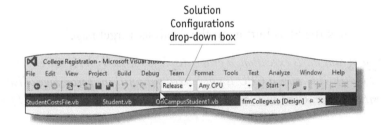

FIGURE 11-37

STEP 2 Click Analyze on the menu bar and then click Performance Profiler.

A Report tab opens and displays the Analysis Target page (Figure 11-38).

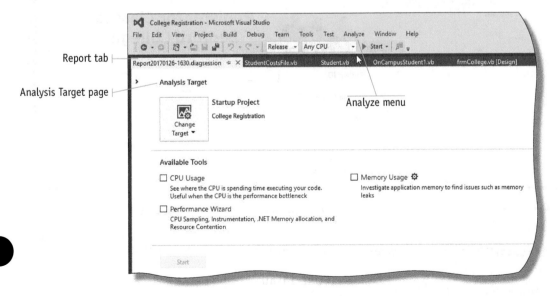

FIGURE 11-38

STEP 3 Check the CPU Usage check box to see where the CPU is spending time executing your code.

The CPU Usage check box is checked (Figure 11–39).

FIGURE 11-39

STEP 4 Click the Start button on the Analysis Target page.

After the program starts execution, a graph displays the load on the CPU processors (Figure 11-40). Typically, a CPU is not maxed out until the percentage of load reaches 80 percent or higher. Continue the program and watch the load on the CPU processors.

FIGURE 11-40

Program Design

As you have learned, the requirements document identifies the purpose of the program being developed, the application title, the procedures to be followed when using the program, any required equations and calculations, any conditions that must be tested, notes and restrictions that must be followed by the program, and any other comments that would be helpful to understanding the problem. The requirements document for the College Registration Costs application is shown in Figure 11-41.

REQUIREMENTS DOCUMENT

Date Submitted:	August 29, 2019
Date:	
Application Title:	College Registration Costs
Purpose:	This Windows application allows a user to enter student registration information for Bedford College and then calculates the student registration costs.
Program Procedures:	In a Windows application, the user enters the student ID, student name, and number of units (credits), selects an off-campus or on-campus resident status, selects housing and board if resident status is on-campus, and then selects a major. When the user clicks a button, the application calculates the semester costs and records the information in a log file.
Algorithms, Processing, and Conditions:	1. The user first enters the student ID, student name, and number of units.
	2. The user selects either off-campus residence or on-campus residence. If on-campus residence is selected, the user indicates the housing/board selection (Cooper Dorm, Craig Hall, or Julian Suites). The user then selects the student's major from a list.
	3. When the user clicks a button, the program calculates the semester costs and writes a log file.
	4. A Clear Form button should be available to clear the form and place the insertion point in the Student ID text box.
	5. The course cost is $450.00 per unit.

FIGURE 11-41 (continues)

6. The formula to calculate semester course costs is the number of units times the cost per unit.

7. If the student is an on-campus resident, the following housing/board costs must be added to the course costs: Cooper Dorm, $2,900.00 per semester; Craig Hall, $3,400.00 per semester; Julian Suites, $4,000.00 per semester.

8. The log file is a text file that contains the Student ID, the Student Name, the Major, and the semester costs. It should be a comma-delimited file.

Notes and Restrictions:

1. The student ID must be a complete Social Security number.

2. The student name cannot be left blank and must begin with an alphabetic character.

3. The number of units must be a numeric value of 1 through 24.

4. A major must be selected. The majors available are App Development, Biology, Business, Chemistry, Programming, Liberal Arts, Mathematics, Physics, Sociology, and Technology Education.

5. The housing/board selections should not be displayed in the window unless the user selects the on-campus resident status.

6. When the user clicks the button to calculate costs and the program determines that an error occurred during data entry, a message box is displayed and the user must enter valid data before continuing.

7. Off-campus residency is the default selection; if a student is an on-campus resident, Cooper Dorm is the default selection.

Comments:

1. Obtain an image for this program from CengageBrain.com. The name of the picture is college.

2. The program should use a three-tier structure with presentation, business, and persistence classes.

FIGURE 11-41 (continues)

The Use Case Definition for the application is shown in Figure 11-42.

USE CASE DEFINITION

1. The user enters the student ID, the student name, and the number of units.
2. If necessary, the user selects off-campus or on-campus resident status using radio buttons. If on-campus residency is selected, the housing/board choices are displayed. If necessary, the user selects the housing/board choice.
3. The user selects a major from a list.
4. The user clicks the Calculate Costs button.
5. The program calculates and displays the semester costs, including the cost of housing/board if appropriate.
6. The program writes a log of the student registration costs.
7. If necessary, the user clicks the Clear Form button to clear the form of data and place the insertion point in the Student ID text box.

FIGURE 11-42

Design the Program Processing Objects

You will recall that an event planning document is a table that specifies which objects in the user interface will cause events, the action taken by the user to trigger each event, and the event processing that must occur. In addition, an event planning document is required for each object in the program that is called from another object. The event planning documents for the College Registration Costs program are shown in Figures 11-43 through 11-46 on page 686.

EVENT PLANNING DOCUMENT

Program Name: College Registration Costs	Developer: Corinne Hoisington	Object: frmCollege	Date: August 29, 2019
OBJECT	**EVENT TRIGGER**	**EVENT PROCESSING**	

btnCalculateCosts	Click	Declare Student object
		Declare OnCampusStudent object
		Declare Boolean InputError indicator
		If student ID mask is not full
		    Display message box with error
		        message
		    Clear student ID masked text box
		    Place focus on student ID masked
		        text box	

FIGURE 11-43 (continues)

OBJECT	EVENT TRIGGER	EVENT PROCESSING

		Set input error indicator to true
		Else If student name text length
		    < 1 or first character in text
		    box less than "A"
		  Display message box with error
		    message
		  Clear student name text box
		  Place focus on student name text
		    box
		  Set input error indicator to true
		Else If number of units is not numeric
		  Display message box with error
		    message
		  Clear number of units text box
		  Place focus on number of units
		    text box
		  Set input error indicator to true
		Else If number of units is not 1–24
		  Display message box with error
		    message
		  Clear number of units text box
		  Place focus on number of units
		    text box
		  Set input error indicator to true
		Else If major selected index < 0
		  Display message box with error
		    message
		  Place focus on major combo box
		  Set input error indicator to true
		End If
		If no input error
		  If off-campus radio button
		    checked
		    Instantiate student object with
		      arguments
		    Set costs label visible property
		      to true
		    Call student compute costs
		      procedure
		    Display student costs
		  Else
		    Instantiate on-campus student
		      object with arguments
		    Set costs label visible property
		      to true

		Call on-campus student compute costs procedure Display student costs End If

FIGURE 11-43 (continues)

OBJECT	EVENT TRIGGER	EVENT PROCESSING
radOnCampus Radio Button	Selected	Make housing/board group visible
radOffCampus Radio Button	Selected	Make housing/board group not visible
btnClearForm	Click	Clear student ID masked text box Clear student name text box Clear number of units text box Set major combo box selected index to −1 Set major combo box text property to "Select a Major" Set off-campus radio button checked property to true Set Cooper radio button checked property to true Set housing/board group visible property to false Set costs label visible property to false Place focus on student ID masked text box

FIGURE 11-43 (continued)

EVENT PLANNING DOCUMENT

Program Name: College Registration Costs	Developer: Corinne Hoisington	Object: objStudent (Student class)	Date: August 29, 2019
OBJECT	**EVENT TRIGGER**	**EVENT PROCESSING**	
New(student ID, student name, major, units)	Class constructor	Set student ID equal to passed student ID Set student name equal to passed student name Set major equal to passed major Convert number of units passed to Integer	
ComputeCosts	Function procedure call	Cost = units * cost per unit Instantiate objStudentCostsFile object Write the student record Return the cost	

FIGURE 11-44

EVENT PLANNING DOCUMENT

Program Name: College Registration Costs	Developer: Corinne Hoisington	Object: objOnCampusStudent (OnCampusStudent class)	Date: August 29, 2019
OBJECT	**EVENT TRIGGER**	**EVENT PROCESSING**	
New(student ID, student name, major, units, Cooper Boolean, Craig Boolean, Julian Boolean)	Class constructor	Call base class constructor (student ID, student name, major, units) Set Cooper Boolean to passed Cooper Boolean Set Craig Boolean to passed Craig Boolean Set Julian Boolean to passed Julian Boolean	
ComputeCosts	Function procedure call	If Cooper housing Set housing cost = Cooper cost Else If Craig housing Set housing cost = Craig cost Else If Julian housing Set housing cost = Julian cost End If Cost = (units * cost per unit) + housing cost Instantiate objStudentCostsFile object Write the student record Return the cost	

FIGURE 11-45

EVENT PLANNING DOCUMENT

Program Name: College Registration Costs	Developer: Corinne Hoisington	Object: objStudentCostsFile (StudentCostsFile class)	Date: August 29, 2019
OBJECT	**EVENT TRIGGER**	**EVENT PROCESSING**	
New(student ID, student name, major, costs)	Class constructor	Set student ID equal to passed student ID Set student name equal to passed student name Set major equal to passed major Set costs equal to passed costs	
WriteRecord	Function procedure call	Define stream writer for append text file Write student ID with comma Write student name with comma Write major with comma Write costs with line return Close text file	

FIGURE 11-46

Guided Program Development

To design the user interface for the College Registration Costs application and enter the code required to process each event in the program, complete the steps in this section.

Phase 1: Design the Form

1

- **Create a New Windows Project** Open Visual Studio and then close the Start page. Click the New Project button on the Standard toolbar. Begin a Windows Forms App project and name the project CollegeRegistration.

- **Name the Form Object** Select the Form object. Change the (Name) property of the Form object to frmCollege.

- **Assign a Title to the Form Object** With the frmCollege object selected, change the Text property to College Registration Costs.

- **Change the Form Class Name** In the Solution Explorer window, right-click Form1.vb, select Rename on the shortcut menu, and change the class name to frmCollege.vb.

• **Create the User Interface** Using the skills you have acquired in this course and referencing the requirements document in Figure 11-41 on pages 681, create the user interface for the frmCollege object, as shown in Figure 11-47. The heading is Tahoma font, bold, 24 points, and Navy font color. All other fonts are Tahoma, regular, 12 points.

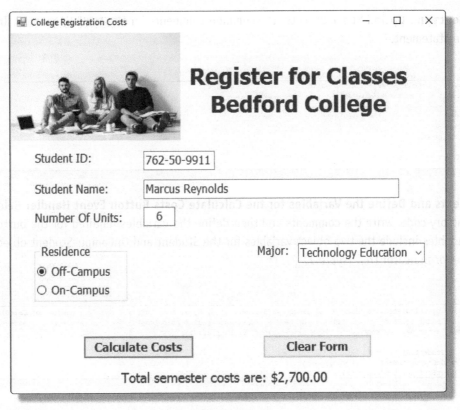

FIGURE 11-47

iStockphoto.com/mediaphotos

Phase 2: Code the Application

2

- **Open the Calculate Costs Button Event Handler** On the Windows Form object in the Design window, double-click the Calculate Costs Button object.

- **Enter Comments and Option Strict On** Enter the common comments for the frmCollege class. Include the Option Strict On statement.

HINT

```
1   ⊟' Program:       College Registration Costs
2    ' Developer:     Corinne Hoisington
3    ' Date:          August 29, 2019
4    ' Purpose:       This program calculates the registration costs for a college student. It also records the costs in a text file.
5
6     Option Strict On
7
8   ⊟Public Class frmCollege
9
```

- **Enter Comments and Define the Variables for the Calculate Costs Button Event Handler** Below the event handler introductory code, write the comments and then define the variables required for the button event handler. The variables include the two object variables for the Student and OnCampusStudent objects and the Boolean input error indicator (*ref: Figure 11-7*).

HINT

```
10   ⊟   Private Sub btnCalculateCosts_Click(ByVal sender As System.Object, ByVal e As System.EventArgs) Handles btnCalculateCosts.Click
11            ' This Calculate Costs button click event handler edits the  registration(costs) form to ensure it contains valid data.
12            ' Then, after passing control to the business class, it displays the cost.
13
14            Dim objStudent As Student
15            Dim objOnCampusStudent As OnCampusStudent
16            Dim InputError As Boolean = False
```

● **Enter the If...ElseIf Statement to Check the Input Data** Enter the code to check the input data, as documented in the program requirements and event planning document (*ref: Figure 11-7*).

HINT

```
17
18          ' Is student ID entered properly
19    ⊟     If txtStudentID.MaskFull = False Then
20              MsgBox("Enter your Student ID in the Student ID box", , "Error")
21              txtStudentID.Clear()
22              txtStudentID.Focus()
23              InputError = True
24              ' Is student name entered properly
25          ElseIf txtStudentName.TextLength < 1 Or txtStudentName.Text < "A" Then
26              MsgBox("Enter your name in the Student Name box", , "Error")
27              txtStudentName.Clear()
28              txtStudentName.Focus()
29              InputError = True
30              ' Is number of units entered properly
31          ElseIf Not IsNumeric(txtNumberOfUnits.Text) Then
32              MsgBox("Enter the units in the Number of Units box", , "Error")
33              txtNumberOfUnits.Clear()
34              txtNumberOfUnits.Focus()
35              InputError = True
36              ' Has 1-24 units been entered
37          ElseIf Convert.ToInt32(txtNumberOfUnits.Text) < 1 Or Convert.ToInt32(txtNumberOfUnits.Text) > 24 Then
38              MsgBox("Units must be 1 - 24", , "Error")
39              txtNumberOfUnits.Clear()
40              txtNumberOfUnits.Focus()
41              InputError = True
42              ' Has a major been selected
43          ElseIf cboMajor.SelectedIndex < 0 Then
44              MsgBox("Please select a major", , "Error")
45              cboMajor.Focus()
46              InputError = True
47          End If
48              ' If no input error, process the registration costs
```

● **Enter the Code to Call the Appropriate Function Procedure in the Appropriate Object** If the input data is correct, enter the code to instantiate the Student class object or the OnCampusStudent class object and then call the ComputeCosts function in the appropriate object. Be sure to include the correct arguments for the New statement for each new object (*ref: Figure 11-20*).

HINT

```
48          ' If no input error, process the registration costs
49        If Not InputError Then
50          If radOffCampus.Checked Then
51            objStudent = New Student(txtStudentID.Text, txtStudentName.Text, Convert.ToString(cboMajor.SelectedItem),
52                txtNumberOfUnits.Text)
53            lblCosts.Visible = True
54            lblCosts.Text = "Total semester costs are: " & (objStudent.ComputeCosts()).ToString("C2")
55          Else
56            objOnCampusStudent = New OnCampusStudent(txtStudentID.Text, txtStudentName.Text, Convert.ToString(cboMajor.SelectedItem),
57                txtNumberOfUnits.Text, radCooperDorm.Checked, radCraigHall.Checked, radJulianSuites.Checked)
58            lblCosts.Visible = True
59            lblCosts.Text = "Total semester costs are: " & (objOnCampusStudent.ComputeCosts()).ToString("C2")
60          End If
61        End If
62      End Sub
```

● **Write the Code for the Off-Campus Radio Button CheckedChanged Event** Write the code to hide the HousingBoard Group.

HINT

```
64   ⊟   Private Sub radOffCampus_CheckedChanged(ByVal sender As System.Object, ByVal e As System.EventArgs) Handles radOffCampus.CheckedChanged
65           ' This event handler is executed when the Off Campus radio button is selected. It hides the Housing/Board radio buttons
66
67           grpHousingBoard.Visible = False
68
69       End Sub
```

● **Write the Code for the On-Campus Radio Button CheckedChanged Event** Write the code to make the HousingBoard Group visible.

HINT

```
71   ⊟   Private Sub radOnCampus_CheckedChanged(ByVal sender As System.Object, ByVal e As System.EventArgs) Handles radOnCampus.CheckedChanged
72           ' This event handler is executed when the On Campus radio button is selected. It makes the Housing/Board radio buttons visible
73
74           grpHousingBoard.Visible = True
75
76       End Sub
```

● **Write the Code for the Clear Form Button** Write the code to clear the form and place the focus on the Student ID text box, as defined in the event planning document (*ref: Figure 11-43*).

The frmCollege code is completed (Figure 11-48).

```
1    ' Program:       College Registration Costs
2    ' Developer:     Corinne Hoisington
3    ' Date:          August 29, 2019
4    ' Purpose:       This program calculates the registration costs for a college student. It also records the costs in a text file.
5
6    Option Strict On
7
8    Public Class frmCollege
9
10       Private Sub btnCalculateCosts_Click(ByVal sender As System.Object, ByVal e As System.EventArgs) Handles btnCalculateCosts.Click
11           ' This Calculate Costs button click event handler edits the  registration(costs) form to ensure it contains valid data.
12           ' Then, after passing control to the business class, it displays the cost.
13
14           Dim objStudent As Student
15           Dim objOnCampusStudent As OnCampusStudent
16           Dim InputError As Boolean = False
17
18           ' Is student ID entered properly
19           If txtStudentID.MaskFull = False Then
20               MsgBox("Enter your Student ID in the Student ID box", , "Error")
21               txtStudentID.Clear()
22               txtStudentID.Focus()
23               InputError = True
24               ' Is student name entered properly
25           ElseIf txtStudentName.TextLength < 1 Or txtStudentName.Text < "A" Then
26               MsgBox("Enter your name in the Student Name box", , "Error")
27               txtStudentName.Clear()
28               txtStudentName.Focus()
29               InputError = True
30               ' Is number of units entered properly
31           ElseIf Not IsNumeric(txtNumberOfUnits.Text) Then
32               MsgBox("Enter the units in the Number of Units box", , "Error")
33               txtNumberOfUnits.Clear()
34               txtNumberOfUnits.Focus()
35               InputError = True
36               ' Has 1-24 units been entered
37           ElseIf Convert.ToInt32(txtNumberOfUnits.Text) < 1 Or Convert.ToInt32(txtNumberOfUnits.Text) > 24 Then
38               MsgBox("Units must be 1 - 24", , "Error")
39               txtNumberOfUnits.Clear()
40               txtNumberOfUnits.Focus()
41               InputError = True
42               ' Has a major been selected
43           ElseIf cboMajor.SelectedIndex < 0 Then
44               MsgBox("Please select a major", , "Error")
45               cboMajor.Focus()
46               InputError = True
47           End If
48           ' If no input error, process the registration costs
49           If Not InputError Then
50               If radOffCampus.Checked Then
51                   objStudent = New Student(txtStudentID.Text, txtStudentName.Text, Convert.ToString(cboMajor.SelectedItem),
52                       txtNumberOfUnits.Text)
53                   lblCosts.Visible = True
54                   lblCosts.Text = "Total semester costs are: " & (objStudent.ComputeCosts()).ToString("C2")
55               Else
56                   objOnCampusStudent = New OnCampusStudent(txtStudentID.Text, txtStudentName.Text, Convert.ToString(cboMajor.SelectedItem),
57                       txtNumberOfUnits.Text, radCooperDorm.Checked, radCraigHall.Checked, radJulianSuites.Checked)
58                   lblCosts.Visible = True
59                   lblCosts.Text = "Total semester costs are: " & (objOnCampusStudent.ComputeCosts()).ToString("C2")
60               End If
61           End If
62       End Sub
63
64       Private Sub radOffCampus_CheckedChanged(ByVal sender As System.Object, ByVal e As System.EventArgs) Handles radOffCampus.CheckedChanged
65           ' This event handler is executed when the Off Campus radio button is selected. It hides the Housing/Board radio buttons
66
67           grpHousingBoard.Visible = False
68
69       End Sub
70
71       Private Sub radOnCampus_CheckedChanged(ByVal sender As System.Object, ByVal e As System.EventArgs) Handles radOnCampus.CheckedChanged
72           ' This event handler is executed when the On Campus radio button is selected. It makes the Housing/Board radio buttons visible
73
74           grpHousingBoard.Visible = True
75
76       End Sub
77
78       Private Sub btnClearForm_Click(ByVal sender As System.Object, ByVal e As System.EventArgs) Handles btnClearForm.Click
79           ' This event handler is executed when the user clicks the Clear Form button. It resets all objects on the user interface.
80
81           txtStudentID.Clear()
82           txtStudentName.Clear()
83           txtNumberOfUnits.Clear()
84           cboMajor.SelectedIndex = -1
85           cboMajor.Text = "Select a Major"
86           radOffCampus.Checked = True
87           radCooperDorm.Checked = True
88           grpHousingBoard.Visible = False
89           lblCosts.Visible = False
90           txtStudentID.Focus()
91
92       End Sub
93
94    End Class
95
```

FIGURE 11-48

(continues)

3

● **Create the Classes Required for the Remainder of the Program** Right-click the name of the project (CollegeRegistration) in the Solution Explorer, point to Add on the shortcut menu, and then click Class on the shortcut menu. Add the Student.vb class. Use the same technique to add the OnCampusStudent.vb class and the StudentCostsFile.vb class (*ref: Figure 11-13*).

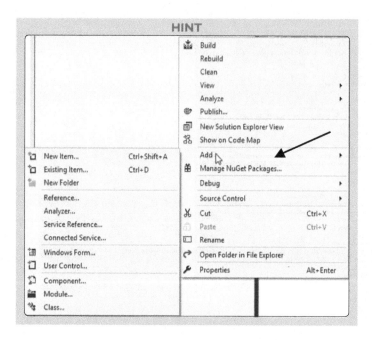

● **Enter Comments and Option Strict On for the Student Class** Display the Student class code window. Enter the common comments for the Student class. Include the Option Strict On statement.

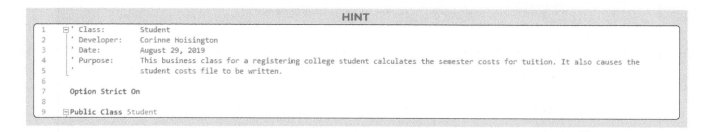

• **Define the Class Variables for the Student Class** Define the class variables for the Student class, including the declaration for the StudentCostsFile object. Remember that the variables should be declared with Protected access because they are used in the OnCampusStudent subclass.

```
                              HINT
 9    ⊟Public Class Student
10
11          'Class variables
12          Protected _strStudentID As String
13          Protected _strStudentName As String
14          Protected _strMajor As String
15          Protected _intUnits As Integer
16          Protected _decCost As Decimal
17          Protected _decCostPerUnit As Decimal = 450D
18
19          Dim objStudentCostsFile As StudentCostsFile
```

• **Write the Student Class Constructor** Write the code for the Student class constructor based on the requirements shown in the event planning document (*ref: Figure 11-22*).

```
                              HINT
21    ⊟    Sub New(ByVal strStudentID As String, ByVal strStudentName As String, ByVal strMajor As String, ByVal intUnits As String)
22              ' This subprocedure is a constructor for the Student class. It is called when the object is instantiated with arguments
23
24              'The following code assigns the arguments to class variables
25              _strStudentID = strStudentID
26              _strStudentName = strStudentName
27              _strMajor = strMajor
28              _intUnits = Convert.ToInt32(intUnits)
29
30          End Sub
```

• **Write the Code for the ComputeCosts Overridable Function Procedure** Write the code to calculate the cost, instantiate the object for the StudentCostsFile class, call the procedure to write the file, and return the cost.

```
                              HINT
31
32    ⊟    Overridable Function ComputeCosts() As Decimal
33              ' This function computes the registration costs, writes a record in the student costs file, and returns the registration costs
34
35              'Calculate cost
36              _decCost = _intUnits * _decCostPerUnit
37
38              'Write the student record
39              objStudentCostsFile = New StudentCostsFile(_strStudentID, _strStudentName, _strMajor, _decCost)
40              objStudentCostsFile.WriteRecord()
41
42              'Return the calculated cost
43              Return _decCost
44
45          End Function
46
47    End Class
```

(continues)

The Student class code is completed (Figure 11-49).

```
1    ⊟' Class:        Student
2     ' Developer:    Corinne Hoisington
3     ' Date:         August 29, 2019
4     ' Purpose:      This business class for a registering college student calculates the semester costs for tuition. It also causes the
5     '               student costs file to be written.
6
7      Option Strict On
8
9    ⊟Public Class Student
10
11        'Class variables
12        Protected _strStudentID As String
13        Protected _strStudentName As String
14        Protected _strMajor As String
15        Protected _intUnits As Integer
16        Protected _decCost As Decimal
17        Protected _decCostPerUnit As Decimal = 450D
18
19        Dim objStudentCostsFile As StudentCostsFile
20
21    ⊟   Sub New(ByVal strStudentID As String, ByVal strStudentName As String, ByVal strMajor As String, ByVal intUnits As String)
22            ' This subprocedure is a constructor for the Student class. It is called when the object is instantiated with arguments
23
24            'The following code assigns the arguments to class variables
25            _strStudentID = strStudentID
26            _strStudentName = strStudentName
27            _strMajor = strMajor
28            _intUnits = Convert.ToInt32(intUnits)
29
30        End Sub
31
32    ⊟   Overridable Function ComputeCosts() As Decimal
33            ' This function computes the registration costs, writes a record in the student costs file, and returns the registration costs
34
35            'Calculate cost
36            _decCost = _intUnits * _decCostPerUnit
37
38            'Write the student record
39            objStudentCostsFile = New StudentCostsFile(_strStudentID, _strStudentName, _strMajor, _decCost)
40            objStudentCostsFile.WriteRecord()
41
42            'Return the calculated cost
43            Return _decCost
44
45        End Function
46
47      End Class
48
49
50    ▎
```

FIGURE 11-49

4

● **Enter Comments and Option Strict On for the OnCampusStudent Class** Display the OnCampusStudent class code window. Enter the common comments for the OnCampusStudent class. Include the Option Strict On statement and the Inherits statement, which indicates that the OnCampusStudent class inherits from the Student class.

```
HINT
1     ' Class:        OnCampusStudent
2     ' Developer:    Corinne Hoisington
3     ' Date:         August 29, 2019
4     ' Purpose:      This business class for registering an on-campus college student calculates the semester costs, including tuition
5     '               and housing. It also causes the student costs file to be written.
6
7     Option Strict On
8
9     Public Class OnCampusStudent
10        Inherits Student
```

● **Define the Class Variables for the OnCampusStudent Class** Define the class variables for the OnCampusStudent class, including the declaration for the StudentCostsFile object. The variables should be declared with Private access.

```
HINT
12        ' Class variables
13        Private _Cooper As Boolean
14        Private _Craig As Boolean
15        Private _Julian As Boolean
16
17        Dim objStudentCostsFile As StudentCostsFile
```

● **Write the OnCampusStudent Class Constructor** Write the code for the OnCampusStudent class constructor based on the requirements shown in the event planning document (*ref: Figure 11-28*).

```
HINT
19    Sub New(ByVal StudentID As String, ByVal StudentName As String, ByVal Major As String, ByVal Units As String,
20            ByVal Cooper As Boolean, ByVal Craig As Boolean, ByVal Julian As Boolean)
21        ' This subprocedure is a constructor for the Student class. It is called when instantiated with arguments
22
23        MyBase.New(StudentID, StudentName, Major, Units)
24
25        'The following code assigns the arguments to class variables
26        _Cooper = Cooper
27        _Craig = Craig
28        _Julian = Julian
29
30    End Sub
```

(continues)

● **Write the Code for the ComputeCosts Overriding Function Procedure** Write the code to define the variables, determine the housing/board cost, calculate the semester cost, instantiate the object for the StudentCostsFile class, call the procedure to write the file, and return the semester cost.

HINT

```
32          Overrides Function ComputeCosts() As Decimal
33              ' This function computes the registration costs, writes a record in the student costs file, and returns the registration costs
34
35              'Define variables
36              Dim HousingCost As Decimal
37              Const cdecCooperHousingCost As Decimal = 2900D
38              Const cdecCraigHousingCost As Decimal = 3400D
39              Const cdecJulianHousingCost As Decimal = 4000D
40
41              'Calculate the cost
42              If _Cooper Then
43                  HousingCost = cdecCooperHousingCost
44              ElseIf _Craig Then
45                  HousingCost = cdecCraigHousingCost
46              ElseIf _Julian Then
47                  HousingCost = cdecJulianHousingCost
48              End If
49
50              _decCost = (_intUnits * _decCostPerUnit) + HousingCost
51
52              'Write the student record
53              objStudentCostsFile = New StudentCostsFile(_strStudentID, _strStudentName, _strMajor, _decCost)
54              objStudentCostsFile.WriteRecord()
55
56              'Return the calculated cost
57              Return _decCost
58
59          End Function
60
61      End Class
```

The OnCampusStudent class code is completed (Figure 11-50).

```
1    ' Class:        OnCampusStudent
2    ' Developer:    Corinne Hoisington
3    ' Date:         August 29, 2019
4    ' Purpose:      This business class for registering an on-campus college student calculates the semester costs, including tuition
5    '               and housing. It also causes the student costs file to be written.
6
7    Option Strict On
8
9    Public Class OnCampusStudent
10       Inherits Student
11
12       ' Class variables
13       Private _Cooper As Boolean
14       Private _Craig As Boolean
15       Private _Julian As Boolean
16
17       Dim objStudentCostsFile As StudentCostsFile
18
19       Sub New(ByVal StudentID As String, ByVal StudentName As String, ByVal Major As String, ByVal Units As String,
20             ByVal Cooper As Boolean, ByVal Craig As Boolean, ByVal Julian As Boolean)
21          ' This subprocedure is a constructor for the Student class. It is called when instantiated with arguments
22
23          MyBase.New(StudentID, StudentName, Major, Units)
24
25          'The following code assigns the arguments to class variables
26          _Cooper = Cooper
27          _Craig = Craig
28          _Julian = Julian
29
30       End Sub
31
32       Overrides Function ComputeCosts() As Decimal
33          ' This function computes the registration costs, writes a record in the student costs file, and returns the registration costs
34
35          'Define variables
36          Dim HousingCost As Decimal
37          Const cdecCooperHousingCost As Decimal = 2900D
38          Const cdecCraigHousingCost As Decimal = 3400D
39          Const cdecJulianHousingCost As Decimal = 4000D
40
41          'Calculate the cost
42          If _Cooper Then
43             HousingCost = cdecCooperHousingCost
44          ElseIf _Craig Then
45             HousingCost = cdecCraigHousingCost
46          ElseIf _Julian Then
47             HousingCost = cdecJulianHousingCost
48          End If
49
50          _decCost = (_intUnits * _decCostPerUnit) + HousingCost
51
52          'Write the student record
53          objStudentCostsFile = New StudentCostsFile(_strStudentID, _strStudentName, _strMajor, _decCost)
54          objStudentCostsFile.WriteRecord()
55
56          'Return the calculated cost
57          Return _decCost
58
59       End Function
60
61    End Class
62
63
```

FIGURE 11-50

(continues)

5

● **Enter Comments and Option Strict On for the StudentCostsFile Class** Display the StudentCostsFile class code window. Enter the common comments for the StudentCostsFile class. Include the Option Strict On statement.

HINT

```
1    ⊟ ' Class:       Student Costs File
2      ' Developer:   Corinne Hoisington
3      ' Date:        August 29, 2019
4      ' Purpose:     This class represents the Student Costs File. The WriteRecord procedure writes a comma-delimited student costs file that
5      '              contains the Student ID, Student Name, Major, and Student Costs.
6
7      Option Strict On
8
9    ⊟Public Class StudentCostsFile
```

● **Define the Class Variables for the StudentCostsFile Class** Define the class variables for the StudentCostsFile class. The variables should be declared with Private access.

HINT

```
11        ' Class variables
12        Private _strStudentID As String
13        Private _strStudentName As String
14        Private _strMajor As String
15        Private _decStudentCosts As Decimal
```

● **Write the StudentCostsFile Class Constructor** Write the code for the StudentCostsFile class constructor based on the requirements shown in the event planning document.

HINT

```
17    ⊟    Sub New(ByVal StudentID As String, ByVal StudentName As String, ByVal Major As String, ByVal Costs As Decimal)
18              ' This sub procedure is the constructor for the StudentCostsFile class.
19
20              ' The following code assigns the arguments to class variables
21              _strStudentID = StudentID
22              _strStudentName = StudentName
23              _strMajor = Major
24              _decStudentCosts = Costs
25
26         End Sub
```

• **Write the Code for the WriteRecord Sub Procedure** Write the code to define the variable. Then, in a Try-Catch block, declare an IO StreamWriter, write the comma-delimited record in the file, and close the file (*ref: Figure 11-36*).

HINT

```
28        Sub WriteRecord()
29            ' This subprocedure opens the StudentCosts output text file and then writes a record in the comma-delimited file
30
31            Dim strNameandLocationOfFile As String = "d:\StudentCosts.txt"
32
33            Try
34                Dim objWriter As IO.StreamWriter = IO.File.AppendText(strNameandLocationOfFile)
35
36                objWriter.Write(_strStudentID & ",")
37                objWriter.Write(_strStudentName & ",")
38                objWriter.Write(_strMajor & ",")
39                objWriter.WriteLine(_decStudentCosts)
40                objWriter.Close()
41
42            Catch ex As Exception
43                MsgBox("No device available - program aborted", , "Error")
44                Application.Exit()
45
46            End Try
47
48        End Sub
49
50    End Class
```

(continues)

The StudentCostsFile class code is completed (Figure 11-51).

```
1     ' Class:        Student Costs File
2     ' Developer:    Corinne Hoisington
3     ' Date:         August 29, 2019
4     ' Purpose:      This class represents the Student Costs File. The WriteRecord procedure writes a comma-delimited student costs file that
5     '               contains the Student ID, Student Name, Major, and Student Costs.
6
7     Option Strict On
8
9     Public Class StudentCostsFile
10
11        ' Class variables
12        Private _strStudentID As String
13        Private _strStudentName As String
14        Private _strMajor As String
15        Private _decStudentCosts As Decimal
16
17        Sub New(ByVal StudentID As String, ByVal StudentName As String, ByVal Major As String, ByVal Costs As Decimal)
18            ' This sub procedure is the constructor for the StudentCostsFile class.
19
20            ' The following code assigns the arguments to class variables
21            _strStudentID = StudentID
22            _strStudentName = StudentName
23            _strMajor = Major
24            _decStudentCosts = Costs
25
26        End Sub
27
28        Sub WriteRecord()
29            ' This subprocedure opens the StudentCosts output text file and then writes a record in the comma-delimited file
30
31            Dim strNameandLocationOfFile As String = "d:\StudentCosts.txt"
32
33            Try
34                Dim objWriter As IO.StreamWriter = IO.File.AppendText(strNameandLocationOfFile)
35
36                objWriter.Write(_strStudentID & ",")
37                objWriter.Write(_strStudentName & ",")
38                objWriter.Write(_strMajor & ",")
39                objWriter.WriteLine(_decStudentCosts)
40                objWriter.Close()
41
42            Catch ex As Exception
43                MsgBox("No device available - program aborted", , "Error")
44                Application.Exit()
45
46            End Try
47
48        End Sub
49
50    End Class
51
52    |
```

FIGURE 11-51

Summary

In this chapter, you have learned to create multiple classes using the three-tier program structure and to incorporate inheritance into your program.

Knowledge Check

1. The purpose of _____ is the separation of processing and hiding data within different classes.

2. What are the names of the three tiers in a three-tiered program structure? What occurs in each of the three tiers?

3. What property can you use to specify the sequence of objects that will be selected when the user presses the TAB key?

4. What property is used to ensure that the user has entered only numbers in a flight number MaskedTextBox object?

5. In a three-tiered program structure, which tiers are allowed to communicate with each other?

6. Identify the three steps to create a new class in a Visual Basic program.

7. When is a class constructor executed?

8. Write the code to instantiate the objAthlete object based on the Olympic class.

9. Write the code to instantiate the objEscapeRoom object based on the Escape class and to pass the following values to the object: City, RoomTheme, Cost, GroupSize. Write the New statement in the Escape class.

10. Write a statement to call the TrainTicket procedure in the objOffPeak object assigned to the variable decTrainCost.

11. Explain the benefits of using separate classes in a program.

12. Complete the following sentence: Inheritance allows one class to inherit _____ and _____ from another class.

13. Describe the difference between a base class and a subclass when using inheritance.

14. What entry must be included in the Class statement of a subclass?

15. What is the first statement that must be coded in a subclass constructor?

16. What is an overridable procedure? Why is it used?

17. In a class, can an attribute be referenced that is not defined in the class? How is this attribute reference resolved?

18. Rewrite the following names in a comma-delimited text file format:

    Aragorn

    Bilbo Baggins

    Boromir

    Frodo

    Gandalf

    Pippin

19. When an IO.StreamWriter is created, what does the IO.File.AppendText entry mean?

20. Which procedure in the IO.StreamWriter class writes a field and begins a new line, or record, in the text file?

1. The code in Figure 11-52 executes when a button is clicked on a Windows Form object. Identify what will happen when a single error occurs. What happens if two errors occur at the same time? What happens if three errors occur at the same time?

```
16              Dim InputError As Boolean = False
17
18              ' Is student ID entered properly
19              If txtStudentID.MaskFull = False Then
20                  MsgBox("Enter your Student ID in the Student ID box", , "Error")
21                  txtStudentID.Clear()
22                  txtStudentID.Focus()
23                  InputError = True
24                  ' Is student name entered properly
25              ElseIf txtStudentName.TextLength < 1 Or txtStudentName.Text < "A" Then
26                  MsgBox("Enter your name in the Student Name box", , "Error")
27                  txtStudentName.Clear()
28                  txtStudentName.Focus()
29                  InputError = True
30                  ' Is number of units entered properly
31              ElseIf Not IsNumeric(txtNumberOfUnits.Text) Then
32                  MsgBox("Enter the units in the Number of Units box", , "Error")
33                  txtNumberOfUnits.Clear()
34                  txtNumberOfUnits.Focus()
35                  InputError = True
```

FIGURE 11-52

Debugging Exercises *continued*

2. Examine the following code and make any corrections required.

CALLING CLASS

```
62 Dim objSubClass As New SubClass(txtLastName, _
63     txtNumberOfDependents)
```

OBJSUBCLASS

```
4 Sub New (ByVal LastName)
```

3. Correct the following code.

```
4 Dim objWater As WaterName
5 WaterName = New WaterName
```

4. Referencing Exercise 3 above, correct the following statement:

```
22 lblWater = GetWater.objWater
```

Program Analysis

1. What is the output of the code in Figure 11-53?

```
            2 references
28      ⊟   Sub WriteRecord()
29              ' This subprocedure opens the StudentCosts output text file and then writ
30
31              Dim strNameandLocationOfFile As String = "e:\StudentCosts.txt"
32
33              Try
34                  Dim objWriter As IO.StreamWriter = IO.File.AppendText(strNameandLocat
35
36                  objWriter.Write(_strStudentID & ",")
37                  objWriter.Write(_strStudentName & ",")
38                  objWriter.Write(_strMajor & ",")
39                  objWriter.WriteLine(_decStudentCosts)
40                  objWriter.Close()
41
42              Catch ex As Exception
43                  MsgBox("No device available - program aborted", , "Error")
44                  Application.Exit()
45
46              End Try
47
48          End Sub
```

FIGURE 11-53

(continues)

2. Analyze the code in Figures 11-54a, 11-54b, and 11-54c. What is the output of the code?

```
17          Dim objCustomer As Customer
18          Dim objInternetCustomer As InternetCustomer
19
20          objCustomer = New Customer
21          objInternetCustomer = New InternetCustomer
22
23          MsgBox.Show(objInternetCustomer.CustomerFunction())
```

FIGURE 11-54a

```
1 Public Class Customer
2
3     Function CustomerFunction() As String
4         Return "Customer function"
5     End Function
6
7     Overridable Function OverridableCustomerFunction() As String
8         Return "Overridable customer function"
9     End Function
10
11
12 End Class
13
```

FIGURE 11-54b

```
1 Public Class InternetCustomer
2     Inherits Customer
3
4     Function InternetCustomerFunction() As String
5         Return "Internet customer function"
6     End Function
7
8     Overrides Function OverridableCustomerFunction() As String
9         Return "Overrode the customer overridable function"
10     End Function
11
12 End Class
13
```

FIGURE 11-54c

3. Analyze the code in Figures 11-55a, 11-55b, and 11-55c. What is the output of the code?

```
17          Dim objCustomer As Customer
18          Dim objInternetCustomer As InternetCustomer
19
20          objCustomer = New Customer
21          objInternetCustomer = New InternetCustomer
22
23          MsgBox.Show(objInternetCustomer.InternetCustomerFunction())
```

FIGURE 11-55a

```
1  Public Class Customer
2
3      Function CustomerFunction() As String
4          Return "Customer function"
5      End Function
6
7      Overridable Function OverridableCustomerFunction() As String
8          Return "Overridable customer function"
9      End Function
10
11
12 End Class
13
```

FIGURE 11-55b

```
1  Public Class InternetCustomer
2      Inherits Customer
3
4      Function InternetCustomerFunction() As String
5          Return "Internet customer function"
6      End Function
7
8      Overrides Function OverridableCustomerFunction() As String
9          Return "Overrode the customer overridable function"
10     End Function
11
12 End Class
13
```

FIGURE 11-55c

Complete one or more of the following case programming assignments. Submit the program and materials you create to your instructor. The level of difficulty is indicated for each case programming assignment.

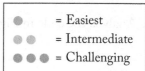

● = Easiest
●● = Intermediate
●●● = Challenging

1 ●
HOME SECURITY CAMERAS

Design a Windows application and write the code that will execute according to the program requirements in Figure 11-56 and the Use Case Definition in Figure 11-57 on the next page. Before writing the code, create an event planning document for each event in the program. The completed Windows Form object and other objects in the user interface are shown in Figure 11-58 on page 710.

REQUIREMENTS DOCUMENT

Date Submitted: July 18, 2019

Date:

Application Title: Home Security Camera Protection Plan

Purpose: This Windows application allows the user to select a monthly security subscription plan from Home Secure Vision, which sends you live video when motion is detected.

Program Procedures: From a Windows application, a user enters her name, home address, and zip code. The user also selects a monthly subscription plan for Home Secure Vision. These plans do not include a one-click response to call the police. To add complete coverage features, users can select whether they have a single motion detection camera or four motion detection cameras for complete home security, and whether they are interested in adding one-click police response to their monthly subscription plan.

Algorithms,   1. The user enters her name, address, and zip code.
Processing, and   2. The user selects a monthly subscription plan:
Conditions: • Motion Detection Coverage, $3.99 a month
                             • Motion Detection plus two-way communication, $4.99 a month
                             • Outdoor Waterproof Coverage, $6.99 a month
                         3 The user must select whether she plans to have a single camera (no change in cost) or four cameras ($2.99 extra per month).
                         4. The user must select whether she wants an add-on feature for one-click police response, which costs another $2 per month.
                         5. After the user selects the one-click police response option, the Email text box appears. The user must enter her email address.
                         6. In a comma-delimited text file, the program keeps a log of the selected plan. The file should contain the user's name, zip code, plan, one-click response option, and monthly cost.

FIGURE 11-56 (continues)

Case Programming Assignments *continued*

Notes and Restrictions:	Validate data that the user enters using accepted standards. The zip code must have only five numbers.
Comments:	1. Obtain an image for this program from CengageBrain.com. The name of the picture is camera. 2. The program should use a three-tiered structure with presentation, business, and persistence classes.

FIGURE 11-56 (continued)

USE CASE DEFINITION

1. The user views the opening screen, which displays an image.
2. The user enters her name, address, and zip code.
3. The user selects a desired monthly security subscription plan from a drop-down list.
4. The user selects the radio button that corresponds to the number of devices she wants.
5. The user selects whether she wants to add one-click response from a drop-down list.
6. The user clicks the Calculate Cost button to view the cost of the monthly subscription plan.
7. The program writes a record of the subscription plan and monthly cost total.
8. A Clear Form button is available to clear the form.

FIGURE 11-57

(continues)

Home Security Cameras

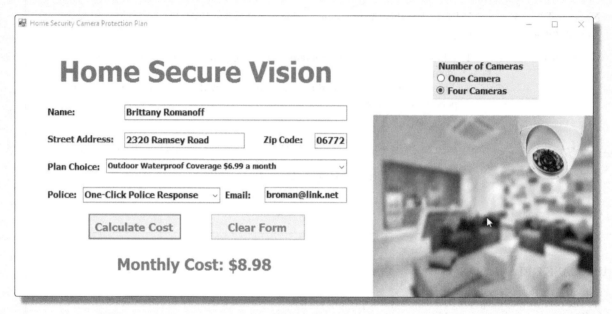

FIGURE 11-58

2 MINI COOPER DEALERSHIP

Design a Windows application and write the code that will execute according to the program requirements in Figure 11-59 and the Use Case Definition in Figure 11-60. Before writing the code, create an event planning document for each event in the program. The completed Windows Form object and other objects in the user interface are shown in Figure 11-61 on the next page.

REQUIREMENTS DOCUMENT

Date Submitted:	July 15, 2019
Date:	
Application Title:	Mini Cooper Dealership
Purpose:	This Windows application allows the user to add cars to the inventory of a Mini Cooper car dealership. The program displays the sticker price for each car and allows the user to display the entire inventory.
Program Procedures:	In a Windows application, a user enters the vehicle number, model, year, mileage, and standard price for a Mini Cooper that is being placed in the inventory of the car dealership. In addition, the user selects the car's color from a list of colors and indicates whether the vehicle is a convertible. The program creates the sticker price for the car and writes a record for the car in the inventory text file.
Algorithms, Processing, and Conditions:	1. The user enters the vehicle number, model, year, mileage, and standard price for a used car being placed in inventory.
	2. The user selects the car color from a list of 17 common car colors, including black, dark gray, and red.
	3. The user indicates whether the car is a convertible.
	4. The program calculates the sticker price for the car on the used car lot.
	5. If the car is a convertible, a 26 percent surcharge is added to the sticker price calculated in step 4 to determine the total sticker price.
	6. After the user enters all the data and clicks a button, the sticker price is displayed.
	7. When the button is clicked, the program also writes a comma-delimited text file that records the new entry into the inventory. The record includes the vehicle number, model, year, mileage, and sticker price.
	8. At anytime, the user can click the Display Inventory menu item on the File menu to display the records in the inventory text file. In a separate window, the vehicle number, make, model, year, mileage, and sticker price should be displayed in a list for every car in the inventory.
Notes and Restrictions:	Validate data that the user enters using accepted standards.
Comments:	1. Obtain an image for this program from CengageBrain.com. The name of the picture is mini.
	2. The program should use a three-tiered structure with presentation, business, and persistence classes.

FIGURE 11-59

(continues)

Mini Cooper Dealership

USE CASE DEFINITION

1. The user views the opening screen, which displays an image.
2. The user enters the vehicle number, vehicle model, year, mileage, and price.
3. The user selects a desired color from a drop-down list.
4. The user selects the Convertible check box if appropriate.
5. The user clicks the Sticker Price button to enter the car into the inventory.
6. The program displays the sticker price and writes a record in the inventory text file.
7. A Clear Form button is available to clear the form.

FIGURE 11-60

FIGURE 11-61

3 ●●
BANK ACCOUNT PROJECTION

Design a Windows application and write the code that will execute according to the program requirements in Figure 11-62. Before designing the user interface, create a Use Case Definition. Before writing the code, create an event planning document for each event in the program.

REQUIREMENTS DOCUMENT

Date Submitted:	July 12, 2019
Date:	
Application Title:	Bank Account Projection
Purpose:	This Windows application calculates and displays the expected values of different types of bank accounts held for one year by current customers of Tenth Street Regional Bank.
Program Procedures:	In a Windows application, a user enters her name and current account number, selects one of five types of accounts, and then enters the amount to be placed in the account. The program calculates the projected value of the account after one year, assuming that the user makes no other deposits or withdrawals.

Algorithms, Processing, and Conditions:

1. The user enters her name and current account number.
2. The user identifies the type of account being considered. The types of accounts are Regular Savings, Checking, 1-year CD, 2-year CD, and 5-year CD.
3. The user enters the amount to be deposited. The minimum amount is greater than $1,000.00.
4. When the user clicks a button, the program calculates and displays the value of the account after one year.
5. The value of the account is based on the following: Regular Savings, 1.75% interest; Checking, $25.00 per month service charge; 1-year CD, 1.85% interest; 2-year CD, 2.30% interest; 5-year CD, 2.37% interest.
6. A comma-delimited text file is kept for each account inquiry. The text file contains the account number, the amount to be deposited, and the type of account selected.
7. The user can click a button to clear the form.

Notes and Restrictions:	Validate data that the user enters using accepted standards.
Comments:	1. Use the web to find an appropriate image for the user interface. 2. The program should use a three-tiered structure with presentation, business, and persistence classes.

FIGURE 11-62

4   COLLEGE BOOKSTORE ACCESS CODES

Design a Windows application and write the code that will execute according to the program requirements in Figure 11-63. Before designing the user interface, create a Use Case Definition. Before writing the code, create an event planning document for each event in the program.

REQUIREMENTS DOCUMENT

Date Submitted:	August 12, 2019
Date:	
Application Title:	College Bookstore Access Codes
Purpose:	This Windows application calculates the costs of college software access codes from a bookstore.
Program Procedures:	In a Windows application, a user selects one of five software access codes to purchase from a list. The user enters the buyer's credit card number and expiration date and identifies whether the buyer is a student. The program calculates the cost of the access codes. It also keeps a log of purchases.
Algorithms, Processing, and Conditions:	1. The user enters the buyer's credit card number and expiration date. 2. The user identifies the app the buyer is purchasing. 3. The five software semester access codes and their prices are: Visio $14.99, QuickBooks $24.99, Project $17.99, Power Bi $9.99, and Speed Type $29.99. 4. For each package, a discount applies if the buyer is a student. The discounts are: Visio, 6%; QuickBooks, 8%; Project, 8%; Power Bi, 5%; Speed Type, 2%. 5. After entering the information, the user can click the Final Total button to determine the amount to be charged to the credit card. 6. The user can click a button to clear the form. 7. The program writes a comma-delimited text file to keep track of all software purchases. The text file contains the credit card number, the name of the app purchased, the discount amount, and the total amount. 8. At anytime, the user can click the Daily Total button to have the program calculate and display the amount of sales that have been recorded in the text file.
Notes and Restrictions:	Validate data that the user enters using accepted standards.
Comments:	1. Use the web to find an appropriate image for the user interface. 2. The program should use a three-tiered structure with presentation, business, and persistence classes.

FIGURE 11-63

Case Programming Assignments

5
•••
HOME RENTAL INVESTMENT

Create a requirements document and a Use Case Definition document and then design a Windows application based on the case project shown in Figure 11-64. Before writing the code, create an event planning document for each event in the program.

Create a three-tiered Windows application that calculates the return on investment of buying a rental home in certain cities. For example, if you buy a home for $100,000 in Ocala, Florida, and the home earns an average of 10.23% in rental return per year, your return on investment after five years would be $51,500.00. The buyer should enter their name, the number of rental years, the city, and home price. The user can select a rental home location and rate of return from the following list:

- Memphis TN 12.38%
- Ocala FL 10.23%
- Atlanta GA 9.70%
- Phoenix AZ 8.77%
- Ogden UT 8.44%

Write a comma-delimited text file to record each sale. The text file should contain all the entered information. The minimum acceptable home price allowed is $10,000.

FIGURE 11-64

Case Programming Assignments

6 ●●● COMMUNITY APPLICATION

Create a requirements document and a Use Case Definition document and then design a Windows application based on the case project shown in Figure 11-65. Before writing the code, create an event planning document for each event in the program.

> You have been asked to locate computer users on your campus or within your community, determine an application they need, and then write the application. Work with your users to develop and implement the application.

FIGURE 11-65

Unicode

The 256 characters and symbols that are represented by ASCII and EBCDIC codes are sufficient for English and western European languages (see Figure A-1 on the next page), but do not provide enough characters for Asian and other languages that use different alphabets. Further compounding the problem is that many of these languages use symbols, called ideograms, to represent multiple words and ideas. One solution to the problem of accommodating universal alphabets is Unicode. Unicode is a 16-bit coding scheme that can represent all the world's current, classic, and historical languages in more than 65,000 characters and symbols. In Unicode, 30,000 codes are reserved for future use, such as ancient languages, and 6,000 codes are reserved for private use. Existing ASCII coded data is fully compatible with Unicode because the first 256 codes are the same. Unicode is implemented in several operating systems, including Windows 10, Windows 8, Windows 7, Mac OS X, and Linux. To view a complete Unicode chart, see www.unicode.org.

UNICODE KEYBOARD CHARACTERS				
Decimal	**Hexadecimal**	**Octal**	**Binary**	**Character**
32	20	040	00100000	
33	21	041	00100001	!
34	22	042	00100010	"
35	23	043	00100010	#
36	24	044	00100100	$
37	25	045	00100101	%
38	26	046	00100110	&
39	27	047	00100111	'
40	28	050	00101000	(
41	29	051	00101001	)
42	2A	052	00101010	*
43	2B	053	00101011	+
44	2C	054	00101100	,
45	2D	055	00101101	-
46	2E	056	00101110	.
47	2F	057	00101111	/
48	30	060	00110000	0
49	31	061	00110001	1
50	32	062	00110010	2
51	33	063	00110011	3
52	34	064	00110100	4
53	35	065	00110101	5
54	36	066	00110110	6
55	37	067	00110111	7
56	38	070	00111000	8
57	39	071	00111001	9
58	3A	072	00111010	:
59	3B	073	00111011	;
60	3C	074	00111100	<

FIGURE A-1 (continued)

Decimal	Hexadecimal	Octal	Binary	Character
61	3D	075	00111101	=
62	3E	076	00111110	>
63	3F	077	00111111	?
64	40	100	01000000	@
65	41	101	01000001	A
66	42	102	01000010	B
67	43	103	01000011	C
68	44	104	01000100	D
69	45	105	01000101	E
70	46	106	01000110	F
71	47	107	01000111	G
72	48	110	01001000	H
73	49	111	01001001	I
74	4A	112	01001010	J
75	4B	113	01001011	K
76	4C	114	01001100	L
77	4D	115	01001101	M
78	4E	116	01001110	N
79	4F	117	01001111	O
80	50	120	01010000	P
81	51	121	01010001	Q
82	52	122	01010010	R
83	53	123	01010011	S
84	54	124	01010100	T
85	55	125	01010101	U
86	56	126	01010110	V
87	57	127	01010111	W
88	58	130	01011000	X
89	59	131	01011001	Y
90	5A	132	01011010	Z

FIGURE A-1 (continued)

Decimal	Hexadecimal	Octal	Binary	Character
91	5B	133	01011011	[
92	5C	134	01011100	\
93	5D	135	01011101	]
94	5E	136	01011110	^
95	5F	137	01011111	]
96	60	140	01100000	,
97	61	141	01100001	a
98	62	142	01100010	b
99	63	143	01100011	c
100	64	144	01100100	d
101	65	145	01100101	e
102	66	146	01100110	f
103	67	147	01100111	g
104	68	150	01101000	h
105	69	151	01101001	i
106	6A	152	01101010	j
107	6B	153	01101011	k
108	6C	154	01101100	l
109	6D	155	01101101	m
110	6E	156	01101110	n
111	6F	157	01101111	o
112	70	160	01110000	p
113	71	161	01110001	q
114	72	162	01110010	r
115	73	163	01110011	s
116	74	164	01110100	t
117	75	165	01110101	u
118	76	166	01110110	v
119	77	167	01110111	w
120	78	170	01111000	x

FIGURE A-1 (continued)

Decimal	Hexadecimal	Octal	Binary	Character
121	79	171	01111001	y
122	7A	172	01111010	z
123	7B	173	01111011	{
124	7C	174	01111100	|
125	7D	175	01111101	}
126	7E	176	01111110	~
127	7F	177	01111111	DEL

FIGURE A-1

Naming Conventions

The table in Figure B-1 displays the common data types used in Visual Basic 2017 with the recommended naming convention for the three-character prefix preceding variable names of the data type.

Data Type	Sample Value	Memory	Range of Values	Prefix
Integer	48	4 bytes	−2,147,483,648 to +2,147,483,647	int
Double	5.3452307	8 bytes	−1.79769313486232E308 to +1.79769313486232E308	dbl
Decimal	3.14519	16 bytes	Decimal values that may have up to 29 significant digits	dec
Char	'?' or 'C'	2 bytes	Single character	chr
String	"The Dow is up 0.03%"	Depends on number of characters	Letters, numbers, symbols	str
Boolean	True or False	Typically 2 bytes; depends on implementing platform	True or False	bln

FIGURE B-1

The table in Figure B-2 displays the less common data types used in Visual Basic 2017 with the recommended naming convention for the three-character prefix preceding variable names of the data type.

Data Type	Sample Value	Memory	Range of Values	Prefix
Byte	7	1 byte	0 to 255	byt
Date	April 22, 2019	8 bytes	0:00:00 (midnight) on January 1, 0001 through 11:59:59 PM on December 31, 9999	dtm
Long	345,234,567	8 bytes	−9,223,372,036,854,775,808 to +9,223,372,036,854,775,807	lng
Object	Holds a reference	4 bytes (32-bit) 8 bytes (64-bit)	A memory address	obj
Short	16,567	2 bytes	−32,768 to 32,767	shr
Single	234,654.1246	4 bytes	$-3.4028235E+38$ to $-1.401298E-45$ for negative values and $1.401298E-45$ to $3.4028235E+38$ for positive values	sng

FIGURE B-2

Form Object Naming Conventions

The table in Figure B-3 displays the prefix naming conventions for Form objects. The three-letter prefixes used before variables names especially are helpful when you use IntelliSense.

Object Type	Prefix	Object Type	Prefix
Button	btn	ListBox	lst
Calendar	cld	MenuStrip	mnu
CheckBox	chk	NumericUpDown	nud
ComboBox	cbo	PictureBox	pic
CompareValidator	cmv	RadioButton	rad
DataGrid	dgd	RangeValidator	rgv
DateTimePicker	dtp	RegularExpressionValidator	rev
DropDownList	ddl	RequiredFieldValidator	rfv
Form	frm	TextBox	txt
GroupBox	grp	ValidationSummary	vsm
Label	lbl		

FIGURE B-3

INDEX

Note: **Boldface** page numbers indicate key terms.